George Washington.
From an Oil Painting by Rembrandt Peale.

RECORDS

OF THE

REVOLUTIONARY WAR:

CONTAINING

THE MILITARY AND FINANCIAL CORRESPONDENCE
OF DISTINGUISHED OFFICERS;

NAMES OF THE OFFICERS AND PRIVATES OF REGIMENTS, COMPANIES,
AND CORPS, WITH THE DATES OF THEIR COMMISSIONS
AND ENLISTMENTS;

GENERAL ORDERS OF WASHINGTON, LEE AND GREENE
AT GERMANTOWN AND VALLEY FORGE;

WITH A LIST OF
DISTINGUISHED PRISONERS OF WAR; THE TIME OF THEIR
CAPTURE, EXCHANGE, ETC.

TO WHICH IS ADDED
THE HALF-PAY ACTS OF THE CONTINENTAL CONGRESS; THE REVO-
LUTIONARY PENSION LAWS; AND A LIST OF THE OFFICERS OF
THE CONTINENTAL ARMY WHO ACQUIRED THE RIGHT TO
HALF-PAY, COMMUTATION, AND LANDS.

BY W. T. R. SAFFELL,

COUNSELLOR, AND AGENT FOR REVOLUTIONARY CLAIMS.

THIRD EDITION.

BALTIMORE:
CHARLES C. SAFFELL,
224 WEST FAYETTE STREET.
1894.

Notice

In many older books, foxing (or discoloration) occurs and, in some instances, print lightens with wear and age. Reprinted books, such as this, often duplicate these flaws, notwithstanding efforts to reduce or eliminate them. The pages of this reprint have been digitally enhanced and, where possible, the flaws eliminated in order to provide clarity of content and a pleasant reading experience.

Copyright © 1894, Charles C. Saffell

Originally published
Baltimore
1894

Reprinted by:

Janaway Publishing, Inc.
732 Kelsey Ct.
Santa Maria, California 93454
(805) 925-1038
www.JanawayGenealogy.com

2011

Printed with:

Index to Saffell's List of Virginia Soldiers in the Revolution

by
J. T. McAllister
1913

ISBN: 978-1-59641-232-3

Made in the United States of America

PREFACE.

As great numbers of the descendants of Revolutionary officers and soldiers are, at this time, eagerly in search of information relative to the service of their ancestors, for purposes of profit and satisfaction as well as of history; and, as many of them reside at places where nothing of the kind can be had without considerable difficulty and expense, I have thought it my proper duty to place my collections within the reach of all interested.

In so doing, I am not without a strong reason to induce a belief that they will be of some considerable historical interest in indicating the different locations and movements of the army, and in showing the whereabouts of individual officers, regiments, detachments, and corps, as well as in giving the precise dates of important events; and as the financial difficulties of the infant Republic in 1780 has been a subject of great interest, both in history and in legislation, new light is thrown upon it by the correspondence dated in that year.

As the Congress of the United States, the Court of Claims, and the Executive Departments are constantly engaged in the legislation upon, and in the investigation and adjustment of, claims against the United States for military service, I am convinced that much of the matter included in my collections, especially the correspondence of officers, and the list of their deaths, will serve as an important guide to individuals in asserting their claims, and as a protection of the interests of the government in adjusting them.

PREFACE.

They will, also, be found useful in answering at once, and without trouble, the thousands of letters to members of Congress from their constituents, asking information relating to military service, pensions, and the Pension and Bounty Land Laws of the Revolution.

In preparing this work, I have availed myself of the free use of "Irving's Life of Washington," "Lossing's Field Book of the Revolution," and "McSherry's History of Maryland," which, I am free to acknowledge, are the best and most accurate works extant, on their respective subjects, and should be owned by every reader in the land.

W. T. R. S.

CONTENTS.

LETTERS.

	PAGE.
Gen. Richard Montgomery, to Col. Timothy Bedel	17—23
do. do. Proclamation to the Canadians	26
Col. Benj. Hinman, to Colonel Bedel	18
Gen. Philip Schuyler, do. do.	18
Aide. John Macpherson, do. do.	20
Com. Noah Phelps, do. do.	23
Col. James Livingston, do. do.	24
Gen. David Wooster, do. do.	28
Col. James Holmes, do. do.	28—29
Col. Robert Troup, do. do.	31
do. to Johnston and Howell	38
Gen. Horatio Gates, to Col. Bedel	38
Secretary Richard Peters, to Col. Edward Antill	30
do. do. to Commissioners of Accounts.	32
Capt. Jotham Drury, to Col. John Lamb	30
Col. Jonathan Trumbull, to do.	74
Gen. David Waterbury, to Continental Commissioners	31
Com. Gen. Elias Boudinot, to Capt. Alexander Graydon	32
Col. Matthais Odgen, to Lieut. L. J. Costigin	33
Pres. John Jay, to William Palfrey, Paymaster-General	33
Paym'r-Gen. John Pierce, to William Palfrey, Paym'r-Gen. 66, 70, 73, 75, 76, 79	
do. do. do. do. 80, 81, 84, 85	
do. do. Paym'r-Gen. Jonathan Burrall..38, 43, 46, 48, 53	
do. do. Continental Congress... 42, 57, 64, 99, 101, 104, 105	
do. do. Paym'r-Gen. Thomas Reed.......43, 45, 46, 49, 82	
do. do. Gen. Wm. Heath	44
do. do. Col. Jeduthan Baldwin	45
do. do. Col. Donald Campbell	45
do. do. Paym'r-Gen. Joseph Clay	48, 52, 70
do. do. Col. Udny Hay, Quarterm'r-Gen	49, 72
do. do. Paym'r-Gen. William Bedlow	52
do. do. Board of Treasury..... 54, 58, 61, 62, 64, 85, 86, 113	
do. do. Col. R. H. Harrison	62
do. do. U. S. Lottery	74
do. do. Mr. Hubbard, of Conn	77
do. do. Hon. Thomas McKean	100
do. do. Col. Israel Shreeve	110
do. do. Thomas Harwood, Esq.	111
do. do. John Neufville, Esq.	111
do. do. Aud. Joseph Howell	112
do. do. Gen. Allen Jones	113
Gen. Count Cassimir Pulaski, to Auditors	33
Col. Joseph Carleton, do.	34
Aud. James Johnston, to Board of Treasury	34

CONTENTS.

				PAGE.
Paym'r-Gen. Jonathan Burrall, to Board of Treasury				39
do.	do.	Paym'r-Gen. John Boreman		39
do.	do.	do.	John Pierce	40, 46, 51
do.	do.	do.	Joseph Clay	41, 47, 56
do.	do.	do.	Benj. Steele	51
do.	do.	do.	Thomas Reed	53
do.	do.	do.	Benj. Harrison	54, 61
do,	do.	do.	Gov. Richard Caswell	57
Capt. J. Baldesqui, to Continental Congress				35, 36
Paym'r-Gen. Thomas Reed, to Paym'r-Gen. John Pierce				50
Joseph Bullock,		do.	do.	73
Sharp Delaney,		do.	do.	73
Col. John Sherman,		do.	do.	94
Hon. Hugh Williamson,		do.	do.	97
Gen. Henry Jackson,		do.	do.	97
Gen. George Partridge,		do.	do.	98
Gen. Jedediah Huntington,		do.	do.	98
Gen. Otho H. Williams,		do.	do.	105
Gen. Mordecai Gist,		do.	do.	106
Aud-Gen. Chris. Richmond,		do.	do.	101
Col. John E. Howard,		do.	do.	102
Col. Samuel Carlton,		do.	do.	107
Gen. Lachlin McIntosh,		do.	do.	110
Capt. George L. Turberville,		do.	do.	108
Paym'r-Gen. William Palfrey,		do.	do.	71
do.	do.	to Board of Treasury		67, 68, 72
do.	do.	to Paym'r-Gen. Thomas Reed		67
do.	do.	to Mr. Jared Saxton		69
do.	do.	to Major Clark		108
Com'ry Paul Woolfolk,	to Com'ry William Porter			88, 89, 90
Quarterm'r-gen. H. Morris,	do.	do.		88
Com'ry J. Pryor,		do.	do.	90, 92
do. Edward Moore,		do.	do.	91
Aide-de-Camp James Fairlee, do.		do.		91
Gen. Anthony Wayne and others, to Com'ry William Porter				94
Quarterm'r-Gen. Udny Hay, to Ebenezer Stevens				95
Com'ry-Gen. Samuel Hodgdon, to		do.		96
Major Bartholomew Von Heer, to Col. Josiah Harmar				96
Aud. Gen. John Nicholson,	to Aud. Joseph Howell			99
Capt. Joseph Morrill,		do.	do.	99
Aud. Gen. Edward Dunscomb,	do.	do.		113
Com'ry Joseph Dawson,		do.	do.	138
Major John Stagg,		do.	do.	139
Aud. Robert Denny,		do.	do.	141
Col. William Barton,		do.	do.	141
Col. Thomas F. Jackson,		do.	do.	142
Lieut. Thomas H. Condy, to Mr. Simmons				142
Aud. Joseph Howell, to Hon. James Madison				139
do.	William Simmons			136
do.	R. J. Vanden Broeck			137
do.	Secretary of War			137
John Deming, of Mass., to	do.			120

CONTENTS.

			PAGE
John Wright, Esq., to Comptroller			118
Capt. Robert Walker, to Col. Eleazer Oswald			103
Cor. A. Throckmorton, to Aud-Gen. A. Dunscomb			106
Capt. John Buckanan, to Congress			102

REGIMENTS.

Colonel Joseph Cilley's	New Hampshire	Regiment		143
do. William Douglass'	Connecticut	do.		152
do. Christopher Green's	Rhode Island	do.		153
do. Israel Angell's	do.	do.		154
do. Ebenezer Stevens'	New York Artillery	do.		155
do. Lewis Dubois'	do.	Infantry	do.	161
do. Peter Gansevoort's	do.	do.	do.	168
do. John Lamb's	do.	Artillery	do.	171
do. Arthur St. Clair's	Penn.	Infantry	do.	183
do. Joseph Wood's	do.	do.	do.	183
do. Anthony Wayne's	do.	do.	do.	196
do. William Irvine's	do.	do.	do.	202, 215
do. Charles Armand's Legion				219
do. Lewis Nicola's	Invalid	Regiment		222
do. Otho H. Williams'	Maryland	do.		234
do. John Gunby's	do.	do.		235
do. Peter Adams'	do.	do.		235
do. Thomas Woolford's	do.	do.		236
do. Benjamin Ford's	do.	do.		236
do. Lewis Weltner's	German	do.		237
do. Charles G. Griffith's	Flying-Camp	do.		237
do. Josiah C. Hall's	do.	do.		238
do. Thomas Ewing's	do.	do.		238
do. William Richardson's	do.	do.		239
do. Moses Rawling's	Rifle,	do.		240
do. Charles Harrison's	Staff and Artillery	do.		241
do. Daniel Morgan's	11th and 15th Virginia	do.		256
do. do.	Rifle	do.		268
do. Alex. Spottswood's	Virginia	do.		270
do. William Heath's	do.	do.		276
do. John Gibson's	Western Frontier	do.		280
do. Nathaniel Gists'	Virginia	do.		285
do. Henry Lee's	Legion, (officers)			288
do. Francis Marion's	South Carolina Regiment			290

CAPTAINS' COMPANIES.

Captain David Arrell,	Virginia	Infantry		277
do. Morgan Alexander,	do.	do.		270
do. Robert Adams,	Pennsylvania	do.		205
do. John Alexander,	do.	do.		218
do. William Alexander.	do.	do.		218
do. John Blackwell,	do.	do.		278
do. Reuben Briscoe,	do.	do.		279
do. Benj. Biggs,	do.	do.		284
do. Thomas Bell,	do.	do.		286
do. Alex. Breckenridge,	do.	do.		287
do. Richard Baker,	South Carolina	do.		290
do. William Brown,	Maryland	Artillery		227

CONTENTS.

				PAGE
Captain	Nathaniel Burrell,	Virginia	Artillery	242
do.	Thomas Baytop,	do.	do.	251
do.	Peter B. Bruin,	do.	Infantry	262
do.	Samuel Booker,	do.	Artillery	265
do.	William Butler,	Pennsylvania	Infantry	189
do.	Stephen Bayard,	do.	do.	190
do.	John Brisban,	do.	do.	191
do.	Lewis Bush,	do.	do.	205
do.	Jacob Bauer,	do.	do.	221
do.	Stephen Buckland,	New York	Artillery	156
do.	Jonathan Brown,	do.	do.	174
do.	Rudolph Bunner,	Pennsylvania	Infantry	185
do.	Thomas Blackwell,	Virginia	do.	262
do.	William Brattan,	Pennsylvania	do.	215
do.	John C. Carter,	Virginia	Artillery	249
do.	Whitehead Coleman,	do.	do.	252
do.	James Calderwood,	do.	Infantry	256
do.	Thomas Craig,	Pennsylvania	do.	187
do.	Thomas Church,	do.	do.	196
do.	Buller Claiborne,	Virginia	do.	270
do.	Richard Dorsey,	Maryland	Artillery	230
do.	Richard Davis,	do.	Riflemen	240
do.	John Dandridge,	Virginia	Artillery	247
do.	Nathaniel Donnell,	New York	do.	157
do.	Thomas Dunbar,	South Carolina	Infantry	293
do.	Philip De Bois Bevier,	New York	do.	164
do.	Jost Driesbach,	Pennsylvania	do.	219
do.	Amos Emerson,	New Hampshire	do.	148
do.	Samuel Eddens,	Virginia	Artillery	250
do.	Ebenezer Frye,	New Hampshire	Infantry	149
do.	Isaac Farwell,	do.	do.	150
do.	Persifer Frazer,	Pennsylvania	do.	198
do.	Jeremiah Gilman,	New Hampshire	do.	144
do.	Henry Goodwin,	New York	do.	166
do.	Philip Griffith,	Maryland	Riflemen	240
do.	Charles Gallahue,	Virginia	Infantry	257
do.	James Gray,	Virginia	Infantry	266
do.	John Gregory,	do.	Artillery	266
do.	David Grier,	Pennsylvania	Infantry	211
do.	Philip Graybell,	do.	do.	222
do.	John Gist,	Virginia	do.	285
do.	Peter Gray,	South Carolina	do.	291
do.	Samuel Hawes,	Virginia	do.	275
do.	Thomas Hall,	South Carolina	do.	292
do.	John Henry,	Virginia	Artillery	253
do.	John Huling,	Pennsylvania	Infantry	193
do.	Samuel Hay,	do.	do.	203
do.	Nathaniel Hutchins,	New Hampshire	do.	151
do.	Amos Hutchins,	New York	Artillery	163
do.	John F. Hamtramck,	do.	Infantry	167
do.	Cornelius T. Jansen,	do.	do.	169
do.	William Johnson,	Virginia	do.	258

CONTENTS. 8

				PAGE
Captain	Strother Jones,	Virginia	Infantry	285
do.	John C. Jones,	Maryland	do	227
do.	John Johnson,	New York	do.	167
do.	Thomas Lee,	do.	do.	165
do.	John Lacey,	Pennsylvania	do.	197
do.	Gabriel Long,	Maryland	Riflemen.	268
do.	Samuel Lapsley,	Virginia	Infantry	285
do.	Philip R. F. Lee,	do.	do.	279
do.	John McDowell,	Pennsylvania	do.	217
do.	Richard Mason,	South Carolina	do.	294
do.	Daniel Mazyck.	do.	do.	294
do.	Everard Meade,	Virginia	do.	271
do.	Moses McLean,	Pennsylvania	do.	213
do.	John F. Mercer,	Virginia	do.	276
do.	Francis Muir,	do.	do.	287
do.	Charles Motte,	South Carolina	do.	291
do.	Thomas Moultrie,	do.	do.	292
do.	John Marshall,	Virginia	do.	267
do.	Amos Morrill,	New Hampshire	do.	146
do.	Andrew Moodie,	New York	Artillery	172
do.	Gershom Motte,	do.	do.	173
do.	Samuel Montgomery,	Pennsylvania	Infantry	216
do.	George Nicholas,	Virginia	do.	273
do.	Noah Nichols,	New York	Artillery Artificers..	160
do.	John Nelson,	Pennsylvania	Riflemen	181
do.	Count de Ottendorf,	do.	Infantry	219
do.	Anthony Post,	New York	Artillery Artificers..	175
do.	Valentine Peyton,	Virginia	Artilley	277
do.	Robert Powell,	do.	Infantry	278
do.	John Peyton,	do.	do.	279
do.	Charles Porterfield,	do.	do.	259
do.	James Pendleton,	do.	Artillery	246
do.	Alex. Parker,	Pennsylvania	Infantry	217
do.	William Pierce,	Virginia	Artillery	242
do.	Adrian Proveaux,	South Carolina	Infantry	290
do.	William Rippey,	Pennsylvania	do.	208
do.	Thomas Robinson,	do.	do.	194
do.	John Reese,	do.	do.	192
do.	George Rice,	Virginia	Artillery	264
do.	Drury Ragsdale,	do.	do.	245
do.	Bernard Romans,	Pennsylvania	do.	178
do.	James Rosecrans,	New York	Infantry	161
do.	Albert Roux,	South Carolina	do.	291
do.	Winthrop Sargeant,	Massachusetts	Artillery	177
do.	George Sylez,	New York	Infantry	168
do.	James Steuart,	do.	Artillery	163
do.	William Scott,	New Hampshire	Infantry	145
do.	Simon Sartwell,	do.	do.	143
do.	William Smith,	Virginia	do.	261
do.	Anthony Singleton,	do.	Artillery	244
do.	Alex. L. Smith,	Maryland	Riflemen	240
do.	Anthony Selins,	Pennsylvania	Infantry	220

CONTENTS.

				PAGE
Captain	Abraham Smith,	Pennsylvania	Infantry	207
do.	Joseph Smith,	Virginia	do.	236
do.	Uriah Springer,	do.	do.	283
do.	William Sanford,	do.	do.	274
do.	John Paul Schott,	Pennsylvania	do.	221
do.	Francis Taylor,	do.	do.	273
do.	Thomas Tebbs,	do.	do.	272
do.	James Taylor,	do.	do.	200
do.	Jeremiah Talbot,	do.	do,	214
do.	Thomas Wills,	Virginia	do.	263
do.	James A. Wilson,	Pennsylvania	do.	210
do.	Robert Wilson,	do.	do.	215
do.	John Wait,	New Hampshire	do.	147
do.	John Winslow,	New York	Artillery	159
do.	Josiah Wool,	do.	do.	175
do.	Samuel Watson,	Pennsylvania	Infantry	183

AMERICAN PRISONERS.

			PAGE
Capture of General Charles Lee			308
do.	do.	Lord Sterling,	306
do.	do.	John Sullivan	308
do.	do.	Benjamin Lincoln	308
do.	do.	William Moultrie	309
do.	do.	James Irvine	309
do.	Colonel Ethan Allen		309
do.	do.	Nicholas Lutz	309
do.	do.	Michael Swope,	310
do.	Major	George Tudor	310
do.	do.	Thomas L. Byles	311
do.	do.	John Poulson	311
do.	Adjt.	John Johnson	311
do.	do.	Daniel Kennedy,	312
do.	Engineer Ferdinand J. S. De Brahm		312
do.	Baron Charles De Frey		312
do.	Captain Henry Bedinger		393
do.	do.	William Crawford	312
do.	do.	John Richardson	312
do.	do.	Bateman Lloyd	313
do.	do.	Robert Sample,	313
do.	do.	Thomas McIntire	313
do.	do.	Robert Caldwell	314
do.	do.	James Moore	314
do.	do.	Matthew Knox	314
do.	do.	Samuel Culbertson	315
do.	do.	John McDonald	315
do.	do.	Alex. Graydon	315
do.	do.	John Stotesbury	316
do.	do.	Robert Patton	316
do.	do.	James Elliott	316
do.	Lieut.	Matthew Bennett	316
do.	do.	Robert Brown	317
do.	do.	Louis J. Costigin	317
do.	do.	Joseph Martin	317

CONTENTS. 10

			PAGE.
Capture of	Lieut.	William Young	317
do.	do.	John V. Hyatt	318
do.	do.	Zachariah Shugart	318
do.	do.	Hezekiah Davis	318
do.	do.	Andrew Robertson	318
do.	do.	John Irwin	319
do.	do.	Thomas Wynn	319
do.	do.	Jonathan Smith	319
do.	do.	Robert Darlington	319
do.	do.	Samuel McClellan	320
do.	do.	Warner Wynn	320
do.	Surgeon David Love		320
do.	Ensign John Thomson		320
Prisoners at Three Rivers			297
do.	Long Island		297
do.	Putnam's Retreat		297
do.	Fort Washington		298
do.	Exchanged by John Adams		320
do.	do.	Abraham Skinner	321

NOTES ON THE SERVICE OF

PAGE.	PAGE.
Capt. Dohickey Arundel.........390	Col. Uriah Forest.............385
Col. George Baylor..............385	Lieut. Henry Field............392
do. Mordecai Buckner.........386	Dr. Corbin Griffin.............389
Capt. Thomas Blackwell........387	Lieut. Robert Green............389
Lieut. Edmund Brooke..........388	do. Thomas Gordon...........392
Capt. George M. Bedinger......389	Surg. David Gould............. 392
do. Peter Bernard.............391	Capt. William E. Godfrey......395
Maj. John Brent..............391	Lieut. Edmund Gamble.... 395
Lieut. Francis T. Brooke... 391	Dr. Francis L. B. Goodwin.....397
Capt. John Blair 391	Rev. David Griffith............396
Ensign William B. Bunting....391	Col. Robert H. Harrison.........385
Lieut. Daniel Bedinger..........391	Lieut. Joseph Hold.............392
do. Isaac Bowman..........395	Capt. William Harrison..... 397
Ensign James Broadus..........396	do. Abraham Hite............398
Capt. Henry Bedinger...........398	Capt. Samuel Jones.............395
Col. William Crawford.........386	Lieut. Samuel Jones............397
do. Richard Campbell.........386	Col. Thomas Knowlton.........387
Dr. William Carter..............388	Com'y Henry King..............395
Capt. Buller Claiborne ... .388	Capt. Reuben Lipscomb.........392
Lieut. Seth Chapin..............389	do. Thomas H. Luckett....... 392
do. Ezra Chapman.... 395	Maj. Daniel Leet 392
Capt. Mayo Carrington.........398	Capt. Jonathan Langdon........392
Rev. John Cordell...............391	do. James Mayson...... 386
Capt. John DeTreville.......... 390	Gen. Hugh Mercer..............386
Maj. Matthew Donovan.........391	Capt. Ambrose Madison........393
Capt. James Davis...............391	do. Joseph Micheaux..........393
Maj. Edmund Dickinson........392	Lieut. Richard Muse............393
Capt. William Davenport.......396	Capt. John Morton 396
do. John Davis.................396	Lieut. John McKinley...........394
Lieut. John Emerson............389	do. Michael McDonald........394

CONTENTS.

	PAGE.		PAGE.
Lieut. James Morton	398	Adjt. Simon Summers	394
Capt. Everard Meade	388	Ensign Clement Sewell	396
Lieut. Richard Nowell	390	Col. John H. Stone	896
Capt. William Nelson	389	Capt. Nehemiah Stokeley	397
do. David Noble	397	Ensign John Spitfathom	398
Col. Richard Parker	386	Capt. John Spottswood	389
do. Charles Porterfield	386	Col. John Thornton	385
Lieut. William Price	388	do. William Taliaferro	387
do. Eli Parsons	390	Lieut. John Taylor	388
Capt. Richard Pendleton	393	Cornett William Teas	388
Surg. Shubell Pratt	393	Surg. Charles Taylor	394
Col. Isaac Reed	387	Capt. Benjamin Timberlake	394
Capt. John Roberts	387	do. Augustus Willett	385
Surg. William Rumney	393	Lieut. Thomas Wallace	389
Capt. Samuel Ranson	397	do. Thomas Wishart	389
Col. Willis Reddick	397	do. John Wilson	394
Capt. Hebard Smallwood	393	do. Charles Yarborough	394

PROMISES AND CONTRACTS OF THE CONTINENTAL CONGRESS.

Land Act of August 14, 1776	401
do. September 16, 1776	403
Half-pay Act May 15, 1778	403
do. November 24, 1778	404
do. May 22, 1779	404
do. August 24, 1780	404
do. October 3, 1780	405
do. do. 21, 1780	405
do. November 28, 1780	405
do. January 17, 1781	406
do. May 8, 1781	406
do. May 26, 1781	406
do. December 31, 1781	406
Commutation Act of March 22, 1783	407
do. May 16, 1783	409
do. January 28, 1784	409
do. February 11, 1784	409
Interest Act of June 3, 1784	410
Commutation Act of March 8, 1785	410
do. August 11, 1790	410
Officers entitled to half-pay	411-438
Remarks on the half-pay acts, &c	439
Court of Claims on half-pay, &c	454
Congress on the half-pay	445
Petitions in 1810 for half-pay	444
Senator Crittenden on the half-pay	449
Senator Seward	451
Chief Justice Gilchrist	458
Baird's heirs vs. United States	454
Wirt's opinion	448-458
Commentaries on the half-pay bill	449

CONTENTS. 12

CINCINNATI SOCIETY.
PAGE.
Description of... 468
Constitution of.. 471
Officers of... 477
Members of the New York Society... 478
    do.   Pennsyvania do. 483
    do.   Maryland   do. 488

VIRGINIA HALF-PAY, LAND, ETC.
Remarks on... 490
Act of Congress, September 13, 1783.. 490
Virginia Bounty Lands.. 494
Act of May 1779.. 494
    do. October 1779... 495
    do.   do.   1780.. 496
    do. May 1782.. 497
    do. October 1782... 497
    do.   do.   1783.. 497
    do.   do.   1784.. 497
Governor's Proclamation.. 498
Officers who received land from Virginia................................... 500
Act of May 1779 (half-pay).. 506
    do. November 1781.. 509
    do. July 5, 1832... 509
Payments per Act of July 5, 1832.. 511

REVOLUTIONARY PENSION LAWS.
Act March 18, 1818... 512
do. May 15, 1828... 514
do. June 7, 1832... 518
do. July 4, 1836... 522
do. July 7, 1838... 523
do. July 29, 1848.. 524
do. February 3, 1853... 525

REVOLUTIONARY OFFICERS.
Extensive list of deaths, with notes....................................... 526
Pensioned Officers... 537
Conclusion... 554

GENERAL INDEX.

Artillery, of N. Y., 19.
Allen, Col. Ethan, 20, 302.
Arnold, Benedict, at Quebec, 22, 28, 76.
Antil, Col., 30.
Ambassdor, French, 38.
Audebert, Philip, 77.
Arrangement of Light Dragoons, 93.
Alexander, William S., 110, 113.
Acres of land, to officers, 494.
Armand, Col., 531.
Armstrong, Gen. John, 531.
Ashe, Gen., 532.

Brig. Gen. Starke, at Bennington, 332.
Brown, Maj., 19, 22.
Boucherville, 28.
Boudinot, Elias, Com. Gen. Pris. 32, 307, 532.
Beatty, John, do. 307.
Brooks, John, Com. of Issues, 307.
Bradford, Thomas, Com. of Pris. 307.
Bradford, William, Com of Musters, 532.
Baldesqui, J. Capt., 32, 33, 34, 36, 38.
Boze, Lieut. Col., killed, 33.
Baldwin, Col. Jeduthan, 45.
Burrall, Jonathan, 46, 47, 51, 53, 55.
Blount, Mr., D. M. P. Gen., 50.
Brook, George, Treasurer of Va. 61.
Boreman, John, D. M. P. Gen. 64.
Bigham, Lieut., 77.
Bevins, Lieut., 77.
Bard, John, Capt., 83.
Brown, William, Capt., 86.
Buchanan, John, Capt., 102, 104.
Burk, William, 139.
Bowdoin, James, 300.
Baskinridge, N. J., 301.
British Prison-ships, 305.
Bland, Col., 532.
Brooks, Col. Eleazer, 532.
Baxter's Flying Camp, 317.

Bullitt, Dept. Adjt. Gen., orders of, 325.
Bennington, Battle of, 332.
Battle of Sept. 19, 1777, 343.
Burgoyne's Surrender, 348.
Broadhead, Col. Daniel, 227.
Boundaries of Mil. Districts, 408.
Brandon, Alex., tried for horse stealing, 329.
Biddle, Clement, appointed Com. of Forage, 381.
"Black Bull," 305.

Caughnawaga Castle, 19.
Chambli, 25, 26.
Campbell, Col., 26, 45, 69.
Crane, Col., John, 30, 135.
Costigin, Lieut. Lewis J., 33.
Carleton, Joseph, Sec. of War, 34.
Coleman, Lieut. Wyatt, 54.
Clay, Joseph, D. P. M. Gen., 56.
Chase, Col., 69.
Clark, Gen. George R., 532.
Corse, Capt. John, 83.
Condy, T. H., 97.
Cadwallader, Col. Lambert, 299.
Cadwallader, Gen. John, 532.
Cornwallis, Lord, 302.
Commissaries of Prisoners, 307.
Chesterfield Arrangement, Va., Line, 384.
Colors of Officers, 325.
Claims against Virginia, 399.
Commutation, officers entitled to, 411, 438.
Constitution of Cincinnati Society, 471.
Cincinnati Society, officers, 477.
Commissions of Va. officers, 288.
Court of Claims, 454.
Continental money, &c., stolen, 359.
Courtlandt, Col., Superintends the sick, 364.
Clinton, Gen. James, 533.

Dugan, Capt. Thomas, 23, 24, 85.
Drury, Capt. Jotham, 30.

GENERAL INDEX. 14

DeKalb, Baron, 64, 65, 101, 105, 529.
Dobb's Ferry, 76.
Dirkes, Col., 82.
De Pontiere, Lewis, 83.
D'Estiang, Count, 295.
De Heister, Gen., 297.
Depreciation, Maryland list, 232.
Dates of Va. Commissions, 288.
Discharged men of Stevens' Artillery, 151.
Discharged men of Gansevoort's Regiment, 168.
Elmore, Major, 19, 24, 26.
Easton, Col., 21, 28.
Elliott, Mrs., 295.
Elizabethtown, prisoners at, 320.
Events in the lives of Officers, 526.

Frazer, Gen., slain, 348.
Fossett, Capt., 24.
Freeman, Capt. Lieut., 30.
Fanning, Charles, Lieut., 48.
Fitzhugh, Perrigrine, Cornet, 82.
Flowers, Philip, 138.
Finley, Capt. Ebenezer, 141.
Fort Washington, 241, 298.
Foreign Officers, 478.
Flying Camp, 237.
Ford, Lieut., appointed Adjt. to Lamb's Regiment, 356.

Gates, Gen. Horatio, 31.
Graham, Col., 44.
Green Gen. Nathaniel. 82, 93.
Godly, George, Wag. Master, 88.
Gilliland, James, Capt.
Green's Orders, 341.
Germantown, Battle of, 345.
German Regiment, Md., 237.
Green, William, Captain. 325.
Gansevoort, Colonel, Peter, 533.
Gibson, Colonel John, 533.
Gibson, Colonel George, 533.

Hinman, Colonel, 17, 18.
Holmes, Colonel James, 28, 29.
Heath, Gen. William, 44, 50, 51, 530.
Hill, Major, 44.
Henderson, Mr. Paymaster, 49.
Harrison, Benjamin, D. P. M. Gen. 50, 58.
Hodgdon, Samuel, Q. M. Gen., 51.
Hand, Brigadier-general, 52.
Hillegas, Mr., 68.

Hall, Colonel David, 83.
Harrison, Col. Charles and Staff, 86, 241.
Hay, Col. Udny, A. Q. M. Gen., 95.
Hughes, John, Lieutenant, 97.
Hazen, General Moses, 118.
Hawes, Colonel Samuel, 138.
Horry, Major, 295.
Howe, Sir William, 302.
Howe, Lord George, 303.
Harcourt, Colonel John, 306.
Howard, Colonel John E. 533.
Howercraft, Sergeant, tent of, 373.
Halletts, Independent Co., 330.
Hull, Capt., tried for gaming, 351.
Hubley, Colonel, tried, 382
Huntington, Gen. Jedediah, 533.

Irvine, General William, 536.
Isle-aux Noix, 17.

Johnson, Colonel Francis, 534.
Jackson, Colonel James, 533.
Jagur, Sergeant, 30.
Jay, John, President, 33.
Johnston, James, Auditor, 34.
James, Colonel, 92.
Jasper, William, Sergeant, 295.

Knox, General, 142, 528.
Kelly, Timothy, 325.
King's Creek, 325.
Kennebec Expedition, 20.
  do. River, 27.
Kennon, Mr., Paymaster, 87.
Kilpatrick, George, trial of, 331.
Keene, Lawrence, appointed A. D. C., 371.

Land Warrants unlocated, 500.
La Prairie, 17, 19, 21, 23.
Livingston, James, Col. 20, 28, 24, 108.
Longueille, 23.
La Come, St. Luke, 28.
Lake George, 28, 29.
Lamb, Colonel John, 30.
Long Island, tories, 31.
Lafayette, Marquis, 31, 529.
Lenox, 32.
Lincoln, General, 47, 83.
Lyman, James, 47.
Lawrence, John, Treas. of Com. 67.
Livingston, Col. Henry B., 99.
Lewis, Brig. Gen., Orders of, 324.

GENERAL INDEX.

Lee, Gen. Charles, Orders of, 325.
Lacy, General John, 534.
Lee, Colonel Henry, 534.
Legislature of Virginia, Cession of Lands, 494.
Lutterloth, Henry E., appointed D. Q. M. G., 381.
Ludeman, Lieutenant, 83.
Laurens, Colonel John, 83.

Montgomery, General Richard, Proclamation, 26.
McPherson, aid-de-camp, 20, 22.
Montreal, 21, 22.
Motte, Colonel, 25, 26.
Mansfield, Captain, 30.
Moylan, Colonel Stephen, 49, 52.
McDougall, General, 49, 529.
Mifflin, General, 70, 581.
Machin, Thomas, 71, 72.
Mohawk River, 73.
McMordle, Rev. Robert, 79.
Morris, Colonel Lewis, 82.
Muhlenberg, Gen. Peter, 90, 91, 534.
McRoberts, Mr., F. C. M. S., 92.
Mytinger, Jacob, Captain, 96.
Marshall, Lieut. Benjamin, 97.
McLane, Major Allen, 101.
Marbury, Joseph, Captain, 102, 105.
Magill, Charles, Colonel, 105.
Moodie, Andrew, Captain, 107.
Motte, Captain Gershom, 107.
Magaw's Regiment, 139.
McClure, Captain James, 141.
Martyrs, Imprisoned, 306.
McAllister's Flying Camp, 317.
Montgomery's Flying Camp, 318.
March through Philadelphia, 334.
Monmouth, Battle of, 383.
Military Land District, Ohio, Kentucky, and Tennessee, 490.
Mifflin, Jon., appointed D. Q. M. G., 381.
Mederas, Captain, tried for forgery, 359.
"Mittens," stolen, 373.
Moultrie, General, 527.
Meigs, Colonel R. J., 534.
Morgan, Colonel Daniel, 534.
Marion, General Francis, 536.

Nourse, Joseph, Asst. Aud. Gen. 45.
New York, Prisoners, 321.

Nash, General, burial of, 346.
Nagle, Colonel, Tea Party, 373.
Nixon, Colonel, family abused, 352.

Ogden, Colonel Matthias, 33.
Ottendorf, Major, 108.
Orendorf, Christian, Lieut., 137.
Officers died in service, 411, 438.
Officers, foreign, 437.
Order of march to Swedes' Ford, 342.

Parsons, Gen. Samuel H., 534.
Phelps, Noah, Col., Bedel's Commissary, 21, 23, 24, 25.
Prescott, General, 28.
Peters, Richard, Secretary of War, 30, 32.
Pulaski, General, 32, 37, 56, 535.
Palfrey, Col. William, 38, 39, 40, 47, 50, 54, 56.
Pickering, Col. Timothy, 71, 84, 534.
Pryor, Major J., 89.
Pepin, Lieutenant, 103.
Putnam, General, 111, 530.
Procter's Artillery, 141.
Petition of Revolutionary Martyrs, 306.
Prisoners of Cadwallader's Reg't 310.
Pay-table of Revolutionary Army, 376, 378.
Prisoners taken by Col. Brown, 343.
Powell, Wm., tried, 383.

Queen's Creek, 325.

Rangers, New Hampshire, 17.
River Onion, mouth of, 17, 18.
Robinson's House, 22.
River Sorel, 28.
Redman, Capt., tried, 383.
Reed, Thomas, A. P. M. Gen., 43, 51
Regnier, Col., 44, 100.
Ramsey, Nathaniel, Col., 82.
Roxburg, Capt., 106.
Russell, Thomas C., 111, 113.
Rahl, Col., 302.
Roe, Gally, 325.
Russell, Wm., Wag. Mr. Gen. 325.
Roe, Jesse, Capt., trial of, 329.
Recruiting in Pennsylvania, 225.
Regiments of Maryland, 234.
Report on Virginia lands, 490.
Regulations for guard, 286.

GENERAL INDEX.

Schuyler, Gen., 17, 28, 530.
Shepherd, Lieut., 19.
Smith, Capt., 19.
Sackett, Capt., 44.
Smith, Lieut. Larkin, 52.
Scott, Gen., 54, 58.
Schott, Capt., 63.
Stelle, Mr., D. P. M. Gen., 82.
Spencer, Wm., Ensign, 83.
Steuben, Baron, 89, 530.
Swift, Gen., 94.
Stewart, Col., 98.
Smallwood, Gen., 106, 535.
Stirling, Lord, 142, 529.
Swope's Flying-Camp, 315.
Supernumerary Officers, 384.
Spy hanged, 368.
Society of Cincinnati, 468.
Soldiers tried for mutiny, 391.
Schuylkill riot, 350.
Stray Horses, 350.
Shanks, Thomas, a spy hanged, 367.
St. Clair, Gen., 528.
Spencer, Gen., 530.
Starke, Gen., 531.

Thomas, Gen. John, 529.
Tinnis' House, 347.
Ticonderoga, 22.
Troup, Col. Robert, 31, 38.
Travers, Capt., 38.
Tucker, Joseph, P. M., 44.
Tupper, Col. Benjamin, 52.
Towles, Col. Oliver, 52, 138.
Trumbull, Jonathan, P. M. Gen., 53.

Turberville, John, 107.
Tudor, Col. William, 136.
Tariff of exchange, prisoners, 304.
Thorndike vs. United States, 457.
Treaty of Hopewell, 499.

Van Renssalaer, James, 27.
Valley Forge, last days at, 378.
Van Schaick, Colonel Goosse, 535.
Varick Col., Richard, 536.
Varnum, General, 536.

Warner, Colonel Seth, 19, 27.
Wooster, Gen. David, 26, 28, 530.
Waterbury, General David, 31.
Williams, Captain, 46.
Woolford, General, 46.
White, Moses, P. M., 48.
Washington, Gen., 51, 136, 526.
Washington, Col. William, 136, 535.
Washington, Gen., orders of, 324, 383.
Woodson, Tarleton, Major, 137.
Watts' Flying Camp, 319.
Weedon, Gen. George, orders of, 341.
Wilcox, Edward, Quartermaster, trial of, 331.
White Clay Creek, 339.
Washington's clock work, 346.
Wayne, General, trial of, 347, 535.
Walker, James, deserts his wagon, 361.
Webb, Lieutenant, tried, 368.
Williams, General O. H., 535.
Willett, Colonel Marinus, 535.

PART I.

CORRESPONDENCE
OF
DISTINGUISHED OFFICERS
OF THE
REVOLUTIONARY WAR,
COMMENCING IN 1775.

SHOWING THE DIFFERENT LOCATIONS AND MOVEMENTS OF THE ARMY, AND THE FINANCIAL CONDITION OF THE COUNTRY IN 1780.

TICONDEROGA, August 19, 1775.

SIR:—I request you will cause the three companies of New Hampshire Rangers under your command to march with all dispatch to the mouth of Onion River, taking care to give the General such timely notice as may enable him to furnish them with provisions and boats, and such further orders as he may judge expedient. I am, sir, your most humble servant,

RICHARD MONTGOMERY, Brig'r Gen'l.

COL. BEDEL,
Of the New Hampshire forces.

TICONDEROGA, August 31, 1775.

SIR:—This will be delivered you by an officer of Col. Hinman's regiment, together with a boat, which I hope will be sufficient to carry you and his parties to Isle-aux-Noix, where you will join me without delay. Should the boat be insufficient to carry all the men, you will try to procure craft there; and if none are to be had, you will send a few men to this place to the commanding officer, acquainting him with what number of men may be left, that he may dispatch boats to you for their transportation. I am, sir, your humble servant,

PH. SCHUYLER.

COL. BEDEL, Onion River.

TICONDEROGA, Sept. 16, 1775.

SIR:—I received yours of the 14th, informing me of your arrival at the Onion River with a number of men; also of the insufficiency of the boats, and your request for more from this place.

I am obliged to inform you that it is not in my power at present to send them, as the whole of the boats went on from thence this day. Notwithstanding I do all in my power to furnish boats to forward the men as they come to hand, there are now about five or six companies lying here and a number at Fort George. How the General expects me to forward the troops I know not. I should think best to send down to the army for boats, and some craft for provisions; otherwise I think the army must retreat for want. unless we send provisions instead of men.

I am, sir, your obedient servant,

BENJAMIN HINMAN.

COL. BEDEL, at Onion, or elsewhere, on Lake Champlain.

CAMP NEAR ST. JOHNS, Sept. 19, 1775.

SIR:—I have this instant received yours. The party is now preparing to carry you some flour and intrenching tools. Young troops are not so expeditious as could be wished. I will send the money by the commanding officer. Somebody must be employed to act as commissary to purchase provisions. As far as my money will go, they shall be paid directly. If the Paymaster does not join us before that happens, they must give us credit, for I have but little. Have you a party at La Prairie?

In haste, your most obedient servant,

RICHARD MONTGOMERY, Brig'r Gen'l.

COL. BEDEL, northward of St. John.

CAMP NEAR ST. JOHNS, Sept. 20, 1775.

SIR:—I have the pleasure to acquaint you of the arrival of the New York Artillery Company, and every instant I look for a considerable reinforcement of other troops. The paymaster-general has also arrived, with cash.

Be so good as to send off a trusty Indian or Canadian to the Caughnawaga Castle with the string of wampum (which the bearer will deliver to you) and the following message:

"Brethren, when I had the pleasure of seeing your chiefs, in my camp near St. Johns, after our treaty of friendship and neutrality was concluded, I told them there was a present from the twelve United Colonies for the Caughnawaga tribes, consisting of £400, York money; but that my treasurer was not arrived with the money; that I expected him soon, and promised to let you know when he came. Conformable to my promise, I take the first opportunity of acquainting you that the money is ready, and I desire to know when you will come to receive it."

You have, I suppose, appointed a trusty Commissary. He must keep his accounts with the utmost exactness, and be upon his oath, as every ration of provisions must be accounted for.

Should Colonel Warner want a little cash for his people, I can now give it to him.

I hope there is the strictest discipline kept up, that our friends may have no reason to complain of us.

I make no doubt that you have a good lookout towards La Prairie. Should regular troops venture into those roads, I think your woodmen will give a good account of them. Should you have any accounts of their bringing artillery with them, it will be necessary to fell timber across the roads.

Tell Major Elmore that I desire Lieutenant Sheppard, who acted as officer of marines on board of one of the vessels, may come this day to our camp—he being wanted here as an evidence with respect to Captain Smith.

I would wish to see Major Brown, if he can be spared for a few days.

I have taken your corned beef, which you shall be reimbursed for, with thanks. I wish for a return of the people under your command, particularly Major Brown's party, as, perhaps, there may be some missing.

I am, sir, your obedient servant,
RICHARD MONTGOMERY.

Col. BEDEL, north side St. Johns.

CAMP SOUTH SIDE ST. JOHNS, Sept. 24, 1775.

SIR :—It is impossible to send you a *marqué*. Perhaps by applying to some of the regiments you are acquainted with you may get one.

Mr. Fink will deliver you twenty half Johanneses, amounting to sixty-four pounds seven shillings, for which he has given his receipt. By the General's order,

JOHN MACPHERSON, Aid-de-Camp.

Col. BEDEL, north side St. Johns.

CAMP SOUTH SIDE ST. JOHNS, Sept. 25, 1775.

SIR :—I send to acquaint you that the garrison have a considerable party bringing timber out of the woods not far from your advanced guard. We judge they are preparing to lay the ways for a vessel ready to be launched. Pray, don't let them carry on this work undisturbed. Their covering parties are regulars, I think. I have information from a prisoner, who was taken attempting to go into the fort on your side, that he carried verbal orders for the garrison to attempt an escape to Quebec. For God's sake, have an eye over them, and send an express to Allen, if he be not yet arrived. It might prevent the success of the Kennebec expedition, should this garrison get down safe.

We have a battery of two twelve-pounders just ready to play on the ship-yards with hot shot. Our mortar-battery will be ready before night.

I have just received yours by Mr. Livingston. I approve exceedingly of your plan, if it can be done without risk of weakening your present post, which might facilitate the escape of the garrison. If you go to Montreal, pay the utmost attention to good order. I am, sir, with earnest wishes for your success,

      Your obedient servant,

           RICHARD MONTGOMERY.
Col. BEDEL.

      CAMP NEAR ST. JOHNS, Sept. 28, 1775.

SIR:—I have just been favored with yours. You do not tell me how many men you have. I should imagine you were sufficiently strong. However, I send you to-morrow, according to your desire, Easton's regiment. I shall send you money by that opportunity. You have nothing to do but send for money when you want it. This I have told you before.

I don't know which is the oldest officer, you or Colonel Easton Should he be the eldest, you will impart to him all such instructions as you have received. I would wish you to keep a good officer and party on the other side, to watch the garrison when they attempt to retire. It is much more probable they will march on that side than on yours, where the difficulties to encounter are much greater.

    I am, sir, your obedient servant,

          RICHARD MONTGOMERY.
Col. BEDEL, north side St. Johns.

      CAMP NEAR ST. JOHNS, Sept. 29, 1775.

SIR:—The young gentleman who brought up the rum to your post some days since, promised to get a quantity of necessaries for our men. When he arrives, or if they can be gotten at La Prairie, those who are absolutely in want of them must have them; but it must be on credit for some time, or for Continental money, as the hard money must be kept to pay for provisions.

You will please order your detached parties to send in their accounts soon, that I may see how money is laid out, for I think it goes away fast. Cannot Mr. Phelps discharge the contractor's business at all the posts, that I may have accounts on this head only with one person?

I must observe to you that I understood from you, at Ticonderoga, that your men were completely equipped for the field. I do not know what footing the troops of your province are on. I shall, therefore, be obliged to make a charge against New Hampshire for any money advanced to them, till I shall have received instructions from the Continental Congress.

If there are any stores still remaining of those taken by Major Brown let me have a return of them, that I may give orders for their distribution.

I am, sir, with anxious wishes for your success,
Your most obedient servant,
RICHARD MONTGOMERY.

Col. BEDEL, north side St. Johns.

(ENDORSED.)

The Canadians complain that your Commissary treats them roughly. The General desires that they may be kindly treated, and those employed supplied with provisions.

JOHN MACPHERSON, Aid-de-Camp.

CAMP NEAR ST. JOHNS, Oct. 2, 1775.

SIR :—Last night I received yours. The cannon shall be ready this evening, if you will send a party for them to go down in the boat, as also the ammunition. They may go down with the greatest safety from the enemy. We had a whale-boat with a few men landed the other night at Mr. Robinson's house, and brought away the glass-doors—a proof that they had no look out on the water.

The mutiny of the Canadians I treat as a joke, nor do I see how two pieces of cannon should change their minds, if it were so. I wait for a large mortar and a considerable reinforcement, to take post on a hill to the westward, with most of my artillery, in order to destroy their defences and make my approaches. The troops must now be on their way.

The report of Arnold's arrival in Quebec seems to gain ground. I think it extremely probable. I imagine it will throw a damp on the people of Montreal.

Let a small party, if possible, be kept at Longueille. Do send me a keg or two of wine.

     I am, sir, your obedient servant,
          RICHARD MONTGOMERY.
Col. BEDEL, north side St. Johns.

      CAMP SOUTH SIDE ST. Johns, Oct. 4, 1775.

SIR:—To the best of my recollection, I have already answered you on the subject of provision for the Canadians. Those who are our friends must certainly be supported. Any guns you can purchase you will deliver to such Canadians as may be depended upon, taking a receipt for the delivery of them. It will be necessary to be upon your guard against imposition, otherwise a man may sell you his own gun and obtain it from you again by the intervention of a friend. You must therefore consult Captain Dugan or Mr. Livingston, or some other person acquainted with the parties concerned. You may send the sick you mention when you please. I wish you would send some rum and some wine for the sick. The expedition against the schooner did not succeed. I hope you got the boat our people let go down the rapids.

     I am, sir, your most obedient servant,
          RICHARD MONTGOMERY.
Col. BEDEL, north side St. Johns.

         LA PRAIRIE, Oct. 4, 1775.

SIR:—After due regards, I have found but one hogshead of rum at this place for sale, which costs *four livres* per gallon by the hogshead, which is the highest price I ever gave for rum in my life; but knowing the necessity of the army, I have bought the same. You know that I had no money when I left your camp—I am stayed as a pledge for the same. Please to let the General know it, and send me me some money by some good man, as I may never go off the ground until I pay for the same. Also army there want some supplies, and our camp will soon want. I am going to Longueille to buy some more rum, if I can find it. I shall be glad of haste in this affair, and you will oblige,   Your humble servant at command,
          NOAH PHELPS.
Col. BEDEL.

AT MR. HAZEN'S, OPPOSITE ST. JOHNS, }
October 5, 1775.

DEAR SIR :—Just now arrived here a small reinforcement of Canadians, but no provisions. Flour we can make but little use of here; and if we mean to open an intrenchment here, it will require twenty men at least to furnish us with bread, rum, &c., constantly. The Canadians are far from being content, and unless they can be supplied with provisions they will drop off by degrees, and all my art will not prevail to make them stay. I beg you will pay attention to this and endeavor to furnish us with beef, bread, &c.

You must be sensible it would be a dishonor to me to begin an intrenchment, battery, &c., and be obliged to quit it for want of provisions. Major Elmore promised me some camp-kettles, but has not been as good as his word. We have only two in the camp, and beg you will send us five or six, and you will oblige

Your most obedient servant,

JAMES LIVINGSTON.

Col. BEDEL, below the rapids, St. Johns.

CAMP SOUTH SIDE ST. JOHNS, Oct. 5, 1775.

SIR :—I send you by Captain Fossett £212 17s. 1d., York money. You will pay for what shoes and stockings I have not paid for (I paid for those purchased by Thomas Dugan), and furnish Mr. Phelps with whatever money may be wanting. As for the £60 you desire, I must tell you hard cash is very scarce, and I would therefore, be glad if you could defer giving your men any money. If they must have necessaries, supply them as sparingly as possible, until we get more cash ; for if we have not ready money to pay for provisions, we shall be ill supplied. Take what you want on credit, if you can. I am surprised to hear the rum is expended. There was a great deal bought. I am afraid it is used too freely a great deal. Our situation absolutely requires it, but I must confess I am uneasy at such an expenditure. You have not sent any wine for the sick or the officers here.

I am, sir, your most obedient servant,

RICHARD MONTGOMERY.

Col. BEDEL, north side St. Johns.

OF THE REVOLUTIONARY WAR.   25

CAMP SOUTH SIDE ST. JOHNS, Oct. 13, 1775.

SIR:—I have been just favored with yours, inclosing your returns, &c. I have great pleasure in telling you that your orders are those of an officer of experience and attention to his duty. It is not your fault, I believe, that you have been frequently obliged to repeat them. But I must again observe that in your letter of the 6th inst. you have confessed that "several officers have refused giving an account of stores taken from the enemy. Those officers you should certainly have brought to justice. Your Commissary has also palpably disobeyed your order of the 26th September, where you forbid him to draw wine on any order but that of the commanding officer or doctor. It is to little purpose to give orders if offenders are not called to account. The ignorance of the common soldier may sometimes excite mercy, but the officer cannot plead in the same manner, and I am therefore of opinion you should begin with him. The Commissary *must* be answerable for a great part of the wine to the public. It has not been disposed of according to your orders or my intentions.

Be so good as to have the guard re-established at Chambli. It has not been taken away by my orders, as I recollect.

I am, sir, your most obedient servant,

RICHARD MONTGOMERY.

Col. BEDEL, north side St. Johns.

CAMP SOUTH SIDE ST. JOHNS, Oct. 26, 1775.

SIR:—I have this instant been favored with yours, and am pleased to hear the nine-pounder and royals are arrived at your post, with the gin. Have you a place to land the cannon? Let them be mounted, if you think they can be drawn to the battery on their own carriages. If that is thought difficult, a large sled must be made for that purpose, and the cannon must be drawn on the sled to the battery and there mounted. Consult Col. Mott on this matter. I shall send almost everybody from hence to your post. Indeed, I shall go myself. Mr. Phelps must be informed our numbers to be victualled at your post will be doubled at least. Some go to-day. Send some trusty Cana-

dians to take down two twelve-pounders this night. I would
not choose to begin our works until we are well able to maintain them. You know the distance is small, and no obstacle in
the way. The garrison can be with us in fifteen minutes. Let
there be plenty of fascines, plank for platforms, and sleepers. In
short, let Col. Mott take care that nothing is wanting. Tomorrow I hope to send a considerable corps of troops. Let Col.
Campbell's stores remain at your post till further orders. I
agree with you it will be expedient to disturb the enemy when
we begin.

If the works our people raised against Chambli be not already destroyed, it should be done immediately. Write to the
Commandant.

      I am, sir, your obedient servant,
          RICHARD MONTGOMERY.
Col. BEDEL, north side St. Johns.

     CAMP SOUTH SIDE ST. JOHNS, Oct. 27, 1775.

SIR :—I think it exceedingly necessary that General Wooster
should be accommodated with a house. You will, therefore be
so good as to have one got ready for him. I am told that which
Major Elmore occupies is the most suitable. Should any repairs be found necessary, do let them be done immediately, as
the General will be there to-day.

     I am, sir, your most obedient servant,
         RICHARD MONTGOMERY.
Col. BEDEL, north side St. Johns.

GENERAL MONTGOMERY'S PROCLAMATION.

          November 15, 1775.

The General embraces this happy occasion of making his acknowledgment to the troops for their patience and perseverance
during the course of a fatiguing campaign. They merited the
applause of their grateful countrymen. He is now ready to fulfil the engagements of the public. Passes, together with boats
and provisions, shall be furnished upon application, from the

commanding officers of regiments, for such as choose to return home, yet he entreats the troops not to lay him under the necessity of abandoning Canada; of undoing in one day what has been the work of months; of restoring to an enraged, and hitherto disappointed enemy, the means of carrying on a cruel war into the very bowels of their country. Impressed with a just sense of the spirit of the troops; their attachment to the interests of the United Colonies; and of their regard to their own honor, he flatters himself that none will leave him at this critical juncture but such whose affairs or health absolutely require their return home.

He has still hopes, notwithstanding the advanced season of the year, should he be seconded by the generous valor of the troops, hitherto highly favored by Providence, to reduce Quebec, in conjunction with the troops which have penetrated by the Kennebec River, and hereby deprive the ministerial army of all their footing in this important province.

Those who engage in this honorable cause shall be furnished completely with every article of clothing requisite for the rigor of the climate, blanket-coats, coats, waistcoat and breeches, one pair of stockings, two shirts, leggins, sacks, shoes, mittens, and a cap, at the Continental charge, and one dollar bounty. The troops are only requested to engage to the 15th of April. They shall be discharged sooner if the expected reinforcement arrives before that time.

JAMES VAN RENSSELAER, Aide-de-Camp.

MONTREAL, NOV. 16, 1775.

SIR:—You will proceed down the river with Lieutenant-colonel Warner's regiment and your own corps, keeping as close to the enemy as an attention to the safety of the troops under your command will admit of. The circumstances and situation of things must point out how you are to act. I have it much at heart to harass the enemy in their retreat, and if possible to get possession of any or all their vessels, especially that with the powder. All public stores, except ammunition and provisions, shall be given to the troops who take them. Above all, I am anxious to secure the persons of the Governor and General Prescott, and also to release Mr. Walker, and any other prisoners who may be on board.

Should the enemy be so fortunate as to pass the Sorel, you will attend them at a convenient distance until you join Colonel Arnold, if that can be done. I shall follow with the artillery and main body of the army as fast as possible.

If the enemy be passed the Sorel, Colonel Easton will embark his artillery and proceed along with you. I furnish you with cash for provisions, etc., for the use of the troops under your command.

Your most obedient servant,
RICHARD MONTGOMERY.

HEAD-QUARTERS, MONTREAL, December 4, 1775.

SIR:—I am informed that St. Luke La Come is exceedingly ill, not able to cross the lake, therefore you will permit him to return to Boucherville.

I am, sir, your most obedient humble servant,
DAVID WOOSTER, Brig. Gen.

Col. BEDEL.

TICONDEROGA, December 16, 1775.

SIR:—When General Schuyler left this post he gave me the following instruction—"If the prisoners from St. Johns should not be able to reach this place by water, you will send to them to come on by land, leaving the baggage, with an inventory thereof, with the commanding officer at that post, to be forwarded as soon as it can." The above instruction related to the prisoners that have been already sent forward. To pursue the same method with those under your command, is as proper a mode as any I can recommend. Lake George is passable with boats. They are at present employed for important purposes.

The committee from Congress left this post the first instant. I shall afford you all the assistance in my power, consistent with orders from General Schuyler.

I am, sir, your very humble servant,

Col. TIMOTHY BEDEL.   JAMES HOLMES, Col. and Com.

TICONDEROGA, December 18, 1775.

SIR:—The batteaux are detained for the purpose of carrying the prisoners across Lake George, agreeable to your request; and other important business is omitted, which I have the General's express commands to prosecute, if you intend to tread the path the General has chalked out.

Please to make all dispatch possible, otherwise I cannot detain the boats, as I shall be answerable for disobeying the General's orders: not only so, the boats will be frozen in. Your answer is earnestly requested.

I am, sir, your very humble Servant,
JAMES HOLMES,
Col. commanding at this point.

Col. TIMOTHY BEDEL, at Crown Point.
(By John Row, a Sergeant.)

TICONDEROGA, Dec. 20, 1775.

SIR:—Yours of the 18th instant I received yesterday afternoon. The person who brought it tired his horse, is the reason why it came so late to hand. Three horse-sleds are all that are in my power. The roads are so bad that it is impossible for them to come till the lake is frozen over, that they can come on the ice.

I am, sir, your humble servant,
JAMES HOLMES.

Col. BEDEL, at Crown Point.

WAR OFFICE, BALTIMORE, Feb. 24, 1777.

SIR:—Congress having received intelligence of the enemy's being reinforced in New Jersey very coniderably, it becomes absolutely necessary, both for the preservation of the army under General Washington, and to check the progress of our cruel and remorseless invaders, that he be joined immediately by all the forces which can possibly be procured. You have the resolve of Congress on that head, inclosed by direction of the Board of War, with which they request you will instantly comply, by sending all the men raised in your regiment. Let them bring what arms, blankets, and clothes they have or can by any means obtain, and the deficiency will be supplied at Philadelphia or Head-quarters. Let nothing delay your immediate march, either by companies or parts of companies, as you can get them together, as the safety of our country much depends on the exertions of its army at this trying period; and it is hoped no care or pains of yours will be wanting, when all we hold dear and valuable demand them.

I have the honor to be your very humble servant,

Lieut. Col. ANTILL, RICHARD PETERS, Secretary.

BOSTON, April 27, 1777.

SIR:—I received your letter dated the 6th, which came to hand on the 20th, requesting a return of the company under my command, to which, sir, I send the same inclosed. I have enlisted ten men at Boston, which you will see in the return, who have gone to Peekskill and received their States' bounty. Colonel Crane says he will exchange them for men his officers enlisted at Gorsey and York, as soon as his arrival at camp. I think it likely I can enlist a considerable number more of men if I am furnished with money. I have received but six hundred dollars, and have borrowed one hundred and thirty since. My officers have received no money for recruiting. I let Captain-lieutenant Freeman have two hundred dollars of my recruiting money at Morristown, which makes me two hundred and twenty dollars out of my own money for recruiting.

I have sent Mr. Jagur, one of my sergeants, with this return, and if you think proper I should tarry any longer on the recruiting business, send me your orders and four or five hundred dollars by him, and his receipt shall make me answerable for the money.

I have not known of any appointment of one first-lieutenant and one second-lieutenant. Your appointment of them will satisfy me.

Captain Mansfield sends his compliments to you, and has not time to write, as the bearer is waiting. The clothing is almost ready, and he expects to march on Friday. If you can purchase any flannel for waistcoats it would be better, for we can't get but one hundred.

Sir, I am your humble servant,

JOTHAM DRURY, Capt. of Artillery.

Col. JOHN LAMB, N. Y. Artillery.

STANFORD, August 25, 1777.

GENTLEMEN:—It may be remembered that I sent the expense of my raising a regiment of men to go to Long Island to disarm the tories by order of Congress, and at the same time I desired you, gentlemen, to let me know if there would be any wages allowed to the men that were raised for that purpose after engaged, until discharged by Congress; and Mr. Davenport told me it was your minds for me to send the pay bounty in, and you would consider the same as you should find it right. I have collected the pay-rolls in as good order as I could from the several captains, and have made out a regimental pay-roll from the same, and send both for your consideration. The time was but short they stood engaged; but the temper of soldiers is to not lose any time, and they are often troubling me about their pay for that service, so I should like it as a favor if you would let me know, as soon as you conveniently can, whether you allow any thing or not. I thought it would not be worth while for me to come to Hartford, as you, gentlemen, could consider it as well without me as with me; and it would be some expense and trouble to come to Hartford; and as for my own part, I want nothing for my time nor trouble while I was engaged.

I am, gentlemen, your most obedient servant,
DAVID WATERBURY, Jr.

Continental Commissioners at }
Hartford, Conn.　　　　　　 }

ALBANY, Feb. 23, 1778.

DEAR COLONEL:—The Marquis de La Fayette, who is appointed to command an expedition into Canada, has something of importance to communicate to you, which he cannot do without seeing you. I am therefore in his name to request you would repair to Albany with all expedition, that the public business may not suffer by any delay.

I am, dear colonel, your humble servant,
ROBERT TROUP,
Aid-de-Camp to Major-general Gates.

COL. BEDE, commanding at Coos. }
　(By express)　　　　　　　　}

CAMP, VALLEY FORGE, April 15, 1778.

Sir:—Having had a personal interview with Capt. Lenox, you may depend on his being among the first of those who are hereafter exchanged. I ought to have announced your exchange to you long ago, as it has taken place ever since January last, but my attention has been so taken up with the greater distresses our unhappy prisoners, that it slipped my memory, except putting it in general orders.

The inclosed will be the most convincing evidence of the transaction, on which I heartily congratulate you.

I am, sir, your very humble servant,

ELIAS BOUDINOT, Com. Gen. Prisoners.

Capt. ALEXANDER GRAYDON,
3d Pa. Reg't.

WAR OFFICE, November 9, 1778.

GENTLEMEN:—Capt. Baldesqui, Paymaster to Pulaski's Legion, is very necessary to the General in carrying on the detail of his corps. He has written very pressingly for Capt. Baldesqui's joining him; but this cannot be done, as he is waiting for the settlement of his accounts, which have been presented to you for that purpose.

You will see by the resolves of Congress for raising this corps, what articles Gen. Pulaski was to find at a stipulated price. His Legion was received by order of Congress, and in general these articles had been provided. If there are any papers in our possession which will be necessary for your information, they shall be sent to you; and I am to request that, if not inconsistent with your other engagements, you will be pleased to dispatch Capt. Baldesqui, who now makes a demand for another advance, which the Board do not think it right to recommend until they are satisfied by your certificate of the expenditure of the sums already received. Gen. Pulaski says it was impossible for him, from the rapid rise of prices, to comply with his engagements to Congress; and therefore provided the articles enumerated at the current prices, and agreeably to this the accounts are made out. You will judge of the propriety of this.

I am, with great respect, your obedient servant,

Commissioners of Accounts.　　　　　　　　RICHARD PETERS.

ELIZABETHTOWN, Dec. 20, 1778.

SIR :—Mr. Lewis Johnston Costigin, of the city of New Brunswick, N. J., was appointed a first-lieutenant in the first regiment of Jersey, in the year 1775, and served in said regiment until the new arrangement for the eighty-eight battalions, when he was again continued as first-lieutenant, and taken prisoner and remained so for upwards of two years, in which time he was left out in the new arrangement of the army. And I likewise certify that he has not drawn either pay or rations in the first Jersey regiment from his last appointment, from the 13th day of November, 1776, to the 18th day of December, 1778, inclusive; as witness,

MATHIAS OGDEN, Col. 1st N. J. Reg't.

[No Address.]

PHILADELPHIA, Jan. 31, 1779.

SIR :—You will receive, herewith inclosed, a copy of an act of Congress of the 30th inst., directing the Paymaster of the Board of War to transmit to you a certain sum of money for the current expenses of the army.

I am, sir, your most obedient servant,

JOHN JAY, President.

COL. WM. PALFREY.

YORKTOWN, March 27, 1779.

GENTLEMEN :—By a resolve of Congress, I am ordered to South Carolina with my Legion, and to leave Capt. Baldesqui, Paymaster of the Corps, to settle my accounts with you concerning said corps. Some receipts were lost in the hands of Lieutenant-colonel Boze, who has been killed at Egg Harbor; but I hope that will make no great difficulties, being persuaded you do depend enough on my honor to pass over such matter. I hope also you will be kind enough to dispatch Capt. Baldesqui as soon as you possibly can, and I will remain, with much gratitude and esteem.

Your most obedient and very humble servant,

C. PULASKI, General.

To the Gentlemen Auditors of the
Army, Esquires, at Camp.

WAR OFFICE, April 19, 1778.

SIR :—At the request of Capt. Baldesqui, I now inclose for your inspection a copy of the payments made to Count Pulaski and himself, for the pay and other expenses of the Legion, amounting to 183,500 dollars; the charges in the abstract will show the purposes for which the sums respectively were advanced. The last sum of 35,000 dollars was paid only a few days ago to General Pulaski for the recruiting services of his Legion. It will therefore be out of the power of Capt. Baldesqui to account at present for the above sum, he having had no returns from the General that show how it has been expended. I am, gentlemen, your obedient servant,

Auditors of Accounts. JOSEPH CARLETON, Secretary.

PHILADELPHIA, May 15, 1779.

GENTLEMEN :—The accounts of General Count Pulaski and Capt. Baldesqui have been carefully examined, amounting to 105,111$\frac{11}{90}$ dollars, and compared with as many vouchers as are produced; but as many are wanting—such as muster-rolls and receipts for several articles, and some articles for large sums are guessed at, as will appear by his remarks herewith,—I find that I cannot settle said accounts, they not being agreeable to the resolves of Congress and orders of the Board of Treasury. It appears that the General and Paymaster have received at sundry times 181,286 dollars. The General, in a letter to the Auditors of the 27th of March, mentions that some receipts were lost by Colonel Boze, who was killed at Egg Harbor, but hopes that will make no difficulty, as he is persuaded we shall depend on his honor to pass over that matter.

The accounts of Capt. Baldesqui, amounting to 44,706$\frac{11}{90}$ dollars, are not agreeable to the resolves of Congress or Board of Treasury—he having not produced any receipts for either officer or private, instead of which, he produces certificates at the bottom of each account, that the account is true and exact, and that the amount of each has been paid by his Paymaster—from all which it appears that these accounts as rendered cannot be settled. JAMES JOHNSTON, Auditor.

Board of Treasury.

PHILADELPHIA, July 28, 1779.

The Honorable Gentlemen, Members of Congress:

I went to Camp a few days after General Count Pulaski's departure for South Carolina, for the purpose of settling the accounts of the Legion with the Auditors of the Army, according to the resolution of the honorable Congress.

The Auditors told me they had so much business in hands at that time that they did not believe they could be able to look over said accounts before three weeks or a month, in consequence whereof I determined to go to Boston, as I had some business there. I gave to said Auditors all the papers I received from Count Pulaski concerning the Legion, together with all the payments made by me to the officers and privates, and told them we should settle at my coming back.

I happened to be sick during my stay at Boston, which obliged me to be absent longer than I thought I should have been; and found at my arrival at camp the Auditors had already visited the accounts, and made such report to the Treasury Board as to induce you, gentlemen, to pass a resolve, which has since been published in the newspapers, which seems greatly to my disadvantage.

General Count Pulaski had begun his expenses for his Legion three months before I was appointed in it, and at that time almost all the business had been done by him, or some of the officers of his corps, who were so negligent as to lose several vouchers, which are now missing. This is a thing, gentlemen, I cannot help. Count Pulaski confesses it himself by a letter he wrote to the Auditors of the Army, which letter I delivered them; and besides this, I add here a general receipt from Count Pulaski, by which he does acknowledge I have given him an exact account of all the sums whatever I received for him, by order of the honorable Congress, during all the time I have been appointed in his corps.

This is, gentlemen, the present situation of the accounts of the Legion; and though some of the vouchers have been lost, they are true and as exact and regular as I could possibly make them. I am furthermore certain that Count Pulaski has laid out for the Legion at least fifty thousand dollars of his own money, which are not mentioned in his accounts. However, gentlemen, should the regularity with which public business ought to be transacted not permit you to fully trust Count Pulaski's honor, in respect of the vouchers which have been lost, please to order the accounts to be settled in the manner you will think it the most right and best; and as to the deficiency, whatever that shall be found in the said accounts, I know Count Pulaski well enough to be certain that he will pay it as soon as he will be informed thereof.

As to my own accounts concerning the payments made to the officers and privates personally by me, the Auditors of the Army pretend also they are not regular, because I did not take a receipt from each of the privates to whom money was advanced. This might have been done very easily, but I did not think it was necessary nor very regular, because the greater part of them could not write their names. I therefore chose to keep their accounts as we are accustomed to do it in France—that is, to pay the troops in the presence of the captain of each company, and to make him certify the pay-rolls, together with the colonel and the general, which has been strictly done.

I hope, gentlemen, you will consider that a foreigner cannot be acquainted with the customs of your country as well as yourselves, and you will please to take the necessary steps so as the Auditors of the Army may settle my accounts on the footing they now stand.

I am in hopes, also, gentlemen, that by a future resolve of Congress the effect of the former may be annulled. I mean that of the 10th of June, which I suppose was made through mistake, since it may induce the public to think I have misbehaved.

I am, gentlemen, your most obedient servant,

J. BALDESQUI.

TREASURY OFFICE, Aug. 3, 1779.

GENTLEMEN:—The Board have received your letters of the 29th May, and 10th and 14th of July last, with their several inclosures. In answer to them I am instructed to inform you that the accounts of Mr. Kennon, Paymaster to the 6th Virginia regiment, must be settled with you, as there are no Continental Auditors in Virginia.

The Board are extremely sorry that any of the regimental Paymasters should be so lost to a sense of duty to the public and their own reputations as to resign before they have settled their accounts. You are to call upon them to join the army immediately, in order to adjust them with you; and if they neglect to attend for that purpose, their names will be reported to Congress as defaulters.

The Board flatters themselves that this evil will be prevented in future, as the Commander-in-chief will not accept their resignations without certificates from you of their accounts being settled.

The inconveniences arising from the allowance granted to officers for purchasing drums, fifes, and cockades, are unavoidable. Justice requires that they should be reimbursed. The Board, therefore, think proper to leave you at liberty to make such allowances for those articles to officers whose accounts are adjusted, as particular circumstances may render expedient.

It is the opinion of the Board that the officers sent to superintend the hospitals are comprehended in the resolve of Congress allowing three dollars per day to officers on command, not incidental to their duty, and are of course entitled to the same allowance.

The Board are desirous that the pay of the clerks in your office should be adequate to their services, but recommend it to them to wait till the first of October next, when it is hoped the value of the money will be more fixed, and a regulation take place upon just and equitable principles.

As the expense of horses and forage at this time is enormous, applications for horses on long marches should be made to the Commander-in-chief.

I inclose you an act of Congress of the 29th ult., and an order of the Board of this day, together with a copy of a memorial to

Congress of Capt. Baldesqui, respecting his accounts as Paymaster to Count Pulaski's Legion, and also the accounts of Count Pulaski for money he has advanced to the Legion—which several papers I transmit you for your government in settling said accounts.

I am, gentlemen, your most obedient and very humble servant,

ROBERT TROUP, Secretary.

Messrs. JOHNSON and BOWELL, Auditors.

PROVIDENCE, August 24, 1779.

SIR :—Capt. Travers is returned from Philadelphia, and will soon be with you, after he shall have seen the new French Ambassador at Boston. I beg you will send him again into Canada and endeavor that no private dissensions obstruct the service.

I am convinced of your zeal in our cause, and wish to have it in my power to prove to you that I am with sincerity,

Sir, your most obedient humble servant,

HORATIO GATES.

To Col. BEDEL, at Coos.

MORRISTOWN, Jan. 2, 1780.

DEAR SIR :—By this conveyance you have my monthly accounts for November and December. The balance is much less than what appears in the return—having advanced to several Paymasters and other persons, by the general orders, about 120,000 dollars, in part of warrants which I design not to charge before the whole are paid. This reduces the real sum on hand to about 150,000 dollars—a sum which makes but a small figure in this office, and evinces the necessity of a further supply, as the troups are now four months in arrears, three of which I design to pay on the arrival of the money I have lately requested.

I am, dear sir, yours sincerely,

JOHN PIERCE, Dep. Pay. Gen.

JONATHAN BURRALL, Asst. Pay. Gen.

PHILADELPHIA, Jan. 3, 1780.

GENTLEMEN :—I inclose you a copy of a warrant which the

Board of War have this day drawn, for 150,000, dollars which I cannot answer without a further supply. As I have not more than 50,000 in hand, I should think it best that a warrant be granted for at least 200,000 dollars, as the remainder will undoubtedly be wanted before the end of the month.

I have the honor to be, gentlemen,
Your obedient servant,
J. BURRALL, Asst. Pay. Gen.

Honorable Board of Treasury.

PHILADELPHIA, Jan. 4, 1780.

SIR :—Yours of the 14th of November to Colonel Palfrey came to my hands in his absence.

I sent you under the care of Mr. Coffing, 150,000 dollars. You will be pleased to send Colonel Palfrey a receipt, as usual.

The many pressing demands on the treasury has prevented me from obtaining the money earlier. As there is but one man to carry the money, I cannot send the books you requested. I should think you would not need any, except one to enter the monthly returns in, as they are entered in this office. On the receipt of your returns, it is not expected, and indeed there can be no advantage in your keeping a waste-book and ledger. The Deputy Paymaster-general at camp does not keep any. I have not yet received any returns from you. I shall expect them on the return of the bearer of this.

I am your obedient servant,
J. BURRALL.

JOHN BOREMAN, Esq.,
Dep. Pay. Gen. at Fort Pitt.

PHILADELPHIA, Jan. 5, 1780.

SIR :—You will herewith receive one million of dollars, forwarded under the care of Messrs. White, Gray, and Hunt, escorts. The demands on the treasury have been so pressing, and so many warrants waiting, that I have not been able to procure the money sooner, although the warrant for it was granted the 12th December. I likewise send you my account of advances in December.

The discharged privates were paid in certificates from the Regimental Paymasters, and it is probable they will not be included in the rolls. If so, it will save you the trouble of making the stoppage. I have not yet received your return for November, and have concluded it must have miscarried. The Board of Treasury have ordered Mr. Reed to repair to Peekskill or West Point. They tell me they shall send a copy of the order to his Excellency or to you by this opportunity, to be forwarded to him.

I am, sir, your humble servant,

J. BURRALL.

JOHN PIERCE, Esq.

PHILADELPHIA, Jan. 7, 1780.

SIR :—I forwarded you two millions on the 22d ult., under the care of an escort, by whom I also sent the Journals of Congress from the 1st of January to the 26th August, 1779, which I believe contain all the alterations of pay which concern your department since the established pay of the army, per resolves of Congress of May 27, 1778.

I have since received yours of the 27th of September and 10th of November to Colonel Palfrey, inclosing a receipt from Mr. Lucas. The money he has not delivered, and your returns.

As you are considered Deputy Paymaster-general for the southern army, it makes no difference what State you are in, and there can be no necessity for your keeping separate accounts.

No pay is yet fixed for any person in the Paymaster-general's department. We are assured it shall be honorable, and rely on the justice of Congress to make it so; and expect, whenever it is fixed, it will commence from May last.

I now send you, per express, a draft on the Governor of South Carolina for two millions of dollars, which, together with the sum lately forwarded, I hope will be more than sufficient to pay all arrearages. You will please acknowledge the receipt of the draft by the return of the bearer. I likewise inclose you an account of money advanced to the troops who are ordered to your department, which you will be pleased to stop if they make their next settlement with you. When the General grants a warrant for a sum to be advanced for any special purpose, there can be no occasion for the Auditors to inspect it; but it should be entered in their books, as it is probable the person will account for the expenditure of it with them.

The musters must always be delivered to you by the Regimental Paymasters with the pay-rolls, that you may compare them, and certify the sums due. They afterwards go to the Auditors to be examined; and are both left, and the warrant only (in which the purpose for which it is paid should be specified) left with you. This is the practice in the main army. By a resolve of Congress a certificate is necessary from the Deputy Paymaster-general where they received pay last, specifying the time to which the regiment has been paid; but it has sometimes been dispensed with. Indeed, there cannot be much danger of a whole regiment drawing pay for the same month twice, as we cannot suppose all the officers who sign the different rolls would concur in it. With single persons, or small detachments, it ought not to be dispensed with if it can be avoided.

Since writing the above, Congress have drawn on the Commissioners of the Continental Loan Office in South Carolina for 200,000 dollars, to be transmitted to you, which draft I likewise inclose you.

I am, sir, your most obedient servant,

J. BURRALL, Asst. Pay. Gen.

JOSEPH CLAY, Esq.,
Dep. Pay. Gen. Southern Dep't.

MORRISTOWN, Jan. 8, 1780.

SIR:—It is now seven months since I have had the appointment as Deputy Paymaster-general to the main army, and during that time have not mentioned to the Congress that no allowance has been given me or my department.

It is hard to sacrifice the best part of a person's life in a service where he is not certain what reward he shall receive, or that it will be equal to the sacrifices he makes, the attention he pays to the business, or its importance in the general scale.

Besides, in the choice of assistants, gentlemen, whose abilities and character will answer the importance of the trust, will rarely venture to leave a certain income for one which is unknown; which, perhaps, may be less than what they would have reason to hope in any other station—for which reasons, I would wish that the pay of my department was stated, and that the advantages which shall accrue to us may be known, that I may be enabled to continue gentlemen already in the department, and engage others which shall be equal to the business.

The variety which passes through my hands is too great for the few employed, and I wish to have sufficient assistance to transact every part of it with the greatest exactness.

I have observed a resolve of Congress, of December the 28th, that all letters to officers of the line and general officers, which come by post, should be free. I would wish to know if the gentlemen who are in the staff of the army were designedly excluded.

In the course of my business I am necessarily involved in considerable postage; but independent of that, as I partake in common with the other officers in the public service, a distinction held out between us implies a demerit somewhere, which I should be unwilling to own, and which I do not believe the honorable Congress ever intended.

Having the most perfect reliance in the justice of the Congress, who, I do not doubt, will give every encouragement to the department which they merit, I would beg leave to subscribe myself, with the most perfect esteem and respect.

   Your Excellency's most humble servant,
             JOHN PIERCE.
To the President of Congress.

            MORRISTOWN, Jan. 9, 1780.

DEAR SIR:—You may see by the inclosed letters, that his Excellency has thought proper to have you pay the troops during this winter at West Point. It is supposed you have a sum of money on hand. I would be much obliged to know how much, as I am directed to furnish you with a small sum from my chest, to enable you to discharge the pay of the troops to the first of November. His Excellency particularly desires you to lose no time in coming to that post. The troops have suffered sufficiently, without the addition of want of money. I shall send you a number of warrants in favor of Paymasters in that department, as also an account of stoppages, as soon as I hear of your arrival. I have stopped the money you desired, which I shall transmit to you at West Point.

Your obedient servant,
JOHN PIERCE.

THOMAS REED, Esq., Albany.

MORRISTOWN, Jan. 12, 1780.

DEAR SIR :—The money which I received the other day was not sufficient to pay the troops for a longer time than the first of October—which payment has already exhausted the chest. His Excellency directed me to reserve 800,000 dollars for Mr. Reed, which I shall send him in a few days. Had the other million arrived with the last, it would have made the troops contented for considerable time; but now November and December must be paid together, and I am fearful that the contingencies of clothing, recruiting, &c., will make it necessary that a larger sum than has been requested should be sent. I wish, however, to have that forwarded as soon as possible, and to know when I may expect it, that the business may be regulated accordingly.

I am, sir, your obedient servant,
JOHN PIERCE.

J. BURRALL, Asst. Pay. Gen.

MORRISTOWN. Jan. 16, 1780.

SIR :—By his Excellency's direction, I have sent in the care of Lieutenant Sherman 250,000 dollars, for the use of the troops under your command, to be delivered to Thomas Reed, Esq., Deputy Paymaster-general, who, it is expected, by this time has arrived from Albany. If he has not, I should take it as a particular favor if the money could be lodged in your care until his arrival. Our necessities are so great that a larger sum could not be sent from the department. It is hoped Mr. Reed has a sum on hand, which he will bring from Albany; and that both these will be sufficient to discharge the arrears of the army to the 1st of November, the time to which the troops are paid in this department.

I am, sir, your most obedient humble servant,

JOHN PIERCE.

Major-general HEATH.
(By Lieut. Sherman.)

MORRISTOWN, Jan. 16, 1780.

DEAR SIR :—By Lieutenant Sherman you will receive 250,000 dollars, which, with the sum you have already in hand, will enable you to pay to the 1st of November, the time to which the troops are paid in this department.

I believe his Excellency expects you to pay on Major-general Heath's warrants. I waited on him for directions on that point, and his secretary informed me that the General thought that the best mode of preceedings.

You will note that the subsistence lately given to the army does not include militia, who remain yet at 10 dollars. For that reason, I have enclosed the abstract and pay-rolls of Colonel Graham's regiment, being made out at 100.

I have advanced 700 dollars to Major Hull, of the 8th Massachusetts regiment: the order on the Paymaster is inclosed, which you will oblige me to receive.

I have in my hands, for stoppages made for you from Lieutenant Betts, 110 dollars, Colonel Regnier, 290 dollars, and Captain Sackett 260, which, when you receive Major Hull's, will remain a balance of 60 dollars due me.

I have advanced by his Excellency's warrant 10,000 dollars to Ensign Joseph Tucker, Paymaster of the 7th Massachusetts regiment, on account of the pay of the regiment, which when you stop, as well as any other money advanced by me, I should take as a particular favor to be informed, so that I may give the necessary credit on my books. I have made a memorandum of the alterations on the abstracts of the regiments for which warrants are granted, and now inclosed you, that the Paymasters may be acquainted with them, and rectify their copies.

I am, sir, your obedient servant,

JOHN PIERCE.

THOMAS REED, Esq.

PAY OFFICE, MAIN ARMY, Jan. 18, 1780.

SIR:—I have received an order from Joseph Nourse, Assistant Auditor-general, dated the 17th of December, ultimo, wherein he writes that the Board of Treasury have directed him to inform the Paymaster-general, that on the settlement of Colonel Donald Campbell's accounts, late Deputy Quartermaster-general in the northern department, by the auditors at Albany, he stands indebted to the United Stetes £553 5s. 11d., New York currency, equal to 1383$\frac{21}{90}$ dollars, which balance is charged by the Auditor-general to his account.

The Board direct that the Paymaster-general forthwith demand the same, and make report thereof to the President of the Board: in compliance with which I would be much obliged for your answer, that I may communicate the same agreeable to the above.

I am, sir, with sentiments of esteem,

Your most obedient servant,

JOHN PIERCE, Dep. Pay. Gen.

Col. JEDUTHAN BALDWIN and }
Col. DONALD CAMPBELL.

MORRISTOWN, Jan. 21, 1780.

DEAR SIR:—Yours of the 11th I have received. I am sorry you have to meet with so many difficulties in procuring money, which is much wanted here, as the chest is entirely empty, and a number of regiments remain unpaid for September and October. I am now convinced that I shall want another sum forwarded to me before November and December can be paid.

I have made the requisition you desire on Colonel Donald

Campbell and Colonel Jeduthan Baldwin. The latter has favored me with an answer, a copy of which I inclose.

I am, sir, your obedient servant,

JOHN PIERCE.

J. BURRALL, Esq., Philadelphia.

PAY OFFICE, PHILADELPHIA, Jan. 21, 1780.

SIR :—I received yours of the 12th inst., and forward you one million of dollars, agreeable to your request, under the care of Mr. Hunt and others, escorts, which I hope will be sufficient to pay the troops for November and December. Mr. Reed has yet a considerable sum on hand, which he will undoubtedly carry to Peekskill with him. I am not certain how much, but I believe about 800,000 dollars.

I am, sir, your humble servant,

J. BURRALL.

JOHN PIERCE, Esq.

MORRISTOWN, Jan. 28, 1780.

SIR :—Under the care of Captain Williams I send you 50,000 dollars for the purpose of paying the Continental bounty to men enlisted during the war.

The low state of the chest renders it impossible to part with a large sum. November and December being now due, I shall pay those months to this department in a few days. Perhaps it would be well for you to make an immediate return to Philadelphia for what money may be wanting to pay to that time, as you cannot be furnished with any more from this chest; and the sum you now have, we are fearful, will not be sufficient to discharge all the demands in the department.

I am, dear sir, yours sincerely,

JOHN PIERCE.

THOMAS REED, Esq.

PAY OFFICE, PHILADELPHIA, Jan. 29, 1780.

SIR :—I wrote you the 22d ult., per escorts, who carried 200,000 dollars for your department; and the 7th inst., per express, inclosing two drafts—one on the Governor of South Carolina for 2,000,000, and the other on the Commissioners of the Loan Office for 200,000 dollars; and likewise an account of money advanced to the troops who are on their way to South Carolina.

I now inclose you copies of two warrants for 350,000 dollars, advanced to General Woodford, for which he is to account with the Auditors in your department, as directed in the warrants.

I beg the favor of you to give General Lincoln (or the Commander-in-chief in the department) copies of them, and likewise the Auditors for their direction in making the settlement.

I am, sir, your obedient servant,

J. BURRALL.

JOSEPH CLAY, Esq., Dep. Pay. Gen.

MORRISTOWN, Feb. 3, 1780.

SIR:—Inclosed is my account for January, by which may be seen the low state of cash in the chest. There are several regiments yet unpaid, which will require near 300,000 dollars to complete the payment, without taking in the addition of clothing and other occurrent demands. I wish therefore to have 500,000 dollars sent me, by which I shall be barely able to satisfy those which are the most necessary and most urgent, especially the recruiting service; and, supposing an exchange takes place, some part of pay and subsistence of the officers who are prisoners. As I am convinced the treasury is almost exhausted, it gives me pain to make so frequent and large demands for the department; yet the necessities of the troops, their sufferings and services, at least claim this attention, which makes me hope that this sum may be also granted and forwarded immediately, especially when we consider that it must give a dissatisfaction to one part of the army to remain so far behind when the others are paid. There have been several advances by Colonel Palfrey to a James Lyman of the 4th Pennsylvania regiment. On comparing the payments with each other, it appears he must have received twice for the same time. That it may be rectified, if a mistake has happened, I enclose you the account as it stands on Colonel Palfrey's advances.

I am, sir, your most obedient servant,

JOHN PIERCE.

J. BURRALL, Esq., Philadelphia.

MORRISTOWN, Feb. 8, 1780.

SIR:—A warrant (No. 4910) for 24,958 $\frac{98}{90}$ dollars for the payment of the 4th Connecticut regiment for November and December, in favor of Lieutenant Charles Fanning, was lost by him and has never been found, since which he got another from his Excellency of the same tenor, which I have paid. I should be glad, as some villian may present it to you for payment, you would detain it in your hands.

I credited the public 300 too much, the 28th of January, for money which was received of Captain Moses White, Paymaster to Colonel Hazen's regiment, which you will please to notice, as I shall charge the public for it in my next account.

I have made out an account of advances against those regiments gone to the Southern department. The stoppages were never made here, as they were never charged in the rolls. Will you superscribe my letter inclosing the account, and forward the same to the deputy in that department?

I wait with some impatience to hear from you if any more money is soon to be expected.

I am, sir, your obedient servant,

JOHN PIERCE.

J. BURRALL, Esq., Philadelphia.

MORRISTOWN, Feb. 8, 1780.

SIR:—Inclosed I transmit you several advances against the regiments of the Virginia and North Carolina lines, who have lately joined your department, for which stoppages are to be made on the settlement of their respective accounts. I suppose there are other stoppages against those lines; but as they were not prior to the department being placed on the present establishment, I am not furnished with the accounts.

I have the honor to be your most obedient servant,

JOHN PIERCE.

JOSEPH CLAY, Esq., Dep. Pay. Gen.

MORRISTOWN, Feb. 8, 1780.

SIR :—I inclose you an account of advances against Colonel Moylan's regiment, which remain unsettled. Mr. Henderson, the Paymaster of the regiment, disputed the justness of the stoppage being made, as he had mislaid the pay-rolls, or left them at Philadalphia, which I conclude by this time he has been able to obtain, and the difficulty removed. I have inclosed also an account of surplusage of clothing against the second Massachusetts regiment for 1777; also a bundle of accounts I received from Mr. Burrall last spring for spirits delivered at West Point, and ordered to be stopped by General McDougal; but as his Excellency never directed it to be done, they remain unsettled.

I remain your obedient servant,
JOHN PIERCE.

THOMAS REED, Esq., New Windsor.

MORRISTOWN, Feb. 9, 1780.

SIR :— As I conclude you are detained by business from giving us the pleasure of your company in this town, and possibly may not have an opportunity this winter, I could wish you would do me the favor to send the warrants you have taken up for me by some careful hand, to whom I will deliver your receipt.

I am about settling my accounts, and can proceed no further without those vouchers. The difficulty in obtaining money from the public treasury has occasioned my chest to be empty the greater part of the winter, for which reason I have been asked several times at head-quarters if that sum was returned.

I make no doubt, sir, but yourself and Mrs. Hay are enjoying every happiness which results from integrity and virtue ; and can only add, that none among the circle of your acquaintance wishes more than myself for its continuance. You will please to present my best regards to your lady, and believe me to be, with sincerity,

Your obedient servant,
JOHN PIERCE.

Col. UDNEY HAY, Dep. Qr. Mr. Gen.,
Peekskill.

PAY OFFICE, PHILADELPHIA, Feb. 9, 1780.

GENTLEMEN :—I inclose you a copy of a letter from Mr. Pierce, who requests a further sum of 500,000 dollars to complete the payment of the main army to January 1st. I likewise inclose you a letter from Mr. Blount, Deputy Paymaster-general in North Carolina, who is out of cash. Benjamin Harrison, Deputy Paymaster-general in Virginia, informs me that his chest is also empty; but the necessities of the two latter seem not to be very pressing.

I am, gentlemen, with due respect,
Your very humble servant,
J. BURRALL, Ass't Pay. Gen.

Honorable Board of Treasury.

NEW WINDSOR, Feb. 12, 1780.

DEAR PIERCE :—I arrived here the 1st inst., and found at General Heath's quarters 250,000 dollars, and a few days after I received per Lieutenant Williams 50,000 dollars. I have given General Heath a receipt for the first, and to Lieutenant Williams one for the latter sum. This 300,000 dollars, with what I brought with me, is not sufficient to answer all the demands in this quarter. However, I will do the best I can. I have made a return to Philadelphia for the sum I think necessary to pay the troops their November and December pay, which I expect along in about a fortnight.

My business is very brisk, therefore you must excuse this scrawl. The first leisure shall be more particular, only let me add, and I hope you will join me in my prayer, and that is, to implore the fates to blast the authors of my removal from Albany. Cursed at New Windsor is an equal curse, and I give it to them with all my heart.

In haste, I remain yours sincerely,
THOMAS REED.

JOHN PIERCE, Esq.

PAY OFFICE, PHILADELPHIA, Feb. 12, 1780.

SIR :—In the absence of Colonel Palfrey, who is gone to Boston, I have regularly received your returns to the last of December.

I should have answered your questions concerning the subsistence of the staff of the army, state troops, militia, &c., had Congress enabled me to do it; but they have not yet extended the subsistence, allowed by the resolve of the 18th of August, to any but those specified in that resolve, except those mentioned in the inclosed list. If by the state troops you mean those of the sixteen battalions, which were raised at the request of General Washington, after the eight battalions formed, they are undoubtedly entitled to the same subsistence as the others. With regard to the militia, I can give no answer.

Your very humble servant,
J. BURRALL.

BENJAMIN STELLE, Esq.

PAY OFFICE, PHILADELPHIA, Feb. 14, 1780.

SIR:—I send you 500,000 dollars per Messrs. Saxton and Hunt, escorts. I likewise send 75 quills, some wax, and the Journals of Congress to December 31, 1779. I wrote you yesterday by Mr. Hodgdon.

I am, sir, your obedient servant,
J. BURRALL.

JOHN PIERCE, Esq.

PAY OFFICE, PHILADELPHIA, Feb. 21, 1780.

GENTLEMEN:—I inclose you a letter from Mr. Reed, Deputy Paymaster-general for the troops under the command of General Heath, who requests 500,000 dollars to enable him to pay off the troops in that department.

I have the honor to be your obedient servant,
J. BURRALL.

Honorable Board of Treasury.

MORRISTOWN, Feb. 27, 1780.

SIR:—Yours of the 8th ult. and 16th inst. are now before me I am obliged to you for attending to Colonel Campbell's letter and the stoppages. The following expenses for recruiting men during the war, I believe you have never had transmitted to you:

Sept. 30, 1779—Paid by Mr. Pierce to Patrick Bennett, for recruiting the 4th regiment of light-dragoons, to be accounted for by Colonel Moylan, ... $5,000
Jan. 16, 1780—Paid by ditto to Colonel Benjamin Tupper, 11th Massachusetts regiment, for recruiting, . . 4,000
Jan. 7, 1780—Paid by Colonel Palfrey, Paymaster-general, to Lieutenant Henry Willis, of the 4th regiment of light-dragoons, for recruiting, ... 4,000
Jan. 7, 1780—Paid by ditto to Lieutenant Larkin Smith, of the same regiment, for recruiting, ... 4,000

Making in all, ... $17,000

I am your obedient servant,

JOHN PIERCE.

WM. BEDLOW, Esq.

MORRISTOWN, MARCH 1, 1780.

SIR :—Since mine of the 8th ultimo, I have advanced money to the following persons in your department:

Feb. 17, 1780—James Legar, 1st North Carolina regiment, for pay and subsistence from March 1, 1779, to January 23, 1780, being then discharged, ... $195
Feb. 28, 1780—Brigadier-general Hand, for Martin Medder and William Earles, privates in the 18th Virginia regiment, for pay and subsistence from May 1, 1778, to Nov. 1, 1779, 276
Feb. 29, 1780—Major Oliver Towles, 6th Virginia regiment, a prisoner on parole, on account, ... 1500

Making in all $1971

I am, sir, your most obedient servant,

JOHN PIERCE.

JOSEPH CLAY, Esq., Southern Department.

MORRISTOWN, March 1, 1780.

SIR :—By this conveyance you will receive my account current for February. I am now preparing to pay the army the two last months, which will require 1,500,000 dollars. This sum

I wish to have forwarded before the end of the present month—your particular attention to which will oblige

Your most obedient servant,
JOHN PIERCE.

J. BURRALL, Esq., Philadelphia.

PAY OFFICE, PHILADELPHIA, March 1, 1780.

GENTLEMEN :—By a resolve of Congress of the 29th May last, it was directed that returns should be made to the Paymaster-general of all money which has been advanced for the pay, &c., of the Continental army in the different departments, that the proper charges might be made in his books, in pursuance of which most of the accounts have been collected. But on examining the general account of payments made by Mr. Trumbull, late Paymaster-general in the Northern department, which is lodged in this office, I find it does not in every instance particularly specify the purpose for which the payment was made. I cannot therefore proceed to enter them in the paymaster-general's books until I can obtain the vouchers to his accounts, which are lodged in the Commissioners' office at Albany. I must therefore request that the Commissioners may be directed to forward them to this office as soon as possible. A further supply of cash is wanted for this office, as the chest is nearly empty, and there are demands on it daily. Two hundred thousand dollars will be sufficient.

I have the honor, gentlemen, to be, with the greatest respect, your very humble servant,

J. BURRALL, Ass't Pay. Gen.

Honorable Board of Treasury.

PAY OFFICE, PHILADELPHIA, March 2, 1780.

SIR :—I received yours of the 5th ultimo about three weeks after the date, and made application to the Board of Treasury for the sum you request; but the treasury being low, I could obtain only 300,000 dollars, which I send you, under the care of Messrs. White and Gray, escorts. I likewise send you some paper and sealing-wax.

I am, sir, your humble servant,
J. BURRALL.

THOS. REED, Esq., New Windsor.

PHILADELPHIA, March 14, 1780.

SIR :—In the absence of Colonel Palfrey, who is gone to Boston, I have regularly received your monthly returns to the 31st December, 1779, and duly noticed them. Your favor of the 10th ult. to Colonel Palfrey, requesting a supply of money to pay the troops under the command of General Scott, did not come to hand till yesterday. I laid it before the Treasury Board this day and have not yet had an answer; but as the treasury is very much exhausted, and the troops for whose pay you requested it (they conclude) have marched before this time, I rather think they will not spare any money for your department at present, as there are other demands more pressing. I will let you know as soon as I get their answer.

I have advanced to Lieutenant Wyatt Coleman, of the 1st Virginia State regiment, eight hundred dollars, on account of his pay and subsistence, by a warrant from the Board of War, which he, or the Paymaster of the regiment, is to repay into your hands. You will please receive the same and place it to the credit of the United States.

I am your obedient servant,

J. BURRALL.

BENJAMIN HARRISON, Esq.,
Dep. Pay. Gen. in Virginia.

MORRISTOWN, March 18, 1780.

GENTLEMEN :—The military chest in the main army being almost exhausted, I have to request a further supply of 1,500,000 dollars for the purpose of paying the months of January and February, which are now become due. I could wish to have this supply as early as possible, and shall do myself the honor to wait on the Board this morning on the subject.

I am, gentlemen, your most obedient servant,

JOHN PIERCE.

Honorable Board of Treasury.

(ENDORSED.)

At a council of war, March 17, 1780—Resolved, That Jonathan Burrall, Esq., Assistant Paymaster-general, do immediately attend to the duties of his office in Walnut street.

PAY OFFICE, PHILADELPHIA, March 20, 1780.

GENTLEMEN :—Mr. Pierce, Deputy Paymaster-general for the main army, informs me 1,500,000 dollars is wanting for the payment of the troops for the months of January and February, which he requests may be forwarded to him as soon as possible.

I have the honor to be, with the greatest respect,

Your obedient servant,

J. BURRALL.

Honorable Board of Treasury.

PAY OFFICE, PHILADELPHIA, March 20, 1780.

SIR :—I received your favor of the 29th January to Colonel Palfrey, acknowledging the receipt of 2,000,000 dollars, and my letter of the 22d December, which accompanied it, and inclosing your returns for November and December. I have since written you twice ; one on the 27th of January, by express, inclosing two warrants in your favor, and the other on the 29th, by post, which 1 hope you have received.

I now enclose you three warrants of Congress, which I have endorsed to you ; one of George Webb, Esq., Treasurer of the State of Virginia, for 1,200,000, another of the Governor of North Carolina, and the third on the Governor of South Carolina—the two latter for 900,000 dollars each. The Board of Treasury inform me that it is not expected that either of the States have sufficient money on hand to discharge the warrant immediately ; but it is their intention that the money which is raised in those States for the use of the United States, should be applied for the use of your department as soon as collected, for which purpose it was necessary that you should have warrants ready ; but it will be useless to send for it until you can obtain information of its being ready, when you will take such methods to get it forwarded as you shall judge most expedient.

I shall write to the Governor of North Carolina and the Treasurer of Virginia, advising them of such warrants being sent you and request them to give you the earliest notice when the money may be obtained, and I should advise you to do the same on your receiving the warrants. If any money is advanced by you to officers or others, who are acting in another department, on account of their pay, it is expected you will transmit an account thereof to the Deputy Paymaster-general of the department to which they belong, that he may make the necessary stoppage. It is undoubtedly expected that you should be accountable for the conduct of your assistants and clerks who are appointed by you.

As to the pay that will be allowed them, I can say nothing, as no pay is yet fixed for any person in the Paymaster-general's department. As soon as Colonel Palfrey arrives from Boston, I expect this matter will be adjusted—I hope, to the satisfaction of all who are employed in the department. In the mean time, you can advance your assistants some money on account of their present necessities, but not include it in your monthly returns until the pay is known. I inclose you a letter from the Deputy Paymaster-general of the main army, with his account of money advanced to the Virginia troops, who are gone to your department. It is not probable that many of the persons charged in his account will settle, or be included in any settlement made with you. If any of them should, you will please to make the necessary stoppage, and credit it to the United States in your monthly accounts. It will be necessary to give the auditors an account of the money advanced for recruiting.

It is contrary to an express resolve of Congress that any officer should receive pay in two capacities, except additional pay to paymasters, adjutants, quartermasters, brigade majors, &c.

The infantry of Count Pulaski's Legion are to receive the same pay as cavalry.

I am, sir, your obedient servant,

J. BURRALL.

JOSEPH CLAY, Esq., Southern Department.

PAY OFFICE, PHILADELPHIA, March 21, 1780.

SIR :—A warrant on your Excellency for 900,000 dollars was issued by Congress on the 16th inst., payable to my order, which sum is to be transmitted to Joseph Clay, Esq., Deputy Paymaster-general for the army under the command of General Lincoln, for the use of the military chest in that department. As I was informed by the Board of Treasury that there was not a probability of there being a sufficient sum in the treasury of your State to answer it immediately, I have endorsed the warrant and sent it to Mr. Clay, and must beg your Excellency to give him or General Lincoln the earliest information when the money or part of it may be obtained.

I have the honor to be your Excellency's most obedient servant.   J. BURRALL, Ass't. Pay Gen.

His Excellency RICHARD CASWELL,
Governor of North Carolina.

PHILADELPHIA, March 25, 1780.
To the Congress of the United States.

That your memorialist has been in the service of the United States as an Assistant Paymaster-general from the 10th day of February, 1776, to 1st June, 1779, since which he has had the honor to serve, by an appointment of Congress, as Deputy Paymaster-general for the main army. Your memorialist would beg leave to represent that, by reason of the depreciation of the currency, the pay, while he was an assistant, became very inadequate to his unavoidable expenses, by which means he has been obliged to involve himself considerably in debt, and has greatly impaired his private fortune; that the pay and other allowances of his present appointments have never been stated either for himself or his assistants; but he has served from that time, relying on the justice and generosity of Congress to give him the compensation which his services may be deemed to merit, taking from time to time such sums from the chest as were sufficient to support himself and his assistants in their expenses; by means of which he finds, as he is now closing the settlement of his accounts, the sum which he has taken is so large that he cannot compute the same without having the pay of his department stated, that it may be charged the public. Your memorialist would beg leave further to request that from the particular situation of private affairs, as well as a willingness to retain in the service the gentlemen who have already assisted him in the business, a state of uncertainty at this time as to the allowances which are to be given the department, will be extremely disagreeable.

Your memorialist would therefore request that the honorable Congress would take his case into their consideration, and grant him such allowance for his past services as they shall deem proper, and affix the pay and other allowances of his department, equal to the importance and weight of the business which passes through his hands.

I have the honor to be your most obedient servant,

JOHN PIERCE.

PAY OFFICE, PHILADELPHIA, March 29, 1780.

GENTLEMEN :—I received a line from Mr. Clarkson, returning a letter from Benjamin Harrison, Deputy Paymaster-general in Virginia, of the 10th of February, and directing me to make an estimate of money wanted to pay the troops in Virginia.

As I do not know how many regiments General Scott's brigade consists of, I have nothing certain whereon to found an estimate; but by the best information I can get from the Board of War, it consists of three Continental regiments; besides, which, there are two State regiments, who, on their arrival in Virginia, were subject to the orders of the Governor.

The first of April there will be four months' pay due them, and if the whole five regiments are to be paid by the Continental Paymasters, it will require 200,000 dollars.

I have the honor to be your obedient servant,

J. BURRALL, Ass't P. M. Gen.

Honorable Board of Treasury.

PHILADELPHIA, April 5, 1780.

GENTLEMEN:—Understanding that my memorial to Congress, which was referred to your Board, has not been reported on, and that there is some hesitation as to its being determined upon at this time, I thought it might not be improper to lay before you some reasons in addition to those in the memorial, which induce me to wish to have it settled *now*, and the principles which may be adopted for that purpose.

When the Congress made the appointments, they directed that the Board of Treasury should report the pay; after which it was resolved it should be suspended until the 1st of October last, at which time Colonel Palfrey's was stated, and his allowance made without mine being fixed; and having served almost a year without any thing, I think it is reasonable that mine should be known. My assistants being in the same situation, and on some accounts worse, are determined to leave the service unles they can receive their pay; and it is extremely hazardous for me to advance them what of right they ought to receive, because, in case it is not allowed, I must refund it; and it is as hard for them to serve with less than what they ought to have, as they have families to maintain, and their expenses run so high. Hitherto the fluctuation of our currency has rendered it improper that any establishment should take place; but now the resolution of Congress of the 18th ult. has fixed the standard, and the objection that the resolve has not yet been adopted by the several States, I think has no force, because that the recommendations of Congress with regard to finances at this time must be complied with, or our public credit ceases, and the common bond of our union will be dissolved. I hope, indeed, there is not a doubt in the mind of any person but that it will be complied with. We ought therefore to act and reason from so necessary a principle as granted. The department being disconnected from any other, an establishment of the pay of it cannot affect the others of the army, as the whole will soon be taken up on the same plan. They have, indeed, not the same reason to complain: theirs is, while mine never has been, stated. The campaign opening very soon, is an additional reason, because the duty of the office will require my presence at camp, and I cannot give my attendance here at another time; and it is extremely disagreeable to confine one's self so constantly as the duty of the office requires, undergoing the solicitude of mind inseparably attending the payment of so much money without knowing what are the advantages he shall receive. Indeed, I have a right to expect it shall be determined. I think that as several States are to make good the depreciation to their officers, or give some other equivalent satisfaction, or lose them, the same justice ought to begin to those under Congress, especially when they have been in my situation, who have been so long in the service on a simple pay, and had no other advantages for a maintenance. I am, indeed, encouraged to expect this from the allowance already made to several of the officers of Congress.

With regard to my present pay, I think, as the duty of the department is more than twice as large as nearly all the other Deputies together on the continent, and the same in every other circumstance as belonged to the Paymaster-general prior to the present establishment, which is now on a more extensive scale, that the pay and other allowances ought to be the same as given formerly to the Paymaster-general.

In order that the fluctuation of the currency may not affect either myself or the public, I believe the most just and proper method would be to establish my pay in *hard money*, which I ought to receive in the currency of the United States at the value at which the same passes in exchange, or at the rate which shall be affixed by Congress. I conclude the late act of Congress states it at 40 for 1, at which rate it is very reasonable I should receive my pay, though much below the current exchange, as the money is *considered* of that value, and will probably be *really* so as soon as that act shall have an operation.

The rations of the Paymaster-general before the new arrangement, as well as of the several Deputies, were six per day. I do not apprehend any objection but that mine should be equal with theirs.

The pay and rations of my assistants I wish may go on the above principles, being the same reasons for both. I have here *asked* for only the same as has been given before. It is hard for an individual to suffer in his private fortune for a depreciation while he is in the service. The pay at best is small, but the depreciation has made it almost nothing; and I desire to be placed on the same footing in my present pay as those who have gone before me in the business, the same service always deserving the same reward.

The dignity of Congress requires that every officer of theirs should be on a respectable footing, and what I desire is nothing to what the Quartermaster's and Commissary's departments have received.

I feel myself interested in the determination of your honorable Board. My love for the service, and my wishes to promote the public good as far as is in my power, make me wish to continue in the office, but I cannot, with justice to myself, unless I have a generous consideration for my services.

I have the honor to be, gentlemen, your most obedient servant,

JOHN PIERCE.

Honorable Board of Treasury.

PAY OFFICE, PHILADELPHIA, April 5, 1780.

SIR:—I have obtained a warrant on George Brook, Esq., treasurer of the State of Virginia, for 100,000 dollars, which I inclose to you for the use of your department. I fear you will not be able to get the money immediately, but as there is none in the treasury, your chest cannot be supplied in any other way. You will please acknowledge the receipt of this warrant by post.

I am, sir, your humble servant,

J. BURRALL.

BENJAMIN HARRISON, Esq. }
Dep. P. M. Gen. in Virginia. }

PHILADELPHIA, April 6, 1780.

GENTLEMEN:—I have received your favor of yesterday desiring an estimate of the expenses of the department in my care. There are three assistants necessary to transact the business under me. Their pay is forty dollars per month, and three rations per day when money was good.

There are some contingent expenses in the department, which, as they are not the object of the present inquiry of the Board, are not necessary to mention.

I am, gentlemen, your obedient servant,

JOHN PIERCE.

Honorable Board of Treasury.

PAY OFFICE, PHILADELPHIA, April 7, 1780.

GENTLEMEN:—I am under the necessity of requesting a supply of money for the military chest at West Point. The troops in that department have pay due them from the 1st of November, and the last sum of 300,000 dollars which was sent there will be chiefly expended in paying the arrears of clothing and bounty to men who have enlisted "for during the war."

It will require at least 800,000 dollars more to pay the troops to the last of February.

I have the honor, gentlemen, to be your obedient servant,

J. BURRALL.

Honorable Board of Treasury.

PHILADELPHIA, April 9, 1780.

GENTLEMEN:—I imagine there will be about seven millions of dollars expended in my department for the present year. The army being diminished, it will not take so much hereafter. —— per cent. will be little enough for the maintenance of myself and assistants, with two rations per day for myself and one for each of the assistants, and keeping for my horses.

The public, I expect, will provide the incidental charges of the department, such as expenses, transportation, necessaries for the use of the office, &c.

I am, gentlemen, your obedient servant,

JOHN PIERCE.

Honorable Board of Treasury.

PHILADELPHIA, April 10, 1780.

SIR:—I have unfortunately been detained here much longer than I expected, and without the consolation of success in my business. On my arrival, I made a return for a million and a half of dollars to pay the army for January and February, and have received only 500,000 dollars, being the whole that was in the treasury! This sum I have now forwarded, as I am informed the Maryland division are marching, and will probably want their pay.

I am sorry that I have no reason to expect a further sum in any short time. I shall have the pleasure to breathe camp air in a few days.

I am, sir, your obedient servant,

JOHN PIERCE.

Col. R. H. HARRISON.

PAY OFFICE, PHILADELPHIA, April 12, 1780.

GENTLEMEN:—Captain Schott, who commands an independent corps stationed at Wyoming, is waiting in town for their pay, which is due from September last, and amounts to more than I have on hand. Having lent Mr. Carleton 40,000 dollars at the request of the Board of War, I have been in daily expectation of receiving it from him, which would have prevented this application, but he now informs me that there is no probability of his being able to repay it soon. I must therefore request the honorable Board to grant a warrant for 50,000 for the use of the chest at this place, there being several other demands besides Captain Schott's. But if that sum cannot be spared, I should be glad of 20,000 dollars, which will be sufficient to pay him. I hope this last sum at least may be obtained, as Captain Schott's returning without the money would occasion much uneasiness in the corps, who have six months' pay due; and the expense of another journey from Wyoming would be considerable.

I have the honor to be, gentlemen, your obedient servant,

J. BURRALL, A. P. M. Gen.

Honorable Board of Treasury.

PHILADELPHIA, April 18, 1780.

GENTLEMEN:—I would beg leave to observe to the honorable Committee of Congress that the pay of the Deputy Paymaster-generals at first was 50 dollars per month and 6 rations, equal to a Colonel's; that in January, 1777, a Colonel's pay being raised to 75 dollars, the Deputies were made the same. As the depreciation continued in that year the pay was enlarged. The ideas of Congress, I conclude, were to keep the pay and other allowances equal to a Colonel's, and which is perhaps the most just and proper mode to be established now; but as the office which I now hold was not then created, a new rule ought to be adopted in my case. On inquiry into the duty and importance of the office, you will find it the same, in every circumstance, as formerly fell to the share of the Paymaster-general; and I would ask if nearly the same allowances as were formerly given him ought not to be made me? His pay at first was 100 dollars per month; some time in 1777 it was raised to 150. Cannot that serve as a foundation to reason from? And is it not reasonable that the same duty should receive the same reward?

I am, gentlemen, your obedient servant,
JOHN PIERCE.

Hon. Committee of Congress.

PHILADELPHIA, April 22, 1780.

GENTLEMEN :—If the regiments in the service will hereafter be as strong as they have been, their pay will be about 3,000 dollars a month, and their present subsistence about 7,600 dollars. The Maryland line being marched, there remains in the main army 35 regiments. As to the contingencies of the department, it is impossible to determine the sum which will be paid, as they depend, except the pay of the General Staff, on unforeseen circumstances.

I have the honor to be your obedient servant,
JOHN PIERCE.

Honorable Board of Treasury.

PAY OFFICE, PHILADELPHIA, April 27, 1780.

GENTLEMEN :—The Board of War have directed me to make application for 230,000 dollars to pay two warrants which they have drawn on me this day; one in favor of Major-general Baron De Kalb for 200,000 dollars, for the purpose of defraying the expenses of the Maryland troops on their march to the southward, and the other in favor of Major Lee for 30,000, to defray the expenses of his corps.

These warrants the Board of War desire may be paid as soon as possible, that the troops may not be delayed in marching.

I have the honor to be your obedient servant,
J. BURRALL.

Honorable Board of Treasury.

PAY OFFICE, PHILADELPHIA, May 3, 1780.

GENTLEMEN :—I have lately received a letter from Mr. Boreman, Deputy Paymaster-general at Fort Pitt, requesting a further supply of cash to pay the troops in his department. There are at that post two regiments and three independent corps, the monthly pay of which will amount to about 80,000 dollars. The troops are so much in arrears that 150,000 dollars will be necessary to pay them to the usual time, and I must request you will report a warrant for that sum. The Board will also be pleased to report a warrant in my favor for 500,000 dollars to answer the drafts of the Board of War. There are now lying in my office two drafts from them; one in favor of the Baron De Kalb for 200,000 dollars, and another in favor of Major Lee for 30,000 dollars. These sums are greatly wanted to forward the march of the troops destined for Carolina.

I would also beg leave to repeat my request that the Board would take some effectual measures that I may be furnished with the accounts and vouchers which have been settled by the Deputy Paymaster-general, and lodged in different offices, without which it will be impossible for me to complete the public books in the manner prescribed by the resolve of Congress passed May 29, 1779. I am particularly in want of the vouchers of Mr. Trumbull's accounts, which were settled with the Commissioners at Albany, and lodged in their office. These gentlemen have been repeatedly applied to, but have constantly refused to send them, by which means the business of my office has been retarded and great loss may accrue to the public by the Auditors of the Army not being seasonably supplied with the proper accounts, which cannot be completed until all the vouchers necessary for forming them are deposited in my office.

I would further beg leave to submit to the Board the propriety of continuing a Deputy at the two posts of Rhode Island and Boston. There are no Continental troops at the latter place except a few invalids and at the former only a few State troops. The distance between Providence and Boston being only forty-five miles, one person could certainly do the business of the whole.

I have the honor to be, with great respect, your obedient servant,   J. BURRALL.

Honorable Board of Treasury.

MORRISTOWN, May 6, 1780.

SIR :—I arrived here yesterday evening, nothing material occurring on my journey. I find the greatest want of money among the officers and soldiers, and could wish for the satisfaction that exertions may be made to obtain a supply. By the estimate annexed, you will see what sum will be sufficient to pay from the 1st of January to this day, being at least 1,500,000 dollars.

Perhaps some favorable circumstance may enable you to obtain the money, which I would forward as soon as possible.

Estimate of pay and subsistence of the main army from January 1 to May 1, 1780.

35 regiments at 11,000 for 4 months, . . .	1,540,000
Contingencies will amount to	150,000
	1,690,000
Balance remaining on hand, per account rendered for April, ... 228,621	
Money paid to the Quartermaster-general's department, by his Excellency's desire to be returned, ... 30,922	
	197,699
Wanting to pay the army . . .	1,492,301

I am, sir, with respect and esteem, your obedient servant,

JOHN PIERCE.

WM. PALFREY, Esq., Paymaster-general.

PAY OFFICE, PHILADELPHIA, May 9, 1780.

GENTLEMEN :—Agreeably to the direction of the honorable Board, signified by the Secretary, I now inclose you an estimate of the sum necessary for the pay of the army to the period you mention, as nearly as I can ascertain it from the information I have received of their numbers. The Board perhaps are not informed that the returns of the army do not come officially before me, neither can I procure them from the Board of War, unless by a positive resolve of Congress for the purpose. Therefore all estimates furnished by me must be very vague and uncertain. The order on the Loan Office in Boston cannot be procured in less than three weeks or a month, even if the money should be ready there, and I should be very glad to be informed by your honorable Board in what manner and under what escort it is to be sent to camp.

I have the honor to be, with the highest respect, your obedient servant.

       WILLIAM PALFREY, P. M. Gen.
Honorable Board of Treasury.

      PAY OFFICE, PHILADELPHIA, May 10, 1780.

SIR :—Inclosed I send you a draft on John Lawrence, Esq., treasurer of the State of Connecticut, for 864,836 dollars, to pay the arrears of the troops in your department. The great difficulty of obtaining money has been the occasion of this supply being delayed. I therefore hope you will lose no time in getting the amount of this draft from Connecticut.

In the month of February you made a stoppage from the 7th Massachusetts regiment, the amount of which, nor the person by whom advanced, do not appear on your returns, which mode of stopping is directly contrary to your instructions. Instead of deducting from the pay-rolls and charging the balance, you should charge the whole pay-roll, and give credit for the stoppage made. This rule you will please strictly to observe in future.

I am sorry that I am obliged to frequently to complain of your want of punctuality in forwarding your monthly returns. You are now in arrears for March and April, which I beg you will send by the first opportunity. I am very confident that the business of your office is not so great as to prevent you making your returns regularly at the end of every month.

I beg you will present my compliments to Mr. Bedlow and his worthy family. It has not been in my power to send him the *red cake-ink* he requested.

    I am, sir, you most humble servant,

THOMAS REED, Esq. } WILLIAM PALFREY.
Dep. P. M. Gen., New Windsor. }

PAY OFFICE, PHILADELPHIA, May 11, 1780.

GENTLEMEN :—Mr. Hillegas is indebted to me 10,000 dollars, balance of a warrant granted in my favor for the purpose of answering the drafts of the Board of War. He has just informed me that there are 16,000 in the hands of Mr. Smith, Continental loan officer, arising from the sale of bills of exchange, which he cannot appropriate to the payment of my balance without the particular direction of your honorable Board.

As the money is extremely wanted for the purpose for which it was granted, I must request you will be pleased to give to Mr. Hillegas directions accordingly, and I am, with the greatest respects, gentlemen,

Your obedient servant,

WILLIAM PALFREY, P. M. Gen.

Honorable Board of Treasury.

PAY OFFICE, PHILADELPHIA, May 13, 1780.

GENTLEMEN :—The Secretary of your honorable Board acquainted me that warrants have been reported in my favor for 2,000,000 dollars, accompanied with a request that I would "inform them when it shall be in my power relative to their payment." As the Board have not acquainted me with the particular offices or States on which the warrants are drawn, it is out of my power at present to give a proper answer to the question. I will do myself the honor to wait on the honorable Board at 12 o'clock, and give them all the information in my power.

I am, gentlemen, your obedient servant,

WILLIAM PALFREY.

Honorable Board of Treasury.

PAY OFFICE, PHILADELPHIA, May 14, 1780.

SIR :—Inclosed you have sundry warrants, with which you are to immediately proceed to the several offices and apply for payment. When you receive the money, you are to return with the same to camp, and deliver to John Pierce, Esq., Deputy Paymaster-general there, one million of dollars. The remainder you are to deliver to me at this office. If you should not be able to procure payment for the whole of these warrants, you will get as much as you possibly can, and proceed with it to camp, keeping a particular account of what part you do receive, which must be indorsed on the warrants. You will take triplicate receipts from Mr. Pierce for whatever sum you pay him.

As the army is greatly in want of the money, I would recommend to you to use all possible dispatch, and I am
Your obedient servant,
WM. PALFREY, P. M. Gen.
Mr. JARED SAXTON, escort.

PAY OFFICE, PHILADELPHIA, May 15, 1780.

SIR:—I have just received from the honorable President of Congress a draft on your office for the purpose of paying the army, which I shall forward to-morrow by an escort. As the troops are greatly in arrears, and the money very much wanted I thought it necessary to give you this notice, that seasonable provisions may be made, and the messenger meet with no detention.

I, am, sir, with great esteem, your obedient servant,
WILLIAM PALFREY.

To JOHN LAWRENCE, Treasurer of Connecticut—296,421$\frac{53}{90}$.
   HENRY GARDNER,   "   Massachusetts Bay—430,000.
   GIRARDUS BANEKER, "   New York—237,333.
   JOSEPH CLARK, Commissioner of the Continental Loan Office, Rhode Island—888,912$\frac{27}{90}$
   His Excellency, President of the Supreme Executive Council of the Commonwealth of Pennsylvania—647,333.

PAY OFFICE, MAIN ARMY, May 15, 1780.

SIR:—Inclosed is a copy of an answer from Colonel Donald Campbell, to a requisition made by me in consequence of an order for that purpose from the Board of Treasury, for a balance due from him to the United States.

I have waited on General Greene on the subject of wheelwrights' stores, who altogether refuses to do any thing in the matter. He says the business, being transacted before his appointmemt, must be settled with Colonel Chase, and included in his accounts while under General Mifflin. I have therefore inclosed the papers, as they will be of no further service here.

I am, dear sir, your obedient servant,

JOHN PIERCE.

Col. WM. PALFREY, P. M. Gen.

PAY OFFICE, MAIN ARMY, May 19, 1780.

SIR :— The Maryland line and several other regiments having marched from the main army for the southward, I inclose you several charges against them, for which stoppages or settlements ought to be made. In case any of the regiments do not fall into your department, it may, perhaps, be proper for you to transmit the charges to the Deputy Paymaster-general in whose department they are paid.

I am, sir, your obedient servant,

JOHN PIERCE.

JOSEPH CLAY, Esq.,
Dep. Pay. Gen., South Carolina.

PAY OFFICE, MAIN ARMY, May 20, 1780.

SIR :— In your absence, I transmitted to Mr. Clay an account against the Virginia regiments, and now inclose you a letter, in which is contained the charges against the Maryland line and the other regiments marched to the southward. I have left it open that you may give such directions with them, as you think proper, and would be obliged that you would seal and forward it.

My presence with the army occasions me the unhappiness of my seeing and hearing their wants, and makes me urge the matter of money. There are gentlemen now waiting with warrants sufficient to take off the sum Colonel Pickering has negotiated, which I wish may come soon. I am tired of seeing their faces. The army being so long in arrears, and the campaign about commencing, I hope will be deemed sufficient reasons to attend to us. I am convinced of the utter impossibility of getting more money; but, however, hope that some unforeseen circumstances may enable you to do it.

I am, with respect, your most obedient servant,

Col. WM. PALFREY, P. M. Gen.

JOHN PIERCE.

PAY OFFICE, PHILADELPHIA, May 24, 1780.

SIR :—Your several favors of the 6th and 7th inst. came duly to hand, and no time was lost in making the proper applications for a supply of money for the use of your department ; but such is the great scarcity of that now valuable article, that I have not been able to procure one farthing for the many warrants which have been passed by Congress in my favor. I have done everything in my power to obtain it, and I have sent expresses to the Eastern States to collect all that can be got there, which I have ordered to be forwarded on to you. I have likewise a prospect of obtaining 200,000 dollars here in the course of ten days or a fortnight, but not sooner.

It gives me real pain that any obstruction should arise in the supplies of my department; but such is the exigence of the times that it cannot be avoided. When the wheels of the new system lately adopted by Congress are set in motion, I am in hopes the pay and supplies of the army will run on as smoothly as heretofore. In the mean time, that patience and perseverance which has formed so shining a part of their character must be exercised a few weeks longer.

I beg you will present my most respectful compliments to his Excellency, and acquaint him with the contents of this letter, and assure him at the same time that no exertions of mine shall be wanting to forward on the supplies the moment they can be obtained.

I am, with real esteem, your obedient servant,

WILLIAM PALFREY, P. M. Gen.

JOHN PIERCE, Esq., D. P. M. Gen.

MORRISTOWN, May 29, 1780.

SIR :—By the bearer, Captain Machin, you will receive one box, containing five smaller boxes, which I received from the Treasury Board, and by the advice of the Committee of Congress now send to your care to be forwarded as speedily and as safely as possible—you getting receipts for them on delivery. The boxes are directed to,—Mr. Lawrence, Loan Office, Hartford, Conn.; Mr. Appleton, Loan Office, Boston, Mass.; Mr. Clark, Loan Office, Providence, R. I.; Mr. Yates, Loan Office, Albany, N. Y.; Mr. Gilman, Loan Office, Exeter, N. H.

I am, sir, with esteem, your obedient servant.

JOHN PIERCE.

Col. UDNY HAY,
Dep. Qr. Mr. Gen., at Fishkill.

MORRISTOWN, May 29, 1780.

Received of John Pierce, Deputy Paymaster-general, one box, containing five smaller boxes, said to contain public books from the Treasury Office, which I am to deliver to Colonel Hay, Deputy Quartermaster-general at Fishkill, having signed two receipts for the same.

THOMAS MACHIN.

PAY OFFICE, PHILADELPHIA, May 30, 1780.

GENTLEMEN:—A friend of mine has written to me to procure him about 9000 dollars in bills of exchange on Spain—the money for which he will pay at ten days' sight; and at the present rate of exchange will produce 360,000 dollars, and may be delivered in camp in thirty days after the bills are sent from here. In the present scarcity of cash and necessity of the army, I thought it my duty to communicate this matter to your honorable Board, and to request you will be pleased to report a warrant in my favor on the Continental Loan Office in this city, and direct that the same may be paid in bills of exchange on Spain.

I am, with the utmost respect, your obedient servant,

WILLIAM PALFREY, P. M. Gen.

Honorable Board of Treasury.

MORRISTOWN, June 1, 1780.

SIR:—Yours of the 24th ult. I have received, and am sorry there are so many obstacles in obtaining money, which no exertions of ours, I am sensible, will be able to overcome. By this conveyance you will receive my monthly account for May. The balance which appears to be on hand has beeen paid to his Excellency's directions for discharged men, and to officers on account, in the manner as in inclosed memoranda, which I shall deduct from the warrants on payment.

The 200,000 dollars you mention to be sent will be well not to have known to any person when it comes, as it will not answer in any measure towards the payment of the troops, and his excellency will apply it to some particular purpose.

We are fearful from the accounts from New York that Charleston is in the hands of the enemy. The country on the Mohawk River is destroyed by the Indians.

I am, sir, your obedient servant,
JOHN PIERCE.

Col. PALFREY, P. M. Gen.

LOTTERY OFFICE, PHILADELPHIA, June 26, 1780.

SIR:—We are particularly called upon by the Treasury for a state of the lottery, in order to ascertain the cash lodged in the different loan offices.

We therefore request you will furnish us as soon as possible with a complete state of your account for all the three classes, inclosing us vouchers for tickets delivered the Governor and President, and for cash paid to the Loan officer, which will enable us immediately to comply with the above requisition of the Treasury.

The prize lists will be furnished in a few days, when we shall, without loss of time, forward them, with the necessary directions for completing the fourth class which we expect daily from Congress.

Your obedient humble servants,
JOSEPH BULLOCK, } Managers.
SHARP DELANCY,

JOHN PIERCE, Esq.

PAY OFFICE, MAIN ARMY, July 13, 1780.

GENTLEMEN:—Yours of the 26th ult., requesting me to furnish a state of my account for the three classes, and inclose you the vouchers, I have received. In regard to the two first classes, I have already made a settlement in your office with

Mr. French, and delivered him my accounts and vouchers. The third class I send an account of inclosed. As those unsold were delivered to your office at Philadelphia, and the money I received for those credited by me in my account with the public, I have not forwarded you the vouchers. It will oblige the army to have the prize list sent on as soon as possible.

The Managers of the United States Lottery,
                                    In account with John Pierce.

To 346 tickets unsold and delivered at their lottery, March 20, 1780, ... Dollars	10,380
To cash received for sale of tickets, ...	42,542
To 1 ticket, No. 4248, which drew 500 dollars in 2d class, taken in tickets in 3d class, ...	500
To 12 tickets, which drew 30 Dollars each in 2d class, renewed in 3d class, ...	360
To ½ per cent. for sale of 1454 tickets, ...	218
Dollars	54,000

CREDIT.

By 1800 tickets of the 3d class, received for sale at 30 dollars, 54,000

I am, gentlemen, with respect, your obedient servant,
                                                JOHN PIERCE.
Manager U. S. Lottery.

LEBANON, July 20, 1780.

SIR:—Agreeably to your request, I have examined my brother the late Commissary-general's books, and find nothing charged to you for rations due before the 1st of January, 1777. Without more formality, I suppose this will be a sufficient certificate with the Paymaster-general.

With much sincerity of regard, I am, dear sir,
                Your most obedient servant,
                                    JONATHAN TRUMBULL, JR.
Col. JOHN LAMB, of Artillery, Fishkill.

PAY OFFICE, MAIN ARMY, July 20, 1780.

SIR :—By this conveyance you will receive my account current for June, which, by reason of our moving situation, I was not able to send you sooner; also my accounts for March, April, May, and June, and a general account current from my appointment to the beginning of this month, which complete a year's vouchers delivered your office. I wish to have an examination and settlement of them entered into, and the necessary acquittance transmitted to me, if the whole are found just and proper. I have also inclosed a bundle of vouchers belonging to Mr. Reed, which I think unnecessary to hazard any longer at camp.

I am, sir, your obedient servant,

JOHN PIERCE.

WM. PALFREY, Esq., P. M. Gen.

PEEKSKILL, August 1, 1780.

SIR:—I wrote you the 25th ult., since which I have received the last sum of money, and receipted for it to-day. I had not time to complete counting it before the march of the army. Some of it was without any bills, and very much confused. The General has already taken between six and seven hundred thousand dollars from the chest for the use of the Quartermaster-general's department. Nothing that could be said in the matter would have any effect. The service, they said, at head-quarters required it, and Congress either would not or could not supply that department as they ought. Probably more will be taken from me for the same pursose. It yet appears to me that some part of the army may refuse taking the money.

The Pennsylvania line desire to have their depreciation made up, and that at 60 instead of 40 for 1, *and to receive money that other people will take from them, and in such quantities that it may answer some purpose.* Nothing but the General's order would induce some of the regiments to take it. The 1000 I found as you say, I have included in my receipt. You mention that some of this money is to be particularly appropriated for the subsistence of the army. I suppose it is intended to make out the abstracts as formerly where the pay is included with it. They are now made out in that manner, and cannot be separated; and indeed I do not see the necessity of it.

All our Continental troops are now joined. The Jerseys and West Point are to be defended by militia. We are proceeding towards New York, and probably may make an attack on it. It is now but thinly garrisoned. If it is not attended with success, at least the march of our army that way will recall the enemy back from New England. I find the New England regiments are very much strengthened by recruits.

We shall certainly want more money, and hope you will be able to obtain it. The army being so large now, it will take a greater sum than was at first imagined. The importance of the campaign requires that the General should be supplied with money for exigencies, or perhaps operations may entirely cease.

I am out of quills, and will be much obliged to have some forwarded me.

I am, sir, your most obedient servant,

JOHN PIERCE.

Col. WM. PALFREY, P. M. Gen.

TAPPAN, August 11, 1780.

SIR:—Our almost constant movement occasions a delay in my returns. I have at last made out the one for July, which is inclosed. By the returning escort, I send you some bundles containing my own and Mr. Reed's vouchers, which I hope you have received. Our army arrived here on Tuesday last. We are throwing up a work or fort at Dobb's Ferry, possibly to secure a communication there, and fix one step further towards New York.

General Arnold has a large garrison of militia at West Point; and on the approach of the French towards New York, we shall undoubtedly have a very large army. This points out the necessity of being well supplied in cash. It would be better to have something valuable; but as that cannot be the case, I wish to see the *shadow* of it.

I am, sir, your obedient servant,

JOHN PIERCE.

Col. WM. PALFREY, P. M. Gen.

CAMP ORANGETOWN, Aug. 13, 1780.

SIR :—My department being the only one in the staff composed by gentlemen from the State of Connecticut, and under circumstances in which we cannot procure more supplies than what are in common with the army, at the same time partaking with them in the same service, with their discouragements and disadvantages, makes me desire to draw from the State a portion of those refreshments and supplies forwarded the army. In case no depreciation is made up to us by the State, I will refund the amount of what is received in the same proportion with other officers. This method, I conceive, will be attended with no ill consequences, as there is no other person with the army who can claim it as a precedent.

Justice points out the propriety of the States dealing out her benefits with some liberality to all her children who are equally deserving.

By Mr. Lyttle's desire, I write you on the subject, who thinks you will be able to give the necessary order for the purpose.

I am, sir, your obedient servant,
JOHN PIERCE.

Mr. HUBBARD,
State Store-keeper, Connecticut.

CAMP, Sept. 1, 1780.

SIR :—Yours of the 4th ult. came to hand yesterday, and I am much obliged for the quills, as I want them exceedingly. The money was taken for the Quartermaster-general when the British were gone eastward, and our moving for New York. The exertions of that department were then indispensably necessary, and having no other resource, his Excellency was obliged to draw from the chest, or the army must have halted.

In the list of payments made by you, I observe two advances said to be made in April, one to Lieutenant Bigham, and the other to Lieutenant Bevins—similar accounts of the same date I have received from you before. I suppose there has not been two advances of the same kind to them in this month. I wish Mr.

Audibert would put down the regiments the persons belong to to whom you make advances, as there are several in this last account that I cannot tell where charges ought to be made.

I have paid the army as far as the money has gone for January, February and March; my cash is now exhausted, and I want about 400,000 dollars to complete the payment. The army would not receive it but on account, which was accordingly entered into the warrants to be so, agreeable to a resolve of Congress of the 10th of April last. Many of the regiments being mustered for a longer time than the 1st of April in one roll, a separation could not be made in this case. The General directed me to include the whole in one warrant, and give the Paymaster a certificate for the sum over the 1st of April to be paid with the rest of the army, which is the reason that the balance in the inclosed account current for August appears to be in my favor. I have called for the pay-rolls and abstracts of the army up to the 1st of August, for examination, which will be completed for payment in a few days.

I wish that there is a possibility the money may be obtained, as we shall then complete the time the army are to be paid in this money—and the army will now receive it. Perhaps waiting a longer time will raise another broil, which will not be so easily appeased as the late one.

I send you by Colonel Forrest 632⅔ dollars of Maryland, Pennsylvania, and Delaware money, which came with the last you sent. As it will not pass here, I would be obliged to you to receive or exchange it for other money.

I am, sir, your obedient servant,

JOHN PIERCE.

To the Paymaster-general.

HACKENSACK, OLD BRIDGE, Sept. 10, 1780.

SIR:—With my last monthly account, I requested a further sum to complete my payments to the 1st of April, since which several unexpected demands have appeared, and will require more to discharge them than what I then imagined. Indeed, I hope no obstacle will arise to prevent your obtaining a sufficiency for the payment of the army to the 1st of August, when it seems the millennium of our currency is to take place.

Some time last year I received your orders not to pay Mr. McMordie, of the Pennsylvania troops, any longer, as Mr. Rogers was appointed Chaplain to the third brigade. Mr. McMordie, in July last, received an appointment to the first brigade, and now requests his pay as Chaplain to the 11th regiment, from the time his pay was stopped to his new appointment, which regiment I suppose he never saw during that time, nor indeed labored very much in any vineyard towards gathering into the sheepfold. I have not paid him until I can know where he was discharged from the regiment, or I have some further direction in the matter.

Mr. Reed was with me to-day, who, being unable to maintain himself, wishes to leave the service. As the money which has yet passed through my hands has not been half sufficient to defray the charges of the department, much less must be coming to him. Nothing would have induced me to continue, but the hopes that the army would be paid in better money, by which the per cent. allowed me would be more valuable. If that is not the case, I must leave the department considerably in debt to the public. I wish Congress thought with me, that it is their interest to be generous to their honest and faithful servants. Can there be a greater inducement to a person to be dishonest, than to find amidst his sacrifices that he is denied the means of appearing in character, and maintaining himself like a gentleman?

I am, sir, your obedient servant,

JOHN PIERCE.

COL. WM. PALFREY, P. M. Gen.

HACKENSACK, OLD BRIDGE, Sept, 15, 1780.

SIR :—Since the derangement of the Mustering Department there have been no persons pointed out by Congress for the performance of that duty, nor any reward given the officers who have done it by the desire of the General; the consequence of which is, that the troops have been mustered in a very irregular and imperfect manner, and the advantage arising from the musters, being a check to the pay-rolls, is almost wholly lost. I wish, sir, that you would represent the matter, that some persons may be particularly pointed out by Congress, who will consider it as their inclination and duty to transact the business of the department.

The army being to be paid in the new money after the 1st of last month, I am at a loss what allowance is to be given many of the officers, particularly the extra pay and subsistence to aides, brigade-majors, inspectors, paymasters, adjutants, clothiers, quartermasters, &c.; also the pay of surgeons and surgeons' mates all which has been stated after the 1st January, 1777. Indeed, I wish to have the pay of the whole army sent me, which I want now, as the pay-rolls and abstracts cannot be made out before this is known.

I have sent Mr. Burrall all the receipts I have taken up of yours, amounting to 10,072 dollars; the balance due me is 5,472 dollars. Money being so much wanted in the department, makes me wish you to pay him that sum on his delivering up the receipts. I have inclosed you a list of what remains behind. As some of the regiments are at the southward, it is impossible that I should be able to keep up the whole.

I am, sir, your obedient servant,
JOHN PIERCE.

Col. WM. PALFREY, P. M. Gen.

ORANGETOWN, Oct. 8, 1780.

SIR :— Since that of the 11th of August I have not been honored by any of yours. On my part I have written you the 11th of August, and the 1st, 10th, and 15th ult., which I should be happy at least to have acknowledged, that in case of failure I may write again. Inclosed you have my accounts for September. My situation is very unhappy, on account of the want of money in the army.

I am, sir, with respect and friendship, yours,
JOHN PIERCE.

Col. WM. PALFREY, P. M. Gen.

PAY OFFICE, MAIN ARMY, Nov. 7, 1780.

SIR :—I returned yesterday from a short furlough, but unfortunately missed your letter which was forwarded for me. I am sorry you meet with so many difficulties in obtaining the money for the army, and I can assure you their uneasiness increases, which will produce in a few days a remonstrance to Congress. I am happy, however, they do not think the blame lies in your department, but believe they attribute it to the right source. You will note that there is due more than 400,000 dollars to several regiments for January, February and March ; that the pay and subsistence of the whole army, as well as contingencies, are due in old money after that time to the 1st of August; and that the army have *some reason* to expect that two months pay may be *advanced* in the new money after that time; all of which, if received soon, will make them contented and happy, but the want of it will probably have a very contrary effect. I mentioned to you, some time since, a desire to have the pay of the army, as it stands since 1st of August, sent me, which I wish may be done soon, as well as any other directions in the making out of the rolls, that I may bring up my examinations since that time ready for payment. It is with pleasure I see the late arrangement of Congress adopted by the army with cheerfulness, and am persuaded we shall be ready long before the 1st of January to drop into the settled form. The officers who retire will expect to receive their pay before they leave camp ; and it will be political to pay the soldiers also on their discharge.

The Assembly of Connecticut are apportioning their quota of troops into districts, who are each to raise a soldier for three years, or during the war ; and in case of refusal, one is to be hired, and the amount levied from the district, agreeable to their grand list. They will call in their own money, lay a tax on continental, and another on provisions, or hard money.

I am, sir, your obedient servant,

JOHN PIERCE.

Col. WM. PALFREY, P. M. Gen.

PAY OFFICE, Nov. 7, 1780.

SIR :—I am to congratulate you on the situation in which I have just heard you have entered. Your immediate partner I am acquainted with, and wish each of you every happiness that arises from so tender and endearing a connection.

Cannot you let me have your note from the Treasurer of Connecticut? I want money so much that I would do almost any thing for some. I have a friend at Hartford who can catch the money as fast as it comes to the treasury. If you want any of it, when I get some, I will let you have it; and any authority you desire shall be procured, for the transfer either from Colonel Palfrey, the treasury, or General Washington. If you will let me have the note it will oblige me to have it sent immediately, or if not, your answer.

I am, dear sir, yours, sincerely,

JOHN PIERCE.

THOS. REED, Esq.

PAY OFFICE, MAIN ARMY, Nov. 8, 1780.

SIR :—Since mine of the 19th May ult., I have received yours of the 6th of the same month. The several advances since that time may require your attention, either in stopping or transmitting to some other department, which are as follows:

Dec. 31, 1779—Paid by Col. Palfrey, to Lieut. Col. Dirkes,
    his pay from Nov. 5. 1778, to Dec. 31, 1779, . . 2,964
    Pay and subsistence for January, 1780, . . . 460
    Ditto, for February and March, 1780, ... 920
    Ditto, from March to June, 1780, ... 1,380
April 5, 1780—Paid by Mr. Stelle, D. P. M. Gen., for the Rhode Island Department, to Lieut. Col. Lewis Morris, Aid-de-Camp to Gen. Sullivan, now to Gen. Greene, on account, ... 120
May 2, 1780—Paid by myself, to Lieut. Col. Nathaniel Ramsay, of the Maryland Line, a prisoner on parole, on account, ... 2,500
July 5, 1780—Paid by myself, to Lieut. Col. Lewis Morris, Aid-de-Camp to Major Gen. Greene, on account, . 2,000

July 11, 1780—Paid by Col. Palfrey, to Lieut. Ludeman,
for pay and subsistence for March and April, . .   232
July 11, 1780—Paid by Col. Palfrey, to Lieut. Col. John
Laurens, on account of his expenses when sent to
Philadelphia by Gen. Lincoln, . . , . .   2,000
July 25, 1780—Paid by Col. Palfrey, to Capt. John Corse,
of the Delaware regiment, for difference of pay and
subsistence between a Captain and Lieutenant, from
January 26, 1778, to March 1, 1780, . . • .   1,107
August 4, 1780—Paid by Col. Palfrey, to Cornet Perregrine Fitzhugh, of Baylor's Dragoons, . . .   2,700
August 13, 1780—Paid by myself, to Ensign William
Spencer, of the 8th Va. regiment, on account of his
pay, per the hands of Mr. Williams, . . .   800
August 14, 1780—Paid by myself, to Lieut. Col. Oliver
Towles, a prisoner on parole, on account, . . .   4,000
August 22, 1780—Paid by Col. Palfrey, to Col. David Hall
of the Delaware regiment, ...   4,000
August 29, 1780—Paid by myself, to Capt. John Bard, of
the second Georgia battalion, a prison on parole,
on account, ...   1,500
August 30, 1780—Paid by Col. Palfrey, to Lewis De Pontiere, of Pulaski's Legion, for pay and subsistence
from Feb. 1 to July 1, ...   1,250
October 2, 1780—Paid by myself, to Jacob Collins, a private in the 2d Maryland regiment, for two years'
pay and one year's subsistence, while in the hospital
at Albany, ...   280

I am, sir, your obedient servant,
JOHN PIERCE.

JOSEPH CLAY, Esq., Southern Army.

PAY OFFICE, MAIN ARMY, Nov. 8, 1780.

SIR:—Inclosed I transmit you my last month's account, and a letter of stoppages in the Southern department, which I wish you to forward.

Money! money! money! or rather the want of it, is the word. It will oblige me much to hear what prospects you have of obtaining any.

I am, with much respect and friendship, yours,

JOHN PIERCE.

Col. PALFREY, P. M. Gen.

HEAD-QUARTERS, Nov. 17, 1780.

SIR :—Colonel Pickering has just informed me you wrote him you design to resign, and that you are going to France. You are sensible sir, of the delicacy of my situation, my length of service, and if I have any, my merit, and I could wish for your friendship and influence to succeed you, if you think proper.

I suppose I ought to take your place; and if I fail in my attempt, I am determined to resign, which will be at this time disagreeable, as I have sacrificed so much that I had, perhaps, better give up the whole of my time to the public. You will excuse my haste, and believe me to be, with sincerity,

Your most obedient servant,

JOHN PIERCE.

Col. WM. PALFREY, P. M. Gen.

PAY OFFICE Nov. 18, 1780.

SIR :—I feel a degree of regret in parting with so valuable a friend and principal, whose ability and inclination can never be replaced by another. Should the person you mention be appointed, his exertions will not be wanting, however he may fall short in point of *genius*. I take this opportunity, sir, to acknowledge the many and repeated obligations I lay under to you, and can at present only return them by wishing you every happiness and prosperity.

I cannot find that I ever received of you a million of dollars on the 11th of September, 1779, which you will perceive to be the case on the examination of my returns. The first was July 24th, the next, October 6th, and the next, November 30th. I have sent a blank receipt, which you will fill up properly, as I suppose you mistook the date in your letter. I have inclosed you the account you desired. I have taken up one receipt more, that from Thomas Dugan for 403¼ dollars, which I have sent Mr. Burrall.

I have not money enough to ride out of camp, and cannot therefore see you now; but if the appointment takes place, I shall go immediately for Philadelphia.

I am, dear sir, your obedient servant,

JOHN PIERCE.

Col. WM. PALFREY, P. M. Gen.

PAY OFFICE, Nov, 28, 1780.

GENTLEMEN :—I would beg leave to represent that the extra pay given officers of the line, who are aides-de-camp, brigade-majors, regimental-paymasters, clothiers, adjutants, and quartermasters, has been stated since the first of January, 1777, the time to which the resolution of Congress of the 12th of August last has retrospect in determining the pay of the army. In case this extra pay was fixed higher on account of the depreciation, it ought then to have a new stating; but if it was designed to be made up as good money, it ought then, perhaps, stand as it is. I am informed that some of the States have considered it as hard money, and made up the depreciation accordingly.

As the accounts of the army, since the first of August last, are at a stand for this to be determined, I would be obliged, gentlemen, for your attention in the matter.

1 have the honor to be your obedient servant,

JOHN PIERCE.

Hon. Board of Treasury.

PHILADELPHIA, Dec. 20, 1780.

SIR :—Inclosed you have a warrant in my favor on the Treasurer of Connecticut, and another on the Treasurer of Rhode Island—both endorsed to you.

As you are present at Hartford, I make no doubt of your being able to obtain the money there, and wish, after you have been informed where that from Rhode Island can be had, you will send an express for it, if you cannot get it easier. You see I presume on your friendship, which I have experienced so often, and do not doubt but you will be happy to serve me. Mr. Reed has a note from the Treasurer of Connecticut for more than 800,000 dollars. I have written him to let me have it. He says I may, on delivering him a part.

Will you ask the Treasurer how much of it he can advance, and when the whole can be paid? If the sum is worth receiving, I will get the note and send it to you.

I am, dear sir, yours sincerely,

JOHN PIERCE.

J. BURRALL, Esq. }
By Mr. McCall. }

PAY OFFICE, Dec. 26, 1780.

GENTLEMEN:—Captain William Brown, of Colonel Charles Harrison's regiment of artillery, who has been stationed at Fort Schuyler, is now on his march with his company to join the Southern army. Not being furnished with money to defray his expenses, he is obliged to call for the pay of the company, which is due since the 1st of January last, amounting to August 1st, in the old money, to 12,375 dollars, and from that time to the 1st inst. to 2,636 dollars in the new emissions, warrants for which the Board of War have granted on me. As I am unsupplied in cash, I thought it not improper to request, if the money can be obtained, that your honorable Board will report in my favor on the Treasurer to enable me to pay him.

I am, gentlemen, your obedient servant,

JOHN PIERCE.

Honorable Board of Treasury.

The following is a list of Captain Brown's company who are to be paid:

William Brown, Captain.
James Smith, Captain-lieutenant.
James McFaddon, First do.
John Carson, Second do.
Thomas Stanley, Cadet.
John Stanley, Volunteer.
John Staples, Sergeant.
(Given him a certificate of pay to Dec. 20, 1780.)

Henry Slack, Sergeant.
Thomas Barber, do.
Charles Stewart, do.
Patrick Cochran, do.
Alex. A. Mackay, do.
(Deserted Oct. 20, 1780.)
Arthur Carnes, Corporal.
Tamolin Spencer, do.

John Radcliff, Corporal.
Thomas Fanning, do.
Michael Hawke, do.
Samuel J. Nelme, do.
Thomas Condron, Bombardier.
Michael O'Brien, do.
William Jones, do.
Philip O'Bryan, do.
John Connolly, Gunner.
John Vaughn, do.
John Slack, do.
James Welch, do.
James Whalen, do.
James Brooks, Drummer.
Peter Minor, jun., Fifer.
Isaac Burton, Matross.
Thomas Brown, do.
(October 1, 1780.)
Ignatius Butler, Matross.
Robert Campbell, do.
James Compton, do.
James Cole, do.
Hugh Champlin, do.
John Evans, do.
John Fitzgerald, sen. do.
John Fitzgerald, jun, do.
Mark Goldsboro'. do.
Ignatus Griffin, do.
Jonathan Gill, do.
William Huckersen, do.
Edward Hennissey, do.
Henry Higgs, do.

Daniel Harvey, Matross.
William Harney, do.
Francis Johnson, do.
Peter Lawrence, do.
Joshua Lovely, do.
Robert Livingston, do.
(Recruited Nov. 15, 1780, "for during the war.")
Peter Mayner, sen., Matross.
William Moran, do.
(Recruited Nov. 29, 1780, for during the war.)
Mays Nevin, Matross.
Benjamin Palmore, do.
Francis Popham, do.
Samuel Popham, do.
(Given him a certificate of pay to Dec. 20, 1780.)
Joseph Pogue, Matross.
Peter Robinson, do.
Thomas Smith, do.
Reuben Scott, do.
John Saunders, do.
(Given him a certificate of pay to Dec. 20, 1780.)
James Simonds, Matross.
(Recruited Nov. 13, 1780, for during the war.)
William Stalker, Matross,
(Recruited Nov. 15, 1780, for during the war.)
James Taylor, Matross.
David Young, do.
Michael Hawke, do.
(Exchanged for Thomas Brown, October 1, 1780.)
George Baker, Matross.
(Executed by sentence of Court Martial, Nov. 2, 1780.)

NOTE.—This company belonged to the Maryland line.

COWPER'S MILLS, Va., March 19, 1781.

SIR:—Mr. Bacon will deliver you sixty-three guns to be repaired. Some of them are very good guns, and may be made fit for service with very little labor. I think it would be most advisable to examine all the arms, and have those got in order first which are in want of the least repairs.

I received yours of the 15th respecting the box of flints. I have got them, but did not know what number the box contained.

I hope you will be shortly able to furnish the army with a number of guns. The wagon that brings the damaged arms may be left to transport the repaired arms to the different posts where they may be wanted.

I am, sir, your obedient servant,

PAUL WOOLFOLK, Cond. M. Stores.

Mr. W. PORTER, at Broadwater.

BABB'S FIELDS, Va., April 2, 1781.

SIR:—The bearer, Wagon-master George Godby, waits for a load of provisions. Dispatch him and the others as soon as possible. I desired Mr. Adkins to give you a horse and let him have the order.

I shall send you one quire of paper the first opportunity. At present every thing is packed up.

I am yours obediently,

H. MORRIS, Ass't Qr. Mr. Gen.

W. PORTER, C. M. Stores, Broadwater.

CAMP NEAR SCOTT'S, Va., April 10, 1781.

SIR:—By a brigade of wagons and guard, you will receive a very considerable quantity of stores, that are given up by the militia who have served their tours of duty. You will please to take them in and make out an exact inventory of what are delivered to you. On account of the large number received, and what I expect to take in for several days, render it impossible for me to send a list of those articles at this time; but when matters are in a more settled situation, I shall make out a just list of what you may from time to time receive. It is the General's desire that all the cartridges which are in their boxes should be taken out and put in boxes which you will have made for that purpose. From the scarcity of cartridges, you cannot be too careful of those you will receive. You will observe that nearly all the guns are loaded.

In a few days the better half of our militia will be discharged, and I expect to see you at Broadwater very shortly, in company with the remaining part of our army.

I am your friend and obedient servant,

PAUL WOOLFOLK, Ass't Com. Mil. Stores.

Mr. WM. PORTER,
Com. Mil. Stores at Broadwater.

PRINCE GEORGE COURT-HOUSE, Va., April 13, 1781.

SIR :—After much trouble with bad wagons, I have at length arrived at this place with all the stores taken from Broadwater and below. For fear cartridges should be wanted below, I have sent down one box containing 117 dozen. The wagons will get to Broadwater by Sunday evening.

I imagine the General has given you further directions respecting the removal of the military stores. You will make yourself acquainted with his intentions relative thereto, and dispatch those wagons, and others you may have got, with all expedition.

I am, sir, your obedient servant

PAUL WOOLFOLK, A. C. M. Stores.

MR. WM. PORTER, C. M. S. Broadwater.

BLAND'S TAVERN, Va., April 21, 1781.

SIR :—You will receive by four wagons a quantity of damaged arms, sent up from Broadwater. You will dispose of them agreeably to the directions you receive from the Baron Steuben or Major Pryor. The number is not ascertained, being those you had an account of below.

I am, sir, your obedient servant,

PAUL WOOLFOLK, A. C. M. Stores.

WM. PORTER, C. M. Stores.

CHESTERFIELD COURT-HOUSE, Va., April 25, 1781.

SIR :—By two wagons you will receive 230 guns, which were taken from Petersburg yesterday. I believe them to be a part of the arms taken from Broadwater. You will charge me with two guns, which I furnished the militia with yesterday. Those are the whole left in Petersburg. On my way down, I met with General Muhlenburgh, Cabin Point, and returned again to Prince George. Mr. Robert Smith is sent down to remove all the stores remaining at Broadwater. I gave him your letters and instructions for what you were in want of at that place. I am now on my way to Richmond. Mr. Edward Moore is appointed to act below in my place.

     I am, sir, your obedient servant,
        PAUL WOOLFOLK, A. C. M. Stores.
Mr. PORTER,
C. M. Stores, Powhatan C. H.

     CHESTERFIELD COURT-HOUSE, VA., April 25, 1781.

SIR:—The bearer waits on you with a wagon for the following ammunition, viz: 100 sixth-round cartridges, 50 six-pound canister cartridges, 24 Port-fires, and 100 sixth tubes.

You have not been explicit enough in your return. You mention 18 boxes of cannon cartridges, but do not mention the size, though I think there must be the sixth among them. If not, send express for those to Goochland Court-house. Tubes are at the last mentioned place. Do not detain the whole for a deficiency of a part, but send off what you have immediately, and the balance will follow as soon as possible down the road leading to this place or where you may hear the army is.

There has been a pretty severe action this afternoon at Petersburg. The enemy have possession of that place, and our army has retreated to a few miles below this, and are to march tomorrow morning at four o'clock up to this place, and further up the road if necessary. Our men behaved exceedingly well, but overpowered by numbers, were obliged to retire. Our loss was about fifty killed and wounded, and the enemy's considerably more by every account.

If you have any musket-cartridges, send them also. Be as expeditious as possible, as we are nearly out of ammunition.

     I am, sir, your most obedient servant,
        J. PRYOR, Field Com. Mil. Stores.
Mr. Wm. Porter,
Com. Mil. Stores, Powhatan.

CAMP, COAL-PIT, VA., April 30, 1781.

SIR :—I received by the wagoner the articles mentioned in your letter, and have also sent you 59 muskets, 57 bayonets, 39 cartridge-boxes, part of a barrel of damaged cartridges and bullets, and two barrels of powder. The powder and bullets I received at Petersburg, which you will receive. The bayonets, cartridge-boxes, and muskets are all damaged ; also some of them you sent are not fit for use. I have never seen Smith since I came down, but will make inquiry for pork, &c. I will speak to the General for the armorers, and I am, with esteem,

Your obedient servant,

EDWARD MOORE, C. M. Stores.

Mr. W. PORTER, C. M. Stores.

CHESTERFIELD COURT-HOUSE, VA., May 5, 1781.

SIR :—You will take under your charge five wagons, containing 400 stand of arms, complete with bayonets, &c., 200 leather cartridges, two hundred tin canisters, and two thousand flints, and you will proceed immediately to Suffolk. Immediately on your arrival, you will acquaint General Muhlenburgh of it. You will not by any means deliver any of the above articles without General Muhlenburgh's particular order. You will set out from this place this evening, or to-morrow morning very early, so that you may arrive at Suffolk by the 8th instant.

By order of Major-general Steuben.

JAMES FAIRLIE, Aid-de-Camp.

WM. PORTER, C. M. Stores.

RICHMOND, May 6, 1781.

SIR :—Yours dated yesterday, at Carter's Ferry, just came to hand. I am happy to hear you have got a shop and set the armorers to work. As they are fixed, they may remain where they are till further orders, and continue to repair arms with all expedition. Colonel Davis' orders, I think, were very proper, only I do not suppose he knew a large quantity of powder will be immediately wanted for a battery of four 24-pounders and four 18-pounders, at Hood's Creek.

I have called on Captain Brown for the balls and every other necessary that must be brought down immediately. I would wish you to send down all the cannon ammunition fit for service, musket ammunition, arms in repair with bayonets fitted to them and an equal number of cartridge-boxes, sky-rockets, and port-fires, and tubes, if you have any, to Westham, addressed to Mr. McRoberts, Field Commissary of Military Stores, whom I have appointed as such, and I will direct some person to receive them.

The loose balls are of no use in camp. You will therefore send them to the laboratory at Goochland Court-house, taking a receipt for them ; and all the other military stores you will have carried up to Point of Fork, and deposited in some secure house under the eye of some careful person who will take charge of them. You will send all the empty cartridge-boxes you may have, or can procure, to the laboratory, to pack cartridges in, to be sent down to the army, they being much wanted, barrels having been made use of for the want of them.

After you have done what is above required, you will make Mr. Gray, who I suppose is at the head of the armory, responsible for the arms, &c., left in his care, and press him to push their repairs as much as possible—then you may go home to Broadwater, and have all the arms, &c., in that quarter, brought immediately up—those in repair to be left with the new levies at Chesterfield Court-house, and the damaged ones carried up to Colonel James's or the armory for repairs.

I did expect a complete return of all the stores you have in charge, as well as the horse-accoutrements I requested you to take charge of. You may re-deliver them to the Quartermaster, as they are not in your department, and render him an account of your issues of them, and show him your authority for so doing.

You will please to be very particular in this, and send me a similar account of them.

I am, sir, your obedient and humble servant,

J. PRYOR, Com. Gen. Mil. Stores.

Mr. W. PORTER, C. M. S., Carter's Ferry.

November 9, 1782.

SIR:—Pursuant to the orders of Major-general Greene, of the 2d and 3d days of November, 1782, we have formed the 1st and 3d regiments of dragoons, now serving in the State of South Carolina, into five troops, agreeably to an order of the Secretary of War, to be commanded by the following officers, viz:

George Baylor, Colonel, commissioned January 8, 1777.
William Washington, Lieutenant-colonel.
John Swan, Major, commissioned October 21, 1780.
Churchill Jones, Captain, do. June 1, 1777.
John Watts, do. do. April 7, 1778.
William Barrett, do. do. May, 1779.
William Parsons, do. do. November, 1779.
John Hughes, do. do. March 31, 1781.
Ambrose Gordon, 1st Lieut., commissioned December, 1779
John Linton, do. do. May, 1780.
Henry Bower, do.
Francis Whiting, do.
Chas. Yarborough, do.
James Merriweather, 2d. Lieut.
John Harris, do.
George White, do.
Philip Stewart, do.
William Fitzhugh, do.
—— Nelson, Paymaster.
Charles Scott, Cornet.
Jasper Hughes, do.
John Massey, do.
John Perry, do.
John Walters, do.
Robert Rose, Surgeon.
John Wallace, do.
——Vaughn, Surgeon's Mate.

Doctor Rose being sick at present, and unable to do immediate duty, Doctor Wallace is arranged to do the duty of Surgeon to the regiment until the recovery of Dr. Rose.

It is the opinion of the Board that a Court of Inquiry be, as soon as possible, ordered to determine the rank of the officers, to the end that the dates of their commissions may be inserted in the arrangement. We have arranged the officers of the 1st and 8d regiments to a command in the five troops, in proportion to the number of troops in each corps, from the principle of their being entitled to promotion regimentally.

     Your obedient servants,
      ANTHONY WAYNE, B. G.
      JOHN SWAN, Major L. D.
      CHURCHILL JONES, Captain L. D.

(No Address.)

          NEW HAVEN, Jan. 10, 1783.

SIR :—The circumstances of my business render it impossible for me to receive any part of the securities now to be issued to the army. The late 4th Connecticut regiment has no agent appointed to receive theirs. I wish they might be delivered to Mr. Beers, as the principal part of the officers and men belong to this county.

The 2d Connecticut regiment I suppose General Swift will receive, as he is agent ; otherwise I should like them also delivered to Mr. Beers, in order that the several charges made against individuals mighty be rightly understood from my accounts.

I shall, after the securities are issued to the several regiments, apply to your office with my accounts stated for settlement.

I conclude that the accounts made out by Mr. Clark, for 1783, as well as those I handed you, are rightly understood, so that the securities can be issued to the two regiments at the time the other regiments in the Connecticut line receive theirs, as no advice has been received to the contrary.

I send my account by Mr. Beers for the extra pay as Paymaster, which was to be paid in Morris' notes, or money for those who attended to the settlement of accounts. Likewise, the amount due for subsistence, I should receive it as a particular favor to have it paid him.

     I am your obedient servant,
          JOHN SHERMAN.

JOHN PIERCE, P. M. Gen.

POUGHKEEPSIE, N. Y. May 17, 1783.

SIR :—I was honored with yours of the 8th inst. I remember exceedingly well having a bundle of papers from you, on account of expenses attending the transportation of cannon to Farmington, but cannot recollect the amount; and as these vouchers shared the same fate with almost the whole of my other papers, I do not esteem myself at liberty to give any new vouchers until Congress has pointed out some general course by which my conduct ought to be regulated in all such cases.

I am, with greatest respect, sir,
Your most obedient, humble servant,
UDNY HAY, D. Q. M. Gen.

Col. EBENEZER STEVENS.

PHILADELPHIA, June 3, 1783.

SIR :—This morning I received your letter relative to the money advanced you to pay for the transportation of the ordnance and stores from Albany to Farmington.

I must inform you that immediately on my return, I made up my account for every farthing received by me, and gave it you; soon after which it was examined and approved by the Auditors at Albany, and referred to Colonel Hay, as being in his department, for settlement—at which time I delivered you every paper relative to the transaction, and have never since seen any of them. Having done with them entirely, the receipt given you was cancelled; and you having delivered the papers to Colonel Hay, who also examined and admitted them, 'exonerates you from blame by his misfortune. He repeatedly offered you a discharge, and I always thought you had it, and that the whole matter was settled long since. Colonel Hay, upon application, will certainly certify that the whole was settled, which I suppose will be satisfactory.

With regard to the pay received by me and my department, you will find it by examining the abstracts; but I will send you a copy of the account as it stands between us, from which you can extract any sums that ought to be charged the public which remain unaccounted for.

You will see that I have accounted with you for all that I ever received, except the money for the transportation, which, having settled with you on my return, closed the transaction on my part—nor have I a scrap of paper on the subject. Having done the business for you, and the examination having been made and approved, I conceived myself as exonerated, and made no register of the matter.

Brother Ben will sail in a few days for the Cape. He presents abundance of love.

    With affection, I remain yours,
            SAMUEL HODGDON.
Col. EBENEZER STEVENS.

           RAEDING, Decemper 24, 1783.

DEIR SIR:—I schold Dack it as a graet faver, you wold be so kint and to Ender My Name and Capt. Jacob Mytinger of my Troop in the Boock of Society of Sencinates for whech we have Laft a Monts Pay whet the Pay Master Generale of the arMy, and hafe encloset a Certificat from the Pay Master Generale, whech mentionet that the Money may be Trowen as Sun the order is Broeduset. I schall be Blaessed to you, you will Rid me a Lader and Mentionet what Money must be send for Endrens, if der is any oder Exbenses, yöu will be so Kint as to lad us Know. My Seff and Capt. Mytinger will Comply whet what you schalle Tin proper,

  Sir, I Remin whet the Gradest Estim
    Your Efectiont frend and M. H. S.
         BARTHW. VON HEER,
          Major Light Dragoons.
Col. HARMER, at Mrs. Srunk's Tavern,
 Second Streed, Philadelphia.

          ANNAPOLIS, Jan. 1, 1784.

SIR:—About the time we adjourned from Princeton I received a line from you, to which you would probably have discovered before this time that I had paid every attention possible; but there have not since that time been nine States represented in Congress. Your concerns are delayed with the most important ones of the nation.

On the application of some foreign officers for some immediate pay, a committee was appointed some time ago, of which I am chairman. The journals ought to show what has and what has not been promised or done for the foreign officers who have been in our service; but there are many different opinions as to the manner in which our executive officers construe the meaning of those journals.

Be so good as to inform me, whether in settling the accounts of foreign officers who have been in our service they have been allowed half-pay. If half-pay has been allowed to any of them, whether it has been indiscriminately allowed to those who had and those who had not taken the oath of fidelity to the United States.

I have the honor to be your obedient servant,

HUGH WILLIAMSON.

JOHN PIERCE, Esq.

COMPTROLLER-GENERAL'S OFFICE, Jan. 30, 1784.

SIR :—The State has paid to Lieutenants Benjamin Marshall, John Hughes, and —— Morrison, of the Pennsylvania Line, the sum of one hundred and forty-six dollars and two-thirds of a dollar, each, being for 5¼ months' pay, which you will please to charge them with at the settlement of their accounts.

I am your friend and very humble servant,

JOHN NICHOLSON, Aud. Gen.

JOSEPH HOWELL, Esq.

BOSTON, Nov. 18, 1784.

SIR :—Your favor of the 18th September, by Captain Thomas H. Condy, I have received. I am exceedingly disappointed that Captain Condy was not able to settle my accounts, as he was fully empowered by me for that purpose. I flatter myself that by this time you have been able to find my account, with the vouchers. If they are not already examined, I request you to have them taken up the first opportunity after the receipt of this, as I am very anxious to have them adjusted. A line from you, by the post, on this subject, will lay me under a particular obligation.

I am, with great esteem, your obedient servant,

JOHN PIERCE, Esq., P. M. Gen.

HENRY JACKSON.

TRENTON, Dec. 11, 1784.

SIR :—I should be very much obliged to you to inform me, whether, by the orders of Congress, the widow or children of a Major-general who lost his life in the service is entitled to the half-pay of a Major-general for seven years, or to that of a Colonel only.

There is a dispute in the State of Massachusetts which is suspended on the decision of this question.

If you think the case clear, your opinion, with the grounds of it, will no doubt give satisfaction; but if you are in any doubt, I shall apply to Congress for an explanation of those acts.

I am with the highest esteem, your obedient servant,

GEORGE PARTRIDGE.

Col. JOHN PIERCE, P. M. Gen.

NORWICH, Dec. 16, 1784.

SIR :—Since I wrote you last, respecting my ration accounts (an answer to which I have not had the pleasure, although Mr. Brown tells me you wrote me by Mr. Lovell), I recollect that I signed them in a form that might answer for a discharge in full : and should you leave the office, it might be concluded by your predecessor that the accounts were settled and paid. I presume that the act of Congress of the 3d of June supersedes the necessity of Colonel Stewart's vouchers.

If it appears so to you, I will be much obliged to you to pay the balance due me on those accounts to Mr. Pelatiah Webster, and beg the favor of him, in my behalf, to send it to me by some convenient opportunity, or to bring it when he next comes to Norwich.

I am, dear sir, with great regard, your humble servant,

JEDEDIAH HUNTINGTON.

JOHN PIERCE, P. M. Gen., Philadelphia.

NEW YORK, Dec. 24, 1784.

SIR :—I am under the necessity of requesting the favor of you to examine the muster-rolls of the Invalid Corps ; and in Captain Woelport's company you will find a man by the name of Simon Peterson, who was formerly a soldier in the 4th New

York regiment, commanded by Colonel Henry B. Livingston. The said Peterson was sent to Simsbury Hospital when the regiment lay at Wyoming, in October, 1779, and he was invalided from that place the latter part of that year, or in 1780, on account of a bayonet having been run through his foot. He served in the Invalid Corps until 1783, when he was legally discharged on pension, but unfortunately lost his discharge, and by that means was deprived of his depreciation, pension, and all other emoluments which are due to him from the State of New York, unless he can make it appear he served in the Invalid Corps after he left the New York line. After you have examined the rolls, you will be kind enough to send such a certificate back by Mr. Horton, the bearer, as will serve as a voucher for the Auditors of the State of New York, which is all they require.

Your obedient servant,
JOSEPH MORRELL.

JOSEPH HOWELL, Esq., Philadelphia.

NEW YORK, August 2, 1785.

SIR :—The Commissioner for settling the army accounts, to whom was referred the petition of James Gilleland, late a Captain in the corps of Sappers and Miners, begs leave to report—that notwithstanding Captain Gilleland has stated in his petition that he served in the army to the end of the war, it appears by the returns of the corps and by the records of the War Office, that he resigned his commission on the 9th day of October, 1782—which resignation, in the opinion of your Commissioner, debars him from the benefits of the resolution of Congress of the 16th September, 1776, granting lands, and of October 21st, 1780, granting half-pay for life to such officers as shall continue in service to the end of the war; that there is still due to James Gilleland some arrears of pay and subsistence, certificates for which will be issued to him on his application.

I have the honor to be your obedient servant,
JOHN PIERCE.

President of Congress.

NEW YORK, August 2, 1785.

SIR:—In answer to your note respecting the special paid to the officers of the army in the years 1782 and 1783, I beg leave to inform you that there has not been any advanced by a State to any of the lines to my knowledge on account of their pay, but the sum has been furnished by the United States under the arrangement of the Office of Finance, and I believe by no particular resolution of Congress. The sum intended to be advanced to the army under these regulations has been two months for officers of higher grades in 1782, and four months for the line in general in 1783, which was advanced in notes of the Superintendent of Finance, payable in six months to the Northern army, and by bills at thirty and sixty days' sight for the Southern army. The Northern lines are completely paid, and there are considerable arrears, which I am endeavoring to ascertain with precision, now due to the Southern troops.

I have the honor to be your obedient servant,

JOHN PIERCE.

Hon. THOMAS MCKEAN.

NEW YORK, August 10, 1785.

SIR:—The Paymaster general, to whom was referred the petition of Pierre Regnier de Rousse, late a Lieutenant-colonel in the fourth and second New York regiments, praying the depreciation on his pay, begs leave to report that it appears the petitioner resigned his commission on the 24th day of March, 1780; that by the resolutions of Congress of the 10th day of April and of the 8th day of August, 1780, and of the 15th of May and 12th of August, 1783, this allowance appears to be altogether restricted to the officers in the service on the 10th day of April, 1780; that Mons. Regnier conceives himself entitled to claim his depreciation, particularly as he was a foreigner previous to the war, expecting that a distinction would be admitted between foreign and domestic officers; which principle the Paymaster-general humbly conceives to be improper, and not justified by any usage or resolution of Congress. He therefore submits the following resolve: That Mons. Regnier, having resigned his commission prior to any promise of depreciation, cannot, agreeable to the principles adopted by Congress in such cases, be entitled to this allowance.

JOHN PIERCE, P. M. Gen.

President of Congress.

ANNAPOLIS, August 15, 1785.

SIR:—I had a letter from Major Allen McLane, late of Lee's Legion, in answer to one I wrote him on the subject of an advance by the State of Maryland, in which he requests the same may be charged to the United States, to be accounted for by him on final settlement; and although I have already transmitted the account to your office, I have thought proper to mention the matter again, lest that might have been mislaid. The sum charged to Major McLane is £187 10, new emission, received in March, 1781, at the rate of 8¼ for 1, is £57 13 10, specie, for which sum please to charge him, and give the State of Maryland credit therefor. The certificates for horses taken, and purchased by Major McLane within this State, have all been taken up and liquidated by the State, and will be charged to the United States in general account.

In answer to your letter of the 14th July, on the subject of the advance to the Baron De Kalb, I have to inform you that I never received any money from him, nor did I ever hear of his taking up any money for the purposes you mention until I received your letter. As soon as I receive answers to the inquiries I have set on foot touching this business, I will write to you again thereon.

With highest regard, I am your obedient servant,

C. RICHMOND, Auditor-general.

JOHN PIERCE, Esq. New York.

BALTIMORE, August 18, 1785.

SIR:—I have delayed answering yours of the 14th July, expecting to be able to give you some information respecting the expenditure of the money received by the Baron De Kalb. I have not yet met with any person that can give me any information on the subject, more than that the Baron was known to have a large sum of money in his hands for the purpose of marching the troops to the southward, and that Captain Joseph Marbury, Quartermaster for the detachment, received part of it for the use of his department. I make no doubt but he has, or can account for what he received. He is now in Virginia. I will write to him on the subject, if an opportunity offers. I think, from considering the circumstances of the army, that but a small part of the money could have been expended. It soon became useless in procuring any thing whatever for the army, and recourse was had to other means for subsistence. With respect to arrearages of clothing, I doubt whether the army ever received it.

I am your most obedient servant,

J. E. HOWARD.

JOHN PIERCE, Esq., P. M. Gen., New York.

NEW YORK, August 19, 1785.

GENTLEMEN:—The petition of John Buchanan, citizen of the State of New York, most respectfully showeth, that your petitioner was one among the first of the inhabitants of the State who avowed an opposition to the arbitrary measures of the British Government, and was honored with the command of a company of his fellow-citizens upon the first arrangement of the militia in this city, in the year 1775; that early in the year 1776, your petitioner was employed by the Commander-in-chief, and by other Generals, in many confidential and difficult services, which he has had the happiness to execute to their satisfaction, and was in the year 1777 appointed a superintendent of the water-craft on the Hudson River; that in the month of January, 1778, your petitioner being, with the boats under his command, at Tarrytown, far advanced of the enemy, and stationed for their greater security in their winter cantonments, was apprised that a party of the enemy were approaching with an intent, among other objects, to destroy the boats and guard under his command, but he had the good fortune to either kill or make prisoners the whole of the party, although in the action he was wounded, and thereby not only disabled from service for a considerable time, but has in a great measure lost the use of his right arm forever; that as soon as your petitioner was able to withdraw himself from the hospital, he again entered upon his duty, and on the 3d of February, 1779, was appointed by General McDougall to a very troublesome and confidential service, and stationed at the garrison at West Point, which appointment was afterwards confirmed by General Washington, and in this station your petitioner remained to the close of the war; that all the pay and subsistence of your petitioner was equal to that of a Captain in the line of the army; yet, from the frequent changes in the Quartermaster-general's department, or causes which he knows not, there is due to him his pay from the 21st of August, 1778, to the 4th of August, 1780, and his subsistence for the same space of time, except while he was in the hospital; and there is also due to him the depreciation of his pay from the 1st of September, 1777, to the said 21st of August, 1778.

Your petitioner is therefore constrained to present his case to your honorable body, not doubting but that he will meet with that justice and favor which those who have faithfully served their country are entitled to; and in proof of the facts which he has herein set forth, he is ready to produce the most substantial vouchers.

JOHN BUCHANAN.

Honorable Congress of the United States.

NEW YORK, August 22, 1785.

SIR:—On examination of the claims of Lieutenant Pepin for the five years' full pay in lieu of half-pay for life, I find that he held a regular military commission in Colonel James Livingston's regiment; that he was returned with sundry other officers on the 23d June, 1779, in the musters of the regiment, as a supernumerary, and furloughed under that idea for twelve months, which furlough, by a certificate of General Gates and Colonel Livingston, appears to have taken effect; that his pay as a supernumerary officer was drawn as far as the rolls can be procured, which is up to January 1, 1780; that in the year 1780 he received a pass from one of the Aides of the Commander-in-chief as a *late Lieutenant* of Livingston's regiment; that he did duty in Malcolm's regiment in October, 1780, and was seen with the infantry in 1780; that he has settled his accounts of depreciation at the Treasury up to July 31, 1780. On which evidence, I am of opinion his military commission in the army of the United States was totally extinct on his becoming supernumerary; that he has received in his settlement, and the money he has drawn in his regiment, more than to the amount of the year's pay promised to supernumeraries at that time; and that therefore, as there was then no other promise, he can have no claim, as a late officer of Colonel Livingston's regiment, to any further allowance to half-pay or commutation.

The certificates that he produces, that he did duty afterwards in other corps, cannot, in my opinion, be construed as conferring another appointment on him as an officer, such appointment being derived immediately from Congress. They prove, indeed, that he served as a volunteer, and may entitle him to any allowances given to such characters; but as the grant of commutation is founded entirely on actual appointments, it is necessary that he prove such appointment was given to him again after leaving his late regiment.

This opinion considers his right only as an officer, but should those of a Canadian be distinct from the rest of the army, it may not be properly founded.

I have the honor to be you obedient servant,

JOHN PIERCE.

President of Congress.

NEW YORK, August 29, 1785.

SIR :—The commissioner for settling the army accounts, to whom was referred the petition of John Buchanan, lately employed in the Quartermaster's department, begs leave to report —That his prayer for depreciation cannot at present be granted, Congress having in no instance giving it to officers in that department; that his claim to pay and rations from August

21, 1778, to August 4, 1780, appears properly to come under the consideration of the commissioner appointed for settling the accounts of the Quartermaster's department who is already invested with sufficient authority to finally liquidate the same; that his claim for a proper allowance for his maintenance, in consequence of a wound received in battle, arises from simple testimony, produced by him, that he received this wound in his right arm and shoulder in meritorious service, wherein he, with eighteen boatmen under his command, killed and took prisoners a party of twenty-five British new levies; and that this wound has almost totally deprived him of the use of that right arm. Your commissioner therefore submits that he be considered as comprehended within the benefits of the ordinance of Congress of June 7, 1785, providing for those that have been disabled in the service, in the same manner as if he had been a Captain in the line.

I have the honor to be your obedient servant,

JOHN PIERCE.

President of Congress.

BALTIMORE, Sept. 20, 1785.

SIR :—I was from home when your letter of the 14th July was left at my office. It is not in my power to give you any satisfactory account of the money received by the Baron De Kalb in the year 1780. Captain Marbury of the Maryland line acted at that time as Quartermaster to the Maryland division of the army, and probably received some part of it; but I think it improbable that the regimental clothiers, forage-masters, or commissaries had much of it in their hands; they were constantly with the troops, and we seldom encamped where there was anything to purchase. In my opinion, the Baron expended the principal part of the money, or left it in Philadelphia, for clothes and other articles to be forwarded.

I am your obedient servant,

O. H. WILLIAMS.

JOHN PIERCE, Esq., New York.

CHARLESTON, S. C., Sept. 15, 1785.

SIR:—I have to acknowledge the receipt of your favor of the 14th July, and am sorry I cannot furnish you with the information you wish, having none of the orderly books or papers relating to that campaign by me. I do not recollect the names of the staff officers you suppose the money might have been advanced to, but believe Captain Joseph Marbury was the Deputy Quartermaster and Captain Roxburg the Commissary, both of the Maryland line.

General Smallwood is now in Maryland, to whom I would recommend you to apply for information, and make no doubt he can acquaint you fully on the subject.

I have the honor to be, with respect, your obedient servant,
MORDECAI GIST.

JOHN PIERCE, Esq., New York.

DECEMBER 15, 1785.

SIR:—Some time last summer I inclosed a furlough given to me by Colonel Baylor, wherein he mentions I had one from General Greene, which I know he kept when he granted mine. Be pleased to be so very good as to say what can be done. Colonel Charles Magill will bring whatever you may honor him with.

I am, sir, yours,
ALBION THROCKMORTON.

ANDREW DUNSCOMB, Esq., Richmond, Va.

STRATFORD, April 18, 1786.

SIR:—I received yours of the 8th inst. Agreeably to your request, as also that of General Lamb's, I have forwarded to Mr. Bull a return of the men in my company who received the State bounty of £10, with my attestation thereon; likewise I have inclosed a similar return to you with General Lamb's account on the back—that is, a copy, being taken from his account stated with me and balanced, as will appear. This contains the whole of the bounty received from State or Continent. I have all the men's receipts to show for the receipt of the same, except John Fite's, who, I am pretty positive, received said bounty of £10 of Lieutenant Hughes, but I do not find his receipt: said Hughes had the note of me for that purpose. That makes the twenty-five recruits which I paid said bounty to, agreeably to which General Lamb credited me at the time, as you will see. Also you will perceive I paid, or delivered to Captain Andrew Moody, four of said notes, for which he has credited me in his accounts. This, sir, comprehends the whole. I am inclined to believe that Captain Mott, as well as Moody, has a number of these notes.

I am, dear sir, with respects to your family,

Your obedient servant,

ROBT. WALKER, late Captain of Artillery.

Col. ELEAZER OSWALD, New York.

SALEM, July 21, 1786.

SIR:—Inclosed you will receive my account with the United States, and I must request your kind attention to it. By reason of sickness, I have delayed my account to this time, but hope you will be able to settle it; and if any vouchers are necessary, please to inform me. But I must inform you that as I lost my baggage on the retreat from Ticonderoga, my receipts were all lost. I have the original minutes, which I then kept in my journal agreeable to each receipt. Having the journal in my pocket at that time, I preserved it. I have inclosed Paymaster Ebenezer Storer's certificate. Please to bear in mind that by the act of Congress interest is to be allowed from April, 1779.

I am, sir, your most obedient servant,

SAMUEL CARLTON, Lieut. Col.

JOHN PIERCE, Esq., P. M. Gen., New York.

RICHMOND, July 23, 1786.

SIR:—Understanding that your office closes on Saturday, and finding that my claim as Aid-de-camp to General Lee cannot be liquidated here, I have ventured to solicit the favor of you to examine into its merits, and forward the result as speedily as possible.

I was appointed as Aid to General Lee in May, 1778, and continued until his suspension. I was at that time a Captain in the 15th Virginia regiment.

My father, John Turberville, has a claim for a wagon, team, and negro, which were impressed in 1778, and never returned to him. If this will serve to stay his claim, I will forward on the exhibits to prove the impressment, &c., which, if they were not at a distance, should be forwarded by this post.

I have the honor to be, with much esteem, your obedient servant,

GEORGE L. TURBERVILLE.

JOHN PIERCE, Esq., P. M. Gen., New York.

JULY 31, 1786.

SIR:—In consequence of orders received from the Board of Treasury, I settled Major Ottendorff's account, August 8, 1777, and paid him a balance of 516$\frac{9}{90}$ dollars. After the account was settled, I received a charge against him of 200 dollars advanced him by Mease & Caldwell, which the Major promised to account for when the receipt was produced. I applied to Mease & Caldwell for the same, who told me these receipts were lodged with the Treasury Board, and the matter still remains unsettled for that sum only.

The Major says he has pay due him which will more than answer for that sum. You will please therefore to examine into the same, and if you think proper, settle with him accordingly.

I am yours,

WILLIAM PALFREY.

Major CLARK.

SAVANNAH, ———.

SIR:—I am inclined to think you will find it extremely difficult, if not impossible, to settle the accounts of the Georgia line of the late army, so as to do equal justice to the individuals and the United States, by the mode you have hitherto adopted, unless you take up the whole of their accounts from the beginning of their respective services, with those parts of the Quartermaster's and Commissary's departments, as each of them were entitled to, as they have already made them out themselves, and settled them in that manner with the Auditor of the State: for which I offer the following reasons, which I presume must justify you in any deviation you are obliged to make from your general instructions, and as you will find cannot suit this State.

First, Because, by the distance of this State from Congress the little attention paid to it for some time, the neglect of men in office, and the uncertainty of conveyance, the several resolves and recommendations of Congress did not reach it to be put into execution in due time, prior to the 29th of December, 1778, when the State, and nearly the whole line of it, fell into the hands of the British, and were chiefly lost ever after.

Second, Because, that after the capture of Savannah, and while the State of Georgia continued in the hands of the enemy, there was no regular government existing in the State, and therefore impossible they could take up any directions or recommendations from Congress respecting regulations, recruiting, supplies, depreciation of pay, &c., for their line of the late army as other States have done, until July, 1782, when the British evacuated Savannah; and every officer, during that unfortunate period, who had been at large, or were released from imprisonment, being driven from their country and property, took an active part in the other States, as they respectively found an opportunity: and they look to Congress alone to make good their engagements, as the State they belonged to was rendered incapable.

And lastly, Because, by an act of the Legislature of Georgia, passed at Augusta, 29th July, 1783, the first time they had leisure and opportunity to take up the business, all accounts of officers and soldiers of the Georgia line of the State, which were certified by any person authorized by Congress, or other authority under them, that such accounts as would be passed to the credit of the State with the United States, should be taken as cash in payment of all public sales, with an allowance of 12¼ per cent. in such payments, provided they were tendered within twelve months after the date of the act; and was with some difficulty prolonged twelve months more the last session—therefore the individuals must be capital losers, without any benefit to the United States, unless their accounts are taken up immediately, and altogether prior to the first of August, 1780, when Congress took upon themselves to make up all deficiencies, as well as since that period—and as the State of Georgia was singularly unfortunate, though not for want of exertions, and rendered incapable of doing it before.

I am, sir, your most obedient humble servant,

LACHLIN MCINTOSH,
Late Brig. Gen. Commanding the Georgia Line.

JOHN PIERCE, Esq., P. M. Gen.,
   at Mrs. Minis's, Savannah.

NEW YORK, Jan. 8, 1787.

SIR:—I have delayed the gentleman who handed me your letter of the 80th ult. until this day, in order that I might myself survey the whole muster-rolls of your regiment, and obtain a thorough information of all the circumstances that attend the recruiting of it; and have now, from a consideration of these and the statement contained in your letter, formed an opinion that I shall not be justified, on the evidence before me, in making an allowance for your advances to your officers beyond what you have received from the public, if even they can be admitted to that amount.

I hope, sir, that your knowledge of my character will lead you to believe, that in the decision I am influenced by no other principles but what I conceive to be my duty, and that there appears to me an absolute necessity, before your claim can be admitted, that you obtain the approbation of Congress.

I am, dear sir, your obedient servant,

JOHN PIERCE.

COL. ISRAEL SHREEVE.

RICHMOND, VA., May 18, 1787.

SIR:—There was a large sum of Maryland paper money, which was issued under the act of Congress of March or April, 1780, left by an accident, in the year 1781, in the hands of a Mr. William S. Alexander, who acted as Quartermaster at Hillsboro' in North Carolina; after which, I am informed that it came into the hands of a Mr. Thomas Commander Russell, lately residing at Charleston.

This latter man has been attempted to be found, but cannot. His wife says that he has gone a long way off—but where, she cannot tell. I am therefore of opinion he may be in Maryland, to dispose of the money. I give you this information, therefore, that you may be watchful, that in case any person should be known to be disposing of such money, you may inform me in this city, and also the Board of Treasury, as soon as possible, or take any other steps you may think advisable.

I am your obedient servant,

JOHN PIERCE.

THOMAS HARWOOD, Esq.,
Maryland Loan Office.

RICHMOND, VA., May 18, 1787.

SIR:—I have but now received your letter of April 15th, and am much surprised at the intelligence it contains.

I wish you to find if this Russell has not come this way, or into this State. From some circumstances I am led to suppose that he, or some agent for him, is now selling this money. If you can trace him out, and give me any information about him, you will oblige me by communicating the same at this place, where I shall remain until about the first of August.

I am, sir, your obedient servant,

JOHN PIERCE.

JOHN NEUFVILLE, Esq.

RICHMOND, May 18, 1787.

SIR:—Your letter of the 7th inst., with its inclosures, has arrived.

I am so much engaged in the State's business, that I have not attended to Dr. Bond's claim sufficiently to form an opinion on it. I am doing some other business for him with this State, and will write to him on both, when I have accomplished this. I rather think his pay ought to be extended to January, 1785.

I do not well recollect what opinion I had formed respecting General Putnam's demands; but this I remember, that it appeared to me that he must be charged with the 3,000 dollars he gave his note for to Mr. Bedlow, or for so much of it as is unaccounted for. It did not appear to me clearly that he was entitled to his rations, because he did no actual duty, and his pay and commutation appeared as sufficient compensation to him. Pay, I considered as equivalent to services, and rations, to expenses in that service, which he would not be at while at home. It occurs to me, however, that the idea struck me that his confinement by sickness might make a difference, though I believe it did not in his case. You must take the opinion of the Treasury or Comptroller, and do as you think proper, remembering, in case the allowance is made, there must be clear proof that he drew no rations during the time.

I conclude that the duplicates to General Huntington's papers are as good as originals. His case, I suppose, must be referred to Congress.

I wish you to lay the copy of Mr. Neufville's letter before the Board of Treasury, and request information from the Board if they have heard from Alexander, and where he is. In the meantime, as I am now but a little more than a hundred miles from the place where he acted as Quartermaster, I shall endeavor to find him out.

I want from you copies of his receipt to the express, and of Mr. Clay's attested account-current with him. You will find them in my letter to Mr. Neufville or to the Board of Treasury, when I first informed them of this money. It is uncertain when my business here will be closed. My compliments to Mrs. Howell.

Since writing the above, I imagine I have got a clue to find out where the man is who has, or has had, the public money in his hands which was lodged with Alexander. I wish you therefore to advise with the Board, and obtain such legal authority as will enable me to prosecute Alexander, in case I find it necessary. His original receipt is in Mr. Nourse's office, among my vouchers. Clay's attested account is among his papers, in Mr. Nourse's office. Your immediate attention to this may be of importance.

I am, sir, your obedient servant,

JOHN PIERCE.

JOSEPH HOWELL, Esq.

RICHMOND, May 21, 1787.

SIR:—I take the liberty to request you to inform me if a William S. Alexander, or a Thomas Commander Russell, can be found in your State, and where?

My reasons for troubling you on this occasion are, that I have *good evidence* that a large sum of the public money is in one or both their hands, and that they are appropriating it to their private purposes, and that in case they are found, it is essential that they are not alarmed by any notice of my pursuit of them.

As Mr. Alexander may be known at Hillsboro', you will oblige the public very essentially, if you have a correspondent there, by writing to him for this information, which I wish to have communicated to me, in this city, as soon as possible.

I am, sir, your obedient servant,
JOHN PIERCE.

Gen. ALLEN JONES.

NEW YORK, Sept. 13, 1787.

GENTLEMEN:—In the letter which I did myself the honor to write to the Board, on the 3d inst., I informed the Board that Mr. Clay knew that the money which I there referred to was lodged in Alexander's hands for him, and that therefore it was his neglect that he did not secure it for the use of the public; but having since examined more minutely into Mr. Clay's letters and returns, I find that he has not only received this money from Alexander, but acknowledges, in express terms, that he considers himself accountable for it.

I have the honor to be your obedient servant,
JOHN PIERCE.

Honorable Board of Treasury.

RICHMOND, Feb. 18. 1788.

SIR:—Extreme hurry of business has prevented my sending you the return desired until now—it must also plead for the manner in which it is drawn, as I had not time to give a more official look to the writing.

I am, with much regard, your obedient servant,
ANDREW DUNSCOMB.

JOSEPH HOWELL, Esq.

Return of men belonging to and considered as part of the quota of the State of Virginia in Hazen's, Lee's, Armand's, and Invalid corps. Those entitled to land are marked *.

HAZEN'S CORPS.

*John Taylor, Major.
*Tarleton Woodson, Major.
*Richard Edmonston, Sergeant.
*William Easton,   "
*John Walden, Corporal.
*Cornelius Bearly, "
*James McGeorge, Private.
*Ralph Moore,   "

*John Percival, Corporal.
*Edward Brooks, Private.
*William O'Neil,   "
*Michael Hailstock, Drummer.
*Michael McGomery, Lieutenant.
*Reuben Taylor, Captain.
*James Campbell, Private.
*Charles Galloway, "

LEE'S LEGION.

*Mark Kenton, Sergeant.
*Thomas Hogan,   "
William Strother, "
*John Alexander,   "
Charles Moorehead, "
*Julias Hite,   Corporal.
Richard Marshall, "
John Hopper,   "
James White,   "
*Richard Johnson, "
*Joseph Braun,   "
Richard Hall,   "
*Andrew Coon, Trumpeter.
William Haynes, Private.
*Ephraim Andrew,   "
*William Burke,   "
*James Bland,   "
*John Barber,   "
*Robert Furgeson,   "
John Fennell,   "
John Purcell,   "
*James Swart,   "
Joseph Tankersley, "
*Benjamin Tyler,   "
John Walden,   "
*John Brannan,   "
William Groves,   "
Charles Owens,   "
*William Halbert,   "

Joseph Owens,   Private.
Samuel Thompson, "
*Thomas Almond, "
*John Green,   "
William Rogers,   "
*Andrew Brann,   "
George Foster,   "
*William Binns,   "
William Huff,   "
*William Hailey,   "
*Thomas Thornhill, "
*William Lewis,   "
Randolph McDaniel, "
William Loden,   "
*William Bransford, "
*William Bigbee,   "
William Dennis,   "
*Daniel Gray,   "
John Fleace,   "
*Brothers Thompson, "
*John Brett,   "
*John Wiggonton,   "
*Silas Johnson,   "
*John Gardiner,   "
*Samuel Avery,   "
*William Garner,   "
Berry Shields,   "
David Partello,   "
Robert Meydon,   "

OF THE REVOLUTIONARY WAR.

Robert Fishkin,	Private.	William Carpenter,	Private.
*Green Robinson,	"	Daniel Hailey,	"
Andrew Tosh,	"	Darien Henderson,	Qr. Mr's Sergeant.
*Robert Welch,	"		
Daniel Campbell,	"	John Champe, Sergeant.	
Thomas Chapman,	"	Robert Paver,	"
Richard Cooper,	"	John Mitchell,	"
*Thomas Fisher,	"	Wm, B. Harrison,	"
Redman Cruze,	"	*John Briggs,	Private.
Thomas Whitlock,	"	John Wheeler,	"
James Selcock,	"	James Wheeler,	"
James Hutchinson,	"	Benjamin Strother,	"
Jacob Lynn,	"	*William Buckley,	"
*Wheedon Smith,	"	George Newman,	"
David Hambrich,	"	John Sorrell,	"
*John Morris,	"	Joseph Davidson,	"
Richard Riely,	"	Peter Crawford,	"
Thomas Jones,	"	Henry Aires,	"
*William Hunt,	"	John Myers,	"
*Godfrey Smith,	"	John Zachary,	"
James Wood,	"	Thomas Hattaway,	"
Tandy Holman,	"	*Ranson Bridges,	"
Francis Ramsay,	"	Elijah Walbrow,	"
John Richmond,	"	Isaac Mooney,	"
Benjamin Jackson,	"	John Johnson,	"
Isaac Fanchaw	"	Minor Smith,	"
James Thompson,	"	Conrad Patterson,	"
*Charles Bryan,	"	Joseph Asberry,	"

ARMAND'S CORPS.

*William Bawcut,	Sergeant.	*William Abnor,	Private.
*John Nunelay,	"	*Thomas Davis,	"
*Jacob Hiliff,	"	*John Collins,	"
*Detrich Geisekus,	"	*Thomas Somerset,	"
*Jesse Farmer,	Corporal.	*William Thomson,	"
*Lewis Dupont,	"	*Solomon Alexander,	"
*Frederick Wattsbach,	"	*John Smith,	"
*John Lloyd,	Farrier.	*Richard Piles,	"
*Robert Teate,	"	*Peter Walker,	"
*Gothiel Glass,	Trumpeter.	*Godrell Lively,	"
*James Jenkins,	Wagoner.	*Henry Brider,	"
*John Rock,	Private.	*William Spencer,	"
*Samuel Young,	"	*Jacob Lawrence,	"

116   CORRESPONDENCE OF OFFICERS

*Nathan Glasby,	Private.
*Robert Strahan,	"
*Joseph Gray,	"
*Samuel Wells,	"
*William Bennett,	"
*John Thompson,	"
*John Smith,	"
*John Steele,	"
*James Busby,	"
*William Davis,	"
*Bowlin Coates,	"
*Nathan Farmer,	"
*Henry Howard,	"
*James Ramsay,	"
*James Nash,	"
*Thomas Collins,	"
*John Watts,	"
*John Buzby,	"
*George Walker,	"
*Joseph Harton,	"
*Pressley Anderweek,	"
*John Baumaster,	"
*George Mayor,	"
*Jones Jordan,	"
*James Ramsay,	"
*John Bryan,	"
*Lewis Langene,	"
*Andrew Le Burn,	"
*Matthew Duchene,	"
*Lewis Bellbose,	"
*John Le Barre,	"
*John Connor, jun.,	"
*John Mills,	"
*John O'Briant	"
*William Carr,	"
*Clement Green,	"
*Thomas Dove,	"
*Henry Jacobs,	"
*Edward Newton	"

John Jones, Sergeant.
William Roach, "

*John Elliott,	Private.
*Benjamin Toltman,	"
*John Calligan,	"
*Peter Jackson,	"
*John Burdoin,	"
*Mark Woods,	"
*Richard Chapman,	"
*James Paul,	"
*James Key,	"
*Michael La Rochelle,	"
*John Ville,	"
*Arnold La Rekausance,"
*John Conner, sen.,	"
*Charles Brussell,	"
*John Mowlt,	"
*James Adams,	"
*George Doughty,	"
*Michael Hardoffer,	"
*William Davis,	"
*Barney Connor,	"
*William Marshall,	"
*James McClean,	"
*John Smith,	"
*Stephen Gendell,	"
*John Goodwin,	"
*Anthony La Rue,	"
*Joseph De Court,	"
*Peter Sans Quartier,	"
*John F. Slicker,	"
*William Dowlins,	"
*Charles Milling,	"
*Duncan Young,	"
*Christian Shrawder,	"
*John Nalton,	"
*John Wright,	"
*Michael La Motte,	"
*Nicholas Coquette,	"
*Francis Fleury,	"
*John Waters,	"

GIBB'S GUARDS.

William Jones,	Private.
William Harris,	".

OF THE REVOLUTIONARY WAR.   117

John Edge,	Private.	Spencer Hill,	Private.
Joseph Parker,	"	Henry Pullen,	"
Shedrack Painstone,	"	Raleigh Christian,	"
William Coram,	"	John Smith,	"
Frederick Young,	Sergeant.	Reaps Mitchell,	"
Henry Randolph,	Corporal.	William O'Neale,	"
John Bell,	Private.	Williamson Place,	"
Robert Wadsworth,	"	John Dawes,	"
Thomas Allen,	"	Willmore Cooper,	"
William Palmer,	"	Andrew Harrison,	"
John King,	"	William McIntire,	"
James Timberlake,	"	Thomas Howl,	"
James Johnson,	"	Lewis Flemiston,	"
Pendleton Isbell,	"	Henry Perry,	"
John Bodine,	"	John Stockdell,	"
John Sterne,	"	Miles Brown,	"
Abram Vansickle,	"		

INVALID CORPS.

*Miles Cardiff,	Corporal.	*John Meurdugh,	Private.
*John Massey,	"	*Andrew McGuire,	"
*Wm. Bedwerth,	"	*Edward Johnson,	"
*Abram Levi,	Private.	*Robert Beakham,	"
*Abraham Nettles,	"	*James Wright,	"
*Archibald Rowan,	"	*Patrick McCline.	"
*William Woodford,	"	*James Wheaton,	"
*Joseph West,	"	*James Gordon,	"
*Charles Lenox,	"	*William Posey,	"
*Luke Brady,	"	*Joel Harlow.	"
*Michael Drake,	"	*Peter Collings,	"
*John Corbett,	"	*James Rodley,	"
*Barnhard McGaw,	"	*James Anderson,	"
*Lewis Holmes,	"	*William Morgan,	"
*Smith Steven,	"	*Samuel Hodgin,	"
*Alex. Dukey,	"	*Robert Clark,	"
*Edward Harriss,	"	*Cornelius McGomery,	"
*John Martin,	"	*Joseph Robnett,	"
*Thomas Brown,	"	*John Wilson,	"
*James Shaw,	"	*Henry Lawson,	"
*Dennis Diskill,	"	*John Smith,	"

Those not marked are three years men.

JANUARY 8, 1790.

SIR :—I have carefully examined the accounts of General Moses Hazen against the United States, as stated and reported by the late Mr. Pierce, and find in that statement every allowance which the acts of Congress and the rules of the department will admit, and I might add, all that equity and good conscience require.

The first material objection, I understand, made by General Hazen to the transit of his account in its present form, is the reduction of a balance, unaccounted for in the old emissions of Continental currency, at the rate of 20 for 1, the exchange in June, 1779, instead of a depreciation of 40 for 1, in January, 1780.

The inclosed paper, No. 1, is an arrangement of the sums received by General Hazen in old emissions, and their subsequent appropriations, and shows that the adoption of the scale in June, 1779, is going as far in favor of the claimant as justice to the United States will admit, and proves that considerable sums remained in his possession at the time of his demands for further supplies.

The next objection of consequence to the statement, is the liquidation of a payment made by him into the hands of the Deputy Paymaster-general in the year 1780, insisting that it should be opposed to the charges for old emissions received. If sir, this had been a payment of money, and it would appear even possible that it was a proportion of the sums received from the treasury of the United States, then justice might give her sanction to the demand; but the inclosed paper, No. 2, will show that no part of it was money, but, on the contrary, was warrants drawn by the Commander-in-chief in favor of sundry officers for extra service in 1780, and those warrants dated nearly at the same time in which they were received by the Deputy Paymaster-general.

General Hazen also insists on the propriety of opposing to the sums in old emissions charged him, the amount of a certificate granted by Clement Biddle, Esq., in 1780, for forage due him.

Upon this I may add, sir, that Mr. Pierce's liquidation of it is in exact conformity with the rules and forms established in all the offices of the United States. Warrants drawn by the Commander-in-chief are reduced to specie by the scale of depreciation at the date of the warrant. Quartermasters' and Commissaries' certificates are liquidated upon the same principles, without inquiry into the time of furnishing the articles, or performing the service for which these certificates issued. It will remain for the Comptroller of the Treasury to say whether General Hazen's particular service to his country will authorize a departure from rules of office so long established, and which have received the approbation of so great a variety of officers.

The account in which there is the greatest difference between General Hazen's expectancy and Mr. Pierce's admissions, is for recruiting, he charging and insisting upon an allowance for 841 men, said to be recruited in 1781 and 1782, at 20 dollars for each.

Upon the most exact and critical examination of the muster-rolls, only 186 of them appear mustered in those years.

If, sir, the practice of the army had been that an officer producing a man, and having him mustered, was sufficient to entitle the officer to the bounty of twenty dollars and the premium for enlisting him, then the same rule must consequently be applied to this claim; but I believe, sir, that very different was the practice.

The officer was required to produce the enlistments with the receipt of the recruit for his full bounty. In case of the accidental loss of these enlistments and receipts, recurrence was had to the muster rolls, which, with the officer's deposition to the truth of the several charges, were considered as sufficient to the passage of his account. I am not sure that General Hazen has declared his having paid the bounty charged in his account; but if he does, the papers contain such a weight of evidence to the contrary, as must, in the opinion of every impartial and disinterested person, entirely invalidate his testimony.

The method adopted by Mr. Pierce in ascertaining the bounty paid by General Hazen is shown in the papers. He had in possession five accounts of General Hazen's officers, exhibiting the actual disbursements in recruiting 129 men. These amounted to nine hundred and fourteen dollars, averaging little more than seven dollars for each recruit, and would produce thirteen hundred and eighteen dollars for 186 men, calculating at the same rate. Although this cannot be positive for more than 129 men, yet the testimony of the officers affords the strongest presumptive evidence that no greater than a proportionate sum was paid for the remainder.

There appears a charge against General Hazen of 26,692$\frac{20}{90}$ dollars, old emissions: included in the account of Mr. Chinn, Paymaster to the regiment, a receipt of General Hazen's appears for 15,269 dollars, dated in October, 1779. A part of the above sum, and the other payments, are stated by Mr. Chinn to have been made in 1778. These, I am of opinion, remain to be debited to General Hazen, as they do not appear to have been introduced into the account-current stated by Mr. Pierce.

It appears from the proceedings of Congress of 26th April, 1785, that the accounts of General Hazen were referred, for final adjustment, to the Board of Treasury. Although they did not formerly report their decision upon the charges, yet I believe, upon inquiry, it will be found there was an entire coincidence of opinion between that honorable Board and Mr. Pierce.

The foregoing is a reference to papers and evidence, I suppose, most essential to the Comptroller in his examination of the account.

JOHN WRIGHT.

To the Comptroller.

BOSTON, May 9, 1791.

SIR:—Your favor of the 18th of April, inclosing objection to some officers and soldiers charged by the State, as appears by the Commissioners of army accounts to be paid to men who were omitted at a certain time in the returns, or were never mustered, has been received.

To the settlement with the Massachusetts line of the Continental army, I have been one of the Committee from the beginning, and can assert from my knowledge that the Committee were very careful and attentive that no officer or soldier should be considered in the line of depreciation for the first three years, or for their pay in 1780, but those that, by the returns from the Colonels or Commanders of regiments to the Committee, stood fair to be considered in respect of pay; that no officer that was not by the return honorably discharged, or no soldier that was returned deserted, should ever be considered in the line of depreciation, or the same charged to the United States as receiving pay: and if any mistake took place in this respect, it did arise from the officer's returns, for the returns of the officers were the foundation on which the Committee proceeded in making the settlement with officers or soldiers. You must note that the Committee, in settling with the army for the first three years, presumed that all officers and soldiers received from the United States the nominal sum of their wages in camp, and accordingly charged them with the real value, and this was deducted from the whole amount of their wages—whatever the balance was after this deduction, was charged the United States.

In the settlement for the year 1780, the General Court ordered the Committee to credit the officers and soldiers with the depreciation for their not receiving this nominal sum in camp in season, and as it became due with interest thereon, which, for a private soldier that served the whole of the first three years, amounted to £6 1 3, which sum he had credit for in the settlement for 1780, in addition to his pay for service in 1780, which was also charged the United States, with his pay for the time of service.

I shall now proceed to give you the information respecting those officers and soldiers which you mention to me were objected to.

CORRESPONDENCE OF OFFICERS

The First, or Vose's Regiment.

Jonathan Norton, private, returned in Capt. Hancock's Co. as serving the whole three years.

Henry Rasnor, private, returned in Capt. Hancock's Co. as invalided, but made up in the regiment.

Pierce Moran, private, returned in Capt. Hunt's Co. as invalided, but made up in the regiment.

Peter Lahare, private, returned in Capt. Hunt's Co. as serving from May 17, 1777, to Dec. 31, 1779.

Arthur Day, private, returned in Capt. Hunt's Co. invalided, but made up in the regiment.

Daniel Preble, private, returned in Major Coggswell's Co. as died July 15, 1779.

Daniel Bradley, private, returned in Capt. Cushing's Co. as died Nov. 11, 1777.

Daniel Vicory, private, returned in the Lieut. Colonel's Co. as serving the whole time.

Daniel Dyer, private, returned in the Lieut. Colonel's Co. as serving the whole three years.

Asa Hatch, private, returned in the Lieut. Colonel's Co. as deserted July 4, 1779, returned to his duty in 1780, per Col. Vose's certificate.

James Wesson, private, returned in Major Coggswell's Co. as deserted, but returned to his duty, and enlisted for during the war.

The Second Regiment.

Josiah Blood, Corporal, returned in the Colonel's Co. discharged Feb. 1, 1779.

William Waterman, private, returned in 3d Co. as died Feb. 15, 1777.

Enoch Stocker, private, returned in 3d Co. as invalided.

Abner Hall, private, returned as serving the whole time.

Benoni Barrell, private, returned in 4th Co. as discharged May 12, 1778.

The Third Regiment.

Ebenezer Priest, private, returned in Capt. Summer's Co. as on command with Qr. Mr. Gen. at Boston.

Justin Day, private, returned in Capt. Flower's Co. as serving the whole time from April 18, 1778.

Abel Hancock, private, returned in Capt. Cotton's Co. as invalided.

Josiah Lyon, Sergeant, returned in Capt. Foster's Co. as invalided.

Stephen Whiting, Sergeant, returned in Capt. Foster's Co. as killed July 22, 1777.

The Fourth Regiment.

Ebenezer Brewster Gould, Lieutenant, returned by Col. Shepard as 1st-Lieut. in his regiment, Jan. 1, 1777, to April 12, 1778.

Nathaniel Gale, private, returned in Capt. Learnard's Co. as serving from Jan. 1, 1777, to Jan. 1, 1778.

Gershom Whiting, private, returned in Capt. Field's Co. as died Nov. 20, 1777.

Jacob Renard, private, returned in Capt. Field's Co. discharged after serving 26 days.

John Herrick, private, returned in Capt. Moore's Co. as serving the whole time.

Moses Town, private, returned in Capt. Moore's Co. as invalided.

Charles Flacaty, private, returned as taken prisoner June 20, 1777.

John Bowers, private, returned in Capt. Field's Co. as died July 1, 1777: his allowance for delay of payment makes the difference.

The Fifth Regiment.

Benjamin Jacobs, private, returned in Capt. Gardner's Co. as discharged Oct. 24, 1777.

Butler Everett, private, returned in Capt. Mose's Co. as discharged Oct. 15, 1777.

Daniel Gilson, private, returned in Capt. Mose's Co. as discharged Oct. 24, 1777.

Josiah Mills, private, returned in Capt. Mose's Co. as discharged Oct. 24, 1777.

John Conn, private, returned in the Colonel's Co. as transferred to Col. Smith's regiment May 15, 1777.

James Gray, private, returned in the Colonel's Co. as invalided, but made up in the regiment.

Samuel Winship, private, returned in the Colonel's Co. as discharged Aug. 1, 1777.

Barney Ryan, private, returned in the Colonel's Co. from March 30, 1779, to Dec. 31, 1779.

Thomas Whaling, private, returned in Capt. Benson's Co. as discharged Sept. 5, 1777.

Nathaniel Pease, private, exchanged for John Webb, August 28, 1777, in Capt. Whipple's Co.

The Sixth Regiment.

Eliakim Danforth, Ensign, returned in the 6th regiment as resigned March 1, 1779.

Ebenezer Crane, private, returned in Capt. Speer's Co. as discharged Jan. 11, 1778.

Edmund Britt, private returned in Capt. Holden's Co. as serving the whole time from Jan. 1, 1777, to Jan. 1, 1780.

John Dean, private, returned in Capt. Holden's Co. as died July 18, 1777.

Daniel Deland, private, returned in Capt. Holden's Co. as invalided.

Jesse Fowler, private, returned in Capt. Holden's Co. for the whole time.

Jacob Holliday, private, returned in the Colonel's Co. as discharged Sept. 19, 1779.

Benajah Woodbury, private, returned in the Colonel's Co. as serving the whole time to December 31, 1779.

Nathan Beard, private, returned in 7th Co. as invalided.

Benjamin Baldwin, do.   do.   do.   do.
Jonathan Frost,   do.   do.   do.   do.

The Seventh Regiment.

John Woodman, Sergeant, returned in Capt. Lane's Co. to Oct. 10, 1779, and then promoted to an officer.

John Cole, private, returned in Capt. Lane's Co. for the whole time.

Charles Hudsom, private, returned in Capt. Lane's Co. as taken prisoner Nov. 10, 1778, and charged with £50 8 10 as pay.

Robert Pasco, private, returned as being in Boston Jail May 12, 1777.

Joseph Appleby, private, returned in Capt. Lane's Co. as serving from Feb. 28, 1778, to Dec. 31, 1779.

Richard Tilly, private, returned in the 3d Co. as discharged Sept. 2, 1777.

Daniel Dana, private, returned in Capt. Day's Co. as taken prisoner July 31, 1777.

Sylvanus Burke, private, returned in Capt. Day's Co. as discharged Nov. 11, 1777.

Luke Day, private, returned in Capt. Day's Co. as discharged Nov. 11, 1779.

Jessie Cole, private, returned in Capt. Day's Co. as discharged Nov. 11, 1779.

Abiger Richmond, private, returned in Capt. Day's Co. as discharged Sept. 15, 1777.

Abijah Addition, private, returned in Capt. Reed's Co. as serving to December 31, 1779.

James Parmeter, private, returned in Capt. Reed's Co. as serving to December 31, 1779.

Thomas Ross, private, returned in Capt. Reed's Co. as invalided.

Edward Dascon, private, returned in Capt. Lane's Co. as serving the whole time.

The Eighth Regiment.

David Hill, Sergeant, returned in Capt. Burnam's Co. as died Sept. 2, 1778.

James Kittle, private, returned in Capt. Burnam's Co. as died Feb. 15, 1778.

William Bunton, private, returned in Capt. Burnam's Co. as deserted after serving 9 months.

Daniel Whallin, private, returned as a deserter, after 8 month's 6 days' service.

Michael McLaughlin, private, returned as a deserter, after serving 12 days.

Peter Ross, private, returned in Captain Burnam's Co. as a deserter, after 15 months' 18 days' service.

Daniel Gray, private, returned in Capt. Burnam's Co. as died Aug. 5, 1778.

Luther Topliff, private, returned in Capt. Burnam's Co. as serving the whole time.

Stephen Varnum, private, returned in Capt. Cleveland's Co. as died May 30, 1777.

James Bailey, Sergeant, returned in Capt. Bancroft's Co. as serving the whole time.

George Lord, private, returned in Capt. Wiley's Co. as died Oct. 8, 1777.

The Ninth Regiment.

Stephen Elbridge, Qr. Mr's. Sergeant, returned in the Major's Co. as serving the whole time.

Joseph Gray, private, returned in Capt. Watson's Co. as serving the whole time.

John Matterson, private, returned in Capt. Watson's Co. as discharged May 1, 1778.

Samuel Maxfield, private, returned in Capt. Dix's Co. as discharged Dec. 24, 1777.

William Gordon, private, returned in Capt. Blanchard's Co. as invalided.

Seth Sturdivant, private, returned in 2d Co. as serving the whole time.

John Newcomb, private, returned in Capt. Carr's Co. as deserted March 1, 1778.

The Tenth, or Marshall's Regiment.

Seth Delino, Sergeant, returned in Lieut. Colonel's Co. as taken prisoner.

OF THE REVOLUTIONARY WAR.   127

Henry Blasdell, private, returned in the Colonel's Co. as died May 7, 1777.
Edmond Horton, private, returned in the Colonel's Co. as invalided.
Ebenezer Bowman, Private, returned in the 1st Co. as died April 20, 1777.
William Condell, private, returned in the 1st Co. for the whole time.
Peter Franklin, private, returned in the 1st Co. as died April 21, 1777.
Abel Moon, private, returned in the 1st Co. as died April 1st, 1777.
Richard Barnard, private, returned in the 2d Co. as invalided.
Elisha Munsell, private, returned in 2d Co. as Invalided.
Silas Carter, private, returned in 3d Co. as discharged June 20, 1777.
Levi Carter, private, returned in the 3d Co. as hiring a man to take his place Sept. 1, 1779.
John Conway, private, returned in the 4th Co. as invalided.
Samuel Payson, private, returned in the 4th Co. as taken prisoner July 6, 1777.
Colburn Barrett, private, returned in the 5th Co. as died Nov. 30, 1777.
Esperana Litchfield, private, returned in the 5th Co. as died May 1, 1778.
Joseph Vinal, private, returned in the 5th Co. for the whole time.
Nathan Crosby, private, returned in the Major's Co. as died July 6th 1777.

The Eleventh, or Col. Benj. Tupper's Regiment.

John Skillings, Captain, returned by Col. Tupper for the time he is made up.
Peter Martin, private, returned in Capt. Abbott's Co. as drafted into Gen. Washington's Life Guards.
Sampson Faye, Private, returned in Captain Abbott's Co. as serving from July 29, 1779, to Dec. 31, 1779.
William Watkins, private, returned in Capt. Abbott's Co. as serving from July 29, 1779, to Dec. 31, 1779.

John Lovejoy, private, returned in Capt. Abbott's Co. as died Oct. 13, 1778.

Amos Knowlton, private, returned in Capt. Abbott's Co. as died June 30, 1778.

Daniel Lampson, private, returned in Capt. Porter's Co. for the whole time.

Richard Lee, private, returned in Capt. Porter's Co. as died May 1, 1777.

John Smith, private returned in Capt. William Greenleaf's Co. for the whole time.

Solomon Aubirc, private, returned in Capt. Greenleaf's Co. as died Oct. 4, 1778.

Daniel Collings, private, returned in Capt. Greenleaf's Co. as died Dec. 7. 1777.

Syphax Carey, private, returned in Capt. Greenleaf's Co. as died Dec. 15, 1777.

Jacob Lunt, private, returned in Capt. Greenleaf's Co. for the whole time.

William Lewis, private, returned in Capt. Greenleaf's Co. for the whole time.

Newport Richardson, private, returned in Capt. Greenleaf's Co. for the whole time.

John Askins, private, returned in Capt. Greenleaf's Co. for the whole time

John Annis, private, returned in Capt. Greenleaf's Co. for the whole time.

John Fielding, private, returned in Capt. Greenleaf's Co. for the whole time.

John Hutchinson, private, returned in Capt. Greenleaf's Co. for the whole time.

Oliver page, private, returned in Capt. Greenleaf's Co. as discharged Nov. 15, 1777.

Nathan Filburt, private, returned in Capt. Page's Co. as died Jan. 15, 1778.

Abraham Doyle, private, returned in Capt. Page's Co. as invalided.

William Rea, private, returned in Capt. Page's Co. for the whole time.
Jerome Hutchins, private, returned in Capt. Page's Co. for the time he is made up for.
William McKinney, Sergeant, returned in Capt. Clark's Company as promoted to Ensign, April 8, 1777.
Reuben Clough, private, returned in Capt. Clark's Co as died Oct 1, 1777.
Jonathan Lumbard, private, returned in Capt Clark's Co. as taken prisoner July 7, 1777.
Philander Smith, private, returned in Capt. Clark's Co. as died Oct. 20, 1777.
James Snow, private, returned in Capt. Francis' Co. as discharged May 28, 1777.
Joshua Hatch, private, returned in Capt. Francis' Co. as discharged Jan. 21, 1778.
John Whoston, private, returned in Capt. Francis' Co. as discharged May 20, 1777.
Tobias Pillsbury, private, returned in Capt. Marbury's Co. as invalided, and discharged Dec. 21, 1779.
Reuben Libby, private, returned, in Capt. Maybury's Co. as invalided.
Bartholomew Thompson, private, returned in Capt. Maybury's Co. as discharged Jan. 19, 1778, by order of Maj. Gen. Heath.
William Sayer, private, returned in Capt. Maybury's Co. as died July 1, 1778.
John Lombs, private, returned in Capt. Clark's Co. as died July 7, 1777.
James Ryon, private, returned in Capt. Maybury's Co. as taken prisoner July 7, 1777.
Hannaniah Clark, private, returned in Capt. Maybury's Co. as taken prisoner, and died March 1, 1779.
Ebenezer Chase, private returned in Capt. Maybury's Co. as discharged May 28, 1778.
John Miller, private, returned in Capt. Maybury's Co. as discharged May 28, 1778.

Thomas Jones, private, returned in Capt. Maybury's Co. as died July 7, 1777.
Benj Bailey, private, returned in Capt. White's Co. as taken prisoner July 7, 1777.
Thomas Foot, returned in Capt. White's Co. as discharged January 1, 1779.
Jonathan Osburn, private, returned in Capt. White's Co. as died Oct. 15, 1779.
Timothy Pratt, private, returned in Capt. White's Co. as killed July 7, 1777.
Richard Poor, private, returned in Capt. White's Co. as taken prisoner July 7, 1777.
John Shannon, private, returned in Capt. White's Co. as killed July 7, 1777.
David Thompson, private, returned in Capt. White's Co. as killed July 7, 1777.
William Wilson, private, returned in Capt. White's Co. as taken prisoner July 7, 1777.
Thomas Wilham, private, returned in Capt. White's Co. as killed July 7, 1777.
John Stone, private, returned in Capt. White's Co. as died May 10, 1777.

The Twelfth Regiment.

Timothy Whiting, Dep. Qr. Mr. General, made up in Sproat's Reg., agreeable to his discharge signed by Col. Udny Hay.
Jonathan Milbury, private, returned in Colonel's Co. as discharged Nov. 3, 1779.
Benjamin Beary, private, returned in the Major's Co. as taken prisoner July 6, 1777.
Asa Hutchins, private, returned in Capt. Means' Co. as taken prisoner July 7, 1777.
Edward Davis, private, returned in Capt. Means' Co. as discharged July 1, 1777.
John Godfrey, private, returned in Capt. Means' Co. as died April 25, 1779.

Joseph Keeter, private, returned in Capt. Means' Co. as taken prisoner Dec. 1, 1777.
Zacheus Nixon, private, returned in Capt. Means' Co. as died May 18, 1777.
Job Reamond, private, returned in Capt. Means' Co. as died Feb. 5, 1777.
Demp Squearis, private, returned in Capt. Means' Co. as a prisoner Dec. 7, 1778.
Thomas Bickford, private, returned in Capt. Hitchcock's Co. as invalided.
Noah Taylor, private, returned in Capt. Hitchcock's Co. for the whole time, but sick in the hospital till he died Dec. 1, 1780.
Abel Whitney, private, returued in Capt. Sewell's Co. as discharged Aug. 12, 1777.
Richard Hines, private, returned in Capt. Burbank's Co. as discharged July 15, 1778.
Thomas Harmon, private, returned in Capt. Burbank's Co. as serving the whole time.
Elias Starbird, private, returned in Capt. Burbank's Co. as killed July 7. 1777.
Jacob Smith, private, returned in Capt. Burbank's Co. as taken prisoner July 7, 1777.
Abraham York, private, returned in Capt. Burbank's Co. as taken prisoner July 7, 1777.
Peter Pease, Sergeant, returned in Capt. Williams' Co. as discharged Dec. 1, 1779.
Simeon Woodworth, private, returned in Capt. Williams' Co. as died June 10, 1778.

The Thirteenth Regiment.

Isaac Burton, Lieutenant, returned by Col. Smith as serving in his regiment to Sept. 9, 1777, and then resigned.
Joshua Chase, Surgeon's Mate, returned by Col. Smith as serving from Jan. 1, 1777, to June 28, 1777.
John Storey, private, returned in the Colonel's Co. as serving the whole time.

John Glass, private, returned in Capt. J. K. Smith's Co. from Oct. 23, 1778, to Dec. 81, 1779.

Peter Marshall, private, returned in Capt. J. K. Smith's Co. as discharged Nov. 5, 1778.

Samuel Vose, private, returned in Capt. Ebenezer Smith's Co. for the whole time.

John Shaysbirck, private, returned in Capt. Ebenezer Smith's Co. as exchanged March 15, 1779.

John Millon, private, returned in Capt. Ebenezer Smith's Co. from March 16, 1779, to Dec. 81, 1779.

Jonathan Hemmenway, private, returned in Capt. Allen's Co. as serving the whole time.

Abiezer Washburn, private, returned in Capt. Allen's Co. as died Nov. 17, 1777.

John Hensell, private, returned in Capt. Woodbridge's Co. as a deserter.

John Kent, private, returned in Capt. Woodbridge's Co. as died June 1, 1778,

William Moon, private, returned in Capt. Woodbridge's Co. as serving from May 15, 1779, to Dec. 81, 1779.

Benjamin Ballard, Sergeant, returned in Capt. Page's Co. for the whole time.

William Gould, private, returned in Capt. Page's Co. for the whole time.

Cavenah Haskell, private, returned in Capt. Page's Co. as died May 20, 1777.

Jacob Jones, private, returned in Capt. Page's Co. as discharged Sept. 1, 1777.

Joshua Wiltham, private, returned in the Major's Co. as serving the whole time.

Henry Leland, private, returned in the Major's Co. as serving the whole time.

Timothy Nokes, private, returned in the Major's Co. as died June 18, 1778.

Fortune Homer, private, returned in the Major's Co. as died April 18, 1777.

Robert Murphy, private, returned in the Major's Co. as left sick at Albany Oct. 1, 1777.

James Garrish, private, returned in Capt. Smart's Co. as died May 29, 1777.

Benjamin Robbins, private, returned in Capt. Smart's Co. as died May 20, 1778.

Samuel Wimble, private, returned in Capt. Smart's Co. as died May 20, 1777.

The Fourteenth Regiment.

Seth Cottle, Sergeant, returned in Capt. Turner's Co. as serving the whole time.

Jonathan Elms, Corporal, returned in Capt. Turner's Co. as serving the whole time.

Samuel Bennet, Corporal, returned in Capt. Redding's Co. as discharged Dec. 1, 1778.

Samuel Ellis, Corporal, returned in Capt. Wadsworth's Co. for the whole time.

William Shune, private, returned in Capt. Redding's Co. as serving from March 25, 1779 to Dec. 31, 1779.

Asa Fuller, private, returned in Capt. Wadsworth's Co. as died Sept. 15, 1779.

Sylvanus Hall, private, returned in Capt. Wadsworth's Co. as serving the whole time.

Samuel Newell, private, returned in Capt. Wadsworth's Co. as died June 10, 1778.

Joshua Finkham, private, returned in the 3d Co. as discharged March 11, 1778.

John Beake, private, returned in the 3d Co. as died Jan. 1, 1778.

William Allen, private, returned in the 3d Co. as died Jan. 31, 1778.

Jonathan Ball, private, returned in the 4th Co. for the whole time.

Zebedee Sears, private, returned in the 4th Co. as died Dec. 10, 1778.

Jonathan Halloway, private, returned in the 4th Co. as killed June 9, 1777.

James Cole, private, returned in the 5th Co. as invalided.
Jane Keeler, private, returned in the 5th Co. as died May 28, 1777.
Vernon Toby, private, returned in the 5th Co. as died May 14, 1777.
Labor Linis, private, returned in the 5th Co. as discharged August 20, 1779.
Benjamin Lumber, private, returned in the 5th Co. as invalided.
James McClbb, private, returned in the 5th Co. as invalided.
Joseph Nicholson, private, returned in the 5th Co. as invalid.
Jere Jae, private, returned in the 5th Co. as died May 28, 1777.
George Shem, private, returned in the 6th Co. as died July 14, 1777.
William Haskell, private, returned in the 6th Co. as died May 2, 1777.
Moses Tob, private, returned in the 6th Co. as died Dec. 20, 1777.
Richard Thomas, private, returned in the 6th Co. as died Jan. 4, 1778.
Ansel Gours, private, returned in the 6th Co. as died Dec. 3, 1777.
Zecheus Eddy, Sergeant, returned in the 6th Co. as died June 9, 1777.
Jonathan Sanders, Sergeant, returned in the 7th Co. as killed July 7, 1777.
Nathan Fane, private, returned in the 7th Co. to June 18, 1777.
Joseph Chamberlain, private, returned in the 7th Co. for the whole time.
Lot Bly, private, returned in the 7th Co. as died March 1, 1778.
Jabez Brooks, Sergeant, returned in the 8th Co. as serving the whole time.
John Strong, private, returned in the 8th Co. as died Feb. 10, 1778.
Nathan Barry, private, returned in the regiment and made up by Col. Bradford's certificate.

The Fifteenth Regiment.

Timothy Calton, private, returned in Capt. Smith's Co. as serving the whole time.

William Wyman, private, returned in Capt. Smith's Co. as serving the whole time.

Daniel Cole, private, returned in Capt. Smith's Co. as serving the whole time.

Prentiss Russell, private, returned in Capt. Barnes' Co. as exchanged Oct. 1, 1777.

Silas Wyman, private, returned in Capt. Barnes' Co. as killed Aug. 5, 1779.

Richard Wesson, private, returned in Capt. Monroe's Co. as died Aug. 20, 1777.

George Knight, Drummer, returned in Capt. Ellis' Co. as invalided.

Samuel Barret, private, returned in Capt. Brown's Co. as serving from March 11, 1779, to Dec. 31, 1779.

The Sixteenth Regiment.

Bano Brown, Sergeant, returned in Capt. Brown's Co. as serving to Dec. 31, 1779.

Allen Turner, private, returned as serving in the Lieut. Col.'s Co. the whole time.

Asa Ware, private, returned in H. Jackson's regiment from Col. Lee's regiment, invalided, serving the whole time.

John Gragg, private, returned in H. Jackson's regiment from Col. Lee's regiment, and invalided.

Col. John Crane's Artillery.

Jere Niles, Lieutenant, returned by Col. Crane as Captain-lieutenant in his regiment from Jan. 1, 1777, resigned Sept. 9, 1778.

Payne Downs, Sergeant, returned in Capt. Cook's Co. made up by Col. Crane's certificate for the time of service, being to Feb. 28, 1779.

Martin Norwich, Bombardier, returned in Capt. Donnell's Co. as killed at Tarry Town, July 15, 1778.

James Day, Gunner, returned in Capt. Winslow's Co. as discharged by Gen. Gates, Dec. 31, 1777.

Alexander Perkins, Matross, returned in Capt. Lillie's Co. as serving to Dec. 31, 1778.

Oliver Tidd, Matross, returned in Capt. Treadwell's Co. as serving the whole time.

Deranged Officer.

William Tudor, Lieutenant-colonel, is returned as Lieut. Col. of Col. Hendley's regiment, as resigned April 9, 1778, per Gen. Heath's certificate.

Major *Gibb's* Corps.

Michael Titcomb, Corporal, said to be in Gen. Washington's Life-Guards, and was made up for his depreciation by a special resolve of court.

Charles King, Sergeant-major, made up for his depreciation by a certificate from William Washington, Lieut. Col.

Michael Caswell, Fifer, made up for his depreciation by a discharge from William Washington, Lieut. Col. of Light Dragoons.

Nathaniel Potter, private, returned by Major Gibbs as commanding-general of Washington's Guards.

The above is a true copy from the returns lodged in this office.

JOHN DEMING,
One of the Committee for settling with the Massachusetts Line of the Continental Army.

[No address.]

Nov. 2, 1791.

SIR:—You will receive by the hands of Colonel Israel Shreeve his account against the United States for recruiting the late Second Regiment of New Jersey, in the years 1777, '78, and '79. As Mr. Pierce made some objection to the passage of this account, I have been the more particular in the examination of the evidence in support of the charges; and am fully of opinion that the balances now reported are justly due to Colonel Shreeve.   I am, sir, your obedient servant,

JOSEPH HOWELL.

Mr. WM. SIMMONS.

PAY OFFICE, NOV. 4, 1791.

SIR:—I have attended to the several matters contained in your letter of the 2d inst.

On examining the muster-roll of the late Virginia line, I find Nathaniel Lucas was commissioned a lieutenant the 28th September, 1776, and was deranged on the 1st of October, 1778. The musters are silent in respect to any promotion; but as the musters of the Virginia Line are *exceedingly imperfect*, and as Col. Wood was one of the senior officers of that line, I am of opinion that his evidence should be admitted.

You will inform the Secretary of War, that Mr. Lucas has no credit on the books of this office for one year's pay as a supernumerary officer, and that in consequence of delaying an application for this pay he is foreclosed by the act of limitation.

I am, sir, your obedient servant,

JOSEPH HOWELL.

R. J. VANDEN BROECK, Esq.

NOVEMBER 11, 1791.

SIR:—On appealing to the muster-rolls of General Hazen's regiment, it appears that Major Tarleton Woodson was furloughed in December, 1781, the term not mentioned; and on the muster for March, 1782, taken on the 1st of April following, it is noted opposite his name, "furlough expired, March 1, 1782;" after which Major Woodson does not appear either on the musters, or in the accounts of the regiment. The regiment consisted of ten companies in 1782, and eight in 1783. No promotion appears to have taken place in consequence of Major Woodson's leaving the regiment.

I am, sir, your obedient servant,

JOSEPH HOWELL.

Hon. Secretary of War.

REGISTER'S OFFICE, Nov. 16, 1791.

SIR:—Lieutenant Christian Orendorff, of the sixth Maryland regiment, has made application at this office to know whether there is any charge against him on the books of the Treasury. I have examined the records of the Department, and cannot find that any settlement has taken place with him. He alludes to an arrearage of pay and rations due to him while he was a prisoner.

If you can point out any particular reference which may be obtained in this office that will show light on the nature of his claim, it shall be attended to.

I am your obedient servant,
JOSEPH DAWSON.

J. HOWELL, Esq., Acting P. M. Gen.

PAY OFFICE, NOV. 16, 1791.

SIR :—The muster-rolls of the late German Regiment express that Philip Flowers was enlisted November 1, 1776, for the war, and was killed October 4, 1777. On reference to a list of balances paid by the Paymaster of this regiment, it appears the sum $1\tfrac{5}{90}$ dollars was returned to the Paymaster-general as due to Flowers, which sum is still due the estate at a depreciated rate, therefore not worthy of notice. The heirs of the deceased are not entitled, agreeably to the existing acts of Congress, to depreciation; but I am clearly of opinion they are to the proportion of lands.

I have carefully examined the record of the Pennsylvania line, formed from the musters, and cannot find the name of Phineas *Kuhn*, or *Coon*. I am apprehensive, if there was one of that name died in service, that he must have been in the hospital for some time, and was omitted in the musters, which was too frequently the case.

I am your obedient servant,
JOSEPH HOWELL.

Hon. Secretary of War.

PAY OFFICE, NOV. 17, 1791.

SIR :—It appears by the arrangement of the late line of Virginia, that Oliver Towles was a Lieutenant-colonel in the fifth Virginia regiment, and was arranged as such to the First Regiment in the year 1783. But it is further remarked on this arrangement, that Lieutenant-colonel Oliver Towles retired, and that Lieutenant-colonel Samuel Hawes took his place. There being but one regiment, a settlement could only take place with one of them; and in consequence of the application of Lieutenant-colonel Hawes, the Assistant Commissioner settled with him to Nov. 15, 1783. Lieutenant-colonel Towles now comes forward with a claim for his pay in 1783, which I presume cannot be granted.

I am, sir, your obedient servant,

J. HOWELL.

Hon. Secretary of War.

WAR OFFICE, Nov. 22, 1791.

SIR:—I am directed by the Secretary of War to transmit you the inclosed petition of Thomas Jenny and Andrew Dover, late officers in Colonel Magaw's regiment, and who were taken prisoners at Fort Washington in 1776. The Secretary requests you will please to examine their claims, and report your opinion accordingly.

I am, sir, your humble servant,

JOHN STAGG.

JOS. HOWELL, ESQ.

PAY OFFICE, Nov. 24, 1791.

SIR:—Agreeably to your request I have examined the musters of the late Virginia line, from which it appears that there was a William Burk enlisted in the Third Regiment on the 16th of February, 1778, for one year, and was discharged from the Fifth Regiment, Feb. 16, 1779. There also appears a William Burk in the Seventh Regiment, who was mustered in that regiment in December, 1778, for the war; and in the Eleventh Regiment there is also a William Burk, mustered in May, 1777, for the same term; the 11th regiment being incorporated with the 7th in or about November, 1778, it may be presumed that they are one and the same person.

It further appears that there was a William Burk in the Sixth Regiment, who enlisted Dec. 7, 1776, and a William Burk in the Tenth Regiment, who appears to have been enlisted on the same day for the war. I believe the 10th regiment was incorporated with the 6th in 1778. It is therefore probable that they are one and the same person.

By the accounts of the State of Virginia for depreciation of pay to her line, it appears that four of the name were settled with, viz:

William Burk, for 18 months' service,	£36 0	0
William Burk, from Jan. 1 to Dec. 31, 1777,	103 19	8
William Burk, do. do.	102 3	11
William Burk, from March 19 to Dec. 31, 1777,	19 1	10

I have also examined the settlements made by the Assistant Commissioner of Army Accounts for Virginia, and find that he settled with one William Burk of Colonel Lee's Legion. This man, exclusive of certificates issued, had 16 dollars specie due him, which sum, with others, was put into the hands of John Hopkins, Esq., and is probably the sum which is now claimed, and paid to his order or some one of the name.

I wish to remark to you that, if the present applicant did not belong to Colonel Lee's Legion, he has no claim on the United States for specie or other pay, that I can find by any record in this office.

I am, sir, your obedient servant,

JOSEPH HOWELL.

Hon. JAMES MADISON.

AUDITOR'S OFFICE, ANNAPOLIS, Nov. 26, 1791.

DEAR SIR:—I am favored with yours by John Bennett of Lee's Legion, and have made inquiry respecting his finals. Mr. White has lodged none with the Executive, except such as have been issued to the Maryland line in his own name. If Mr. White exhibited no vouchers for the settlement of the certificates from Mr. Dunscomb, I see no chance at this time to come at the certainty whether any part has been applied to the purposes for which it was issued. I imagine you can furnish him with the account as stated by Mr. Dunscomb to enable him to resort to Mr. White's estate. He alleges he never received his depreciation. It has been paid here. Cannot you refer to the vouchers and let him know to whom the same was paid? The checks in my office do not give the information.

I shall be much obliged to you for a copy of Captain-lieutenant Ebenezer Finley's account as stated and settled in your office as an officer of the Maryland Artillery, and also as Deputy Judge-advocate of the Southern army. Mr. White procured me a copy once for his executor, which I delivered; but by some means the persons concerned in the adjustment of his estate cannot agree on the principles, and the first copy cannot now be produced.

Whatever charge may attend this business, I will direct some of my friends in your city to discharge the debt immediately.

I am really sorry to hear of our friend Richmond's illness. I hope by this time he has recovered much. My compliments to him and Knapp, and believe me to be,

Most sincerely, your friend and humble servant,

ROBERT DENNY.

JOSEPH HOWELL, Esq.

NEW YORK, Nov. 28, 1791.

SIR:—The bearer hereof, Lewis Bramer, says he was a private in Captain James McClure's company of artillery in Colonel Proctor's regiment, and that he was mustered as such and drew his rations accordingly. Captain McClure, on the other hand, contends that Bramer was employed by him in the capacity of his servant, and that he, as his master, is entitled to the depreciation certificates made out for Bramer, and that he claims, in pursuance of some resolution of Congress which gives the servants' pay to their masters.

You will greatly oblige me by letting me know how Bramer stands on the muster-rolls, or by any other information with which you can favor me, that may enable me to determine how far Bramer is entitled to his depreciation.

Captain McClure has *actually received* the certificates which were made out in Bramer's name.

I am, with great respect, your most obedient servant,

W. BARTON.

JOSEPH HOWELL, Esq.

NEW YORK, Nov. 6, 1794.

SIR:—Although I have not the honor of being personally acquainted with you, I take the liberty to ask a very particular favor, in which you may oblige me very much, being induced to make this request to you, as I presume it comes under your department in the War Office.

Mr. McEwen will present you this, and attend to everything necessary on my part.

What I want is an official certificate that I was returned, and considered as part of the quota of New York in the British war. My commission is dated November 15, 1779, in the Second Regiment of Light Dragoons, as a Lieutenant. Soon after, I was appointed Adjutant to said regiment, and in 1781, Aid-de-camp to Major-general Lord Sterling, and was always with Captain Hoogland and the several dragoons returned to the State of New York, where we had our depreciation of pay made up, until, by an arrangement of Congress, the whole cavalry was made legionary, and affixed to particular States.

Respectfully, your humble servant,
THOMAS FREDERICK JACKSON.

Maj. HOWELL.

BOSTON, May 9, 1795.

SIR:—In the year 1786, General Knox granted me a warrant, at the War Office, for 850 dollars. There being no money to satisfy the demand at that time, it has remained in that office ever since. General Knox has assured me, that upon his arrival at this place, upon application through you, the demand would be satisfied. Your attention to the business will much oblige,

Your obedient, humble servant,
THOMAS H. CONDY,
Late Lieut. Mass. Line.

Mr. SIMMONS.

PART II.

NAMES, RANK, DATES OF COMMISSIONS, AND TIME OF ENLISTMENT OF THE OFFICERS AND PRIVATES OF COL. JOSEPH CILLEY'S NEW HAMPSHIRE REGIMENT, FROM NOV. 8, 1776, TO JAN. 1, 1779.

Joseph Cilley, Colonel, commissioned Apr. 2, 1777. Served to the end of the war.
George Reed, Lieutenant-colonel. Transferred to 2d regiment.
Jeremiah Gilman, Lieutenant-colonel.   Commissioned September 20, 1777.
William Scott, Major.   do.   do.
Jeremiah Gilman, do.   do.   do.
Benjamin Kimball, Paymaster and Lieutenant,   do.   December 30, 1778.
Jeremiah Pritchard, Adjutant and Lieutenant.   do.   January 1, 1778.
Josiah Munro, Quartermaster and Lieutenant.   do.   August 21, 1778.
John Hale, Surgeon.   do.   May 2, 1777.
Jonathan Pool, Surgeon's Mate.   do.   do.

THE FIRST COMPANY.

Simon Sartwell, Captain. Commissioned as Lieutenant, November 8, 1776. Promoted to Captain, December 1, 1778.
Joshua Thompson, Lieutenant. Commissioned as Ensign, November 8, 1776. Promoted to Lieutenant, March 4, 1778.

Non-commissioned Officers for Three Years.

Hubard Carter, Sergeant. Appointed January 1, 1777.
Morris Millet,   do.   do.   do.
John Jordan,   do.   do.   do.
Ripley Bingham,   do.   do.   November 13, 1776.
John Joiner, Qr. Mr. Sergeant.   do.   November 19, 1776.
James Cochran, Corporal.   do.   January 1, 1777.
Daniel Sterns,   do.   do.   May 1, 1777.
Stephen Abbott, Drummer.   do.   January 1, 1777.

OFFICERS AND PRIVATES

Privates for Three Years.

	Enlisted.		Enlisted.
John Allen,	Jan. 1, 1777.	Samuel Sanderson,	Jan. 1, 1777.
David Addoms,	do.	Ephraim Stevens,	do.
Isaac Addoms,	Mar. 10, 1778.	Michael Silk,	do.
Benjamin Beavins,	Feb. 1, 1777.	James Shail,	do.
Nathaniel Bartlett,	May 1, 1777.	Loring Thompson,	May 1, 1777.
Thomas Bates,	Mar. 13, 1778.	Jacob Taylor,	Mar. 21, 1778.
John Clark,	May 1, 1777.	Jonathan Wellock,	Feb. 15, 1777.
John Cowdry,	April 21, 1777.	William White,	Jan. 1, 1777.
John Combes,	April 11, 1777.	John Willace,	Mar. 27, 1778.
Moses Chase,	May 1, 1777.	Ebenezer Williams,	Mar. 10, 1778.
Philemon Duset,	do.	Joseph Burley,	Mar. 15, 1778.
Thomas Davis,	April 21, 1777.	William Cowen,	Mar. 1, 1778*
John Dole,	May 18, 1777.	John Alds,	Mar. 1, 1778.
William Darrah,	Dec. 30, 1777.	Samuel Ayers,	Mar. 10, 1778.
Ralph Ellenwood,	April 3, 1778.	Samuel Boyd,	Mar. 1, 1778.
Ebenezer Hills,	April 21, 1777.	Samuel Bates,	May 15, 1778.
Thomas Kimball,	June 1, 1778.	Thomas Capren,	April 11, 1778.
John Millet,	Jan. 1, 1777.	Joel Rice,	May 1, 1777.
William Man,	April 1, 1777.	Jacob Rice,	Jan. 1, 1778.
Nathaniel Man,	do.	John Willsgrove,	Jan. 1, 1777.
Abel Merrill,	do.	Asa Sterns,	May 1, 1777.
James Moore,	Jan. 1, 1777.	Abner Wise,	do.
John Matthews,	do.	Thomas McNeal,	do.
William Pettigrew,	Mar. 18, 1778.	Samuel Morrison,	do.
Joel Royce,	May 1, 1777.	Thomas Whitlock,	do.

THE SECOND COMPANY.

Jeremiah Gilman, Lieutenant-colonel. Commissioned September 20, 1777.
Benjamin Kimball, Lieutenant. Commissioned November 8, 1776. Made Paymaster, December 20, 1778.
Daniel Clapp, Lieutenant. Commissioned November 8, 1776.
Thomas Blake, Ensign. Commissioned November 8, 1776. Promoted to Lieutenant, May 11, 1778.

Non-commissioned Officers for Three Years.

Isaac Gibbs, Sergeant.	Appointed March 10, 1777.		
Robert Miller,	do.	do.	February 17, 1777.
Samuel Hews, Corporal.	do.		April 8, 1777.
Stephen Jennings,	do.	do.	May 12, 1777.
Asa Lovejoy, Drummer.		do.	February 1, 1777.
			Sick since Oct. 27, 1778.

OF THE REVOLUTIONARY WAR. 145

Privates for Three Years.

	Enlisted.		Enlisted.
Nathaniel Andrews,	May 15, 1777.	Abel Lovejoy,	Feb. 1, 1777.
Isaac Boynton,	April 10, 1777.	Matthias Miller,	Feb. 17, 1777.
Nathaniel Bugby,	April 22, 1777.	Robert Mason,	Mar. 17, 1778.
Benjamin Burnett,	Feb. 17, 1777.	Thomas Newman,	Mar. 1, 1777.
William Connick,	Feb. 1, 1777.	Nathaniel Patton,	Feb. 1, 1777.
Jonathan Conant,	April 22, 1777.	James Roose,	do.
Edward Carter,	Feb. 1, 1777.	David Sanderson,	do.
Nathan Davis,	Mar. 17, 1778.	Seth Thompson,	April 18, 1777.
Lemuel Dean,	Mar. 8, 1777.	Medad Taylor,	Mar. 17, 1778.
Ralph Emerson,	April 10, 1777.	Jonathan Wright,	April 22, 1777.
Edward Evans,	Feb. 1, 1777.	David Wright,	do.
Daniel Fuller,	Mar. 1, 1777.	Phinehas Wright,	do.
David Gibbs,	Mar. 10, 1777.	Thomas Hardy,	April 26, 1778.
Joshua Gibbs,	Mar. 1, 1777.	Jonathan Morse,	April 20, 1778.
Simeon Goold,	Feb. 1, 1777.	Reuben Blood,	Unknown.
William Hale,	April 10, 1777.	Simon Blood,	do.
George Knox,	May 10, 1778.	Wilder Willard,	do.

THE THIRD COMPANY.

William Scott, Captain and Major. Commissioned September 20, 1777.
Moody Dustin, First-Lieutenant.   do.   November 8, 1776.
Bazaleel Howe, Second-Lieutenant.   do.   November 8, 1776.

Non-Commissioned Officers for Three Years.

Thomas Stickney, Sergeant. Appointed February 20, 1777.
William Richardson, do.   do.   January 1, 1777.
Robert Miller,   do.   do.   February 17, 1777.
William Lang, Corporal,   do.   February 18, 1777.
Thomas Whittock, Drummer.

Privates for Three Years.

	Enlisted.		Enlisted.
Samuel Ayres,	Mar. 10, 1778.	Jacob Downing,	Jan. 20, 1777.
David Bryant,	Nov. 12, 1776.	John Dorman,	Jan. 20, 1778.
Samuel Boyd,	Mar. 1, 1778.	Noah Emery,	April 10, 1777.
Samuel Bates,	Feb. 15, 1777.	Samuel Fugard,	Nov. 13, 1776.
Abner Bingham,	Mar. 10, 1777.	Nathan Glines,	Jan. 9, 1777.
John Cross,	Jan. 10, 1778.	James Gilmore,	April 24, 1777.
Ephraim Cross,	April 25, 1777.	Timothy Harrington,	Nov. 14, 1776.
Thomas Capron,	April 11, 1778.	Walter Hains,	May 15, 1777.
David Dickey,	do.	John Hillsgrove,	Unknown.

OFFICERS AND PRIVATES

	Enlisted.		Enlisted.
Moses Hutchins,	Nov. 16, 1776.	John Read,	May 18, 1777.
Samuel Morris,	Unknown.	William Simson,	Jan. 1, 1777.
Peter Jenkins,	April 7, 1777.	Asa Stearns,	May 1, 1777.
James Lamb,	Mar. 10, 1777.	Thomas Severance,	Mar. 21, 1777.
Thomas McNeal,	Unknown.	James Simonds,	Unknown.
Jonathan McKoy,	Mar. 11, 1778.	Adam Thompson,	Feb. 1, 1777.
Nathaniel Powers,	Feb. 13, 1778.	John Vance,	April 28, 1777.
Jethro Pattingal,	Mar. 6, 1777.	William Walker,	May 8, 1777.
Jonathan Pattingal,	April 9, 1777.	Wilder Willard,	April 21, 1777.
Reuben Robarts,	Nov. 4, 1776.	Abner Wise,	Unknown.
Joel Royce,	May 1, 1777.	Daniel Yong,	Jan. 27, 1778.

Privates for Two Years.

John Alds,	Mar. 1, 1778.	Jonathan Palmer,	April 20, 1778.
Hugh Jemerson,	April 19, 1778.	Jacob Royce,	Jan. 1, 1778.
Francis Mitchell,	April 13, 1778.	Abiel Walton,	July 1, 1778.
Nathaniel Patton,	Jan. 1, 1778.		

THE FIRST CAPTAIN'S COMPANY.

Amos Morrill, Captain. Commissioned November 8, 1776. Promoted to Major. Served to the end of the war.

Nathaniel McColley, First-Lieutenant. Commissioned November 8, 1776. Furloughed for 60 days from November 4, 1778, by General Poor.

Jonathan Willard, Second-Lieutenant. Commissioned as Ensign November 8, 1776. Promoted to Lieutenant January 10, 1778.

Bazaleel Hower, Second-Lieutenant. Commissioned November 8, 1776. Served to the end of the war.

Non-commissioned Officers for three Years.

Samuel Wells, Sergeant. Appointed November 13, 1776.
Benjamin Cotton, do. do. April 1, 1778,
Thomas Scott, do. do. July 31, 1778.
Samuel Whidden, Corporal. do. March 8, 1777.
Theophilus Cass, do. do. Unknown.
Benjamin George, do. do. March 1, 1777.

Privates for Three Years.

	Enlisted.		Enlisted.
John Ash,	Unknown.	Jonathan Cilley,	Nov. 12, 1776.
Joshua Blodget,	Mar. 14, 1777.	Robert Cunningham,	April 20, 1777.
Benjamin Butler,	Dec. 5, 1777.	William Cook,	May 17, 1777.
Cæsar Barnes,	Unknown.	Solomon Chapman,	Unknown.

OF THE REVOLUTIONARY WAR.   147

	Enlisted.		Enlisted.
Benjamin Dowe,	Unknown.	Timothy Martin,	Mar. 8, 1777.
James Dickey,	Mar. 4, 1777.	Andrew McIntire,	do.
Joshua Damford,	Unknown.	John McIntire,	do.
Philip Flanders,	do.	William Nealy,	Unknown.
Thomas George,	Mar. 1, 1777.	James Orr,	Mar. 8, 1777.
Isaac George,	do.	Zadoc Read,	Unknown.
Nathaniel Grimes,	Feb. 17, 1778.	John W. Robertson,	do.
Joseph Grant,	Mar. 5, 1778.	Samuel Sinkler,	Jan. 21, 1777.
Joseph Hesselton,	Feb. 12, 1777.	Joshua Sinkler,	Dec. 1, 1777.
Jonathan Hessleton,	Unknown.	Peter Stevens,	Unknown.
Elisha Hutchinson,	April 20, 1778.	Alexander Smith,	do.
Levi Hutchinson,	do.	Ephraim Stevens,	Mar. 1, 1777.
Moses Locke,	Unknown.	Peter Wells,	Unknown.
Samuel Locke,	do.	Joseph York,	do.
Nathaniel Molton,	do.	Adam Thompson,	Feb. 1, 1777.
Florence McColley,	do.	Benj. Pettingall, died Dec. 3, 1778.	

THE SECOND CAPTAIN'S COMPANY.

Jason Wait, Captain. Commissioned November 8, 1776. Furloughed by Gen. Poor for 60 days from December 22, 1778.

Jeremiah Pritchard, Lieutenant. Commissioned November 8, 1776. Furloughed by Gen. Poor for 60 days from December 22, 1778.

Jonathan Perkins, Ensign. Commissioned July 29, 1777. Promoted to Lieutenant. Served to the end of the war.

Non-commissioned Officers for Three Years.

Josiah Burton,	Sergeant.	Appointed, unknown.
Sylvester Wilkins,	do.	do.	February 1, 1777.
Richard Roberson,	do.	do.	February 2, 1777.
Ripley Bingham,	do.	do.	November 13, 1776.
Robert Parker, Corporal.		do.	April 9, 1777.
Hezekiah Clark, Drummer.		do.	April 21, 1777.

Privates for Three Years.

	Enlisted.		Enlisted.
Elijah Avery,	April 9, 1777.	Ebenezer Forgood,	Jan. 7, 1777.
Samuel Allen,	Unknown.	Henry Harris,	Jan. 9, 1777.
Elisha Addams,	April 16, 1777.	Simon Hutchins,	do.
William Brown,	Nov. 22, 1776.	David Johnson,	Feb. 16, 1777.
John Bishop,	Unknown.	Francis Joiner,	Nov. 13, 1776.
Joseph Davis,	Dec. 16, 1776.	John Lapish,	Unknown.
Charles Dority,	Unknown.	William McGee,	Dec. 10, 1776.

OFFICERS AND PRIVATES

	Enlisted.		Enlisted.
John McGee,	Dec. 10, 1776.	Benjamin Smith,	April 9, 1777.
John McClintock,	Mar. 15, 1777.	Nathan Tuttle,	do.
James Merrill,	Nov. 17, 1776.	Reuben Wheeler,	Dec. 1, 1777.
Enoch Moss,	Feb. 2, 1777.	George Wilson,	Feb. 3, 1777.
Nathaniel Needham,	Mar. 1, 1777.	Rufus Walton,	Mar. 10, 1777.
Benjamin Perkins,	Feb. 2, 1777.	Stephen Ward,	do.
Richard Richardson,	April 3, 1777.	Thomas Wilson,	Unknown.
James Rider,	Unknown.	Lewis Wisso.	Nov. 14, 1776.
Isaac Smith,	April 9, 1777.	Daniel Ritter,	April 17, 1777.

Privates for Two Years.

Asaph Butler,	April 1, 1778.	Alpheus Kingsley,	April 1, 1778.
Walter Geers,	Mar. 16, 1778.	Jedediah Rice,	Jan. 22, 1778.
Charles Geers,	Feb. 19, 1778.	Joseph Right,	April 1, 1778.
Thomas Hunt,	do.	Henry Stevens,	Mar. 22, 1778.
Eleazer Howard,	Jan. 22, 1778.	Tyler Spafford,	Feb. 19, 1778.
Solomon Harris,	Mar. 22, 1778.	(Deserted Dec. 25, 1778.)	

THE THIRD CAPTAIN'S COMPANY.

Amos Emerson, Captain. Commissioned November 9, 1776.

Josiah Munro, First-Lieutenant and Quartermaster. Commissioned as Lieutenant November 8, 1776; appointed Qr. Mr., August 21, 1778. Promoted to Captain and served to the end of the war.

Simon Merrill, Second-Lieutenant. Commissioned November 8, 1776. Promoted to Lieutenant, September 19, 1777.

Non-commissioned Officers for Three Years.

Jonathan Burrows,	Sergeant.	Appointed	Jannary 1, 1777.
Israel Ingalls,	do.	do.	January 27, 1777.
Sanders Bradbury,	do.	do.	April 1, 1777.
William Richardson,	do.	do.	January 1, 1777.
John Manning,	Corporal,	do.	April 17, 1777.
Jeremiah Towl,	do.	do.	April 3, 1777.
Nathaniel Batchelder,	do.	do.	March 20, 1777.
Paul Woods,	Fifer.	do.	Unknown.

Privates for Three Years.

	Enlisted.		Enlisted.
Samuel Aiken,	April 3, 1777.	Charles Booles,	Feb. 2, 1778.
Noah Buswell,	Jan. 31, 1777.	Thomas Fuller,	April 2, 1777.
John Barron,	May 12, 1777.	Thomas Grush,	Mar. 23, 1777.
Simeon Butterfield,	Mar. 1, 1777.	Duncan Grant,	April 4, 1777.

OF THE REVOLUTIONARY WAR.   149

	Enlisted.		Enlisted.
Samuel Holt,	Mar. 14, 1777.	Jonathan Nock,	Mar. 10, 1777.
Charles Hanson,	Jan. 1, 1777.	John Perry,	Feb. 19, 1777.
Peter Honey,	April 18, 1777.	Jonathan Powers,	Jan. 15, 1777.
David Hunt,	Jan. 1, 1778.	William Powell,	June 15, 1777.
Zacheus Hunt,	Feb. 2, 1778.	John Rowe,	April 15, 1777.
Reuben Hall,	Mar. 14, 1777.	David Smith,	Mar. 14, 1777.
Jesse Heath,	April 25, 1777.	Benjamin Taylor,	April 17, 1777.
John Kent,	Feb. 2, 1778.	Daniel Woods,	do.
Eliphalet Manning,	April 15, 1777.	Benjamin Smith,	Mar. 14, 1777.
Barnard Merrill,	April 4, 1777.	Henry True,	April 3, 1777.
John McClellan,	April 1, 1777.	Daniel Shirley,	do.

THE FOURTH CAPTAIN'S COMPANY.

Ebenezer Frye, Captain. Commissioned November 8, 1776. Served to the end of the war.

Asa Senter, Lieutenant. Commissioned November 8, 1776. Served to the end of the war.

Joshua Thompson, Ensign. Commissioned November 8, 1776. Promoted to Lieutenant. Served to the end of the war.

Non-commissioned Officers for Three Years.

Jeremiah Holtman, Sergeant.	Appointed November 15, 1776.	
Samuel Thompson,	do. do.	May 3, 1777.
Robert Hodgert,	do. do.	March 24, 1777.
Thomas Stickney,	do. do.	February 5, 1777.
William Leevy, Corporal.	do.	April 5, 1777.
Jonas Cutting,	do. do.	November 14, 1776.
Joseph Marsh,	do. do.	April 7, 1777.
Joseph Polly, Drummer.	do.	April 1, 1777.

Privates for Three Years.

	Enlisted.		Enlisted.
James Boyes,	Nov. 14, 1776.	Samuel Eyers,	April 28, 1777.
James Brown,	April 1, 1777.	Robert Forrest,	Mar. 16, 1778.
Bishop Coster,	April 9, 1777.	George Galt,	Nov. 14, 1776.
James Campbell,	April 26, 1777.	John Head,	Nov. 13, 1776.
Thomas Colburn,	Jan. 15, 1777.	Thomas Haynes,	April 15, 1777.
Zebulon Colbie,	Jan. 10, 1777.	John Hall,	Mar. 12, 1778.
Samuel Dalton,	Feb. 1, 1777.	Ichabod Martin,	Nov. 13, 1776.
William Dickey,	April 9, 1777.	Alexander McMaster,	do.
John Douglass,	April 17, 1778.	John McMurphy,	April 20, 1777.
Samuel Danford,	April 27, 1778.	Thomas Mathews,	April 25, 1777.

OFFICERS AND PRIVATES

	Enlisted.		Enlisted.
John Mack,	May 2, 1777.	John Riddle,	Mar. 7, 1778.
Thomas Muchemore,	Jan. 23, 1777.	Edward Smith,	April 17, 1777.
Daniel McCoy,	Mar. 11, 1778.	Bartholomew Stevens,	Feb. 1, 1777.
Thomas McLaughlin,	Mar. 12, 1778.	John Sampson,	Nov. 13, 1776.
Joseph McFarland,	April 28, 1777.	Solomon Todd,	April 28, 1777.
George McMurphy,	April 7, 1777.	James Thompson,	Nov. 14, 1776.
Joseph Mack,	April 2, 1777.	Prince Thompson,	May 15, 1777
Joseph Norris,	Mar. 4, 1778.	Robert Wilson,	April 1, 1777.
John O'Brion,	April 9, 1777.	James Wilson,	do.
Nathan Plummer,	April 7, 1777.	Samuel Walton,	April 9, 1777.
Thomas Riddle,	Mar. 23, 1777.		

THE FIFTH CAPTAIN'S COMPANY.

Isaac Farwell, Captain. Commissioned November 8, 1776. Served to the end of the war.

William Hutchins, Lieutenant. Commissioned November 8, 1776.

Jonathan Willard, Ensign. Commissioned November 8, 1776. Promoted to Lieutenant, January 10, 1778.

Non-commissioned Officers for Three Years.

Levid Adams,	Sergeant.	Appointed February 1, 1777.
Ephraim Foster,	do.	do. do.
Gilbert Caswell,	do.	do. July 8, 1777.
Ira Evans,	Corporal.	do. November 16, 1776.
Abner Preston,	Drummer.	do. February 1, 1777.
Thomas Dodge,	Fifer.	do. May 14, 1777.

Privates for Three Years.

	Enlisted.		Enlisted.
Joel Andrews,	Jan. 1, 1778.	James Hawkley,	Mar. 1, 1777.
Jonas Adams,	Feb. 1, 1777.	William Hewett,	Feb. 1, 1778.
David Abrahams,	Unknown.	Sylvanus Hastings,	Jan. 1, 1778.
Joseph Burk,	Feb. 9, 1777.	Page Harryman,	May 19, 1777.
John Clark,	Feb. 3, 1777.	Giles Keley,	April 18, 1777.
Bunker Clark,	Feb. 1, 1777.	Jonathan Kelly,	Nov. 27, 1776.
Benjamin Critchett,	Feb. 18, 1777.	William Leatten,	Unknown.
Moses Farnsworth,	Feb. 1, 1777.	Ebenezer Mathews,	Mar. 12, 1778.
Thomas Gilmore,	Nov. 14, 1776.	Isaac Mitchell,	Unknown.
Silas Gill,	Feb. 1, 1777.	Timothy Newton,	do.
Matthew Greer,	Mar. 16, 1776.	Thomas Osgood,	Mar. 12, 1778.
John Grout,	May 1, 1777.	William Pritchard,	Nov. 16, 1776.
Nathaniel Hays,	Feb. 1, 1777.	Samuel Phelps,	Nov. 15, 1776.

OF THE REVOLUTIONARY WAR.   151

	Enlisted.		Enlisted.
Simeon Powers,	Unknown.	Abner Thurston,	Unknown.
Noah Porter,	Jan. 1, 1778.	Joseph Tucker,	Feb. 3, 1778.
Philip Peters,	May 1, 1778.	William Taggert,	Feb. 4, 1778.
John Pike,	Unknown.	Ithamar Wheelock,	Feb. 1, 1777.
Lemuel Royce,	Feb. 4, 1777.	Aaron Adams,	Mar. 12, 1778.
Paris Richardson,	Mar. 13, 1778.	John Cross,	Jan. 1, 1778.
Samuel Sisco,	Feb. 17, 1777.	Moses Hutchins,	Nov. 16, 1776.
William Sisco,	May 1, 1778.	Nathaniel Powers,	Mar. 13, 1778.
John Simonds,	Jan. 1, 1778.	James Simonds,	Unknown.
Silas Simonds,	do.	John Pettengill,	April 9, 1777.
Levi Simonds,	Feb. 13, 1778.		

THE SIXTH CAPTAIN'S COMPANY.

Nathaniel Hutchins, Captain. Commissioned April 3, 1777. Served to the end of the war.

Daniel Clapp, Lieutenant. Commissioned November 8, 1777.

Non-commissioned Officers for Three Years.

Eliphalet Quimby,	Sergeant.	Appointed April 5, 1777.
Samuel Caldwell,	do.	do. July 3, 1777.
Gilbert Caswell,	do.	do. July 8, 1777.
Amos Barns,	do.	do. January 21, 1778.
William Lang,	Corporal.	do. February 18, 1777.
John Chadwick,	do.	do. April 6, 1777.
Johnthing Conner,	do.	do. April 8, 1777.
Benjamin Williams,	do.	do. April 6, 1777.
Samuel Stocker,	Drummer.	do. April 10, 1777.
Daniel Creesy,	Fifer.	do. do.

Privates for Three Years.

	Enlisted.		Enlisted.
James Boles,	July 14, 1777.	Thomas Easman,	July 8, 1777.
William Bachelor,	Jan. 10, 1777.	Thomas Flanders,	Feb. 10, 1777.
Enos Chelis,	May 7, 1777.	Jacob Flanders,	do.
Samuel Cammett,	Mar. 1, 1777.	Elijah Fairfield,	April 17, 1777.
Moses Colby,	May 11, 1777.	William Frankfort,	July 9, 1778.
Thomas Cammet,	April 16, 1777.	Thomas George,	April 17, 1777.
Joshua Church,	April 12, 1777.	Antona Gilman,	Jan. 1, 1777.
John Cooper,	do.	Charles Greenfield,	April 1, 1777.
Stephen Dustin,	April 10, 1778.	William Hodskins,	April 6, 1777.
James Doud,	Unknown.	Enoch Hoyt,	July 3, 1777.
James Eagerly,	April 14, 1777.	Jonathan Judkins,	April 11, 1777.

152   OFFICERS AND PRIVATES

	Enlisted.		Enlisted.
Stephen Lord,	Feb. 24, 1777.	Jonathan Webster,	Mar. 7, 1777.
John Larabee,	Nov. 25, 1776.	Thomas Jamerson,	Feb. 22, 1778.
John Smart,	April 7, 1777.	Moses Sanborn,	April 27. 1778.
John Sweet,	April 16, 1777.	Ephraim Sargeant,	do.
Caleb Smart,	April 7, 1777.	William Powell,	do.
Jonathan Stevens,	do.	Samuel Powell,	do.
Benjamin Sweet,	April 16, 1777.	Asa Heath,	do.
James Sherer,	April 6, 1777.	Ephraim Cross,	April 25, 1778.
Jonathan Sawyer,	April 4, 1777.	John Dorman,	Jan. 20, 1778.
Joseph Sanborn,	Nov. 22, 1776.	Thomas Severance,	Mar. 21, 1777.
Henry Thompson,	Nov. 24, 1776.	Reuben Roberts,	Nov. 24, 1776.
Ezra Turner,	Mar. 5, 1777.		

NAMES, RANK, AND DATES OF COMMISSIONS OF THE OFFICERS OF COL. WILLIAM DOUGLAS' CONNECTICUT REGIMENT, RAISED BY THE STATE IN JUNE, 1776, TO JOIN THE CONTINENTAL ARMY IN NEW YORK.

William Douglas, Colonel. Commissioned June 20, 1776.
James Arnold, Lieutenant-colonel. Commissioned June 20, 1776.
Phinehas Porter, Major. Commissioned June 20, 1776.
Benjamin Trumbull, Chaplain. Commissioned June 24, 1776.
Samuel Barker, Adjutant. Commissioned June 20, 1776.
Jonah Clark, Quartermaster. Commissioned June 22, 1776.
Jared Potter, Surgeon. Commissioned July 3, 1776.
Witham Gould, Surgeon's Mate. Commissioned July 3, 1776.
Daniel Abbott, Armorer. Commissioned July 8, 1776.

Captains Commissioned June 20, 1776.

Nathaniel Johnson,	Jonas Prentice,
Edward Russell,	Jacob Brackett,
Samuel Peeks,	Nathaniel Bunnell,
John Lewis,	Cornelius Higgins.

NOTE.—The sum of £7,847 16s. 2½d. was paid by Ebenezer Huntington, Deputy Paymaster-general, for the services of this regiment until the 29th December, 1776, when they were discharged by Major-general William Heath. Jonah Clark, Quartermaster, acted as Paymaster of the regiment for the time. It does not appear that any of those officers served after this, in the Continental Line, to the end of the war.

OFFICERS AND PRIVATES OF COL. CHRISTOPHER GREENE'S RHODE ISLAND REGIMENT, AS IT STOOD MAY 1, 1779.

Christopher Greene, Colonel.
John Holden, Adjutant.
Samuel Ward, Major.
Peter Turner, Surgeon.
John Parish, Surgeon's Mate.
John Cook, Quartermaster.
Ebenezer Flagg, Paymaster.

CAPTAINS.

John S. Dexter,
Elijah Lewis,
Thomas Arnold,
Ebenezer Flagg,
Thomas Cole.

LIEUTENANTS.

Zephaniah Brown,
Daniel Pierce,
Elias Thompson,
John Holden,
David Johnston,

ENSIGNS.

Edward Slocum,
Joseph Cornell,
Charles Pierce,
Cornelius Russell,
Elias Thompson,
John Cooke.

SERGEANTS.

Henry Davis,
John Smith,
Samuel West,
George Sisson.
Ebenezer Talbert,
Asa Lewis,
Samuel Cranston,
Seth Fisher,
Joseph Brown,
William Hutton,
William Kipp,

Thomas Taylor,
James Ross,
George Popple,
Eldridge Spink,
Benajah Davis.

CORPORALS.

Prince Simons,
Thomas Stafford,
Alexander Love,
William Parks,
David Potter,
George Potter,
Ebenezer Slocumb.

PRIVATES.

Edward Anthony,
Benedict Aron,
Bristol Arnold,
Richard Allen,
Joseph Boyer,
Jack Burrows,
Primus Babcock,
Hampton Barton,
Abram Bemon,
Prince Bucklin,
Job Burton,
Africa Bush,
Frank Bourn,
Cato Barrister,
James Carpenter.
Prince Childs,
William Cooper.
John Charles,
Jack Coddington,
Newport Champlin
James Clark,
Prince Case,
Prince Gardiner,
Perry Green,
Thomas Nichols,
Cæsar Updike,

John Watson,
Jack Minthorn,
Mingo Rodman,
Jacob Hazzard,
Peter Daily,
Milford Dick,
Cæsar Wheaton,
Ichabod Northrup,
Thomas Amos,
Cato Green,
William Green,

Henry Tabor,
Boston Wilbur,
Reuben Roberts,
Prince Rodman,
Thomas Spencer,
Josias Soule,
Primus Watson,
James Daily,
Gideon Harry,
Landon Hall,
John Pump.

NAMES AND RANK OF THE OFFICERS OF COL. ISRAEL ANGELL'S RHODE ISLAND CONTINENTAL REGIMENT IN 1779, AND OTHER OFFICERS OF THAT STATE.

Israel Angell, Colonel.
Jeremiah Olney, Lieutenant-colonel.
Simeon Thayer, Major.
Thomas Waterman, Lieutenant and Adjutant.
Samuel Tenny, Surgeon.
Elias Cornelius, Surgeon's Mate.

CAPTAINS.
William Allen,
William Tew,
Stephen Olney,
Coggeshall Olney,
William Humphrey,
William Littlefield,
Thomas Hughes.

LIEUTENANTS.
Thomas Waterman,
Dutee Jerauld,
Joseph Wheaton,
John M. Greene,
David Sayles,
Ebenezer Macomber,
Benj. L. Peckham,
John Hubbard,
Oliver Jenks.

ENSIGNS.
William Pratt,
Joseph Masury,
John Rogers,
Jeremiah Greenman.

Other Regiments.

Christopher Lippett, Colonel.
Adam Comstock, Lieut.-colonel.
William Tyler, Adjutant.
Benjamin Bourn, Quartermaster.

CAPTAINS.
Arthur Fenner,
Simeon Martin,
David Dexter.

Nathan Blackmar,
Loring Peck,
John Carr,
Thomas Gorton,
Benjamin Hoppin,
Christopher Dyer,
Thomas Arnold,
Lemuel Bailey,
William Jones.

OF THE REVOLUTIONARY WAR. 155

LIEUTENANTS.	ENSIGNS.
Gilbert Richardson,	Amos Gilson,
Reuben Hewitt,	David Melville,
Thomas Noyes,	Benjamin Burn,
William Belcher,	Philip Martin,
Peleg Hoxie,	John Holden,
Abram Turtelot,	John Cowen,
Jacob Williams,	William Pullen,
Ichabod Prentice,	Caleb Mathews,
Alexander Thomas,	Brinton Bliss,
Gilbert Grant.	Joseph Reed.

Officers in the Early Part of the War.

CAPTAINS.	LIEUTENANTS.
Christopher Manchester,	Malachi Hammet,
Caleb Gardner,	Augustus Stanton,
Peter Church,	Walter Palmer,
Job Pierce,	Charles Lippett,
Thomas Wells,	Paul Hannington,
William Barton,	James Smith,
James Wallace,	Lemuel Bailey,
Charles Dyer,	
Samuel Philips,	
Josiah Gibbs,	John Rogers,
Benjamin Dimond.	John Holden,
Benjamin Frye.	Samuel Stevens.

NAMES, RANK, DATES OF COMMISSIONS, AND COMMENCEMENT OF SERVICE, OF THE OFFICERS AND PRIVATES OF COLONEL EBENEZER STEVENS' COMPANIES OF NEW YORK ARTILLERY.

Commissioned Officers.

Ebenezer Stevens. Commissioned as Lieutenant of Infantry, May 8, 1775; as Captain of Artillery, December 6, 1775; as Major of Artillery, November 9, 1776: and as Lieutenant-colonel of Artillery, April 30, 1778.

Samuel Hodgdon. Commissioned as Commissary of Military Stores, February 1, 1777; and as Commissary-general of Military Stores, February 11, 1778.

Hezekiah Whetmore, Adjutant. Commissioned February 1, 1777. Resigned September 6, 1778.

John Winslow, Paymaster and Captain. Commissioned as Captain, June 8, 1777; as Paymaster, June 1, 1778. Resigned November 5, 1778.

William Wheeler, Surgeon. Commissioned September 4, 1777. Resigned January 8, 1779.

Josiah Watrous, Surgeon's Mate. Commissioned September 4, 1777. On command at West Point from November 8, 1778, to January 8, 1779, when he resigned.

Benjamin Bartlett, Conductor. Commissioned January 9, 1777. On command in Connecticut, August 8, 1778.

Jasper M. Gidley, Conductor. Commissioned June 1, 1777. On command at West Point, August 8, 1778.

James Boyer, Conductor. Commissioned April 24, 1778.

FIRST COMPANY.

Stephen Buckland, Captain. Commissioned November 9, 1776; furloughed by General Washington from October 30, 1778, for five weeks. On command in Connecticut, May, 1778; and at West Point, January, 1779.

William Johnston, Captain-lieutenant. Commissioned November 9, 1776. On command at West Point in January, 1779.

Constant Freeman, First-lieutenant. Commissioned November 9, 1776. On command at West Point, January 17, 1779. Served to the end of the war in Crane's Artillery.

George Ingersol, Second Lieutenant. Commissioned November 9, 1776; joined Crane's Artillery in 1779; and served to the end of the war in Massachusetts.

Isaac Barber, Second-lieutenant. Commissioned November 9, 1776. At West Point, January, 1779. Joined Crane's Artillery.

David Deming, Second-lieutenant. Commissioned February 1, 1777. At West Point, January 17, 1779.

Non-commissioned Officers for the War.

Alexander Campbell, Sergeant-major. Appointed June 16, 1777.

John Degrove,	Sergeant.	do.	November 13, 1776.
Edward Blake,	do.	do.	January 8, 1777.
Jeremiah Shea,	do.	do.	March 19, 1777.
Henry Morto,	do.	do.	August 9, 1777.
John Blunt,	do.	do.	do.
Alexander Campbell,	do.	do.	November 19, 1776.
Roger Taylor,	Corporal.	do.	January 3, 1777.
James Yates,	do.	do.	do.
William Anderson,	do.	do.	January 4, 1777.
John Skerrett,	do.	do.	January 3, 1777.
Anthony Kelly,	do.	do.	August 9, 1777.
Richard Northover,	do.	do.	November 17, 1776.
Samuel Denny,	do.	do.	May 14, 1777.
William Loudon,	Drum-major.	do.	November 11, 1776.
Henry Crombie,	Drummer.	do.	February 20, 1777.
Robert Sloan,	Fifer.	do.	February 7, 1777.

OF THE REVOLUTIONARY WAR. 157

Bombardiers for the War.

	Appointed.		Appointed.
Francis Kline,	Nov. 14, 1776.	Thomas Parker,	Aug. 9, 1777.
Neal McNeal,	do.	William Balyer,	May 10, 1777.
Henry Defreest,	do.		

Gunners for the War.

Edward Ahern,	Nov. 17, 1776.	William Farden,	Mar. 24, 1777
John Bitters,	Jan. 20, 1777.	(Taken prisoner July 6, 1777.)	
John Granger,	May 24, 1777.	John Kenny,	Mar. 24, 1777.
William Gortley,	May 10, 1777.	(Reduced July 21, 1777.)	
John Teen,	Aug. 9, 1777.		

Matrosses for the War.

Edward Bird,	Dec. 20, 1776.	John Love,	Dec. 22, 1776.
Edward Brown,	Jan. 24, 1777.	(Missing since July 6, 1777.)	
Benjamin Cleveland,	Nov. 16, 1776.	Thomas Flemming,	Nov. 14, 1776.
Samuel Denny,	July 21, 1777.	(Missing since July 6, 1777.)	
William Dorkham,	Jan. 25, 1777.	Henry Morto,	July 21, 1777.
John Green,	Jan. 2, 1777.	(Promoted to Serg. Aug. 9, 1777.)	
Henry Graham,	Aug. 1, 1777.	John Blunt,	July 21, 1777.
Stephen Hays,	Jan. 28, 1777.	(Promoted to Serg. Aug. 9, 1777.)	
John Harvey,	Jan. 20, 1777.	Anthony Kelly,	May 14, 1777.
William Hunter,	do.	(Promoted to Corp. Aug. 9, 1777.)	
John Kenny,	July 21, 1777.	Thomas Parker,	July 21, 1777,
Peter Meredith,	Jan. 27, 1777.	(Promoted to Bomb. Aug. 9, 1777.)	
John McIndoe,	Jan. 1, 1777.	John Teen,	May 7, 1777.
John Nickle,	Jan. 4, 1777.	(Promoted to Gun. Aug 9, 1777.)	
Gregory O'Brine,	Jan. 29, 1777.	Jeremiah Coughland,	Feb. 4, 1777.
John Pewshew,	Jan. 18, 1777.	(Deser'd to the enemy, July	
James Russell,	Jan. 13, 1777.	5, 1777.)	
Jabez Spencer,	Nov. 15, 1776.	Daniel McIntosh,	Jan. 6, 1777.
John Shobee,	Jan. 18, 1777.	(Deser'd to enemy July 5, 1777.	
Jacob Visbee,	Jan. 4, 1777.	Enos Line,	Nov. 15, 1776.
George Wilson,	Jan. 5, 1777.	(Deserted July 9, 1777.)	

THE SECOND COMPANY.

Nathaniel Donnell, Captain. Commissioned as Second-lieutenant in Captain Bernard Romans' Pennsylvania Artillery, March 25, 1776. Promoted to First lieutenant May 15, 1776, and promoted to Captain in Major Stevens' corps November 9, 1776. Served to end of the war.

Thomas Vose, Captain-lieutenant. Commissioned November 9, 1776, and served with Stevens and Crane to the end of the war.

Joseph Perry, First-lieutenant. Commissioned November 9, 1776. In service at Pluckermin, January 17, 1779.

OFFICERS AND PRIVATES

Daniel McLane, Second-lieutenant. Commissioned Nov. 9, 1776. Wounded in 1778, and furloughed by Gen. Gates. On command at Springfield, January 17, 1779. Served to the end of the war. (See Penn.)

Joseph Driskill, Second-lieutenant. Commissioned Nov. 9, 1776. On command at Fishkill in May, 1778, and on furlough in Maryland, Jan. 17, 1779.

Andrew H. Tracey, Second-lieutenant. Commissioned June 1, 1777. Resigned September 15, 1778.

Non-commissioned Officers for the War.

Asa Copland, Sergeant-major.
Nathaniel Champlin, Sergeant.
Silas Barber, do.
John Cockel, do.
James Wilsey, do.
Lot Howse, do.
Henri Schineman, do.
Wm. Loudon, Drum-major.

Benoni Harris, Fifer.
Miles Hubbard, Corporal.
Matthew Hopkins, do.
Emanuel Fokey, do.
John Harwood, do.
Ephraim Cook, do.
John Gartsee, do.

Bombardiers for the War.

Joseph Huckey,
Gail Cole,
Thomas Shepard,

Jacob Whitter,
William Tolley.
John McCormitt.

Gunners for the War.

Alexander Brinton,
George Wood,
Peter Mooney,
John A. Kemper,

Richard Vanorman,
Matthew Green,
James Sinnix.

Matrosses for the War.

Joseph Allen,
Matthew Asterman,
Francis Bertho,
Samuel Brown,
Patrick McDormitt,
John McCoy,
Hugh Jones,
John Kransz,
William Kelly,
George Oglesby,
Robert Robinson
Peter Vunth,

John Boudinot,
Pattricius Band,
Charles Burman,
James Douley,
John Dewitt,
John Good,
Michael Geer,
John Kester,
Emanuel Lewis,
John McMurdough,
James Sinnix,
George Hanley.

OF THE REVOLUTIONARY WAR.   159

THIRD COMPANY.

John Winslow, Captain. Commissioned June 8, 1777. Resigned November 5, 1778. Lieutenant Thomas Barr took his place.

Thomas Barr, Captain-lieutenant. Commissioned as Third-lieutenant in Capt. Romans' Pennsylvania Artillery, March 28, 1776; promoted to Second-lieutenant, May 15, 1776; on command with Gen. Schuyler till November 9, 1776, when he was promoted to Captain-lieutenant in Major Stevens' corps. On duty January 17, 1779.

Jacob Kemper, First-lieutenant. Commissioned November 9, 1776. Served to the end of the war. (See N. J.)

Jacob Welch, Second-lieutenant. Commissioned November 9, 1776. Resigned November 5, 1778.

Richard Hunnewell, Second-lieutenant. Commissioned February 1, 1777. Resigned November 25, 1778.

John Liswell, Second-lieutenant. Commissioned February 1, 1777. On duty January 17, 1779.

Non-commissioned Officers for the War.

Ephraim Milton,	Sergeant.	Appointed March 21, 1777.	
Charles Newcomb,	do.	do.	do.
John Jackman,	do.	do.	do.
John Pocock,	do.	do.	do.
Henry Stevens,	do.	do.	do.
George Barron,	Corporal.	do.	do.
William Hayden,	do.	do.	March 22, 1777.
Dennis Hogan,	do.	do.	do.
Jeremiah Smith,	do.	do.	August 15, 1777.

Bombardiers for the War.

	Appointed		Appointed
Thomas McDowle,	Aug. 15, 1777.	Benjamin Hunt,	Aug. 15, 1777
Neal Campbell,	do.	John Robinson,	do.
Benjamin Cleveland,	do.	John McKay,	do.

Gunners for the War.

Robert Hawkins,	Aug. 15, 1777.	Matthew Thompson,	Aug. 15, 1777.
Michael Moore,	do.	John McKenzie,	do.

Matrosses for the War.

John Brown,	Daniel Elmore,
Lawrence Bolong,	John Moore,
Lewis Cary,	Christian Moore,
Peter Elino,	James Murphy,

160   OFFICERS AND PRIVATES

Ephraim Sufferance,
John Simme,
George Zimmerman,
Reese Pugh,
(Taken prisoner July 7, 1777.)
Anthony Francis,
David Franks,
Charles Hewitt,
John Jones,

Clark Lacroix,
Archibald Nelson,
Francis Pickard,
Alexander Ross,
John Redinbacker,
Christian Willing,
John Cantlion,
(Deserted August 8, 1777.)

ARTILLERY ARTIFICERS BELONGING TO COL. EBENEZER STEVENS' CORPS, AS IT STOOD FROM DEC. 16, 1776, TO OCT. 1, 1778.

Noah Nichols, Captain. Commissioned November 9, 1776.
Nathaniel Call, Captain of Cartridge Makers. Commissioned December 19, 1777. Resigned September 10, 1778.
Thomas Patton, Foreman of Smiths. Commissioned December 15, 1777.
Bela Nichols, Quartermaster. Commissioned July 11, 1778.
Joseph Olmstead, Lieutenant. Commissioned November 22, 1776.

Privates for Three Years.

	Enlisted		Enlisted
Jonathan Bates	Feb. 2, 1777.	Augustus Pierce,	Feb. 23, 1777.
Ebenezer Burrell,	Mar. 6, 1777.	Jenkins Palmer,	Mar. 8, 1777.
Alden Burrell,	do.	Nathaniel Peck,	Mar. 10, 1777.
Seth Badcock,	Mar. 17, 1777.	James Stoddard,	Feb. 2, 1777.
Samuel Bunn,	Feb. 19, 1777.	Oliver Stetson,	Mar. 2, 1777.
Jonathan Bradford,	Mar. 15, 1777.	John Sears,	do.
Charles Curtis,	Mar. 2, 1777.	Benjamin Stevens,	Mar. 20, 1777.
Sylvanus Cook,	Mar. 15, 1777.	Samuel Stetson,	Mar. 2, 1777.
Israel Cowing,	Feb. 14, 1777.	Gershom Spear,	Feb. 19, 1777
Benjamin Colemore,	Mar. 6, 1777.	Peter Sears,	Mar. 2, 1777.
Edward Dammon,	do.	Thomas Wood,	Jan. 9, 1777.
Daniel Edwards,	Mar. 20, 1777.	James Sutter,	Jan. 23, 1777.
Samuel Freeman,	Mar. 3, 1777.	(For two years.)	
Josiah Fuller,	Mar. 15, 1777.	Boylston Potter,	Dec. 15, 1776.
Gershom Howe,	Mar. 24, 1777.	(For two years.)	
Abner Holmes,	Mar. 15, 1777.	Stephen Rogers,	Jan. 22, 1777.
John Hutter,	Mar. 3, 1777.	(For during the war.)	
Lemuel Horton,	Mar. 20, 1777.	John Thorp,	Nov. 27, 1776.
Ebenezer Jackson,	Mar. 13, 1777.	(For during the war.)	
Melzor Joy,	Feb. 2, 1777.	William Smith.	Feb. 22, 1777.
John Karkar,	Dec. 16, 1776.	(For during the war. Taken prisoner July 6, 1777.)	
Levi Man,	Mar. 6, 1777.		

OF THE REVOLUTIONARY WAR. 161

NAMES OF THE DISCHARGED OFFICERS AND PRIVATES OF CAPT. EBENEZER STEVENS' COMPANY OF ARTILLERY IN 1776, WHO LEFT SERVICE AT TICONDEROGA JANUARY 1, 1777.

David Cook, Captain-lieutenant.
Samuel Dogget, Lieutenant.
Robert Carver, Lieutenant and Quartermaster.
John Baker, Sergeant.
Samuel Walker, do.
Thomas Chaffie, do.
Isaac Jacobs, Corporal.
Squire Howe, Bombardier.
Benoni Simmons, do.
Nathaniel House, do.
James Fowler, Bombardier.
Benjamin Wade, Gunner.
Jerod Joy, do.
John Steward, do.
John Butterworth, Matross.
Elijah Brant, do.
Peleg Damond, do.
Elisha Joy, do.
Ezekiel Wallis, do.
Jacob Muckler, Drummer.

NAMES, RANK, DATES OF COMMISSIONS, AND TIME OF ENLISTMENT OF THE OFFICERS AND PRIVATES OF COL. LEWIS DUBOIS' NEW YORK REGIMENT, AS IT STOOD AT WHITE PLAINS, JULY 22, 1778.

Lewis Dubois, Colonel. Commissioned June 25, 1776; on furlough by General Gates in July, 1778; at the battle of Klock's Field in 1780; and at the capture of Fort Montgomery the 6th October, 1777.

Jacobus Bruyn, Lieutenant-colonel. Commissioned June 26, 1776; taken prisoner at Fort Montgomery October 6, 1777.

Samuel Logan, Major. Commissioned June 26, 1776; taken prisoner at Fort Montgomery October 6, 1777. Served to the end of the war.

Henry Dubois, Adjutant. Commissioned November 21, 1777.

Nehemiah Carpenter, Quartermaster. Commissioned November 21, 1776; taken prisoner at Fort Montgomery October 6, 1777.

Samuel Townsend Paymaster. Commissioned November 21, 1776; on furlough by Captain Rosecrans.

John Gano, Chaplain. Commissioned November 21, 1776; promoted to Brigade Chaplain.

Samuel Cook, Surgeon. Commissioned November 21, 1776. Served to end of the war.

Ebenezer Hutchinson, Surgeon's Mate. Commissioned June 12, 1778.

FIRST COMPANY.

James Rosekrans, Captain. Commissioned November 21, 1776; promoted to Major, and served to the end of the war.

Henry Dodge, First-lieutenant. Commissioned November 21, 1776. Served to the end of the war.

Samuel Dodge, Second-lieutenant. Commissioned November 21, 1776; taken prisoner at Fort Montgomery October 6, 1777. Served to the end of the war.

Henry Swartwout, Ensign. Commissioned November 21, 1776; taken prisoner at Fort Montgomery October 6, 1777. Served to the end of the war.

Non-commissioned Officers for Three Years.

		Appointed	
John Christy,	Sergeant.	January 1, 1777.	
Abraham Johnston,	do.	do.	do.
Eleazer Lusy,	do.	do.	do.
Samuel Hull,	do.	do.	do.
James Robinson,	Qr. Mr's. Sergt.	do.	do.
Joseph Gleason,	Drum-major.	do.	do.
David Philips,	Drummer.	do.	do.
Abraham Goodwin,	Fife-major.	do.	do.
Depuy Rosecrans,	Fifer.	do.	do.
William Walcott,	Corporal.	do.	do.
John Jee,	do.	do.	April 4, 1777.

Privates for Three Years.

	Enlisted.		Enlisted.
Jeremiah Bundy,	Jan. 1, 1777.	William Niver,	May 10, 1777.
Joseph Brooks,	do.	Timothy Riden,	Jan. 1, 1777.
Francis Bevins,	do.	William Russell,	do.
John Crum,	May 21, 1778.	George Robinson,	do.
Ezra Darling,	Jan. 20, 1777.	John Southard,	Jan. 28, 1777.
John Darling,	do.	Harmonicus Springsteen, do.	
John Delameter,	do.	Elijah Stansbury,	May 18, 1777.
Christopher Decker,	do.	Reuben Smith,	Feb. 12, 1777.
Martinus Decker,	do.	Abner Smith,	May 20, 1778.
Richard Dodge,	do.	John Thayer,	Jan. 1, 1777.
William Frost,	Feb. 5, 1777.	George Tenegar,	May 26, 1777.
Henry Geraldeman,	do.	James Thornton,	do.
John Gibbons,	do.	Isaac Utter, Sen.,	Feb. 17, 1777.
Caleb Glean,	do.	Isaac Utter, Jr.,	Feb. 20, 1777.
Nathaniel Hollister,	do.	Gilbert Utter,	do.
John Harwood,	do.	Andrew Vantyning,	Jan. 1, 1777.
Griffin Jones,	do.	Peter Vermilyea,	May 20, 1778.
Prince Johnson,	May 19, 1778.	Richard Williams,	May 11, 1777.
Thomas Johnson,	do.	Robert Waddel,	May 26, 1777.
Joseph Johnson,	do.	Richard Williams,	do.
Paul Kiesley,	do.	Josiah Ward,	do.
Joshua Lake,	Jan. 28, 1777.	Gilbert Edwards, des. June 28, 1778.	
Evert Letz,	April 13, 1777.		
John Lounsbury,	do.	Samuel Gardner, des. July 7, 1778.	
Henry Lewis,	do.	John B. Keyser, des. June 30, 1778.	
Benjamin Meynema,	May 10, 1777.	John Storm, deserted July 9, 1778.	

OF THE REVOLUTIONARY WAR. 163

SECOND COMPANY.

James Stewart, Captain. Commissioned November 21, 1776. Served to the end of the war.
Alexander McArthur, Lieutenant. Commissioned November 21, 1776. Taken prisoner at Fort Montgomery October 6, 1777.
John McClaughrey, Ensign. Commissioned November 21, 1776. Taken prisoner at Fort Montgomery, October 6, 1777.
John Reid, Sergeant. Appointed January 1, 1777.
John Lovett, Corporal. do. do.

Privates who formed the Company, January 1, 1777.

Walter Booker,	Daniel Monison,
Conrad Cunite,	William Malcalf,
Daniel Carrigan,	Patrick Monow,
Volker Dow,	Jeremiah Richie,
Thomas Fitzgerald,	Thomas Russell,
James Gillasby,	Robert Robertson,
George Hasbrook,	John Stump,
Samuel Hopper,	Thomas Smally,
James Humphrey,	Joseph Smith,
James Heller,	Isaac Samson.
Abraham Hepp,	

THIRD COMPANY.

Amos Hutchings, Captain. I cannot get any information relative to the commission of this Captain, nor his service; but it appears he lost his life in the service June 23, 1778.
Patton Jackson, Lieutenant. Commissioned November 21, 1777. Taken prisoner at Fort Montgomery October 6, 1777.
John Furman, Second-lieutenant. Commissioned November 21, 1776. Captured at Fort Montgomery October 6, 1777. Served to the end of the war.

Non-commissioned Officers for Three Years.

Seth Stalker, Sergeant. Appointed February 12, 1777.
James Pride, do. do. August 12, 1776.
Jasper Allen, Drummer. do. January 1, 1777.
John Factor, Fifer, do. do.
John Wilson, Corporal, do. do.

Privates for Three Years from January 1, 1777.

Samuel Langdon,	John Rhoads,
Roger Latimore,	Philip Richards,
Peter Hopper,	Thomas Jones,

164   OFFICERS AND PRIVATES

Joseph Jones,
Benjamin Latemore,
John Secor,
Malatiah Weeks,

John Wills,
John Allison,
Lawrence Bonker,
John Allison, jun.

FOURTH COMPANY.

Philip De Bois Bevier, Captain. Commissioned November 21, 1776. Served to the end of the war.

Michael Connolly, First-lieutenant. Commissioned November 21, 1776. On command at New Windsor in 1778. Served to the end of the war

Daniel Birdsall, Second-lieutenant. Commissioned November 21, 1776. On command at Wallkill, in 1778, after clothing, &c.

Non-commissioned Officers for Three Years.

Ebenezer Burnett,	Sergeant.	Appointed	December 10, 1776.
James Hannah,	do.	do.	April 6, 1777.
Henry Hornbish,	do.	do.	April 12, 1777.
Jasper Prior,	do.	do.	March 12, 1777.
Joseph Case,	Corporal.	do.	July 26, 1776.
Nathan Tupper,	do.	do.	January 1, 1777.
William Pembroke,	do.	do.	February 7, 1777.
James Peresonus,	do.	do.	February 27, 1777.
William Whitehead,	Drummer.	do.	December 1, 1776.
William Cooke,	Fifer.	do.	July 1, 1777.

Privates for Three Years.

Enlisted.			Enlisted.
William Bloomer,	Feb. 1, 1777.	Silas Leonard,	June 21, 1778.
John Blaws,	Dec. 1, 1776.	John McAnarny,	Aug. 2, 1776.
James Bishop,	April 9, 1777.	John McLean,	Dec. 1, 1776.
Asa Crawfoot,	do.	Robert Milligan,	do.
Lemuel Chapman,	Feb. 1, 1777.	Joseph Mitchell,	Feb. 1, 1777.
Jacob Cline,	Aug. 4, 1777.	William Nelson,	Mar. 11, 1777.
Nehemiah Cheshire,	do.	Daniel Osben,	June 26, 1776.
Moses Dimond,	Jan. 25, 1777.	Jonathan Penny, sick at Newburg.	
William Dimond,	do.	William Russell,	Jan. 1, 1777.
Daniel Flanagan,	Aug. 28, 1777.	William Riston,	do.
John Fulton,	Mar. 31, 1777.	Thomas Shurkey,	Dec. 1, 1776.
John Hendrickson,	Dec. 1, 1776.	David Smith, jun.,	Feb. 7, 1777.
Wm. Hankerson,	Jan. 5, 1777.	David Smith, sen.,	do.
William Hollet,	Jan. 17, 1777.	John Slouter,	April 13, 1777.
George Hollet,	Jan. 18, 1777.	Jesse Smith,	do.
Caleb Jewet,	Feb. 1, 1777.	Abraham Traverse,	Jan. 1, 1777.
Andrew Kyser,	Aug. 4, 1777.	Peter Tilton,	Mar. 1, 1777.
John Kyser,	do.	Samuel Townsend,	April 15, 1777.

OF THE REVOLUTIONARY WAR. 165

Enlisted.		*Enlisted.*	
Absalom Townsend,	April 15, 1777.	Edward Welsh,	May 19, 1777.
Gysbert Vandemark,	Aug. 10, 1776.	Patrick Dirking, returned from captivity July 22, 1778.	
Abraham Wilson,	Aug. 12, 1776.		
Henry Wilsey,	Jan. 30, 1777.		

FIFTH COMPANY.

Thomas Lee, Captain. Commissioned November 21, 1776. Served to June 23, 1778, and either died or resigned.

Henry Pawling, First-lieutenant. Commissioned November 21, 1776; taken prisoner October 6, 1777; promoted to Captain June 23, 1778. Served to the end of the war.

Samuel English, Second-lieutenant. Commissioned November 21, 1776. Served to the end of the war.

James Johnson, Ensign. Commissioned November 21, 1776; promoted to Lieutenant. Served to the end of the war.

Non-commissioned Officers for Three Years.

Corneles Tarbush,	Sergeant.	Appointed	December 25, 1776.
Isaac Lent,	do.	do.	December 23, 1776.
Richard Hawkey,	do.	do.	May 14, 1778.
Corneles Vandermark,	do.	do.	September 4, 1777.
Peter Snyder,	do.	do.	December 25, 1777.
Francis Vantine,	Corporal.	do.	June 1, 1777.
Nathaniel Banker,	do.	do.	June 11, 1777.
Samuel Hawall,	do.	do.	September 4, 1777.
David Gregg,	do.	do.	January 9, 1778.
Syles Horton,	Drummer.	do.	March 1, 1778.
Elijah Parker,	Fifer.	do.	September 4, 1777.

Privates for Three Years.

Enlisted.		*Enlisted.*	
Adam Brannon,	April 5, 1777.	Joseph Geones,	April 20, 1776.
Jeremiah Briggs,	Jan. 1, 1777.	John Homer,	Dec. 25, 1777.
Josiah Buckby,	do.	Henry Hawkey,	May 14, 1778.
Samuel Curran,	Nov. 16, 1776.	Philip Kerbenger,	May 4, 1776.
John Coleman,	Jan. 20, 1777.	William Lane,	Dec. 16, 1776.
Isaac Danielson,	Dec. 25, 1776.	John Lockwood,	July 1, 1777.
Michael Fowler,	May 6, 1778.	Daniel Loder,	do.
Hezekiah Gregg,	Dec. 26, 1776.	Ebenezer Landers,	April 5, 1777.
Gideon Goodshed,	Dec. 25, 1776.	William Lawrence,	Dec. 26, 1776.
Michael Gwin,	Dec. 27, 1776.	John McClarning,	do.
Samuel Goslin,	July 1, 1777.	Philip Muckeloony,	April 27, 1778.
Seth Gilbert,	do.	Jonathan Newman,	May 4, 1778.

166   OFFICERS AND PRIVATES

	Enlisted.		Enlisted.
Joshua Philips,	Dec. 16, 1776.	Abraham Shear,	Feb. 20, 1777.
John Peck,	Dec. 27, 1776.	Nehemiah Sheroden,	April 21, 1778.
Matthias Randal,	Dec. 28, 1776.	John Talladay,	Dec. 15, 1776.
Daniel Robinson,	Jan. 1, 1777.	Joshua Tucker,	do.
Jacob Ramson,	June 20, 1777.	Robert Vantine,	Jan. 1, 1777.
William Strait,	Dec. 25, 1776.	Garret Vanhuser,	Dec. 26, 1777.
Henry Strait,	do.	Joseph Vansant,	June 25, 1777.
Ezekiel Simmons,	do.	Isaac Vantine,	May 15, 1778.
Evarts Slawter,	do.	Titus Vanderdunk,	May 13, 1777.
Marvel Slutt,	Jan. 1, 1777.	Isaac Williams,	Dec. 26, 1776.
Abraham Skeet,	Jan. 1, 1778.	Samuel Weed,	do.
Henry Scouten,	Jan. 1, 1777.	James Wood,	do.
Thomas Smith,	Feb. 28, 1777.	John Whitehead,	do.
Abraham Sleet,	Feb. 9, 1777.	Jacob West,	Jan. 1, 1777.
George Shafer,	Dec. 26, 1776.		

THE SIXTH COMPANY.

Henry Goodwin, Captain. Commissioned November 21, 1776; captured at Fort Montgomery October 6, 1777. Served to the end of the war.

Solomon Pendleton, First-lieutenant. Commissioned November 21, 1776. Captured at Fort Montgomery October 6, 1777, and was still a prisoner December 1, 1780.

Ebenezer Motte, Second-lieutenant. Commissioned Nov. 21, 1776; captured at Fort Montgomery October 6, 1777. Served to the end of the war.

Abraham Leggett, Ensign. Commissioned November 21, 1776; captured at Fort Montgomery October 6, 1777. Served to the end of war; was made Lieutenant.

Non-commissioned Officers for Three Years.

Henry Schoonmaker, Sergeant.	Returned from captivity July 22, 1778.
Jonathan Baylis,	do.	Appointed March 4, 1777.
John Alaben,	do.	do.	do.
John Christy,	Corporal.	do.	do.
Daniel Johnson,	do.	do.	do.
Joseph Anderson,	do.	do.	do.
David Goodwin,	Drummer,	do.	do.

Privates for Three Years. Joined March 4, 1777.

Holmes Austin,	Prince Danford,
Lemuel Bartlett,	Peter Holmes,
Jacob Craft,	James Hunter,
Nathan Dubois,	William Mooney,
Abraham Delancey,	Abraham Mooney,

OF THE REVOLUTIONARY WAR. 167

John Nicolls,
Stephen Nicolls,
Jeremiah Simkins,
Richard Stephens,
Abraham Seymore,

Elias Thompson,
Jacob Tobias,
Jacob Van Geleder,
Frederick Wemire.

THE SEVENTH COMPANY.

John F. Hamtramck, Captain. Commissioned November 21, 1776. Served to the end of the war.
Francis Hanmer, Lieutenant. Commissioned November 21, 1776. Served to the end of the war.

Non-commissioned Officers for Three Years.

William Barken,	Sergeant.	
Benjamin Lawrence,	do.	
Alexander Humphrey,	do.	Appointed April 23, 1777.
Joseph Pribble,	do.	Deserted July 22, 1778.
John Wandell,	do.	
William Sole,	do.	Appointed June, 14, 1777.
John Hains, Drummer.	do.	do.
Thomas Russell, Fifer.	do.	Feb. 21, 1778.

Privates for Nine Months from June 14, 1778.

Russel Brockaway.
John Babcock.
Elisha Berry.
Ebenezer Cummins.
Ephraim Eaton.
Moses Gee.
Joshua Griffin.
Jeremiah Griffith.
John Hasom.

Emanuel Heneky.
Elisha Millard.
Ephraim Quan.
John Ripley.
James Slaven.
James Shaw.
Obadiah Thorn.
William Selle.
Joseph Vanote.

THE EIGHTH COMPANY.

John Johnson, Captain. Commissioned November 21, 1776. Served to the end of the war.
Henry W. Vandeburg, First-lieutenant. Commissioned Nov. 21, 1776. Served to the end of the war.
James Betts, Second-lieutenant. Commissioned November 21, 1776.
Henry J. Vandeburg, Ensign. Commissioned November 21, 1776.

Non-commissioned Officers for Three Years.

John Furdon, Sergeant.
Levi Watson, do.
Versal Dickinson, do.
James Taller, do.

Samuel Combes, Corporal.
Peter Combes, do.
Joshua Hunt, Drummer.
James Ransom, Fifer.

Privates for Three Years.

James Betts, Jr.,
Amos Beach,
John Bonker,
James Bishop,
Ambrose Benedict,
Bartholomew Bonker,
John Culp,
John Combes,
Amos Denton,
Jacob Eakby,
James Forgason,
James Gready,
William Hews,
Henry House.

Jonathan Oakley,
Thomas Palmerton,
John Pepper,
Jonathan Rose,
James Russell,
Robert Sweet,
George Thomas,
Jacob Wilbur,
Stephen Wheeler,
Ichabod Wilbur,
Stephen Smith,
John Chamberlain, Sergeant, returned from captivity, July 22, 1778.

NAMES, RANK, &C., OF COLONEL PETER GANSEVOORT'S COMPANY IN THE THIRD NEW YORK REGIMENT, AS IT STOOD IN WINTER QUARTERS AT ALBANY, FROM DEC. 1, 1778, TO MARCH 15, 1779.

Peter Gansevoort, Colonel. Commissioned November 21, 1776. Served to the end of the war, from 1781, under a commission from the State of New York. Died July 2, 1812.

George Sylez, Captain-lieutenant. Commissioned November 21, 1776. Served during the war.

Peter Magee, Ensign. Commissioned November 21, 1776. Promoted to Lieutenant. Served to the end of the war.

Non-commissioned Officers for Three Years.

Robert Weldon, Sergeant-major.
Francis Jackson, Quartermaster's Sergeant.
Conradt Friday, Drummer.
Andrew Gardiner, Fife-major. Appointed January 1, 1777.
Daniel Dawson, Fifer.

Sylvanus Seely,	Sergeant.	Appointed January 1, 1777.	
Jonathan Hunter,	do.	do.	April 24, 1777.
Samuel Gilbert,	Corporal.	do.	December 6, 1776.
Nathaniel Mecker,	do.	do,	December 1, 1776.
Daniel Owens,	do.	do.	do.

Privates for Three Years.

Peter Anthony,
John Anthony,

Nicholas Bovie,
John Borden,

OF THE REVOLUTIONARY WAR.   169

Eliphalet Cassells,
Benjamin Cowdry,
Joseph Demont,
Thomas Gregg,
John Goodcourage,
Adam Harter.
William Harvey,
John Hurley,
Frederick Huffner,
Christian Kiesburg,
James Lighthall,

Lancaster Lighthall,
John McFarlin,
James Patterson,
John Ross,
Solomon Smith,
John Thompson,
John Van Sice
Roger Wabby,
Joseph White.
Francis Willet,
Michael Zeaster.

	Enlisted.		Enlisted.
John Burke,	June 9, 1777.	Eli Pixley,	Jan. 1, 1777.
Sylvanus Craddock,	July 5, 1777.	Chalken Pratt,	Dec. 18, 1776.
William Grumsby,	Dec. 3, 1776.	Richard Robertson,	Dec. 1, 1776.
Hendrick Hines,	Jan. 5, 1779.	Samuel Shirts,	Jan. 1, 1777.
Jonathan Klock,	Jan. 1, 1777.	Samuel Suller,	Dec. 17, 1776.
Bartley Murray,	Dec. 1, 1776.	William Whitham,	Jan. 1, 1777.
Edward Parker,	Dec. 29, 1776.	Nicholas Loux,	Jan. 29, 1779.

NAMES, RANK, DATES OF COMMISSIONS, AND TERMS OF SERVICE OF THE OFFICERS AND PRIVATES OF CAPTAIN CORNELIUS T. JANSEN'S COMPANY, BELONGING TO COLONEL PETER GANSEVOORT'S NEW YORK REGIMENT, FROM NOVEMBER 21, 1776, TO JANUARY 1, 1781, WHEN IT CAMPED AT FORT EDWARD.

Cornelius T. Jansen, Captain. Commissioned November 21, 1776. Served to the end of the war.

Nanning Vanderheyden, First-lieutenant. Commissioned November 21, 1776. At Fort Schuyler, June 1, 1778, on duty.

Moses Yeomans, Second-lieutenant. Commissioned November 21, 1776. Sent on the recruiting service from April 1, 1778.

Benjamin Bogardus, Lieutenant. Commissioned November 21, 1776. Transferred to the Major's Company, August 1, 1780.

Josiah Bagley, Ensign. Commissioned November 21, 1776. Promoted to Lieutenant, January 7, 1780. Transferred to the Major's Company. Served during the war.

John Spoor, Ensign. Commissioned November 21, 1776. On command at Stillwater, May 19, 1779.

Jeremiah Van Rensselaer, Ensign. Commissioned November 21, 1776. On furlough at Albany from January 9 to July 5, 1780. Acted as Paymaster in 1780. Transferred to the Lieutenant-colonel's Company. Promoted to Lieutenant, and served to the end of the war.

OFFICERS AND PRIVATES

Non-commissioned Officers for During the War.

Samuel Abby,	Sergeant.	Appointed February 6, 1777.
John Burkaus,	do.	do. May 13, 1777.
Alexander McDougall,	do.	do. February 26, 1777.
Jacob Sax,	do.	do. November 27, 1777.

(Took the place of John Burkaus, who was promoted to Ensign, Feb. 17, 1778.)

Benjamin Wearing, Corporal.	Appointed November 27, 1776.
Christian Shriver,	do.	do. do.
Joseph Ladd,	do.	do. do.
Nathan Upright, Drummer.	do. February 16, 1777.
John McKinsey, Fifer.	do. November 29, 1776.

Privates for During the War.

	Enlisted.		Enlisted.
Peter Adley,	Feb. 19, 1777.	John McHenry,	Feb. 26, 1777.
Henry Ademy,	Nov. 29, 1776.	(Deserted Feb. 27, 1777.)	
Joseph Bailey,	Dec. 10, 1776.	Joseph Hughes,	Feb. 22, 1777.
George Blawer,	Nov. 12, 1776.	(Died Mar. 9, 1777.)	
John Black,	Feb. 18, 1776.	Alexander Campbell,	April 5, 1777.
John Briggs,	Nov. 12, 1776.	(Deserted April 13, 1777.)	
Nicholas Cassady,	Mar. 13, 1777.	Ephraim Seamans,	Dec. 2, 1776.
John Corragill,	April 8, 1777.	Deserted April 26, 1777.	
Francis Cranbury,	Mar. 8, 1777.	Adam Dornberry,	June 16, 1777.
Joseph Evans,	Nov. 12, 1776.	(Deserted June 22, 1777.	
William Gifford,	Dec. 2, 1776.	Pervis Austin,	Feb. 28, 1777.
Thomas Herrett,	Nov. 28, 1776.	(Discharged July 19, 1777, by	
John Limbaker,	Feb. 25, 1777.	General Schuyler.)	
John Miles,	Dec. 2, 1776.	James Cansman,	April 18, 1777.
Christopher Mentz,	Jan. 5, 1777.	(Deserted April 26, 1777.)	
Cornelius McDermott,	Dec. 1, 1776.	Stephen Tuttle,	Mar. 22, 1777.
Christopher Queen,	Nov. 12, 1776.	(Discharged by the Muster-	
Albert Rose,	April 4, 1777.	master as unfit.	
Joseph Russell,	Nov. 12, 1776.	Barnhart Minnick,	June 31, 1779.
Isaac Seamans,	Nov. 28, 1776.	Uriah Owens,	Mar. 21, 1779.
Christian Shriver,	Nov. 12, 1776.	Timothy Canfield,	April 18, 1778.
Jacob Shyler,	Feb. 26, 1777.	James Fowls,	Dec. 8, 1776.
George Upright,	April 19, 1777.	Arthur Hurley,	April 3, 1778.
John Wallace,	Feb. 20, 1777.	Evert Lansing,	Jan. 12, 1777.
Joel Freaze,	Dec. 1, 1776.	Moses Lent,	April 25, 1778.
(Deserted Dec. 2, 1776.)		Robert Ryon,	April 11, 1778.
John Vandank,	Feb. 16, 1777.	James Sheels,	Feb. 28, 1777.
(Deserted Feb. 17, 1777.)		Esau Wilbur,	April 30, 1778.
Jesse Hoft,	Feb. 25, 1777.	Henry Weaver,	Nov. 26, 1776.
(Deserted Feb. 26, 1777.)		John Forrigh,	Nov. 27, 1777.

OF THE REVOLUTIONARY WAR.   171

	Enlisted.			*Enlisted.*
Hercules Lent,	Mar. 27, 1778.		Perry Bennet,	May 9, 1779.
Robert Leonard,	May 30, 1778.		Ephraim Blawer,	Mar. 17, 1780.
Charles Bennet,	May 5, 1779.			

Discharged Men, &c.

Nicholas Cassady, discharged March 13, 1780.
George Upright,   do.   April 16, 1780.
Joseph Evans, prisoner with the enemy April 16, 1780.
John Limbaker, wagoner with the army.
Samuel Abby, died October 5, 1780.
Jacob Sax, discharged November 27, 1780.
Timothy Canfield, on a horse-guard in Dutchess county, in December, 1780.
Joseph Edes, in the Armory in Albany, December, 1780.
Henry Weaver, transferred to the Major's Company July 13, 1780.

James Mulholland,	do.	do.	do.
Isaac Yeomans,	do.	do.	do.

Esau Wilbur, died August 7, 1780.
John Pitman, died January 9, 1780.

Evert Lancing,	discharged January 12, 1780.
James Sheels,	do.	February 8, 1780.
Nathan Upright,	do.	February 16, 1780.
John Wallace,	do.	February 18, 1780.
Alexander McDougall,	do.	February 26, 1780.
George Blawers,	do.	February 10, 1780.
William Gifford,	do.	do.

Francis Crambury, taken prisoner August 24, 1778.
Hercules Lent, discharged November 3, 1778.

This company was at Fort Schuyler in 1777 and 1778, and bravely defended it against St. Leger; at Saratoga in March 1779; at Albany from December, 1778, to May, 1779; at Canajoharie in June, 1779; at the camp near Morristown in the winter of 1779 and spring of 1780; at the Highlands of the Hudson July, 1780; and in winter-quarters at Fort Edward, January 1, 1781.

NAMES, RANK, DATES OF COMMISSIONS, AND OTHER NOTES OF COLONEL JOHN LAMB'S REGIMENT OF NEW YORK ARTILLERY, FROM JANUARY 1, 1777, TO MARCH 4, 1779.

John Lamb, Colonel. Commissioned January 1, 1777. Served to the end of the war.
Eleazer Oswald, Lieutenant-colonel. Commissioned January 1, 1777. Left the service in July, 1778, soon after the battle of Monmouth.

OFFICERS AND PRIVATES

Isaac Hubbell, Adjutant. Commissioned April 1, 1777.
William Fenno, Quartermaster. do. March 5, 1777.
John Dutton Crimshier, Paymaster. do. July 1, 1777.
Caleb Austin, Surgeon's Mate. do. January 1, 1777.
Anthony Post, Captain of Artificers. do. do.
Garret Brower, Lieut. of Artificers. do. do.
Samuel Johnson, Foreman. do. do.

COMPANY NO. 1.

Andrew Moodie, Captain. Commissioned January 1, 1777. Served to the end of the war.
Daniel Gano, Captain-lieutenant. Commissioned January 1, 1777.
Joseph Ashton, Lieutenant. Unknown.
George Lecraft, do. do.
Andrew McFarlane, Sergeant. do.
Cornelius Swartwout, Lieutenant. Supernumerary in 1778.

Thomas Kelton, Sergeant.	Unkn.		Wm. Buchanan, Bombard'r.	Unkn.	
Abel Pettie,	do.	do.	John Hammond,	do.	do.
Thomas Vallance,	do.	do.	Hugh Crocast,	do.	do.
Thomas Munro,	do.	do.	Thomas Preston, Gunner.		do.
Moses Latta,	do.	do.	Robert English,	do.	do.
Edward Hayne,	do.	do.	John Sullivan,	do.	do.
William Nichols, Corporal.	do.		Alexander McKoy,	do.	do.
Israel Smith,	do.	do.	John Patterson,	do.	do.
James J. Slack,	do.	do.	Cornelius Vanderhof, Drum'r.		do.
Hugh Lindsey, Bombardier.	do.		James Pembrook, Fifer.		

Matrosses.

John Rhodes,	Thomas Thorp,
David Hanmore,	Alexander Young,
Robert Wigham,	Samuel Miller,
James Van Garder,	William Cunningham,
Alexander Moffit,	Christopher Medler,
John Douglas,	James Brown,
William Graham,	David Pembrook,
James Sherer,	James Little,
William Swan,	John Decker,
Thomas Griffith,	William Darby,
Hugh McCall,	Hugh Pauley,
John Kelly,	John Garnett,
Francis Postle,	Gideon Chase,
Patrick Connell,	John Decker,
David Corben,	James Boyd,

OF THE REVOLUTIONARY WAR. 173

COMPANY No. 2.

Gershom Mott, Captain. Commissioned January 1, 1777. Served to the end of the war.
Joseph Thomas, Captain-lieutenant. Commissioned January 1, 1777.
Isaac Hubbell, Lieutenant.   do.   do.
Isaac Guion,   do.   do.   February 1, 1777.
Francis Shaw,   do.   do.   February 1, 1777. Resigned February 10, 1779.
Peter Woodward, do.   do.   February 1, 1777.
Jos. Van Emburg, Sergeant. Unkn.   John Rowen, Bombardier. Unkn.
Lewis Felton, Corporal.   do.   John Revere,   do.   do.
Samuel Longley, Drummer.   do.   John Mahony, Gunner.   do.
Michael Rockford, Fifer.   do.   Joseph Emerson, do.   do.
James Johnston, Bombardier. do.   Joshua Bishop, do.   do.

Matrosses for Three Years.

William Robertson,   Abraham Myers,
Jesse Brown,   John Youkse,
Joseph Vericul,   John Russell,
John Sunderlin,   Ambrose Laddow,
Thomas Kerney,   George Bishop,
John Cogan,   Robert Richardson,
Robert Fowler,   David Storm,
Jacob Wilsie,   George Harris,
Jacob Hicks,   Abraham Dutcher,
John David,   John Smith.

COMPANY No. 3, FROM JANUARY 1, 1777.

Samuel Lockwood, Captain.   Joseph Travers, Corporal.
Henry Waring, Capt. Lieut.   William Waters,   do.
James Brewster, Lieutenant.   Thomas Winters, Bombardier.
Stephen Alling,   do.   Israel Henna,   do.
Samuel Whiting,   do.   Hercules Wissells, do.
Jeremiah Finch, Sergeant.   Timothy Lockwood, Drummer.
Charles Knapp,   do.   Joseph Fletcher, Gunner.
Edward Rich,   do.   Medd. Marshall,   do.
John Townd,   do.   Abraham Haise,   do.
Elijah Tilden, Corporal.   Samuel Johnson,   do.
Jared Lockwood,   do.

Matrosses for Three Years.

Samuel Knapp,   David Lockwood,
Peter Betts,   James Vissels,
John Burley,   Samuel Finch,
Jonathan Adams,   Theodorus Parsons,

174 OFFICERS AND PRIVATES

John Reed,
Justus Whitney,
Nathaniel Holmes,
Moses Lockwood,
Elijah Whiting,
Elijah Meed,
David Slater,

Joseph Goreham,
Samuel Meed,
Daniel Adams,
Isaac Davis,
William Townd,
Edmund Swaney,
Thomas Sanders.

COMPANY NO. 4, FROM JANUARY 1, 1777.

Robert Walker, Captain.
Samuel Welb, Capt. Lieut.
James Hughes, 2d Lieut.
William Hubbell, do.
John Benjamin, Sergeant.
Samuel Stowe, do.
John Smyth, do.
Enos Jones Prindle, Corporal.

John Peet, Corporal,
Jeremiah Hyne, Bombardier.
Jesse Smyth, do.
Richard Williams, Gunner.
Joshua Hinkley, do.
Samuel Wakelin, do.
John Wilcox, Drummer.
Joseph Ransford, Fifer.

Matrosses for Three Years.

Ebenezer Hastings,
Matthew St. John,
Samuel L. Brooks,
Peter Garrison,
Eli Nicholas,
Henry Cutler,
David Barlow,
Robert Simmons,

Eliakim White,
Benjamin Dean,
Benoni Gardner,
Stephen Mix,
Andrew Porter,
John Clark,
David Sellick,
Robert Morris.

COMPANY NO. 5, FROM JANUARY 1, 1777.

Jonathan Brown, Captain,
Ephraim Fenno, Capt. Lieut.
Caleb Brewster, First-lieutenant. Severely wounded in the service. Congress, per act 11th August, 1790, allowed him $348.57 for expenses, and $16⅔ per month for pension, provided he refund his "commutation."
Oliver Lawrence, Second-lieut.
William Cebra, do.
Timothy Mix, Sergeant.
David Clark, do.
Charles Veck, do.
Isaac Fish, do.
Hiel Peck, do.
Gabriel Leverish, do.

William Heacock, Corporal.
Solomon Barnes, do.
Yale Todd, do.
Elias Willcocks, do.
Edmund Parker, do.
Cornelius Brack⊕, Bombardier.
Samuel Pribble, do.
Timothy Wilmot, do.
Benjamin Smith, do.
Abraham Barns, Gunner.
Zebulon Benton, do.
Isaac Foot, do.
Walter Wilmott, do.
David Stone, do.
Obadiah Hill, do.
Jesse Peck, Drummer and Fifer.

Matrosses for Three Years.

Isaac Cooper,
Samuel Champion,
Samuel Frasier,
Abel Jacobs,
Ebenezer Lines,
James Moody,
John Pierpont,
Elmore Russell,
Patrick Snow,
Samuel Turney,

Thaddeus Barns,
Thomas Rumbloo,
Samuel Squires,
Taber Smith,
James Thomas,
John Twitchell,
Gideon Webb,
Stephen Whelton,
Abel Mallet,
Joel Wilmott.

Company No. 6, from January 1, 1777.

Josiah Wool, Captain.
William Stevens, Capt. Lieut.
Elisha Harvey, 2d Lieut.
Amariah Vose, Sergeant.
Cornelius Stagg, do.
Samuel Pearsons, Gunner.

William Thompson, Gunner.
John Day, Matross.
James Silve, do.
William Bacon, do.
Thomas Shehan, do.
Amos Eastwood, do.

Company No. 7, from January 1, 1777.

Theodore Thomas Bless, Captain.
 Served to the end of the war.
Thomas Machin, Capt. Lieut.
Thomas Gee, Sergeant.
James McGuffie, do.
John Buchanan, do.
Joseph Halstead, do.

James McBride, Corporal.
Daniel Thorn, do.
William McBride, Bombardier.
Peter States, do.
James Scofield, do.
John Murphy, Gunner.
William Ockennan, do.

Matrosses.

George Clark,
John Cunningham,
Enos Hegerdy,
Samuel Woodruff,

James Whitmore,
Jeremiah Randall,
Israel Coleman,
John Nelson.

Names and Rank of Captain Anthony Post's Artificers attached to Colonel John Lamb's New York Artillery, by order of Brigadier-General Knox, January 1, 1777.

Anthony Post, Captain.
Garret Brower, Lieutenant.   Samuel Johnson, Foreman.

OFFICERS AND PRIVATES

Privates.

David Shaddel,
Abraham Brower,
Thomas Dolphin,
Thomas Harrison,
Thomas Whitman,
Ebenezer Byrom,
Joseph Clark,
Abel Burgess,
Azariah Willis,
John Bachelder,
Benjamin Fuller,
Oliver Chapman,
Jonathan Bills,
Abner Burrows,
Silas Huntington,
Timothy White,
Theodore Burnham,
Moses Boynton,
Eleazer Burnett,
Nathan Burrows,
William Walker,
Moses Samson,
Consider Chapman,
Job Eaton,
Samuel White,

Isaac Townson,
Thomas Willys,
Abiathar Elmore,
Ashbel Fox,
Nathaniel Holmes,
Woodbridge Balcher,
Abraham Forster,
Zechariah Forster,
Cotton Dickinson,
Nathan Field,
Sylvanus Waters,
David Knapp,
Jeremiah Randall,
Amos Lockwood,
Jonathan Childs,
John Pollard,
Benjamin Hatch,
John Wild,
Benjamin Gilman,
Elihu Cook,
Amariah Cushman,
Ephraim Dunlap,
Edward Allen,
Alexander Mills,
Edward Lockwood.

NAMES OF CAPTAIN GERSHOM MOTT'S COMPANY OF COLONEL JOHN LAMB'S ARTILLERY, AS IT STOOD AT PLUCKAMIN, MARCH 4, 1779.

Gershom Mott, Captain. On furlough.
Joseph Thomas, Captain-lieutenant.
Isaac Hubbell, First-lieutenant.
Isaac Gion, Second-lieutenant.
Peter Woodward, do. do. On command.
Joseph Van Emburg, Sergeant. Appointed March 18, 1777.
Robert Britt, do.
Nathaniel Higgins, do.
Joseph Emerson, do.
Jesse Brown, Corporal.
William Nelnit, do.
John Revere, Bombardier. Appointed March 18, 1777.
Joshua Bishop, Gunner. do. February 22, 1777.

OF THE REVOLUTIONARY WAR. 177

Gabriel Bishop,	Matross.	Appointed February 22, 1777.
Abraham Dutcher,	do.	do.	September 8, 1777.
John David,	do.	do.	September 23, 1777.
Jacob Hicks,	do.	do.	February 24, 1777.
Ambrose Laddow,	do.	do.	February 25, 1777.
Abraham Myer,	do.	do.	February 24, 1777.
John Russell,	do.	do.	do.
Robert Richardson,	do.	do.	August 21, 1777.
Jacob Wilsie,	do.	do.	July 22, 1777.
John Yurkse,	do.	do.	July 24, 1777.

John Mahony,	Samuel Langley, Drummer.
William Robertson,	John Cogan,
John Sunderlin,	Richard Dale,
Joseph Varicul,	Joseph Hunt.

NAMES, RANK, &C., OF CAPTAIN WINTHROP SARGENT'S COMPANY OF ARTILLERY BELONGING TO THE REGIMENT COMMANDED BY COLONEL JOHN CRANE OF MASSACHUSETTS, AS IT STOOD NOV. 1, 1778.

Winthrop Sargent, Captain. Stationed on Quaker Hill.
Daniel Parker, Captain-lieutenant. Resigned October 25, 1778.
James Hall, First-lieutenant.
John Cooper, Second-lieutenant.
Joseph Bliss, Second-lieutenant. Annexed to Capt. Sargent Oct. 1, 1778, and on command at Providence, R. I.
Samuel Bass, Second-lieutenant. Transferred to Capt. Eustis, October 1, 1778.
Reuben Jagger, Sergeant.
William Young, do. Appointed May 19, 1778.
John Tucker, Corporal. do. May 15, 1777.
Nathaniel Bowen, Corporal. Annexed to Captain Sargent November 1, 1778. On command at Providence.
John Rusher, Corporal. Appointed November 23, 1777. Transferred to Capt. Eustis, November 1, 1778.
Nathan Fuller, Gunner. Appointed March 29, 1777.
John Sanders, Drummer. do. June 7, 1777.
Temple de Corsta, Fifer. do. March 11, 1777.

Matrosses.

	Enlisted.		*Enlisted.*
Cornelius Bergen,	April 16, 1877.	David Austin,	Unknown.
Thomas Bagnell,	May 24, 1778.	William Burt,	do.

178   OFFICERS AND PRIVATES

	Enlisted.		Enlisted.
Justin Boice. Annexed to Captain Sargent, Nov. 1, 1778.		Michael Kirklin,	Unknown.
		Peter Le Baugh,	Jan. 24, 1778.
Philip Brooks,	Mar. 2, 1778.	John Neale,	Unknown.
Lewis Carra,	Jan. 18, 1778.	Ephraim Kidlen,	May 13, 1777.
Nicholas Le Clair,	Mar. 24, 1778.	Peter Rosier,	Mar. 28, 1778.
Mark Le Carra,	Jan. 18, 1778.	John Diott,	Jan. 18, 1778.
Peter David,	Nov. 1, 1778.	Joseph Flott,	Nov. 1, 1778.
John Gillon,	Unknown.	Samuel Vickory,	Unknown.
Jacob Germon,	do.	Elijah Vickory,	do.
John Gillard,	do.	William Young,	do.
Bartholomew Hurley,	do.	John Hamilton,	do
John Hooper,	May 13, 1777.	John Stewart,	do.

NAMES, RANK, DATES OF COMMISSIONS, AND TIME OF ENLISTMENT OF THE OFFICERS AND PRIVATES OF CAPT. BERNARD ROMANS' PENNSYLVANIA ARTILLERY, FROM FEB. 8, 1776, TO NOV. 28, 1776, WHEN ENCAMPED AT TICONDEROGA.

Bernard Romans, Captain. Commissioned February 8, 1776.
Gibbs Jones, Captain-lieutenant. Commissioned February 9, 1776. Promoted to Captain Nov. 9, 1776, in Major Stevens' corps, N. Y.
Matthew Whitlow, First-lieutenant. Commissioned February 14, 1776. Resigned May 15, 1776.
Nathaniel Donnell, Second-lieutenant. Commissioned March 25, 1776; promoted May 15, 1776, to First-lieutenant; promoted Nov. 10, 1776, to Captain in Major Stevens' corps.
Thomas Barr, Third-lieutenant. Commissioned March 28, 1776. Promoted to 2d lieutenant May 15, 1776; and ordered on command with Gen. Schuyler.
John Druitt, Third-lieutenant. Commissioned May 15, 1776. Dismissed July 30, 1776.
Andrew Caldwell, Third-lieutenant. Commissioned Nov. 6, 1776.
John Druitt, Conductor. Appointed March 25, 1776. Promoted to Lieutenant May 15, 1776.
Andrew Caldwell, Conductor. Appointed May 15, 1776. Promoted to Lieutenant November 6, 1776.
Andrew Foster, Sergeant. Appointed February 9, 1776.
Benjamin Whitlow, Sergeant. Appointed Feb. 9, 1776. Discharged May 27, 1776.
John Melchoir Adam. Sergeant. Appointed Feb. 11, 1776.
John Martin Ludwick, Sergeant. Appointed Feb. 18, 1776.
Adam Handell, Sergeant. Appointed May 27, 1777. Reduced to Corporal August 24, 1776.
James Turbett, Sergeant. Appointed August 24, 1776.

OF THE REVOLUTIONARY WAR. 179

Andrew Caldwell, Sergeant. Appointed May 4, 1776.
Joseph Buffingham, Corporal. Appointed Feb. 14, 1776. Deserted April 5, 1776.
John Brookins, Corporal. Appointed Feb. 20, 1776.
Andrew Caldwell, Corporal. Appointed Feb. 20, 1776. Promoted to Sergeant May 4, 1776.
Adam Handell, Corporal. Appointed Feb. 11, 1776. Promoted to Sergeant May 27, 1776.
George Moore, Corporal. Appointed April 8, 1776. Deserted to the enemy June 19, 1776.
Isaac Collard, Corporal. Appointed May 29, 1776.
John Chambers, Corporal. Appointed July 7, 1776. Died Aug. 20, 1776.
James Turbett, Corporal. Appointed July 6, 1776. Promoted to Sergeant August 6, 1776.
James Hooper, Corporal. Appointed Aug. 24, 1776.
James Hooper, Bombardier. Appointed Feb. 10, 1775. Promoted to Corporal Aug. 24, 1776.
John Harman, Bombardier. Appointed Feb. 18, 1776. Joined Capt. Donnen's Company Nov. 21, 1776.
Isaac Collard, Bombardier. Appointed Feb. 19, 1776. Promoted to Corporal May 29, 1776.
James Turbett, Bombardier. Appointed May 15, 1776. Promoted to Corporal July 6, 1776.
John Chambers, Bombardier. Appointed March 12, 1776. Promoted to Corporal July 6, 1776.
John Creed, Bombardier. Appointed May 26, 1776. Drummed out July 6, 1776.
James Wiltsey, Bombardier. Appointed May 29, 1776. Joined Capt. Donnell Nov. 11, 1776.
Jedediah Lippincott, Bombardier. Appointed August 24, 1776. Sick in camp Nov. 28, 1776.
James Dowling, Bombardier. Appointed Oct. 1, 1776.
Phillip Sullivan, Bombardier. Appointed April 8, 1776. Deserted to the enemy June 19, 1776.
James Creed, Gunner. Appointed Feb. 15, 1776. Promoted to Bombardier May 26, 1776.
William Dutton, Gunner. Appointed Feb. 15, 1775. Deserted to the enemy June 17, 1776.
William Stephens, Gunner. Appointed Feb. 18, 1776.
James Turbett, Gunner. Appointed Feb. 20, 1776. Promoted to Bombardier May 15, 1777.
John Nesselrode, Gunner. Appointed Feb. 20, 1776. Deserted May 20, 1776.
Ludwick Hoofer, Gunner. Appointed Feb. 20, 1776.
Paul Hausman, Gunner. Appointed Feb. 22, 1776. Deserted May 20, 1776.
Eliakim Stoops, Gunner. Appointed March 1, 1776.
Jedediah Lippincott, Gunner. Appointed March 3, 1776. Advanced to Bombardier Aug. 24, 1776.
William Reynolds, Gunner. Appointed March 7, 1776. Deserted April 9, 1776.
James Dowling, Gunner. Appointed March 26, 1776. Advanced to Bombardier Oct. 1, 1776.
Archibald McGinnis, Gunner. Appointed April 17, 1776.
John Cockle, Gunner. Appointed Oct. 1, 1776. Joined Capt. Donnell Nov. 11, 1776.
Patrick McDermott, Gunner. Appointed Oct. 1, 1776.

OFFICERS AND PRIVATES

William Campbell, Fifer. Appointed April 18, 1776. Deserted April 22, 1776.
John Spencer, Fifer. Appointed May 12, 1776. Taken away by Col. Maxwell, June 20, 1776,
John Burchell, Drummer. Appointed Feb. 10, 1776.
James Simpson, Drummer. Appointed March 28, 1776. Deserted April 9, 1776.
William Loudon, Drummer. Appointed May 11, 1776. Joined Capt. Donnell Nov. 11, 1776.

Matrosses.

Christopher Bugley, enlisted May 13, 1776. Taken away by Capt. Reese June 1, 1776.
Thomas Britt, enlisted March 25, 1776. Deserted April 9, 1776.
James Campbell, enlisted May 4, 1776. Died Nov. 26, 1776.
John Carroll, enlisted May 7, 1776. Deserted June 4, 1776.
John Clark, enlisted May 7, 1776. Deserted June 9, 1776.
John Cockle, enlisted April 18, 1776. Advanced to Gunner Oct. 1, 1776.
Baltus Collins, enlisted April 3, 1776. Discharged Sept. 1, 1776.
Michael Conlon, enlisted Feb. 10, 1776. Killed or captured June 20, 1776.
John Crone, enlisted March 4, 1776. Discharged Sept. 10, 1776.
William Debow, enlisted Feb. 20, 1776. Died Nov. 24, 1776.
John Falkender, enlisted May 4, 1776. Missing June 6, 1776.
James Farrell, enlisted Feb. 20, 1776. Killed or captured June 20, 1776.
George Gardiner, enlisted May 4, 1776.
Richard Gesper, enlisted Feb. 10, 1776. Discharged Oct. 1, 1776.
John Granger, enlisted May 5, 1779. Joined Capt. Donnell Nov. 18, 1776.
John Green, enlisted May 4, 1776. Deserted Nov. 12, 1776, but captured by Col. Patterson.
Adam Handell, enlisted August 24, 1776.
John Harris, enlisted March 3, 1776. Deserted April 5, 1776.
William Halton, enlisted March 4, 1776. On command at Philadelphia.
Martin Heindler, enlisted April 3, 1776. Deserted July 20, 1776.
John Hindman, enlisted May 4, 1776.
William Hollis, enlisted April 5, 1776. Died May 81, 1776.
James Hurley, enlisted Feb. 20, 1776.
Cornelius Keaton, enlisted May 13, 1776. Died Sept. 16, 1776.
Frank Leland, enlisted May 4, 1776.
Patrick McDermott, enlisted March 26, 1776 Advanced to Gunner Oct. 1, 1776.
Archibald McGinnis, enlisted Feb. 25 1776. Advanced to Gunner Apr. 18, 1776.
John McCoy, enlisted Feb. 19, 1776. Joined Capt. Donnell Nov. 11, 1776.
Michael McNulty, enlisted March 26, 1776.
Martin Norwich, enlisted April 4, 1776.
John Philips, enlisted May 26, 1776. Drummed out July 6, 1776.
Frederick Powell, enlisted April 5, 1776. Discharged Nov. 25, 1776.
James Powers, enlisted Feb. 15, 1776.
Abraham Preble, enlisted Feb. 10, 1776. Discharged June 6, 1776.
Hopkins Rice, enlisted March 24, 1776. Deserted April 22, 1776.
Hugh Robbins, enlisted May 4, 1776.
Benjamin Robinson, enlisted May 5, 1776. Deserted June 28, 1776.
John Rode, enlisted March 25, 1776. Deserted April 22, 1776.
Daniel Shanlee, enlisted Feb. 16, 1776. Died July 6, 1776.
Matthew Shipe, enlisted Feb. 25, 1776.
Robert Smith, enlisted Feb. 20, 1776.
John Sutherland, enlisted April 25, 1776. Died Sept. 24, 1776.

OF THE REVOLUTIONARY WAR.   181

Nicholas Thomas, enlisted May 4, 1776.
Henry Welsh, enlisted March 7, 1776.
George Weymer, enlisted March 26, 1776. Deserted April 22, 1776.
Anthony Weaver, enlisted May 4, 1776.
Martin Yeost, enlisted May 4, 1776.
Michael Young, enlisted Feb. 19, 1776.

NAMES, RANK, DATE OF COMMISSIONS, AND TIME OF ENLISTMENT OF THE OFFICERS AND PRIVATES OF CAPT. JOHN NELSON'S COMPANY OF PENNSYLVANIA RIFLEMEN IN THE REGIMENT COMMANDED BY COL. JOHN PHILIP DE HAAS, AS IT STOOD FROM JAN. 30 TO NOV. 30, 1776.

John Nelson, Captain. Commissioned January 30, 1776.
William Oldham, First-lieutenant. Commissioned January 30, 1776.
Adam Ott, Second-lieutenant. Commissioned January 30, 1776.
Robert McCullam, Second-Lieutenant. Commissioned January 30, 1776. Resigned July 12, 1776.
Joseph Archer, Second-lieutenant. Commissioned July 12, 1776.
Richard Price, Sergeant. Appointed February 15, 1776. Died at Fort George, October 30, 1776.
Thomas Hartley, Sergeant. Appointed February 7, 1776.
Andrew Smith,   do.   do.   February 9, 1776.
Robert McKown,   do.   do.   February 7, 1776.
John Carr,   do.   do.   October 30, 1876.
Edward Preston, Corporal.   do.   February 15, 1776. Died Sept. 20, 1776.
Joseph Bonner,   do.   do.   February 22, 1776.
Jesse Brown,   do.   do.   February 21, 1776.
John Fugate,   do.   do.   February 13, 1776.
John Carr,   Corporal. Appointed September 21, 1776. Promoted October 31, 1776, to Sergeant.
Thos. Nelson, sen., do.   do.   October 31, 1776.

Privates.

	Enlisted.		Enlisted.
Francis Bower,	Feb. 19, 1776.	James Caldwell,	Feb. 18, 1776.
Thomas Bird,	Feb. 28, 1776.	John Cunningham,	Feb. 17, 1776.
(Deserted May 2, 1776.)		(Furloughed by Gen. Gates.)	
Robert Brooks,	Feb. 7, 1776.	John Carr,	Feb. 14, 1776.
(Deserted May 2, 1776.)		(Promoted Corporal Sept. 21, 1776.)	
Edward Bradley,	Mar. 1, 1776.	Joseph Collins,	Feb. 15, 1776.
(Sick in hospital.)		(Deserted Mar. 15, 1776.)	
Barnet Campbell,	Feb. 10, 1776.	Isaac Coffman,	Feb. 9, 1776.
(Sick in hospital.)		(Deserted April 1, 1776.)	

OFFICERS AND PRIVATES

	Enlisted
John Cox,	Feb. 20, 1776.
Valentine Clipper,	Feb. 21, 1776.
(Deserted May 2, 1776.)	
John Corbett,	Feb. 28, 1776.
(Furloughed by Gen. Gates.)	
William Campbell,	Mar. 5, 1776.
John Carmickle,	Mar. 8, 1776.
Thomas Downey,	Feb. 10, 1776.
Morgan Davis,	Feb. 12, 1776.
Jacob Deal,	do.
Philip Ditch,	Mar. 12, 1776.
John Downey,	Mar. 14, 1776.
Charles Eastley,	Feb. 7, 1776.
(Deserted April 14, 1776.)	
Christian Eversole,	Feb. 8, 1776.
Robert Edmunston,	Feb. 19, 1776.
Nicholas Easter,	Mar. 8, 1776.
(Deserted March 18, 1776.)	
Henry Eakle,	Feb. 17, 1776.
Joseph Fitch,	do.
Samuel Fisher,	Feb. 10, 1776.
(Deserted March 27, 1776.)	
George Flack,	Feb. 19, 1776.
Abraham Forsyth,	Mar. 11, 1776.
Christian Fuller,	Feb. 22, 1776.
John Gowns,	Feb. 18, 1776.
(Deserted May 2, 1776.)	
Andrew Gutting,	Mar. 13, 1776.
Jasper M. Gidley,	Feb. 15, 1776.
(Joined Donnell's Artillery Co. Nov. 21, 1776.	
Michael House,	Feb. 6, 1776.
George Harris,	Feb. 7, 1776.
Michael Harrigan,	Feb. 10, 1776.
Henry Holland,	Feb. 11, 1776.
William Hand,	Feb. 23, 1776.
William Holt,	Mar. 17, 1776.
James Johnson,	Feb. 10, 1776.
Samuel Jameson,	Mar. 22, 1776.
William Kirkpatrick,	Feb. 17, 1776.
(Furloughed to Maryland.)	
James Kelly,	Feb. 9, 1776.

	Enlisted
Isaac Lemon,	Feb. 19, 1776.
(Deserted May 6, 1776.)	
William Love,	Feb. 23, 1776.
(Deserted March 12, 1776,)	
Robert Mullady,	Feb. 7, 1776.
(Deserted April 2, 1776.)	
Daniel McCulloh,	Feb. 9, 1776.
(Killed at Fort Ann May 29, 1776.)	
Thomas McGuire,	Feb. 12, 1776.
Daniel McGuire,	Feb. 19, 1776.
Evan Morgan,	Mar. 1, 1776.
Arthur Murphy,	Feb. 14, 1776.
John Mitchell,	do.
(Deserted April 14, 1776.)	
William McManus,	Feb. 19, 1776.
Thomas Nelson, jun.,	Oct. 25, 1776.
Andrew Nelson,	do.
Thomas Nelson, sen.,	Feb. 10, 1776.
(Promoted to Corp. Oct. 31, 1776.)	
Samuel Nixdorff,	Mar. 7, 1776.
Abraham Onsell,	Feb. 10, 1776.
John O'Brian,	Feb. 19, 1776.
(Deserted May 2, 1776.)	
Emanuel Phyfar,	Feb. 16, 1776.
Tobias Pooder,	Feb. 5, 1776.
Morris Roach,	Feb. 12, 1776.
James Rawlston,	Feb. 7, 1776.
George Renick,	Feb. 14, 1776.
(Deserted March 14, 1776.)	
Thomas Reed,	Feb. 20, 1776.
John Stonemyer,	Feb. 2, 1776.
Michael Stuckey,	Feb. 19, 1776
(Deserted May 2, 1776.)	
William Smith,	Feb. 24, 1776.
John Smith,	Feb. 10, 1776.
(Deserted May 2, 1776.)	
John Slusoer,	Mar. 6, 1776.
(Furloughed by Gen. Gates.)	
George Tingle,	Mar. 9, 1776-
(Deserted April 22, 1776.)	
William Teel,	Feb. 12, 1776.
John Williams,	Mar. 14, 1776.

OF THE REVOLUTIONARY WAR. 183

Enlisted.   *Enlisted.*
James Wallace,   Feb. 12, 1776.   John Wolf,   Feb. 13, 1776.
(Acting as butcher at Mount In-   Richard Wells,   Feb. 26, 1776.
dependence.)   George Trippner,   Feb. 21, 1776.

NAMES, RANK, DATES OF COMMISSIONS, AND TIME OF ENLISTMENT OF THE OFFICERS OF CAPT. SAMUEL WATSON'S COMPANY, IN THE BATTALION COMMANDED BY COL. ARTHUR ST. CLAIR AND COL. JOSEPH WOOD OF PENNSYLVANIA, FROM JAN. 5, 1776, TO NOV. 25, 1776.

Samuel Watson, Captain. Commissioned January 5, 1776. Died May 21, 1776.
Thomas L. L. Moore, Captain. Commissioned May 21, 1776.
John Chilton, First-lieutenant. Commissioned Jan. 5, 1776. Resigned Nov. 11, 1776.
Henry Epley, First-lieutenant. Commissioned Nov. 11, 1776.
James Montgomery, Second-lieutenant. Commissioned Jan. 5, 1776. Promoted to First-lieutenant May 21, 1776.
Benjamin Miller, Ensign. Commissioned Jan. 5, 1776. Promoted to Second-lieutenant May 21, 1779.
James Englis, Ensign. Commissioned Sept. 20, 1776.
Morris McMahon, Sergeant. Appointed Jan. 26, 1776. Deserted April 10, 1776.
James Anderson, Sergeant. Appointed Jan. 30, 1776.
Robert Gibson,   do.   do.   do.
John Watson,   do.   do.   Feb. 3, 1776. Disch'ged Oct. 27, 1776.
Bates Dorsey,   do.   do.   June 12, 1776.
Thomas Kelly,   do.   do.   Oct. 12, 1776.
John Toy,   Corporal.   do.   Jan. 28, 1776.
Bates Dorsey,   do.   do.   Feb. 1, 1776. Promoted June 12, 1776.
William Smith,   do.   do.   Feb. 5, 1776.
John Steel,   do.   do.   Feb. 3, 1776.
Thomas Kelly,   Corporal. Appointed June 12, 1776. Promoted Oct. 28, 1776.
William Atchison, do.   do.   Sept. 10, 1776.
Francis Grenades, Drummer.   do.   March 1, 1776.

Privates.

Enlisted.   *Enlisted.*
James Arthur,   Feb. 2, 1776.   James Applegate,   Feb. 6, 1776.
John Adams,   Feb. 12, 1776.   (Deserted April 10, 1776.)
William Adams,   Feb. 8, 1776.   John Armour,   Jan. 24, 1776.
Parmer Adams,   Jan. 24, 1776.   (Missing June 8, 1776.)
Benjamin Adair, Feb. 8, 1776.

OFFICERS AND PRIVATES

Enlisted.

William Atchison, Feb. 8, 1776.
(Promoted Sept. 10, 1776.)
John Buck, Feb. 7, 1776.
John Battersby, Feb. 13, 1776.
John Book, Feb. 18, 1776.
(Deserted April 7, 1776.)
Daniel Brown, Feb. 6, 1776.
(Deserted April 8, 1776.)
Samuel Beatty, Jan. 25, 1776.
John Claig, Feb. 9, 1776.
John Clemens, Feb. 5, 1776.
(Deserted March 29, 1776.)
John Carr, Feb. 5, 1776.
(Died Oct. 10, 1776.)
John Clendennen, Feb. 11, 1776.
Allen Casada, Jan. 28, 1776.
James Chart, Feb. 6, 1776.
William Cannon, Jan. 28, 1776.
(Died July 11, 1776.)
John Cooler, Feb. 1, 1776.
(Deserted April 8, 1776.)
John Carmichael, Jan. 22, 1776.
Michael Dinger, Jan. 31, 1776.
Griffith Ford, Feb. 15, 1776.
Daniel Fallon, Feb. 8, 1776.
John Flesning, Jan. 31, 1776.
John Ford, Feb. 8, 1776.
John Forgey, Jan. 22, 1776.
John Finney, Jan. 26, 1776.
William Flanagan, Jan. 28, 1776.
(Deserted April 8, 1776.)
Thomas Garner, Feb. 6, 1776.
John Graham, Jan. 20, 1776.
(Deserted April 6, 1776.)
Archibald George, Feb. 4, 1776.
(Deserted April 6, 1776.)
Michael Gorman, Mar. 3, 1776.
Samuel Hunter, Feb. 7, 1776.
Richard Harper, Feb. 11, 1776.
(Deserted March 14, 1776.)
John Hutchinson, Feb. 8, 1776.

Enlisted.

Daniel Harley, Feb. 6, 1776.
(Died Oct. 23, 1776.)
James Hagerty, Feb. 19, 1776.
Isaac Harley, Feb. 23, 1776.
(Deserted March 10, 1776.)
William Haney, Feb. 4, 1776.
(Deserted April 8, 1776.)
Edward Jennings, Feb. 2, 1776.
William Imlay, Feb. 1, 1776.
Thomas Kelly, Feb. 4, 1776.
(Promoted June 12, 1776.)
Timothy Kelly, Jan. 29, 1776.
Joseph Kegan, Feb. 17, 1776.
Richard Lovett, Feb. 5, 1776.
(Died July 9, 1776.)
Thomas Lunny, Jan. 28, 1776.
John Montgomery, Feb. 17, 1776.
Daniel Martin, Feb. 1, 1776.
Henry Mustard, Feb. 4, 1776.
Thomas McKean, Feb. 9, 1776.
Thomas McIlvaine, Feb. 12, 1776.
John McCune, Feb. 12, 1776.
William Marrow, Feb. 13, 1776.
John Madole, Jan. 28, 1776.
Joseph Mathews, Feb. 29, 1776.
(Deserted March 22, 1776.)
Robert McDonald, Jan. 21, 1776.
(Discharged Sept. 25, 1776.)
William Miller, Feb. 8, 1776.
James McLaughlin, Jan. 22, 1776.
Daniel O'Brien, Feb. 2, 1776.
(Deserted April 2, 1776.)
George Porter, Feb. 3, 1776.
Henry Pemberton, Jan. 22, 1776.
(Died Oct. 2, 1776.)
James Parker, Jan. 25, 1776.
(Discharged Oct. 7, 1776.)
Edward Price, Jan. 22, 1776.
(Deserted April 14, 1776.)
John Quin, Feb. 10, 1776.
(Missing June 8, 1776.)

OF THE REVOLUTIONARY WAR. 185

	Enlisted		*Enlisted*
James Robinson,	Feb. 17, 1776.	John Winslow,	Feb. 9, 1776.
John Reed,	do.	(Deserted March 15, 1776.)	
James Reed,	Jan. 28, 1776.	William Williamson,	Feb. 16, 1776.
John Rankin,	Jan. 25, 1776.	(With Dr. McCrae.)	
John Smith,	Feb. 8, 1776.	John Watkins,	Feb. 3, 1776.
Christian Smith,	Feb. 6, 1776.	(Discharged Sept. 25, 1776.)	
William Shehan,	Feb. 12, 1776.	James Workman,	Feb. 8, 1776.
Matthew Thornson,	Feb. 19, 1776.	(Deserted April 8, 1776.)	
Benjamin Thornson,	Jan. 31, 1776.	Jesse Ward,	Jan. 22, 1776.
(Died Oct. 1, 1776.)		Samuel Webb,	Jan. 23, 1776.
Joseph Worrell,	Jan. 25, 1776.	(Deserted April 8, 1776.)	
(Deserted April 26, 1776.)		Joshua Yeomans,	Jan. 22, 1776.
		(At Crown Point.)	

NAMES, RANK, DATE OF COMMISSIONS, AND TIME OF ENLISTMENT OF THE OFFICERS AND PRIVATES OF CAPTAIN RUDOLPH BUNNER'S COMPANY IN COL. ARTHUR ST. CLAIR'S AND COL. JOSEPH WOOD'S PENNSYLVANIA BATTALION, FROM JAN. 5 TO NOV. 25, 1776.

Rudolph Bunner, Captain. Commissioned January 5, 1776. Promoted to Captain Craig's Company, November 11, 1776.

Samuel Moore, Captain. Commissioned November 11, 1776.

Thomas Moore, First-lieutenant. Commissioned January 5, 1776. Promoted May 21, 1776.

James Montgomery, First-lieutenant. Commissioned May 21, 1776.

John Marshall, Second-lieutenant. Commissioned November 11, 1776.

Ezra Bartleson, Second-lieutenant. Commissioned January 5, 1776. Discharged June 19, 1776.

George Ross, Ensign. Commissioned January 5, 1776. Resigned July 21, 1776.

James Armstrong, Ensign. Commissioned May 21, 1776. Promoted November 11, 1776.

Abner Dunn, Ensign. Commissioned November 11, 1776.

Jacob Pope, Sergeant. Appointed February 11, 1776. Died June 13, 1776.

Samuel Randecker, Sergeant. Appointed January 20, 1776. Missing at Three Rivers, June 8, 1776.

Henry Knight, Sergeant. Appointed Jan. 18, 1776. Deserted April 17, 1776.

William Wallace, do. do. Jan. 20, 1776. Qr. Mr.'s Sergeant.

Richard Ellis, Sergeant. Appointed June 13, 1776.

Lewis Grant, do. do. March 1, 1776. Discharged Oct. 1, 1776.

Christy Patterson, do. do. June 8, 1776. do. Nov. 23, 1776.

OFFICERS AND PRIVATES

Thomas Holmes, Sergeant. Appointed April 17, 1776.

Richard Ellis,	Corporal.	do.	Jan. 24, 1776.	Promoted June 12, 1776.
Lewis Grant,	do.	do.	Feb. 26, 1776.	do. Mar. 4, 1776.
Matthias Cline,	do.	do.	Feb. 11, 1776.	Reduced July 1, 1776.
Christo'r Patterson,	do.	do.	do.	Promoted June 8, 1776.
John Kerr,	do.	do.	March 7, 1776.	
John Williams,	do.	do.	Oct. 2, 1770.	
Jacob Thomas,	do.	do.	June 13, 1776.	
Jacob Clatter,	do.	do.	July 1, 1776.	
Patrick Fox,	do.	do.	March 8, 1776.	Drummer.

Privates.

	Enlisted.		Enlisted.
Joseph Banks,	Jan. 28, 1776.	Thomas Green,	Feb. 13, 1776.
James Barber,	Jan. 30, 1776.	(Deserted Feb. 18, 1776.)	
Martin Bender,	Feb. 5, 1776.	David Green,	Feb. 12, 1776.
John Cole,	Feb. 23, 1776.	(Died June 22, 1776.)	
(Missing June 8 at Three Rivers.)		David Gorman,	Feb. 12, 1776.
Joseph Crafts,	Feb. 15, 1776.	(Deserted Mar. 8, 1776.)	
(Died July 8, 1776.)		Thomas Henderson,	Jan. 24, 1776.
James Curran,	Mar. 9, 1776.	(Missing June 8, 1776.)	
(Missing June 8 at Three Rivers.)		William Harris,	Feb. 24, 1776.
John Curran,	Mar. 9, 1776.	Jacob Hunter,	Jan. 31, 1776.
David Collins,	Jan. 26, 1776.	William Hoofnagle,	Feb. 5, 1776.
Jacob Clouts,	Feb. 14, 1776.	(Died July 1, 1776.)	
(Deserted April 8, 1776.)		Josiah Hall,	Jan. 30, 1776.
Israel Connolly,	Feb. 15, 1776.	(Discharged Sept. 28, 1776.)	
William Colston,	Mar. 1, 1776.	Thomas Holmes,	Feb. 9, 1776.
Thomas Currin,	do.	(Promoted April 17, 1776.)	
(Missing June 8 at Three Rivers.)		Samuel Hall,	Mar. 8, 1776.
Matthais Cline,	July 1, 1776.	Daniel Hannah,	Mar. 5, 1776.
Fenis Coons,	Mar. 1, 1776.	(Died June 7, 1776.)	
Owens Claney,	do.	George Hansel,	Mar. 1, 1776.
Jacob Clatter,	do.	(Discharged Oct. 16, 1776.)	
(Promoted July 1, 1776.)		Thomas Isburter,	Jan. 23, 1776.
William Dixon,	Feb. 26, 1776.	(Missing at Three Rivers June 8.)	
James Ellison,	Feb. 16, 1776.	Samuel Ireton,	Feb. 14, 1776.
Andrew Foster,	Feb. 20, 1776.	John Kives,	Jan. 23, 1776.
(Deserted Mar. 11, 1776.)		John Keve,	Mar. 7, 1776.
James Gorman,	Jan. 30, 1776.	(Promoted March 7, 1776.	
Michael Grouse,	Feb. 3, 1776.	Daniel Kooger,	Mar. 7, 1776.
(Discharged Oct. 11, 1776.)		Samuel Mellon,	Mar. 23, 1776.
Lawrence Griffy,	Feb. 22, 1776.	Thomas Morgan,	Mar. 8, 1776.

OF THE REVOLUTIONARY WAR. 187

	Enlisted		Enlisted
Peter Miller,	Mar. 6, 1776.	George Smyth,	Jan. 17, 1776.
Joshua Morrin,	Jan. 22, 1776.	(Discharged Oct. 16, 1776.)	
Abraham Moyer,	Feb. 24, 1776.	Aaron Smallwood,	Mar. 12, 1776.
Thomas McCully,	Jan. 29, 1776.	Jacob Thomas,	Feb. 7, 1776.
John Morris,	Mar. 1, 1776.	(Promoted June 13, 1776.)	
(Missing June 8 at Three Rivers.)		Jonathan Wright,	Jan. 25, 1776.
Joseph Norman,	Feb. 15, 1776.	John Williams,	Feb. 2, 1776.
Richard Nixon,	do.	(Promoted Oct. 2, 1776.)	
Thomas Owen,	Jan. 25, 1776.	Obadiah Wright,	Feb. 14, 1776.
(Discharged Sept. 30, 1776.)		(Died July 31, 1776.)	
Peter Polar,	Feb. 15, 1776.	John White,	Jan. 24, 1776.
(Deserted April 17, 1776.)		(Died July 15, 1776.)	
Jacob Price,	Feb. 18, 1776.	Michael Williams,	Feb. 6, 1776.
(Deserted Feb. 18, 1776.)		(Missing June 8 at Three Rivers.	
Francis Quinn,	Jan. 25, 1776.	Elijah Walter,	Mar. 9, 1776.
Nathaniel Richards,	Feb. 4, 1776.	Reuben Wiley,	Mar. 1, 1776.
Thomas Roberts,	Feb. 16, 1776.	(Died Sept. 21, 1776.)	
(Died July 23, 1776.)		Richard Willis,	Mar. 1, 1776.
Nicholas Smeal,	Jan. 25, 1776.	(Missing June 8 at Three Rivers.)	
Daniel Shuttle,	Feb. 7, 1776.	John Young,	Jan. 23, 1776.
John Stump,	Feb. 1, 1776.		

NAMES, RANK, DATES OF COMMISSIONS, AND TIME OF ENLISTMENT OF THE OFFICERS AND PRIVATES OF CAPT. THOMAS CRAIG'S COMPANY, COL. ST. CLAIR'S PENNSYLVANIA BATTALION, FROM JAN. 5 TO NOV. 28, 1776.

Thomas Craig, Captain. Commissioned Jan. 5, 1776. Promoted Sept. 7, 1776.
Rudolph Bunner, Captain. Commissioned Sept. 7, 1776.
Andrew Kachline, First-lieutenant. Commissioned Jan. 5, 1776. Discharged June 21, 1776.
Isaac Budd Dunn, First-lieutenant. Commissioned July 4, 1776.
John Craig, Second-lieutenant. Commissioned Jan. 5, 1776. Promoted Nov. 11, 1776.
James Armstrong, Second-lieutenant. Commissioned Nov. 11, 1776.
Thomas Park, Ensign. Commissioned Jan. 5, 1776. Discharged June 20, 1776.
Abraham Dull, Ensign. Commissioned Oct. 25, 1776.
Robert Marshall, Sergeant. Appointed Jan. 7, 1776. Discharged July 12, 1776.

Peter Smith,	do.	do.	Jan. 15, 1776. Promoted Nov. 11, 1776.
Abraham Horn,	do.	do.	Jan. 5, 1776.
Abraham Dull,	do.	do.	Jan. 19, 1776. Promoted Oct. 25, 1776.
Christian Shouse,	do.	do.	July 13, 1776.

OFFICERS AND PRIVATES

John Carey,	Sergeant.	Appointed Oct. 25, 1776.	Discharged Nov. 21, 1776.	
John McMichael,	do.	do.	Nov. 21, 1776.	
John Minor,	do.	do.	Jan. 13, 1776.	Drummer.
George Gangwar,	do.	do.	Jan. 13, 1776.	Fifer. Reduced Oct. 11, 1776.
Stephen Fuller,	do.	do.	Oct. 11, 1776.	Fifer.
Christian Shouse,	Corporal,	do.	Jan. 15, 1776.	Promoted July 13, 1776.
John Carey,	do.	do.	Jan. 5, 1776.	Promoted Oct. 25, 1776.
Peter Bijll,	do.	do.	Jan. 17, 1776.	Deserted April 8, 1776.
Henry Powelson,	do.	do.	Feb. 10, 1776.	Deserted April 12, 1776.
John McMichael,	do.	do.	April 8, 1776.	Promoted Nov. 21, 1776.
Robert Shearer,	do.	do.	April 12, 1776.	
James Surney,	do.	do.	Nov. 21, 1776.	
Samuel Mow,	do.	do.	July 13, 1776.	

Privates.

	Enlisted		Enlisted
Anthony Assur,	Jan. 14, 1776.	John McMichael,	Jan. 27, 1776.
John Ackerd,	Jan. 29, 1776.	(Promoted April 8, 1776.)	
John Boyer,	Sept. 1, 1776.	Conrad Minges,	Jan. 10, 1776.
Adam Branthuver,	Jan. 13, 1776.	Christian Miller,	Jan. 8, 1776.
Peter Bowerman,	do.	Samuel Mow,	Jan. 8, 1776.
Jacob Bijel,	Feb. 2, 1776.	(Promoted July 13, 1776.)	
Alex. Cunningham,	Jan. 15, 1776.	Mathias Miller,	Mar. 22, 1776.
Batler Crist,	Jan. 8, 1776.	Samuel Ney,	Jan. 13, 1776.
Josiah Crane,	Jan. 12, 1776.	Leonard Nagle,	do.
Thomas Dobbs,	do.	Henry Sharer,	Jan. 24, 1776.
(Deserted April 12, 1776)		Peter Smith,	Jan. 10, 1776.
Peter Daily,	Jan. 10, 1776.	John Shannon,	Jan. 28, 1776.
(Deserted March 17, 1776.)		Thomas Shaffer,	do.
Daniel Deyley,	Jan. 22, 1776.	Philip Smith,	Mar. 6, 1776.
John Davis,	Feb. 3, 1776.	John Darling,	Feb. 3, 1776.
(Missing since the engagement at Three Rivers, June 8, 1776.)		(Deserted March 13, 1776.)	
		Evan Davis,	Jan. 7, 1776.
Evan Evans,	Jan. 10, 1776.	(Missing since the engagement at Three Rivers, June 8, 1776.)	
Jacob Davenspeck.	Feb. 17, 1776.		
David Darling,	Feb. 3, 1776.	Peter Fleck,	Jan. 8, 1776.
John Docher,	Feb. 14, 1776.	Henry Freedly,	do.
Leonard Labar,	Mar. 12, 1776.	Daniel Foulk,	Jan. 17, 1776.
Melchir Labar,	do.	Philip Groob,	Jan. 24, 1776.
Robert Morey,	Jan. 19, 1776.	Samuel Grimes,	Mar. 13, 1776.
David Minon,	Jan. 8, 1776.	(Missing since the battle at Three Rivers, June 8, 1776.)	
Lawrence Marr,	Jan. 13, 1776.		
John Marr,	Jan. 22, 1776.	George Gangwer,	Oct. 4, 1776.
John Mock,	do.	John Hindman,	Jan. 22, 1776.

OF THE REVOLUTIONARY WAR.

	Enlisted.		Enlisted.
Frederick Horn,	Jan. 8, 1776.	Jonathan Richards,	Feb. 2, 1776.
John Hubler,	Jan. 17, 1776.	(Deserted Feb. 25, 1776.)	
Leonard Hans,	Jan. 18, 1776.	Timothy Rogers,	Jan. 11, 1776.
Ludwick Hoofman,	Feb. 21, 1776.	Abraham Rinker,	Jan. 13, 1776.
Wm. Hirkle,	Feb. 28, 1776.	Conrad Reiswick,	Feb. 2, 1776.
Martin Jost,	Jan. 8, 1776.	George Stirner,	Jan. 13, 1776.
George Huntsman,	Jan. 29, 1776.	Peter Standley,	Jan. 15, 1776.
George Kuns.	Jan. 13, 1776.	David Stinson,	Jan. 15, 1776.
(Died Aug. 6, 1776.)		Robert Shearer,	Jan. 31, 1776.
Michael Kuns,	do.	(Promoted April 12, 1776.)	
Charles King,	Jan. 17, 1776.	James Sweeny,	Feb. 8, 1776.
(Deserted March 12, 1776.)		(Promoted Nov. 21, 1776.)	
Nicholas Kautsman,	Feb. 10, 1776.	James Thompson,	Jan. 15, 1776.
George Phass,	Feb. 10, 1776.	Jacob Wise,	Jan. 13, 1776.
Jacob Powels,	Feb. 14, 1776.	Robert Wilson,	Feb. 26, 1776.
Daniel Reyley,	Feb. 18, 1776,	Faltey Yeisly,	Jan. 14, 1776,
Thomas Ransey,	Jan. 27, 1776.	Stophel Prang,	Jan. 13, 1776.

NAMES, RANK, AND DATES OF COMMISSIONS OF THE OFFICERS OF CAPT. WILLIAM BUTLER'S COMPANY OF COL. ST. CLAIR'S AND COL. WOOD'S PENNSYLVANIA BATTALION, WITH A LIST OF THE PRIVATES, FROM JANUARY 5 TO NOVEMBER 25, 1776, AS THEY STOOD AT TICONDEROGA.

William Butler, Captain. Commissioned Jan. 5, 1776. Promoted Oct. 7, 1776.
James Chrystie, Captain. Commissioned November 11, 1776.
Thomas Butler, First lieutenant. Commissioned January 5, 1776.
Charles Seltze, Second-lieutenant. Commissioned January 5, 1776. Dropped September 20, 1776.
George McCully, Ensign. Commissioned January 5, 1776. Promoted to Lieutenant September 20, 1776.
Nathan McMillon, Ensign. Commissioned September 20, 1776.

Sergeants.

Robert McCully,	Hugh McClarren,
Thomas Jack,	Thomas Carrell.

Corporals.

George McKee,	John Kelso,
Abraham Bennet,	William Webb.

Privates.

John Brown,	John Conner,
Elijah Branch,	James Calaghan.

Charles Coil,
James Craig,
William Cowley,
John Carothers,
Amos Davis,
Robert Davis,
Robert Dixon,
Bryan Doyle,
William Ewin,
Robert Futhy,
George Fleming,
Henry Fleming,
James Forbes,
Andrew Gordan,
David Hanna,
James Hamilton,
John Henry,
Patrick Heron,
Hugh Jones,
Garret Jordan,
James Kinsey,
William Kyle,
James Kenedy,
John Lindsey,
Patrick Laferty,

William Lucas,
Edward Lear,
William Martin, jun.,
James McConnel,
Matthew McCord,
Thomas McFaddon,
James McGill,
Dennis McCarrel,
William Mathews,
Dennis Myre,
John McKenzie,
William Martin, sen.,
John McMillion,
Edward Navel,
William Paterson,
Jonathan Roberts,
Isaac Roddy,
George Rucraft,
James Sweeny,
John Sutherland,
John Slover,
John Smith,
Isaac Stimble,
Robert Varner,
Samuel Wilson,

NAMES, RANK, AND DATES OF COMMISSIONS OF THE OFFICERS OF CAPT. STEPHEN BAYARD'S COMPANY IN COL. ST. CLAIR'S PENNSYLVANIA BATTALION, WITH A LIST OF THE PRIVATES, FROM JANUARY 5, 1776, TO NOVEMBER 25, 1776.

Stephen Bayard, Captain. Commissioned January 5, 1776.
James Chrystie, First-lieutenant. Commisssoned January 5, 1776.
John Craig,   do.   do.   November 11, 1776.
Isaac Budd Dunn, Second-lieutenant. Commissioned January 5, 1776. Promoted July 4, 1776.
James Black, Ensign. Commissioned January 5, 1776. Promoted July 4, 1776.
John Marshall, do.   do.   November 11, 1776.
James Oates,   do.   do.   do.

Sergeants.

John Shepherd,
Barney Philips,
Andrew Cosgroove,

Joseph Points,
Thomas Boyd.
Thomas Jones.

OF THE REVOLUTIONARY WAR.   191

Drum and Fife.

John Maxwell, | George Docherty.

Corporals.

Thomas Boyd, | James Barret,
Thomas Jones, | Patrick Brown.
Thomas Wood,

Privates.

Patt Allen, | Patt Lockey,
John Baggs, | William Leech,
James Burris, | Charles McKinley,
Benjamin Black, | William McClair,
Patrick Brown, | Daniel McElvoy,
Alex. Campbell, | Thomas Murphy,
William Cox, | Robert McClennon,
Andrew Cosgrove, | Andrew McConnell,
Robert Coyle, | William Martin,
John Duffield, | Connel McFadin,
William Dougherty, | Wm. McCracken,
Patt Donohoe, | John Quigg,
John Hollis, | James Ruttledge,
John Holliday, | James Thompson,
Thomas Harkins, | Robert Wiley,
Patt Johnson, | Aaron Work,
Joseph English, | John Weary.
George Greer,

NAMES, RANK, AND DATES OF COMMISSIONS OF THE OFFICERS OF CAPTAIN JOHN BRISBAN'S COMPANY, COL. ST. CLAIR'S PENNSYLVANIA BATTALION, WITH A LIST OF THE PRIVATES, FROM JANUARY 5 TO NOVEMBER 25, 1776.

John Brisban, Captain. Commissioned January 5, 1776. Furloughed by Gen. Gates from November 25, 1776.

John Gross, First-lieutenant. Commissioned January 5, 1776.

Charles Seitze, Second-lieutenant. Commissioned January 5, 1776.

William Chambers, Second-lieutenant. Commissioned January 5, 1776. Resigned July 5, 1776.

John Evans, Ensign. Commissioned January 5, 1776. Died June 20, 1776.

George Boss,   do.   do.   July 4, 1776.

Sergeants.

Joseph Gournie, | Daniel Bloom,
James Hagan, | Joseph Biggs.

OFFICERS AND PRIVATES

Corporals.

William Carman,
Evan Evans,

William Peacock,
Ulrich Whitman.

Drum and Fife.

Joseph Hall,

Charles Haney.

Privates.

Thomas Allen,
Samuel Blair,
Jacob Bayard,
Robert Bayley,
John Boyd,
Edward Cummings,
John Craiger,
George Campbell,
Frederick Deamer,
James Dority,
Charles Ferguson.
James Gwinn,
Dominick Hand,
Abraham Henry,
John Hogan,
Thomas Jones,
Henry McLaughlin,
Christopher Hannon,
Neal McKenzie,
Alex. McGugan,
Constant McMagan,
John Holmes,

James Montgomery,
Patrick McAnally,
James McPick,
John McGill,
Barnabas McMagan,
Adam Moore,
James McCormick,
John Ogan,
John Oxford,
Christian Pemperton,
James Ross,
Patrick Rodgers,
Hugh Reed,
Richard Short,
Robert Stewart,
Hugh Shannon,
Ludwig Shortley,
Lawrence Sloan,
John Sloan,
James Stewart,
William Ulit,
Adam Wilhelm.

NAMES, RANK, AND DATES OF COMMISSIONS OF THE OFFICERS OF CAPT. JOHN REESE'S COMPANY OF COL. WOOD'S PENNSYLVANIA BATTALION, WITH A LIST OF THE PRIVATES FROM JAN. 5 TO NOV. 25, 1776.

John Reese, Captain. Commissioned Jan. 5, 1776. Recruiting from Nov. 25, 1776.

Samuel Moore, First-lieutenant. Commissioned Jan. 5, 1776. Promoted Captain Nov. 11, 1776.

Ross Currie, First-lieutenant. Commissioned Jan. 5, 1776. Captured by the enemy June 8, 1776, at Three Rivers.

Daniel St. Clair, Ensign. Commissioned Sept. 20, 1776. On recruiting service.

OF THE REVOLUTIONARY WAR. 193

Henry Eppile, Ensign. Commissioned Jan. 5, 1776. Promoted Lieutenant Nov. 11, 1776.
George Hoffner, Ensign. Commissioned Jan. 5, 1779. Promoted Second-lieutenant Nov. 11, 1776.
Mordecai Davis, Ensign. Commissioned Jan. 5, 1776. Died Aug. 12, 1776.

Sergeants.

| Samuel Coulter, | Methusalah Davis. |
| David Filson, | Adam Hamilton. |

Corporals.

| Michael Waite, | Andrew Moore, |
| Thomas Meredith, | Michael McMillian. |

Privates.

James Alexander,	John Johnson,
James Baggs,	James Johnson,
Christopher Buckle,	Mordecai James,
Abraham Couldren,	William Marr,
Hugh Divinney,	Thomas McClosky,
Jacob Drumheller,	John McManors,
Edward Edwards,	Abraham Nunn,
Hugh Edwards,	William Otty,
George Forguer,	Isaac Pearsel,
John Faulkner,	John Reese,
Benjamin Gilmore,	William Ramage,
William Gallaher,	William Ramsey,
Daniel Gallaher,	James Robinson,
Enos Graham,	George Sanxton,
George Gardner,	Jonathan Scott,
John Hull,	George Scott,
Patrick Hand,	Philip Sheer,
John Jordan.	Thomas Williams.

NAMES, RANK, AND DATES OF COMMISSIONS OF THE OFFICERS OF CAPT. JOHN HULING'S COMPANY, OF COL. ST. CLAIR'S PENNSYLVANIA BATTALION, WITH A LIST OF THE PRIVATES FROM JAN. 5 TO NOV. 25, 1776.

John Huling, Captain. Commissioned Jan. 5, 1776. Furloughed from Oct., 1776, by Gen. Gates.
William Bird, First-lieutenant. Commissioned Jan. 5, 1776. Captured by the enemy at Three Rivers, June 8, 1776.
William Craig, Ensign. Commissioned Jan. 5, 1776. Promoted Second-lieutenent July 4, 1776.

OFFICERS AND PRIVATES

Ross Currie, Second-lieutenant. Commissioned Jan. 5, 1776. Promoted Nov. 11, 1776.

George Haffner, Ensign. Commissioned July 4, 1776. Promoted Nov. 11, 1776.

Sergeants.

John Young,	James Lowes,
Frederick Funk,	Barney Ferrill.

Corporals.

Joseph Riddle,	John Gordon,
Allen Nixon,	Neal Anderson.

James Mitchell, Drummer.

Privates.

Frederick Almond,	Jacob Koch,
Philip Albright,	Michael Kail,
Moses Baldwin,	Paul Larkin,
William Black,	Hugh McCardel,
Abraham Cooper,	Edward McKee,
James Crookshank,	John Randal,
Nathaniel Dickey,	Peter Reese,
Peter Daniel,	Michael Reed,
Mathias Dair,	Henry Rork,
John Evans,	Robert Bennet,
Michael Fagan,	Henry Shoup,
John Fair,	Peter Stone,
Joseph Gabel,	Peter Servey,
John Gorley,	John Steel,
John Goodman,	Christopher Stoutsman,
John Hide,	Herman Sundock,
John Husick,	Peter Walburn.

NAMES, RANK, AND DATES OF COMMISSIONS OF THE OFFICERS OF CAPT. THOMAS ROBINSON'S COMPANY, OF COL. ANTHONY WAYNE'S PENNSYLVANIA BATTALION, WITH A LIST OF THE PRIVATES FROM JAN. 5 TO NOV 26, 1776, AS IT STOOD AT TICONDEROGA.

Thomas Robinson, Captain. Commissioned Jan. 5, 1776. Sick in Pennsylvania.

John Christy, First-lieutenant. Commissioned Jan. 5, 1776.

William Moulder, Second-lieutenant. Commissioned Jan. 5, 1776. Resigned Oct. 1, 1776.

Job Vernon, Second-lieutenant. Commissioned Oct. 1, 1776.

Thomas Wallace, Ensign. Commissioned Jan. 5, 1776. Resigned Oct. 1, 1776.

George North, Ensign. Commissioned Oct. 1, 1776.

OF THE REVOLUTIONARY WAR. 195

Sergeants.

Thomas Merchant,　　　　Joseph Gray,
James Grubb,　　　　　　Mathias Amos.
David Valleau, killed or captured at Three Rivers, June 8, 1776.

Corporals.

Richard Mathews,　　　　Samuel Miller,
Robert Anderson,　　　　John Murdock.

Drum and Fife.

George Moll,　　　　　　William Stone.

Privates.

George Bullock,　　　　　James Lord,
George Bowin.　　　　　Amos Longfellow,
Daniel Burns,　　　　　　William Lynch,
Joseph Bryant,　　　　　William Lammy,
Christopher Bench,　　　John Loughrey,
William Crane,　　　　　Nathan Motts,
Samuel Casky,　　　　　John Moder,
Abraham Chapman,　　　John Moore,
Richard Carridon,　　　　Morgan McCafferty,
James Deveny,　　　　　Benjamin McMurray,
John Deveny,　　　　　　John Mathers,
Isaac Dawson,　　　　　Joseph McBride,
Jeremiah Dawson,　　　George Nox,
Casper Driver,　　　　　Jonathan Phips,
Samuel Dickson,　　　　Robert Owens,
John Dunn,　　　　　　William Russell,
Jacob Dill,　　　　　　　Thomas Riely,
William Davice,　　　　Peter Senear,
George Eaton,　　　　　John Tanyard,
Humphrey Edmondson,　John Talbott,
Alexander Finley,　　　Richard Statton,
Patrick Green,　　　　　Benjamin Smith,
Thomas Glenn,　　　　　John Tagert,
Edward Gobbans,　　　　John Wilson,
John Hill,　　　　　　　Robert Webb,
Nathan Horner,　　　　　James Williams,
Thomas James,　　　　　Benjamin Webb.
Timothy Kerley,

OFFICERS AND PRIVATES

NAMES, RANK, AND DATES OF COMMISSIONS OF THE OFFICERS OF CAPTAIN THOMAS CHURCH'S COMPANY, OF COL. WAYNE'S PENNSYLVANIA BATTALION, WITH A LIST OF THE PRIVATES, FROM JANUARY 5, TO NOVEMBER, 26, 1776.

Thomas Church, Captain. Commissioned January 5, 1776.
James R. Reid, First-lieutenant.   do.   do.
Charles C. Beatty, Second-lieutenant. do.   do.
Job Vernon, Ensign. Commissioned January 5, 1776. Promoted to Lieutenant in Captain Robinson's Company, October 1, 1776.
Alexander Martin, Ensign. Commissioned October 1, 1776,

Sergeants.

William Bigham,   Samuel Widner,
Robert Low,   John McMakan.

Corporals.

Peter Fennakel,   Thomas Bigham,
Jacob Moyer,   Everhart Ferrihan.

Drum and Fife.

Adam Kibler,   —   Charles Leonard,

Privates.

Peter Bitting,   Thomas Heffernan,
Jacob Brindle,   Edward Hagan,
Laban Boger,   Timothy Nowland,
Henry Barnhart,   Connell Kenedy,
Jarvis Burford,   Richard Kelly,
John Bruffy,   William Kerr.
George Beavar,   John Lankister,
John Bigham,   John Little,
Henry Craig,   Michael McCorthy
Henry Crips,   Benjamin Michael,
Jacob Consil,   Robert McIntire,
Patrick Conner,   Michael McGee,
Christian Coplin,   James McKinley,
John Craig,   John McKinley,
William Delany,   Daniel McLeroy,
Jacob Derr,   William McGahey,
John Dieter,   Archibald McNeil,
Malchom Forrest,   Andrew McFarran,
John Gibson,   William Morrow,
John Gilliland,   Thomas McIntiney,
Gotleib Hoffman,   Charles McGahan,

OF THE REVOLUTIONARY WAR.

Robert McDonal,
Robert Martin,
James McGinnes,
John McCreary,
Joseph Neal,
John Nickle,
Robert Neal,
Benjamin Pack,
Henry Pensinger,
John Reyney,
William Ray,
Henry Sharlack,

John Smith,
George Seeds,
Charles Semple,
Robert Shepard,
James Smith,
Thomas Sharp,
Robert Wood,
James Woods,
Robert Wright,
Samuel Whitman,
John Wooleber,
John Williamson.

NAMES, RANK, AND DATES OF COMMISSIONS OF THE OFFICERS OF CAPTAIN JOHN LACEY'S COMPANY OF COLONEL WAYNE'S PENNSYLVANIA BATTALION, WITH A LIST OF THE PRIVATES, FROM JANUARY 5, TO NOVEMBER 1, 1776.

John Lacey, Captain. Commissioned January 5, 1776.
Samuel Smith, First-lieutenant. Commissioned January 5, 1776.
Michael Ryan, Second-lieutenant. Commissioned January 5, 1776.
John Bartley, Ensign. Commissioned Jan. 5, 1776. Promoted Oct. 1, 1776.
James Forbes, Ensign. Commissioned October 1, 1776.

Sergeants.

William Hood,
Andrew Oliphant,

William Randle,
Samuel Elliot.

Corporals.

Stafford Graham,
John Peter,

John Bailey,
Samuel Morris.

Drum and Fife.

John McCowen,

David Palmer.

Privates.

Jacob Anderson,
James Anderson,
James Agnew,
Moses Aikson,
John Bodenham,
William Camagy,
James Cummings,
Thomas Corbett,

Henry Clotter,
Arthur McCrea,
Anthony McClellan,
Abednego Davis,
Thomas Dickinson,
Samuel Fegan,
John Gibson,
Thomas Gordon,

OFFICERS AND PRIVATES

Samuel Hare,	Robert Redman,
Peter Jones,	John Randle,
Francis Kelly,	George Sawyers,
Robert Lawrence,	Thomas Service,
Aaron Lockard,	Benjamin Stagg,
Robert Leason,	George Saville,
John Laschom,	John Smith,
John May,	Zecheus Smith,
Daniel Millhuff,	William Steel,
Thomas Maloy,	Jeremiah Sullivan,
John May.	Thomas Thompson,
Torrence McManes,	James Thomas,
Isaac Meason,	James Weady,
Richard Moore,	William Welch,
Robert McGaudy,	Philip Williams,
John Noble,	David Wesner,
Samuel Nief,	Charles Wallington,
David Nelson,	Moses Whalen,
Nicholas Redin,	John Sidders.

NAMES, RANK, DATES OF COMMISSIONS, AND TIME OF ENLISTMENT OF THE OFFICERS AND PRIVATES OF CAPTAIN PERSIFOR FRAZER'S COMPANY OF COL. WAYNE'S PENNSYLVANIA BATTALION, FROM JANUARY 5 TO NOVEMBER 26, 1776.

Persifor Frazer, Captain. Commissioned Jan. 5, 1776. Promoted Sept. 24, 1776.
Joseph Potts, Captain. Commissioned October 12, 1776.
Benjamin Bartholomew, Captain. Commissioned January 5, 1776.
Isaac Seely, Second-lieutenant. Commissioned January 5, 1776.
Levi Griffith, Ensign. Commissioned January 5, 1776.

Sergeants.

	Appointed.		Appointed.
Edward Buckley,	Jan. 10, 1776.	William McGee,	Jan. 30, 1776.
Daniel Harris,	Jan. 22, 1776.	Edward Verner,	Feb. 2, 1776.

Corporals.

	Appointed.		Appointed.
Joshua Davis,	Jan. 19, 1776.	James Long,	Feb. 2, 1776.
(Drowned Aug. 1, 1776.)		John Taylor,	Jan. 19, 1776.
Evan James,	Feb. 7, 1776.	Abram Wood,	Aug. 1, 1776.

OF THE REVOLUTIONARY WAR.   199

Drummers.

Appointed.

Abraham Butler, Jan. 21, 1776.
 (Discharged April 19, 1776.)
John McCarter, April 19, 1776.
 (Returned to ranks July 1, 1776.)

Appointed.

Robert McIntire, July 1, 1776.
 (Died Nov. 1, 1776.)
Abram Muskall, Nov. 1, 1776.
William Kline, Fifer, Jan. 22, 1776.

Privates.

Enlisted.

James Adams, Feb. 5, 1776.
 (Deserted July 10, 1776.)
George Atkinson, Jan. 17, 1776.
Joseph Becket, April 8, 1776.
Philip Bolton, April 6, 1776.
James Berry, Feb. 17, 1776.
Thomas Burns, Jan. 30, 1776.
John Boyles, Feb. 28, 1776.
Alexander Boggs, Jan. 22, 1776.
John Bartholomew, Feb. 19, 1776.
 (Deserted July 10, 1776.)
Philip Bostol, Jan. 31, 1776.
John Blackwood, Mar. 21, 1776.
Patrick Conner, Feb. 22, 1776.
Lawrence Connolly, Feb. 1, 1776.
Thomas Cloward, Feb. 14, 1776.
 (Died Feb. 15, 1776.)
Patrick Carroll, Jan. 15, 1776.
William Cruddicks, Feb. 7, 1776.
 (Deserted Mar. 12, 1776.)
John Corry, Feb. 20, 1776.
William Cane, Feb. 10, 1776.
John Cligner, Mar. 17, 1776.
 (Deserted May 1, 1776.)
Charles Calhoun, April 29, 1776.
 (Died Nov. 20, 1776.)
James Dailey, Feb. 27, 1776.
John Dobbins, April 3, 1776.
 (Deserted May 1, 1776.)
Paul Ellis, Jan. 23, 1776.
Thomas Guin, Feb. 4, 1776.
John Harvey, Feb. 15, 1776.
George Herbster, May 9, 1776.
 (Deserted July 10, 1776.)

Enlisted.

David Harris, Jan. 22, 1776.
 (Discharged April 19, 1776.)
John Harrington, Jan. 16, 1776.
James Innis, Feb. 7, 1776.
John Ingram, Feb. 1, 1776.
 (Discharged May 1, 1776.)
Thomas Junkin, Jan. 22, 1776.
 (Discharged April 19, 1776.)
Francis Jones, Jan. 21, 1776.
 . (Discharged April 20, 1776.)
Patrick Joyce, Mar. 21, 1776.
Jacob Kirrigan, Feb. 1, 1776
 (Discharged April 1, 1776.)
Peter King, Jan. 16, 1776.
Caleb Kenedy, Jan. 10, 1776.
 (Died Jan. 18, 1776.)
Timothy Kelly, Jan. 25, 1776.
Christopher Kelly, Jan. 21. 1776.
Patrick Lynn, Feb. 24, 1776.
William Lyons, Jan. 31, 1776,
John McCulloh, Feb. 5, 1776.
Joseph McCormick, Jan. 27, 1776.
Zebulon Morland, Feb. 8, 1776.
 (Claimed by Col. Maxwell.)
William McGuire, Jan. 25, 1776.
Charles McGarrel, Jan. 31, 1776.
John McCarter, Feb. 8, 1776.
 (Promoted to Drummer April 19.)
James McDonald, Jan. 16, 1776.
Patrick Martin, Jan. 25, 1776.
Robert Mercer, do.
Samuel McCully, Feb. 8, 1776.
Hugh McLaughlin, Feb. 8, 1776.
John Murtland, Feb. 1, 1776.

OFFICERS AND PRIVATES

Enlisted.

John Miller,	Feb. 1, 1776.
(A servant, discharged.)	
Joshua Matin,	Jan. 23, 1776.
(Discharged May 1, 1776.)	
Samuel McGowen,	April 29, 2776.
John McLaughlin,	April 22, 1776.
Peter McDonald,	Feb. 8, 1776.
(A servant, discharged.)	
William Nelson,	Jan. 31, 1776.
(Died Nov. 18, 1776.)	
John Nuby,	Feb. 15, 1776.
Joseph Norman,	Mar. 21, 1776.
Thomas Owen,	Jan. 31, 1776.
William O'Neal,	Jan. 16, 1776.
(Discharged April 19, 1776.)	
Peter O'Brien,	May 9, 1776.
(Deserted July 10, 1776.)	
John Parker,	Jan. 29, 1776.
David Powell,	Jan. 26, 1776.
Samuel Pedrick,	April 6, 1776.
(Deserted May 1, 1776.)	
William Rowls,	Jan. 30, 1776.
Hezekiah Ragg,	Jan. 16, 1776.
John Ramsey,	Mar. 25, 1776.
Tobias Shields,	Jan. 21, 1776.
Samuel Smiley,	Jan. 19, 1776.

Enlisted.

Michael Smith,	Jan. 18, 1776.
John Steward,	Mar. 19, 1776.
Daniel Swiney,	April 1, 1776.
(Deserted Oct. 10, 1776.)	
John McCarter,	July 1, 1776.
Robert McIntire,	do.
William Toland,	Feb. 2, 1776.
(Died Sept. 26, 1776.)	
John Tanner,	Jan. 19, 1776.
William Trego,	Jan. 29, 1776.
(Confined, and left with General Washington's army.)	
David Thomas,	April 17, 1776.
John Watson,	Feb. 4, 1776.
(Deserted July 10, 1776.)	
Alexander Wright,	Jan. 16, 1776.
(Deserted July 1, 1776.)	
John Wilson,	Feb. 1, 1776.
John Wolf,	Jan. 26, 1776.
Abraham Wood,	April 6, 1776.
(Promoted Aug. 1, 1776.)	
James Young,	April 13, 1776.
(Deserted July 11, 1776.)	
John Young,	April 22, 1776.
(Deserted May 1, 1776.)	
John Walker,	July 1, 1776.

NAMES, RANK, DATES OF COMMISSIONS, AND TIME OF ENLISTMENT OF THE OFFICERS AND PRIVATES OF CAPT. JAMES TAYLOR'S COMPANY, OF COL. WAYNE'S PENNSYLVANIA BATTALION, FROM JAN. 5 TO NOV. 26, 1776.

James Taylor, Captain. Commissioned January 5, 1776.
Michael Kimmel, First-lieutenant. Commissioned January 5, 1776.
Thomas Boude, Second-lieutenant. Commissioned January 5, 1776.
Ezekiel Letts, Ensign. Commissioned January 5, 1776. Resigned Oct. 11, 1776.
John Harper, Ensign. Commissioned October 12, 1776.

Sergeants.

Appointed.

Francis Ruth,	Jan. 20, 1776.
James McCullock,	Jan. 27, 1776.
Robert Anderson,	Jan. 27, 1776.

Appointed.

John Lindsey,	Jan. 27, 1776.
(Deserted July 1, 1776.)	
Joseph Simeral,	July 2, 1776.

Corporals

Appointed			Appointed	
Alexander McHatton,	Jan. 27, 1776.	Robert Ross,	Mar. 1, 1776.
Nathaniel McGill,	Jan. 28, 1776.	Samuel Giffen,	Feb. 10, 1776.

Drummers

Elias Peters,	Jan. 30, 1776.	James Graham,	Jan. 29, 1776.
(Reduced to ranks June 25.)		(Dead Gen. Hospital.)	
John Connolly,	June 25, 1776.		

Privates

Enlisted			Enlisted	
James Anderson,	Feb. 1, 1776.	Evan Evans,	Feb. 7, 1776.
Humphrey Andrews,	Jan. 26, 1776.	(Deserted Feb. 19, 1776.)	
David Armstrong,	Feb. 10, 1776.	John Fisler,	Jan. 31, 1776.
(Deserted July 1, 1776.)		(Deserted Feb. 19, 1776.)	
Michael Arthur,	Jan. 30, 1776.	John Fitzgerald,	Feb. 5, 1776.
Thomas Baxter,	Feb. 1, 1776.	(Deserted July 5, 1776.)	
Thomas Benderman,	Jan. 29, 1776.	William Fleming,	Jan. 31, 1776.
Zecharias Boyce,	Jan. 30, 1776.	William Gibson,	Jan. 27, 1776.
John Bowman,	Jan. 22, 1776.	Ryncer Gibbert,	Jan. 12, 1776.
James Britain,	Feb. 1, 1776.	John Gilbreth,	Jan. 29, 1776.
Alexander Brown,	Feb. 14, 1776.	(Deserted June 29, 1776.)	
Samuel Carson,	Jan. 25, 1776.	Paul Gilmore,	Jan. 29, 1776.
James Coffeld	Feb. 7, 1776.	Thomas Gould,	Jan. 27, 1776.
John Connolly,	Mar. 12, 1776.	Thomas Griffith,	Feb. 6, 1776.
(Promoted Drummer, June 25.)		Christian Grim,	do.
James Conner,	Feb. 8, 1776.	Christian Hague,	Feb. 10, 1776.
(Died Oct. 24, 1776.)		(Deserted Feb. 19, 1776.)	
James Cornelius,	Jan. 25, 1776.	David Hailey,	Jan. 29, 1776.
John Cornelius,	Jan. 12, 1776.	Charles Hanagan,	Jan. 30, 1776
Kerry Copland,	Mar. 1, 1776.	David Hayes,	Feb. 10, 1776.
John Dailey,	Feb. 1, 1776.	(Died Nov. 20, 1776.)	
James Dale,	Jan. 30, 1776.	Samuel Hughes,	Mar. 26, 1776.
William Davidson,	Mar. 23, 1776.	John Jones,	Feb. 4, 1776.
Daniel Denjel,	Feb. 5, 1776.	Thomas Kelly,	Jan. 29, 1776.
Cornelius Devinny,	Jan. 31, 1776.	William Leadly,	Jan. 31, 1776.
Joseph Dew,	Feb. 7, 1776.	James Letts,	Jan. 12, 1776.
John Dieffenderffer,	Jan. 30, 1776.	John Logan,	Jan. 29, 1776.
John Dobbins,	Feb. 3, 1776.	(Deserted Feb. 18, 1776.)	
Robert Dobbins,	Jan. 25, 1776.	Joseph Mashman,	Feb. 3, 1776.
Dennis Dougherty,	Feb. 7, 1776.	Jacob Mayer,	Feb. 5, 1776.
John Dunn,	Feb. 1, 1776.	Jacob Miller,	Feb. 4, 1776
James Dysart,	Jan. 27, 1776.	Michael Miller,	Feb. 6, 1776.

OFFICERS AND PRIVATES

	Enlisted.		Enlisted.
William Morgan,	April 10, 1776.	James Ridings,	Feb. 6, 1776.
Richard Morris,	Feb. 1, 1776.	William Rogan,	Jan. 30, 1776.
William McAy,	Jan. 25, 1776.	John Ross,	Jan. 25, 1776.
Thomas McCallian,	Jan. 25, 1776.	John Rudicil,	Feb. 10, 1776.
John McCann,	Jan. 20, 1776.	(Deserted Jan. 9, 1776.)	
William McClusky,	Jan. 29, 1776.	Thomas Scott,	Jan. 28, 1776.
Joseph McConnell,	Feb. 1, 1776.	(Deserted Feb. 20, 1776.)	
William McConnell,	Jan. 25, 1776.	Christopher Sipe,	Feb. 6, 1776.
George McCord,	Feb. 1, 1776.	Archibald Shanks,	Feb. 12, 1776.
John McCowan,	Jan. 24, 1776.	John Sharp,	Jan. 25, 1776.
Malcom McDonald,	Feb. 1, 1776.	Mathew Simpson,	Feb. 16, 1776.
William McDonald,	Jan. 23, 1776.	(Deserted Feb. 20, 1776.)	
John McKinney,	Jan. 30, 1776.	Andrew Sinnet,	Jan. 30, 1776.
John McClelland,	Jan. 28, 1776.	Joseph Simeral,	Jan. 25, 1776.
Samuel McMurray,	Mar. 13, 1776.	(Promoted Sergeant, July 2.)	
Daniel McNeal,	Feb. 1, 1776	John Spear,	Feb. 1, 1776.
Robert McPike,	Feb. 5, 1776.	Walter St. John,	Feb. 8, 1776.
Alexander Nelson,	Jan. 24, 1776.	Leonard Stone,	Jan. 30, 1776.
Felix O'Neal,	Jan. 4, 1776.	(Deserted Feb. 20, 1776.)	
Arthur Patterson,	Jan. 25, 1776.	Francis Taylor,	Jan. 29, 1776.
Elias Peters,	June 25, 1776.	Samuel Vogan,	Feb. 1, 1776.
Michael Phink,	Feb. 6, 1776.	John Watson,	Mar. 20, 1776.
Francis Porter,	do.	Andrew Wilson,	Jan. 29, 1776.
Patrick Riley,	Jan. 31, 1776.	John Welt,	Feb. 10, 1776.
(Discharged at Fort George.)		(Deserted Feb. 19, 1776.)	
James Richardson,	Jan. 24, 1776.	Michael Wise,	Feb. 5, 1776.

NAMES, RANK, AND DATES OF COMMISSIONS, OF THE FIELD, STAFF, AND OTHER OFFICERS OF COLONEL WILLIAM IRVINE'S PENNSYLVANIA REGIMENT, WITH A LIST OF THE PRIVATES, AS IT STOOD AT MOUNT INDEPENDENCE, NOVEMBER 28, 1776.

William Irvine, Colonel. Commissioned January 9, 1776. Captured by British troops under General Frazer, June 8, 1776, at Three Rivers, about forty-five miles down the St. Lawrence from the mouth of Sorel River. General Thompson, Colonel Irvine, and about two hundred men were captured here, and about twenty-five slain, by the enemy.

Thomas Hartley, Lieutenant-colonel. Commissioned January 9, 1776.
James Dunlap, Major. Commissioned January 10, 1776.
David Greer, Major. Commissioned June 1, 1776.
John Brooks, Adjutant and Lieutenant. Commissioned January 9, 1776.

OF THE REVOLUTIONARY WAR.   203

Robert Johnson, Surgeon. Commissioned January 9, 1776.
John McDowl, Surgeon's Mate and Lieutenant. Commissioned Jan. 9, 1776.
James Calderwood, Quartermaster. Commissioned January 9, 1776. Promoted to Lieutenant on board the Fleet, August 1, 1776.
William Nichols, Quartermaster. Commissioned August 1, 1776. Resigned November 17, 1776.
Robert Hopes, Quartermaster. Commissioned November 17, 1776, by order of General Gates.

COMPANY No. 1.

Samuel Hay, Captain. Commissioned January 9, 1776.
John Grier, First-lieutenant. Commissioned January 9, 1776. Taken prisoner July 24, 1776.
Alexander Parker, Second-lieutenant. Commissioned January 9, 1776. Promoted June 1, 1776.
Samuel Montgomery, Second-lieutenant. Commissioned June 1, 1776.
William Miller, Ensign. Commissioned January 9, 1776.

Sergeants.

Apppointed.		Appointed.	
John Hughes,	Jan. 29, 1776.	John Foster,	Feb. 1, 1776.
(Promoted June 24.)		(Captured at Three Rivers, June 8.)	
John Faucet,	Jan. 17, 1776.	John Parker,	Jan. 23, 1776.
(Captured at Three Rivers June 8, 1776.)		William Boyd,	June 24, 1776.
		(Taken prisoner July 24, 1776.)	

Corporals.

John Hanna,	Jan. 25, 1776.	William Boyd,	Jan. 25, 1776.
Ezekiel Sample,	do.	(Prom. to Serg't June 24, 1776.)	
Francis Rowdin,	do.	William Bramer,	Jan. 25, 1776.
(Reduced July 24.)		(July 24, 1776.)	

Drummers.

John Drumond,	Jan. 20, 1776.	Elias Mewnham, Fifer,	
John Henry,	Jan. 15, 1776.		Feb. 20, 1776.

Privates.

Enlisted.		Enlisted.	
John Butcher,	Jan. 25, 1776.	Robert Brown,	Feb. 21, 1776.
Andrew Byers,	Jan. 31, 1776.	Abram Boyd,	Feb. 2, 1776.
(Captured June 8, 1776.)		(Captured June 8, 1776.)	
John Boyle,	Feb. 1, 1776.	Samuel Barclay,	Jan. 30, 1776.
(Taken on board the fleet, Oct. 15, 1776.)		William Bamer,	Jan. 25, 1776.
		(Promoted July 24, 1776.)	
William Brimigin,	Feb. 5, 1776.	Darby Bannon,	Feb. 15, 1776.
Patrick Bolden,	Jan. 25, 1776	William Batson,	Jan. 5, 1776.

OFFICERS AND PRIVATES

Enlisted.

George Butler, Feb. 20, 1776.
(Captured June 8, 1776.)
William Blair, Feb. 28, 1776.
(Captured June 8, 1776.)
Samuel Cochran, Feb. 12, 1776.
(Promoted June 9, 1776, to Sergeant, but sick.)
Charles Carlton, Mar. 1, 1776.
James Cochran, Mar. 8, 1776.
(Killed at Three Rivers June 8,'76)
Robert Cunningham, Jan. 23, 1776.
Patrick Demsey, Jan. 26, 1776.
Thomas Dyas, Jan. 26, 1776.
John Dunwoody, Jan. 27, 1776.
(Captured June 8, 1776.)
Edward Davison, Jan. 30, 1776.
Henry Freet, Feb. 1, 1776.
(Wounded.)
John Flaverty, Jan. 28, 1776.
Abel Forsyth, Jan. 31, 1776.
Robert Forsyth, Jan. 26, 1776.
(Deserted May 1, 1776.)
Arthur French, Jan. 30, 1776.
James Graham, 1st, Jan. 26, 1776.
James Graham, 2nd, Feb. 27, 1776.
Timothy Harly, Jan. 31, 1776.
(Captured June 8, 1776.)
Robert Hughes, Jan. 27, 1776.
John Hastings, Jan. 31, 1776.
Robert Hamilton, Feb. 28, 1776.
William Holliday, Jan. 29, 1776.
(Captured July 24, 1776.)
Thomas Hanon, Jan. 28, 1776.
(Captured June 8, 1776.)
John Jamison, Feb. 10, 1776.
(Deserted April 8, 1776.)
James Kearns, Jan. 31, 1776.
Archibald Kennedy, Jan. 23, 1776.
(Sergeant Since Aug. 1.)
Michael Kerr, Jan. 27, 1776.
(Deserted Feb. 28, 1776.)

Enlisted.

William Leech, Jan. 25, 1776.
(Died Nov. 24, 1776.)
Samuel Lowrey, Feb. 28, 1776.
Edward Murphy, Feb. 1, 1776.
Thomas Means, Jan. 25, 1776.
Alex. Mairs, Feb. 1, 1776.
Edward McMullan, Feb. 15, 1776.
James Mitchell, Jan. 25, 1776.
John McMichael, Feb. 8, 1776.
William McIntyre, Feb. 6, 1776.
Adam Martin, Feb. 12, 1776.
(Captured June 8, 1776.)
Hugh McMillan, Feb. 21, 1776.
James Mulloy, Feb. 10, 1776.
Charles McConnell, Jan. 26, 1776.
William McCoy, do.
James McCormick, Feb. 5, 1776.
(Deserted Nov. 15, 1776.)
William McQuown, Jan. 17, 1776.
(Appointed Sergeant, June 10.
Captured July 24, 1776.)
Patrick McCormick, Feb 20, 1776.
James McClaine, Feb. 1, 1776.
Ruday McCoy, Feb. 4, 1776.
Patrick McGalls, Feb. 20, 1776.
(Died at Carlisle, April 1, 1776.)
Daniel McGlaughlin, Feb. 1, 1776.
William McKee, Feb. 27, 1776.
William McKinley, Feb. 20, 1776.
William McDonald, do.
(Killed at Three Rivers June 8.)
Thomas Nelson, Jan. 23, 1776.
(Captured at Three Rivers June 8.)
Robert Neal, Jan. 29, 1776.
Robert Pendergrass, Mar. 14, 1776.
Charles Riley, Jan. 5, 1776.
David Roach, Jan. 25, 1776.
(Died Oct. 12, 1776.)
John Ross, Jan. 29, 1776.
Robert Reah, Feb. 12, 1776.
(Deserted Nov. 26, 1776.)

OF THE REVOLUTIONARY WAR. 205

Enlisted.			*Enlisted.*	
Francis Rowain,	July 24, 1776.	Charles Wright,	Jan. 22, 1776
Michael Trance,	Jan. 26, 1776.	Garret Wagoner,	Jan. 25, 1776.
Joseph Thompson,	Feb. 2, 1776.	Andrew Wilson,	Feb. 1, 1776.
(Wounded and captured July 24.)		Alex. Wilkins,	do.
Alex. Thomas,	Feb. 26, 1776.	John White,	Jan. 25, 1776.
John Thompson,	Jan. 25, 1776.	(Died July 2, 1776.)	
(Deserted March 27, 1776.)			

COMPANY NO. 2.

Robert Adams, Captain. Commissioned Jan. 9, 1776. Killed June 21, 1776.
Lewis Bush, do. do. June 24, 1776.
William Bratton, First-lieutenant. Commissioned Jan. 9, 1776.
William Nichol, Second-lieutenant. Commissioned June 21, 1776.
Samuel McFerran, Second-lieutenant. Commissioned Jan. 9, 1776. Promoted June 21, in Captain Wilson's Company.
James Calderwood, Ensign. Commissioned May 1, 1776. Promoted Aug. 1, on board the Fleet.
Thomas McCoy, Ensign. Commissioned Aug. 1, 1776. Taken prisoner October 1, 1776.
John King, Ensign. Commissioned October 17, 1776.

Sergeants.

Appointed.			*Appointed.*	
James Ewing,	Jan. 25, 1776.	John Smith,	Jan. 25, 1776.
Samuel Woods,	do.	(Reduced May 15, 1776.)	
(Reduced June 2, 1776.)		William Kyle,	May 15, 1776.
John McLiu,	do.	John Orbison,	June 2, 1776

Corporals.

Joseph Byars,	Jan. 25, 1776.	William Renick,	Jan. 25, 1776.
Thomas Lawson,	do.	Josiah Wilson,	June 15, 1776.
(Reduced May 1, 1776.)		Timothy O'Neal,	Sept. 25, 1776.
Alex. Carnaghan,	do.		

Drummer and Fifer.

John Haset,	Jan. 30, 1776.	John Wann,	Jan. 25, 1776.

Privates.

Enlisted.			*Enlisted.*	
Roger Burns,	Jan. 25, 1776.	Richard Brannon,	Jan. 25, 1776.
William Bryan,	do.	(Capt'ed at Three Rivers, June 10.)	
John Burns,	Feb. 14, 1776.	Walker Beatty,	Feb. 3, 1776.
Andrew Burns,	do.	Daniel Blue,	Feb. 3, 1776.
(Capt'ed at Three Rivers, June 10.)		(Waiting on Gen. Schuyler.)	
William Baskins,	Feb. 14, 1776.		

OFFICERS AND PRIVATES

Enlisted.

John Bucket,	Mar. 1, 1776.

(Deserted May 1, 1776.)

James Bullain, Feb. 8, 1776.
(Capt'ed at Three Rivers, June 10.)
John Cachy, Jan. 30, 1776.
Alex. Campbell, do.
Amos. Chapman, Feb. 8, 1776.
Robert Cummins, Jan. 30, 1776.
John Conner, Feb. 1, 1776.
Charles Dugan, Jan. 25, 1776.
John Davis, do.
(Capt'ed at Three Rivers, June 10.)
William Drannon, Feb. 8, 1776.
Edward Denny, Jan. 30, 1776.
(Killed June 10, at Three Rivers.)
George Drue, Feb. 14, 1776.
James Duffy, Jan. 30, 1776.
James Douglas, Mar. 1, 1776.
(Captured Oct. 1, and on parole.)
William Dyer, Mar. 1, 1776.
John Dougherty, Jan. 30, 1776.
James Elliott, Feb. 14, 1776.
Edward Edgarton, do.
John Ewing, Feb. 6, 1776.
Edward Gallaher, Feb. 2, 1776.
Thomas Gillis, Feb. 17, 1776.
Thomas Greer, Jan. 30, 1776.
William Hamilton, Jan. 25, 1776.
(Died Sept. 1, 1776.)
James Hamilton, Jan. 25, 1776.
Hugh Handbury, Jan. 30, 1776.
John Hamilton, Jan. 21, 1776.
James Higgins, Feb. 14, 1776.
David Hall, Feb. 4, 1776.
George Wiseman, Jan. 21, 1776.
William Redstone, Jan. 21, 1776.
Thomas Lawson, May 1, 1776.
(Capt'ed June 10, at Three Rivers.)
Solomon Isaac, Feb. 6, 1776.
(Capt'ed June 10, at Three Rivers.)
Richard Joyce, Jan. 30, 1776.
(Capt'ed June 10, at Three Rivers.)

Enlisted.

James Kenedy, Jan. 30, 1776.
(Capt'ed June 10, at Three Rivers.)
Thomas Killwell, Jan. 21, 1776.
William Kyle, Jan. 30, 1776.
(Promoted Sergeant May 15.)
James Maxwell, Feb. 14, 1776.
Thomas McGee, do.
John McGee, do.
Thomas McIntire, Jan. 21, 1776.
William May, Feb. 22, 1776.
Gilbert McCoy, Feb. 14, 1776.
Thomas McCoy, do.
(Promoted to Ensign May 1, 1776.)
William McGowan, Jan. 30, 1776.
John McCartney, Feb. 2, 1776.
Barnabas McGillagan, Feb. 5, 1776.
James Murkhey, Feb. 6, 1776.
(Deserted May 27, 1776.)
Andrew McGee, Feb. 14, 1776.
Paul McNeal, Feb. 30, 1776.
Michael McConnell, Jan. 30, 1776.
(Capt'ed June 10, at Three Rivers.)
Thomas Morrow, Jan. 25, 1776.
(Taken on the Fleet Oct. 12.)
Hugh McLane, Jan. 25, 1776.
(Capt'ed June 10, at Three Rivers.)
William Mooney, Mar. 1, 1776.
Timothy O'Neal, Feb. 3, 1776.
(Promoted Corporal Sept. 21.)
John Olford, Feb. 4, 1776.
John Obison, Jan. 30, 1776.
(Promoted Sergeant, June 2.)
William Polch, Jan. 30, 1776.
(Died Sept. 22, 1776.)
Jacob Pitzer, Jan. 30, 1776.
James Quigley, Jan. 21, 1776.
William Standup, Feb. 8, 1776.
Joshua Smith, Feb. 1, 1776.
(Capt'ed June 10, at Three Rivers.)
Patt Shockney, Feb. 6, 1776.
James Stenson, May 1, 1776.

OF THE REVOLUTIONARY WAR.   207

Enlisted.

John Swany   Jan. 25, 1776.
(Deserted April 10, 1776.)
James Thompson,   Jan. 21, 1776.
Evan Tomlinson,   Feb. 3, 1776.
Samuel Wood,   Jan. 25, 1776.
(Capt'ed June 10, at Three Rivers.)

Enlisted.

William Waugh,   Feb. 3, 1776.
John White,   do.
Josiah Wilson,   Jan. 30, 1776.
(Promoted Corporal June 15.)
John Ward,   Feb. 2, 1776.

COMPANY No. 3.

Abraham Smith, Captain. Commissioned January 9, 1776.
Robert White, First-lieutenant. Commissioned January 9, 1776. Resigned February 9, 1776.
John Alexander' Second-lieutenant. Commissioned January 9, 1776. Promoted February 10, 1776.
Andrew Irvine, Second-lieutenant. Commissioned February 9, 1776.
Samuel Montgomery, Ensign. Commissioned January 9, 1776. Promoted June 1, 1776.
Samuel Kennedy, Ensign. Commissioned June 1, 1776.

Sergeants.

Appointed.

John Beatty,   Jan. 27, 1776.
Samuel Hamilton,   Jan. 30, 1776.
(Died July 11, 1776.)

Appointed.

Hugh Foster,   Feb. 2, 1776.
William Scott,   Feb. 11, 1776.
William Burk,   July 11, 1776.

Corporals.

William Burk,   Jan. 29, 1776.
(Promoted July 11, 1776.)
George Standley,   Mar. 2, 1776.
(Died in Oct., 1776.)
John Moore,   Feb. 12, 1776.
(Died in Sept., 1776.)
William Campbell,   Feb. 3, 1776.

Seth Richey,   July 11, 1776.
William McCormick, Sept. 25, 1776.
William Drennon,   Oct. 25, 1776.
John Fannon,   Feb. 4, 1776.
(Drummer.)
William Cochran,   Aug. 1, 1776.
(Fifer.)

Privates.

Enlisted.

David Armor,   Feb. 9, 1776.
(Deserted May 14, 1776.)
John Brown,   Feb. 3, 1776.
Patrick Brown,   Feb. 4, 1776.
John Blakeley,   Feb. 22, 1776.
John Brannon,   Mar. 9, 1776.
(Captured July 24, 1776.)
Philip Boyle,   Mar. 9, 1776.
Josiah Cochran,   Jan. 29, 1776.
Robert Craighead,   Feb. 6, 1776.
(Captured at Three Rivers June 9.)

Enlisted.

Anthony Creevy,   Feb. 19, 1776.
William Cochran,   Mar. 2, 1776.
(Promoted Aug. 1, 1776.)
James Dunlap.   Feb. 2, 1776.
Thomas Drennon,   Feb. 12, 1776.
William Downey,   do.
Hugh Drennon,   Feb. 14, 1776.
Daniel Divinney,   Feb. 20, 1776.
(Captured Oct. 12, 1776.)
Patrick Flemming,   Feb. 1, 1776.
William Guin,   Jan. 29, 1776.

OFFICERS AND PRIVATES

	Enlisted.
Alex. Gordon,	Jan. 27, 1776.
Robert Gregg,	Feb. 22, 1776.
Thomas Higgins,	Jan. 30, 1776.
(Captured Oct. 12, 1776.)	
James Holliday,	Feb. 3, 1776.
Thomas Holmes,	Feb. 4, 1776.
John Hendricks,	April 8, 1776.
(Deserted May 28, 1776.)	
Robert Jarret,	Feb. 2, 1776.
Thomas Johnson,	Feb. 12, 1776.
(Captured at Three Rivers June 9.)	
Benjamin Ishmail,	Feb. 12. 1776.
Samuel Love,	Jan. 29, 1776.
George Lucas,	Feb. 10, 1776.
Nicholas Little,	Feb. 14, 1776.
(Captured at Three Rivers June 9.)	
James Lowry,	Feb. 14, 1776.
Daniel McKissock,	Jan. 9, 1776.
John McCollam.	do.
William McCormick,	Feb. 1, 1776.
(Promoted Sept. 25, 1776.)	
Michael McGarra,	Feb. 1, 1776.
(Deserted May 28, 1776.)	
Bryan McLaughlin,	Feb. 2, 1776.
John McFetridge,	do.
John Montgomery,	Feb. 3, 1776.
Michael McMullan,	do.
James McKissock,	do.
Adam McBrea,	Feb. 4, 1776.
Alex. Moore,	do.
John McDowell,	Feb. 5. 1776.
Robert Miller.	do.
Hugh Milligan,	Feb. 7, 1776.
Samuel McBrea,	Feb. 12, 1776.
(Died Aug. 10, 1776.)	

	Enlisted.
Robert McIlno,	Feb. 25, 1776.
Alex. McKenny,	Mar. 4, 1776.
Moses Powell,	Feb. 19, 1776.
(Killed Sept. 6, 1776.)	
Nathaniel Points,	Feb. 2, 1776.
John Rannell,	do.
Seth Richey,	Feb. 4, 1776.
(Promoted July 11, 1776.)	
Patrick Rogers,	Feb. 4, 1776.
John Rannell, jun.,	Feb. 5, 1776.
Peter Runey,	Feb. 9, 1776.
Alex. Reid (sick),	Feb. 26, 1776.
Alexander Reid, 2d,	Mar. 3, 1776.
(Captured at Three Rivers June 9.)	
Barthol. Roharty,	Mar. 9, 1776.
Thomas Smith,	Jan. 29, 1776.
Patrick Silvers,	Feb. 6, 1776.
Thomas Scott,	Feb. 7, 1776.
George Simpson,	Feb. 13, 1776.
Robert Swime,	Feb. 20, 1776.
John Stoops,	Feb. 22, 1776.
Adam Sheaver,	do.
William Stitt,	do.
Peter Sheran.	Mar. 5, 1776.
(Deserted May 14.)	
Charles Tipper,	Jan. 27, 1776.
John Todd,	Jan. 29, 1776.
Michael White,	Feb. 10, 1776.
(Captured at Three Rivers June 9.)	
James White,	Feb. 16, 1776.
John McKingham,	do.
(Captured at Three Rivers June 9.	
John Wilson,	Feb. 18, 1776
John Young,	Feb. 4, 1776.

COMPANY NO. 4.

William Rippey, Captain. Commissioned January 9, 1776.

William Alexander, First-lieutenant. Commissioned January, 9, 1776. Promoted to Captain, June 1, 1776.

Alexander Parker, First-lieutenant. Commissioned June 1, 1776.

John Brooks, Second-lieutenant.   do.   January 9, 1776.

William Lusk, Ensign.   do.   do.

OF THE REVOLUTIONARY WAR.

Sergeants.

	Appointed.		Appointed.
John Hughes,	Jan. 18, 1776.	John McClelland,	Jan. 18, 1776.
Robert Watt,	do.	William Anderson,	do.

Corporals.

	Appointed.		Appointed.
William Gibb,	Jan. 19, 1776.	George Gordon,	Jan. 26, 1776.
(Promoted in August to Capt. Wilson's Co.)		Nathaniel Stevenson,	Jan. 27, 1776.
		Daniel Peterson,	Mar. 26, 1776.
Jeremiah McKiblen,	Jan. 26, 1776.	(Drummer.)	
James McCullough,	do.	Wm. Richards, Fifer, Jan. 18, 1776.	

Privates.

	Enlisted.		Enlisted.
Jacob Anderson,	Feb. 12, 1776.	Robert Haslet,	Feb. 29, 1776.
Robert Barckley,	Jan. 22, 1776.	(Captured June 8, 1776.)	
Bernard Burns,	Feb. 2, 1776.	John Hendry,	Feb. 5, 1776.
(Drummed out May 10.)		William Henderson,	Jan. 18, 1776.
Robert Caskey,	Jan. 29, 1776.	(Discharged April 18, 1776.)	
Henry Caistweight,	Feb. 2, 1776.	James Hervey,	Jan. 18, 1776
Robert Cortney,	do	(Died Aug. 10, 1776.)	
Jacob Christyardenger,	Feb. 1, 1776.	Cumberland Hamilton, Jan. 23, 1776.	
Benjamin Cochran,	Jan. 18, 1776.	Neal Hardon,	Jan. 25, 1776.
(Captured at Three Rivers, June 8.)		(Captured at Three Rivers, June 8.)	
Hugh Cull,	Jan. 24, 1776.	George Hewett,	Feb. 5, 1776.
John Collins,	Feb. 2, 1776.	Jacob Justice,	Jan. 20, 1776.
(Died Nov. 22, 1776.)		Robert Irvine,	Feb. 29, 1776.
William Doucherty,	Feb. 2, 1776.	John Johnston,	Feb. 1, 1776.
John Davison,	Jan. 28, 1776.	Christopher Kechler,	Jan. 29, 1776.
Joseph Divin,	Jan. 18, 1776.	Francis Kain,	Jan. 31, 1776.
Anthony Dawson,	Jan. 27, 1776.	(Died Oct. 24, 1776.)	
Thomas Dycke,	Jan. 26, 1776.	John Kelly,	Jan. 18, 1776.
James Finerty,	Feb. 12, 1776.	William Lowry,	Feb. 1, 1776.
Hugh Forsyth,	Jan. 18, 1776.	Daniel Lavery,	Feb. 19, 1776.
Hugh Ferguson,	do.	David Linsey,	Jan. 18, 1776.
Terrance Falls,	Jan. 31, 1776.	James Lynch,	Jan. 26, 1776.
William George,	Jan. 29, 1776.	John Madden,	Jan. 20, 1776.
Henry Girven,	Feb. 3, 1776.	Josiah McCall,	Feb. 3, 1776.
Thomas Gill,	Feb. 18, 1776.	John McMichael,	Mar. 5, 1776.
Jacob Glouse,	Jan. 31, 1776.	James McComb,	Feb. 1, 1776.
Nathan Hemphill,	Jan. 22, 1776.	William McIntire,	Jan. 31, 1776.

OFFICERS AND PRIVATES

	Enlisted.		Enlisted.
John Moore,	Feb. 1, 1776.	Jabez Rogers,	Feb. 1, 1776.
James Mullan,	Feb. 3, 1776.	(Captured July 24, 1776.)	
Thomas McCall,	Jan. 29, 1776.	Thomas Reed,	Jan. 18, 1776.
Philip Melon,	Mar. 1, 1776.	Robert Robeson,	Jan. 27, 1776.
(Captured July 24, 1776.)		(Captured June 8, 1776.)	
Alexander McNichols,	Feb. 8, 1776.	Basil Regan,	Jan. 18, 1776.
James McCoy,	Feb. 1, 1776.	(Killed June 21, 1776.)	
James McCon,	Jan. 20, 1776.	John Storm,	Jan. 22, 1776.
David McClain,	Jan. 18, 1776.	Henry Scott,	Jan. 31, 1776.
John McDonal,	Jan. 20, 1776.	(Captured June 8, 1776.)	
Daniel McClain,	Jan. 26, 1776.	Alex. Stephenson,	Feb. 12, 1776.
John McGaw,	Feb. 8, 1776.	(Captured June 8, 1776.)	
Charles Melone,	Feb. 5, 1776.	Nathaniel Stephenson,	Jan. 27, 1776.
George McFerson,	Jan. 19, 1776.	(Promoted Nov. 10, 1776.)	
William Nicholson,	Feb. 1, 1776.	James Smiley,	Feb. 5, 1776.
John Ortman,	Mar. 6, 1776.	William Thompson,	Jan. 19, 1776.
John O'Neal,	Jan. 19, 1776.	John Tribel,	Jan. 18, 1776.
Thomas Pratt,	Jan. 18, 1776.	Jacob Trash,	Feb. 1, 1776.
(Captured June 8, 1776.)		John Van Kirk,	Jan. 18, 1776.
Thomas Parsons,	Feb. 1, 1776.	John Winn,	Feb. 2, 1776.
(Captured June 8, 1776.)		John Wright,	Jan. 31, 1776.
Aaron Patterson,	Mar. 6, 1776.	Peter Young,	Feb. 2, 1776.
Charles Rosbrough,	Jan. 22, 1776.	(Deserted April 7, 1776.)	
John Rosbrough,	do.		

COMPANY NO. 5.

James A. Wilson, Captain. Commissioned January 9, 1776. Taken prisoner, July 24, 1776.

Lewis Bush, First-lieutenant. Commissioned January 9, 1776. Promoted in Captain Adams' Company, June 24.

Samuel McFerren, First-lieutenant, Commissioned January 9, 1776. Taken prisoner, June 21, 1776.

William McClelland, Second-lieutenant. Commissioned Jan. 9, 1776. Resigned.

Robert Wilson, Second-lieutenant. Commissioned January 9, 1776.

Joseph Culbertson, Ensign. Commissioned Jan. 9, 1776. Killed June 21, 1776.

John Bush, Ensign. Commissioned June 24, 1776.

Sergeants.

| Robert Phillips, | John Morrison, |
| Robert Morton, | William Gibb. |

Corporals.

| Francis Alexander, | Dennis Hughes, |
| Jonathan Stirling, | Thomas Cavan. |

OF THE REVOLUTIONARY WAR.   211

Drum and Fife.

Thomas Neilson, | John McIlroy.

Privates.

William Alexander,
James Chambers,
Christopher Chisar,
Alexander Cook,
Anthony Cochran,
Dennis Dailey,
William Fletcher,
John Ferris,
Josiah Gilbreath,
Roger Goff,
Alexander Graham,
William Hanna,
Robert Harris,
Arthur Harson,
Joseph Linton,
John Mann,
James McKain,
Henry McChain,
Robert McCormack,
David McCoy,
Samuel McCullough,
Patt McDonald,
James Kirkpatrick,

James McGuire,
Samuel McKey,
James McKinley,
John McGlaughlan,
John McForely,
David Miller,
George Mock,
Joseph Moore,
John Miller,
Robert Murry,
Daniel Murry,
John O'Neill,
John Parker,
George Patrick,
Joseph Pinkerton,
Charles Strong,
John Thompson,
Robert Todd,
Hector White,
Michael Wickard,
William Wiggans,
Joseph Wren,
John Smith.

Company No. 6.

David Grier, Captain. Commissioned January 9, 1776. Promoted Major, June 1, 1776.
William Alexander, Captain. Commissioned June 1, 1776.
John McDowel, First-lieutenant. Commissioned January 9, 1776.
Abdiel McAllister, Second-lieutenant. Commissioned January 9, 1776. Captured June 21, 1776.
William Nichols, Ensign. Commissioned January 9, 1776. Promoted to Capt. Bush's Company, June 21, 1776.
John Hughes, Ensign. Commissioned June 21, 1776.

Sergeants.

Andrew Walker,
John Knox,

Robert Jeffries,
John Hoyman.

OFFICERS AND PRIVATES

Corporals.

James Lawson,
Felix McIlhenny,
(Captured June 8, 1776.)

David Lathen,
Ezra Johnson,
(Captured June 8, 1776.)

Drum and Fife.

James Hamilton,

Mathias Wright,
(Captured June 8, 1776.)

Privates.

William Anguish,
John Brian,
Robert Bond,
James Berry,
George Baker,
George Cooper,
Cornelius Corrigan,
John Clemmons,
Adam Conn,
Archibald Campbell,
John Doice,
Charles Dougherty,
David Davis,
Alexander Eason,
Robert Forsyth,
Joseph Gettis,
James Herkins,
Thomas Hoy,
William Johnston,
Robert Johnston,
James McMullin,
Henry McKissick,
John McCall,
Lawrence Mealy,
William McCoy,
John McDonald,
Samuel McGowan,
Patrick O'Lean,

Peter O'Neal,
James Price,
John Pearcy,
William Quigley,
James Robinson,
Joseph Russell,
Patrick Rooney,
Archibald Shaw,
James Stevenson,
Peter Swartz,
George Swartz,
Philip Shive,
Patrick Scullion,
Peter Sidle,
Francis Shanley,
Michael Shultz,
Peter Seigh,
James Shaw,
Balzer Swank,
Edward Spencer,
John Snider,
Jacob Trace,
Edward Welch,
Joseph Wilson,
Joseph Wead,
William Wilkinson,
Adam Weaverling,
George Worley.

Prisoners captured from this Company.

	Captured.		Captured.
George Conner,	June 14, 1776.	Charles Gyfinger,	June 21, 1776.
John Dougherty,	June 8, 1776.	Peter Grant,	June 8, 1776.
Thomas Delany,	do.	Edw. Hickinbottom,	June 14, 1776.

OF THE REVOLUTIONARY WAR. 213

	Captured.		Captured.
Thomas Kelly,	June 8, 1776.	Dennis Murphy,	June 8, 1776.
James Leison,	do.	Jacob Mathews,	do.
William Mason,	do.	Murtough Redmond,	do.
Mathias Wright,	do.	John Taylor,	do.
Lawrence Mealy,	do.		

COMPANY No. 7.

Moses McLean, Captain. Commissioned January 9, 1776. Taken prisoner June 21, 1776.
Barned Eichelberger, First-lieutenant. Commissioned January 9, 1776.
John Edie, Second-lieutenant. Commissioned January 9, 1776. Taken prisoner June 8, 1776.
Edward Stille, Second-lieutenant. Commissioned January 9, 1776.
John Hoge, Second-Lieutenant. Commissioned January 9, 1776. Taken prisoner June 8, 1776.
Robert Hopes, Ensign. Commissioned January 9, 1776.

Sergeants.

Robert Ralston,	John King,
John Smith,	(Promoted Oct. 17, 1776.)
James Milligan,	Robert Alison,
	(Appointed Oct. 17, 1776.)

Corporals.

Henry Tibbons,	John McGee,
John Walker,	(Appointed Oct. 18, 1776.)
Andrew Miller,	David Sloane,
Hugh Bradley,	(Appointed Oct. 18, 1776.)

Drum and Fife.

Patrick Conner,	Richard Stack.

Privates.

John Adair,	Felix Duffield,
John Brown,	Thomas Dill,
Joseph Barclay,	John Dunlap,
George Blakely,	William Entrican,
John Blair,	Alexander Faith,
William Cochran,	Thomas Graynor,
William Savan,	Matthias Gerard,
Robert Crawford,	William Hughes,
Thomas Chesney,	John Hargle,
James Conn,	James Johnston,
David Cunningham,	Robert Alison,
Patrick Cunningham,	(Promoted Oct. 17, 1776.
William Dingley,	Aaron Jayne,

214   OFFICERS AND PRIVATES

George Johnston,   James Maxwell,
Samuel Kinkaid,   John McWilliams,
Patrick King,   Jacob McFarland,
Wm. King, Artificer,   Christian Morgan,
Joseph Long,   Dennis O'Hara,
Patrick Limerick,   John Patten,
John McGee,   John Patterson,
(Promoted Oct. 18, 1776.)   John Robinson,
William McDonald,   John Simonton,
John McBride,   William Semple,
Neal McGonagle,   Peter Sullivan,
Patrick McGuan,   David Sloane,
Charles Mahon,   (Promoted Oct. 18, 1776,)
Eneas Murray,   Eli Shugart.
Owen McKeeder,

COMPANY NO. 8.

Jeremiah Talbott, Captain. Commissioned January 9, 1776.
John McDonald, First-lieutenant. Commissioned January 9, 1776.
Alexander Brown, Second-lieutenant. Commissioned January 9, 1776.
William Graham, Ensign. Commissioned January 9, 1776.

Sergeants.

John McCollam,   James Cuppels,
John Wilson,   Samuel Mitchell.

Corporals.

William Campbell,   John Chain,
Robert Hunter,   John Reniston.

Drum and Fife.

John Melton,   John Killin.

Privates.

Robert Asten,   Hugh Fairess,
John Bradley,   James Gardner,
William Black,   David Gibson,
John Church,   William Heaslet,
George Coghren,   John Heatherington,
Francis Clark,   Duke Handlon,
Robert Carnahan,   John Higgins,
Charles Connor,   Kern Kelly,
John Campbell,   Stephen Lyon,
Joseph Chambers,   Jacob Lewis,
John Dinning,   Hugh Lilly,
William Evans,   James McFarlan,
John Faulkner,   John Marten,

Robert Mellon,
Benjamin Morrison,
Charles McKown,
Archibald McDonald,
Thomas Mitchell,
Charles Murray,
Patrick Murray,
Matthew McConnell,
Thomas McCreary,
Lawrence McCreary,
Abel Morgan,
Charles McMullin,
Archibald Nickel,
Andrew Pinkerton,
Samuel Power,
John Pollock,
James Quarre,
William Shaw,
Mike Sesalo,
John Shoomaker,
James Sloan,
John Totton,
John Thompson,
Hugh Thompson,
William White,
John White,
John Welch,
Robert Watson,
Isaac Wiley.

FIELD AND STAFF OF COL. WILLIAM IRVINE'S PENNSYLVANIA REGIMENT, AS IT STOOD JULY 31, 1777.

William Irvine, Colonel.
David Grier, Lieutenant-colonel.
Samuel Hay, Major.
John Rose, Surgeon.
Robert Elliott, Adjutant.
James Gamble, Quartermaster.
John Knight, Paymaster.
John Morrison, Sergeant-major.
William McGriggar, Quartermaster's Sergeant.
John Melton, Drum-major.
Richard Stack, Fife-major.

Captains.

Jeremiah Talbott,
William Alexander,
William Bratton,
John McDowell,
John Alexander,
Alexander Parker,
Robert Willson,
Samuel Montgomery.

CAPT. ROBERT WILLSON'S COMPANY, COL. IRVINE'S REGIMENT, AS IT STOOD NOVEMBER 30, 1777.

Robert Wilson, Captain.
John Bush, Lieutenant.
James Williamson, do.
John O'Neal, Sergeant.
James Kilpatrick, do.
William McGrigger, Sergeant.
John Dugan, Drummer.
Josiah Gilbreath, Corporal.
John Gibney, do.
William McMullan, do.

Privates.

John Mann,
Alex. Porter,
John Parker,
William Miles,
John McSorely,
Patrick Black,
Edward McKillan,
Daniel Murray,
James Chambers, 1st,
Richard Cummins,

OFFICERS AND PRIVATES

Hector White,
Joseph Renn,
John Collins,
William Wiggans,

James Moore,
James Chambers, 2d,
Daniel Sullivan,
John McLaughlin,

CAPT. WILLIAM BRATTON'S COMPANY, AS IT STOOD NOV. 30, 1777.

William Bratton, Captain.
Thomas McCoy, Lieutenant.
William Armstrong, Ensign.
Timothy O'Neal, Sergeant.

Amos Chapman, Sergeant.
Thomas Gillis   do.
Edward Steen, Drummer.
John Wann, Fifer.

Privates.

Francis Henry,
Patrick Shocky,
John Print,
Peter Rooney,
James Elliott,
James Simonton,
Edward Edgarton,
John Beatty,
Daniel Dunnivan,

Peter Martin,
Peter Loyd,
David Hall,
Patt. McDonald,
John Ryan,
John McKean,
Fergus Lee,
John Taylor,
Gilbert McCay.

CAPT. SAMUEL MONTGOMERY'S COMPANY, AS IT STOOD NOV. 30, 1777.

Samuel Montgomery Captain.
Samuel Bryson, Lieutenant.
John McGee, Ensign,
William Roberts, Sergeant.
Josias Wilson,   do.

James Maxwell, Sergeant.
Robert Todd,   do.
Charles Riley, Corporal.
Daniel Cogdail, Drummer.
Christian Crow, Fifer,

Privates.

Darby Brannon,
James Maloy,
William McCoy,
Rudy McCoy,
Garret Wagoner,
Samuel McClane,
Thomas Means,
Charles Dongan,
Thomas Johnston,
Thomas Payne,
Edward Davison,
James Graham,
Robert Allice,
William McIntire,
Thomas Dyke,
John Mellon,
Andrew Griffy,

Philip Brown,
John Allen,
Francis Curty,
William McDonald,
Charles McConnell,
William Brinnagan,
Edward McMullan,
John Heathrington,
James McGuire,
Joseph Chambers,
Daniel McGarrigan,
Lawrence Kerry,
John Cavanagh,
John Flinn,
Samuel Perry,
William Roberts.

CAPT. JEREMIAH TALBOTT'S COMPANY, AS IT STOOD NOV. 30, 1777.

Jeremiah Talbott, Captain.
Andrew Irvine, Lieutenant.
Joseph Torrance, do.
John McCollam, Ensign.
William Gibb, Sergeant.

Robert Hunter, Sergeant.
Thomas Whiteley, do.
Hugh Thompson, do.
John Smith, Corporal.

Privates.

Jacob Weaver,
Francis O'Hara,
Charles Conner,
William Foster,
Patt. Murray,
Felix O'Neal,
Charles Kelly,
James Rawls,
Daniel McCarty,
Joseph West,

Hugh Casady,
John McKinley,
Michael Pitzler,
Patt Boyle,
George Coghran,
James Lee,
John Johnson,
Andrew McGrahy,
Edward Hart,
John Curray.

CAPT. ALEXANDER PARKER'S COMPANY, AS IT STOOD NOV. 30, 1777.

Alexander Parker, Captain.
William Lusk, Lieutenant.
John Blair, do.
John Hughes, Ensign.
John Benniston, Sergeant.
George Hewett, do.

James McConn, Corporal.
Michael Madden, do.
George McPherson, do.
Edward McGinnis, Drummer.
William Price, Fifer.

Privates.

John McMichael,
Cumberland Hamilton,
Henry Gawin,
John Carney,
John Dugan,
William Intrican,
Hugh Call,
John Winn,
Michael Shields,
Peter Sheckel,
Andrew Craley,
William Carman,
Thomas McClain,

James Davidson,
Robert George,
Bartholomew McGuire,
Joseph Cenney,
Jacob Clouse,
John Hoar,
John Wright,
John Johnston,
Anthony Spinkhouse,
Robert Elliott,
Thomas Hunt,
John Tribble,
William Nicholson,

CAPT. JOHN MCDOWELL'S COMPANY, AS IT STOOD NOV. 1, 1777.

John McDowell, Captain.
William Miller, Lieutenant.
Robert McPherson, do.
James Milligan, Ensign.
Roger Gaff, Sergeant.

Adam Linn, Sergeant.
Thomas Gainer, do.
William Manly, Corporal.
Paul Conner, Drummer.

OFFICERS AND PRIVATES

Privates.

John Connolly,
James Quin,
Marly Sullivan,
James Welch,
William Bradshaw,
John Fanning,
John McCalloh,
Edward Welch,
Patt McKeehan,
Thomas Chesney,
Patt Keing,
Dennis Murphy,
Bartholomew Mulloy,

Philip Duffield,
Edward Atchison,
Henry Garman.
William Campbell,
Alex. McDaniel,
Daniel Conner,
Samuel Gilmore,
Michael Lenonagan,
John Walch,
George Blackley,
Neal McGunnagle,
James Johnston,
Solomon Silas.

CAPT. JOHN ALEXANDER'S COMPANY, AS IT STOOD NOV. 1, 1777.

John Alexander, Captain.
Robert Peebles, Lieutenant.
William Wilson, Ensign.
William McCormic, Sergeant.

John Nicholson, Sergeant.
Joshua Cochran, Corporal.
Matthew McConnell, do.
Robert Gregg, do.

Privates.

William Bruce,
John Benson,
William Marshall,
John Smith,
Philip Boyle,
Alexander Reid,
John Alexander,
Andrew Pinkerton,
George Patrick,
Thomas Johnston,
John Collins,
Robert Craighead,

John Todd,
Patrick McCue,
John Ford,
James Bonine,
John Hays,
Michael Hogan,
John Quin,
Henry Corman,
James Hamil,
Thomas Pezzy,
Kearns Kelly.

CAPT. WM. ALEXANDER'S COMPANY, AS IT STOOD NOV. 1, 1777.

William Alexander, Captain.
Samuel Kennedy, 1st-lieutenant.
Alexander Russell, 2d do.
Robert McWheeling, Ensign.
John Smith, Sergeant.
Joseph Wade, do.

Matthew Way, Sergeant.
William Gray, do.
George Brown, Corporal.
Joseph Rawlings, do.
James Hamilton, do.
Joseph Templeton, do.

OF THE REVOLUTIONARY WAR. 219

Privates.

James Berry,
John Brains,
Adam Conn,
John McCall,
Patt Rooney,
Cornelius Conigan,
William Wilkinson,
Henry Frett,
John Clemonds,
David Davis,
James Harkins,
James Donovan,

George Worley,
John McGinnis,
William Courtney,
Patt. McCormick,
Timothy Murphy,
William Guthrie,
Patt. McGonaghy,
William Anguish,
James Price,
Richard Henley,
Thomas McConn.

NAMES, RANK, DATES OF COMMISSIONS, AND TIME OF ENLISTMENT OF THE OFFICERS AND PRIVATES OF COL. ARMAND'S LEGION.

Charles Armand (Marquis de la Rouarie), Colonel. Commissioned May 10, 1777.
Count de Ottendorff, Major.
Jost Driesback, Captain. Commissioned February 22, 1777.
Anthony Selin, do. do. December 10, 1776.
—— Bauer, do. do. do.
Lieutenant De Howelman, Quartermaster. Commission Dec. 9, 1776.
John Paul Schott, Captain. Commissioned December 9, 1776.

COMPANY NO. 1.

Jost Driesback, Captain. Commissioned March 3, 1777.
Conrad Latur, First-lieutenant. Commissioned March 3, 1777.
Jacob Glaeton, Lieutenant. Commissioned March 3, 1777.
Henry Beats, Sargeant. Commissioned March 1, 1777.
Daniel Woible, Sergeant. Commissioned February 16, 1777.

Privates.

	Enlisted.		Enlisted.
Jacob Arner,	Feb. 21, 1777.	John Reaty,	Mar. 15, 1777.
John Reity,	do.	Daniel Shitz,	Mar. 31, 1777.
Richard Richardson,	do.	John Keisty,	April 1, 1777.
Peter Gruber,	Feb. 24, 1777.	John Koehler,	April 2, 1777.
Jacob Long,	Feb. 25, 1777.	John Wint,	do.
Jacob Hess,	Feb. 26, 1777.	John Kinkings,	do.
Henry Keck,	do.	George Kearn,	April 5, 1777.
Adam Brandhefer,	do.	Daniel Koad,	April 10, 1777.
Oliver Moles,	Mar. 1, 1777.	Martin Brechel,	April 20, 1777.
Christian Shitz,	Mar. 2, 1777.	John Arner,	do.
Jacob Miller,	Mar. 3, 1777.	Eberhardt Hahl,	April 29, 1777.
Jacob Frey,	Mar. 15, 1777.		

OFFICERS AND PRIVATES

COUNT DE OTTENDORFF'S COMPANY.

	Enlisted.		*Enlisted.*
Johannes Mitchel,	April 20, 1777.	William Toliver,	Feb. 1, 1777.
Hans Georg Klein,	April 21, 1777.	Isaac Haal,	Feb. 8, 1777.
Andreas Sturnburt,	April 6, 1777.	John Walter,	Jan. 28, 1777.
Christian Casseur,	April 7, 1777.	John Green,	Feb. 8, 1777.
Robert Stuart,	April 24, 1777.	James Dreiskoll,	Feb. 10, 1777.
Joseph Outbridge,	April 25, 1777.	Andreas Bengell,	do.
Jacob Hess,	do.	Michael Berry,	do.
Johann G. Neunrich,	April 26, 1777.	John Bengell,	Feb. 20, 1777.
Johannes Hoffman,	April 27, 1777.	George Fill,	Feb. 22, 1777.
George Stepper,	April 27, 1777.	John Thomson,	Feb. 17, 1777.
Philip Weber,	April 28, 1777.	John Schuh,	Jan. 20, 1777.
Henreich Shaffer,	Mar. 1, 1777.	Henreich Bartholome,	Mar. 1, 1777.
Henry Beatz,	do.	John Hawkins,	Jan. 10, 1777.
Jacob Ofner,	Feb. 21, 1777.	John Trow,	Mar. 22, 1777.
Peter Gruver,	Feb. 24, 1777.	Philip Grimm,	Mar. 11, 1777.
Henrich Donich,	do.	Wilhelm Dorn,	Mar. 22, 1777.
Geo. Laughramer,	Jan. 23, 1777.	Henrich Donich,	Dec. 10, 1776.
Charles Geisinger,	Jan. 13, 1777.	Arnold Loos,	Dec. 21, 1776.
Matthias Güntzell,	Mar. 1, 1777.	Jacob Kern,	Dec. 23, 1776.
John Blum,	Jan. 14, 1777.	Edmond Lynch,	Jan. 10, 1777.
Valentine Keyser,	Jan. 17, 1777.	John Morgin,	Jan. 19, 1777.
George Marcks,	Jan. 24, 1777.	James Sorfil,	Jan. 23, 1777.
Jeams Reichway,	Jan. 6, 1777.	Jacob Ferngold,	Feb. 8, 1777.
John Philips,	Jan. 17, 1777.	Christian Fels,	do.
John Roch,	Jan. 25, 1777.	Pierre Triest,	Feb. 7, 1777.
Samuel Murden,	Jan. 27, 1777.	James Brucks,	do.
John Darrel,	do.	John Geisinger,	Mar. 16, 1777.
George Rex,	Jan. 30, 1777.	Alexander Black,	Feb. 9, 1777.
Christopher Bagal,	do.	Adolph Grieslins,	Mar. 1, 1777.

COMPANY NO. 2.

Anthony Selins, Captain.
Lawrence Myers, Lieutenant.
Christian Froelick, do.
Arnold Loose, Volunteer.
Philip Strubine, do.
Henrich De Gevricourt, do.
Henrich Luders, Sergeant.

Henrich Bartolomia, Sergeant.
John Blum, do.
Valentine Keiser, do.
George Marks, Corporal.
John Walter, do.
John Schu, Drummer.
John Tomson, Fifer.

Privates.

Henrich Donig,
Jeams Rigeway,
John Philips,
John Roge,
Samuel Murden,
Mathias Gengill,
John Darrell,
Michael Berry,
William Durn,
John Bengell,

George Rex,
Isaac Haal,
John Green,
Thomas Driswall,
Andrew Bengell,
Daniel Klein,
John Trow,
George Deal,
John Eberts,
William Marks.

COMPANY NO. 3.

John Paul Schott, Captain.
Christian Mancke, Lieutenant.
George Schaffner, Lieutenant.
Fredrich Liebe, Sergeant.
George Dean, Sergeant.

George Langeamer, Sergeant.
Frederich Bargman, Corporal.
David Breckle, do.
John Gedeke, do.
John Woodbridge, Drummer.

Privates.

Tui Cromwell,
George Kearing,
Peter Corback,
Henry Mincks,
Tobias Ritter,
Andony Leopard,
John Haal,

Jacob Phaltzer,
Jacob Reiner,
John Plesch,
Johnson Borwell,
Charles Weels,
Gabriel Vilein,
Nadaniel Johns.

COMPANY NO. 4.

Jacob Bauer, Captain.
Baron De Wehtritz, Lieut.
John Sharp, do.
Jacob Young, Sergeant.

George Bamburg, Sergeant.
John Mannerson, Corporal.
Andrew Homberg, do.
Andrew Ransier, Drummer.

Privates.

Oliver Moles,
George Eirig,
John Sheperd,
Godfrey Niemerich,
Jonathan Lynch,
William Roak,
John Geisel,
John Pattis,
Jacob Shaver,

John Mitchell,
George Klein,
Charles Feidler,
Andrew Reboarg,
Peter Gruber,
John Walsch,
Charles Butner,
Adam Sypert,
Jacob Ferncorn.

OFFICERS AND PRIVATES

NAMES AND RANK OF THE OFFICERS AND PRIVATES OF THE THIRD VACANT COMPANY OF THE GERMAN REGIMENT OF PENNSYLVANIA, COMMANDED BY COL. LEWIS WELTNER, AS IT STOOD AT VALLEY FORGE, IN MARCH, 1778.

Philip Graybell, Captain. Resigned March 12, 1778.
William Rice, First-lieutenant.
Martin Sugart, Second-lieutenant.
William Rumelson, Sergeant.

Frederick Sollars, Sergeant.
George Stouffer, do.
Joseph Hook, Corporal.
Jacob Etter, do.

Privates.

Ferdinand Lorants,
Michael Crowley,
Anthony Miller,
John Schlife,
John Eisell,
Michael Kershner,
John Harley,
Fred. Wm. Haller,
Jacob Myers,
John Schaffer,
Philip Shautz,
Wolgong Ebsberger,
Wendle Laurentz,
Henry Smith,
Nicholas Keiser,
Rudolph Crower,

Joseph Williams,
Abraham Frantz,
George Lighhiser,
David Mumma,
James Caple,
Peter Baker,
Jacob Meily,
John Schryock,
William Craft,
Joseph Striber,
Paul Esling,
George Cretho,
David Finck,
John Smith,
Henry Rumfelt,
Michael Huling,

NAMES AND RANK OF THE INVALID REGIMENT OF PENNSYLVANIA, COMMANDED BY COLONEL LEWIS NICOLA, AS IT WAS DISCHARGED, APRIL, 1783.

Lewis Nicola, Colonel.
Thomas Arnold, Captain.
Moses McFarland, do.
John McGowan, do.
John Riely, do.
Ebenezer Hills, do.
William McHatton, Capt. Lieut.
Jonathan Pugh, Lieut. and Adjutant.
Osgood Carleton, Lieut. and Qt. Mast.
Matthew Maus, Surgeon.
Christopher Taylor, Surgeon's Mate.

Talmadge Hall, Lieut. and Paymaster.
Samuel Gibbs, Lieutenant.
Robert Barnett, do.
William Maynard, do.
Philip Leibert, Captain.
John D. Woelper, do.
William Williams, do.
Leonard Cooper, do.
Eli Sterors, Sergeant-major.
David Hillyer, Qt. Mast.'s Sergeant.
Robert Hunter, Drum-major.

OF THE REVOLUTIONARY WAR. 223

Privates and others.

George Ceely, Sergeant.
Andrew Dunlap, do.
John Sullivan, do.
Andrew Deal, do.
William Wear, do.
James Hunter, Corporal.
Stephen Chapman. do.
Willard Pierce, Corporal.
Ichabod Coe, Fifer.
Thomas Abbott,
Michael Bazel,
Anthony Benford,
Luke Brady,
Jeremiah Belcher,
Thomas Brackett,
Robert Clark,
John Campbell,
Benjamin Cheshire,
Alexander Dickey,
Duncan Frazer,
Peter Fitzpatrick,
Enos Frankinson,
Cato Freeman,
Cash Finney,
Robert Freemoult,
James Foster,
John Groves,
Joseph Harrop,
John Harris,
Jonathan Hubard,
Matthew Kelly,
George Krottle,
Peter Liddington,
Henry Lawson,
Robert Lynn
John Leigher,
Roger McCullough,
Paul McTall,
John McGunghey,
William McAllister,
John McConnell,
John McKewing,
Bazley Moffett,
William Pinnard,
William Ryan,
John Rowland.
Bartlett Robinson,
John Robins,
Lawrence Smith,
John Smith,
Nathan Stiles,
Samuel Thompson,

Edward Tobin,
Peter Thompson,
Edward Welch,
Joseph Welch,
Timothy Conner, Corporal.
William Barkhill, Sergeant.
Edward Franklin, do.
Jonah Malting, Corporal.
John Baily, Drummer.
Robert Baker.
James Barklor,
Peter Collins,
John Dismond,
Joshua Gray,
George Hansell,
John Hackett,
Asa Hays,
Stephen Luddleton,
John Murray,
Mark Martin,
Elisha Munsell,
John Owens,
James Serdon,
Asa Seymour,
John Mundin, Sergeant.
Thomas Gerald, do.
John Price, do.
John Bristol, do.
John Keating, Corporal.
John Mundin, Drummer.
Peter Mundin, do.
Frederick Boardman, Fifer.
Joel Beers,
William Tomlinson,
Michael Berry,
Judah Bills,
Nicholas Bartrum,
Daniel Bragden,
John Corbett,
Barnabas Dougherty,
John Delaguin.
Joseph Freeman,
William Feagan,
John Freelove,
Samuel Hodgins,
Southwick Hubbard,
William Johnston,
Martin Jordan,
James Lipscomb,
David Lincoln,
Lawrence Morfee,
James McCarapher,

OFFICERS AND PRIVATES

John McDonald,
Peter McCoy,
Dan Mansfield,
Patrick Marr,
Rufus Newport,
James Nicholas,
John O'Neal,
John Nutting,
Asa Porter,
Samuel Pike,
William Putrin,
Francis Pollard,
Philip Richardson,
James Rankin,
Zubil Stone,
James Taylor,
Ebenezer Waterman,
Caleb Woods,
Margaret Corbin,
Peter Willard,
Gideon Noble, Corporal.
William Rider,
Moses Boardman,
Edward Bates,
John Neal,
Elijah Davis,
Richard Hubbard,
Thomas Langman,
John Dunovan,
Joseph Chieney,
John Cappy,
Samuel Davis,
Isaac Ebbert,
John Holden,
Thomas Langman,
Andrew McGuire,
Elisha Molton,
Samuel Pith,
John Spencer,
John Demmon,
John Needham, Sergeant.
Joseph Gongon,
Samuel Potter, Sergeant.

John Heath, Corporal.
Samuel Whitney, do.
James Riley, Fifer.
Ben Abro,
Amos Barnes,
John Beardsworth,
Benjamin Bachelor,
John Cannon,
Gershom Corwin,
Michael Cambler,
Timothy Chellas,
Edward Crowell,
John Davidson,
Barnabas Davidson,
James Fuller,
Thomas Goldthraite,
Thomas Glawson,
Samuel Hadlock,
Bazaleel Hamlin,
Richard Hazard,
Tower Hill,
John Hutching,
Rufus Harrington,
Thomas King,
John Knowlton,
Isaac Lovejoy,
William Messer,
Seth Moore,
William Morgan,
William Osburn,
William Pitts,
Robert Patterson,
Lloyd Powell,
John Perkins,
Sieby Richmond,
John Rich,
John Taylor,
Joseph Stacey,
Oliver Simmons,
John Spry,
William Watrous,
Joseph Waterman,
Nicholas Weasel,

OF THE REVOLUTIONARY WAR. 225

Hiber Smith, Sergeant.
Jeremiah Howe, do.
William Coombs, do.
Gerard Craig, Corporal.
Peter Alexander,
Moses Barns,
Peter Babb,
Josiah Braman,
Daniel Barnett,
William Cambell,
Jesse Danforth,
Michael Drake,
Timothy Howard,
Samuel Pottage,
Robert Richardson,
Seth Warren,
James Wraland,
Thomas Nichols,
Caleb Orcutt, Sergeant.
Jeremiah Lord, do.
James Nevice, Corporal.
Daniel McDougall, do.
Charles Perkins, do.
Joseph Wheeler, do.
John Clough, do.
Samuel Sumner, Drummer.
Michael Greene, Fifer,
Thomas Andrews,
Gideon Allen,
Joseph Bryington,
John Brown,
Thomas Clues,
Elisha Cole,
John Cross,
Enoch Curtis,
Stephen Calliff,
John A. Dager,
Zebulon Fuller,
Elias Greenleaf,
Ephraim Goodenough,
Clark Gibbs,

Moses George,
Richard Hill,
Samuel Holmes,
William Hancock,
Samuel Hunt,
Cæsar Hall,
Matthew Jamison,
Epes Jewett,
Ezra King,
Charles King,
Thomas Loveland,
John Ludaman,
Elijah Nutting,
Russell Oliver,
Richard Patten,
Samuel Farrer,
Jonathan Goldthaite,
John McCoy,
Christian Powers,
Edward Powers,
Thomas Reynolds,
Owen Reeck,
Robert Smith,
Elijah Taylor,
Benjamin Ward,
William Welsh,
Cato Wayman,
Elijah Bliss, Sergeant.
Timothy Culver, do.
Jonathan Andrews, Corporal.
Joseph Bond,
Jotham Wood,
Henry McNeal,
John Brannon,
Josiah Brackett,
Phinehas Collar,
Thomas Dakin,
James Fuller,
Stephen Ludlow,
James Phillips,
Landon Sawyer.

NAMES OF OFFICERS OF THE PENNSYLVANIA LINE ENGAGED IN THE RE-CRUITING SERVICE, THE NAMES OF THE REGIMENTS RECRUITED, AND THE AMOUNT PAID FOR RECRUITING.

Nicholas Housaker, Colonel German Regiment..........................£825
Col. William Cook, 12th Pa. Regiment, recruiting in 1776................2825

OFFICERS AND PRIVATES

Lieut. Colonel George Nagle, recruiting	Col. Irvine's Regiment in 1776.		1500
Capt. Matthew Henderson,	do.	same Regiment in 1776........	75
Col. Jos. Wood & Capt. Hellings,	do.	his Regiment in 1776............	187
Capt. John Davis,	do.	do. do.	75
Col. Thomas Hartley,	do.	7th Regiment, do.	1125
Col. Francis Johnston,	do.	4th Regiment, do.	375
Lieut. Amos Wilkinson,	do.	Col. de Haas' Regiment in 1776	200
Lieut. Samuel Talbert,	do.	do. do.	187
Lieut. William Moore,	do.	do. do.	75
Col. Eneas McCoy,	do.	8th Pa. Regiment, do.	3000
Capt. Stephen Bayard,	do.	3d Pa. Regiment, do.	375
Capt. Robert Connelly,	do.	4th Pa. Regiment, do.	112
Capt. Stephen Bayard,	do.	Col. Wood's Regiment, do.	375
Lieut. Colonel George Nagle,	do.	Col. Irvine's Regiment, do.	187
Lieut. Thomas Boude,	do.	Col. Wayne's Regiment, do.	112
Capt. Robert Connolly,	do.	Col.Cadwallader's Regt.,do.	536
Col. William Cook,	do.	his own Regiment, do.	750
Lieut. Thomas B. Bowen,	do.	service in 1777	375
Capt. William Gray,	do.	Col.Cadwallader's Regt.,do.	337
Major Francis Nichols,	do.	1st Regiment, do.	75
Capt. James Parr,	do.	do. do.	75
Lieut. Colonel Henry Beeker,	do.	6th Pa. Regiment, do.	750
Capt. Benjamin Bird,	do.	Col.Cadwallader's Regt.,do.	375
Col. Samuel Cadwallader,	do.	his own Regiment, do.	1500
Capt. Jeremiah Talbott,	do.	7th Pa. Regiment, do.	93
Capt. Francis Nichols,	do.	9th Pa. Regiment, do.	187
Major Persifor Frazer,	do.	4th Pa. Regiment, do.	375
Major Samuel Benezett,	do.	6th Pa. Regiment, do.	1500
Capt. Caleb North,	do.	4th Pa. Regiment, do.	375
Capt. John Pugh,	do.	2d Pa. Regiment, do.	158
Capt. Alex. Ramsey,	do.	his Independent Co., do.	112
Lieut. Colonel David Grier,	do.	7th Pa. Regiment, do.	4500
Lieut. Colonel William Butler,	do.	4th Pa. Regiment, do.	1500
Major Meriam Lamar,	do.	do. do.	937
Col. Adam Hubley,	do.	10th Pa. Regiment, do.	937
Capt. James Lang,	do.	service, do.	375
Capt. William Oldham,	do.	5th Pa. Regiment, do.	375
Col. James Chambers,	do.	1st Pa. Regiment, do.	1500
Capt. Michael Hoofnagle,	do.	8th Pa. Regiment, do.	112
Col. Thomas Craig,	do.	3d Pa. Regiment, do.	281
Lieut. Archibald Campbell,	do.	6th Pa. Regiment, do.	300
Capt. John Riley,	do.	service, do.	150
Capt. Jacob Humphreys,	do.	6th Pa. Regiment, do.	187
Major Samuel Benezett,	do.	do. do.	187
Capt. Samuel Williams,	do.	13th Pa. Regiment, do.	18
Capt. John Harris,	do.	12th Pa. Regiment, do.	356

OF THE REVOLUTIONARY WAR. 227

Major De Ottendorff, for his pay as Adjutant in 1776	£75
Lieut. B. Neilly, for recruiting service in 1779	$300
Capt. Van Swearingen, do. do.	2500
Capt. Samuel Dawson, do. do.	1760

Paid by Colonel Daniel Brodhead.

Joseph Skelton, his pay as Assist. Com. Purchases in 1779	885
Caleb Calvin, his pay as Indian Interpreter, do.	74
John Montour, do. do. do.	115
William Cooper, Ensign, for recruiting, do.	3040
William Brady, his pay as Indian Interpreter, do.	1100
Charles Bradford, his pay as Assistant Qr. Mr., do.	1100

NAMES AND RANK OF THE OFFICERS AND PRIVATES OF CAPTAIN JOHN C. JONES' COMPANY OF THE 7TH MARYLAND REGIMENT, COMMANDED BY COL. JOHN GUNBY, AS IT STOOD JUNE 1, 1778.

John C. Jones, Captain.
Wm. Lamar, First-lieutenant.
Wm. Adams, Second do.
Geoge Ford, Sergeant.
Richard Bryan, Corporal.
James Johnson, do.
Richard Harrison, Fifer.

Privates.

Benjamin Fitzgerald,
Charles Ramsey,
Joseph Hart,
James McGurk,
Alexander Ross,
Benjamin Annis,
Richard Dixon,
John Jeans,
William Parker,
Ignatius Wheeler,
William Love,
Walter Maddox,
William Barrett,
Samuel Purnell,
Thomas Wright,
Joseph Finch.

NAMES, RANK, AND DATES OF COMMISSIONS OF THE OFFICERS OF CAPT. WILLIAM BROWN'S MARYLAND ARTILLERY, WITH A LIST OF THE PRIVATES, AS IT STOOD FROM NOV. 22, 1777, TO FEB. 5, 1778.

William Brown, Captain. Commissioned November 22, 1777.
James Smith, Captain-lieutenant. Commissioned November 22, 1777.
James McFadden, First-lieutenant. Commissioned November 22, 1777.
Clement Skerritt, Second-lieutenant. Commissioned February 5, 1778.
Appointed Quartermaster December 6, 1779.

OFFICERS AND PRIVATES

Non-commissioned Officers who joined the Company Nov. 22, 1777.

Sergeants for Three Years.

Thomas Collins,
John Staples,
James Adams,

Henry Slack,
Thomas Barber,
Patrick Corcoran.

Corporals for Three Years.

Thomas Carpenter,
Charles Sutton,
Charles Steward,

William Roebuck,
Hans Adams,
William Brady.

Drum and Fife for Three Years.

James Brooks,

John Carroll.

Bombardiers for Three Years.

Arthur Carnes,
Thomas Fanning,
John Radcliff,

George Baker,
Tamer Spencer,
Matthew Adams,

Gunners for Three Years.

Michael Hawke,
William Jones,
William Bright,

Thomas Condrall,
James Simmons,
Michael O'Bryan.

Matrosses for Three Years.

John Evans,
Thomas Smith,
Darby Spelcy,
William Hickinson,
Philip O'Brian,
Michael Hughes,
James Moril,
John Fearall,
Robert Campbell,
Francis Popham,
John Dixon,
Jonathan Gill,
John Brigham,
Joseph Poague,
Daniel Havey,
Peter Lawrence,
Patrick Coursey,
Henry Higgs,
Benjamin Patmore,
John Vaughn,
Jerrard Tippelt,
Mays Neville,

John Burke,
John Connelly,
James Carwin,
John Rhodes,
Joseph Deale,
John Slack,
John Saunders,
Francis Johnson,
Ignatius Butler (negro),
William Johnson,
Reuben Scott,
James Welch,
Ignatius Griffin,
James Cole,
Charles Dowde,
James Whaling,
Thomas Carter,
James Royston,
James Compton,
Hugh Champlain,
David Young,
Timothy Connolly.

OF THE REVOLUTIONARY WAR.

John Reynolds,	John Lynch,
Isaac Burton,	Thomas Wilson,
William Dyer,	John Folks,
John Walker,	John Head,
Charles Groome,	Joshua Lovely,
William Connolly,	James Taylor,
Robert Smith,	Edward Jefferson,
Mark Goldsborough,	Daniel Frazier,
John Fitzgerald, sen.,	James Clark,
John Fitzgerald, jun.,	John Traner,
Charles Murat,	Dennis Minor,
James Ford,	Richard Page,
William Davis,	(Deserted Jan. 4, 1778.)

CAPT. WILLIAM BROWN'S COMPANY OF MARYLAND ARTILLERY, AS IT STOOD ON THE HIGH HILLS OF THE SANTEE, AUG. 1, 1781.

William Brown, Captain. On command at Camden. Superintending the Hospital since July 18, 1781.
James Smith, Captain-lieutenant.
James McFadden, First-lieutenant.
Clement Skerritt, Second-lieutenant. On furlough to Maryland.
John Carson, Second-lieutenant. Commissioned May 1, 1779. Transferred to Captain Singleton January 1, 1781.

Sergeants.

Henry Slack,	John Vaughn,
Charles Steward,	Thomas Barber.]
John Slack,	

Corporals.

Michael Hawke,	Thomas Fanning,
Thomas Condron,	Lemuel J. Nelmes,
James Royston,	Tamolin Spencer.
John Radcliff,	

Bombardiers.

Michael O'Brian,	William Jones.
Philip O'Brian,	

Gunners.

James Welch,	James Whalen.
James Morel,	

Drum and Fife.

Peter Mayner,	James Brooks.

OFFICERS AND PRIVATES

Matrosses.

Thomas Brown,	William Davis,
Isaac Burton,	Charles Groome,
Arthur Carnes,	John Head,
John Fitzgerald, jr.,	Charles Muret,
Jonathan Gill,	Thomas Smith,
Henry Higgs,	Charles Sutton,
Daniel Havey,	James Simonds,
Francis Johnston,	Peter Robinson,
Robert Livingston,	Benjamin Patmore.
Joshua Lovely,	James Navin,
John Reynolds,	Mays Nevin,
Peter Lawrence,	William Moran,
James Clark,	Edward Hennessy,
John Evans,	John Fitzgerald, sen.,
Joseph Pogue,	James Henry,
Robert Myers,	(Joined Jan. 18, 1781.)
(From Jan. 1, 1781.)	John Gilman,
John Sellman,	(Joined Jan. 18, 1781.)
(From Jan. 30, 1781.)	Ignatius Butler,
William Stalker,	Francis Popham,
Robert Smith,	(Killed at Augusta.)
David Young,	Thomas Stanley, Cadet.
Reuben Scott,	(Died Aug. 6, 1781.)
Timothy Connolly,	

NOTE.—Captain Brown's Company was located at Valley Forge until June, 1778; at White Plains, July 1778; at Fort Schuyler, August and September, 1780; at High Hills of the Santee, in August, 1781; at Col. Scirvins, January, 1782; and at Bacon's Bridge, S. C., in April, 1782.

NAMES, RANK, AND DATES OF COMMISSIONS OF THE OFFICERS OF CAPT. RICHARD DORSEY'S COMPANY OF MARYLAND ARTILLERY, WITH A LIST OF THE PRIVATES, AS IT STOOD AT VALLEY FORGE JUNE 8, 1778.

Richard Dorsey, Captain. Commissioned May 4, 1777.
Ebenezer Finley, Captain-lieutenant. Commissioned July 4, 1777.
Robert Wilmott, First-lieutenant. Commissioned November 24, 1777.
Nicholas Ricketts, Second-lieutenant. Commissioned December 1, 1777.
Young Wilkinson, Second-lieutenant. Commissioned February 25, 1778.

Sergeants for One Year.

Samuel Thompson,	John Wheeler,
John Howard,	James Rice,
David Walsh,	Robert Thompson.

Corporals for One Year.

Thomas Neilson,
Philip Jones,
David White,

William Delaney,
Thomas Smith,
John Wilkins.

Drummer, Henry Kelliker.

Bombardiers for One Year.

John Pierson,
David Maroney,

Alexander McMullan,
John Clarke.

Gunners for One Year.

Timothy Donovan,
Daniel Donogue,
John Turner,

Thomas Grainger,
John Brady,
John Ackerly.

Matrosses for One Year.

Dennis Flannegan,
Edward Coughland,
James Berry,
Patrick Shoughness,
John Bryant,
John Jallome,
John Sandall,
Howel Lewis,
William Grimes,
William Reed,
William Day,
William Wade,
Frederick Pine,
Andrew Shrink,
Roger O'Donald,
Robert Britt,
John Fitzpatrick,

Hugh McDowell
Richard Wilkinson,
Daniel Redden,
Freeman Newman,
Matthew Kelly,
Daniel Neil,
James Jack,
Thomas Randall,
Michael Connor,
Thomas Pierce,
Mathew McMahan,
John Taylor
Stephen Fennel,
John Handlin,
William Forbes,
Bryan Ferrel,

CAPT. RICHARD DORSEY'S COMPANY OF MARYLAND ARTILLERY, AS IT STOOD IN "CAMP COL. SCIRVIN'S," JAN. 28, 1782.

Richard Dorsey, Captain. Prisoner of War, on parole in Maryland.
James Smith, Captain-lieutenant. Joined from Captain Brown's Company, December 24, 1781.
Ebenezer Finley, Captain-lieutenant.
Robert Wilmott, First-lieutenant. On furlough in Maryland.
James Bacques,   do.   do.   do.
Nicholas Ricketts, Second-lieutenant.   do.   do.

OFFICERS AND PRIVATES

Young Wilkinson, Second-lieutenant. Sick in hospital at Boon's Plantation.
Isaac Rawlins, do. On furlough in Maryland.
John Cheever, do. do. do.

Sergeants for the War.

Jesse Thompson, | Samuel Carter.
William Rawlins, | Richard Lewis,
James Hatton, | William Morgan,
William Cornwall,

Corporals for the War.

James Hammond, | Rawleigh Spinks,
William Hutton,

Bombardiers for the War.

Dennis McCormac, | William Dixon,
William Hillen, | John Clark, Gunner.

Drum and Fife.

Thomas Williams, | Thomas Patten,
Elisha Redman, | Peter Davis,

Matrosses for the War.

Perregrine Askew, | John Prout,
Michael Connor, | Thomas Redman,
Thomas Gleeson, | Thomas Randall,
Cornelius Harling, | Bennet Rayley,
John Ireland, | Andrew Shrink,
Philip Masterson, | John Sandall,
James Neale, | Edward Berry,
Michael O'Farrell, | Benedict Johnson,
John Payne, | John Stanley,
Thomas Bowler, | John Smith,
John Compton, | Daniel Redden,
Philip Jones, | Hugh McDowell,
John Clark, | John Owens.

NAMES AND RANK OF THE OFFICERS AND PRIVATES TO WHOM DEPRECIATION ON THEIR PAY WAS MADE UP BY THE STATE OF MARYLAND, THE TIME PAID FOR, AND THE AMOUNT PAID.

              For Service from   £. s. d.
John B. Ainsworthy, private.......April 22, 1777, to Aug. 1, 1780...... 81 10 4
Robert Britt, Matross............Jan. 1, 1777, to Aug. 1, 1780........ 104 5 3
Mountjoy Bailey, Captain..........Jan. 1, 1777, to Sept. 14, 1780...... 205 12 0

OF THE REVOLUTIONARY WAR. 233

	For Service from	£.	s.	d.
Joshua Broughton, private	Jan. 1, 1777, to Dec. 31, 1779	68	17	9
Thomas Burrows, private	Jan. 1, 1777, to April 4, 1777	8	9	4
Thomas Boarman, private	June 15, 1779, to Aug. 1, 1780	81	17	5
James Carvin, private	Dec. 4, 1776, to Dec. 10, 1779	69	11	5
Nicholas Cissell, private	Jan. 27, 1780, to Aug. 1, 1780	15	1	8
Mordecai Cooley, private	April 26, 1779, to Aug. 1, 1780	35	15	5
Robert Cooley, private	May 20, 1778, to Oct. 6, 1778	8	13	0
William Carroll, private	Mar. 20, 1777, to Jan. 20, 1779	40	9	1
Philip Culloch, Private	Jan. 1, 1777, to Oct. 1, 1777	12	12	9
Bartholomew Callahan, private	Dec. 1776, to Dec. 6, 1779	68	2	0
Michael Connor, Sergeant	Jan. 29, 1777, to Jan. 29, 1780	82	14	11
Cornelius Downey, Corporal	Jan. 15, 1777, to June 28, 1778	30	15	6
Hugh Doyle, Sergeant	Dec. 6, 1776, to Dec. 9, 1779	84	4	8
Thomas Davis, private	Mar. 7, 1777, to Aug. 1, 1780	84	16	8
John Donent, private	April 28, 1777, to April 28, 1780	73	17	8
Dennis Downey, private	Mar. 13, 1777, to April 1, 1780	75	12	4
Edward Edwards, Ensign	Dec. 10, 1776, to Nov. 1, 1777	42	5	0
Benjamin Freshwater, private	June 1. 1779, to Aug. 1, 1780	38	9	6
John Gill, private	May 21, 1777, to Feb. 1, 1779	38	5	4
Leonard Gates, private	June 1, 1778, to Aug. 1, 1780	58	8	4
John Hartlove, private	Dec. 10, 1776, to Aug. 1, 1780	86	0	0
Samuel Hamilton, Sergeant	Dec. 10, 1776, to May 27, 1779	70	16	2
Andrew Hagerty, Fifer	Mar. 13, 1777, to Mar. 13, 1780	79	9	8
Jacob Hazlewood, private	Aug. 9, 1776, to Aug. 9, 1779	55	12	10
William Harper, private	Mar. 19, 1778, to Jan. 9, 1779	19	7	9
John Hall, private	Mar. 18, 1778, to Jan. 24, 1779	20	9	10
Thomas Jones, private	May 1, 1777, to Aug. 1, 1780	81	11	8
Benjamin Johnson, private	Oct. 9, 1778, to Aug. 1, 1780	50	1	4
James Jones, Drummer	April 20, 1779, to Aug. 1, 1780	39	19	5
Lewis Jones, Fifer	April 5, 1779, to Dec. 1, 1779	19	16	7
Benjamin Kidwell, private	May 26, 1778, to Aug. 1, 1780	58	15	0
Patrick Kelly, Corporal	Jan. 1, 1777, to July 24, 1779	64	15	0
John Kline, private	Oct. 12, 1776, to Oct 12, 1779	62	17	9
George Kelly, private	Mar. 14, 1777, to April 14, 1780	74	18	4
Robert Livingston, Matross	Nov. 1, 1779, to Aug. 1, 1780	27	7	1
Francis W. Luckett, Corporal	Dec. 10, 1776, to April 16, 1778	27	2	1
John Lanham, private	Dec. 10, 1776, to Dec. 27, 1779	68	13	2
David Lawler, private	Feb. 5, 1777, to Aug. 1, 1780	83	0	6
Martin Mudd, Sergeant	May 10, 1777, to May 27, 1778	37	1	8
Henry Mudd, Corporal	May 21, 1777, to Nov. 1, 1777	9	9	6
Daniel McIntire, private	Jan. 1, 1777, to Aug. 1, 1780	84	0	0
Ennals Martin, Surgeon's Mate	June 1, 1777, to Feb. 16, 1780	475	10	0
Jacob Miller, private	July 20, 1776, to July 20, 1779	56	15	3
John Mails, private	July 1, 1777, to July 31, 1780	73	11	8
Frederick Mire, private	Dec. 10, 1776, to Dec. 27, 1779	68	13	2

OFFICERS AND PRIVATES

	For Service from	£.	s.	d.
Barney McManus, private	Jan. 1, 1777, to Aug. 1, 1780	86	0	0
Ignatius Martin, private	Mar. 18, 1777, to Aug. 27, 1777	8	5	0
Moses McNew, private	Dec. 10, 1776, to Aug. 1, 1780	63	0	0
Walter Maddox, private	Mar. 9, 1777, to June 28, 1778	30	4	4
James Murphy, private	Mar. 18, 1778, to July 20, 1778	8	0	2
Andrew Malone, private	Jan. 10, 1777, to Jan. 10, 1780	75	8	5
William Ormond, private	May 1, 1777, to July 5, 1778	25	7	1
David Plunkett, Capt. of Dragoons	Jan. 20, 1777, to Mar. 1, 1779	343	9	10
William Parsons, private	April 20, 1777, to Aug. 1, 1780	82	1	8
John Pickering, private	Feb. 13, 1778, to Aug. 1, 1780	65	9	8
Jacob Palmer, private	May 5, 1779, to Aug. 1, 1780	35	1	1
Benjamin Posey, private	Oct. 10, 1777, to Feb. 23, 1779	32	9	6
James Quay, private	Feb. 15, 1778, to July 16, 1779	35	7	2
Henry Quiggins, private	May 30, 1777, to Nov. 16, 1777	9	3	2
John Richardson, Drummer	Mar. 15, 1780, to Aug. 1, 1780	12	6	5
Jacob Strapp, private	Feb. 24, 1777, to Feb. 24, 1780	72	0	2
John Sheridine, private	Mar. 6, 1777, to Mar. 2, 1780	71	17	9
William Spaulding, private	Jan. 1, 1778, to Nov. 26, 1778	21	10	3
Clement Sewell, Ensign	Mar. 4, 1777, to Sept. 14, 1777	63	17	1
William Spalding, private	June 1, 1777, to Dec. 31, 1777	11	14	2
Alexander Scott, Sergeant	Dec. 8, 1776, to Dec. 8, 1779	22	19	0
Elisha Steel, private	Feb. 24, 1777, to Feb. 20, 1780	73	6	2
Roger Skiffington, private	Jan. 10, 1778, to Aug. 1, 1780	67	15	0
Daniel Skelly, Corporal	Dec. 6, 1776, to Dec. 6. 1779	76	0	0
Robert Tongue, private	June 6, 1778, to Aug. 1, 1780	58	0	10
Thomas Taylor, private	Mar. 19, 1778, to Oct. 1, 1778	12	11	4
William Taylor, Sergeant	Mar. 1, 1777, to Jan. 26, 1779	59	2	8
Samuel Taylor, Fifer	April 22, 1778, to Aug. 1, 1780	67	6	3
Zephaniah Williams, private	May 2, 1778, to Aug. 1, 1780	60	7	0
Thomas Yates, Matross	Jan. 1, 1777, to Aug. 1, 1780	82	3	2

Names, Rank, and Dates of Commissions of the Officers of the Five Regiments of Maryland, as they stood June 1, 1781.

FIRST REGIMENT.

Otho H. Williams, Colonel. Commissioned January 1, 1777.
John Stewart, Lieutenant-colonel. Commissioned February 10, 1781.
John Eccleston, Major. Commissioned December 10, 1777.

Captains.

	Commissioned.		Commissioned.
Jonathan Sellman,	Jan. 10, 1777.	William Reily,	Oct. 13, 1777.
Edward Teall,	June 10, 1777.	John Sprigg Belt,	Dec. 15, 1777.

OF THE REVOLUTIONARY WAR. 285

	Commissioned.			*Commissioned.*
Christian Orendorf,	April 1, 1778.		Lloyd Beall,	Feb. 10, 1781
Richard Bird,	June 12, 1780.		Thomas B. Hugo,	June 12, 1781.
George Armstrong,	Feb. 11, 1780.			

Lieutenants.

William Lamar,	Nov. 15, 1777.		Hezekiah Ford,	Aug. 16, 1780.
James Ewing,	May 29, 1778.		John J. Lowe,	Jan. 20, 1781.
Jas. John Skinner,	Sept. 18, 1778.		Edward M. Smith,	Feb. 19, 1781.
Isaac Duvall,	April 10, 1779.		Samuel Edmiston,	Mar. 14, 1781.
John Hamilton,	June 1, 1779.		John Truman,	Mar. 16, 1781.
William Woolford,	Sept. 11, 1779.		Richard Pindell, Surgeon.	
William Raison,	Jan. 26, 1780.		Hezekiah Bayne, Mate.	
Joshua Burgess,	Mar. 11, 1780.			

SECOND REGIMENT.

John Gunby, Colonel. Commissioned April 17, 1777.
John Eager Howard, Lieutenant-colonel. Commissioned March 11, 1779.
John Dean, Major. Commissioned March 11, 1779.

Captains.

Alexander Trueman,	Jan. 1, 1777.		Thomas Mason,	June 8, 1779.
Jonathan Morris,	April 14, 1777.		John Gassaway,	April 2, 1780.
Walker Muse,	June 10, 1777.		Adam Hooper,	Mar. 16, 1781.
William Wilmott,	Oct. 15, 1777.		Samuel McPherson,	April 25, 1781.
John Jordan,	Dec. 26, 1777.			

Lieutenants.

Edward Dyer,	Sept. 10, 1780.		William Murdock.	April 1, 1780.
John A. Hamilton,	Feb. 1, 1778.		Zedekiah Moore,	Sept. 10, 1780.
Christop'r Richmond,	May 27, 1778.		Mark McPherson,	Jan. 1, 1781.
William Adams,	June 8, 1779.		Jacob Crawford,	Feb. 20, 1781.
Nicholas Gassaway,			William Smoot,	Mar. 16, 1781.
Arthur Harris,	Oct. 26, 1779.		James Arthur,	
Thomas Price,	Feb. 11, 1780.		Walter Warfield, Surgeon.	

THIRD REGIMENT.

Peter Adams, Lieutenant-colonel. Commissioned August 1, 1779.
Henry Hardman, Major. Commissioned 29, 1779.
Thomas Lansdale, Major. Commissioned February 19, 1781.

Captains.

Henry Dobson,	Jan. 10, 1777.		James W. Gray,	Dec. 25, 1777.
Joseph Marbury,	Jan. 1, 1777.		Edward Spurrier,	May 20, 1779.
Lilburn Williams,	April 16, 1777.		Benjamin Price,	July 1, 1779.
Robert Chesley,	June 10, 1777.		Richard Waters,	April 7, 1779.
John Smith,	Nov. 9, 1777.			

OFFICERS AND PRIVATES

Lieutenants.

	Commissioned.		Commissioned.
Francis Revelly,	April 15, 1777.	William Pendergast,	Oct. 29, 1779.
James Gould,	Mar. 11, 1778.	Henry Baldwin,	Feb. 11, 1780.
James Winchester,	May 27, 1778.	David Lucket,	April 7, 1780.
Philip Reid,	Oct. 13, 1778.	Walter Dyer,	Sept. 5, 1780.
John Hartshorn,	May 21, 1779.	Nathan Wright,	Jan. 1, 1781.
Regnal Hillary,	July 15, 1779.	John Boone,	April 12, 1781.
Philip Hill,		Levin Denwood, Surgeon.	

FOURTH REGIMENT.

Thomas Woolford, Lieutenant-colonel. Commissioned October 23, 1779.
Levin Winder, Major. Commissioned April 17, 1777.
Alexander Roxburg, Major. Commissioned April 7, 1780.

Captains.

John Lynch,	Jan. 1, 1777.	George Hamilton,	Jan. 25, 1778.
Jacob Brice,	do.	David Lynn,	May 22, 1778.
Henry Gaither,	April 17, 1777.	John Mitchell,	July 15, 1779.
John C. Jones,	Sept. 20, 1777.	Jonathan Gibson,	May 1, 1780.
Richard Anderson,	Nov. 15, 1777.		

Lieutenants.

Nicholas Mangers,	April 15, 1779.	Nathan Smith,	Sept. 15, 1779.
James Simmes,	May 27, 1778.	Edmund Compton,	Feb. 18, 1780.
Peter Hartcastle,	Sept. 14, 1778.	Joshua Rutledge,	May 1, 1780.
Benjamin Garnett,	Oct. 13, 1780.	John Brevett,	Sept. 20, 1780.
William Stoddert,	May 21, 1779.	John McCoy,	Jan. 1, 1781.
Lavasha De la Van Brunne.		Robert Hatherston,	April 25, 1781.
(His widow was pensioned under the act of July 4, 1836, and died in 1837.)		Henry Gassaway,	May 12, 1781.
		William Kelty, Surgeon.	

FIFTH REGIMENT.

Benjamin Ford, Lieutenant-colonel. Commissioned ———— ————.
John Davidson, Major. Commissioned January 12, 1781.
Benjamin Brooke, Major. Commissioned March 16, 1781.

Captains.

William D. Beall,	Jan. 1, 1777.	Perry Benson,	Mar. 5, 1778.
John Smith,	do.	James Somerville,	June 1, 1779.
Edward Oldham,	May 20, 1777.	William Bruce,	Aug. 1, 1779.
Horatio Clagett,	Oct. 10, 1777.	Edward Edgerly,	Sept. 10, 1779.
John Gale,	Dec. 10, 1777.		

OF THE REVOLUTIONARY WAR.

Lieutenants.

	Commissioned.		Commissioned.
James Bruff,	Oct. 7, 1777.	Benjamin Tickle,	Feb. 19, 1780.
Gassaway Watkins,	Sept. 14, 1778.	Roger Nelson,	July 5, 1780.
Jacob Norris,	Nov. 26, 1778.	Thomas Boyd,	Jan. 1, 1781.
John Lynn,	June 1, 1779.	John Sears,	do.
Samuel Hanson,	Aug. 1, 1779.	Henry Clements,	April 25, 1781.
Thomas Rouse,	————.	Adam Jamieson,	June 1, 1781.
Robert Denny,	Jan. 3, 1780.		

Colonel Josiah Carvil Hall, Lieutenant-colonel Nathaniel Ramsey, and Lieutenant-colonel Edward Tillard, became supernumerary on the 1st of Jan., 1781.

OFFICERS OF THE MARYLAND PART OF THE GERMAN BATTALION.
Lodowick Weltner, Lieut. Colonel. Commissioned August 9, 1777.
Charles Baltzell, Captain. Commissioned May 10, 1777.

Christopher Myers,	do.	do.	March 12, 1778.
Michael Boyer,	do.	do.	May 25, 1778.
Martin Sugart,	Lieutenant.	do.	do.
Jacob Gomath,	do.	do.	January 4, 1778.
David Morgan,	do.	do.	April 8, 1778.
Jacob Reybold, Ensign.		do.	July 24, 1778.
Alexander Smith, Surgeon.		do.	August —, 1778.

OFFICERS OF THE MARYLAND FLYING CAMP, IN 1776.
Rezin Beall, Brigadier-general.

FIRST BATTALION.
Charles G. Griffith, Colonel.

Henry Shryock, Lieut. Colonel. | Peter Mantz, Major.

Captains.

Edward Burgess,	Jacob Good,
Leonard Deakins,	Eneas Campbell,
Benjamin Spiker,	John Reynolds,
Philip Marony,	Henry Hardman.

Lieutenants.

John Gaither,	Adam Grosh,
Thomas Nowland,	Clement Holliday,
Greenberry Gaither,	Moses Chapline,
Elisha Beall,	Daniel Stull,
John B. Thompson.	Thaddeus Beall.

OFFICERS AND PRIVATES

Elisha Williams,
Richard Anderson,
John Hellen,
John Chiseline,

Peter Adams,
John C. Jones,
Christian Orendorf,
Peter C. Hanson.

Ensigns.

Thomas Edmundson,
John Griffith,
Nicholas Schybert,
William Beatty, jun.,
John Smith,

John Richardson,
David Lynn,
Nathan Williams,
John Rench.

SECOND BATTALION.

Josiah Carvil Hall, Colonel.
William Hyde, Lieut. Colonel.

John Craddock, Major.
Isaac Guest, Quartermaster.

Captains.

Zachariah McCubbin,
John Eager Howard,
John Stevenson,

James Young,
Aquilla Paca,
Bennet Bussy.

Lieutenants.

Thomas Yeates,
Thomas Lansdale,
Edward Oldham,
James Bond,
John B. Hall,
Joshua Miles,

Michael Gilbert,
John Christie,
William Riely,
James Oglebie,
John Smith,
Asahel Hitchcock.

Ensigns.

Thomas Lingan,
Robert Morrow,
Joseph Lewis,

James Tool,
John Patterson,
Aquilla Arnos.

THIRD BATTALION.

Thomas Ewing, Colonel.
John Addison, Lieut. Colonel.
James Eden, Major.

John Dorsey, Surgeon.
William Parran, Quartermaster.

Captains.

Uriah Forrest,
Thomas Hanson,
Belair Posey,
John Brook,
John H. Lowe,
James Disney,

Robert Bowie,
Alexander H. Magruder,
Edward Norwood,
Edward Tillard,
Daniel Dorsey,
Thomas Hammond.

Lieutenants.

Frederick Skinner,
John M. Burgess,
Benjamin Brooks,
William S. Bowie.
Samuel Godman,
Samuel L. Chew,
Joseph Burgess,
Henry Ridgely,
Thomas Mayo,

Nathaniel Willson,
William Duvall,
William D. Beall,
Benjamin Contee,
John W. Dorsey,
John S. Belt,
John Lorah,
Jonathan Sellman,
Joshua Meriken,

Ensigns.

James Somerville,
Horatio Clagett,
William Shircliff,
Alexander Trueman,
Richard Talbott,

John Kilty,
Michael Burgess,
Edward Spurrier,
Andrew Hammond.

FOURTH BATTALION.

William Richardson, Colonel.
Joseph Earle, Lieut. Colonel.
Robert Campbell, Adjutant.

William Hopewell, Major.
Samuel Edmunson, Qr. Master.

Captains.

Joshua George,
Walter Alexander,
Isaac Perkins,
Thomas Smyth,
Philip Fiddeman,

John Dean,
John Dames,
Greenberry Goldsborough,
Zabdiel Potter,
Thomas Burk,

Lieutenants.

William Veasy,
Andrew Porter,
Andrew Falconer,
James Williamson,
John Hawkins,
Thomas L. Emory,
Woolman Gibson,
Thomas W. Lockerman,
Henry Downs, jr.,
Berkit Falcon,

John Stockton,
Harman Arrants,
Jesse Cosden,
Nathaniel Kinnard,
John Neville,
Samuel W. Thomas,
John Thomas, jr.,
Levin Handy,
John Reynolds,
John Lynch.

Ensigns.

Richard Bird,
George Hamilton,
James Henry,

Josiah Johnston,
Thomas Mason,
Samuel Earle.

John Jackson, | Philip Casson,
Perry Benson, | James W. Gray.

NOTE.—The writer is indebted to the History of Maryland by James McSherry, Esq., for the foregoing Maryland officers—that gentleman, and Messrs. Murphy & Co., publishers, of Baltimore, having kindly permitted me to copy them.

NAMES AND RANK OF THE MARYLAND RIFLE COMPANIES UNDER LIEUT. COL. MOSES RAWLINGS, AS THEY STOOD MAY 81, 1777.

FIRST COMPANY.

Alex. Lawson Smith. Captain. | Joshua Saunders, Sergeant.
William Bradford, Lieutenant. | Isaac Rose, Corporal.
John Thompson, Sergeant. | John Howe, do.
Matthew Alexander, do. | Thomas Lively, Fifer.

Riflemen.

William Andrews, | Henry Rowlin,
Josias Kimball, | William Catterill,
Samuel Power, | John Leviston,
John Cooper, | William Pritchard,
Patrick McCann, | John Irons,
John Debruler, | William Cooper,
Charles Baker, | Jesse Corbitt,
John Coltman, | Thomas Dearmott,
Thomas Smith, | Reuben Ross,
Abraham Watson, | John Crocket,
James Dennison, | Patrick Quinn.

SECOND COMPANY.

Philip Griffith, Captain. | Elijah Evans, Lieutenant.
Adamson Tannehill, Lieutenant. |

Riflemen.

John Carr, | Peter Dyche,
Joshua Burton, | Patrick Lemon.
John Johnston, |

THIRD COMPANY.

Richard Davis, Captain. | John Burk, Private.
John McBride, Drummer. | Jonathan Shepard.
Patrick Kirby, Private. |

OF THE REVOLUTIONARY WAR. 241

FOURTH COMPANY.

Thomas Bell, Captain.
John Ford, Corporal.
James Ferguson, do.
Bryan Davenport, Private.

William Batton,
Peter Trust,
Patrick Collins,
Charles Saffell.

NOTE.—These rifle companies were present at the attack on Fort Washington, on the 16th November, 1776, by the English forces under Sir William Howe. For some considerable length of time, the deadly fire of these riflemen, aided by a three-gun battery, kept the left column of the Hessians and Waldeckers, under General Knyphausen, entirely at bay. At length, their rifles becoming so foul from incessant firing, they were compelled to give ground. The fort was, after a desperate resistance on the part of the Americans, surrendered to the British, who took about 2,800 American prisoners, among whom were many of these riflemen, which circumstances so thinned their ranks, that in the summer of 1777 they were incorporated into other companies.

NAMES, RANK, DATES OF COMMISSIONS, AND TIME OF ENLISTMENT OF THE FIELD, STAFF, NON-COMMISSIONED OFFICERS, AND PRIVATES OF COL. CHARLES HARRISON'S VIRGINIA AND MARYLAND REGIMENT OF ARTILLERY, AS IT STOOD FROM NOV. 30, 1776. TO APRIL, 1782.

Charles Harrison, Colonel. Commissioned Nov. 30, 1776. Served to the end of the war.
Edward Carrington, Lieutenant-colonel. Commissioned Nov. 30, 1776. Served to the end of the war.
Christian Holmer, Major. Commissioned Nov. 30, 1776. Served to the end of the war.
William Camp, Adjutant. Commissioned March 16, 1778.
Richard Waters, Adjutant. Commissioned Sept. 21, 1778. Served as Lt. and Adjt. to the end of the war.
Ambrose Bohannon, Paymaster. Commissioned June 1, 1778. Served as Lt. and Paymaster to the end of the war.

Jervis Adams,	Quartermaster.	Commissioned	Nov. 21, 1777.
Clement Skerrett,	do.	do.	June 6, 1779.
Thomas Chrystie,	Surgeon.	do.	April 1, 1778.
Jonathan Calvert,	Surgeon's Mate.	do.	Nov. 30, 1776.
Alex. Lajournade,	do.	do.	Mar. 15, 1778.
Thomas Parr,	Fife-major.	Appointed	Nov. 30, 1776.
Robert Hart,	Drum-major,	do.	do.
John Coale,	Sergeant-major.	do.	do.
Griffith Evans,	Qr. Mr.'s Sergeant.	do.	do.

COMPANY NO. 1, AS IT STOOD AT VALLEY FORGE, JUNE 3, 1778.

William Pierce,	Captain.	Commissioned	Nov. 30, 1776.
Samuel Coleman,	1st Lieut.	do.	June 15, 1778.
Thomas Dix,	do.	do.	Jan. 15, 1778.
William Fraizer,	Capt. Lieut.	do.	Nov. 30, 1776.
Henry Punter,	Sergeant.	Appointed.	June 17, 1777.
Christopher Stoakes,	Corporal.	do.	Jan. 30, 1777.
Francis Ratliff,	do.	do.	Dec. 20, 1776.
William Elliott,	Bombardier.	do.	Dec. 30, 1776.
John May,	do.	do.	Dec. 23, 1776.
Hugh Robinson,	Gunner.	do.	Dec. 20, 1776.
John Harris,	do.	do.	Nov. 8, 1776.
William Fleming,	do.	do.	Dec. 23, 1776.
Isaac Freeman,	Drummer.	do.	Dec. 26, 1776.

Matrosses for Three Years.

Enlisted.

Holman Snead,	Dec. 31, 1776.	Thomas Figg,	Dec. 20, 1777.
Joseph Eaton,	Jan. 6, 1777.	Richard Jenkins,	Jan. 15, 1777.
Henry Shackelford,	Dec. 24, 1776.	James Bray,	Sept. 4, 1777.
James Garland,	Dec. 31, 1776.	William Bartley,	April 18, 1777.
Mag. Shackleford,	Dec. 28, 1776.	John Kelly,	Sept. 19, 1777.
John Bishard,	Dec. 31, 1776.	William Kelly,	Jan. 19, 1778.
John Howard,	Jan. 16, 1777.	William Walker, deserted.	
John Lutredge,	Jan. 1, 1777.	James Morgan,	sick in Virginia.
Robert Belvin,	Mar. 23, 1777.	John Hughes, Serg't,	do.
William Hart,	Mar. 18, 1777.	Jesse Hughes,	do.
James Stewart,	Mar. 10, 1777.	James Alexander, Corp.,	do.
David Shelton,	April 20, 1777.	Thomas Brooke,	do.
Presley Anderwig,	June 14, 1777.	John Rosser,	do.

NOTE.—The above company was incorporated in Capt. Samuel Edden's.

COMPANY NO. 2, AS IT STOOD AT VALLEY FORGE, JUNE 3, 1778.

Nathaniel Burwell, Captain, and Aid-de-Camp to Brigadier-general Robert Howe. Commissioned November 30, 1776. Served to the end of the war.
John Blair, Captain-lieutenant. Commissioned November 30, 1777.

William Camp,	First-lieutenant.	do.	November, 30, 1777.
William Stevenson,	do.	do.	June 15, 1778.
Thomas Grubbs,	Sergeant.	Appointed	December 20, 1777.
Samuel Cross,	do.	do.	January 7, 1777.
William Emmons,	Corporal.	do.	December 20, 1776.
Edward Shacklett,	do.	do.	January 28, 1777.
James Johnson,	do.	do.	January 4, 1777.
Burwell Bacon,	Bombardier.	do.	January 17, 1777.
Richard Routon,	do.	do.	February 9, 1777.

OF THE REVOLUTIONARY WAR. 243

Lewis St. John,   Gunner.   Appointed March 4, 1777.
Richard Spratliff, do.   do. December 20, 1777.
Jesse Peal,   Fifer.   do. December 14, 1777.
Thomas Wells,   Drummer.   do. December 24, 1777.

Matrosses for Three Years.

	Enlisted.		Enlisted.
Thomas Chuning,	Feb. 11, 1777.	Charles Lawman,	Jan. 10, 1777.
Thomas Cross,	June 1, 1777.	Elias Jones,	Jan. 12, 1777.
Aaron Ball,	Feb. 4, 1777.	John Jenkins,	Jan. 15, 1777.
Alexander Childress,	Feb. 6, 1777.	Samuel Dyer,	Jan. 2, 1777.
John Harris,	Jan. 12, 1777.	Benjamin Kidd,	April 15, 1777.
Thomas Elmore,	Jan. 7, 1777.	Major Callahan,	Nov. 22, 1777.
William Hains,	Feb. 8, 1777.	Walker Williams,	Jan. 28, 1777.
Thomas Alphin,	Feb. 3, 1777.	Edward Connolly,	Dec. 20, 1776.
Abraham Pickett,	Feb. 9, 1777.	John Spencer,	June 1, 1776.
Reuben Hughes,	Jan. 14, 1777.	(Turned over to 1st Va. Reg't.)	
Francis Dyer,	Feb. 1, 1777.	Thomas Adderson,	Jan. 20, 1777
John Bushiel,	Feb. 9, 1777.	(Deserted May 25, 1778.)	
Charles Gunter,	Feb. 7, 1777.	Adam Smith. (Proved to be a de-	
Alexander Kersey,	Mar. 8, 1777.	serter from another regiment.)	

CAPT. NATHANIEL BURWELL'S COMPANY, AS IT STOOD AT SMITH'S CLOVE, JULY 2, 1779.

Nathaniel Burwell, Captain, and Aid to General Howe.
John Blair, Captain-lieutenant.
William Stevenson, First-lieutenant.
Samuel Cross, Sergeant. Appointed November 30, 1777.
William Emmons, do.   do.   September 21, 1778.
Edward Shacklett, do.   do.   March 1, 1779.
James Johnson, Corporal and Artificer, in Philadelphia.
Richard Routon, Corporal. Appointed September 1, 1778.
Burwick Bacon, Bombadier.   do.   do.
Lewis St. John,   do.   do.   do.
Richard Spratliff,   do.   do.   do.
Reuben Hughes, Gunner.   do.   do.
Thomas Cross,   do.   do.   do.
John Jenkins, Gunner and Wagoner. Appointed Sept. 1, 1778.
Jesse Peal, Fifer. Appointed December 14, 1777.

Matrosses for Three Years.

	Enlisted.		Enlisted.
Thomas Chuning,	Feb. 11, 1777.	Alexander Childress,	Jan. 6, 1777.
Aaron Ball,	Feb. 4, 1777.	(Wagoner.)	
Nathaniel Hughes,	Feb. 14, 1777.	Thomas Alphin,	Feb. 3, 1777.

OFFICERS AND PRIVATES.

	Enlisted		Enlisted.
John Harriss, (Wagoner.)	Jan. 12, 1777.	Edward Taylor, John Bushell,	Dec. 10, 1776. Feb. 9, 1777.
Richard Shearwood,	Feb. 15, 1777.	Charles Gunter,	Feb. 7, 1777.
Abraham Pigott,	Feb. 9, 1777.	Frederick Hall,	Dec. 22, 1777.
Abraham Smithey, (Wagoner.)	Jan. 14, 1777.	Alexander Kinsey, Charles Lawman,	Mar. 8, 1777. Jan. 10, 1777.
Francis Dyer,	Feb. 1, 1777.	Elisha Jones,	Jan. 12, 1777.
Major Callahan,	Nov. 22, 1777.	Samuel Dyer,	April 15, 1777,
Walter Williams,	Jan. 28, 1777.	Benjamin Kidd,	do.
Thomas Grubbs, (Wagoner.)	Dec. 20, 1776.	Thomas Elmore,	Jan. 7, 1777.

COMPANY NO. 3, AS IT STOOD AT VALLEY FORGE, JUNE 3, 1778.

Anthony Singleton, Captain. Commissioned Feb. 1, 1777. Served to the end of the war.

Ambrose Bohannon, Captain-lieutenant. Commissioned January 12, 1777. Appointed Paymaster June 1, 1778. Served to the end of the war.

Wm. Miller, First-lieutenant. Commissioned Jan. 13, 1777. Sick in Virginia.

Henry Wallace, Second-lieutenant. Commissioned March 1, 1778. do.

William Piggot, Sergeant. Appointed December 20, 1776.

John Oliver,	Corporal.	do.	do.
Beriah West,	do.	do.	do.
Robert Finney,	Bombardier.	do.	do.
Elias Boyer,	do.	do.	do.
William Langham,	Gunner.	do.	January 24, 1777.
George Fritts, Drummer.		do.	December 20, 1776.
Morris Bowers, Fifer.		do.	September 8, 1777.

Matrosses for Three Years.

	Enlisted.		Enlisted.
Master Adkerson,	Feb. 10, 1777.	Thomas Tabor,	July 15, 1777.
Richard Sanford,	April 5, 1777.	Edward Linegar, (Sick in camp.)	Mar. 24, 1777.
John Randolph,	Nov. 3, 1777.		
Charles Williams,	April 1, 1777.	Philip Bowers, (Sick in camp.)	Feb. 4, 1777.
Lewis Bowdry,	April 4, 1777.		
John Webb,	Aug. 24, 1777.	Thomas O'Neal, (Sick in camp.)	Feb. 1, 1777.
Oliver Yarnton,	Feb. 12, 1777.		
James Sparham,	Feb. 1, 1777.	John Cashell, deserted Apr. 25, 1778.	
Drury Wilkerson,	Nov. 24, 1777.	Wm. Meacham, sick in Virginia.	
Benj'n Blankership,	Feb. 17, 1777.	Peter Jones,	do.
William O'Neal,	Jan. 11, 1777.	Thomas Jones.	do.
James Chamberlain,	Nov. 24, 1777.	M. Richerson,	do.
Artes Bennet,	Feb. 8, 1777.	Benjamin Hudson,	do.
Philip Evans,	Feb. 1, 1777.	John Cornelius,	do.

OF THE REVOLUTIONARY WAR. 245

Thomas Sanford, sick in Virginia.
William Sanford, do.
Thomas Doleman, do.
Reuben Atkinson, sick in Virginia.
Josiah Cornelius, do.

CAPTAIN ANTHONY SINGLETON'S COMPANY OF ARTILLERY, AS IT STOOD AT SMITH'S CLOVE, JULY 1, 1779.

Anthony Singleton, Captain. Sick in quarters.
Ambrose Bohannan, Captain-lieutenant and Paymaster.
Samuel Bradford, First-lieutenant. Commissioned January 13, 1777.
Benjamin Mosely, Second-lieutenant. Commissioned April 9, 1779.
William Piggot, Sergeant. Appointed December 20, 1776.
William Mitcham, Sergeant. Appointed February 10, 1777.
Griffith Evans, Sergeant. Appointed February 1, 1777.
John Oliver, Sergeant. Appointed December 20, 1776.
Peter Jones, Sergeant and Wagoner. Appointed December 20, 1776.
Beriah West, Sergeant. Appointed December 20, 1776.
Robert Finney, Bombardier. Appointed December 20, 1776.
Elias Boyer, Bombardier. Appointed December 20, 1776.
William Langham, Bombardier and Wagoner. Appointed January 24, 1777.
Morning Richardson, Gunner. Appointed February 19, 1777.
George Fritts, Drummer. Appointed December 20, 1776.
Morris Bowers, Fifer. Appointed September 8, 1777.

Matrosses for Three Years.

	Enlisted.		Enlisted.
Major Atkinson,	Feb. 10, 1777.	Edward Linegar,	Mar. 24, 1777
Reuben Atkinson,	Mar. 4, 1777.	(Sick at Pluckemin.)	
(Wagoner.)		Thomas O'Neal,	Feb. 1, 1777
Lewis Bowdree,	Mar. 4, 1777.	William O'Neal,	Jan. 11, 1777.
Benja'n Blankership.	Sept. 17, 1777.	Richard Sanford,	Mar. 5, 1777.
Artes Bennet,	Feb. 8, 1777.	Thomas Sanford,	Feb. 9, 1777.
(Wagoner.)		James Sparham,	Feb. 1, 1777.
Philip Bowers,	Feb. 4, 1777.	(Sick at Pluckemin.)	
Josiah Cornelius,	Mar. 24, 1777.	John Webb,	Aug. 14, 1777.
James Chamberlain,	Nov. 21, 1777.	Drury Wilkinson,	Mar. 4, 1777.
Thomas Doleman,	Mar. 10, 1777.	Oliver Yarrington,	Feb. 12, 1777.
Philip Evans,	Feb. 4, 1777.	Francis Houge,	Dec. 6, 1778.
Thomas Evies,	July 8, 1777.	William Sanford,	Mar. 5, 1777.

COMPANY NO. 4, AS IT STOOD AT PLUCKEMIN, JULY 16, 1779.

Drury Ragsdale, Captain. Commissioned February 7, 1777.
William Godman, Captain-lieutenant. Commissioned January 1, 1778.
Richard Waters, First-lieutenant. Commissioned January 13, 1777. Appointed Adjutant, September 21, 1778.

246   OFFICERS AND PRIVATES

William Darvil, Second-lieutenant. Commissioned February, 7, 1777.

Alexander Petrie, Sergeant.   Appointed July 15, 1777.
Major Lipscomb,   do.   do.   July 30, 1777.
John Cowels,   do.   do.   August 28, 1778.
John Lipscomb, Corporal.   do.   July 21, 1777.
Samuel Johnson,   do.   do.   do.
Johan Flishner,   do.   do.   Unknown.
James Waters,   do.   do.   do.
Elias Langham, Bombardier.   do.   do.
Julius Comer,   do.   do.   January 1, 1777.
Notley Maddox,   do.   do.   Unknown.
James McDorman, Gunner.   do.   January 1, 1778.
William Lial,   do.   do.   August 1, 1777.
James Barnes,   do.   do.   Unknown.
John Porter, Drummer,   do.   do.
John Ketlar, Fifer.   do.   do.

Matrosses for Three Years.

	Enlisted.		Enlisted.
Charles Broach,	Dec. 21, 1777.	James Harding,	Unknown.
John Grant,	Dec. 20, 1776.	Edward Peek,	do.
William Hagley,	Sept. 21, 1777.	James House,	do.
William Russell,	Jan. 21, 1777.	Thomas Ives,	do.
Thomas Bates,	Unknown.	John Jones,	do.
James Beavers,	do.	John Riland,	do.
Joseph Clayton,	do.		

COMPANY NO. 5, AS IT STOOD AT VALLEY FORGE, JUNE 3, 1778.

James Pendleton, Captain. Commissioned February 7, 1777.
John Prior, Captain-lieutenant. Commissioned February 13, 1777.
Richard Waters, First-lieutenant. Commissioned January 13, 1777.
James Didlake, Sergeant.   Appointed December 20, 1776.
Thomas Hood, Corporal.   do.   do.
Thomas Ward, Bombardier.   do.   do.
James Bartley,   do.   do.   February 28, 1777.
John Jordan, Gunner.   do.   December 20, 1776.
James Lloyd,   do.   do.   February 13, 1777.
Christian Bland, Drummer.   do.   March 20, 1777.
Phil. Johnson, Fifer.   do.   April 1, 1777.

Matrosses for Three Years.

	Enlisted.		Enlisted.
Ed. Clark,	Jan. 22, 1777.	Beverly Spencer,	Jan. 30, 1777.
William Barns,	do.	George Ogden,	Feb. 8, 1777.
Matthew Allen,	Feb. 2, 1777.	Samuel Sandifer,	April 3, 1777.

OF THE REVOLUTIONARY WAR. 247

	Enlisted.			Enlisted.
Samuel Wilkins,	Jan. 3, 1777.	James Furlough,		June 3, 1777.
James Musgrove,	Jan. 18, 1777.	(Wagoner.)		
Zechariah Nance,	Feb. 19, 1777.	Peter Smith,		Mar. 20, 1778.
Isaac Kenny,	Mar. 5, 1777.	(Deserted May 1, 1778.)		
Fielding Barrom,	Feb. 15, 1777.			

CAPT. JAMES PENDLETON'S COMPANY OF ARTILLERY, AS IT STOOD AT "CAMP NEAR CHESTER," JULY 9, 1779.

James Pendleton, Captain.
John Prior, Captain-lieutenant, and Aid-de-Camp to Maj. Gen. Lord Sterling.
Samuel K. Bradford, First-lieutenant. Commissioned Jan. 13, 1777, and annexed to Capt. Singleton's Company June 1, 1777.

Justinian Cartwright,	Sergeant-major.	Appointed	Mar. 1, 1779.
James Hines,	Qr. Mr.'s Sergeant.	do.	Aug. 15, 1778.
James Didlake,	Sergeant.	do.	Dec. 20, 1776.
Thomas Hood,	do.	do.	do.
Robert Hart Hunter,	Drum-major.	do.	Unknown.
Thomas Parr,	Fife-major.	do.	do.
Phil. Johnson,	Drummer.	do.	do.
Matthew Allen,	Corporal.	do.	Nov. 1, 1778.
Thomas Ward,	do.	do.	do.
James Alexander,	do.	do.	Unknown.

Matrosses for Three Years.

William Barnes, enlisted January 22, 1777.
Christian Bland, do. March 20, 1777.
John Farlough, do. June 3, 1777. (Wagoner to Col. Harrison.)
Phil. Johnson. (Reduced from Drummer, June 1, 1779.)
Isaac Kimmey. (Driver to ammunition-wagon.)
John Kelly, } (Sent to Providence, R. I., to join Captain Pierce's Com-
William Kelly, } pany, June 1, 1779.)
James Sandifer, enlisted April 3, 1777. (Driver to a field piece.)
Beverly Spencer, do. January 30, 1777. (Wagoner.)
William Powell, do. in General Knox's Guard.

COMPANY NO. 6, AS IT STOOD AT VALLEY FORGE, JUNE 4, 1778.

John Dandridge,	Captain.	Commissioned	Feb. 1, 1777.
Michael McNemera,	First-lieutenant.	do.	Jan. 1, 1778.
Walter Richardson,	Second-lieutenant.	do.	Mar. 4, 1778.
William Meredith,	Captain-lieutenant.	do.	Jan. 13, 1777.
Justinian Cartwright,	Sergeant.	Appointed	Dec. 20, 1776.
Robert Scott,	Corporal.	do.	do.
Elias Wingate,	do.	do.	do.

248   OFFICERS AND PRIVATES

Thomas Robinson,	Corporal.	Appointed	Dec. 20, 1776.
James Hines,	do.	do.	do.
Joseph Ball,	Bombardier.	do.	Jan. 22, 1777.
William Freeman,	do.	do.	Dec. 20, 1776.
Thomas Leigh,	Gunner.	do.	Feb. 10, 1777.
Thomas Coleman,	do.	do.	Jan. 27, 1777.
Charles Nelmes,	do.	do.	Mar. 10, 1777.
John Cottey,	Fifer.	do.	Dec. 20, 1776.
Thomas Wilkins,	Drummer,	do.	Mar. 28, 1777.

Matrosses for Three Years.

	Enlisted.		Enlisted.
Thomas Carter,	Mar. 10, 1777.	Samuel Henderson,	Dec 28, 1776.
Joseph Lock,	do.	William Fitzhugh,	Mar. 17, 1777.
John Fisher,	Feb. 1, 1777.	Edward Dean,	Mar. 1, 1777.
Sill Welsh,	Feb. 4, 1777.	James Sullivan,	do.
Benj. Welch,	do.	John Jones,	Feb. 4, 1777.
George Walker,	do.	Peter Layland (deserted), do.	
John Alexander,	Mar. 10, 1777.	John Gray,	do. Feb. 2, 1777.
Robert Bryon,	Dec. 20, 1776.	William Dinny,	do Mar. 10, 1777.
Wm. Worthington,			

CAPT. JOHN DANBRIDGE'S COMPANY OF ARTILLERY, AS IT STOOD AT SMITH'S CLOVE, JULY 4, 1779.

John Danbridge, Captain. Absent on leave.
Walter Richardson, Second-lieutenant.

Sergeants.

Thomas Robinson, | Charles Nelmes.

Corporals.

Robert Scott, | Thomas Leigh.
Elias Wingate,

Bombardiers.

William Freeman, | Thomas Coleman.

Gunners.

Thomas Carter, | Joseph Lock.

Drum and Fife.

Thomas Wilkins, | John Cottey.

Matrosses.

John Alexander,	William Hutton,
Robert Bryron,	George Rice, (Wagoner).
James Sullivan,	George Walker,
Edward Deans,	Michael Welch,
John Fisher,	Sill Welch,
William Fitzhugh,	Benj. Welch,
Samuel Henderson	John Jones,

OF THE REVOLUTIONARY WAR. 249

COMPANY NO. 7, AS IT STOOD AT VALLEY FORGE, JUNE 3, 1778.

John Champe Carter, Captain.		Commissioned	Oct. 30, 1777.
William Poythress, First-lieutenant.		do.	Nov. 20, 1777.
Robert Dandridge, Second-lieutenant.		do.	Oct. 30, 1777.
Martin McKennon, Sergeant.		Appointed	Dec. 20, 1776.
Jacob Diener,	do.	do.	do.
William Suttle,	Corporal.	do.	do.
William Summers,	Bombardier.	do.	do.
William Cook,	do.	do.	do.
Reuben Griffith,	do.	do.	Dec. 20, 1776.
Nell Brown,	Gunner.	do.	Jan. 27, 1777.
John Adams,	do.	do.	Jan. 30, 1777.
Henry Pursell,	do.	do.	do.
Bejamin Shurles,	do.	do.	Jan. 27, 1777.
Uriah Brock,	Fifer.	do.	Feb. 1, 1778.
Charles McAllister,	Drummer.	do.	Jan. 30, 1777.

Matrosses for Three Years.

	Enlisted.		Enlisted.
Luke Bullin,	Dec. 16, 1776.	William Sollers.	April 4, 1777.
Henry Middleton,	Dec. 22, 1776.	William Shannon,	Aug. 8, 1777.
John Wren,	Jan. 11, 1777.	William Dichie,	Jan. 5, 1777.
Jeremiah Levy,	April 1, 1777.	Isham Burns,	Sept. 4, 1777.
Robert Kelly,	Jan. 23, 1777.	Henry Hazel,	April 16, 1777.
William Chevis,	Jan. 27, 1777.	David Wilson,	Dec. 10, 1776.
Gideon Wing,	Feb. 10, 1777.	(Died May 10, 1778.)	
William Powers,	Feb. 6, 1777.	Nicholas Dorsey,	Jan. 1, 1777.

CAPT. JOHN CHAMPE CARTER'S COMPANY, AS IT STOOD AT "CAMP NEAR CHESTER," JULY 9, 1779.

John C. Carter, Captain.
Thomas Dix, Captain-lieutenant. Commissioned Jan. 15, 1778.
William Poythress, First-lieutenant. Commissioned Nov. 20, 1777.

Sergeants.

Martin McKennon,	William Cook,
Jacob Diener,	William Summers, Corporal.

Bombardiers.

Nell Brown,	John Adams.

Gunners.

Henry Middleton,	Benjamin Shurles, acting as Guard
William Chevis,	to General Knox.

Drum and Fife.

William Shannon,	Uriah Brock.

OFFICERS AND PRIVATES

Matrosses.

Robert Brown,	Matthew Ellis,
Joseph Bishop,	Reuben Griffith,
Isham Burns,	Robert Kelly,
Luke Bullins,	Jeremiah Levey,
Nicholas Dorsey,	Laurence McDonald,
William Dichie,	Charles McCallister,
William Powers,	William Suttles,
William Sollers,	Gideon Wing.
John Wren,	

COMPANY NO. 8, AS IT STOOD AT VALLEY FORGE, JUNE 8, 1778.

Samuel Eddens, Captain. Commissioned January 1, 1778.
Lewis Booker, Captain-lieutenant. Commissioned January 13, 1777.
Richard Hill, First-lieutenant. Commissioned October 20, 1777.
Abraham Cole, Second lieutenant. Commissioned November 30, 1777. Sick in Virginia.
John Chick, Sergeant. Sick in Virginia.

Christian Francis,	Corporal.	Appointed	December 20, 1776.
William Machie,	do.	do.	do.
Augustine Lawless,	Bombardier.	do.	February 10, 1777.
Christian Cawthorn,	do.	do.	January 11, 1777.
Charles Powell,	do.	do.	January 9, 1777.
James Gentry,	do.	do.	January 11, 1777.
Richard Croxton,	Gunner.	do.	February 10, 1777.
Richard Rogers,	do.	do.	January 5, 1777.
George Anderson,	Drummer.	do.	February 15, 1777.
John Sneed,	Fifer.	do.	January 20, 1777.

Matrosses for Three Years.

	Enlisted.		Enlisted.
Joseph Clark,	Feb. 9, 1777.	William Vaughan,	Feb. 10, 1777.
John Denton,	Jan. 29, 1777.	(Sick in camp.)	
Charles Lyle,	Dec. 20, 1776.	John Wilds,	Sept. 24, 1777.
Charles Morgan,	Jan. 10, 1777.	(Sick in camp.)	
Isaac Wessen,	Sept. 15, 1777.	Richard Parker,	Feb. 10, 1778.
Benjamin Lawson,	Sept. 24, 1777.	(Sick in camp.)	
William Cremer,	April 10, 1777.	William Bibb,	Unknown.
John Lyle,	Jan. 31, 1777.	(Sick in camp,	
Jacob Peale,	Jan. 27, 1777.	Solomon Hall,	do.
Edward Sage,	Aug. 1, 1777.	(Sick in camp.)	

OF THE REVOLUTIONARY WAR. 251

CAPT. SAMUEL EDDENS' COMPANY OF ARTILLERY, AS IT STOOD AT SMITH'S CLOVE, JULY 4, 1779.

Samuel Eddens, Captain. On command at Providence.
Lewis Booker, Captain-lieutenant.
John Carson, Second-lieutenant. Commissioned May 1, 1779. Joined Captain Brown's Maryland Company.
Christian Cawthorn, Sergeant. Appointed October 1, 1778.
Charles Powell, do. do. do.
Christopher Francis, Corporal. do. December 20, 1776.
Augustine Lawless, do. Driver to a piece of Artillery.
William Michie, do.
James Gentry, do. do. January 1, 1779.
Richard Rogers, Gunner.
John Sneed, Fifer.
George Anderson, Drummer.

Matrosses.

Zechariah Bowls,   Jacob Peal,
Joseph Clark,   James White,
William Creimer,   John Wells,
Benjamin Lawson,   Isaac Wesson,
Charles Morgan,   (Piece Driver.)

COMPANY NO. 9, AS IT STOOD AT VALLEY FORGE, JUNE 3, 1778.

Thomas Baytop, Captain. Commissioned February 5, 1778.
William Fleming Gaines, Captain-lieutenant. Commissioned Oct. 20, 1777.
Holland Haynie, First-lieutenant. Commissioned November 30, 1777.
William Stevenson, Second-lieutenant. do. September 30, 1777.
James Tyrie, do. do. April 23, 1778.
Gawin Hamilton, Sergeant. Appointed December 26, 1776.
John Cooper, do. do. February 15, 1777.
James Tucker, do. do. May 1, 1777. Furloughed to Virginia.
James Bailey, Corporal. do. February 3, 1777.
James Sharpe, do. do. December 20, 1776.
William Alexander, do. do. do.
Jesse Dillon, Bombardier. do. do.
William Foster, do. do. February 8, 1777.
Richard Carle, Drummer. do. April 28, 1777.
John Williams, Fifer. do. May 11, 1777.

Matrosses for Three Years.

	Enlisted.		Enlisted.
John Hopper,	Jan. 31, 1777.	John Roach,	April 5, 1777.
William Powel,	Jan. 8, 1777.	Henry Lacy,	Feb. 22, 1777

OFFICERS AND PRIVATES

	Enlisted.		Enlisted.
Dale Carter,	Aug. 23, 1777.	Peter Springfield,	Jan. 19, 1777.
John Graves,	Dec. 20, 1776.	William Gentry,	Nov. 12, 1777.
John Morgan,	July 20, 1777.	Valentine Bethel,	Jan. 9, 1777.
Michael Sullivan,	Dec. 20, 1776.		

COMPANY NO. 10, AS IT STOOD AT VALLEY FORGE, JUNE 8, 1778.

John Henry Captain. Commissioned February 7, 1777.
William Meredith, Captain-lieutenant. Commissioned January 18, 1777.
Thomas Fenn, First-lieutenant. do. do.
Matthew Drury, Sergeant. Appointed December 20, 1776.

James Christian,	do.	do.	do.
William Smith,	do.	do.	do.
Warren Parker,	Corporal.	do.	do.
Lemuel Carter,	do.	do.	June 17, 1778.
William McTyre,	Bombardier.	do.	February 6, 1777.
John Dunn,	do.	do.	January 20, 1777.
John Jones,	Gunner.	do.	January 27, 1777.
Thomas Wotten,	Drummer.	do.	January 6, 1778.
Thos. Campbell,	Fifer.	do.	July 16, 1777.

Matrosses for Three Years.

	Enlisted.		Enlisted.
Richard Henson,	Jan. 27, 1777.	Bartlett Leigh,	June 1, 1777.
George Gray,	Jan. 7, 1777.	Samuel Drury,	Jan. 19, 1777.
William Ferrell,	Feb. 1, 1777.	George Richerson,	Jan. 31, 1777.
John Allen,	Feb. 2, 1777.	Thomas Smith,	Feb. 9, 1777.
William Powell,	Jan. 4, 1777.		

THE ABOVE COMPANY, AS IT STOOD AT "CAMP NEAR CHESTER," JULY 9, 1779.

Whitehead Coleman, Captain. Commissioned August 15, 1778.
William Meredith, Captain-lieutenant.
Thomas Fenn, First-lieutenant. Promoted to Captain-lieutenant in Captain Pierce's Company in Rhode Island, June 18, 1779.
Robert Dandridge, Second-lieutenant. Commissioned October 30, 1777.

Matthew Drury, Sergeant.	Warren Parker, Corporal.
James Christian, do.	Samuel Carter, do.
William Smith, do.	William McTyre, do.

Bombardiers.

John Dunn,	Thomas Campbell, Fifer.
John Jones,	John Allen, Gunner. Enlisted
Thomas Wooton, Drummer.	Feb. 2, 1777.

OF THE REVOLUTIONARY WAR. 253

Matrosses.

Richard Henson,
William Ferrell,
George Gray,
Fielding Barram,
Bartlett Leigh,
Samuel Drury,
John Lynch,
James Clark,
Mark Goldsberry,
Darby Spelcy,
Timothy Conly,
Charles Murritt,
John Sanders,

John Rhodes,
Charles Groome,
John Fitzgerald,
John Aspinwall,
Thomas Carter,
John Reynolds,
James Taylor,
John Folkes,
John Head,
Robert Smith,
Ignatius Griffin,
James Compton,

LIST OF THE OFFICERS AND PRIVATES OF COL. CHARLES HARRISON'S REGIMENT OF ARTILLERY, WHO WERE DISCHARGED AND FURLOUGHED FROM THE PARK OF ARTILLERY, AT MORRISTOWN, IN 1780.

Nathaniel Burwell,	Captain.	On furlough.
John Blair,	Lieutenant.	do.
William Stevenson,	do.	do.
William Pierce,	Captain.	do.
Samuel Coleman,	Lieutenant.	Absent—sick.
Walker Richardson,	do.	On furlough.
Lewis Booker,	do.	do.
Drury Ragsdate,	Captain.	On furlough to Virginia.
Whitehead Coleman,	do.	do.
William Meredith,	Lieutenant.	do.
Robert Dandridge,	do.	do.
John C. Carter,	Captain.	do.
Thomas Dix,	Lieutenant.	do.
William F. Gaines,	do.	do.
Holland Hainey,	do.	do.
Anthony Singleton,	Captain.	do.
Ambrose Bohannan,	Lieut. & P. M.	do.
Samuel K. Bradford,	Lieutenant.	do.
Martin McKennon,	Sergeant.	Deserted April 1, 1780.
John Roach,	Corporal.	Discharged April 10, 1780.
George Fritts,	Drummer.	do. do.
Thomas Neal,	Matross.	Furloughed to Virginia.
James Chamberlain,	do.	do. do.
Richard Sandford,	do.	Discharged Mar. 10, 1780.
Thomas Doleman,	do.	do. do.

OFFICERS AND PRIVATES.

Edward Lenegar,	Matross.	Furloughed to Virginia.	
Lewis Bowdry,	do.	Discharged Mar. 10, 1780.	
Josiah Cornelius,	do.	do.	do.
Reuben Atkinson,	do.	do.	do.
Samuel Sandford,	do.	do.	do.
Drury Williamson,	do.	Furloughed to Virginia.	
Gideon Wing,	do.	Deserted April 1, 1780.	
William Sollers,	do.	Discharged April 10, 1780.	
Peter Springfield,	do.	Deserted April 1, 1780.	
James Hines,	Sergeant.	Discharged April 10, 1780.	
Robert Hart,	Drum-major.	Furloughed to Virginia.	
Thomas Parr,	Fife-major.	Deserted April 1, 1780.	
Charles Nelmes,	Sergeant.	Discharged Mar. 10, 1780.	
James Stewart,	Gunner.	do.	do.
Thomas Carter,	do.	do.	do.
William Hart,	Matross.	do.	do.
Joseph Lock,	Gunner.	do.	do.
Robert Belvin,	Matross.	do.	Mar. 23, 1780.
David Skelton,	do.	do.	April 10, 1780.
John Alexander,	do.	do.	Mar. 10, 1780.
Lewis St. John,	Bombardier.	do.	do.
Alexander Kersey,	Matross.	do.	do.
Benjamin Kidd,	do.	do.	April 10, 1780.
James McDorman,	do.	do.	do.
John Fleshner,	Matross.	do.	do.
Isaac Kimmey,	do.	do.	do.
Samuel Sandifer,	do.	do.	do.
William Johnson,	do.	Furloughed to Maryland.	
Samuel Drury,	do.	Furloughed to Virginia.	
John Lynch,	do.	Sick at Pluckemin.	
James Harding,	do.	do.	do.
Fielding Barrom,	do.	Furloughed to Virginia.	
John Kittler,	do.	Sick at Pluckemin.	
Christopher Stoakes,	Sergeant.	Discharged Jan. 10, 1780.	
James McGarland,	Matross.	do.	do.
John Howard,	do.	do.	do.
William Bartley,	do.	do.	Feb. 7, 1780.
Samuel Cross,	Sergeant.	do.	Jan. 10, 1780.
Edward Shacklet,	do.	do.	do.
Burwell Bacon,	Corporal.	do.	do.
Richard Bouton,	do.	do.	do.
Reuben Hughes,	Bombardier.	do.	do.
Thomas Cross,	Gunner.	do.	do.
Thomas Chewning,	Matross.	do.	Feb. 22, 1780.
Aaron Ball,	do.	do.	Feb. 7, 1780.
Nathan Hughes	do.	do.	Jan. 10, 1780.

OF THE REVOLUTIONARY WAR.

Alexander Childress,	Matross.	Discharged Jan. 10, 1780.	
John Harris,	do.	do.,	Jan. 12, 1780,
Richard Sharwood.	do.	do.	Feb. 22, 1780.
Thomas Alphin,	do.	do.	Feb. 7, 1780.
Abraham Piggat,	do.	do.	Feb. 22, 1780.
Robert Smithey,	do.	do.	Jan. 10, 1780.
Francis Dyer,	do.	do.	Feb. 4, 1780.
Walter Williams,	do.	do.	Jan. 10, 1780.
John Bushell,	do.	do.	Feb. 22, 1780.
Charles Gunter,	do.	do.	Jan. 10, 1780.
Elisha Jones,	do.	do.	do.
John Elmore,	do.	do.	do.
Charles Lorman,	do.	Furloughed to Virginia.	
Samuel Dyer,	do.	do.	
Thomas Coleman,	Bombardier,	Discharged Jan. 10, 1780.	
John Fisher,	Matross.	do.	Feb. 7, 1780.
George Walker,	do.	do.	do.
Sill Welch,	do.	do.	do.
Christopher Cawthron,	Sergeant.	do.	Jan. 10, 1780.
Charles Powell,	do.	do.	do.
James Gentry,	Corporal.	do.	do.
Richard Croxton,	Bombardier.	do.	Feb. 22, 1789.
William Baughan,	do.	do.	do.
Richard Rogers,	Gunner.	do.	Jan. 10, 1780.
John Sneed,	Fifer.	do.	do.
Zechariah Bowles,	Matross.	do.	do.
Joseph Clark,	dd.	do.	do.
Jeremiah Clark,	do.	do.	do.
John Lyle,	do.	do.	do.
Charles Morgan,	do.	do.	do.
Charles Lyle,	do.	Furloughed to Virginia.	
Thomas Barber,	Sergeant.	Acting Com. Mil. Stores.	
Roger O'Donald,	Matross.	Furloughed to Pluckemin.	
Reuben Scott,	do.	Wagoner of forage.	
Matthew Adams,	Corporal.	Transferred to N.Y. Artillery	
James Adams,	Sergeant.	do.	do.

NOTE.—The Maryland Artillery, under Captains Brown and Dorsey, were joined to Colonel Harrison's regiment in 1778, and continued to do duty in this regiment to the close of the war. These companies are given in a former place.

NAMES AND RANK OF THE FIELD, STAFF, AND OTHER COMMISSIONED OFFICERS AND PRIVATES OF COL. DANIEL MORGAN'S 11TH AND 15TH VIRGINIA REGIMENTS, INCORPORATED, AS THEY STOOD FROM MAY 31, 1777, TO NOVEMBER 30, 1778.

Daniel Morgan, Colonel.
Abraham Buford, Colonel from May 15, 1778.
John Cropper, Lieut. Colonel, from May 15, 1778.
Gustavus B. Wallace, Lieut. Col.
David Stephenson, Major.
Philip Slaughter, Captain, and Paymaster from June 1, 1778.
Samuel Jones, Lieut. and Paym'r.
Albridgeton Jones, Adjutant.

Robert Porterfield. Lieut. and Adjutant.
John Barnes, Lieut. and Qr. Mas'r.
Mace Clements, Surgeon.
Joseph Davis, do.
John Crute, Quarterm'r's Serg't.
William Death. do.
Charles Erskine, Sergeant-major.
Thomas Pollock, do.
Robert Sharman, Fife-major.

COMPANY NO. 1, AS IT STOOD IN MAY, 1777.

James Calderwood, Captain. Commissioned January 19, 1777.
Thomas Lucas, First-lieutenant. do. January 23, 1777.
Thomas Burd, Second-lieutenant. do. do.
William Hood, Ensign. do. do.
Elijah Rippey, Sergeant. Appointed February 11, 1777.
James Weir, do. do. February 20, 1777.
William Kane, do. do. May 6, 1777.
John Foster, Drummer. do. March 20, 1777.
John Shields, Fifer. do. May 4, 1777.

Privates.

	Enlisted.		Enlisted.
John Brittain,	Mar. 14, 1777.	Joseph Bates,	May 3, 1777.
John Haines,	do.	George Cotton,	April 29, 1777.
William Howell,	Mar. 19, 1777.	John Ryan,	May 4, 1777.
Peter Mitchell,	Mar. 20, 1777.	Bernard Gorman,	do.
John Dempsey,	April 1, 1777.	Thomas Sheridan,	April 25, 1777.
Thomas Nevines,	April 24, 1777.	Daniel Halley,	May 4, 1777.
Daniel Robinson,	April 20, 1777.	James Barton,	April 27, 1777
John Davis,	April 4, 1777.	William Fiely,	April 30, 1777.
Thomas Neyland,	April 1, 1777.	Joseph Ellerton,	April 18, 1777.
Matthias Abell,	Feb. 15, 1777.	John McDowell,	Feb. 20, 1777.
Samuel King,	Feb. 17, 1777.	John Doyle,	Feb. 5, 1777.
John McKay,	Feb. 26, 1777.	James Ryan,	Feb. 28, 1777.
William Richison,	Feb. 20, 1777.	Richard Mudd,	Feb. 10, 1777.
Richard Hutchison,	Mar. 29, 1777.	John Connolly,	Feb. 14, 1777.

OF THE REVOLUTIONARY WAR. 257

	Enlisted.		*Enlisted.*
Philip Bassett,	Feb. 23, 1777.	Joseph Bramford,	Feb. 16, 1777.
William Lucas,	Mar. 26, 1777.	Michael Grew,	May 4, 1777.
George Ogleby,	April 25, 1777.		

COMPANY NO. 2, AS IT STOOD IN MAY, 1777.

Charles Gallahue, Captain.   Robert Young, Lieutenant.
Died May 24, 1777.   Charles Tyler, Ensign.
Joseph Davis, Lieutenant

Sergeants.

| Thomas Roberson, | John H. Johnson, |
| Francis Langfitt, | Robert Mills. |

Corporals.

| Richard Marshall, | Aquilla Narvel, |
| John Quint, | Yelverton Reardon. |

Drum and Fife.

| John Farrell, | Robert Shearman |

Privates.

Isaac Davis,	William Trusfield,
Benjamin Gray,	William Smith,
Moses Wickliffe,	James Thompson,
Benjamin Wickliffe,	Thomas Bryan,
William Suddoth,	Edward Wilson,
Terrance Conner,	George Whately,
James Brower,	John Robertson,
Arrington Wickliffe,	George Winter,
Stephen King,	William Henry,
John Mattingly,	William Pope,
William Grant,	Robert Holliday,
Roger McMahon,	Robert Clark,
William Cotrell,	Peter Lowry,
Peter Fullam,	Duncan Cowen,
James Evans,	John Armond,
James Clerk,	Leander Murphy,
George White,	Thomas Skinner,
Henry Dogan,	John H. Crosson,
Zephaniah Posey,	Samuel Guy,
James Ebb,	Daniel Rich,
George Gilmore,	James Gilbert,
Charles Cunningham,	David Mason,
John Dickerson,	John Harley,
Joseph Roberts,	Francis Gray,
Amos Spencer,	George Marlow.
William Bird,	

OFFICERS AND PRIVATES

COMPANY NO. 8, AS IT STOOD JUNE 1, 1777.

William Johnston, Captain.
William Powell, Lieutenant.
Robert Porterfield, do.
John Townes, Ensign, from Nov. 25, 1776.

Sergeants.

Peyton Powell,
Archibald Botts,
William Oldrid,
Michael Loysett.

Corporals.

John Means,
William Palmer,
Shadrack Reader,
John McCart,
John Harriss, Drummer.

Privates.

John Cahill,
Andrew Harrison,
John Stanton,
John Hurley,
William Hunt,
John Pasgoe,
James Nicholls,
Nicholas White,
Thomas Welch,
Christian Fitzimmons,
Thomas Organ,
Richard Woodham,
Matthew Donnovan,
John Winder,
Francis Nix,
Richard Conner,
John Beavan,
Richard Matthews,
John Feagan,
Reuben Bearley,
Samuel Hart,
Nicholas Loyde,
John Martin,
Thomas Miller,
John Thomas,
Peter Read.

THE ABOVE COMPANY, AS IT STOOD NOVEMBER 1, 1778.

William Johnston, Captain.
Robert Porterfield, Lieutenant, and Adjutant in the Light-horse.
John Crittenden, Lieutenant.
Timothy Feely, do.

Sergeants.

Peyton Powell,
John Bruce,
John Lyon,
Michael Loysett,
Samuel Flaugherty
Archibald Botts.

Corporals.

John Means,
Shadrack Reader,
John Godbolt,
John Kearns,
John McCart,
John Harris, Drummer.

Privates.

Samuel Sparks,
James Thompson,
Nicholas White,
John Stanton.

OF THE REVOLUTIONARY WAR.   259

Aaron Paul,
Michael McEnnolly,
William Burk,
David Phillips,
James Nicholas,
Thomas Jeffs,
George Hanshaw,
George Shackelty,
John Smith,
Edward Marlow,
John McMullen,
Job Jenkins,
William Hunt,
Peter Gilham,
Richard Addison,
John Johnson,
Michael Shea,
Benjamin Bogan,
Robert Stakes,
James Heatly,
Alexander Strickland,
Joseph Fox,
Thomas Sherry,
William Gamble,
Thomas Miller,
Thomas Welch,
John Bartley,

John Thomas,
William Campbell,
John Read,
Thomas Smith,
Michael Donnovan,
Hugh Glass,
John Kahill,
Joseph White,
James Lynch,
John Halfpain,
Patrick Welch,
Andrew Harrison,
Thomas Jones,
Robert Blair,
Timothy Shain,
Thomas Roberts,
Richard Connor,
James Maloy,
Thomas Ogan,
John Feagan,
Daniel Dulin,
Richard Woodham,
James Bowing,
Robert Mitchell,
John Lovell,
William Groves,
Daniel Kent.

COMPANY NO. 4, AS IT STOOD JUNE 1, 1777.
Charles Porterfield, Captain.

Sergeants.

William Edmondson
George Greenway,

James Dunbar,
Solomon Fitzpatrick.

Corporals.
William Jenkins,

Anthony Maidy, Drummer.

Duncan Mead, Fifer.

Privates.

John Heth, Cadet.
David Cole,
Michael Redman,
John Qnaintance,
Richard Evans,
John Hickey,
James O'Bryan,

John Roberts,
Abraham Brewer,
John Melone,
Joshua Haycroft,
William Hodge,
Joseph Harris,
John Quinn,

OFFICERS AND PRIVATES

John Tomlin,
William Hinds,
Anthony Madden,
James Romaine,
John Holly,
Nathaniel Harper,
Jeremiah Connell,
Abel Romaine,
Christopher Buly,
Samuel Johns,
George Harris,
Moses Plain,
James Cassenbury,
James Allenworth,
Robert Severe,
John Kelly.

Thomas Stutherd,
Patrick Daily,
John Phillips,
Lewis Stump,
Andrew Everhart,
Andrew Drake,
Baptist Russell,
Aaron Redman,
John Alright,
William Atchison,
John Ously,
David Pugh,
Archibald Finley,
Alexander Dressdell,
John Collett.

COL. MORGAN'S RIFLEMEN, WHO WERE INCORPORATED AND SERVED WITH CAPT. PORTERFIELD'S COMPANY.

Elias Toland, Corporal. | Roly Jacobs, Corporal.

Privates.

Daniel Davies,
Humphrey Becket,
Solomon Veal,
Christopher Duncan,
Absalom Crown,
John Anderson,
Richard Rounsifer,
Edward Clevinger,
Jacob Stump,

William Bartlett,
David Ray,
John Adams,
John Robinson,
Samuel Middleton,
Abraham Groves,
John Hopewell,
James Giles,
William Jacobs.

THE ABOVE COMPANY OF CAPT. PORTERFIELD, AS IT STOOD NOV. 30, 1778.

Charles Porterfield, Captain,
Philip Slaughter, Lieutenant, and Paymaster.
David Williams, Lieutenant.

Sergeants.

William Edmundson,
James Dunbar,
Tobias Bourk,
Barnard Rogers,

Isaac Brown,
William Jenkins,
John Collett.

Corporals.

John Campbell, | Benjamin Sutton,

OF THE REVOLUTIONARY WAR.

Thomas Gaines,
Anthony Madden,
John Potts,

William Copeland,
William Hogg,
Anthony Byrom, Drummer.

Privates.

John Wood,
Augustus Berry,
Clement Richards,
Adam Sheets,
Thomas Hernly,
Rowland Sutton,
James Holmes,
Sylvester Hurly,
Jonathan Potts,
David Potts,
James Noland,
Archibald Finley,
Alex. Dindell,
Peter Barrand,
John Tomlin,
Jeremiah Connell,
Nathaniel Henper,
Edwin Clevenger,
John Kelly,
Joshua Haycraft,
George Wolf,
Zachary Butts,
William Roe,
Thomas Lee,

Henry Tinchman,
John Bell,
James Fitzgerald,
Thomas Stutherd,
John Cowgill,
Felty Fish,
Robert Green,
Thomas Mitchell,
John Strickland,
Lewis Stump,
Michael Murphy,
John Phillips,
William Elcheson,
William Bills,
Daniel Collett,
Moses Plain,
William Hinds,
Andrew Everhart,
William Whiteall,
John Dempsey,
Aaron Redman,
William Beason,
William Hicks,
Edwin Toe.

COMPANY NO. 5, AS IT STOOD JUNE 1, 1777.
William Smith, Captain.

Isaiah Larks, Lieutenant.

Thomas Thomas, Ensign.

Sergeants.
Isaac Brown,
Jonathan Owsly,
Thomas Owsly.

Corporals.
John Pruce,
Randall Morgan,
Matthew Byram.

Privates.

Timothy Kennedy,
Thomas McDonald,
David Phillips,
Thomas Boberts,
William Copeland,
David Potts,

Joseph Thornton,
Henry Purcel,
James M. Warren,
Edward Holmes,
William Whitehall,
Edward Marlow.

OFFICERS AND PRIVATES

Tobias Burgh,
Isaac Fleetwood,
Johathan Potts,
Joseph Daniels,
John Nugent,
John McMaklan,

Benjamin Kock,
George Spencer,
John Olvason,
Anthony Forrest,
(Discharged May 21, 1777.)

COMPANY NO. 6, AS IT STOOD JUNE 1, 1777.

Thomas Blackwell, Captain.
John Marshall, 1st Lieut.

James Wright, 2d Lieut.
Thomas Ransdell, 3d Lieut.

Sergeants.

John Morgan,
Samuel Phillips,

John Anderson,
Joseph Garner.

Corporals.

Edward Fielding,
Thomas Lawler,

Thomas Rycroft,
William Sudduth.

John Bates, Drummer.

Privates.

John Lawless,
John Williams,
Spencer Edwards,
John Lee,
Benjamin Kenton,
John Grant,
Daniel Grant,
John Mitchell,
John Laws,
John Hasty,
Clement Hasty,
Mach. Robinson,
James Ash,
Bayles Stone,
Richard Harvey,
Edward Ransdell,

Richard Broadus,
William Shumate,
John Straughn,
Charles Gainer,
John Phillips,
William Dennis,
Thomas Bates,
William Heally,
David Harris,
Samuel Elliott,
Charles Morgan,
Charles Duncan,
William Kearns,
John Crytser,
Simon Barry.

COMPANY NO. 7, AS IT STOOD JUNE 1, 1777.

Peter Bryn Bruin, Captain.
George Calmes, 1st Lieut.

Charles Magill, 2d Lieut.
Timothy Feely, Ensign.

Sergeants.

James Flaherty,
William Death,

John Early,
Daniel Carson.

James Fowdle, Cadet.

OF THE REVOLUTIONARY WAR.   263

Privates.

Benjamin Bogan,
William Burk,
John Bartley,
Job Jenkins,
Robert Blair,
John Halfpenny,
James Beetly,
Richard Addison,
Curtis Hill,
James Bowen,
George Handshaw,
John Kearly,
James Molloy,
John Burk,
John Carey,
John Campbell,
Dennis Jarrel,
William Gamble,
Hugh Glass,
William Legget,
John Crumm,
William Castle,
Christian Roony,
Michael McAnally,

Aaron Paul,
Robert Stokes,
Timothy Shehan,
Michael Shee,
Samuel Sparks,
John Sherry,
George Sheckelty,
James Thompson,
Joseph White,
Charles Wiltshire,
Thomas Jeffs,
John Johnston,
John Meade,
John Lovell,
William Groves,
Richard Black,
John McGuire,
Samuel Glynn,
James Davis,
Mathew Bevins,
James Talman,
Joseph Vance,
Peter Karland,
John Lyon.

COMPANY NO. 8, AS IT STOOD NOV. 30, 1778.

Thomas Wills, Captain. | Luke Cannon, Lieutenant.

Sergeants.

Henry Prudon,
William Trabue,

Frederick Nance.

Corporals.

Benjamin Rucks,
Bradford Cox,

John Murfrey.

Drum and Fife.

Thomas Gale, | Charles Broadfield.

Privates.

Cornelius Rind,
Joshua Perkins,
Samuel Murfrey,
Benjamin Ash,
Daniel Jones,
Charles McEntire,

Murdock McKinsey,
John Edwards,
Richard Johnson,
James Casey,
David Turner,
Obadiah Bullock.

OFFICERS AND PRIVATES

William Morris,
Jesse Kelly,
Aaron Woosley,
John Everett,
William Rose,
Robert Dison,
Walter Rand,
Daniel Goff,
Alexander Scurlock,
Burwell Flood,
John Morris,
William Creaton,
Claiborne Andrews,
John Connant,

George Blankership,
Isham Grow,
William Belcher,
James Crook,
Lawrence Ward,
John Toles,
William Guy,
Charles Lucas,
Joseph Handley,
Stephen Dyson,
Peter Maginnis,
Daniel Mullan,
James Walden,
Bartholomew Cyrus.

COMPANY NO. 9, AS IT STOOD NOV. 30, 1778.

George Rice, Captain.
James Wright, 1st Lieut.

John Barnes, 2d Lieut. and Qr. Mr.
Richard Marshall, Serg't Major.

Sergeants.

David Parker,
William Davis,

Aquilla Narvell.

Corporals.

Benjamin Wickliffe,
William Waller,
John Parkson, Fifer.
Joseph McMahon, do.

Henry Shaugh,
John Ferrill, Drummer.
John Welch, do.

Privates.

George McMahon,
William Henry,
William Cottrell,
John Bolden,
William Lewis,
John Mathews,
John Critchfield,
Thomas Shores,
Thomas Shivers,
James Evans,
George Winter,
Samuel Guy,
Robert Holliday,
Michael Malone,
Charles Cunningham,
Leander Murphy,

William Cole,
Terrance Conner,
Thomas Bryan,
John Melvin,
John Mattingly,
Moses Wickliffe,
William Suddoth,
James Brown,
James Parks,
William Gibbs,
Philip Freeman,
John Midson,
Henry Clung,
William Grant,
John Armond,
James Thompson,

OF THE REVOLUTIONARY WAR. 265

Robert Young,
Daniel Rich,
Henry Dogan,
Zephaniah Posey,
James Clark,
Matthew Martin,
John Evans,
Joseph Stillwell,
Amos Spencer,
Thomas Ashley,
Thomas Parsons.

John Stephens,
James Luck,
Enoe Lyon,
Thomas Crumley,
George White,
Benjamin Gray,
Edward Wilson,
John Quint,
Peter Fullam,
Francis Gray.

COMPANY NO. 10, AS IT STOOD NOV. 30, 1778.

Samuel Booker, Captain. | Lawrence Butler, Lieutenan

Sergeants.

Daniel Vasser, | William Cock.

Corporals.

James Ryalls, | Samuel Ryalls.

John Lewis, Drummer.

Privates.

Joel Vasser,
James Hinds,
Lewis Pugh,
Thomas Bridgeman,
Littleton Gaskins,
John Spence,
Levin Clark,
Joshua Hundly,
Benoni Lipscomb,
Bennet McGery,
Andrew Pable,
Joseph Robison,
John Dunaway,
Matthew Webb,
John Brawner,
John McKinsey,
William Buford,
John Tillory,
Henry Bird,
Moll Wilday,
Henry Spence,
Israel Singleton,
Abraham Davis,

Elisha Wyatt,
Benj. Bartlett,
John Algood,
Isaac Proctor,
John Kem,
Jesse Gaskins,
William Jeffrace,
Matthew Jackson,
Elijah Blundell,
John Parris,
Joseph Singleton,
John Lawrence,
James Frazier,
John Webb,
William Curtiss,
William Sebra,
John Nelson,
Jeffrey Palmer,
Charles Edwards,
John Derry,
Peter Howard,
James Spence,
Robert Ord.

OFFICERS AND PRIVATES

COMPANY NO. 11, AS IT STOOD NOV. 30, 1778.

James Gray, Captain.

Samuel Jones, Lieut. and Paym'r. | Thomas Davis, Ensign.

Sergeants.

Robert Craddock, | Richison Booker
Willis Wilson, | Henry Tillar.
Spratley Simmons, |

Corporals.

Micajah Holt, | Thomas Trent.
Benjamin Sublett, |

Drum and Fife.

James Curtis, | Thomas Weatherly.

Privates.

Henry Craddock, | Bartlett Holmes,
William Neal, | Thomas Pope,
James League, | Asa Cawley,
Lewis Story, | John Nunnally,
Morning Lipscomb, | George Lovell,
John Speed, | Moore Lumpkin,
Anthony P. Walter, | Richard Taylor,
Jerry Basham, | Moses Woosley,
Edmund Clements, | Stephen Stacey,
Jerry Bentley, | Stephen Freeman,
George Belcher, | Benjamin Newton,
Edward Belcher, | John Chaffin,
Edmund Absalom, | Isham Whitt,
Kirby Portis, | Joseph Whitaker,
Francis Smith, | Isaac Morris,
Jesse Bryant, | Robert White,
David Maiden, | Bobert Harrison,
Richard Day, | Caleb Hill,
Joseph Covender, | William Shett,
Robert Belcher, | John Quinn,
Thomas Lipscomb, | Robert Mush,
William Jenkins, | David Evans,
John Barker, | Jesse Hall,
William Woosley, | John Redwood,
William Madison, | Randall Reese,
Daniel Story, | Edmund Massey,

COMPANY NO. 12, AS IT STOOD NOV. 30, 1778.

John Gregory, Captain, | Thomas Holt, Lieutenant.
David Mason, do. |

OF THE REVOLUTIONARY WAR.   267

Sergeants.

Burwell Wilks,
Jacob Pain,
Isham Felts,
Lewis Best,

William Pryor,
George Hunt,
John Walters.

Corporals.

Joseph Hews,
Thomas Goodrum,
Bernard Wilkinson,
John Henderson,

John Slate,
Patrick Lynch,
John Newell.

Drummers.

Thomas Butler,
William Pearce.

David Mangum,
Edmund Edwards, Fifer.

Privates.

John Pearce,
William Green,
John Cleveland,
Ben. Wharton,
Chris. James,
Fennel Baker,
John Early,
Stephen Turner,
William Tomlinson,
John McKenny,
Jerry Ingram,
John Williams,
Michael Booth,
Hart. Barham,
John Hunter,
Jesse Kirkland,
James Dick,
Thomas Wilkerson,
William Whaley,
Michael Upchurch,

John Soden,
James Oast,
Sol. Kinsey,
Henry Williams,
David Dunn,
Jesse Nichols,
Matthew Russell,
George Russell,
Drury Thompkins,
Richard Edmunds,
Williamson Simmons,
James Simmons,
William Ward,
John Singleton,
Benjamin Matthews,
Peter Lynch,
Job Gaskins,
Andrew Harrison,
Tarlton Oldmond,
John Tuder.

LIEUT. COL. JOHN CROPPER'S COMPANY OF COL. MORGAN'S REGIMENT, ATTACHED TO GENERAL WOODFORD'S BRIGADE, AS IT STOOD NOVEMBER 30, 1778.

John Cropper, Lieut. Colonel.
Jno. Marshall, Capt. On furlough.

Thomas Ransdell, First-lieut.
John Townes, Second-lieut.

OFFICERS AND PRIVATES.

Sergeants.

Samuel Phillips,
Thomas Lawler,
William Cox,

Nathaniel Quarles,
George Flack,
John Anderson.

Corporals.

Edward Fielding,
Thomas Rycroft,
James Duffey,

Robert Watterson,
Simon Butt,
John Bates, Drummer.

Privates.

Spencer Edwards,
Kedar Dobbs,
William Roland,
Timothy Wood,
James Bailey,
Jesse Jones,
George Long,
John Huffman,
Abden Duff,
William Healy,
Alexander Rynalds,
Richard Broadus,
William Shumate,
William Dolbey,
Henry Matthias,
Matthew McDougle,
Joseph Davis,
Holliday Rival,
Howell Underhill,
Alexander Campbell,
William Leversage,
Charles Dunn,
William Creamore,
John Hastey,
John Laws,
William Kearns,

George Rose,
Henry Simmons,
Richard Harvey,
John Phillips,
John Fagg,
John Lee,
William Hardy,
David Harris,
Joshua Stafford,
Adam Cormack,
Levi Whitehurst,
John Bibbey,
George Sampson,
Thomas Banks,
Joseph Carter,
Seth Williams,
Isaiah Symes,
Daniel Haily,
Abraham Hill,
Nathan Millington,
John Lawless,
John Ore,
John Mitchell,
John Crytser,
Samuel Elliott,
William Flora.

COL. MORGAN'S COMPANIES OF RIFLEMEN, AS THEY WERE INCORPORATED, AND AS THEY STOOD JUNE 1, 1777.

Gabriel Long, Captain,
Philip Slaughter, Lieutenant.

James Harrison, Lieutenant.
Reuben Long, Ensign.

Corporals.

James Edrard,
John Campbell,

Daniel Hartley,
Nicholas Long,

Privates.

Evans Long,
John Harrison,
John Wood,
Augustine Barry,
James Hoomes,
John James,
Thomas Carrier,
Samuel McCurkle,
George Wolf,
Rowland Sutton,
Benjamin Sutton,
Clark Wise,
Robert Green,
James Noland,
John Cowgill,
Isaiah Corbin,
William Tandy,

William Roe,
Thomas Gaines,
Anthony Garnett,
William Howell,
Vincent Howell,
Burren Moore,
Thomas Wright,
John Thomas,
Jesse Wilhite,
James Harris,
Jacob Smith,
Isaac Miller,
Henry Holdway,
William Loyd,
James Wilson,
Patrick Harrison.

CAPT. SHEPHERD'S RIFLEMEN, JUNE 1, 1777.
Elert Hogland, Sergeant.

Privates.

Richard Evans,
Thomas Mitchell,

Felty Fritz,
Adam Sheets,

CAPT. WEST'S COMPANY OF RIFLEMEN, JUNE 1, 1777.
William Davis, Sergeant.

Privates.

Henry Tinchman,
Clement Richards,
James Bryan,

Martin Murphy,
Daniel Williams,
Joseph Sampson,

CAPT. BRADY'S RIFLE COMPANY JUNE 1, 1777.
John Barnes, Ensign.

Sergeants.

Robert Rankin,

John Burriss.

Privates.

William Cole,
William Lewis,
Charles Bealer,
Michael Malone,

John Evans,
John Bolden.
John Strickland,
Robert Fields.

NAMES AND RANK OF THE FIELD, STAFF, AND OTHER COMMISSIONED OFFICERS AND PRIVATES OF COLONEL ALEXANDER SPOTTSWOOD'S 2D VIRGINIA REGIMENT, AS IT STOOD FROM JANUARY TO JUNE, 1777.

Alexander Spottswood, Colonel.
Richard Parker, Lieut. Colonel.
Benjamin Day, Adjutant.
Ambrose Madison, Paymaster.
Robert Bell, Quartermaster.

Robert Andrews, Chaplain.
John Markham, Major.
James Wallace, Surgeon.
William Graham, Surgeon's Mate.

COMPANY NO. 1, AS IT STOOD MARCH 1, 1777.
Buller Claiborne, Captain.

John Worsham, First-lieutenant. | John Kennon, Second-lieutenant.

Sergeants.

George Burroughs,
Joseph Crook,
Lovell Harrison, Corporal.

John Cole,
John Crawford.
Patrick O'Hara, Drummer.

Privates.

Richard Bonner,
Rowland Kirkland,
Isham Browder,
John Stacy,
John Parker,
Frederick Young,
Reaps Mitchell,
Alexander Kear,

John Teate,
Henry Barker,
Barney Sykes,
Joseph Harrison,
Thomas Fisher,
Frederick Hobbs,
James Gordon,
Frederick Hobbs,

COMPANY NO. 2, AS IT STOOD MARCH 1, 1777.

Morgan Alexander, Captain.
Marquis Calmes, 1st Lieut.

Thomas Catlett, 2d Lieut.
Daniel Ragin, Ensign.

Sergeants.

Richard Patridge,
Patrick Hagerty,

John Thompson,
Thomas Trapp.

Corporals.

John McCullock,
Ledford Puller,

Henry Parrish,
Philip Ragin.

Privates.

Vaughn Jump,
John Ashby,

Priesly Loven,
Ephraim Doughrah.

Moses Baaer,
Aaron O'Bannon,
Samuel Trivet,
Alexander Keith,
George Blackmore,
Joseph Drinker,
Michael Monohon,
Thomas Bishop,
James Gassaway,
Moses Johnson,
Brice Ragin,
Stacy Wilson,
John Bowen,
Adam Byas,
William Cole,
John Breedlove,
Daniel McGowan,
Leonard Johnson,
Thomas Simmons,

Arthur Fenton,
Francis Nichols,
John Corking,
John Gassaway,
John Reid,
James Brown,
Jesse Balles,
John Brent,
James Thomas,
Jeremiah Harrigan,
William Reed,
Solomon Bishop,
William Dollar,
William McKentree,
George Smith,
Thomas Blackmore
Jacob Antill,
Charles Roan.

COMPANY NO. 3, AS IT STOOD MARCH 1, 1777.

Everard Meade, Captain.
Wood Jones, 1st Lieut.

John Ogilby, 2d Lieut.
Henry Moss, Ensign.

Sergeants.

Woodlief Thomas,
Robert Jones,

Francis Mallory,
Miles Gibbs.

Corporals.

William Porter,
Burwell Jackson,

Daniel Dunnavant,
John Porter.

Privates.

Philip Dunnavant,
Leonard Dunnavant,
Claiborne Dunnavant,
Edward Gibbs,
William Maiden,
Shedrack Clay,
Solomon Clay,
Hezekiah Seay,
Josiah Lussy,
Jacob Davis,
Joseph Roach,
Thomas Webster,
Isaac Belcher,

John Sadler,
Reuben Compton,
William Garrett,
Thomas Belcher,
James Seay,
Edward Booker,
Jaby Deaton,
Joshua Worsham,
Thomas Elmore,
Jacob Belcher,
Archibald Compton,
John Tucker,
Thomas Bowers,

OFFICERS AND PRIVATES

Samuel Hunt,
Thomas Robertson,
Richard Alderson,
John Spinner,
Thomas Brooks,
George Deaton,
Edward Belcher,
Joshua Hood,
Robert Mann,
Richard Wray,
Robert Bradshaw,
John Hood,
Barnard Roberts,
Henry Worsham,
George Vasser,
James Chappell,
Joel Shelton,
Joseph Stubbs, Drummer.

Herod Gibbs,
George Moody,
Peter Dyer,
Robert Ferguson,
Thomas Burton,
James T. Carr,
Joel Belcher,
William Belcher,
Joseph Eskridge,
Joseph Pollard,
James Taylor,
Nathan Davies,
John Cavender,
Obediah Hubbard,
Edward Hobson,
John Cossens,
Shedrack Lussy,
Thomas Mansfield, Fifer.

COMPANY NO. 4, AS IT STOOD APRIL 30, 1777.

Thomas Tebbs, Captain.
Peyton Harrison, Lieutenant. Commissioned February 25, 1777.
Valentine Harrison, Lieutenant.
Erasmus Gill, appointed Sergeant Aug. 28, 1776, and Ensign Nov. 28, 1776.

Sergeants.

John Hall,
Simon Horn,

Joseph Hough.

Corporals.

Levy Talbert,
James Dollar,

Adam Goff,
Alex. Smith, Drummer.

Privates.

Henry Palmer,
William Elliott,
George Williams,
John Cox,
William Rhodes,
James Dawson,
John Price,
Richard Price,
Charles Land,
Thomas Heatherly,
James Hardy,
Robert Preston,

James Farron,
William Denny,
Richard Bradley,
Thomas Hughes,
Evan Thomas,
Thomas Pennell,
Samuel Dunlap,
Thomas Splaune,
Cattesly Farron,
Henry Bush,
John Carroll,
Robert McWilliams.

OF THE REVOLUTIONARY WAR. 273

Francis Drishell,
Adonijah Davidson,
Philip Goff,
William Haller,
John Warner,
John Hildrup,
Patrick McIvory,
James Kidd,
John Reardon,
John Dunlap,
Elijah Henwood,
John Strother,

James Duvlin,
William Dawbin,
John McKensey,
Richard Fryer,
William Harris,
William McIntosh,
William Cannary,
Thomas Conner,
John Saunders,
William Farrow,
John Caddell,
Thomas Forbes.

COMPANY NO. 5, AS IT STOOD APRIL 1, 1777.

George Nicholas, Major.
John Holder, Lieutenant.

Samuel Cobbs, Lieutenant.

Sergeants.

Jeremy Parker,
Nathaniel Robertson,

Richard Claiborne,
John Bevins, Drum-major.

Corporals.

James Hix,
Francis Merryman,

Richard Jenkins.

Privates.

John Childress,
Jesse Bowling,
Nathan Gemmels,
Jacob Seay,
James Harper,
Robert Lowe,
William Booton,
James Robertson,
Thomas Merryman,
Robert Dickerson,
Henry Claiborne,
James Slate,
William Dillon,

James Morgan,
William Waters,
David Harfield,
Uriah Coulter,
Henry Hix,
Zechariah King,
William Jones,
George Williams,
John Moss,
James Strother,
Peter Dean,
Dudley Ballard,
William Woody.

COMPANY NO. 8, AS IT STOOD APRIL 1, 1777.

Francis Taylor, Captain.
William Taylor, First-lieutenant.

Francis Cowherd, Second-lieut.
James Burton, Ensign.

Sergeants.

Samuel Clayton,
James Broadus,

James Welch,
Robert Dawson.

274   OFFICERS AND PRIVATES

Corporals.

James Quin, | Thomas Shelton,
Evan Bramham, | John Bourn.

Jeremiah Cox, Drummer.

Privates.

Achilles Foster, | Joseph Hervey,
Henry Russell, | Shedrack Hill,
George Brooks, | Benjamin Dawson,
Ransdell Abbott, | Thomas Morris,
William Medley, | John Finnet,
William Ward, | Thornberry Bowling,
Thomas McClenahan, | James Dearing,
Robert White, | Thomas Breedlove,
Andrew Harrison, | Jacob Burrows,
Stephen Ham, | Elisha Estes,
Elijah Deer, | Perry Patterson,
Leonard Sale, | William Davis,
John Almand, | Humphrey Shay,
Gerard Morton, | William Martin,
Elisha Hawkins, | John Snow,
Robert Chandler, | Thomas Flennan,
James Brown, | Lewis Pines,
John Chowning, | Joel Foster,
John Gillock, | James Jackson,
Samuel Warren, | Thomas Ballard,
William Morris, | James Beazley,
Joseph Thomas, | William Turner,
James Long, | Edward Broadus,
Henry Barnett, | James Gibbons,
Turner Thompson, | John Johnson,

COMPANY NO. 7, AS IT STOOD MARCH 1, 1777.

William Sanford, Captain. | Joseph Archer, Lieutenant,
Alexander Parker, Lieutenant. | Thomas Parker, Ensign.

Sergeants.

William Eskridge, | Presley Sanders,
James Sanford, | Richard Sanford.

Corporals.

Jesse Brewer, | Joseph Smith.

Privates.

George Williams, | Rowly Harris,
William Chilton, | Tarpley Nash,
Daniel McChinney, | Henry Chilton.

OF THE REVOLUTIONARY WAR.   275

John Anderson,
William Silence,
John Cave,
Robert Sisson,
Richard Murry,
John Dunnaway,
Vincent McKinney,
George Davis,
William Hudson,
Francis Moore,
William Holmes,

John Holmes,
John White,
John Jackson,
Griffy Matthias,
George Allison,
William Marshall,
William Gowden,
John Marvel,
James Johnson,
George Hill,
Read Hutt.

COMPANY NO. 8, AS IT STOOD JUNE 1, 1777.
Samuel Hawes, Captain.

Thomas Jones, First-lieutenant. | James Upshur, Second-lieutenant.

Sergeants.

Thomas Downer,
Michael Long,

Thomas Parker,
John Gravatt.

Corporals.

Jeremiah Long,
James Croncher,

Samuel Boutwell,
George Muse.

Privates.

Thomas Ramsey,
Sylvester Hughes,
Virgil Poe,
John Vaughn,
Jesse Poe,
Jonathan Smith,
Richard Key,
John Sullinger,
Richard Chewning,
John Yarboro',
Thomas Livingston,
Reuben Allen,
William Griffin,
John Carter,
Willender Riddle,
Richard Ridle,
Obadiah Carter,
Rush Hudson,
Benjamin Robertson,
William Davis,
Humphey Davis,
Andrew Long,

George Murran,
Charles Brown,
Samuel Taylor,
Francis Golman,
James Baxter,
Cager Chapman,
Mark Bowler,
Benjamin Herndon,
James Sacrey,
Isaac Sacrey,
John V. Smith,
Harden Tuning,
George Marshall,
Clayborn Durret,
Joseph Flipper,
Landon Carter,
Jesse Woodruff,
Presley Cox,
William Marshall,
William Carter,
William Coates,
William Scandle,.

OFFICERS AND PRIVATES

NAMES AND RANK OF THE FIELD, STAFF, AND OTHER COMMISSIONED OFFICERS, AND THE PRIVATES OF THE 3D VIRGINIA REGIMENT, COMMANDED BY LIEUT. COL. WILLIAM HETH, AS IT STOOD FROM SEPTEMBER, 1777, TO MAY, 1778.

Thomas Marshall, Colonel.
William Heth, Lieut. Colonel, from April 1, 1777.
Chas. West, Major, from Feb. 1, 1777.
John Hawkins, Adjutant.
William Mountjoy, Paymaster.
Hezekiah Turner, do.
James Hansbrough, Quartermas'r.
Thomas Lawler, do.

David Griffith, Chaplain.
David Griffith, Surgeon.
Charles Land, Surgeon's Mate.
James Primm, Qr. Mr.'s Sergeant.
Chárles Whiteman, do.
Arthur Lind, Sergeant-major.
Richard Beal, do.
Edward Harris, Drum-major.
Daniel McCarty, Fife-major.

COMPANY NO. 1, AS IT STOOD FEB. 1, 1778.
John F. Mercer, Captain.

Sergeants.

James Prim,
George Jones,
George Patten,

Jeremiah Thindall
Daniel James,
John King,

Corporals.

Thomas Burris,
Burn Harris,
William Oliver,

David Price,
John Rogers,
John Nicholson.

Privates.

Samuel Young,
Charles Lambert,
James Holliday,
William Bland,
John Tate,
John Ethrington, sen.,
John Ethrington, jun.,
Edward McGinnis,
James Templar,
John Bridges,
Malleroy Adams,
James Kearns,
Thomas Moss,
Michael Rogers,
George Collop,
James Shepard,

Aaron Reynolds,
James Lee,
Robert Burn,
William Spender,
Francis Hughes,
William Sutherland,
William Sugars,
Daniel Mathews,
John Scott,
John Wells,
John Ayres,
John Thrailkill,
George Armstrong,
William Posey,
George Smith,
Robert Alvey.

OF THE REVOLUTIONARY WAR. 277

COMPANY NO. 2, AS IT STOOD MARCH 1, 1778.

David Arrell, Captain. | Arthur Lind, Ensign.

Sergeants.

Thomas Clack, | George Gordon.

Corporals.

William Wright, | Paul Tanner.
James Grimes, |

Drum and Fife.

John Bates, | Abraham Hammersly

Privates.

John Salter, | John Browers,
Benjamin McFarland, | Samuel Mason,
William Sollers, | Daniel Hayley,
George Johns, | John Lawler,
James Alverson, | Daniel Wright,
George Jeffrey, | James Dukins,
John Munroe, | Thomas Reed,
William Williams, | Joseph Bowen,
John Kelshaw, | Robert Allen,
John Athinson, | William Russell,
Andrew Monroe, | Thomas Holland,
William Kent, | William Bryant,
Dennis Shea, | James Wilkes,
Dennis McGuire, | Andrew Alexander,
Robert Godfrey, | Michael Drake,
Robert Bowling, | Arthur Stephenson,
William Gibbs Wallace, | William Williamson,

COMPANY NO. 3, AS IT STOOD MARCH 1, 1778.

Valentine Peyton, Captain. | William Gimber, Corporal.
Isham Keith, Lieutenant. | Walter Young, Fifer.
Hick Crosby, Sergeant. | William Bell, Drummer.

Privates.

Thomas Rutherford, | George Gully,
John Goley, | Thomas Fox,
—— McRector, | John Coppage,
Samuel Cox, | James Fleming,
James White, | William Jones,
Richard Sheerer, | Edward Riley,
William Elsmore, | Charles Barker,
Alexander Patten, | Jacob Pool,

OFFICERS AND PRIVATES

Jeremiah Stacy,
John King,
Nat. Coleman,
Moses Elmore,
John Felkins,
William Dogans,

Jesse Rose,
William King,
Nat. Lacey,
John Haddocks,
Christian Burn,
John Hastings.

COMPANY NO. 4, AS IT STOOD APRIL 1, 1778.

John Blackwell, Captain,
Joseph Blackwell, Lieutenant.
William Moore, Ensign.

William Bawcut, Sergeant.
Moses Allen, Corporal.

Privates.

Robert McMicken,
Thomas McClain,
James Tufnell,
John Thomas,
William Moffett,
William Bradford,
Stephen Tomlin,
Samuel Madden,
Daniel Dennington,
William Davis,
William Bailey,
Conner McGuire,
William Turvey,
John Wilkinson,
Morris Blenningham,

John Walker,
Jonathan Crook,
Benjamin Hamrick,
John Walton,
George Russell,
William Davidson,
Robert Doyle,
John Legg,
Robert Wood,
John Riley,
James Mitchell,
Thomas Gliver,
Henry Garrett,
George Cowling,
Peter Dearon.

COMPANY NO. 5, AS IT STOOD APRIL 1, 1778.

Robert Powell, Captain.
James Davis, Lieutenant.
Beverly Roy, Ensign.

Thomas Keane, Sergeant.
James Armstrong, Corporal.

Privates.

John Miller,
Richard Lee,
Charles Blunder,
Richard Jones, the taller,
Richard Jones, the less,
Thomas Brown,
Joseph Team,

William Feris,
Archibald Mitchell,
John Salter,
Lystra Vaughn,
William Breedlove,
Reuben Arthur,
Thomas Rice.

OF THE REVOLUTIONARY WAR.

Company No. 6, as it stood April 1, 1778.

Reuben Briscoe, Captain.
Thomas Hungerford, Lieut.
Thornton Taylor, Ensign.
John Elsmore, Sergeant.

Privates.

John Hines,
William Collins,
Daniel Preston,
Phil. Conner,
Michael Linton,
Aug. McDonald,
John Thompson,

Men discharged from this Company.

Peter Benham, Sergeant.
Charles Lander, do.
John Sidebottom, Corporal.
John Moreland, do.

Privates.

Even Thomas,
Andrew Race,
Charles Tyler,
George May,
James Murray,
William Bruton,
William Adams,
Sebastian Lush,
James McKinnie.

Company No. 7, as it stood April 1, 1778.

John Peyton, Captain.
John Tebbs, Lieutenant.
Henry Micon, Ensign.
John Copin, Sergeant.

Privates.

James Coates,
Luke Brady,
John Wood,
William Lent,
William Baily,
William Connerd,
John Mathews,
John Towers,
Lewis Murphy,
Zealy Colbert,
Jonathan Williams,
Henry Garvey.

Discharged Men.

William Matthews, Sergeant.
John Cullins, Sergeant.

Company No. 8, as it stood Feb. 14, 1778.

Philip Richard F. Lee, Captain.
Benjamin Tinnel, Lieutenant.
Samuel Love, Sergeant.
John Athey, Corporal.

Privates.

Henry Webb,
William Thurman,
Patrick Dorothy,
John Young,
John Russell,
Peter Larru,
Obadiah Philbert,
John Norman,

OFFICERS AND PRIVATES

William Groves, John Alva,
Francis Kendall, John Tillis,
George Florence, Abraham Line.

NAMES AND RANK OF THE FIELD, STAFF, AND OTHER COMMISSIONED OFFICERS OF COL. JOHN GIBSON'S DETACHMENT, WHO SERVED IN THE WESTERN DEPARTMENT, FROM JANUARY 1, 1780, TO DECEMBER 6, 1781, THE TIME HE SURRENDERED THE COMMAND OF THAT DEPARTMENT TO BRIG. GEN. WILLIAM IRVINE, WITH A LIST OF THE RESIGNED, DISCHARGED, AND DEAD FOR THE WHOLE TIME.

John Gibson, Colonel.
Richard Taylor, Major.
Jacob Colman, Ensign and Adjutant, and Lieutenant and Adjutant, from Dec. 1, 1780.
Josiah Tannehill, Ensign, Paymaster, and Clothier; and Lieutenant, Paymaster, and Clothier, from January 1, 1781.
Henry Dawson, Ensign and Quartermaster, and Lieutenant and Quartermaster, from February 22, 1780.
David Holmes, Surgeon.
John Knight, Surgeon's Mate.
Thomas Woods, Sergeant-major.
James Lane, Quartermaster's Sergeant.
John Smith, Drum-major.
William Coxon, Fife-major.
Lewis Thomas, Lieutenant. On detached service.
Lawrence Harrison. do. do.
William Conner, Ensign. do.
John Beck, Ensign. On detached service. Promoted to Lieutenant Mar. 1, 1780.
Uriah Springer, Captain.
Benjamin Biggs, do.

Robert Beall,	Captain.	Resigned	December 31, 1780.
Robert Vance,	do.	do.	do.
George Berry,	do.	do.	do.
Ephraim Relph,	Lieutenant.	do.	February 15, 1780.
John Dent,	do.	do.	November 20, 1780.
Thomas Holliday,	Sergeant.	Discharged	March 7, 1780.
William Dowell,	do.	do.	March 1, 1780.
Henry Bowen,	do.	do.	January 1, 1780.
Thomas Everett,	do.	do.	November 1, 1780.
John Hays,	do.	do.	April 10, 1780.
Benjamin Goodwin,	do.	do.	March 18, 1780.

OF THE REVOLUTIONARY WAR. 281

		Discharged		
John Chambers,	Sergeant.	March 1, 1780.		
Joseph Lemasters,	do.	do.	do.	
William Jenkins,	do.	do.	do.	
Caleb Hale,	do.	do.	do.	
Thomas Chambers,	do.	do.	October 14, 1780.	

Privates.

	Discharged.		Discharged.
James McKinney,	Mar. 1, 1780.	John Cleveland,	June 2, 1780.
Benjamin Dane,	do.	Thomas Robinson,	Oct. 28, 1780.
William Gillaspy,	do.	John Woods,	do.
Edward Stoker,	do.	John Dixon,	do.
John Shaver,	Mar. 13, 1780.	John Alexander,	do.
John Haley,	Mar. 15, 1780.	Edward Crutchlow,	Oct. 31, 1780.
James Salter,	do.	George Lefler,	Nov. 1, 1780.
George Emmett,	do.	William Orr,	Nov. 2, 1780.
James Rankins,	do.	Arnold Evans,	Nov. 1, 1780.
Jacob Poisal,	Mar. 27, 1780.	John Aliford,	Dec. 8, 1780.
William Roberts,	Mar. 28, 1780.	Patrick McGuire,	Jan. 2, 1781.
Jesse Clark,	Mar. 7, 1780.	James Manly,	Nov. 2, 1780.
Philip Finn,	April 18, 1780.	James Murphy,	do.
William Brown,	do.	Richard Carty,	Jan. 1, 1781.
Bartholomew Nedley,	April 19, 1780.	William Oakman,	Mar. 1, 1780.
Cornelius Downey,	April 27, 1780.	John Campbell	Nov. 10, 1780.
John McCutchen,	do.	Elijah Veatch,	Jan. 15, 1780.
Daniel Leany,	Sept. 10, 1780.	Hezekiah Linsey,	do.
Daniel Ryanhart,	Oct. 28, 1780.	Edward Wood,	Mar. 1, 1780.
James McMullan,	Nov. 13, 1780.	John Brisby,	do.
Christopher Baker,	Jan. 8, 1781.	James Kelly,	do.
Thomas Bendure,	do.	John Smith,	do.
John Lisk,	do.	Jacob Weatherholt,	do.
James Shaw,	do.	William Wood,	do.
Joseph Blackburn,	Mar. 1, 1780.	William Hunter,	do.
James Watson,	Mar. 9, 1780.	Henry Thomas,	do.
Benjamin Archer,	Mar. 1, 1780.	Freeman Battershell,	do.
Thomas Ricketts,	Mar. 8, 1780.	Hezekiah Clark,	do.
Abraham Booker,	do.	John Custard,	Mar. 8, 1780.
Nicholas Dickert,	Mar. 10, 1780.	John Aldridge,	Mar. 13, 1780.
William McElroy,	April 27, 1780.	Joseph Hiveler,	Mar. 18, 1780.
Peter Parchment,	Dec. 22, 1780.	Anthony Coon,	Mar. 20, 1780.
Simon Bailey,	Jan. 1, 1780.	John Lefevers,	Jan. 15, 1780.
William Bagly,	do.	Thomas Ravenscroft,	Jan. 28, 1780.
Joseph Thomas,	Mar. 1, 1780.	James Tittle,	May 12, 1780.
Elijah Thomas,	do.	Bladen Ashby,	do.
William Owens,	Mar. 8, 1780.	Thomas Brownlee,	June 2, 1780.
James Hicks,	Mar. 1, 1780.	James Gray,	Sept. 20, 1780.

	Discharged.		Discharged.
Samuel Calloway,	Oct. 15, 1780.	John Merick,	July —, 1780.
John Mains,	do.		Killed.
William Owens,	do.	Francis Johnston,	Mar. —, 1781.
Samuel Hutchison,	Oct. 12, 1781.	Thomas Eady,	do.
John Knapp,	Oct. 14, 1781.	John Michell,	July 18, 1781.
James M. Christy,	do.	John Evans,	Nov. 12, 1781.
Robert Penery,	Mar. 1, 1780.		Discharged.
Thomas Whitaker,	Mar. 2, 1780.	John Cowen,	Mar. 28, 1780.
Peter Springer,	Mar. 1, 1780.	Andrew Dunn,	July 6, 1780.
John Hamilton,	do.	William Collis,	do.
John Wheeler,	do.	Edward Evans,	Sept. 10, 1780.
Thomas Kelly,	do.	John Mishwonger,	April 29, 1780.
Jeremiah Archer,	do.	Thomas Mosely,	July 16, 1780.
John Stackhouse,	Mar. 2, 1780.	John Drummond,	do.
Peter Cartwright,	Mar. 10, 1780.	Charles Harvey,	Sept. 19, 1780.
Isaac Ross,	Mar. 18, 1780.	John Watson,	do.
John Brown,	do.	Harman Eakle,	Feb. 17, 1780.
John Brown,	Mar. 15, 1780.	John Allington,	Mar. 4, 1780.
Jacob Walter,	April 8, 1780.	Ralph Morrow,	
Peter Walter,	do.	John Wallace,	Mar. 29, 1780.
William White,	Mar. 1, 1780.	Joshua Still,	Jan. 5, 1780.
Jeremiah Simpson,	June 2, 1780.	Philip Buzan,	Jan. 10, 1780.
Charles Bodkin,	Sept. 10, 1780.	Patrick Kelly,	Mar. 29, 1780.
Simon Coghran,	Sept. 28, 1780.	David Smith,	Oct. 1, 1780.
John Smith,	Mar. 16, 1781.	Daniel Murray,	May 16, 1780.
William English,	Mar. 1, 1780.	Thomas Winn,	May 1, 1780.
Cornelius Johnson,	do.	John Kinard,	April 1, 1780.
Levid Bridgewater,	Mar. 2, 1780.	John Cheany,	May 11, 1780.
Thomas Philips,	Mar. 10, 1780.	George Fitzgerald,	May 24, 1780.
George Harling,	Mar. 18, 1780.	Henry Irons,	May 28, 1780.
James Gunner,	Mar. 13, 1780.	John Gilbert,	June 15, 1780.
Samuel Streets,	do.	Patrick Rogers,	do.
Henry Scott,	Mar. 18, 1780.	John Sullivan,	July 16, 1780.
John Colbert,	do.	Thomas Duggan,	July 20, 1780.
Thomas Walker,	do.	Joseph White,	July 1, 1780.
James Colvin,	Mar. 16, 1780.	James Gray,	Aug. 16, 1780.
Michael Poock,	Sept. 30, 1780.	William Canard,	Mar. 1, 1780.
John Pratt,	Nov. 10, 1780.	Joseph Fuller,	Aug. 1, 1780.
Thomas James,	do.	Brice Ragon,	Mar. 14, 1781.
Robert Beckett,	do.	Robert Broad,	do.
Richard Bilby,	Nov. 24, 1780.	Peter Parker,	do.
Richard Churchfield,	do.	John Smith,	Feb. 1, 1781.
John Cowen,	do.	John Clark,	May 1, 1781.
Adam Dust,	Jan. 1, 1780.	James Dawson,	do.
William Walker,	Mar. —, 1780.	William Douglass,	July 20, 1781.

OF THE REVOLUTIONARY WAR. 283

	Discharged.		Discharged.
Jeremiah York,	July 20, 1781.	John Pearson,	Mar. 1, 1780.
Andrew Anderson,	Aug. 15, 1781.	Ludwick Hart,	Aug. 1, 1780.
George Sutch,	Aug. 1, 1781.	Charles Crawford,	Mar. 30, 1781.
Felix McKinney,	June 4, 1780.	John Needham,	July 15, 1781.

CAPT. URIAH SPRINGER'S COMPANY.

John Harrison, Lieutenant.
Joseph Winlock, Ensign.
John Gibson, do.
John Williams, Sergeant.
Thomas Tannehill, do.
Thomas Moore, do.
William Evans, Corporal.

James Adams, Corporal.
John Hagerty, Corporal, from Jan. 1, 1781.
Isaac Horsfield, Corporal.
John Smith, Drummer.
Thomas Whealy, do.
John Hinds, Fifer.

Privates.

James Cumberford,
John Burnett,
Garret Cavener,
William Barr,
John Britton,
Thomas Hatley,
Alexander McIntosh,
William Harbert,
Richard Roach,
Hyatt Lazier,
Roderick McDaniel,
Richard Carter,
William Smith,
James Reynolds,
William Craig,
Benjamin Broomes,
Philip Henthorn,
Edward Paul,
Samuel Smith,
James Seavell,
Nicholas Carter,
Robert Hughes,
Henry Squires,

John Ross,
Pat. Baity,
William Hansford,
Edward McDonald,
James Smith,
Jacob Conrad,
Henry Vann,
Samuel Osburn,
Thomas Craigg,
James Duffy,
John Gossett,
Charles Evans,
Michael Kairns,
William Bailey,
Richard Sparrow,
David Dunnagan,
Christopher Carpenter,
John Finney,
Robert McCarney,
Matthew Hurley,
Francis Smith,
Michael Smith,
Joseph Row.

Those who joined this Company Jan. 1, 1781.

Nicholas Hagerty,
James Whealy,
Robert Crawford,
John Lockhart,
Lachlin McLane,

Patrick Finnagin,
Eneas McCoy,
Christopher Carpenter,
William Hansford,
Michael Hainy.

OFFICERS AND PRIVATES

William Hickock,
Isaac Stott,
John Young,
George Phelps,

Bryan Cowran,
Charles Brooks,
Robert Hughes,
Francis Mains.

CAPTAIN BENJAMIN BIGGS' COMPANY.

Jacob Springer, Lieutenant.
John Mills, Ensign.
Alexander Fraser, Sergeant.
John Hull, do.
Moses Ward, do.
Samuel Cruswell, Corporal.

John Barnett, Sergeant.
(Joined Feb. 1, 1781.)
William Johannes, Corporal.
Edward Sheppard, do.
(Joined Jan. 1, 1781.)
Thomas McIlwain, Fifer.

Privates.

Jonathan Welsh,
Samuel McCord,
William Overline,
John Rooke,
Robert Bacon,
Thomas Jackson,
John Guttery,
Samuel Lemon,
James Amberson,
James Carr,
John Robeson,
Thomas Buite,
Stephen Winters,
John Shea,
Pat. Thornton,
James Stackpole,
Michael Murphy,
John Riley,
Alex. McAdams,
John Rock,
Peter McCartny,
James Low,
John English,
William Cloyd,
Henry Skinner,
Charles Robinson,
Joseph Fowler,
John Conner,
William Brumagem,
John Morrison,
William Connolly,
William Martin,

David Clark,
John Phillips,
Samuel Reaves,
Clement Gillihan,
Joseph Woods,
John Godfrey,
James Hoorish,
Jacob Adams,
John Cardonas,
William Love,
Isaac Devore,
John Ritchie,
Jacob Buher,
Jacob Rhodes,
Charles Morgan,
John Bean,
Thomas Jones,
John Dougherty,
John Vilet,
John Richeson,
William Woods,
Joseph Denison,
Isaac Halfpenny,
Dennis Selavan,
John Berry,
James Johnson,
James Parlor,
Reuben Abbett,
James Beham,
Edward Walker,
William Brazer,
John Woodman.

OF THE REVOLUTIONARY WAR.

NAMES OF THE CAPTAINS AND PRIVATES OF COLONEL NATHANIEL GIST'S VIRGINIA REGIMENT, IN 1777.

FIRST COMPANY.

John Gist, Captain.

Privates.

David Luckett,
Sherwood Vaughn,
James McEagan,
Edward Joyce,
Dennis Curly,
William Harris,
William Welch,
Michael Madden,
John Connelly,
Archibald Bartlett,
William Knowles,
William Ryan,
Matthew McHugh,

John Lewin,
Thomas Watson,
John Tubbs,
Joseph Lovett,
Joseph Neal,
Walter Hartlett,
Thomas Griffin,
Peter Carbury,
Elisha Darrington,
James Johnson,
Joseph Wilson,
Daniel Spratt,
Samuel Bent.

SECOND COMPANY.

Samuel Lapsley, Captain.

Privates.

Isaac Anglin,
Abram Cutlip,
Edward Thomas,
Thomas Smith,
John Martin,
John Carpenter,
Thomas Kinsey,
John Arnold,
James Smith,
John Hanna,
Elias Roberts,
Thomas Ermin,
John McElhenny,
Julius Blackburn,
Hugh Hughs,

Charles Wymer,
James Gibson,
James Simpkins,
Thomas Price,
James Squires,
John Turbutt,
Solomon Brundage,
William Simpkins,
Garret Simpkins,
John Lee,
James Harris,
John Freeland,
Robert Martin,
Robert Oglesvy,
Humphrey Montgomery.

THIRD COMPANY.

Strother Jones, Captain.

OFFICERS AND PRIVATES

Privates.

John Nelson,
Thomas Harrison,
Josias Stone,
Jacob Johnson,
George Speak,
Henry West,
Wilson Gray,
Edward Clements.
Aaron Simmons,

William Speake,
William Basey,
Joshua Poor,
John Howard,
Matthew Coffer,
Hezekiah Speake,
Owen Scolfield,
Nehemiah Crawford,
Alexander Wallace.

FOURTH COMPANY.
Joseph Smith, Captain.
Privates.

Alexander Monroe,
Patrick Coleman,
Edward Harvey,
John Hillier,
William Mitchell,
James Taylor,
Charles Hagan,
John Parrott,
Daniel Chumly,
Jeffrey Basdell,
Thomas Johnson,
James Solomon,
William Jaco,
Francis Rogers,
Dennis Shay,

William J. Conner,
Peter Pole,
George Moore,
Thomas Taylor,
Jonathan Tinsley,
Michael Yewless,
Michael Dolin,
Emanuel Ebbs,
Nightingale Richardson,
John O. Brian,
Thomas Henry,
Robert McAdams,
John Wooster,
Hugh Barthorn,
Josiah Daniel.

FIFTH COMPANY.
Thomas Bell, Captain.
Privates.

Patrick Shannon,
Thomas Chapman,
James Tate,
Sampson Archer,
David Chambers,
John Stephens,
John Mitchell,
William Kingore,
William McGowan,
John Brown,

James Shields,
James Wilson,
Bartholomew Ragan,
Rousy Merritt,
John Locke,
John Forehand,
Thomas Foster,
Dennis McKinney,
Gordon Kelly,
George Wesfield,

OF THE REVOLUTIONARY WAR. 287

Joseph Hood,
Michael McMasters,
James Lockhart,
Ludwick Miller,
James O'Brian,

Abell Armstrong,
Thomas Conway,
Joseph Kenny,
Martin Sutton.

SIXTH COMPANY.

Alexander Breckenridge, Captain.

Privates.

Alexander Rattray,
Hezekiah Brady,
Peter Parish,
Joseph Smith,
Ambrose Jones,
Smith Thompson,
John Williams,
Hugh McLaughlin,
Richard Spindler,
Thomas Gillaspy,
Benjamin Dawson,
Thomas Snead,
Samuel Savage,

Thomas Curtis,
Daniel White,
Thomas Miller,
Christopher O'Brian,
George Tomlinson,
Richard Pearle,
Hazel McWilliams,
John Sweepstone,
George Lambert,
Thomas Smith,
Thomas Rhodes,
John Cain,
James Squires.

SEVENTH COMPANY.

Francis Muir, Captain and Paymaster of the Regiment.

Privates.

John Linton,
Edward Rineker,
John Spitfathom,
Durret Covey,
Charles Melton,
Thomas Hopewell,
John Sale,
John Wynn,
Daniel Ferguson,
Waitman Reynolds,
Isaac Artiss,
Luke O'Neal,
Caleb Baldwin,
Henry Orem,
Daniel Guilder,

John McDaniel,
William Crosby,
William Haley,
John Gruttage,
Jesse Rineker,
Francis Ravenscroft,
Peter Kittare,
William Nuss,
Thomas Flood,
James Thompson,
Luke Metheny,
Thomas Meruny,
Samuel Patterson,
Timothy Kelly,
John Kirk.

OFFICERS AND PRIVATES

THE EIGHTH, OR THE MAJOR'S COMPANY.

Privates.

James McGee,
Jacob Rump,
John Crook,
Thomas Stevens,
Joseph Williams,
Robert Reynolds,
Christian Hobinstock,
Joshua Clifton,
Levi Powell,
Israel Peterson,
James Oliver,
Frederick Myers,
Benjamin Dawson,

Henry Ringlespauser,
Samuel Jones,
Benjamin Ethol),
Thomas Verdin,
John Knight,
Richard Hill,
Perrigrine Brady,
Joseph Brady,
James Rains,
Henry Rains,
William Foster,
Jesse Davis,
Morris Minnaham.

OFFICERS OF LIEUT. COL. LEE'S LEGION OF CALVARY.

Henry Lee, Lieut. Colonel (Light-horse Harry).
Henry Peyton, Major. Died in service.
Joseph Eggleston, Major.
Alexander Skinner, Surgeon and Lieutenant.
Wm. Winston, Adjutant and Lieutenant.
Patrick Carnes, Captain.
Ferdinand O'Neal, do.
James Armstrong, do.
Matthew Irwin, Surgeon.
Michael Rudolph, Captain.

George Handy, Captain.
Lawrence Manning, Lieutenant.
Peter Johnson, do.
George Carrington,
George Guthrie,
William Lewis, Lieutenant. Died in service.
Robert Power, Cornet.
John Jordan, do.
William Middleton, do.
Albion Throckmorton, do.
William B. Harrison, do.
Clement Carrington, Ensign.
John Champe, Sergeant-major.

A LIST OF VIRGINIA OFFICERS, WITH THE DATES OF THEIR COMMISSIONS, IN 1776.

Captains.

	Commissioned.		Commissioned.
James Johnson,	Feb. 16, 1776.	Thomas Patterson,	Feb. 24, 1776.
Oliver Towles,	do.	William Gregory,	Feb. 26, 1776.

OF THE REVOLUTIONARY WAR.   289

	Commissioned.		Commissioned.
Samuel Hopkins,	Feb. 26, 1776.	Thomas Massie,	Mar. 11, 1776.
Samuel Cabell,	Mar. 4, 1776.	Thomas Hutchins,	Mar. 21, 1776.
Thomas Ruffin,	Mar. 11, 1776.	John Jones,	April 9, 1776.

Lieutenants.

Nicholas Hobson,	Feb. 16, 1776.	Peter Garland,	Feb. 16, 1776.
Nathaniel Fox,	do.	Charles Tutt,	do.
Joseph Curd,	Feb. 24, 1776.	James Burnett,	Feb. 24, 1776.
Peter Dunn,	Feb. 16, 1776.	John Gregory,	Feb. 26, 1776.
Abiah Clay,	Feb. 26, 1776.	Hutchins Burton,	do.
Alexander Rose,	Mar. 4, 1776.	Benj'min Talliaferro,	Mar. 4, 1776.
Billy H. Avery,	Mar. 11, 1776.	William Murray,	Mar. 11, 1776.
John Hockaday,	do.	Richard Appuson,	do.
Henry Williams,	Mar. 21, 1776.	James Conway,	Mar. 21, 1776.
Peter Jones,	April 9, 1776.	William Stark,	April 9, 1776.

Ensigns.

John Stokes,	Feb. 16, 1776.	James Barnett,	Mar. 4, 1776.
Joseph Holliday,	do.	Collin Cock,	Mar. 11, 1776.
John Barksdale,	Feb. 20, 1776.	William Armstead,	do.
John Bell,	Feb. 26, 1776.	Harden Perkins,	Mar. 21, 1776.
William Dawson,	do.	Dinwiddie Goodwin,	April 9, 1776.

Cadets.

Beverly Stubblefield,	Capt. Towles' Co.	Approved Feb. 10, 1776.	
Larkin Smith,	do.	do.	do.
John Chew,	do.	do.	Feb. 14, 1776.
Benjamin Patterson,	Capt. Patterson's Co.	do.	Feb. 27, 1776.
John Baynham,	Capt. Towles Co.	do.	Feb. 28, 1776.
William Parsons,	Capt. Fox's Co.	do.	Mar. 25, 1776.
William Hill,	do.	do.	do.
Edward Irwin,	do.	do.	do.
John Jordan,	Capt. Cabell's Co.	do.	Mar. 26, 1776.
John Clay,	Capt. Hopkins' Co.	do.	Mar. 30, 1777.
James Dillard,	Capt. Cabell's Co.	do.	do.
Philip Holliday,	Capt. Massie's Co.	do.	July 17, 1776.
Samuel Buckner,	do.	do.	Aug. 25, 1776.
Larkin Stanard,	do.	do.	Sept. 1, 1776.

NAMES AND RANK OF THE OFFICERS, AND A LIST OF THE PRIVATES, OF LIEUT. COL. FRANCIS MARION'S SOUTH CAROLINA REGIMENT, AS IT STOOD NOVEMBER 1, 1779.

FIRST COMPANY.

Adrian Proveaux, Captain.
Josiah Kolb, Lieutenant.
Robert Matthews, Sergeant.
(Killed.)
John Burtell, Sergeant.

Noble Barnett, Sergeant.
John Mills, Corporal.
Solomon Long, do.
Enoch Boolk, Drummer.
Jacob George, Fifer.

Privates.

George Hughs,
Alexander Stewart,
James McDaniel,
John Hawkins,
Isaac Chinners,
William Norman,
Archy M. Daniel,
Frederick Hughs,
John Ratford,
John Harper,
William Johnston,
David Vaughn,
Walkinsheer Thompson,
Samuel Cortney,

Rolly Rawlins,
Edward George,
John Thompson,
Philip Thomas,
John White,
John Perry,
Lewis Patrick,
Jacob Benhoist,
John Caddy,
Amos Tubbs,
James Gaskey,
William Phillips,
Samuel Blackford.

SECOND COMPANY.

Richard Baker, Captain.
Alexander Hume, Lieutenant.
(Killed Oct. 9, 1779.)
John Roberts, Sergeant.
Alexander McDonald, do.

Joseph Wilkins, Corporal.
Daniel Andrews, do.
Levi Brown, do.
Silas Gibson, Fifer.

Privates.

Solomon Stapleton,
Benjamin Webster,
Dickerson Green,
John Fenwick,
John Richardson,
Henry Taylor,
Robert Clyatt,
Andrew Adams,
Samuel Horn,
Thomas Hagarthy,
William Connell,

James Castello,
Moses Mace,
Nathaniel Swobb,
Timothy Downing,
George Taylor,
James Russell,
Jonathan Collins,
Adam Meek,
William Waites,
Joshua Morgan,
Lewis Domas.

THIRD COMPANY.

Charles Motte, Captain. Killed Oct. 9, 1779.
Albert Roux, Lieutenant. Captain from Oct. 9, 1779.
Alexander Petrie, Lieutenant.
Christopher Rogers, do.
William Murphy, Sergeant.

George Brewton, Sergeant.
William Jones, Corporal.
William Oliver, Corporal. Killed Oct. 9, 1779.
William Lyon, Corporal.
William Burbridge, Drummer.
Peter Area, Fifer.

Privates.

Benjamin Huggins,
James Fitzsimmons,
Thomas Burbridge,
Matthew Anderson,
John Burbridge,
Jonathan Burbridge,
James Stanton,
Oswald Hackle,
Nathaniel Rogers,
Humphrey Haines,
Robert Penhorn,
William Easton,
Malcolm McFarlan,

John Taylor,
Cornelius Constanstine,
Ralph Ingram,
Joseph Cooper,
Samuel Kinney,
Lewis Powell,
George McCormack,
Francis Farrell,
William Willis,
Thomas Mills,
Hugh Newman,
John Godbolt,
Vincent Maroni.

FOURTH COMPANY.

Peter Gray, Captain.
John Wickom, Lieutenant.
James Gray, do. (Killed Oct. 9, 1779.)
John McDowell, Sergeant.
James Feast, do.

Joseph Turner, Sergeant.
Abraham Bearslick, Corporal.
Thomas Galloway, do.
Samuel Brown, do.
Lewis McClendall, Drummer.
Frederick Lamb, Fifer.

Privates.

Richard Clark,
John Campbell,
Ambrose Bray,
Alexander Ferguson,
Joseph Pain,
Isaac Withersford,
Bartholomew Sline,
Henry Martin,
Joshua Hall,
William Winford,
John Riley,
Abraham Berlean,

Hendrick Kiler,
Jesse Simmons,
Charles Hutton,
William Martin,
Charles Skipper,
Reuben Wales,
Charles Bentley,
John Hyrne.
William Hughes,
John Bewly,
Edward Bambrick,
William Simpson,

OFFICERS AND PRIVATES.

William Leaton,
Moses Childs,
John Peter Allen,

Benjamin Stone,
Thomas Jones,
Robert Launce.

FIFTH COMPANY.

Thomas Hall, Captain.
John Hart, Lieutenant.
(Promoted Aug. 6, 1779.)
James Legare, 2d Lieutenant.
William Henderson, Sergeant.
Reuben Minor, do.

William Harvey, Sergeant.
Robert Raine, Corporal.
George Valley, do.
John Dubose, do.
Philip Fry, Drummer.
Conrad Fitner, Fifer.

Privates.

James Reed,
John Croford,
Thomas Crozer (killed),
John Caton,
Thomas Welch,
Daniel McFarling,
Francis Simson,
Rapes Going,
Enoch Andrews,
William Hasemon,
Benjamin Owens,
Dempher Oldfield,
Solomon Mitchell,
Hugh Holland,
John Proby,

Edward Fry.
Samuel Moet,
Nehemiah Watt,
Thomas Faulder,
Needham Gunter,
John Clements,
Henry Dishes,
Thomas Goodson,
Thomas Davis,
Samuel Henderson,
Thomas Bowan.
James Fitzpatrick.
Benjamin Sergenor,
William Linsey,
John Marlow.

SIXTH COMPANY.

Thomas Moultrie, Captain.
Peter Foissin, Lieutenant.
Stephen Roberts, Sergeant.
Douglass O'Neal, do.
Daniel Green, do.

William Rogers, Corporal.
David Manly, do.
Samuel Murray, do.
Robert Logan, Drummer.
Archibald Robertson, Fifer.

Privates.

William Cade,
Frederick Gowin,
James Grubbs,
Edward Gainey,
Archibald Lamb,
William McAllister,
James Grover,
William Russell,

Abraham Baggett,
Francis Bridges,
Edward Wainwright,
James Hain,
Richard Lackey,
Henry McCall,
John Friday,
Robert Cox,

OF THE REVOLUTIONARY WAR. 293

John Bently,
Moses Groom,
Elisha Tomplat,
James Houston,
Peter Deviney,

James McGowin,
Edward Murphy,
Nicholas Barger,
John Steel,
(Killed Oct. 9, 1779.)

SEVENTH COMPANY.

Thomas Dunbar, Captain.
William Capers, 1st Lieutenant.
Cornelius Van Vielland, 2d Lieutenant. Killed Oct. 9, 1779.
Alexander McDonald. Sergeant-major.
William Jasper, Qr. Master's Sergt. Killed while attempting to plant the American colors on the parapets of Spring Hill redoubt, at

the storming of Sayannah, October 9, 1779.
Henry Webb, Sergeant.
John McDonald, do.
Reuben Dewitt, do.
Harris Dewitt, Corporal.
William Manning, do.
James Sparrow, do.
James Newton, Corporal and Fifer.
Jesse Martin, Drummer.

Privates.

Barnaby Brian,
Joseph Davis,
John Dius,
Aaron Harris,'
William Henson,
John Hampton,
John Holmes,
William Mimms,
James Moody,
Richard Richardson,
Robert Whiley,
James Oliver,
James Leaton,
Robert Gamble,
James Ford,
John Butler,
Frederick Simmons,
Daniel Jordan,
Nicholas Flinn,
John Chavis,
John Martinsharp,
William Chancelly,
Hezekiah Heath,
James Clark,

Kindred Hollisman,
James Jones,
Barrel Jones,
William Wilkinson,
John Francis,
George Carrick,
Thomas Oliver,
William Cook,
Thomas Nute,
David Whily,
Christopher Gamond,
John McBride,
James Scurry,
David Stuart,
John Smith,
Shedrack McClindens,
John Sparrow,
William Cade,
John M. Cade,
John Whitely,
Thomas Stafford,
Joseph Hughes,
Thomas Windsor,
William Clark.

OFFICERS AND PRIVATES

EIGHTH COMPANY.

Richard Mason, Captain.
Paul Warley, Lieutenant.
John Taylor, Sergeant.
John Davis, do.

James Clatworthy, Sargeant.
Thomas Kidwell, Corporal.
William Crapps, Drummer.
Moses Newton, Fifer.

Privates.

John Conner,
William Brown,
Samuel Butler,
Joseph Reeves,
Benjamin Reeves,
Matthew Skipper,
Isaac Herring,
Thomas Rawlins,
William T. Jones,
Matthew Kenedy,
Jeremiah Peters,
Hugh Derberry,
John Thompson,
Anthony Hinds,

Adam Smith,
Peter Rosman,
Michael Peters,
William Ryan,
Charles Burnham,
Stephen Irons,
William Enochs,
Philip Newton,
Thomas Raybold,
William Chaney,
William Dalton,
Henry Savage,
Timothy Green.

NINTH COMPANY.

Daniel Mazyck, Captain.
John Martin, 1st Lieutenant.
George Ogiere, 2d do.
William Wood, Sergeant.
Benjamin Stone, do,
Jacob Kalkoffer, do.

William McCollough, Corporal.
Marmaduke Ethridge, do.
Samuel McMillian, do.
David Parrish, Fifer.
Benj. Booth, do.
John Robinson, Drummer.

Privates.

Hugh Davis,
Rowland Walker,
John Carter,
Benjamin Breeler,
Thomas Poston,
John Smith,
Arthur Colson,
Drury Smith,
John Keith,
William McCullock,
John Breeler,
James Beard,
William Hyde,
Joseph Mallery,
William Clay,

William Pawling,
John Dubose,
Thomas Cowen,
Robert Marker,
Blake Calcott,
William Gunter,
John Skipper,
Edward Brown,
Hector McLane,
Jacob Heigle,
Abram Debraudy,
Christopher Gallington,
John Teague,
Charles Caves,
Frederick Rowland.

NOTE.—This South Carolina Regiment was at the storming of the enemy's works at Savannah, by the American troops under General Lincoln, and the French under Count D'Estaing, on the 9th October, 1779. Captain Motte, of the third Company, and Lieutenant Gray, of the fourth were killed; also Sergeant Matthews, Sergeant Oliver, and Lieutenant Hume, and others.

Count D'Estaing was wounded, and the noble Pulaski was killed. Here, also, Sergeant William Jasper, of Captain Dunbar's Company, so renowned for his feats of daring bravery, while planting the American colors on the parapets of Spring Hill redoubt, was pierced with a ball, and fell into the ditch. Before he died he said to Major Horry, "Tell Mrs. Elliott I lost my life in supporting the colors she presented to our regiment."

BRITISH PRISONS AND AMERICAN PRISONERS.

CAPTURE OF AMERICANS BY THE BRITISH—BRITISH PRISON HOUSES AND PRISON SHIPS—A LIST OF DISTINGUISHED AMERICAN PRISONERS OF WAR—TIME OF CAPTURE, EXCHANGE, ETC.

IN the early part of the Revolutionary war, it happened that the British were often victorious, and successful in the capture of many of the undisciplined Americans. On the 8th, 9th, and 10th of June, 1776, General Frazer, of the British forces overcame the Americans under General Thompson, Colonel St. Clair, Colonel Irvine, and others, at the battle of the Three Rivers, during the invasion of Canada. In this unfortunate skirmish, General Thompson, Colonel Irvine, of Pennsylvania, and about two hundred others, were made prisoners, and the rest pursued through a swamp for several days in great confusion.

At the battle of Long Island, August 27, 1776, General Sullivan was taken prisoner, and at the same battle Lord Stirling surrendered himself to the Hessian General De Heister, with about 1100 men, as prisoners of war. Generals Sullivan and Stirling were confined on board the British ship "Eagle," and the men were confined on Long Island, and on board the enemy's vessels in the Sound. They were subsequently sent to the loathsome prisons in New York city and to the prison-ships at the Wallabout.

At General Putnam's retreat from New York, on the 15th of September, 1776, about three hundred of his men were captured, and on the 11th of October following, General Waterbury, of the Washington Galley, and his crew, were made prisoners by the crew of the British ship "Inflexible."

FORT WASHINGTON SURRENDERED.

On the 16th of November, 1776, Fort Washington, on the east bank of the Hudson, near the city of New York, after a desperate resistance on the part of the Americans, was surrendered by Colonel Magaw of the Pennsylvania line. Mr. Lossing, in in his Field Book, says:

"On the 15th, Howe was informed of the real condition of the garrison and works at Fort Washington, by a deserter from Magaw's battalion, and he immediately sent a messenger with a summons for the commander to surrender, or peril his garrison with the doom of massacre. Magaw, in a brief note, promptly refused compliance, and sent a copy of his answer to Washington at Hackensack. Howe, confident of success, ordered a cannonade to be opened upon the American outworks from two British redoubts, situated on the east side of the Harlem, a little above the High Bridge. The cannonade commenced early on the morning of the 16th, to cover the landing of troops which crossed the Harlem there, preparatory to a combined attack at four different points. Expecting this, Magaw made a judicious disposition of his little force. Colonel Rawlings, with his Maryland riflemen, was posted in a redoubt (Fort George) upon a hill north of Fort Washington, and a few men were stationed at the outpost, called Cock-hill Fort. Militia of the Flying Camp, under Colonel Baxter, were placed on the rough wooded hills east of the fort along the Harlem River, and others, under Colonel Lambert Cadwallader, of Pennsylvania, manned the lines in the direction of New York. Magaw commanded in the fort.

"The plan of attack was well arranged. Knyphausen, with five hundred Hessians and Waldeckers, was to move to the attack on the north simultaneously with a division of English and Hessian troops under Lord Percy, who were to assail the lines on the south. At the same time, Brigadier Matthews, supported by Cornwallis, was to cross the Harlem River with the guards, light-infantry, and two battalions of grenadiers, and land above Fort Washington under cover of the guns on the Westchester Hills, just mentioned, while Colonel Stirling, with the 42d regiment, was to cross at a point a little above the High Bridge. These arrangements were carried out. Knyphausen divided his forces. One division under Colonel Rahl (killed at Trenton seventy days afterwards), drove the Americans from Cock-hill Fort, while Knyphausen with the remainder penetrated the woods near Tubby Hook, and, after clambering over felled trees and other obstructions, attacked Rawlings in Fort Tryon. The fort was gallantly defended for some time, and many of the Hessians were slain. Rawlings was finally forced to yield, and returned to Fort Washington, under cover of its guns, when Knyphausen planted the Hessian flag upon Fort Tryon. In the mean while Percy had crossed near Harlem, swept over the plain, drove in the American pickets at Harlem Cove (Manhattanville), and attacked Cadwallader at the advanced line of intrenchments. Percy's force was eight hundred strong; Cadwallader had only one hundred and fifty men and one eighteen-pounder. Both parties fought bravely, and Percy, yielding, moved towards the American left, behind a wood, and the combat ceased for a while.

"While Rawlings and Cadwallader were keeping the assailants at bay, Stirling and Matthews landed. The latter pushed up the wooded heights, drove Baxter's troops from their redoubt (Fort George) and rocky defence, and stood victor upon the hills overlooking the open field around Fort Washington. Stirling, after making a feigned landing, dropped down to an estuary of the river, landed within the American lines, and rushing up the acclivity by a sinuous road, attacked a redoubt on the summit, and made about *two hundred prisoners*. Informed of this, and perceiving the peril of being placed between two fires, Cadwallader retreated along the road nearest the Hudson, closely pursued by Percy, and battling all the way. When near the upper border of Trinity Cemetery (155th-street), he was attacked on the flank by Colonel Stirling, who was pressing across the island to intercept him. He continued the retreat, and reached the fort, after losing a few killed and about *thirty made prisoners*. On the border of the Cemetery, and near the fort, severe skirmishes took place, and many of the Hessian pursuers were slain. The defence was gallant; but pike, ball, and bayonet, used by five thousand men, overpowered the weakened patriots, and at meridian they were nearly all gathered within the ramparts of the fort. General Howe now sent another summons to surrender. Perceiving resistance to be in vain, Magaw complied, and at half-past one o'clock the British flag was waving where the Union banner was unfurled defiantly in the morning. The garrison, amounting to more than two thousand men, were made prisoners of war, and with these the *jails of New York were speedily gorged*."

Washington, who had been all the time an anxious spectator of the battle from the other side of the Hudson, wept like a child on beholding the retreat to, and surrender of, the fort. He wrote to General Charles Lee, informing him of the surrender of the fort, and of his future plans of operation. Lee replied, and all that he said with respect to the surrender of Fort Washington, was: "Oh, General, why would you be persuaded by men of inferior judgment to your own? It was a cursed affair." Lee was second in command to the Commander-in-Chief, whose speculations as to the future were full of gloomy anticipations.

To James Bowdoin, President of the Massachusetts Council, Lee writes as follows: "I hope the cursed job of Fort Washington will occasion no dejection—the place itself was of no value. For my own part, I am persuaded that if we only act with common sense, spirit, and decision, the day must be our own. Indecision bids fair for tumbling down the goodly fabric of American freedom, and, with it, the rights of mankind. 'Twas indecision of Congress prevented our having a noble army, and on an excellent footing. 'Twas indecision in our military councils which cost us the garrison of Fort Washington, the consequence of which must be fatal, unless remedied in time by a contrary spirit. Inclosed I send you an extract of a letter from the General (*Washington*), on which you will make your comments; and I have no doubt you will concur with me in the necessity of raising immediately an army to save us from perdition. Affairs appear in so important a crisis, that I think the resolves of Congress must no longer too nicely weigh with us. We must save the community in spite of the ordinances of the Legislature. There are times when we must commit treason against the laws of the State for the salvation of the State. The present crisis demands this brave, virtuous kind of treason."*

In December, 1776, our "decisive" General Lee was snugly quartered at a tavern at Baskinridge, N. J., about three miles from his own army, and about twenty miles from the British encampment at Brunswick. Supposing himself perfectly safe, Lee wrote to General Gates about Fort Washington, and rapped the Commander-in-Chief over the knuckles in the following strain: "The ingenious manœuvre of Fort Washington has completely unhinged the goodly fabric we had been building. There never was so dammed a stroke; *entre nous*, a certain great man is most damnably deficient. He has thrown me into a situation where I have my choice of difficulties: if I stay in the province I risk myself and army; and if I do not stay, the province is lost forever." †

We will now see what became of our impetuous and "decisive" Lee. He had just signed his famous letter to General Gates, doubtless presuming he had uplifted a thunderbolt sufficient to demolish General Washington, when suddenly General Wilkinson, who was with him, exclaimed, "Here, sir, are the British cavalry!" "Where?" replied Lee. "Around the house," said Wilkinson. "Where is the guard? Damn the guard—why don't they fire? Do see what has become of the guard," said Lee. Poor Lee, the guards had fled! Colonel Harcourt's dragoons entered the house and took Lee, and conveyed him a

---

* Irving's Life of Washington. † Ibid.

prisoner of war to the British camp. They boasted of having taken the "American Palladium," for they considered Lee the most scientific and experienced of the rebel generals.‡

On the 25th September, 1775, Colonel Ethan Allen, of "Continental Congress" renown, and famous as the captor of Ticonderoga, was himself captured at Montreal, and sent to England to be tried for treason. He was confined there in Pendennis Castle, and, without a trial, he was returned to New York in 1776, a prisoner of war, and was not exchanged until May 6, 1778.

On the other hand, by way of retaliation, the Americans were successful in making some wholesale captures of the British forces. At the battle of Trenton, December 26, 1776, the Americans, under General Washington, succeeded in capturing about 1000 Hessians under Colonel Rahl, among whom were about thirty-two officers. Colonel Rahl was mortally wounded in the confused skirmish with the Americans, and soon after died.

On the 17th October, 1777, General Burgoyne, of the British forces, and his whole army, surrendered to the Americans under General Gates; and on the 19th October, 1781, Lord Cornwallis and his army surrendered to the Americans under General Washington, at Yorktown, Va. The particulars of the above capitulations are too well understood by the American people to require explanation here, but the captives of those two armies were not confined by the Americans in loathsome dungeons, like the infamous British prisons in New York.

On the 13th of January, 1777, General Washington wrote to Sir William Howe as follows: "I am directed by Congress to propose an exchange of five of the Hessian field officers taken at Trenton for Major-general Lee; or, if this proposal should not be accepted, to demand his liberty upon parole within certain bounds, as have ever been granted to your officers in our custody. I am informed, upon good authority, that your reason for keeping him hitherto in a stricter confinement than usual, is, that you do not look upon him in the light of a com-

‡Ibid.

mon prisoner of war, but as a deserter from the British service as his resignation has never been accepted, and that you intend to try him as such by a court-martial. I will not undertake to determine how far this doctrine may be justifiable among yourselves, but I must give you warning that Major general Lee is looked upon as an officer belonging to, and under the protection of the United Independent States of America, and any violence you may commit upon his life and liberty, will be severely retaliated upon the lives and liberties of the British officers, or those of their foreign allies in our hands. I would beg that some certain rule of conduct towards prisoners may be settled; and if you are determined to make captivity as distressing as possible, let me know it, that we may be upon equal terms, for your conduct shall regulate mine."

"I am sorry," writes he to Lord George Howe, on the subject of the naval prisoners, "that I am under the disagreeable necessity of troubling your lordship with a letter, almost wholly on the subject of the cruel treatment which our officers and men in the naval department, who are unhappy enough to fall into your hands, receive on board the prison-ships in the harbor of New York. From the opinion I have ever been taught to entertain of your lordships humanity, I will not suppose that you are privy to proceedings of so cruel and unjustifiable a nature; and I hope that, upon making the proper inquiry, you will have the matter so regulated, that the unhappy persons whose lot is captivity, may not in future have the miseries of cold, disease, and famine, added to their other misfortunes. You may call us rebels, and say that we deserve no better treatment, but remember, my lord, that, supposing us rebels, we still have feelings as keen and sensible as loyalists; and will, if forced to it, most assuredly retaliate upon those upon whom we look as the unjust invaders of our rights, liberties, and properties. I should not have said thus much, but my injured countrymen have long called upon me to endeavor to obtain a redress of their grievances, and I should think myself as culpable as those who inflict such severities upon them, were I to continue silent."

Both Lord Howe and Sir William Howe, in their answers affected to believe that the American prisoners were not severely treated, and appeared ignorant of the brutal tyranny of Cunningham, the provost marshal, over the unfortunate but firmly patriotic prisoners.

Some difficulties and misunderstandings arose relative to the case of General Lee, which put an end to operations with respect to negotiations for the exchange of prisoners, and those on both sides had to suffer on in consequence, and with them, the brave and eccentric captor of Ticonderoga, Ethan Allen.

A tariff for the exchange of prisoners was fixed upon by Major-general Phillips on the part of the British, and a committee of officers, prisoners at New York, on the part of the Americans, in 1779, in which a sergeant was reckoned equal to two privates, an ensign to four, a lieutenant to six, a captain to sixteen, a major to twenty-eight, a lieutenant-colonel to seventy-two, a colonel to one hundred, a brigadier-general to two hundred, a major-general to three hundred and seventy-two, a lieutenant-general to a thousand and forty-four, an adjutant and quartermaster to six, each, a surgeon to six, a surgeon's mate to four, a surgeon of hospitals to sixteen, deputies and assistants to six, each, and all other officers in proportion, to be regulated by their rank in the line.

From September 15, 1776, to November 25, 1783, nearly the entire period of the revolutionary war, New York remained in the hands of the British, and was made the head-quarters of the foulest tyranny over helpless prisoners ever known in the darkest ages of the world. The bastiles of Europe never furnished such a picture. Jerusalem within, besieged by the Romans without, never felt the horrors of the New York prisons; the fear of which stimulated the American nerve to fight with desperation, and die, if he could, rather than be doomed to this awful incarceration. The bones of the martyrs washed, naked and exposed, on the shores of the Wallabout, brought forth fruit unto liberty and constituted a prominent pillar in the glorious fabric of American freedom. These bones inspired the living patriot. Let a monument over them be erected to the skies!

"The new jail," says Mr. Lossing in his Field Book, "was made a provost prison, where American officers, and the most eminent whigs, who fell into the hands of the British were confined. Here was the theatre of Cunningham's brutal conduct towards the victims of his spite. The prisoners were formally introduced to him, and their names, age, size, and rank, were recorded. They were then confined in the gloomy cells, or to the equally loathsome upper chamber, where the highest officials in captivity were so closely crowded together, that when, at night, they laid down to sleep on the hard plank floor, they could change position only by all turning over at once, at the words, *right—left*. Their food was scanty and of the poorest kind, often that which Cunningham had exchanged at a profit for better food received from their friends or the commissariat. Little delicacies, brought by friends of the captives, seldom reached them; and the brutal Cunningham would sometimes devour or destroy such offerings of affection in the presence of his victims, to gratify his cruel propensities.

"Thus for many months gentlemen of fortune and education, who had lived in the enjoyment of the luxuries and refined pleasures of elegant social life, were doomed to a miserable existence, embittered by the coarse insults of an ignorant, drunken Irish master.

"The prison-ships were intended for seamen taken on the ocean, yet some soldiers were confined in them. These lay in Gravesend Bay, and there many of the prisoners taken in the battle near Brooklyn were confined until the British took possession of New York, when they were removed to prisons in the city. In 1778 the hulks of decaying ships were moored in the Wallabout, a sheltered bay on Long Island shore, where the present Navy-yard is. There, in succession, the *Whitby, Good Hope, Scorpion, Prince of Wales, Falmouth, Hunter, Stromboli,* and half a dozen of less note were moored, and contained hundreds of American seamen captured on the high seas. The sufferings of these captives were intense, and at the close of 1779 they set fire to two of them, hoping to secure either liberty or death.

"In 1780 the Jersey was placed in the Wallabout, and used as a prison-ship till the close of the war, when she was left to decay on the spot where her victims suffered.

'The name and character of each prisoner were registered when he first came on board. He was then placed in the hold, frequently with a thousand others, a large portion of them covered with filthy rags, often swarming with vermin. Every morning the prisoners brought up their bedding to be aired, and, after washing the decks, they were allowed to remain above till sunset, when they were ordered below with imprecations, and the savage cry, '*Down, rebels, down!*' The hatches were then closed, and in serried ranks they lay down to sleep, if possible, in the putrid air and stifling heat, amid the sighs of the acutely distressed and the groans of the dying. Each morning the harsh order came below, '*Rebels, turn out your dead.*' The dead were selected from the living; each sewed in his blanket, if he had one, and thus conveyed in a boat to the shore by his companions, under guard, and hastily buried.

"So shallow were the graves of the dead on the shores of the Wallabout, that while the ships were yet sending forth their victims, the action of the waves and the drifting of the loose sand often exposed the bones of those previously buried. Year after year this revolting exhibition might be seen, and yet no steps were taken to preserve the remains of the martyred patriots until 1803, when Samuel L. Mitchell presented a memorial to Congress, in behalf of the Tammany Society of New York, soliciting a tomb for the martyrs. The prayer of the petitioners was not granted, and no further legislative action was had."

At the second session of the twenty-seventh Congress, in 1842, as shown by Report No. 1026, the Common Council of the city of Brooklyn again took this subject in hand, and petitioned the National Legislature to bury, and erect a monument over the bones of the revolutionary patriots who perished in the British prisons and prison-ships in New York. The bones are now deposited in the ground owned in 1842 by Benjamin Romaine, Esq., on Long Island. The committee of Congress to whom this petition was referred, made an adverse report, for fear of establishing a precedent for other similar petitions! Will not this rich, powerful, and independent nation, even at the sacrifice of her last dollar, reconsider the matter, grant the petition, and erect the monument!

The imprisoned, emaciated, and dying patriots, in the dark hours of 1780, when nearly all hope of independence had fled forever, and when the deserter, tory, and traitor stalked over the land in fearful combination, reached forth their skeleton hands, wrote, and bequeathed this task to their countrymen in their dying hours: "If you are victorious, and our country emerges free and independent from the contest in which she is now engaged, but the end of which we are not permitted to see, bury us in her soil, and engrave our names on the monument you shall erect over our bones, as victims who willingly surrendered their lives as a portion of the price paid for your liberties, and our departed spirits will never murmur, or regret the sacrifice we made to obtain for you the blessings you enjoy."

The following is a List of the Principal American Commissaries of Prisoners, with a List of Captured and Imprisoned Officers:

ELIAS BOUDINOT, Commissary-general of Prisoners, appointed in 1776.
JOHN BEATTY, Commissary-general of Prisoners.
ABRAHAM SKINNER,   do.   do.
JOHN ADAMS, Assist.   do.   do.
JOHN BROOKS, Assist. Com. of Issues.
THOMAS BRADFORD, Com. of Prisoners.
LEWIS PINTARD, Agent for the prisoners at New York.
THOMAS FRANKLIN, Agent for the prisoners at Philadelphia.

PRISONERS OF WAR.

CHARLES LEE, MAJOR-GENERAL,

Second in command to the Commander-in-Chief, was captured at Baskinridge, N. J., in December, 1776, by Colonel Harcourt, of the British dragoons. A tory had visited the quarters of General Lee, to complain of the loss of a horse taken by his army, and on learning the whereabouts of the particular quarters of General Lee, the tory rode eighteen miles in the night to inform the British. Lee's quarters were three miles from the encampment of his army. At the time of his capture his guards had stacked arms, and were sunning themselves by the south side of the house, when the British dragoons galloped up, scattered the guards, took Lee, without hat, and in his slippers and blanket-coat, and triumphantly clattering off to the British camp at Brunswick, delivered up their queer-looking specimen of a prisoner. He was exchanged for General Prescott, on the 6th of May, 1778.

MAJ. GEN. LORD STERLING

Was taken prisoner at the battle of Long Island, August 27, 1776, by the Hessians, under General De Heister, and was confined on board the British ship "Eagle" for about one month, when he was exchanged for Governor Brown, of Providence Island, who had been captured by Commodore Hopkins.

MAJ. GEN. JOHN SULLIVAN

Was also captured at the battle of Long Island, August 27, 1776, by the Hessians, under the immediate command of Count Donop, and confined in the "Eagle," with Lord Stirling; but was paroled by Lord Howe, and sent by him to the Continental Congress with a verbal message, desiring a conference with a committee of that body. He remained a prisoner on parole for about three months and was exchanged for General Prescott.

MAJ. GEN. BENJAMIN LINCOLN

Surrendered himself a prisoner of war to Sir Henry Clinton, at the fall of Charleston, May 12, 1780. He remained a prisoner on parole until November of the same year, when he was exchanged, and in the spring of 1781 joined General Washington.

MAJ. GEN. WILLIAM MOULTRIE

Was the second in command at the siege and fall of Charleston. He was, with General Lincoln, taken prisoner May 12, 1780, at the surrender of Charleston. He remained a prisoner on parole for about eighteen months, and returned to Charleston in 1782.

COL. ETHAN ALLEN

Was captured in his attack on Montreal, Sept. 25, 1775, and carried to General Prescott, the commandant of the British post at that place. General Prescott asked him if he was that same Allen who captured Ticonderoga. On being told he was the very man, Prescott shook his cane over his head, put himself in a great rage, called him a rebel, and threatened his neck with a halter. He was exchanged May 6, 1778, as before observed.

BRIG. GEN. JAMES IRVINE,

Of the Pennsylvania militia, was captured in his attack on the British Camp on Chestnut-Hill, near White Marsh, on the 5th of December, 1777. After a short skirmish, all his men fled, and left him wounded on the field. Gen. Irvine was sent to Philadelphia, and put in confinement there. He received fifty dollars from Thomas Franklin, the agent for the prisoners in that city, to cheer him in his dungeon. In January, 1778, he was removed to New York. On the 3d December, 1780, Mr. Skinner, the Commissary-general, advanced him 4,000 continental dollars, which, at the enormous rate of depreciation then existing, profited him but little. He was exchanged June 1, 1781. General Washington, before he was properly acquainted with him, called him *Ewing*, which gave rise to many errors among historians about his name. To settle this question, he will be again referred to in a future page.

COL. NICHOLAS LUTZ,

Of the Pennsylvania Flying-Camp, was captured at the battle of Long Island, August 27, 1776. On the 16th April, 1777, he was admitted to parole within certain bounds, and was exchanged September 10, 1779. He returned to his home at Reading, Pa., where he must have died shortly after, for it does not appear that he ever called on the commissaries of prisoners for anything that may have been due him during his imprisonment and parole.

PRISONERS OF WAR.

Col. Michael Swope,

Of the Pennsylvania Flying-Camp, a Fort Washington prisoner, was captured November 16, 1776. He was released on parole June 23, 1778, but again called into New York on the 8th of August, 1779, where he had to endure the confinement of his fellow-prisoners, martyrs for patriotism. He was exchanged at Elizabethtown, N. J., on the 26th of January, 1781, and returned home to Yorktown, Pa., on foot, a distance of 170 miles. He was very well supplied by Mr. Pintard, at New York, with "Continental dollars," which he readily sold at the rate of seventy-five for one in specie in the spring of 1780! The current exchange of the day was forty for one in specie, but the poor prisoners, robbed of their liberty, money, and life, could not get the advantages of the money market.

Major George Tudor,

Of the 3d Pennsylvania Regiment, commanded by Colonel Lambert Cadwallader, was captured at Fort Washington. At the time of his capture he was a captain, and the following soldiers of his company were taken prisoners with him on the memorable 16th of November, 1776:

Charles Fleming,
John Wright,
James McKinney,
Ebenezer Stille,
Jacob Leinhart,
Abraham Van Gorden,
Peter Daubert,
William Carbury,
John McDowell,
William McKague,
Henry Parker,
James Burns,
Henry Kepler,
Baltus Weigh,
Charles Beason,
Leonard Huber,
John McCarroll,
Jacob Guiger,
John May,
Daniel Adams,
George McCormick,
Jacob Kettle,
Jacob Miller,
George Neason,
James Kearney,
David Sutor,
Adam Bridel,
Christian Mull,
Daniel McKnight,
Cornelius Westbrook,
Luke Murphy,
Joseph Conklin,
Adam Dennis,
Edward Ogden,
William Scoonover,
James Rosencrants.

Those unfortunate and devoted patriots endured the horrors of the prison-ships and prison-houses of New York; nor is it known that they were ever exchanged by a kinder interposition than death. They lived to inscribe their names high up on the sombre walls of their prison, and died martyrs for the cause of American freedom, appealing with their fellow-prisoners to their countrymen that in case American Independence should ever be achieved, a monument would be erected over their bones, which were washed and exposed on the shores of the Wallabout.

Major Tudor was exchanged May 10, 1778, and repaired quickly to join his regiment, then at Schoharie, N. Y.

MAJOR THOMAS L. BYLES,

Of Colonel Lambert Cadwallader's 3d Pennsylvania Regiment, was another of the prisoners of Fort Washington, captured November 16, 1776. He was Captain from the 1st of August, 1776, to June 8, 1777, when he was promoted to Major. He was exchanged March 1, 1778, and hastened to join his regiment at Valley Forge. He died in service on the first day of February, 1779.

MAJ. JOHN POULSON,

Of the 8th Virginia Regiment, was captured October 5, 1777.— He was Captain from July 1, 1777, to May 12, 1779, when he was promoted to Major. He was exchanged November 2, 1780, at Elizabethtown, N. J., and returned to his home in Accomack county, Va. He subsequently joined the army, and served to the end of the war.

ADJUTANT JOHN JOHNSON,

Of Colonel Baxter's Flying-Camp, was captured at Fort Washington, November 16, 1776. He received 3650 Continental dollars and £204 while imprisoned. He was exchanged November 2, 1780; and returned to his home in Buckingham township, Buck's county, Pa., when his military career seems to have ended.

ADJUTANT DANIEL KENNEDY,

Of the 6th Pennsylvania Regiment, was captured April 17, 1778. He was Sergeant from September 1, 1776, to February 15, 1777, when he was promoted to Lieutenant, and to Adjutant the 15th of June, 1777. Prisoners always received promotion according to rule as though they were in active service. Major Samuel Benezet kindly supplied Adjutant Kennedy with money and provisions. It appears that he spent most of the time of his captivity in Philadelphia, and received the special attention of Colonel William Palfrey, Paymaster-general. He was exchanged August 1, 1780.

FERDINAND J. S. DE BRAHM,

Major of Engineers, was captured at the surrender of Charleston, May 12, 1780. He was confined a prisoner in that city, and received cash and supplies to the amount of about 3000 Continental dollars from John Sanford Dart, Deputy Paymaster-general for the Southern Army, and Mr. Fisher, Commissary of Prisoners. He was exchanged April 22, 1781, and appeared in Philadelphia on the 17th of July of that year, where he succeeded in selling his "Continental dollars" at the rate of forty for one in specie.

BARON CHARLES DE FREY,

Captain of light-dragoons in Count Pulaski's Legion. He was captured February 1, 1778, and released July 1, 1778.

CAPTAIN WILLIAM CRAWFORD,

Of the 5th Regiment of Pennsylvania, another Fort Washington captive, taken November 16, 1776. He was Lieutenant from September 1, 1776, to May 1, 1777, when he was promoted to Captain. He received supplies from Lewis Pintard, agent for the New York prisoners, and was exchanged December 18, 1780. He returned to Philadelphia, and subsequently returned to his regiment and served to the end of the war.

CAPTAIN JOHN RICHARDSON,

Of the 5th Regiment of Pennsylvania, another Fort Washington prisoner, taken November 16, 1776. He received supplies from Lewis Pintard, agent of the prisoners at New York, and was exchanged October 31, 1778. He became a supernumerary on the new arrangement of the army in 1778, received "half-pay November 1, 1778, to May 22, 1779, agreeable to a resolve of Congress of November 24, 1778," and "one year's pay allowed to supernumerary officers, agreeable to a resolve of Congress May 22, 1779."

Captain Bateman Lloyd,

Of the 2d Regiment of New Jersey, was captured February 27, 1778. He received his supplies from Lewis Pintard, at New York, and Thomas Franklin, at Philadelphia. He was exchanged at Elizabethtown, N. J., on the 1st of April, 1781, and made his way, 116 miles on foot, to his place of abode in Salem, in that State. All the imprisoned officers were offered their liberty in case they would enlist in the British cause, and the inhuman keepers of their prisons always held this temptation before them. Foul subornation of treason! Lord Howe, where was thy blush?

Captain Robert Sample,

Of the 10th Regiment of Pennsylvania, was captured March 7, 1778. He received his supplies from Thomas Franklin at Philadelphia, and Lewis Pintard and John Adams at New York. He was exchanged November 4, 1780, at Elizabethtown, N. J., and returned to his home, 170 miles, to Bucks county, Pa., but returned to the army, and served to the end of the war. Captain Sample was a fine scholar and a meritorious officer.

Captain Thomas McIntire

Commanded an independent company. The circumstances of his capture and imprisonment appear nowhere on record, yet his name is among the prisoners of 1780. He was Ensign from August 1, 1777, to January 1, 1778, when he was promoted to a Lieutenant; and on the 8th of March, 1779, he was made Captain of an Independent Company, and some part of his time harrassed the confederated savages in the valley of the Wyoming.

Captain Robert Caldwell,

of Colonel Samuel I. Atlee's Regiment. Captain Caldwell and Colonel Atlee were both Fort Washington prisoners. I have met with no particulars of Colonel Atlee's imprisonment and exchange. Captain Caldwell was Lieutenant from September 1, 1776, and was promoted to Captain November 16, 1776, the same day of his capture. He received supplies from Lewis Pintard and Elias Boudinot at New York, and was exchanged April 15, 1779, at Elizabethtown, N. J., and made his way to Philadelphia, a distance of eighty miles. I have no account of his return to the service.

Captain James Moore,

Of Colonel Hall's Delaware Regiment, was captured January 20, 1778. Lewis Pintard to Colonel Hall, under the date of March 4, 1781, states that Captain Moore received from him, by order of John Beatty, Commissary-general of Prisoners, £107 7s. 5d., while a prisoner in New York; and Thomas Franklin says that he advanced him £8 7s. 4½d. at Philadelphia; and John Adams at Elizabethtown says he advanced him 276 Continental dollars. He was exchanged December 7, 1780, at Elizabethtown, and made his way to Dover, in the State of Delaware, a distance of 170 miles. He soon joined his regiment, and dealt out hot revenge on his remorseless captors until the close of the war.

Captain Matthew Knox,

Of Colonel Lambert Cadwallader and Colonel John Shee's 3d Pennsylvania Regiment, was another of the ill-starred Fort Washington prisoners, captured November 16, 1776. He was commissioned as Lieutenant January 5, 1776, and promoted to a captaincy October 11, 1776, in the place of Captain West, promoted to Major. Lewis Pintard advanced him £72 7s. 8d. while a prisoner in New York. He received "half-pay from October 23, 1778, to May 22, 1779, agreeable to a resolution of Congress of the 24th of November, 1778," and "one year's pay allowed to supernumerary officers, agreeable to a resolve of Congress of

May 22, 1779." He was exchanged October 22, 1778, at Elizabethtown, and returned to his home in Philadelphia, a distance of eighty miles, which appears to have closed his military career.

CAPTAIN SAMUEL CULBERTSON,

Of Colonel Montgomery's Regiment of Flying-Camp, a Fort Washington prisoner, was captured November 16, 1776. He was a prisoner, within certain bounds on Long Island, until August 16, 1779, when he was ordered into the the city prisons of New York. Lewis Pintard and Colonel Palfrey supplied him in 1776 and 1777 with money. He was exchanged November 2, 1780, at Elizabethtown, N. J., and made his way, 110 miles, to his place of abode at Yellow Springs, Pa. Captain Culbertson was possessed of fine literary abilities, and military talents.

CAPTAIN JOHN MCDONALD,

Of Colonel Swope's Regiment of Pennsylvania Flying-Camp, was another Fort Washington prisoner, captured November 16, 1776. He was paroled on Long Island, June 28, 1777. I have no account of his place of confinement from the time of his capture to the time of his parole. He was ordered into New York prisons on the 9th of August, 1779, and received supplies from Lewis Pintard, Agent, John Beatty and Abraham Skinner, Commissaries-general of Prisoners, and John Brooks, Assistant Commissary of Issues. He was exchanged at Elizabethtown, N. J., November 2, 1780, and made his way to his home in Yorktown, a distance of 170 miles.

CAPTAIN ALEXANDER GRAYDON,

Of Colonel Lambert Cadwallader's 3d Regiment of Pennsylvania, was also captured at Fort Washington, November 16, 1776. Captain Graydon was confined on Long Island until July 7, 1777, when he was admitted to parole by the enemy, and visited General Washington's camp at Morristown. Colonel Cadwallader kindly supplied Mrs. Graydon, at Reading, with money to the amount of £293 6s. during her husband's imprisonment. Captain Graydon was exchanged by Elias Boudinot,

Commissary-general of Prisoners, on the 15th of April, 1778, at Elizabethtown, from whence he returned to his place of abode at Reading, Pa., a distance of 136 miles. I have no account of his return to the service. He was a gentleman of high literary attainments, and was the author of an exceedingly interesting work entitled "Graydon's Memoirs of the Revolution."

CAPTAIN JOHN STOTESBURY,

Of the 11th and 6th Pennsylvania Regiments, was captured March 10, 1778, and confined in Philadelphia until the 10th of June of the same year, when he was admitted to parole. On the 1st of January, 1779, he was called into New York, and confined there. He was supplied with money, &c., by Thomas Franklin, John Beatty, Lewis Pintard, Thomas Bradford, and John Adams. He was exchanged December 31, 1780, at Elizabethtown, and made his way home to Philadelphia. Captain Stotesbury was a well-educated gentleman, and an efficient officer.

CAPTAIN ROBERT PATTON,

Of the 11th Pennsylvania Regiment, was captured in a skirmish on the 27th October, 1776. He was supplied by Lewis Pintard, John Beatty, and Abraham Skinner, and was exchanged at Elizabethtown, January 3, 1781, and went to his home at Yorktown. He soon returned to the army, and served to the end of the war.

CAPTAIN JAMES ELLIOTT

Commanded an independent company in Pennsylvania. His name is found among the prisoners, but nothing as to the particulars of his capture and exchange. He was Lieutenant from February 27, 1778, and Captain from March 8, 1779. No traces of his service are found beyond August 1, 1780, but circumstances warrant the presumption that he served to the end of the war.

LIEUTENANT MATTHEW BENNETT,

Of Colonel Baxter's Regiment of Flying-Camp, was another

Fort Washington prisoner, captured November 16, 1776. He was imprisoned in the city of New York, and received supplies from Lewis Pintard, and afterwards from John Adams, at Elizabethtown, and was exchanged at the latter place, December 8, 1780. He returned to his place of abode, in Bucks county, Pa.

LIEUTENANT ROBERT BROWN,

Of Colonel Baxter's Flying-Camp, was captured at Fort Washington, November 16, 1776. He was confined in New York, and received supplies from Mr. Pintard, and from the Com. Gen., Mr. Skinner. He was exchanged at Elizabethtown, January 25, 1781, and returned to his home in Northampton county, Pa.

LIEUTENANT LEWIS JOHNSTON COSTIGIN,

Of the 1st Regiment of New Jersey, another Fort Washington prisoner, was captured in a skirmish November 13, 1776, three days prior to the memorable 16th. He was confined in the New York Sugar-house, and received no supplies from the Commissaries. He seems to have been a special object of hate for his royal captors. He received "half-pay, agreeable to a resolve of Congress November 24, 1780," and "one year's pay allowed to supernumerary officers by a resolve of Congress of May 22, 1779." He returned to his place of abode at New Brunswick, N. J., and it appears never afterwards took the field,—all of which is given as stated by a Thomas Lowry of those times.

LIEUTENANT JOSEPH MARTIN,

Of Colonel Baxter's Flying-Camp, was another Fort Washington prisoner, captured November 16, 1776, and confined in New York city. He was supplied by Mr. Pintard and Mr. Bradford with specie and Continental currency, and was exchanged November 2, 1770, at Elizabethtown. He returned to his place of abode, a distance of 150 miles, in Northampton county, Pa.

LIEUTENANT WILLIAM YOUNG,

Of Colonel McAllister's Flying-Camp, a Fort Washington prisoner, captured November 16, 1776. He received his supplies from Mr. Boudinot, Com. Gen. of prisoners, and from Mr.

Adams and Mr. Bradford. He was exchanged December 8, 1780, at Elizabethtown, and returned to his home in Chansford township, York county, Pa., a distance of 166 miles.

LIEUTENANT JOHN VANCE HYATT,

Of Colonel Hall's Delaware Regiment, was captured by the British April 25, 1778. John Beatty, Commissary-general of Prisoners, supplied him with £107 5s. 2d., through the hands of Lewis Pintard, agent for prisoners in New York. Mr. Skinner advanced him cash for 96 weeks' board, and Mr. Bradford, in June, 1781, forked over to him 1000 Continental dollars, which he sold at the rate of 75 for 1 in specie. He was exchanged March 31, 1781, at Elizabethtown, and returned to his home, 140 miles, into the State of Delaware, but subsequently joined his regiment, and served to the end of the war.

LIEUTENANT ZACHARIAS SHUGART,

Of Colonel Swope's Pennsylvania Flying-Camp, was captured at Fort Washington November 16, 1776, and confined in the city of New York. He received supplies from Mr. Pintard and Mr. Bradford, exchanged December 31, 1780, and returned home to Yorktown.

LIEUTENANT HEZEKIAH DAVIS,

Of Colonel Montgomery's Regiment of Flying-Camp, was captured at Fort Washington November 16, 1776, and imprisoned in New York. He received from Mr. Pintard £64 15s. 2d., from Mr. Beatty, £143 7s. 4d., eighty weeks' board from Mr. Skinner, 266 dollars from Mr. Adams, and 1469 dollars from Mr. Bradford. He was exchanged December 8, 1780, at Elizabethtown, and returned to his home in Chester county, Pa.

LIEUTENANT ANDREW ROBINSON.

Of the 11th Pennsylvania Regiment, commissioned September 13, 1776, was captured at Fort Washington November 16, 1776, and confined in New York. He received supplies from Mr. Pintard and others, and a warrant for 1000 dollars from General Washington. He was exchanged January 4, 1781, and returned to his home in Yorktown, Pa.

LIEUTENANT JOHN IRWIN,

Of Colonel Baxter's Regiment of Flying-Camp, was captured at Fort Washington November 16, 1776, and confined in New York. He received supplies from Mr. Pintard and Mr. Beatty, and was exchanged at Elizabethtown February 18, 1781, and returned to his home in Bucks county, Pa.

LIEUTENANT THOMAS WYNN,

Of Colonel Montgomery's Regiment of Flying Camp, was also captured at Fort Washington November 16, 1776, and confined in New York. He received some supplies from the agent for the prisoners in New York; was exchanged at Elizabethtown January 1, 1781, and returned to his home, a distance of 120 miles, in Chester county, Pa.

LIEUTENANT JONATHAN SMITH,

Of Colonel Bowman's 8th Virginia Regiment, was captured October 1, 1777. He was Ensign until April 4, 1778, when he was promoted to a Lieutenant. He was confined in New York, and received the attention of Mr. Pintard; was exchanged December 15, 1780, at Elizabethtown, and returned to his home at Fredericksburg, Va., a distance of 360 miles, but returned to his regiment, and served to the end of the war.

LIEUTENANT ROBERT DARLINGTON,

Of Colonel Watts' Regiment of Flying-Camp, was captured at Fort Washington, November 16, 1776, and was confined on Long Island. He was admitted to parole May 26, 1777, but was ordered into the New York city prisons on the 17th of August, 1779, where he was supplied by Mr. Pintard and Mr. Beatty, and was honored, on the 6th of June, 1777, with a warrant for 167 dollars from his Excellency General Washington. He was exchanged at Elizabethtown on the 14th of May, 1781, and returned to his home in Chester county, Pa. Lieutenant Darlington was an "able officer, a ripe scholar, and polite gentleman."

LIEUTENANT SAMUEL McCLELLAN,

Of Colonel Montgomery's Flying-Camp, was also captured at Fort Washington, November 16, 1776, and confined on Long Island. He was admitted to parole on the 20th of May 1777, but was on the 29th of September, 1779, ordered into the prisons in New York. He received the attention of Mr. Pintard, Mr. Skinner, and Mr. Adams, who furnished him with supplies. He was exchanged Dec. 7, 1780, and returned to his home in Chester county, Pa.

LIEUTENANT WARNER WYNN,

Of Colonel Montgomery's Flying-Camp, was captured at Fort Washington, November 16, 1776, and confined in New York, where Mr. Pintard advanced him £10 10s. 3d. There appears no account of his exchange, and the time of his imprisonment cannot be ascertained beyond May 1, 1777. It would appear that he escaped from the British and joined the Americans in his former company.

DAVID LOVE, SURGEON

To the North Carolina Brigade, appears among the New York prisoners, yet no account of his capture nor exchange can be found. He served as Surgeon from 18th August, 1779, to August 1, 1781, and received 75 dollars per month pay.

ENSIGN JOHN THOMPSON,

Of Colonel Morgan's Pennsylvania Militia, was captured January 3, 1777, and confined in New York, where Mr. Pintard advanced him £64 and 300 dollars. He was exchanged at Elizabethtown, August 26, 1778, and returned to his place of abode in Philadelphia county, Pa.

The following List of American Prisoners were released from Captivity at Elizabethtown, N. J., by John Adams, Commissary of Prisoners, at the date written opposite their names.

John Harper, Brigade Major, Pa., Nov. 4, 1780.
John Wells, Major, 2d Va. Regt., Nov. 8, 1780.
William B. Gifford, Lieutenant, 3d N. J. Regt., Nov. 22, 1780.
Gabriel Blakeney, Lieutenant, Col. Watts' Flying-Camp, Nov. 22, 1780.
John Riley, Lieutenant, Col. Webb's Conn. Regt., Dec. 3, 1780.

PRISONERS OF WAR.

William Robertson, Adjutant, 9th Va. Regt., Dec. 3, 1780.
Joseph Payne, Ensign, 9th Va. Regt., Dec. 3, 1780.
Asa Lay, Lieutenant, Col. Meigs' Conn. Regt., Dec. 3, 1780.
Abraham Stout, Lieutenant, 2d N. J. Regt., Dec. 3, 1780.
Ebenezer West, Adjutant, Col. Ely's Conn. Regt., Dec. 3, 1780.
William Martin, Lieutenant, Col. Proctor's Pa. Artillery, Dec. 4 1780.
James Smith, Lieutenant, Col. Proctor's Pa. Artillery, Dec. 4, 1780.
John Cozens, Captain, N. J. Regt., Dec. 8, 1780.
Samuel McElhatton, Ensign, Col. Watts' Flying-Camp, Dec. 8, 1780.
John Crawford, Lieutenant. Col. Watts' Flying-Camp, Dec. 8, 1780.
Ephraim Hunter, Lieutentant, Col. Watts' Flying-Camp, Dec. 8, 1780.
Henry Clayton, Lieutenant, Col. Swope's Flying-Camp, Dec. 8, 1780.
Benjamin Davis, Lieutentant, Col. Montgomery's Flying-Camp, Dec. 8, 1780.
Hugh King, Lieutenant, Col. Baxter's Flying-Camp, Dec. 8, 1780.
Jacob Mumme, Ensign, Col. Baxter's Flying-Camp, Dec. 8, 1780.
Thomas Warman, Lioutenant, Col. Rawling's Md. Regt., Dec. 8, 1780.
Samuel Fisher, Captain, 2d Regt. Northumberland Militia, Dec. 8, 1780.
Joseph Thompson, Lieut. Col. of Massachusetts, Dec. 8, 1780.
Henry Lyles, Lieutenant, 3d Md. Regt., Dec. 22, 1780.
James Winchester, Lieutenant, 3d Md. Regt., Dec. 22, 1780.
Abraham Watson, Captain, 3d Mass. Regt., Dec. 22, 1780.
Jonathan Maynard, Lieutenant, 7th Mass. Regt., Dec. 22, 1780.
Stephen Townsend, Ensign, 6th Mass. Regt., Dec. 22, 1780.
Thomas Parker, Lieutenant, 9th Va. Regt., Dec. 22, 1780.
Thomas Paine, Lieutenant, 9th Va. Regt., Dec. 22, 1780.
James Anderson, Lieutenant, Col. Hazen's Regt., Dec. 22, 1780.
Ebenezer Carson, Lieutenant, 10th Pa. Regt., Dec 22, 1780.
Jacob Weaver, Captain, 10th Pa. Regt., Dec. 22, 1780.
Levi Bradley, Ensign, 4th Mass. Regt., Dec. 22, 1780.
James Whitlock, Lieutenant, Monmouth Militia, Dec. 22, 1780.
Samuel Culver, Ensign, Col. Cook's Regt., Dec. 22, 1780.
J. Brainard, Lieutenant, 4th Regt. State Troops, Dec. 22, 1780.
John Smith, Lieutenant, Col. Walker's Va. Regt., Dec. 22, 1780.
William Ellis, Major, N. J. Militia, Dec. 22, 1780.
John Weidman, Lieutenant, German Regt., Pa., Dec. 30, 1780.
John Eccleston, Major, 5th Md. Regt., Dec. 30, 1780.
William Hill, Lieutenant, 2d Maryland Regt., Dec. 30, 1780.
Aquilla Giles, Major and Aide-de-Camp to Maj. Gen. St. Clair, Nov. 10, 1780.
Richard Dorsey, Captain, Md. Artillery, a prisoner on parole from the spring of 1781 to the end of the war.

Capt. John Reid acted as escort of the British prisoners from Fort Frederick, in Maryland, to Elizabethtown, N. J., the place of exchange.

The following List of American Officers, prisoners at New York, were exchanged by Abraham Skinner, Commissary-general of Prisoners, on or about the dates opposite their names.

John Ely, Colonel, Connecticut, Dec. 5, 1780.
Nathaniel Ramsay, Lieut. Colonel, Maryland line, Dec. 14, 1780.
Luke Marbury, Colonel, Maryland Militia, March 26, 1781.

James Abbott, Ensign, Ely's Conn. Regt., Dec. 17, 1781.
William Andrews, Lieutenant, Crane's Mass. Artillery, March 19, 1781.
Richard Andrews, Lieutenant, 2d N. C. Regt., March 26, 1781.
George Blewer, Lieutenant, 4th Pa. Regt., Jan. 29, 1781.
Henry Brewster, Lieutenant, Allison's N. Y. Regt., Dec. 17, 1780.
Edward Bulkley, Lieutenant, Webb's Conn. Regt., Dec. 17, 1780.
Gabriel Blakeley, Lieutenant, Col. Watts' Flying-Camp, Nov. 23, 1780.
Charles Clark, Lieutenant, Col. Watts' Flying-Camp, Jan. 29, 1781.
Joseph Cox, Lieutenant, 6th Pa. Regt., Jan. 29, 1781.
Charles Croxall, Lieutenant, 11th Pa. Regt., Nov. 23, 1780.
John Craig, Lieutenant, Col. Baxter's Flying-Camp, Mar. 19, 1781.
Ephraim Douglass, Quartermaster, 8th Pa. Regt., Nov. 27, 1780.
John Duguid, Lieutenant, 3d Pa. Regt., Nov. 10, 1780.
John H. Finley, Lieutenant, 5th Pa. Regt., Jan. 22, 1781.
William Ferguson, Captain, Col. Proctor's Pa. Artillery, Dec. 1, 1780.
Samuel Finley, Lieutenant, Pa. Artillery, Nov. 2, 1780.
James W. Gray, Captain, 5th Md. Regt., Feb. 10, 1781.
Jesse Grant, Lieutenant, Col. Webb's Conn. Regt., Dec. 17, 1780.
George Gilchrist, Captain, 9th Va. Regt., Nov. 2, 1780.
William George, Lieutenant, Rawling's Md. Regt., Nov. 2, 1780.
Erasmus Gill, Lieutenant, 4th Pa. Regt. of Dragoons, Oct. 22, 1780.
John Green, Ensign, Pa. Militia, Mar. 26, 1781.
Elisha Hopkins, Adjutant, Col. Webb's Conn. Regt., Dec. 17, 1780.
Henry Hambright, Captain, Pa. Flying-Camp, Nov. 4, 1780.
Edward Hall, Lieutenant, 16th additional regiment Md., Nov. 5, 1780.
James Janney, Lieutenant, 5th Regt. Pa., Jan. 29, 1781.
James Jones, Lieutenant, Pa. Flying-Camp, Jan. 29, 1781.
Daniel Jamison, Lieutenant, Col. Baxter's Flying-Camp, Mar. 26, 1781.
James Kronkhite, Captain, Col. Drake's N. Y. Regt., Dec. 17, 1780.
Isaac Keeler, Lieutenant, Col. Drake's N. Y. Regt., Mar. 19, 1781.
Thomas H. Lucket, Lieutenant, Md. Line, Nov. 2, 1780.
Samuel Logan, Major, N. Y., Militia, Dec. 21, 1780.
Nathaniel Lawrence, Lieutenant, 2d S. C. Regt., April 18, 1781.
Henry Murfits, Lieutenant, Pa. Flying-Camp, Jan. 29, 1781.
George Mathews, Colonel, 9th Va. Regt., Dec. 5, 1781.
John Mercer, Lieutenant, 1st N. J. Regt., Nov. 6, 1780.
Sands Niles, Ensign, Col. Ely's Conn. Regt., Mar. 19, 1781.
Solomon Pendleton, Lieutenant, Col. Dubois' N. Y. Regt., Feb. 8, 1781.
William Preston, Captain, Pa. Militia Artillery, Jan. 29, 1781.
David Poor, Lieutenant, Col. Hutchinson's Mass. Regt., Dec. 17, 1780.
Nathaniel Pendleton, Lieutenant, Col. Rawling's Md. Regt., Oct. 18, 1780.
Abraham Parsons, Lieutenant, N. J. Militia, Mar. 26, 1781.
Thomas Rouse, Ensign, 2d Md. Regt., Feb. 10, 1781.
Thomas Reed, Ensign, Pa. Flying-Camp, Nov. 4, 1780.
Samuel Rutherford, Ensign, Pa. Flying-Camp, Nov. 4, 1780.
Cornelius Swartwout, Captain, N. Y. Artillery, Dec. 17, 1780.
Henry Swartwout, Lieutenant, Col. Dubois' N. Y. Regt., Dec. 17, 1780.
Roger Staynor, Captain, Pa. Flying-Camp, Nov. 4, 1780.
Smith Snead, Captain, 9th Va. Regt., Nov. 2, 1780.
Andrew Thompson, Ensign, Col. Spencer's Regt., Dec. 17, 1780.
Edward Tillard, Major, Congress Regt., Nov. 2, 1780.
John Willis, Captain, 8th Va. Regt., Jan. 29, 1781.

Ebenezer West, Adjutant, Col. Ely's Conn. Regt., Dec. 3, 1780.
Robert Walker, Lieutenant, Col. Brewer's Regt., April 4, 1781.

NOTE.—The preceding list includes all the principal captive officers of the Continental army who remained in prison any considerable length of time. Many others were captured, but soon exchanged. We have no account of the naval prisoners from which anything like a complete list could be made.

If there is any class of patriots more deserving of the gratitude of a nation than another, it is these captives, who dwelt in dungeons for their country's sake. Their names should be quickly snatched from the verge of oblivion, and inscribed in letters of gold upon the loftiest monument ever erected to perpetuate the memories of a nation's birth.

GENERAL ORDERS AND COURTS MARTIAL

OF THE

COMMANDER-IN-CHIEF, AND OTHER DISTINGUISHED OFFICERS, IN 1776, 1777, AND 1778.

WILLIAMSBURG, April 1, 1776.

For the future, the Quartermaster-general, Commissary, and Wagonmaster, will attend regularly at head-quarters at 10 o'clock, unless detached on public business—a return to be given in of ammunition, ordinance, &c.

The General has observed that detachments of troops march into and out of town without the least ceremony, contrary to all military customs and regulations. The Adjutant-general will post a sufficient number to prevent such irregularities in future. The field-officers of the day will be responsible that no party enter in or march out of the town without previously acquainting the General or commanding officer of the place. Field-officer for to-morrow—Colonel Bucknor. On guard—Captain Massie, Lieutenant Talieferro, Lieutenant Avery, Lieutenant Curd.

By order,

A. LEWIS, Brig. Gen.

WILLIAMSBURG, April 4, 1776.

The Continental Congress has appointed Thomas Bullitt Deputy Adjutant-general, with the rank of Lieutenant-colonel. He is to be obeyed and respected as such. The 6th regiment to be under arms to-morrow at 10 o'clock. Major Green is the field-officer to-morrow.

A. LEWIS, B. G.

ADJT. GEN. BULLITT'S ORDERS.

WILLIAMSBURG, April 4, 1776.

A subaltern and twenty-five men will take the guard at the point of Queen's Creek (now consisting of only a Sergeant and twelve men). The subaltern is to detach from his guard a Corporal and six men to the point of King's Creek, below Mr. Burwell's house. Sentinels must be placed on the point, to give notice of any tenders or enemy's vessels. This subaltern guard to be released weekly.

THOMAS BULLITT, D. A. Gen.

WILLIAMSBURG, May 3, 1776.

As General Lee will remain here but a few days, all returns of guards, fatigues, and duties of every kind, will be given to General Lewis. The captains of the different companies are desired to consign over to Captain William Green, Lieutenant Timothy Kelly, and Josiah Singleton, mate, of the Roe galley, whatever men they have in their respective companies for sea and river service.

William Russell is appointed Wagonmaster-general until the pleasure of Congress is known.

It was established by General Washington, as a mark of distinction, that the general officers, aides-de-camp, and brigade-majors might be known to the soldiers, that a Major-general should wear a purple or blue ribbon, a Brigadier, a pink or light red, the Staff and Adjutant-general, a green, &c.

THOMAS BULLITT, D. A. Gen.

WILLIAMSBURG, May 12, 1776.

As the office of Quartermaster-general in all armies is an office of the highest trust and dignity, and generally honored with a rank in proportion to the trust; and the present Quartermaster-general of the Continental army in Canada having the rank of Colonel, General Lee thinks he shall not do justice to Mr. Finney, whose real activity and abilities, from his short acquaintance, gives him the greatest reason to recommend him to the Congress as a subject on whom they ought to confer some respectable rank. Mr. Finney, until further action of the Congress, is to hold rank as youngest Lieutenant-colonel in the army.

CHARLES LEE.

ORDERS FOR GUARD.

MIDDLEBROOK, June 12, 1777.

The General thinks it necessary to establish the following regulations for guard, and hopes that officers will consider them as the rule of practice, and make themselves well acquainted with them:

When any guard arrives at the post assigned it, the officer's first care must be to place his sentinels properly, according to circumstances. The guard should remain under arms while this is doing, and if it be at an outpost, or anywhere near the enemy, temporary sentries should be placed at a small distance to avoid surprise while the commissioned officer reconnoitres the situation of the post to know where his sentries should be placed for a continuance. This is to be done in case the ground has not been beforehand examined, and particular direction given about the matter, or in case he does not relieve some other guard; but if he relieves another, he is to receive all the orders given to the officer of the old guard, on receiving which, together with those he received from the brigadier and field-officers of the day, he is punctually to observe. If any difference between them arises, he is to obey the latter in preference. He is immediately to send a party under a trusty officer of the old guard to relieve the sentries thereof, who are to return to the guards they belong to. If the guard be of such a nature, as other matters, other than the security of the post, may be intrusted to it, they must be contained in a written report, and an officer of the new, accompanied by an officer of the old, must be sent to take them in charge, comparing the things themselves with the report, and seeing all is right.

The sentries of the old guard having joined it, the offices is to march it back whence it came in the greatest order and decorum, then send off the detachments, under an officer to each, to join their corps, observing regularity on the way. After placing his sentries, the officer of the new guard is to make the men lodge their arms, first giving them the orders necessary to govern their conduct. Care must be taken to lodge their arms in such

ORDERS FOR GUARD. 827

a manner that each man may have recourse to his own in a a moment. In most cases it is best the arms should be grounded on the guard parade during the day. No man to put off his accoutrements on any pretence whatever.

This done, the commanding officer, attended by a couple of men, is to visit all his sentries, to see that they are posted right, and instruct them in the line of their duty. His next care is to take such precaution for the security of his post by forming abatis, digging ditches, and raising parapets, as circumstances require. To guard against a surprise, or repel any sudden attack, he will make himself acquainted, not only with all the great roads leading to the enemy, or army he belongs to, but he should search out every by path and avenue, by which he may the more easily send his parties to reconnoitre the enemy, and make his retreat good in any emergency. He should have scouting parties all day and patrols all night, going towards the enemy in his rear and on his flanks, to give intelligence of their motions, and timely notice of any attempts they may be making. If the notice can be given without firing, it will be best; if not, it must be done by firing—the scouts and patrols retreating by way of the sentries to alarm them.

Visiting rounds should be going all night to see that the sentries are at their posts, alert, and acquainted with every particular of their duty.

The break of day being the most favorable time for an attack or surprise of a guard, officers will be careful not turn out his guard until an hour after sunrise, and to have his visiting rounds and patrols going more than ordinary. From watching through the night, they towards morning grow drowsy and listless, and are the more liable to a surprise. An officer's reputation calls for him to guard against this evil.

A guard is bound to maintain their post as long as possible; but if likely to be overpowered with numbers, it is best to make a skirmishing retreat, firing all the way it goes to give the alarm, and taking advantage of every defile, morass, wood, and every advantageous spot it can find, to delay the enemy. If the enemy do not pursue, but return after having dislodged the guard, it is to resume the post, first taking measures to be sure all is safe.

If two guards are so placed as to have the same object in view, and depend upon each other, they must be attentive to every thing that befall one another, and act in concert. If either is attacked, the other must not only put itself in a posture of defence, but must keep patrols continually going, to bring intelligence of what is doing. If the one attacked retreats, the other must retreat also; if it returns, the other must in like manner. These things depend on circumstances, and the orders of the Brigadier-general and field-officers of the day; and parties of whatever kind coming towards the out-guard are to be stopped by the out-sentries, and notice given to the guard, which in most cases is to be returned out, and the officer in most cases to send a proper person to examine such parties, and give his orders accordingly. All flags must be stopped at the out-sentries, and the officer of the guard to meet them there. If they are charged with letters, or any matters that can be communicated to them, he is to receive them, and transmit them immediately to the Major-general of the day, and his orders receive.

No officer or soldier is to sleep a moment on guard, and no cooking to go on while on guard. The men must either carry their provisions ready dressed, or have them sent to them—the former is preferable. No man is to presume to be out of call without permission from the officer, who is not to suffer more than two to be absent at a time, nor those at the outpost.

In cases of desertions from the outposts, the officer from whose party it happens is to immediately change the countersigns, advertising the other out-guard, who are to conform thereto. He is also to send instantly to acquaint the Brigadier-general and field-officers of the day, and except the out guards paying them honors due them according to their rank and the usages of war, the out-guards to turn out to the Brigadier-gen-

MODES OF PROMOTION.

eral and field officers only. The honors with the drum never to be paid by them. All guards to turn out to receive the *Grand Rounds*—the officer of each to prepare an evening report for the officer of the rounds. All guards when relieved to make a report of every occurrence that may have happened to one of the field-officers of the day, who is to attend at or near the grand parade to receive it when it comes. Arms after this wet weather to be carefully inspected, and put in the best possible order for use.

Brigade Commissaries are to receive their orders from the Commissary-general respecting the mode of supplying their respective brigades in case of a sudden move. The Assistant Quarter-masters are to do the same with Colonel Biddle, that no complaint may arise on a march. Instead of delivering spare ammunition to each brigade, General Knox will furnish the divisions with it. In order to lessen the number of carriages and to convoy it more securely, if the Quartermaster could furnish each brigade with a proper number of scythes for foraging, the horses might be better provided for.

GEORGE WASHINGTON.
JUNE 13, 1777.

At a Court Martial, held the 9th instant, whereof Colonel Marshall was president, Captain Jesse Roe was tried for insulting and ill-treating Mr. Coleclough, Conductor of Wagons, on the march from Morristown. Acquitted and justified by the Court. The General approves the decision, and orders Captain Roe to be released from his arrest with honor.

He also approves the sentence of the same Court Martial, held the 11th instant, before which Alexander Brandon, of the 1st Pennsylvania Regiment was tried for horse-stealing and acquitted. The prisoner to be immediately released from his confinement.

Different modes of promotion having prevailed in the army, productive of disorder and confusion in many instances, the Commander-in-Chief thinks it necessary to establish the following general rule, to prevent all further disputes and inconveniences on this head. All commanding officers to rise regimentally, and according to seniority, until they arrive at the rank of Captain; and from that, in the line of the State they belong to, by seniority also, until they abtain the rank of Colonel. This rule, however, to admit of exceptions, when particular officers signalize themselves by a conduct of extraordinary merit, or when others prove themselves unworthy of preferment by the want of, or neglect of cultivating, any quality requisite to constitute the good officer.

The following men belonging to Captain Hollett's independent company having been sent to camp some time ago and annexed to some corps, the officer commanding the corps in which these men, or any of them, are now doing duty, is required to send a return of them to the Adjutant-general to-morrow morning, viz., Thomas Booker, Samuel Brown, Joseph Petitt, Isaac Green, Charles Clair, Laban Condon, William Caldwell, John Coddington.

GEORGE WASHINGTON.
JUNE 28, 1777.

Major-general for to-morrow,	-	Stevens.
Brigadier-general do.	- -	Woodford.
Field-officers do.	-	{ Lieut. Col. Nelson, Major Richardson.

The usual regiments are to send for their tents, and pitch them where they are now posted. An Orderly Sergeant to attend at head-quarters, as usual.

All chaplains are to perform divine service to-morrow, and on every other succeeding Sunday, with their respective brigades and regiments, when their situations will admit of it, and the commanding officers of corps are to see that they attend. The Commander-in Chief expects an axact compliance with this order, and that it be observed in future as an invariable rule of practice, and every neglect will not only be considered a breach of orders, but a disregard to decency, virtue, and religion.

SENTENCES OF COURTS MARTIAL.

In future, when orders are received at General Weedon's quarters, the orderly-drum will beat the Adjutant's call, that the issuing them to the regiments may not be delayed.

GEORGE WASHINGTON.

JUNE 30, 1777.

A special Court Martial will set to-morrow at 9 o'clock, at the usual place, near General Wayne's quarters, for the trial of Major Stewart, of the 2d Maryland Regiment. Colonel David Hall is appointed president of the court. Jonathan Mifflin and Henry Emanuel Lutterloth are appointed Deputy Quartermasters-general, and Clement Biddle, Commissary of Forage.

GEORGE WASHINGTON.

HEAD-QUARTERS, August 19, 1777.

The following sentences of general Courts Martial, held the 7th, 12th, and 16th inst., of which Colonel Sheldon was president, Edward Wilcox, Quartermaster to Captain Dorsey's Troop, charged with desertion, taking a horse belonging to Colonel Moylan's Regiment, and a trooper with his accoutrements, found guilty, and sentenced to be led round the regiment he belongs to on horseback, with his face towards the horse's tail, and his coat turned wrongside outwards, and that he be then discharged from the army. The Commander-in-Chief approves the sentence, and orders it to be put into execution immediately.

George Kilpatrick and Charles Martin, Sergeants, Lawrence Burne and Enoch Wells, Corporals, Daniel McCarty, Patrick Leland, Philip Franklin, Jacob Baker, Thomas Orles, Adam Rex, Frederick Gaines, Daniel Kainking, Christian Longspit, Henry Winer, and Nicholas Walner, privates in Colonel Moylan's Regiment of Light Dragoons, charged with mutiny and desertion, and adjudged worthy of death—the court esteeming the prisoners, except Sergeant Kilpatrick, objects of compassion, and as such recommend them to the Commander-in-Chief, the General is pleased to grant them his pardon; and the like reasons which led the court to recommend to mercy, joined with others, induces the General to grant this pardon to Sergeant Kilpatrick also. At the same time, the prisoners are to consider their crimes are of a very atrocious nature, and have by the Articles of War subjected themselves to the penalty of death. The remission of their punishment is a signal act of mercy in the Commander-in-Chief, and demands a very great and full return of fidelity, submission, and obedience, in any future military service which he shall assign them. The prisoners are to quit the horse, and enter into the foot-service, in the corps to which they shall be assigned.

Thomas Farshiers and George House, of Colonel Moylan's Regiment, tried by same court, being charged with mutiny and desertion, are found guilty, but some favorable circumstances appearing in their behalf, were sentenced to receive twenty-five lashes on their naked backs, and to be dismissed from horse-service; the Commander-in-Chief approves the sentence, but for the reasons above referred to, and with the like expectations of amendment, remits the penalty of whipping. They will be disposed of in the foot-service.

Thomas Runnals, of Colonel Moylan's Regiment, tried by the same court, being charged, is found guilty, and sentenced to suffer death; the Commander-in-Chief approves the sentence, but the execution of the prisoner is respited till further orders.

Colonel Lawson having already had the command of the Fourth Regiment of Virginia, is to continue in the same command.

Colonel Elliott is appointed to the command of the Sixth Virginia Regiment.

General Greene's Division is to relieve the Provost's and Quartermaster-general's guards this afternoon. The guards to parade by the cross-roads, at 5 o'clock.

GEORGE WASHINGTON.

HEAD-QUARTERS, August 22, 1777.

The Commander-in Chief has the happiness to inform the army of the signal victory obtained to the northward. A part of General Burgoyne's army, about 1500 in number, were detached towards New Hampshire, and advanced with a design to possess themselves of Bennington. Brigadier-general Starke, of the State of New Hampshire, with about 2000 men, mostly militia, attacked them. Our troops behaved in a very brave and heroic manner. They pushed the enemy from one work to another, thrown up on advantageous ground, and from different posts, with spirit and fortitude, until they gained a complete victory over them. The following is a list of the prisoners, killed, and wounded, viz.: one lieutenant-colonel, one Major, five Captains, twelve Lieutenants, four Ensigns, two Cornets, one Judge Advocate, one Baron, two Canadian officers, and three surgeons, thirty-seven British soldiers, three hundred and ninety-eight Hessians, thirty-eight Canadians, and one hundred and fifty-one Tories taken prisoners. The number of the wounded, exclusive of the above, is about eighty. The number of the enemy who had been slain had not been ascertained, but supposed to be about two hundred. Their artillery, consisting of four brass field-pieces, with a considerable quantity of baggage, likewise fell into our hands.

Our loss consisted of about twenty or thirty killed, and perhaps fifty wounded.

The army is to march to-morrow, if it should not rain, in the order appointed—General Greene first, then General Stevens, &c.

GEORGE WASHINGTON.

HEAD-QUARTERS, STANTON, NEAR GERMANTOWN,
August 23, 1777.

Major-general to-morrow,	. . .	Lord Stirling.
Brigadier-general do.	. . .	Scott.
Field-officers do.	. . .	{ Col. Grayson, { Lt. Col. Genny.
Brigade-major do.	. . .	Johnson.

No officer or soldier is to leave the encampment this evening without leave in writing from the Major or Brigadier under whom he acts, and they are desired not to give such leave unless there is apparent cause for it. The army is to move precisely at 4 o'clock in the morning, if it should not rain. The Division commanded by General Wayne is to join its proper place in the line, between Lord Stirling's and General Stevens' Divisions, and it is strongly and earnestly enjoined upon the commanding officers of corps, to make all their men who are able to bear arms, except the necessary guards, march in the ranks, for it is so great a reflection when all orders are disobeyed, and to see such a number of street-rollers (for they cannot be called guards) with the wagons, that it is really shocking.

The army is to march in one column through the city of Philadelphia, going in at and marching down Front-street to Chestnut, and up Chestnut to the Common. A small halt is to be made about a mile this side of the city until the rear is clear up and the line in proper order.

The divisions will march as follows :

Greene's, Stevens', Lincoln's, and Lord Stirling's.

The horse to be divided upon the two wings. Bland's and Baylor's Regiments on the right, and Sheldon's and Moylan's on the left.

The following order of march is to be observed, viz.:

First, a subaltern and twelve light-horse.

Two hundred yards in rear, a complete troop.

Two hundred yards in the rear of the troops, the residue of Bland's and Baylor's Regiments.

One hundred yards in the rear of these, a company of pioneers with their axes, &c., in proper order.

One hundred yards in the rear of the pioneers, a regiment from General Muhlenberg's Brigade, and close in the rear of that regiment all General Muhlenberg's Field Artillery.

This brigade followed by Weedon's, Woolfords, and Scott's in order, with all their field artillery in their respective fronts.

Park of artillery, and the artificers belonging thereto, in the centre.

MARCH THROUGH PHILADELPHIA.

Lincoln's and Lord Stirling's Divisions following, with all their brigade artillery in the rear of their respective brigades.

A regiment from Lord Stirling's Brigade for a rear guard, and to be 150 yards from General Maxwell's Brigade.

Sheldon's and Moylan's Horse, 150 yards in the rear of this regiment.

One troop, 150 yards in the rear of this regiment of horse.

The whole line is to march by sub-divisions at half-distance, the ranks six paces asunder, which is to be exactly observed in passing through the city, and great attention given by the officers to see that their men carry their arms well, and are made to appear as decent as circumstances will admit.

It is expected that every officer without exception will keep his post in passing through the city, and under no pretence whatever leave it; and if any soldier shall dare to leave his ranks he shall receive thirty-nine lashes at the first halting-place afterwards. The officers will be particularly careful of the men, not only in their own divisions but in others also, if they should see an attempt of the kind. They are also to prevent the people from pressing on the troops.

There is to be no greater space between [the divisions, brigades, and regiments than is taken up by artillery, [and is just sufficient to distinguish them.

That the line of march through the city may be as little encumbered as possible, only one ammunition wagon is to attend the field-pieces of each brigade and every artillery park. All the rest of the baggage wagons and spare horses are to file off to the right, to avoid the city entirely, and move on to the bridge at the middle ferry and then halt, but not so far as to impede the march of the troops by preventing their passing them.

Not a woman belonging to the army is to be seen with the troops on their march through the city.

The Wagonmaster-general with all his assistants, together with the Division, Brigade, and Regimental Quartermasters, are to attend the wagons, and assist the field-officers appointed to that duty in preventing any men who are allotted to the wagons from slipping into the city. As the baggage will be but a little time separated from the column, a very few men will be sufficient to guard it, and the General wishes to have as many of them appear in the ranks in the line of march as are able.

The baggage and spare artillery wagons of each brigade, together with the wagons of the artillery park, are to move with the same orders that the brigades, &c., do in the line, that they may more easily unite again when we have passed the city.

The soldiers will go early to rest this evening, as the General expects the whole line will be on their march at the hour appointed. That this may be the case, each brigadier is to appoint patrols to take up all the stragglers from the camp, and all others of the army who do not obey this order.

The Director of the Hospital will order when the sick are to be sent.

The drums and fifes of each brigade are to be collected in the centre of it, and a tune for the quick-step played, but with such moderation that the men may step to it with ease, and without *dancing* along, or totally disregarding the music, as has been too often the case.

The men are to be excused from carrying their camp-kettles to-morrow.   GEORGE WASHINGTON.

HEAD-QUARTERS, Sept. 6, 1777.

The Commissary-general of Prisoners informs the commanding officers of regiments and other corps, that notwithstanding the orders heretofore issued for the purpose, he has received but one small return of prisoners taken by the enemy since his appointment; in consequence of which neglect it will be impossible for him in case of exchange, to pay proper attention to the orders of the different captains at the time.

He further informs them that in future the prisoners will be exchanged according to the return made to him.

ENEMY'S DESIGNS ON PHILADELPHIA. 337

As the baggage wagons are at all times a great encumbrance to the army, and would be particularly in a day of battle, they are in the latter case to be drawn off the field, that the army may not be in the least incommoded by them. It is besides a measure which common prudence dictates; and whenever an action is expected, the Quartermaster-general will immediately wait on the Commander-in-Chief to receive his directions respecting them.

From every information respecting the enemy's designs, and from their movements, it is manifest their aim is, if possible, to possess themselves of Philadelphia. This is their capital object. It is what they last year strove to effect, but were happily disappointed. They made a second attempt at the opening of this campaign, but after vast preparation and expense for the purpose, they abandoned their design and totally evacuated the Jerseys. They are now making their last effort. To come up the Delaware, it seems, was their first intention; but from the measures taken to annoy them in the river, they judged the enterprise that way too hazardous. At length they landed on the eastern shore of Maryland, some little way in the country, but the General thinks they will be again disappointed in their views. Should they push their designs on Philadelphia by this route, their all is at stake. They will put the contest on the event of a single battle. If they are overthrown they are utterly undone—the war is at an end!

Now is the time for our most strenuous exertions. One bold stroke will free the land from rapine, devastation, and burning; and female innocence from brutal lust and violence.

In every other quarter the American arms have of late been rapidly successful. Great numbers of the enemy have fallen in battle and still greater numbers have been taken prisoners. The militia to the northward have fought with that spirit which would have done honor to old soldiers. They bravely fought and conquered! Glory attended them! Who can forbear to emulate their noble spirit? Who is there without ambition to share with them the applauses of their countrymen and of all posterity, as the defenders of liberty, and precursors of peace and happiness to millions in the present and future generations? Two years we have maintained the war and struggled with difficulties innumerable, but the prospect has since brightened and our affairs put on a better face. Now is the time to reap the fruits of all our toils and dangers. If we behave like men, the third campaign will be our last. Ours is the main army. To us our country looks for protection. The eyes of all America and Europe are turned upon us as those by whom the event of the war is to be determined; and the General assures his countrymen and fellow-soldiers that he believes the critical, the important moment is at hand which demands their most spirited exertions in the field. There glory waits to crown the brave! Peace, freedom, and happiness will be the rewards of victory! Animated by motives like these, soldiers fighting in the cause of innocence, humanity, and justice will never give way, but with undaunted resolution press on to conquest! This the General assures himself is the part the American forces now in arms will act, and thus acting, he will insure their success.

GEORGE WASHINGTON.
HEAD-QUARTERS, Sept. 6, 1777.

Major-general to-morrow,	. . . . .	Lord Stirling.
Brigadier-general do.	. . . . .	Scott.
Field-officer do.	. . . . .	Col. J. Parker.
Brigade-major do.	. . . . .	Day.

The General has no doubt that every man who has a due sense of the importance of the cause he has undertaken to defend, and who has any regard to his own honor and the reputation of a soldier, will, if called to action, behave like one contending for everything valuable. But if, contrary to his expectation, there shall be found any officers or soldiers so far lost to all shame as basely to quit their posts without orders, or shall skulk from danger, or offer to retreat before order is given for so doing from proper authority from a superior officer, they are to be instantly shot down as a just punishment to themselves, and for example to others. This order, those in the rear and those in the corps of reserve are to see duly executed, to prevent the cowardly from making a sacrifice of the brave, and by their ill example and groundless tales calculated to cover their own shameful conduct, prevent them from spreading terror as they go. That the order may be well known and strongly impressed on the army, the General positively orders the commanding officer of every regiment to assemble his men and have it read to them, to prevent the plea of ignorance.

The General begs the officers to be attentive to all strange faces and suspicious characters who may be discovered in camp; and if, upon examination of them, no good account can be given why they are there, to carry them to the Major-general for further examination. This is only a necessary precaution, to be done in a manner the least offensive.

The general officers are to meet at five o'clock this afternoon at the brick house by White Clay Creek.

GEORGE WASHINGTON.

BRIGADE HEAD-QUARTERS, Sept. 6, 1777.

Notwithstanding the repeated orders against plundering and burning fences, that abominable practice is still continued, to the eternal shame of the brigade.

Complaints are made that the corn-fields are pillaged without restraint, the fence-rails burnt up, and many other outrages committed by soldiers. To prevent this in future, the officers are once more requested to attend more particularly to the behavior of the men under them, and to punish such as they may see with green corn, unless they can make it appear they bought it; and any fence-rails they may see burning, the mess to which the fire belongs is to be made answerable. The suttlers are ordered to remove immediately from the front of the encampment to some other place.

The Quartermaster's Sergeant will immediately parade the C. C. men of their regiments, and cover up all the filth and nastiness in their respective fronts, and soldiers depositing any more but in the proper place are to receive ten lashes on their bare backs.   GEORGE WEEDON, Brig. Gen.

BATTLE OF BRANDYWINE.

HEAD-QUARTERS, GERMANTOWN, Sept. 12, 1777.

Major-general for to morrow,	. . . . .	Sullivan.
Brigadier-general do.	. . . . .	Weedon.
Field-officers do.	. . . . .	{ Col. Martin, { Major Hay.
Brigade-major do.	. . . . .	Barber.

The General, with peculiar satisfaction, thanks those gallant officers who on the 11th inst. (*battle of Brandywine*) bravely fought in their country's cause. If there are any whose conduct reflects dishonor on soldiership and their names not pointed out to him, he must for the present leave them to reflect how much they have injured their country, how unfaithfully they have proved to their fellow-soldiers; but with this exhortation, that they embrace the first opportunity which may offer to do justice to both and to the profession of a soldier.

Although the events of that day, from some unfortunate circumstances, were not so favorable as could be wished, the General has the satisfaction of assuring the troops that from every account he has been able to obtain the enemy's loss vastly exceeded ours, and he has full confidence that in another appeal to Heaven, with the blessing of Providence, which it becomes every officer and soldier to supplicate, we shall prove successful.

The honorable Congress, in consideration of the gallant behavior of the troops on Thursday last, their fatigue since, and from a full conviction that on every future occasion they will manifest a bravery worthy of the cause they have undertaken to defend, having been pleased to order thirty hogsheads of rum to be distributed among them, in such manner as the Commander-in-Chief shall direct, he orders the Commissary-general of Issues to deliver one gill per day to every officer and soldier while it lasts.

The commanding officer of each brigade, without delay, to send a number of active officers into the city and its environs to pick up and bring to camp all the straggling soldiers whom they may find, as well those belonging to other brigades as their own. Likewise a sergeant from each brigade to the brigade over the Schuylkill to direct the soldiers as they cross where to find their respective brigades.

At roll-calling this afternoon the men are to be charged not to be out of drum-call of their respective brigades, under pain of death, nor the officers, as they value their service and dread cashiering. GEORGE WASHINGTON.

HEAD-QUARTERS, Sept. 13, 1777.

The General takes the earliest opportunity to return his warmest thanks to the officers and soldiers of General Weedon's brigade engaged in the late action for their spirited and soldierly behavior and conduct so worthy, under so many disadvantages, and cannot fail of establishing to themselves the highest military reputation. He thinks himself also under obligations to return his thanks to all other officers and soldiers of his division for their firmness and alacrity which they have discovered upon every occasion, in the course of the day, to engage with the enemy. Though we give them the ground, the purchase has been at much blood—this being by far the greatest loss they ever met with since the commencement of the war.

The General recommends an immediate attention to be paid to the state of the arms and ammunition; and that the arms be put in the best possible order, and the troops be furnished with a full supply of arms, and not less than forty rounds of cartridges per man. NATHANIEL GREENE.

BRIGADE, H. Q., Sept. 13, 1777.

From the motions of the enemy it appearing to his Excellency that our service will for some time continue to be full as active as that we have lately experienced, he has, from that noble spirit which actuates his every movement, by which he wishes to share part in every hardship to which his army is exposed, divested himself and family of every species of baggage, save his blankets.

The Brigadier therefore requests that, though the baggage of the brigade has now joined it, the officers will not think of carrying any more more clothing, &c., than they have hitherto had with them, as he is determined to follow the laudable example of his Excellency. GEORGE WEEDON, Brig. Gen.

HEAD-QUARTERS, GERMANTOWN, Sept. 14, 1777.

The troops are to march to Swedes' Ford in the following order, by subdivisions from right, viz:

    First, two-thirds of the Light Dragoons, from which their commanding officer will detach small parties in front, to reconnoitre on the flanks to a considerable distance.

    Second, a Captain's command from General Smallwood's Brigade, 800 yards in their rear.

    Third, one regiment from same brigade, 200 yards in *their*.

    Fourth, the main body of the army 500 yards in their rear, in the following order, viz.:

        1st. General Sullivan's Division.
        2d. Lord Stirling's   "
        3d. General Wayne's   "
        4th. Park of Artillery.
        5th. General Nash's Brigade.
        6th. General Stevens' Division.
        7th. General Greene's   "

Fifth. the wagons with stores, hospital stores, and commissaries' stores.

Sixth, a rear guard of two regiments from Weedon's Brigade.

Seventh, a Captain's command from these two regiments, at the distance of 200 yards.

Eighth, the remaining third of the Light Dragoons, 500 yards from the foot.

Ninth, a subaltern's command from these Dragoons, at the distance of 500 yards.

The guards in front and rear, and each brigade, to send out small flanking parties on their left. The rear guard of foot, and the Light Dragoons, to pick up all stragglers.

GEORGE WASHINGTON.

BURGOYNE'S SURRENDER.

HEAD-QUARTERS, Sept. 15, 1777.

In future, whenever the men are formed for action, the Sergeants are to be placed in the ranks on the flanks of subdivisions, that their fire may not be lost.

The Brigadiers, or officers commanding regiments, are also to post some good officers in the rear, to keep the men in good order.

If, in any time of action, any man who is not wounded, whether he has arms or not, turns his back on the enemy, and attempts to run away or retreat before orders are given for it, those officers are instantly to put him to death. The man does not deserve to live who basely flies, breaks his solemn engagement, and betrays his country.

GEORGE WASHINGTON.

HEAD-QUARTERS, CAMP AT PENNYBACKER'S MILL,
September 28, 1777.

The Commander-in-Chief has the happiness again to congratulate the army on the success of the Americans to the northward.

On the 19th inst. an engagement took place between General Burgoyne's army and the left wing of ours, under General Gates. The battle began at 10 o'clock, and lasted till night—our troops fighting with the greatest bravery, not giving an inch of ground. Our loss is about 80 killed, and 200 wounded and missing. The enemy's is judged to exceed 1000 killed, wounded, and taken prisoners, and deserters declare that General Burgoyne, who commanded in person, was wounded in the left shoulder. The 62d Regiment was cut in pieces, and the enemy suffered extremely in every quarter where they were engaged. Such was the ardor of our troops, that wounded men, after being dressed, returned to action.

The Commander in-Chief has further occasion to congratulate the troops on the success of a detachment of the northern army, under Colonel Brown, who attacked and carried several of the enemy's posts, and had got possession of several of the old French lines at Ticonderoga.

COL. BROWN CAPTURES THE BRITISH.

Colonel Brown, in those severe attacks, has taken 293 prisoners of the enemy, with their arms, retaken more than 100 of our men, and taken 150 batteaux below the fall in Lake Champlain, and 50 above the falls, including 17 gun-boats, and one armed sloop, besides cannon, ammunition, &c., &c.

To celebrate this success, the General orders that at 4 o'clock this afternoon all the troops be paraded and served with a gill of rum per man, and that at the same time there be discharges of 13 pieces of artillery from the park.

Major-general for to-morrow,	. . . . .	Sullivan.
Brigadier-general do.	. . . . .	Scott.
Brigade-major do.	. . . . .	Peers.
Picket-major do.	. . . . .	Dorson.
Field officers do.	. . . . .	{ Col. Lamb, Maj. Morrill.

GEORGE WASHINGTON.

HEAD-QUARTERS, Oct. 5, 1777.

The Commander-in-Chief returns his thanks to the generals and other officers and men concerned yesterday in the attack on the enemy's left wing, for their spirit and bravery, shown in driving the enemy from field to field,* and although an unfortunate fog, joined with the smoke, prevented the different brigades from seeing and supporting each other, or sometimes even from distinguishing their fire from the enemy's, and some other causes, which as yet cannot be accounted for, they finally retreated, they nevertheless see that the enemy is not proof against a vigorous attack, and may be put to flight when boldly pushed. This they will remember, and assure themselves that on the next occasion a proper exertion of the powers God has given them, and inspired by the cause of freedom in which they are engaged, they will be victorious.

The Commander-in-Chief, not seeing the engagement with the enemy's right wing, desires the general officers to thank those officers and men who behaved with bravery.

GEORGE WASHINGTON.

*Battle at and near Chew's House, or the Battle of Germantown.

BRIGADE ORDERS.

HEAD-QUARTERS, Oct. 6, 1777.

The commanding officers of regiments are, without delay, to send to the Provost for such of their men as have been tried and their sentences have been published.

The battalion of militia from Virginia, commanded by Colonel Runna, is to be attached to General Scott's Brigade.

Brigadier-general Pulaski will make returns of the horse as soon as possible.

John Lawrence, Esq., appointed on the 6th of September as extra Aid-de-Camp to the Commander-in-Chief, is now appointed Aid-de-Camp to him, and is to be obeyed and respected as such.

Thomas Mullans, Esq., appointed on the 3d inst. *to act as* Brigade-major to General Conway, is now, for his gallant behavior on the 4th inst., appointed Brigade-major to General Conway, and is to be respected and obeyed as such.

The commanding officers of corps are every morning to report their strength to the brigadiers or officers commanding, that it may be known daily what stragglers have joined.

Buck-shot shall be put into all cartridges that shall be made hereafter. GEORGE WASHINGTON.

HEAD-QUARTERS, Oct. 7, 1777.

The State Regiment from Virginia is to supply the place of the 9th Virginia Regiment in General Muhlenberg's Brigade, and do duty there till further orders.

John Fardon, of Colonel Hartley's Regiment, found guilty of the crime of desertion, and sentenced, by the general Court Martial, held 25th September last, to suffer death, is to be executed to-morrow at 12 o'clock.

The situation of the army frequently not admitting of Divine Service on Sunday, the Chaplains of the army are forthwith to meet and agree upon some method of performing it at some other time, which method they will make known to the Commander-in Chief. GEORGE WASHINGTON.

CAMP AT PERKIOMING, Oct. 7, 1777.

The General returns his sincere thanks to the officers and soldiers in general of his division for their behavior at the battle of Germantown. Nevertheless, he has the mortification to hear some few behaved ill, who are arrested and reported to his Excellency. The General has the highest confidence in his division, and in the spirit and good conduct of the officers.

He, from the best information, has the mortification to assure the troops that they fled from victory; and he wishes most ardently that the troops may be convinced of the necessity of retreating and rallying likewise, and a partial retreat to change a position is often necessary, and therefore a particular retreat is not to be considered general without the order as such.

Notwithstanding the fog deprived us of the opportunity of seeing how to conduct our own approaches at the enemy's confusion, and giving them a complete rout, which beyond a doubt we should have done if the weather had been clear, nevertheless he has the satisfaction to assure the troops that the enemy suffered very severely.

The arms and ammunition are to be put in order as soon as possible, and everything got in readiness for attack or defence.

NATHANIEL GREENE.

HEAD-QUARTERS, TOAMENSING, Oct. 9, 1777.

Brigadier-general Nash will be interred at 10 o'clock this forenoon, with military honors, at the place where the road where the troops marched on yesterday comes into the great road.— All officers, whose circumstances will admit of it, will attend and pay this respect to a brave man who died in defence of his country.

The execution of John Fardon is postponed till to-morrow at noon.

The general Court Martial, whereof Colonel Brodhead was president, is to sit to-morrow morning at 8 o'clock, at the Horseman's tent, by the park of artillery.

GEORGE WASHINGTON.

HEAD-QUARTERS, TOAMENSING, Oct. 10, 1777.

The Chaplains of the army are to meet to-morrow at 12 o'clock, in the rear of the park of artillery, for the purpose mentioned in general orders of the 7th inst.

The Paymaster-general will attend to the business of his department at General Weedon's quarters at Mr. Tinnis' house.

A Court of Inquiry, consisting of four members and Major-general Lord Stirling, is to sit at 12 o'clock to-day at the President's quarters, to examine into the conduct of Major general Sullivan, in the expedition commanded by him against Staten Island in the month of August last. Major Taylor and other officers who can give information of this matter are to attend. But if the Court see cause to postpone the examination for want of evidence, after hearing what Major Taylor has to urge on that head, they are to do it accordingly. Gen. McDougall, Gen. Knox, Col. Spencer, and Col. Clark are the members.

It is not for every officer to know the principles upon which every order is issued, and to judge how they may and may not be dispensed with or suspended, but their duty to carry them into execution with the utmost punctuality and exactness. They are to consider that military movements are like the working of a clock, and will go equally, regularly, and easily, if every officer does his duty; but without it, be as easily disordered, because neglect from any one, like the stopping of a wheel, disorders the whole. The General therefore expects that every officer will duly consider the importance of the observation, their own reputation, and the duty they owe to their country. He claims it of them, and earnestly calls upon them to do it.

GEORGE WASHINGTON.

HEAD-QUARTERS, TOAMENSING, Oct. 11, 1777.

The Court of Inquiry, of which Lord Stirling is president, now sitting at the President's quarters, is to inquire into the conduct of Brigadier-general Wayne, viz.: that he had timely notice of the enemy's intentions to attack the troops under his command on the night of the 20th ult.; and notwithstanding that intelligence he neglected making a disposition until it was too late either to annoy the enemy or make a retreat without the utmost danger and confusion.* The President will give notice when the Court can enter on the inquiry, and when the parties and evidence are to attend.

GEORGE WASHINGTON.

HEAD-QUARTERS, Oct. 15, 1777.

The General has the repeated pleasure of informing the army of the success of the troops under the command of General Gates over General Burgoyne's army on the 7th inst.

The action commenced at three o'clock in the afternoon, between the pickets of the two armies, which were reinforced on both sides. The contest was warm, and continued till night with obstinacy, when our troops gained the advanced lines of the enemy, and encamped on that ground all night. The enemy fled and left behind them 330 tents, with kettles boiling with corn, 8 brass field pieces, 2 twelve and 6 six pounders, upwards of 200 dead, and the baggage of their flying army. General Frazier is among their slain. Our troops took 550 non-commissioned officers and privates, prisoners, besides Sir Francis Caralback, Aid-de-Camp to General Burgoyne, and a Quartermaster-general, said to be Carleton's, the Commanding Officer of a Foreign Brigade, and an Officer of the British Grenadiers.

GEORGE WASHINGTON.

HEAD-QUARTERS, VALLEY FORGE, May 18, 1778.

Officers for duty to-morrow:

Brigadier-general, ... Patterson.
Lieutenant-colonel, ... Cropper.
Major, ... Conway.
Brigade-major, ... Marvin.
Inspector, from Learned's Brigade.

The Commander in-Chief has the pleasure to inform the army, that the Honorable Congress have been pleased to come to the following resolutions:

---

*The Court pronounced the conduct of General Wayne, on the occasion of the attack referred to. "as every thing that was to be expected from an active, brave, and vigilant officer," and seemed to attach the blame to Colonel Hampton. who, by delay or misapprehension of orders, and an unskillful position of the troops, had exposed them to massacre.—*Irving's Life of Washington.*

RESOLVES OF CONGRESS.

"IN CONGRESS, May 15, 1778.

"*Resolved unanimously,* That all military officers commissioned by Congress, who now are, or hereafter may be, in the service of the United States, and shall continue therein during the war, and shall not hold any office of profit under these States, or any of them, after the conclusion of the war shall be entitled to receive for the term of seven years, if they live so long, one-half of the present pay of such officers,—Provided, that no general officers of the cavalry, artillery, or infantry, shall be entitled to receive more than half the pay of the Colonel of such corps respectively; and provided this resolution shall not extend to any officer in the service of the United States, unless he shall have taken the oath of allegiance to, and shall actually reside within some one of these United States.

"*Resolved unanimously,* That every non-commissioned officer and soldier, who hath enlisted or shall enlist into the service of the United States for and during the war, and shall continue therein to the end thereof, shall be entitled to receive the further reward of 80 dollars at the expiration of the war."

The whole army are directed to prepare, in the best manner possible, for an immediate and sudden movement.

GEORGE WASHINGTON.

HEAD-QUARTERS, VALLEY FORGE, May 19, 1778.

Officers for duty to-morrow:

Brigadier-general, ... Wayne.
Colonel, ... Greene.
Lieutenant-colonel, ... Ballard.
Brigade-major, ... Minnis.

Commanding officers of regiments are to make returns to the Quartermaster-general of the number of tents absolutely wanting in each, for such men as cannot be accommodated consistently with their health and comfort in huts. It will be relied upon, in these returns, that none will make a larger demand than the real situation of their respective regiments requires.— The Quartermaster-general will issue his orders on these returns.

At a general Court Martial, whereof Colonel Bauman was president, held the 18th inst., John Reynolds, artificer in Major Pollard's corps, tried for striking Lieutenant Hemmet, found guilty and sentenced to receive 100 lashes, the Commander-in-Chief approves the sentence and orders it executed on the grand parade to-morrow at guard-mounting.

Samuel Raymond, at the same court, tried for presenting a loaded musket at Lieutenant Hemmet; upon due consideration the court are of opinion that he is guilty of the charge exhibited against him, but the extreme and unpardonable warmth with which the officers conducted themselves, renders the actions of the prisoner in some measure excusable, and operates with the court so strongly in his favor, that they only sentence him to be reprimanded by the commanding officer of the company to which he belongs.

Also John Coffin, tried for abusing Captain Gowerly when attempting to repress a riot on the other side of the Schuylkill, found not guilty and acquitted.

The General approves the sentences, and orders them to take place immediately.

The Brigade and Sub-Inspectors, Majors of Brigade, and Adjutants of the army, will assemble at the Baron Steuben's quarters, at 10 o'clock precisely, where they will receive particular orders.

A stray horse taken up in General Scott's Brigade. Inquire of Captain Killpatrick. Another in General Poor's Brigade. Inquire of Lieutenant Cherry.

Also a number in Colonel Van Schaick's New York Regiment, at Cuckoldstown. GEORGE WASHINGTON.

VALLEY FORGE, H. Q., May 21, 1778.

Officers for duty to morrow:

Brigadier-general,	Varnum.
Lieutenant-colonel,	Reed.
Major,	Moore.
Brigade-major,	McCormick.

The Inspectors, &c., will attend at Baron Steuben's quarters to-morrow, at the hour appointed in the orders of the 19th inst.

If there are any persons in the army who understand making thin paper, such as bank notes are struck upon, they are desired to apply immediately to the orderly office, where they will be shown a sample of the paper. Officers commanding regiments are to publish this in regimental orders.

Mr. Vowles, Adjutant in the 9th Virginia Regiment, is appointed to do the duty of Brigade-major, in General Woodford's Brigade, until further orders.

At a general Court Martial, the 15th inst., whereof Colonel Bowman was president, Captain Cleaveland of Colonel Michael Jackson's Regiment, tried for behaving in an unofficer-like manner in refusing to do a tour of duty when duly notified, found not guilty of the charge exhibited against him, and acquitted with honor. Although Captain Cleaveland ought not to have been warned for duty when returned sick, yet the General cannot applaud the spirit which actuated him in refusing obedience to a positive order, and declining a tour of duty of such a kind as might have been in all appearance easily performed by Captain Cleaveland in his circumstances. Captain Cleaveland is released from his arrest.

At a Brigade Court Martial, whereof Lieutenant-colonel Cropper was president, Captain Edward Hull, of the 15th Virginia Regiment, tried for gaming, when he ought to have been on parade, the 12th inst., unanimously found guilty of that part of the charge exhibited against him relative to gambling, but acquitted of non attendance on parade, and sentenced to be reprimanded by the commanding officer of the brigade, in presence of all the officers thereof.

At the same court, Lieutenant Thomas Lewis, of the same regiment, upon a similar charge, found guilty, and sentenced the same as Captain Hull.

The Commander-in-Chief, however, unwilling to dissent from the judgment of a Court Martial, is obliged to utterly disapprove these sentences, the punishment, in his opinion, being entirely inadequate to the offence. A practice so pernicious in itself as that of gaming, so prejudicial to good order and military discipline, so contrary to positive orders, carried to so enormous a height as it appears, and aggravated certainly, in the case of Lieutenant Lewis, by an additional offence of no trifling military consequence—absence from parade—demanded a much severer penalty than simply a reprimand.

Captain Hull and Lieutenant Lewis are to be released from arrest. GEORGE WASHINGTON.

H. Q., VALLEY FORGE, May 23, 1778.

Officers for duty to-morrow:
Brigadier-general, ... Scott.
Brigade-major, ... Berrien.
Colonel, ... Brewer.
Major, ... Hopkins.

The Auditor's office is removed to James Cloyd's, within a mile and a half of the Paymaster-general's quarters.

At a general Court Martial, the 16th inst., of which Colonel Bowman is president, Lieutenant Edison, of the German Battalion, tried for behaving in a manner unbecoming a gentleman and an officer, in abusing Colonel Nixon's family, unanimously found guilty of the charge exhibited against him, being a breach of Art. 21, Sec. 14, Articles of War, and sentenced to be discharged from the service. The Commander-in-Chief approves the sentence, and orders it to take place immediately.

At a Brigade Court Martial, the 18th inst., Major Wallis president, Lieutenant Marks, of the 11th Virginia Regiment, tried for not attending the parade on the 13th inst., and unanimously acquitted of the charge with honor.

Likewise, Lieutenant William Powell, tried upon the same charge, and acquitted in like manner.

The General observes, that sickness or indisposition is certainly a sufficient excuse for not attending the parade, but it ought to be an established rule, to signify it either personally or in writing, through the Adjutant to the commanding officer of the regiment to which the officer concerned shall belong.

GENERAL ORDERS.

These gentlemen, in not doing this, were deficient in the line of regularity and propriety. Hereafter the excuse shall not be admitted unless this rule be observed, except where any particular circumstances render the observance impracticable, which can rarely happen.

GEORGE WASHINGTON.

H. Q., VALLEY FORGE, May 23, 1778.

Officers for duty to-morrow:
Brigadier-general, ... Patterson.
Colonel, ... Dayton.
Brigade-major, ... Stagg.

Till some further arrangement of the army is made, Major-general Lee is to take charge of the division lately commanded by Major-general Greene, and in case of action or any general move of the army, the three eldest Major-generals present fit for duty, are to command two wings and the 2d line, according to seniority.

Commanding officers of regiments and corps will immediately apply to the Commissary of Military Stores for all the arms and accoutrements wanting for their men.

The Quartermasters of brigades will also make out returns, and apply for orders for ammunition to complete each man with forty rounds and two flints.

All officers are called upon to see that their men's arms and accoutrements are put in the best order possible. They will likewise take particular care that their men have wooden drivers fixed in their pieces at the hours of exercise, to prevent an unnecessary waste of flints. They are not to be absent from camp on any pretence whatever, but be in actual readiness to march at a moment's warning.

GEORGE WASHINGTON.

H. Q., VALLEY FORGE, May 24, 1778.

Officers for duty to-morrow:
Brigadier-general, ... Wayne.
Colonel, ... Patton.
Major, ... Sumner.
Brigade-major, ... Bannister.

BRIGADE COURT MARTIAL.

The general Court Martial, whereof Colonel Bowman is president, is dissolved. Another is ordered to set to-morrow morning at 9 o'clock, to try all such prisoners as shall be brought before it. Colonel Chambers will preside.

Each brigade will give a Captain for the court. All persons concerned will attend.

At a Brigade Court Martial, May 22, 1778, Lieutenant-colonel Cropper, president, Lieutenant Davis, of the 11th Virginia Regiment, tried for encourgaging a soldier to stay away from his regiment, for refusing, when the soldier was sent for by a guard, to let him go to his regiment, and for speaking disrespectfully of the officer who sent the guard a second time; upon mature deliberation, the court are of opinion that he is not guilty of speaking disrespectfully of the officer who sent the guard for Lieutenant Davis, though they are of opinion that his detaining the Sergeant was unwarrantable. But, considering that his error seems to have arose from what he thought was doing his duty, do acquit him.

Lieutenant Davis is ordered to be released from his arrest.

GEORGE WASHINGTON.

H. Q., VALLEY FORGE, May 25, 1778.

Officers for duty to-morrow :
    Brigadier-general, ... Muhlenberg.
    Colonel, ... Swift.
    Lieutenant-colonel, ... Hubley.
    Brigade-major, ... Haskell.

Inspector, to be taken from McIntosh's Brigade.

The Regimental Surgeons will apply to the Flying-hospital store for hog's lard and sulphur. They are to make their returns more punctually on Mondays.

Several guns, packs, and cartridge-boxes, belonging to some soldiers in the army, are left at the orderly office.

The Mustermaster-general and Commissary of Prisoners have removed their quarters to Mr. Evans' house, half a mile north of Sullivan's Bridge, near Perkioming Creek.

SENTENCES OF COURT MARTIAL.

The Regimental Paymasters will give in their abstracts to the Paymaster-general immediately for examination for the month of April.

At a general Court Martial the 1st of May, of which Colonel Febiger was president, Lieutenant Adams of the 10th Pennsylvania Regiment, tried for "ungentlemanly behavior in propagating a report that an officer of the 10th Pennsylvania Regiment had behaved cowardly in the action of Germantown, and when desired by Colonel Hubley to name the officer, for refusing to do it in an unbecoming manner," unanimously found guilty of the charge exhibited against him, being a breach of Art. 21, Sec. 14, Articles of War, and sentenced to be dismissed the service, the Commander-in-Chief approves the sentence, and orders it to take place immediately.

Signals will be given this afternoon in manœuvering by a small field-piece. This notice is given to prevent an alarm.

Lieutenant Ford is appointed to do duty as Adjutant in Colonel Lamb's Regiment of New York Artillery, and is to be respected and obeyed accordingly.

GEORGE WASHINGTON.

H. Q., VALLEY FORGE, May 26, 1778.

Officers for duty to morrow:
Brigadier-general, ... Poor.
Colonel, ... Grayson.
Lieutenant-colonel, ... Weisenfels.
Brigade-major, ... Learned.
Inspector, to be taken from Woolford's Brigade.

The Commander-in-Chief, perceiving that the regimental returns materially differ in the number of *sick absent*, from the hospital reports, notwithstanding these were lodged with the Adjutant-general that the regimental returns might be rectified and adjusted by them, calls upon the commanding officers of regiments to make returns to-morrow to the Adjutant-general, specifying the names of all their sick absent, the places where they are, and the times they were sent to them, that the difference above mentioned may be satisfactorily accounted for. In doing this, the strictest regard is to be paid to the hospital reports.

An Independent Corps, commanded by Captain Selin, are immediately to bury the offal and carrion near the Black Bull.

The Commissary-general of the Staff will in the future apply to the commanding officer of that corps for a party to bury any offal which may be near his stall.

A subaltern, sergeant, corporal, and eight men, with the Commissary of each brigade, are to be sent immediately into the vicinity of their respective brigades to seize the liquor they may find in the unlicensed tippling-houses.

The Commissaries shall give receipts for the liquor they seize, and notify the inhabitants, or persons living in the vicinity of camp that an unconditional seizure will be made of all liquors they shall presume to sell in future.

A flag goes to Philadelphia to-morrow.

GEORGE WASHINGTON.

H. Q., VALLEY FORGE, May 27, 1778.

Officers for duty to-morrow:

    Brigadier-general, ... Varnum.
    Lieutenant-colonel, ... Read.
    Major, ... Murray.
    Brigade-major, ... : . . . Ten Eyck.
    Inspector, from Scott's Brigade.

The commanding officers of regiments are to make returns on Friday next of the arms that were in possession of their respective corps on the 1st November last, of all they have since delivered in, of those they have since drawn, and of those now in actual possession. It is expected they always have exact accounts kept of arms, clothing, camp utensils, &c., furnished their men, as they must be responsible for their due application.

Major general Mifflin, having been permitted by Congress to repair to, and serve in this army, is to take the command of the division late Lincoln's.

The field-officers of regiments who have drawn money from any of the public offices for recruiting their respective corps, are desired as soon as possible to furnish the Auditors of the Army with lists of money advanced by them to their officers for that service.

Captain Turberville is appointed Aid-de-Camp to Major-general Lee till further orders, and is to be respected accordingly.

Officers are to see that the mud plastering around the huts be removed, and every other method taken to render them as airy as possible. They will also have the powder of a musket cartridge burnt in each hut daily to purify the air, or a little tar if it can be procured. The Commissary of Military Stores will provide blank cartridges for that purpose.

GEORGE WASHINGTON.

H. Q., VALLEY FORGE, May 27, 1778.

A general Court Martial, of which Lieutenant-colonel Eleazer Oswald is appointed president, will sit to-morrow at 9 o'clock at the President's quarters, for the trial of such prisoners as shall be brought before them. Captains Wilkerson, Eustis, Von Heer, Kingsbury, Captain-lieutenant McClure, two subalterns from Colonel Crane's Regiment, two from Colonel Lamb's Regiment, and two from Col. Proctor's Regiment, are appointed members; and Captain-lieutenant Ebenezer Finley, Judge-Advocate.

GEORGE WASHINGTON.

H. Q., VALLEY FORGE, May 28, 1778.

Officers for duty to-morrow:

 Brigadier-general, ... Scott.
 Colonel, ... Irvine.
 Lieutenant-colonel, ... Bassett.
 Brigade-major, ... Johnson.

Inspector, from 1st Pennsylvania Brigade.

Commanding officers of brigades in pursuance of former orders to hold themselves in readiness to march, are to apply immediately to the Quartermaster-general for a sufficient number of wagons to transport their baggage, and are to have their respective brigades supplied as completely as possible with camp utensils and necessaries of every kind requisite towards taking the field.

The Commissary will have a quantity of hard-bread and salt meat prepared to issue to the army when called for. As we may expect at every moment to march the army, it is to be prepared in all respects for that purpose.

Guards of every kind are constantly to hold themselves in a collected state with their accoutrements on, and ready to act at a moment's warning. The General forbids all exercise and diversions, such as cause them to disperse and put off their accoutrements, which is equally inconsistent with their safety and good discipline.

A Board of general officers is to set to-morrow morning at 10 o'clock, at General Lee's quarters, to examine into Lieutenant-colonel Regnier's claim of rank in the New York Line, and report their opinion thereon. The other Lieutenant-colonels of that line are to attend. The Commander-in-Chief will lay before the Board the memorial presented by Lieutenant colonel Regnier, with other papers.

A Court of Inquiry will set to-morrow, to examine into the conduct of Lieutenant-colonel Parks, reported to have been absent from camp without leave, and to have been negligent in his duty. All persons concerned will attend. Colonel Johnson is appointed president. Colonel Parker, Lieutenant-colonel Bunner, Lieutenant-colonel Starr, and Major Fenner, will attend as members, at the President's quarters, at 9 o'clock to-morrow morning. GEORGE WASHINGTON.

H. Q., VALLEY FORGE, May 29, 1778.

Officers for duty to-morrow :
    Brigadier-general, ... Huntington.
    Lieutenant-colonel, ... Burr.
    Major, ... Stelle.
    Brigade-major, ... Seely.
    Inspector, from 2d Pa. Brigade.

SENTENCES OF COURT MARTIAL.

The commanding officers of regiments and corps are not, under any pretence whatever, unless duty requires it, to permit their officers or men to be absent from camp, that they may be ready to march at an hour's warning.

At a general Court Martial, Colonel Chambers, president, the 25th inst., Capt. Medaras, of the North Carolina Brigade, tried for forgery. After mature deliberation, the court are of opinion that Captain Medaras is guilty of the charge exhibited against him, but as he could not have been actuated by motives self-interested or injurious to Captain Jones, the gentleman whose name he signed, and as he had been before perfectly acquainted with Captain Jones' sentiments, the court thinking his crime, though he is yet truly blameworthy, alleviated by these circumstances, do sentence him to be reprimanded in general orders.

The Commander-in-Chief approves the sentence, and is much concerned to find that an officer in this army should presume to sign a brother officer's name without his permission. Captain Medaras is ordered to be released from his arrest.

At the same court, William Whiteman, wagoner, tried for desertion, and sentenced to receive sixty lashes, is approved, and ordered to be put into execution to-morrow morning on the grand parade, at guard-mounting.

Also, John Clime, of the 10th Pennsylvania Regiment, tried for desertion, attempting to escape to the enemy, and for stealing a horse, found guilty of both charges, and sentenced to receive 200 lashes, 100 for each crime. The General approves the sentence, and orders it put into execution this evening at roll-call, at the head of the regiment to which he belongs.

Also, John Wood, Sergeant in the 8th Pennsylvania Regiment, tried for desertion and attempting to fly to the enemy, acquitted, and ordered to be released from confinement.

On the night of the 27th inst., James Barry, an inhabitant, was robbed of £160, Continental money, thirteen hard dollars, a diamond ring, silver spoons, buckles, gold buttons, a sword, and some valuable men's and women's wearing apparel, and many other articles.

A REWARD OFFERED.

Fifty Dollars Reward

Will be given to any person that will discover the robbers, that the owner may recover his articles. All officers are desired to order the strictest inquiry to be made, that the villains may be brought to justice, as it is supposed they belong to the army.

GEORGE WASHINGTON.

H. Q., VALLEY FORGE, May 30, 1778.

Officers for duty to-morrow:
Brigadier-general, ... Patterson.
Colonel, ... Bradley.
Brigade-major, ... Marshall.
Inspector, from Poor's Brigade.

The commanding officers of brigades are to appoint a sufficient number of proper officers to be left in charge of the sick, and such others of their respective brigades as will be unable to march with them, in case the army moves from the present camp.

The Regimental Surgeons will make out and lodge with the Surgeon-general of the Flying Hospital, exact returns of the sick belonging to their regiments who shall be left in camp when the army marches.

The Board of general officers, held agreeable to the general order of the 28th inst., have made the following report, viz.: The claims of Lieutenant colonel Regnier and the other Lieutenant-colonels of the State of New York, respecting their standing in rank, being considered, the Board are of the opinion that Lieutenant-colonel Regnier will take rank of those gentlemen on Courts Martial detachments on all duties from the line, but that the command assigned him must be in the line of the State, for notwithstanding Lieutenant-colonel Regnier's rank as Lieutenant-colonel was antecedent to theirs in the line, yet his appointment in that State was posterior. The Commander-in-Chief approves the above report.

At a Brigade General Court Martial, May 27, 1778, Lieutenant-colonel Cropper president, Captain Hull, of the 15th Virginia

Regiment tried, first, for being so far elevated with liquor when on the parade for exercising on the 14th inst., as rendered him incapable of doing his duties with precision; 2dly, for accusing Lieutenant Samuel Jones of not deposing the truth when called on oath to depose against him on the 18th inst.,—acquitted of the first charge, but found guilty of the second, and sentenced to be reprimanded by the commanding officer of the brigade, in presence of all the officers therein. Captain Hull is ordered to be released from his arrest.

At a general Court Martial, May 28, 1778, Colonel Chambers president, Ensign James Walker, of Colonel Gist's Regiment, tried, first, for deserting a wagon he had in his charge at the appearance of one of our Light Horse, and losing his party in his flight; 2dly, for telling several falsehoods in relating the event, when returning to camp: unanimously found guilty of the charges exhibited against him, being breaches of Art. 5, Sec. 18, and Art. 21, Sec. 14 of the Articles of War, and sentenced to be cashiered. The Commander-in-Chief approves the sentence, and orders it to take place immediately.

At the same court, John Lewis, of Colonel Angel's Regiment, tried for threatening to take the lives of several officers of that regiment, found guilty, and sentenced to receive 60 lashes—approved, and ordered to be put into execution at roll-call this evening, at the head of the regiment he belongs to. A quantity of Continental currency, lately found in the hands of Lieutenant Dexter of Colonel Angel's Regiment. The owner may receive the same by proving his property.

Col. Crane's Regiment of Artillery is to be mustered on Monday next at 10 o'clock, Colonel Lamb's and Colonel Proctor's at the same hour on Tuesday, and Colonel Harrison's on Wednesday. The officers will be careful to have their muster-rolls made out correctly, and see that their men have their blankets neatly rolled up, as they must parade with them on.

Captain Brown's and Capt. Dorsey's Companies of Maryland Artillery are annexed to Col. Harrison's Regiment, with which they are to do duty till further orders. GEORGE WASHINGTON.

GENERAL ORDERS.

H. Q., VALLEY FORGE, May 31, 1778.

Officers for duty to-morrow:

Brigadier-general,	Wayne.
Lieutenant-colonel,	Livingston.
Do. do.	Miller.
Brigade-major,	Marvin.

Inspector, from Glover's Brigade.

The Second State Regiment of Virginia is for the present to be annexed to General Muhlenberg's Brigade; and Col. Van Schaick's Regiment, till further orders, is in like manner to be joined to the Second Pennsylvania Brigade, in lieu of the Eighth Pennsylvania Regiment, which is to be detached on other service.

A Surgeon from each brigade is to remain in camp to attend the sick which shall be left behind, under the direction of Dr. Hutchinson, till relieved by surgeons from the General Hospital, when they are to immediately join their respective regiments.

Men with the small-pox, or under inoculation, are to be comprehended in the number of the sick.

Commanding officers of regiments will assist the regimental surgeons in procuring as many women of the army as can be prevailed on to serve as nurses to them, for which they will be paid the usual price. Orderlies are also to be left, one to every 20 sick men, who are to be such as, for want of clothing, from lameness, and the like, are least fit to march with the army, but at the same time capable of this duty. A commissary is likewise to be left to supply the sick with provisions. A commissioned officer to every 50 men is to remain, and a field-officer to superintend the whole.

The arms of the sick in each regiment are to supply, as far as necessary, the deficiency of those unfit for duty. If any remain, they are to be left in care of the officer who stays with the sick. The vaults are to be well covered before the brigades leave the ground.

SENTENCES OF COURT MARTIAL.

Commanding officers of divisions, and all others, are to pay the strictest attention that no woman be suffered, on any pretence, to get into the wagons of the army on the march.

Some hospital tent-poles were delivered at the Quartermaster-general's store through mistake. Those who have them in possession are desired to return them immediately.

At a Brigade Court Martial, whereof Lieutenant-colonel Oswald was president, the 28th, 29th and 30th inst., Sergeant John Nevill, of Colonel Lamb's Regiment, tried for losing a bullock by neglect, when Sergeant of the commissary's guard, was by them unanimously acquitted.

Jonathan Gill, of Capt. Brown's Company, tried for drunkenness at his post, plead guilty and was sentenced to receive 50 lashes.

James Whaling, Drummer of Colonel Proctor's Regiment, tried for desertion and attempting to get into Philadelphia, plead guilty. The court, in consideration of his youth, and his having received no pay or bounty except some clothes, as appeared from Col. Proctor's evidence, do sentence him to receive only 80 lashes.

Michael Nash, of Captain Kingsbury's Company, tried for drunkenness on duty and absenting himself from his guard, plead guilty, and sentenced to receive 50 lashes.

John Gibbons, of Col. Proctor's Regiment, tried for absenting himself from camp without leave, was sentenced to receive 50 lashes.

The General approves the sentences, and orders Sergeant Nevill to be released from his confinement.

Some circumstances appearing in favor of James Whaling, the 80 lashes are remitted. The punishment ordered the others is to be inflicted to-morrow morning at guard-mounting, at the head of the regiments to which they respectively belong.

The Court Martial, whereof Lieutenant-colonel Oswald is president, is dissolved.   GEORGE WASHINGTON.

ORDER OF MARCH.

H. Q., VALLEY FORGE, June 1, 1778.

Officers for duty to-morrow:
  Brigadier-general, ... Muhlenberg.
  Colonel, ... Wigglesworth.
  Major, ... Church.
  Brigade-major, ... Minnis.
  Inspector, from Learned's Brigade.

Colonel Courtlandt is appointed to tarry in camp to superintend the sick left on the ground when the army moves, and to send on the recovered men properly officered to join their respective corps; and Major Marvin will repair to the Yellow Springs and the hospitals near camp, and superintend the sick there. They will apply to the orderly for written instructions.

The following will be observed as a standing model for the order of march, whether of the whole army, a division, brigade, or battalion. It may happen that some changes may be necessary in the strength and number of the advanced, rear, and flank guards, and in the relative distances to each other and to the main body, &c., which are to be determined according to particular circumstances, and which the officers commanding will judge of; but the general principles and rules here laid down, are in all cases to be practised, only with such variations in applying them as different situations may require.

When a battalion receives orders to march, each company forms before its own quarters; the Captain, having inspected into their arms and accoutrements, conducts it to the regimental parade, where the field-officers inspect the whole, form each battalion into eight platoons for charging, agreeable to instructions given, and march it by platoons to the rendezvous. When only one battalion marches, the Colonel orders out an advanced and rear guard, each consisting of one lieutenant, three non-commissioned officers, one drummer, and twenty privates.

A brigade composed of several battalions, has an advanced and rear guard, each consisting of one captain, two subalterns, six non-commissioned officers, and forty or fifty privates.

ORDER OF MARCH.

When the several brigades march together, each brigade furnishes a proportionate number for the advanced and rear guards.

When the whole army marches, the new guards of the day form the advanced guard, and the old ones the rear guard. The new guards being assembled on the grand parade, the Brigadier of the day forms them into a battalion of eight platoons, and the eldest field-officer of the day takes the command of it and marches at the head of the column. The Brigadier of the preceding day, having assembled the old guards, forms them in the same manner, the eldest field-officer taking the command and marching in the rear of the column. The advanced guard should be from 50 to 200 paces in front of the column; each advanced guard should send forward a detachment to serve as an advanced guard to itself, and this detachment should also send out a patrol in front of the others, thus: one captain, two subalterns, six non-commissioned officers, one drummer, and fifty men, will send out a non-commissioned officer and twelve men, and that non-commissioned officer will also advance four men in his front. An advanced guard of one lieutenant and twenty men, will advance one non-commissioned officer and eight men, who will also advance two men in his front. The rear guard will also observe the same rules, sending its detachments in the rear as the advanced guard does in front.

When a brigade, division, or the whole army marches by the right, it is supposed the enemy is on the left, and the contrary. Each battalion will therefore send out on the flank exposed to the enemy one subaltern, two non-commissioned officers, and sixteen men, as a flank-guard, who will march in a platoon by files from the right opposite the centre of the battalion, at the distance of eighty or one hundred yards from the column.

When the army marches in two columns, the right column has its flank-guard on its right, and the left column on its left.

When the army marches in one column, and the position of the enemy is uncertain, guards must be sent on both flanks.—

The advanced, rear, and flank guards must always have their bayonets fixed.

Whenever the ground will permit, the battalions must march by platoons. During the march, each colonel must stay before his battalion, and each captain and subaltern before his platoon: the intervals between the battalions and platoons must be strictly observed during the march.

When there is a creek or defile to pass, the brigadiers must stop till their brigades have passed, and the colonels till their respective battalions have passed. They will take care that the men pass with as large a front and as quick as possible.

The advanced guards having passed, the defile should take such a situation as to be able to see all around, and shall send out patrols 500 paces around. The head of the column will halt before it enters the defile, to let the platoons get half-distance, and when half the column gets through, it halts till the whole has passed, and then continues its march.

When the road will not permit marching by platoons, the march is to be made by four in front, in the following manner, viz: Each officer will divide his platoon into sections; for example, a platoon of sixteen files makes four sections. They will break off by the right or left, each section two paces from the other, and continue the march. If a platoon has fifteen files, the last section will have three files; if fourteen, the last will have four men in one rank; if thirteen files, the last will have five files.

When marching in this order by the right, the officers commanding platoons will be on the left of the first section; the sergeant stays in his place on the right, and the officers and non-commissioned officers who were in the rear will be on the right flank. If they march in this order by the left, the commissioned officer of the platoon remains on the right of the first section, and the others on the left flank, so that by wheeling the sections the platoons will be formed, and each officer and non-commissioned officer will be in his place.

During the march each officer must keep his platoon in order; the officers and non-commissioned officers in the rear must prevent the soldiers from leaving the rank on any account. If the soldiers have occasion for water, the officer must send a non-commissioned officer with some men to fill their canteens, and the non-commissioned officer must bring them back to their platoons immediately. The flank-guard will never suffer any non-commissioned officer or soldier to pass them during the march, and the rear-guard will take care to bring up all stragglers.

A brigade Court Martial is to sit to-morrow morning at nine o'clock, at a tent near the General's house, for the trial of such prisoners as shall be brought before them. Lieut. Colonel Du Plissis is appointed president, Captain Cook, Capt. Lieut. Powers, Capt. Lieut. Coltman, two Captain-lieutenants from Colonel Harrison's Regiment, two subalterns from Colonel Crane's, one from Colonel Lamb's, one from Colonel Proctor's, and two from Colonel Harrison's Regiments, are the members of the court; and Captain Lieutenant Duffy, Judge-advocate.

After Order.—The order for a general Court Martial, of which Lieutenant-colonel Du Plissis was appointed president this day, is countermanded. GEORGE WASHINGTON.

H. Q., VALLEY FORGE, June 2, 1778.

Officers for duty to-morrow:

Brigadier-general,	Poor.
Colonel,	Bowman.
Lieutenant-colonel,	Beauford.
Brigade-major,	Claiborne.

Inspector, from Patterson's Brigade.

At a general Court Martial, of which Colonel Chambers was president, May 29, 1778, Lieutenant colonel Gray, of the 12th Pennsylvania Regiment, tried for ungentlemanlike behavior in entering into private contracts with the soldiers of his regiment for the deficiency of rations, by which means, and other unwarrantable practices, the soldiers are defrauded of a considerable sum of money, found guilty of the charge exhibited against him, being a breach of Art. 21, Sec. 14, of the Articles of War, and sentenced to be cashiered; and agreeable to Art. 22, Sec. 14, his name, place of abode, crime, and punishment, be published in the newspapers in and around camp, and of that particular State from which he came, or in which he usually resides. The Commander-in-Chief approves the sentence, and orders it to take place.

At the same court, Lieutenant Webb, of the 7th Virginia Regiment, was tried for "disobedience of orders, for going on duty in a hunting shirt, after confessing he had a coat; and being desired that if he had no regard to his own appearance to have some for the credit of his regiment, and therefore to not appear in an unofficerlike manner," found guilty, and sentenced to be reprimanded by the officer commanding the regiment to which he belongs, in presence of the officers thereof.

The General approves the sentence, and orders it to be put into execution to morrow morning at roll call.

GEORGE WASHINGTON.

H. Q., VALLEY FORGE, June 8, 1778.

Officers for duty to-morrow:
  Brigadier-general, ... Varnum.
  Lieutenant-colonel, ... Regnier.
  Major, ... Porter.
  Brigade-major, ... McCormick.
Inspector, from Weedon's Brigade.

Thomas Shanks, on full conviction of his being a spy in the service of the enemy, before a Board of general officers held yesterday, by order of the Commander-in-Chief, is adjudged worthy of death. He is therefore to be hanged to-morrow morning at guard-mounting, at some convenient place near the grand parade.

At a general Court Martial, the 1st inst., Colonel Chambers president, Lieutenant Toomy, of Colonel Gist's Regiment, attached to the Third Maryland Brigade, tried for disobedience of orders, found guilty, and sentenced to be reprimanded by the commanding officer of the brigade, in presence of the officers of the brigade to which he belongs. The Commander-in-Chief approves the sentence, and orders it to take place to-morrow morning at roll-call.

When commissions shall be issued to fill the vacancies in the corps of artillery, they will be dated at the time the vacancies happened, according to the usual method.

Officers commanding pieces of artillery are to be very careful that no wagoners are, on any pretence whatever, suffered to lodge in their wagons. Any one found sleeping in a wagon will be punished, and the officer to whom such wagon shall belong shall be called to a severe account.

GEORGE WASHINGTON.

HEAD-QUARTERS, VALLEY FORGE, June 4, 1778.

Officers for duty to-morrow :

Brigadier-general . . . . Scott.
Lieutenant-colonel, ... North.
Major, ... Hawes.
Brigade-major, ... Berrien.
Inspector, from Muhlenberg's Brigade.

The following resolve of Congress, the operation of which has heretofore been prevented by the particular circumstances of the army, is in future to be punctually observed :

"IN CONGRESS, NOV. 19, 1776.

"*Resolved*, That on any sick or disabled non-commissioned officer or soldier being sent to any hospital or sick quarters, the captain or commandant of the troop or company to which he belongs, shall send to the surgeon or director of the said hospital, or give to the non-commissioned officer or soldier, so in the hospital or quarters, a certificate countersigned by the paymaster of the regiment (if he be with the regiment), of what pay is due to such non-commissioned officer or private at the time of his entering the hospital or quarters, and the captain or commandant of the troop or company shall not receive the pay of the said soldier in hospital or quarters, or include him in any pay-abstract during his continuance therein. And in case any non-commissioned officer or soldier shall be discharged from the hospital or quarters as unfit for further service, a certificate shall be given him by the surgeon or director of what pay is then due to him, and the said non-commissioned officer or soldier so discharged shall be entitled to receive his pay at any pay office, or from any paymaster in the service of the United States —the said paymaster keeping such certificate to prevent impositions, and giving the non-commissioned officer or soldier his discharge, or a certified copy thereof, mentioning at the same time that he has been paid. That this resolution be transmitted to the Commanders-in-Chief in the several departments, to be by them given out in orders, and then delivered to the directors of the hospitals in each department, who are to cause the same to be fixed up in some conspicuous place or places in every military hospital, for the information of all concerned."

The commanding officers of regiments are immediately to make returns to the Commissary of Military Stores, of the arms actually wanting in their respective corps to complete the number of men fit for duty in each, agreeable to which the Commissary is further to issue the arms now in store.

All persons whatever are forbid selling liquor to the Indians. If any sutler or soldier shall presume to act contrary to this prohibition, the former will be dismissed from camp, and the latter receive severe corporeal punishment.

On the march, Lieutenant colonel Fleury will be attached to General Lee's Division, Lieutenant-colonel Davis to General Lord Stirling's, Lieutenant-colonel Barber to General Mifflin's, Major Ternant to General Marquis De Lafayette's, Lieutenant-colonel Brooks to General Baron De Kalb's, and as they will not be employed on the march in exercising or manœuvering the troops, they are to fill the office of Adjutant-general, each in his respective division.

GEORGE WASHINGTON.

HEAD-QUARTERS, VALLEY FORGE, June 5, 1778.

Officers for duty to-morrow:
   Brigadier-general, ... Huntington.
   Lieutenant-colonel, ... Vose.
   Major, ... Peters.
   Brigade-major, ... Stagg.
Inspector, from late Conway's Brigade.

A Court of Inquiry, whereof Colonel Wigglesworth is appointed president, will set to-morrow morning at 9 o'clock, at the President's quarters, at the request of Lieutenant-colonel Du Plissis, to inquire into his conduct, on the different occasions mentioned in a letter from the Commander-in Chief to Congress in his behalf, and into the truths of the facts on which the representations contained in it were founded, and of the several matters urged by the officers of artillery to the contrary, in a letter from them to the Commander-in-Chief. All persons concerned will attend. Lieutenant-colonel Dearborn, Lieutenant-colonel Butler, Major Hay, and Major Campbell, are the members of the court.

Captain Lawrence Keene, of the regiment late Patten's, is appointed Aid-de-camp to Major-general Mifflin, and is to be obeyed as such.

A Captain from Weedon's Brigade and a subaltern from the 1st Pennsylvania Brigade, are to repair immediately to the hospitals at the Yellow Springs to relieve Captain Wallace and Lieutenant Swearinger. They will call at the orderly office for instructions.

At a general Court Martial, whereof Colonel Chambers was president, the 27th ult., Lieutenant McDonald, of the 3d Pennsylvania Regiment, tried for "unofficer and ungentlemanlike behavior, in taking two mares and a barrel of carpenter's tools on the lines, which mares he conveyed away, and sold the tools at private sale—and with insulting behavior, in refusing to comply with his arrest." After mature deliberation, the court taking into consideration several circumstances, are unanimously of opinion, that although Lieutenant McDonald is guilty of the facts alleged in the first charge, they do not amount to "unofficer and ungentlemanlike behavior," and do acquit him of it, and likewise of the second.

The Commander-in-Chief is far from being satisfied of the propriety of Lieutenant McDonald's conduct. He knows of no authority under which he had a right to seize the horses in question, and to apply them in the manner he did. He approves still less of the measures taken with respect to the tools.

If the probability of their being carried into the enemy by a disaffected person justifies the seizure, nothing can justify the applying them, as appears to have been intended, to private emolument, to the injury of the right owner, who was an absent and innocent person who had only lodged them in the care of the other during his absence. They ought immediately to have been reported to, and lodged with, the Quartermaster-general. Lieutenant McDonald is released from his arrest.

General Poor's, Varnum's, Huntington's, 1st and 2d Pennsylvania, and late Conway's Brigades, and the Artillery, will receive their pay for the months of February and March this day. Woodford's, Scott's, and the North Carolina Brigades, to-morrow. Glover's, Patterson's, and Learned's, the 7th inst.; Weedon's, Muhlenberg's, and the 1st and 2d Maryland Brigades, the 8th inst.

A general Court Martial in the corps of artillery, of which Colonel Harrison is hereby appointed president, will sit to-morrow morning at 9 o'clock, at the President's tent, for the trial of all such persons as shall be brought before them. Captain Rice, Captain Wells, one Captain, one Captain-lieutenant, and two Lieutenant's from Colonel Harrison's Regiment, two Lieutenant's from Colonel Crane's, one from Colonel Lamb's, and two from Colonel Proctor's Regiments, are the members; and Captain-lieutenant Powars, Judge Advocate.

GEORGE WASHINGTON.

COLONEL NAGLE'S TEA-PARTY.

H. Q., VALLEY FORGE, June 6, 1778.

Officers for duty to-morrow:
  Brigadier-general, ... Patterson.
  Lieutenant-colonel, ... Coleman.
  Major, ... Moore.
  Brigade-major, ... Bannister.
  Inspector, from Huntington's Brigade.

At a general Court Martial, whereof Colonel Chambers was president, the 2d inst., Captain Stake of the 10th Pennsylvania Regiment was tried for "propagating a report, that Colonel George Nagle was seen, on the 15th of May, drinking either tea or coffee in Sergeant Howercraft's tent, with his lady, her mother, the said Howercraft, and his family, to the prejudice of good order and military discipline."

The court having considered the charge and evidence, are unanimously of opinion that Captain Stake's justification in relation to the report of Colonel Nagle's having drunk the tea or coffee as aforesaid is sufficient, and do acquit him of the charge exhibited against him. The General approves the acquittal.

At the same court, Lieutenant Samuel Jones, of the 15th Virginia Regiment, was tried for "concealing, and denying that he had in his possession, a pair of mittens belonging to Capt. Hull; 2dly, for gaming on the 12th of May, and sundry other times; 3dly, for behaving in a manner unbecoming an officer and gentleman in treating Captain Hull with abusive language while under arrest, and endeavoring to incense the officers of his regiment against him."

The court, having considered the charge and evidence, are of opinion that Lieutenant Jones is guilty of the charge exhibited against him, and do sentence him to be discharged from the service.

The General is entirely disposed to believe from the representations he has received in favor of Lieutenant Jones, that he was incapable of having retained the gloves with a fraudulent intention; but as he has been clearly proved to have been guilty of the pernicious practice of gaming, which will invariably meet with every mark of his disapprobation, he confirms the sentence of dismissing Lieutenant Jones.

At the same court, Lieutenant John Roberts, of the 2d North Carolina Regiment, was tried for behaving in a scandalous and infamous manner, and absenting himself from camp without leave. The court, having considered the charges and evidence, are unanimously of opinion that Lieutenant John Roberts is not guilty of the charge exhibited against him, and do acquit him.

The General approves the acquittal, but is sorry to see little personal bickerings between officers, which cannot with propriety be drawn into military offences, made the subjects of Courts Martial.

At a Brigade Court Martial held this day, whereof Col. Harrison is president, George Deloney, of Colonel Crane's Regiment, was tried for desertion, plead guilty, and was sentenced to receive 100 lashes. Also, John Gill, of Colonel Harrison's Regiment, was tried for being drunk on his post, plead guilty, and was sentenced to receive 50 lashes ; but many circumstances appearing in favor of the prisoner, the court recommends him to mercy.

The General approves the above sentences, remits the punishment ordered Gill, and forgives Deloney also, in whose favor some particular circumstances have appeared.

GEORGE WASHINGTON.

H. Q. VALLEY FORGE, June 7, 1778.

Officers for duty to-morrow :
    Brigadier-general, ... Wayne.
    Lieutenant-colonel, ... Haskell.
    Major, ... Mentges.
    Brigade-major, ... Haskell.
    Inspector, from Varnum's Brigade.

The general Court Martial, whereof Col. Chambers is president, is dissolved, and another ordered to sit at the usual place to-morrow for the trial of all such prisoners as shall be brought before it. Col. Livingston will preside. Each brigade will give a captain for the court.

A general Court Martial will sit to-morrow at the Gulf Mill, to try all such persons as shall be brought before them. Lieutenant-colonel Smith will preside. Four captains and eight subalterns, from Colonel Jackson's detachment, will attend as members.

The Court of Inquiry, whereof Colonel Johnson was president, the 29th ult., report as follows : The court duly considering the charge exhibited against Lieutenant-colonel Park, and his defence, are of opinion that he is guilty of having been absent from camp without leave, but that he is not guilty of negligence of duty while in camp. The court taking into consideration the peculiar circumstances of Lieut. Colonel Park's absence, and the punishment he has already endured in consequence of his arrest and suspension from duty, beg leave to recommend him to his Excellency as worthy of acquittal. The General restores Lieut. Col. Park to his command.

The Honorable the Congress have been pleased to come to the following resolutions respecting the establishment of the army, viz.:

In Congress, May 27, 1778.
Establishment of the American Army.
The Infantry.

Resolved, That each battalion of infantry shall consist of nine companies—one of which shall be of light-infantry; the light-infantry to be kept complete by drafts from the battalion, and organized during the campaign into corps of light-infantry. That the battalion of infantry shall consist of—

Pay per month.
- 1 Colonel..............Dollars 75
- 1 Lieutenant-colonel.......... 60
- 1 Major........................ 50
- 6 Captains..............each 40
- 1 Captain-lieutenant........ 26⅔
- 8 Lieutenants...........each 26⅔
- 9 Ensigns................each 20
- 1 Surgeon...................... 60
- 1 Surgeon's Mate............... 40
- 1 Sergeant-major............... 10
- 1 Quartermaster's Sergeant.. 10
- 27 Sergeants...........each 10
- 1 Drum-major................. 9

Pay per month.
- 1 Fife-major..........Dollars 9
- 18 Drums and Fifes......each 7½
- 27 Corporals............each 7½
- 477 Privates..............each 6⅔
- 1 Paymaster to be taken from the line, and to receive in addition to his pay in the line, per mo.. 20
- 1 Adjutant, taken as above, and add'nal pay per mo. 13
- 1 Qr. Master, taken as above, and add'nal pay per mo. 13

Each of the field-officers to command a company. The Lieutenant of the Colonel's company is to have the rank of Captain-lieutenant.

The Artillery.

That a battalion of artillery shall consist of—

Pay per month.
- 1 Colonel............. Dollars 100
- 1 Lieutenant-colonel........ 75
- 1 Major..................... 62½
- 12 Captains..............each 50
- 12 Captain-lieutenants..each 33⅓
- 12 First-lieutenants......each 33⅓
- 36 Second-lieutenants....each 33⅓
- 1 Surgeon..................... 75
- 1 Surgeon's Mate.............. 50
- 1 Sergeant-major............ 11 $\frac{23}{90}$
- 1 Qr. Master's Sergeant,..... 11 $\frac{21}{90}$
- 1 Fife-major................. 10 $\frac{35}{90}$
- 1 Drum-Major................. 10 $\frac{35}{90}$
- 72 Sergeants..............each 10

Pay per month.
- 72 Bombardiers..each, Dolls. 9
- 72 Corporals..............each 9
- 72 Gunners............... each 8⅔
- 24 Drums and Fifes......each 8⅔
- 336 Matrosses..............each 8⅓
- 1 Paymaster to be taken from the line, and to receive in addition to his pay in the line, per mo.. 25
- 1 Adjutant from the line, additional pay per month... 16
- 1 Qr. Master from the line, additional pay per month 16

The Cavalry, or Dragoons.

That a battalion of cavalry shall consist of—

	Pay per month.		Pay per month.
1 Colonel	Dollars 93½	6 Trumpeters	each, Dolls. 10
1 Lieutenant-colonel	75	12 Sergeants	each 15
1 Major	60	30 Corporals	each 10
6 Captains	each 50	374 Dragoons	each 8⅓
12 Lieutenants	each 33⅓	1 Paymaster from the line, and to receive in addition to his pay in the line, per month	25
6 Cornets	each 26⅔		
1 Surgeon	60		
1 Surgeon's Mate	40		
1 Saddler	10	1 Adjutant from the line, additional pay per month	15
1 Trumpet Major	11		
6 Farriers	each 10	1 Qr. Master from the line, additional pay per month	15
6 Quartermast. Sergts,	each 15		

Provosts.

That a provost be established to consist of—

	Pay per month.		Pay per month.
Capt. of Provosts,	Dollars 50	2 Sergeants	each, Dollars 15
4 Lieutenants	each 33⅓	5 Corporals	each 10
1 Clerk	33⅓	43 Provosts or privates	each 8⅓
1 Qr. Master's Sergeant	15	4 Executioners	each 10
2 Trumpeters	each 10		

This corps is to be mounted on horseback, and armed and accoutred as light-dragoons.

That in the *Engineering Department*, three companies be established, each to consist of—

	Pay per month.		Pay per month.
1 Captain	Dollars 50	4 Corporals	each, Dollars 9
3 Lieutenants	each 33⅓	60 Privates	each 8⅓
4 Sergeants	each 10		

That two Aides-de-Camp be allowed to each Major-general, who shall for the future appoint them out of the captains and subalterns. That in addition to their pay in line there be allowed to—

An Aid-de-Camp,	per month	Dollars 24
A Brigade-major,	"	24
A Brigade Quartermaster,	"	15

PAY TABLE.

NOTE.—The pay of the following officers was at different times during the war fixed as follows:

Pay per month.		Pay per month.	
Major-general	Dollars 166	Deputy Director of Hospital.	100
Aid-de Camp	50	Surgeon of Hospital	90
Brigadier-general of cavalry	156¼	Apothecary and Purveyor	92
Brig. General of infantry	125	Stewards of Hospitals	31
Brigade Chaplain	50	Com'ry general of Mil. Stores	83½
Quartermaster-general	166⅜	Field Commissary Mil. Stores	50
Deputy Qr. Mr. Gen. Southern Army	125	Dep'ty Field Com. Mil. Stores	40
Deputy Qr. Mr. Gen. Main Army	75	Commissary of Prisoners	75
		Asst. Com'ry of Prisoners	40
Assistant Qr. Mr. Generals	30	Geographer to the Army	60
Wagonmaster	60	Assistant Geographer	30
Dep. Wagonmaster, Southern Army	50	Judge Advocate	75
		Deputy Judge Advocate	60
Wagon Conductor	20	Clothier-general	250
Adjutant	125	Deputy Clothier-general	75
Deputy Adjutant-general	75	Inspector of Rations	166⅜
Assistant Adjutant-general	50	Riding-master of Cavalry	33½
Clerk to Adjutant-general	40	Geographical Chain-bearer	15
Inspector-general	300	Conductor of Artillery	40
Paymaster-general, in the currency of the day	1166¼	Forage-master	80
		Director of Artificers	40
Deputy Paymaster,general	75	Brigade Inspector, in addition to pay in the line	30
Assist. Paymaster-general	70	Quartermaster-general	80
Director of Hospital	102	Dep. Quartermaster-general	60

All officers will be particular to make themselves well acquainted with the establishment, and govern themselves accordingly. The Commissaries will be particularly observant of what relates to their department until the regiments shall be arranged agreeable to this establishment. The nomination of regimental staff-officers, according to the mode here pointed out, is to be suspended. GEORGE WASHINGTON.

H. Q., VALLEY FORGE, June 8, 1778.

Officers for duty to-morrow:
  Brigadier-general, ... Muhlenberg.
  Lieutenant-colonel, ... Ramsey.
  Major, ... Talbott.
  Brigade-major, ... Alden.
  Inspector, from North Carolina Brigade.

Captain John Mercer, of the 3d Virginia Regiment, is appointed Aide-de-Camp to Major-general Lee, and is to be accordingly respected.

Brigade officer of the day, Captain-lieutenant Meredith. Colonel Harrison gives the orderly to head-quarters, and Colonel Crane to the brigade.   GEORGE WASHINGTON.

H. Q., VALLEY FORGE, June 9, 1778.

Officers for duty to-morrow:
  Brigadier-general, ... Woodford.
  Colonel, ... Smith.
  Major, ... Pauling.
  Brigade-major, ... Johnson.
  Inspector, from Woodford's Brigade.

After the dismission of the old guards, the Brigadier and field-officers of the preceding day are to assemble at the provost-guard and examine into the charges against the several prisoners there, and the circumstances attending them, and to discharge all such as shall appear to be improperly confined, or the length of whose imprisonment may be deemed a sufficient punishment for their crimes, or whose offences are so trifling as to make the process of a general Court Martial unnecessary. They are to send to their brigades and regiments all those who are to be tried by Brigade or Regimental Courts.

Three Captains and nine Lieutenants are wanted to officer the company of sappers. As this corps will be a school of engineering, it opens a prospect to such gentlemen as enter it, and will pursue the necessary studies with diligence, of becoming engineers, and rising to the important employments attached to that profession, such as the direction of fortified places, &c.

The qualifications required of the candidates are that they be *natives*, and have a knowledge of the mathematics and drawing, and are disposed to apply themselves to these studies. They will give in their names at head-quarters.

The army is to take a new camp to-morrow morning at 8 o'clock. The whole is to be in readiness accordingly, and to march to the respective grounds of encampment, which will be pointed out for each division by the Quartermaster-general.

At a Division Court Martial, the 7th inst., Lieutenant-colonel Badlam president, Adjutant Allen, of Colonel Michael Jackson's Regiment, tried for repeated disobedience of orders, and abusive language to Major Hull, and refusing to leave his hut when ordered, was unanimously found guilty of the charges exhibited against him, and sentenced to be discharged from the service.

The Commander-in-Chief approves the sentence, and orders it to take place.   GEORGE WASHINGTON.

H. Q., VALLEY FORGE, June 10, 1778.

Officers for duty to-morrow:
Brigadier-general,	Poor.
Lieutenant-colonel,	Harmar.
Major,	Gaskins.
Brigade-major,	Marshall.

Field-officers for detachment:
Lieutenant-colonel,	Heath.
Major,	Ellison.

For fatigue:
Colonel,	Brewer.
Lieutenant-colonel,	Miller.
Major,	Hopkins.

Colonel Crane gives the orderly to head-quarters, and Colonel Harrison to the brigade.   GEORGE WASHINGTON.

H. Q., VALLEY FORGE, June 11, 1778.

Officers for duty to-morrow:
Major-general,	Lee.
Brigadier-general,	Scott.
Lieutenant colonel,	Brent.
Major,	Tubbs.
Brigade-major,	Minnis.

LAST DAYS AT VALLEY FORGE. 381

Some misunderstanding, and mistakes in consequence, having arisen, with respect to the Major-general's command, the Commander-in-Chief directs, that till a more perfect arrangement can be made under the new establishment, or till further orders on this head, each Major-general is to command the division heretofore assigned him, previous to the late disposition for a march; but in case of an alarm, or any other general movement of the army, the three eldest Major-generals present and fit for duty, are, during the occasion, to command the right and left wings and second line of the army, agreeably to the general order of the 23d May last. The North Carolina Brigade is to supply the place of General Maxwell's and Lord Stirling's Divisions till further orders.

Upon firing the signal-guns for an alarm, the troops are to form immediately in front of their respective brigades, and are to be marched by the senior Major-generals, as above, to their respective alarm-post.

The 1st and 2d Maryland, and Varnum's Brigades, are to draw up in front of their respective encampments, and send to the Commander-in-Chief for orders.

A Major-general is to be appointed for the day, who, with the Brigadier and field-officers on that duty, are carefully to attend to the police and good order of the camp. They are always to be on the grand parade at guard-mounting, and when the guards are marched off, the Major-general will make a distribution of the several duties of the day among the field-officers of it. He is to receive and report to the Commander-in-Chief the remarkable occurrences which happened during his tour of duty, and will attend in an especial manner to the order of the 9th inst., respecting prisoners, as there is reason to believe that many of them are improperly detained in the provost.

All unnecessary waste of timber is to be avoided. The commanding officers will know that their Quartermaster attend particularly to this business.

The Commander-in-Chief having received ample testimony of the general good character and behavior of Lieutenant Jones, who was sentenced to be dismissed from the service by a general Court Martial, which sentence was approved by him on the 6th inst., and being further satisfied by Generals Woodford, Scott, and other officers, that that gentleman is not addicted to the vice of gaming, restores him to his rank and command in the regiment he belonged to, and in the line of the army.

At a Brigade general Court Martial, June 2, 1778, Lieutenant-colonel Adams president, Captain Norwood was tried for refusing to comply with a general order issued expressly for the relief of the troops on picket, founded on the necessity of the case, which at that period could not be otherwise remedied, found guilty of the charge exhibited against him, and sentenced to be privately reprimanded by the officer commanding the regiment to which he belongs.

The Commander-in-Chief utterly disapproves the sentence as altogether inadequate to the offence. The mutinous and dangerous spirit which actuated Captain Norwood, merited, in his opinion, the most exemplary punishment. He is to be released from his arrest.

At a general Court Martial, the 5th inst., Col. Chambers president, Lieutenant-colonel Hubly, of the 10th Pennsylvania Regiment, was tried for "malicious behavior in being the occasion of Colonel Nagle's signing a false return, to the injury of his honor and contrary to good order and military discipline, in the case of Captain Lang, who, as Colonel Hubly told Colonel Nagle, was absent without leave, though he had Colonel Hubly's and General Wayne's orders to remain at Lancaster until the business he was sent on was perfected." After mature deliberation, the court are unanimously of opinion that Lieutenant-colonel Hubly is not guilty, and do acquit him with honor.

The Commander-in-Chief confirms the opinion.

LAST DAYS AT VALLEY FORGE.   883

At the same court, Captain Redman, of the late Colonel Patten's Regiment, was tried for "misconduct on the night of the 11th of last April, in neglecting to guard the passes, by which means Capt. Humphreys was surprised, and not coming to Captain Humphreys' assistance when he was attacked by the enemy." The court are unanimously of opinion, that Captain Redman is not guilty of the first charge exhibited against him, and do acquit him. They are of opinion that Captain Redman is guilty of the second charge, but think that his reasons for not marching to the assistance of Captain Humphreys are sufficient, and do unanimously acquit him with honor.

The Commander-in Chief confirms the opinion of the court.

At the same court, William Powell, soldier in Colonel Angell's Regiment, was tried—1st, for desertion; 2d, for re-enlisting; 3d, for perjury: found guilty, and sentenced to receive 300 lashes, 100 for each crime, and return to Colonel Angell's Regiment.

The Commander-in Chief approves the sentence so far as it extends to 100 lashes.

Likewise Edward Connolly, soldier in Col. Harrison's Regiment of Artillery, was tried—1st, for deserting to the enemy; 2d, for re-enlisting into Col. Weltner's Regiment: found guilty of the charges exhibited against him, and sentenced to receive 200 lashes, 100 for each crime.

The Commander-in Chief approves the sentence the same as Powell's. These sentences to be put into execution to-morrow morning, at the head of the regiments to which they belong.

The grand parade is assigned in front of late Conway's Brigade.   GEORGE WASHINGTON.

NOTE.—About this time it appeared evident that Sir Henry Clinton was about to evacuate Philadelphia, and General Washington and his army at Valley Forge were busy in watching his movements, and preparing if possible, to take any advantage that circumstances might dictate. The American troops under Washington, during their encampment at Valley Forge, had acquired a considerable proficiency in tactics under the Baron Steuben. On the 18th of June, Clinton with his whole army evacuated Philadelphia. Washington sent General Arnold with a force to take possession of the city, broke up his encampment at Valley Forge, and pursued Clinton's army through New Jersey, hoping to strike some blow upon the enemy that would repay him to some extent for his long, inactive, and dreary encampment at Valley Forge. He overtook Clinton's army at Monmouth, on the 28th of June, and engaged in a battle which resulted in the fall of Colonel Monckton, of the Royal Grenadiers, and covered the American arms with glory.

SUPERNUMERARY OFFICERS

AT THE CHESTERFIELD ARRANGEMENT OF THE VIRGINIA LINE, FEBRUARY, 1781; AND NOTES ON THE SERVICES OF DIFFERENT OFFICERS.

Col. William Heath	supernumerary by juniority.	
Col. Levin Joines,	do.	do.
Col. Burgess Ball,	do.	do.
Lieut. Col. John Webb,	do.	do.
Lieut. Col. Richard Taylor,	do.	do.
Lieut. Col. Richard C. Anderson,	do.	do.
Major Thomas Ridley,	do.	by choice.
Major John Hays,	do.	do.
Major Andrew Waggoner,	do.	by juniority.
Major John Gilchrist,	do.	by choice.
Major Thomas Hill,	do.	by juniority.
Major William Taylor,	do.	do.
Major William Mosely,	do.	do.
Major Peter B. Bruin,	do.	do.
Capt. Lieut. William Eppes,	do.	by choice.
Capt. Lieut. John Crittendon,	do.	do.
Capt. Lieut. Arthur Lind,	do.	do.

Captain Richard Stephens, 6th Regiment, superseded.
Captain William Vance, 8th do. do.
Captain John Steed, 4th do. do.
Lieut. David Williams, 8th do. do.
Lieut. Edward Smith, 7th do. do.
Ensign Thomas Holt, 1st do. do.
Ensign Philip Coartney, 1st Regiment, subjected to a court of inquiry.
Ensign Wm. Scott, 4th Regt., subjected to a court of inquiry.
Ensign Spencer Morgan, 7th Regt., do. do.
Ensign Wm. Baylis, 8th do. do. do.

ROBERT H. HARRISON

Entered the army as Aid-de-Camp to General Washington, but soon became his private secretary. On the 5th of June, 1776, Congress resolved that R. H. Harrison, Esq., have the rank of Lieutenant-colonel in the Continental army. He continued in the family of Washington until the spring of 1781, when he left on account of ill health, and was appointed Chief-justice of the General Court of Maryland, March 10, 1781, and held said office until his death, in 1790.

COL. GEORGE BAYLOR

Of the Virginia Dragoons. By a special act of Congress, May 25, 1832, Mrs. Ann D. Baylor, representative, received $19,950.44 as the commutation pay of a colonel of dragoons. Colonel Baylor served to the end of the war, was an officer of great merit, and died in the island of Barbadoes in 1784, where he went for the benefit of his health.

The reader will recollect that on the 27th September, 1778, General Gray, a famous British marauder, surprised Baylor's dragoons while sleeping in a barn at old Tappan, N. Y., and out of one hundred and four persons, unarmed and asleep, sixty-seven were murdered in cold blood, and the rest captured. Seventy horses were also butchered, and Colonel Baylor made a prisoner. The trial and execution of Major Andre also occurred at Tappan.

COL. JOHN THORNTON

Was appointed a Captain in the third Virginia Regiment, February 12, 1776, was promoted to Major March 20, 1777, and in the same year to Lieutenant-colonel. On the invasion of Virginia by Cornwallis in 1781, he commanded a regiment of militia as a Continental officer by order of General La Fayette.

COL. URIAH FORREST,

Of the Maryland Continental Line, was severely wounded in the battle of Germantown, October 4, 1777, which caused the loss of one of his legs. This disabled him from active service, and on the 23d February, 1781, he resigned his commission, and died in April, 1805.

Col. James Mayson,

Of a Regiment of Rangers, raised in the State of South Carolina. By a resolution of Congress of the 24th July, 1776, his regiment was taken into Continental pay. His service cannot be traced beyond the siege of Charleston in 1780.

Col. Mordecai Buckner

Was commissioned Colonel of the 6th Virginia Regiment, February 13, 1776, and was cashiered February 9, 1777.

Col. Richard Campbell

Was commissioned as Captain February 19, 1776, and afterwards promoted to Lieutenant-colonel. He was killed at the battle of Eutaw Springs, in South Carolina, September 8, 1781. His heirs received 1114 acres of land.

Col. William Crawford

Entered the service in 1776, and resigned February 10, 1781. After this he entered the service against the Indians on the western frontier, and was killed by them.

Gen. Hugh Mercer,

Of the Virginia Line, was appointed Colonel to the 3d Virginia Regiment, February 13, 1776, and promoted to Brigadier-general June 5, 1776. He was a brave and accomplished officer, and died January 12, 1777, of wounds received at the battle of Princeton. His heirs received 10,000 acres of land from the State of Virginia, June 24, 1783.

Col. Richard Parker,

Of the Virginia Line, was commissioned Captain in the second Virginia Regiment, January 24, 1776, and afterwards became Colonel of the 8th Regiment. He died at the siege of Charleston, April 24, 1780. His heirs were allowed 6666⅔ acres of land by the State of Virginia, June 4, 1783.

Col. Charles Porterfield

Was commissioned Captain of the 11th Virginia Regiment, February 13, 1776, and served till August 14, 1779, when he was appointed Lieutenant-colonel of the State Garrison Regiment, and was killed at the battle of Camden, August 16, 1780. His heirs received 6000 acres of land from the State, Nov. 18, 1782.

COL. ISAAC REED,

Of the Virginia Line, was appointed Lieutenant-colonel of the 4th Regiment, February 13, 1776, was promoted to Colonel August 18, 1776, and died in service in September, 1778. His heirs received 6666⅔ acres of land from the State.

COLONEL WILLIAM TALIAFERRO,

Of the Virginia Line, was appointed Captain of the 1st Regiment, September 2, 1775, and was soon promoted to Major. He was appointed Lieutenant-colonel, February 1, 1777, and died in service, February 1, 1778. His heirs received 6000 acres of land from the State.

COLONEL THOMAS KNOWLTON

Entered the service 1775, and was very busy at the bombardment of Boston in February, 1776. While the British were playing a theatrical farce called "Boston Blockaded," Major Knowlton and party crossed the mill-dam from Cobble Hill, and set fire to some houses in Charlestown occupied by British soldiers, and the farce suddenly ended in reality. He was commander of the Congress Regiment at the battle of Harlem Plains, September 16, 1776, and was there killed. General Washington said, "He would have been an honor to any country."

CAPTAIN JOHN ROBERTS

Was appointed Captain January 11, 1779, in the Regiment of Convention Guards. The captives of General Burgoyne's army, surrendered at Saratoga October 17, 1777, were called the "Convention Troops." These were marched from the north to Charlotteville, Virginia. On the 5th of March, 1779, he was promoted to Major, and served till May 1, 1781.

CAPTAIN THOMAS BLACKWELL

Became supernumerary on the arrangement of the army at White Plains in September, 1781; and on the 16th of May, 1783, received his pay as Captain to November 1, 1778.

Lieutenant William Price

Served as Sergeant in the 1st Virginia Regiment from 1776, and, in the spring of 1779, was promoted to a lieutenancy, and served to the end of the war. He was discharged at Point of Forks in 1783. His commission was stolen from him while in service. He received his commutation per act 23d March, 1783, and was allowed 2,666⅔ acres of land.

Doctor William Carter

Was a Surgeon in the Continental Hospital at Williamsburg from July, 1776, to the close of the war. He died in the city of Richmond, Virginia, in 1798.

Lieutenant Edmund Brook

Was appointed Lieutenant in Colonel Harrison's Virginia Artillery in February, 1781, and served till the siege of Yorktown, when he left camp on account of sickness, by advice of Captain Coleman.

Lieutenant John Taylor

Served as Lieutenant in the Convention Guards from January 18, 1779, to June 15, 1781, when the regiment was disbanded on account of the general exchange of prisoners. He received 2,666⅔ acres of land November 13, 1832.

Captain Everard Meade

Was commissioned as Captain in the 2d Virginia Regiment, March 8, 1776, and served to May 1, 1780. He was then appointed Aid-de-Camp to Major-general Lincoln, with the rank of Major, and served to near the end of the war.

Cornet William Teas

Served from 1779 to 1781 in Colonel William Washington's Cavalry, and died in 1824. Received no pension.

Captain Buller Claiborne,

Of the Virginia Line, served in Spottswood's 2d Virginia Regiment from the spring of 1776, to 27th of July, 1777. He alleged service as Brigade-major, and Aid-de-Camp to General Lincoln. In 1834 his heirs received 5333⅓ acres of land.

LIEUTENANT JOHN EMERSON

Was a Lieutenant in the 13th Virginia Regiment up to April, 1778. On the 16th of June, 1820, he received 2666⅔ acres of land for services.

LIEUTENANT THOMAS WALLACE,

Of the Virginia Line, was commissioned November 23, 1779, as a Lieutenant in the 8th Virginia Regiment, and served to November 19, 1781, when he received marching orders to join the southern army in the Carolinas.

DOCTOR CORBIN GRIFFIN

Was a Surgeon in the hospital at Yorktown, and continued to serve to the end of the war.

CAPTAIN GEORGE M. BEDINGER

Served as Captain and Indian spy, at Boonsboro', Maryland, from 1775 to 1781.

LIEUTENANT ROBERT GREEN

Was Ensign from 1776, to September 1, 1780; and Lieutenant from July 10, 1781, to December 31, 1781.

LIEUTENANT SETH CHAPIN,

Commissioned as Lieutenant, July 9, 1776, in the 1st Company of Massachusetts Militia, under Colonel Ezra Wood and Capt. Samuel Cragin, and also served in the Continental Line.

CAPTAIN JOHN SPOTTSWOOD

Was commissioned as Captain in the 10th Regiment of Virginia February 20, 1777, and continued to serve till the Chesterfield arrangement, February 12, 1781, when he retired from service as an invalid. He was pensioned, by the State of Virginia, at $200 per annum.

LIEUTENANT THOMAS WISHART

Was a Lieutenant in the 15th Virginia Regiment, served to the surrender of Yorktown, and became supernumerary.

CAPTAIN WILLIAM NELSON

Was Captain of Militia January 25, 1777, September 6, 1779, and June 21, 1781; and was an active, meritorious, and patriotic officer.

LIEUTENANT RICHARD NOWELL

Was Sergeant of Cavalry at the battles of Brandywine and Germantown, and was under General Wayne at Stony Point. He received £90 10s 9d, from the State of Virginia as a Sergeant of Cavalry, was at Morristown with the army in 1780, and promoted to Lieutenant of Cavalry. In 1781 he was an express rider from General Washington to General Greene, and with Colonel Washington's Cavalry at the battle of the Cowpens. For his gallant services he was promoted to Brigade-major, and served to the surrender of Cornwallis. On entering service he was a student at William and Mary College. He was presented with a sword by General Washington for his gallant services. He died January 17, 1800, leaving a widow and five children.

CAPTAIN JOHN DE TREVILLE

Was a French gentleman, and was Captain in the 4th South Carolina Artillery under Colonel Owen Roberts, and was taken prisoner at the surrender of Charlestown, May 12, 1780. He was included in the general exchange of prisoners June 15, 1781.

LIEUTENANT ELI PARSONS

Was commissioned in 1776 as Lieutenant, in Colonel James Clinton's New York Regiment, was subsequently made a Lieutenant in Colonel Crane's Artillery, and was severely wounded at the battle of Germantown, which disabled him from holding rank in the line. He was appointed Commissary of Issues in 1778, and attached to General Knox's Brigade until he received permission to retire, from General Washington, in May, 1779.— Colonel Charles Stewart induced him to remain in service, and take charge of a magazine of provisions at Wyoming for the supply of General Sullivan's expedition against the Indians. He died September 25, 1830.

CAPTAIN DOHICKEY ARUNDELL,

Of the Continental Artillery of Virginia, entered the service February 5, 1776, under General Lewis, as Captain of Artillery, and was killed in the engagement at Gwinn's Island in the Chesapeake Bay, July 8, 1776, by the bursting of a mortar, while attempting to dislodge Lord Dunmore from the island.

CAPTAIN PETER BERNARD

Served two years and two months, ending September 1, 1779, and then resigned.

MAJOR JOHN BRENT

Was commissioned Captain in the Virginia Line February 26, 1776, and resigned as Major May 4, 1778. His commission, with his resignation written on it, is among the Washington papers in the Department of State.

FRANCIS T. BROOKE

Was a Lieutenant and Deputy Quartermaster in Colonel Harrison's Artillery from 1781 to the close of the war. He received 5333½ acres of land from Virginia.

CAPTAIN JOHN BLAIR

Was appointed Lieutenant in Colonel Harrison's Artillery January 13, 1777, was promoted to Captain, and was mortally wounded at the battle of Camden, and died August 18, 1780. His heirs received 4000 acres of land from Virginia.

ENSIGN WILLIAM B. BUNTING

Was commissioned as ensign in the 9th Virginia Regiment February 14, 1776, and died in service April 1, 1777. His heirs received land from Virginia.

LIEUTENANT DANIEL BEDINGER,

Of the Virginia Line on Continental establishment, and entered the service in July, 1776, and continued in actual service till the dismission of the army in South Carolina in 1783.

REV. JOHN CORDELL

Was appointed Chaplain of the 11th Virginia Regiment February 15, 1777, and served to January 1, 1779, and was allowed 6000 acres of land by the State of Virginia.

MAJOR MATTHEW DONOVAN,

Of the 9th Virginia Regiment, died in service in 1777. His heirs were allowed 6893 acres of land by the State of Virginia.

CAPTAIN JAMES DAVIS,

Of the Virginia Line, was appointed August 7, 1776, and became supernumerary September 30, 1778.

Major Edmund Dickinson,

Of the Virginia Line, was appointed Captain in 1776, became Major by promotion, and was killed at the battle of Monmouth June 28, 1778. His heirs received 5333⅓ acres of land from the State of Virginia.

Lieutenant Henry Field,

Of the Virginia Line, was appointed Lieutenant in the 8th Regiment January 26, 1776, and resigned August 3, 1776. He was allowed 2666⅔ acres of land by the State.

Lieutenant Thomas Gordon.

Of the Maryland Line, was appointed February 20, 1777, and resigned July 1, 1778.

Surgeon David Gould

Was a Surgeon of the General Hospital, and served from September 8, 1777, to July 11, 1781.

Lieutenant Joseph Hold,

Of the Virginia Line, was appointed in the 10th Regiment January 12, 1777, and resigned April 1, 1778. He was allowed 2666⅔ acres of land by the State.

Captain Reuben Lipscomb,

Of the Virginia Line, was appointed in the 3d Regiment November 28, 1776, and died in service October 3, 1778. His heirs received 4000 acres of land from the State.

Captain Thomas H. Luckett,

Of Colonel Rawlings'Riflemen, attached to Colonel Morgan's Virginia Riflemen, received 5500 acres of land from the State of Virginia for a service of eight years and four months. He served to the end of the war and received "commutation."

Brigade-Major Daniel Leet

Acted as Quartermaster from January 1, 1777, to October 1, 1777, and as Paymaster from this latter date to September 21, 1778, then as Brigade-major for three months, to December 21, 1778. He received 5333⅓ acres of land from the State of Virginia.

Captain Jonathan Langdon,

Of the Virginia Line, was commissioned as Captain in the 12th

NOTES ON THE SERVICES OF OFFICERS. 393

Regiment September 30, 1776, and resigned November 14, 1776, as appears among the Washington Papers in the department of State.

CAPTAIN AMBROSE MADISON,

Of the Virginia Line, served in the 3d Regiment as Paymaster from February 1, 1777, to August 1, 1778, and as Captain of the Convention Guards, from January 18 to September 23, 1779, and received 4000 acres of land from the State.

CAPTAIN JOSEPH MICHEUX,

Of the Virginia Line, served in the 14th Regiment from February 24, 1777, and resigned December 24 of the same year. He subsequently entered the service, and received 4000 acres of land.

LIEUT. RICHARD MUSE,

Of the Virginia Line, was appointed Lieutenant in the 15th Regiment December 22, 1776, and resigned May 14, 1779. His heirs received 2666⅔ acres of land from the State.

CAPTAIN JOHN MORTON

Was appointed Captain of the 4th Regiment of the Virginia Line February 19, 1776, and resigned March 12, 1777. He received 4000 acres of land from the State.

CAPTAIN RICHARD PENDLETON,

Of the Virginia Line, received 4000 acres of land from the State on the 18th February, 1839, for three years' service.

SURGEON SHUBAEL PRATT,

Of the Virginia Line, received pay as Surgeon from March 12, 1778, to June 12, 1779; and on the 6th June, 1838, his heirs received 6000 acres of land from the State for three years' service.

SURGEON WILLIAM RUMNEY,

Of the Virginia Line, served from March 12, 1778, to March 12, 1780, and received 6000 acres of land.

CAPTAIN HEBARD SMALLWOOD,

Of the Virginia Line, was appointed Captain in Colonel Grayson's Regiment March 4, 1777, and resigned October 6, 1778. He received 4444 acres of land from the State.

SURGEON CHARLES TAYLOR

Served from October 26, 1779, to May 15, 1780, in the Virginia Line, and on the 30th June, 1783, received 6000 acres of land from the State.

CAPTAIN BENJAMIN TIMBERLAKE,

Of the Virginia Line, served as Captain of the Convention Guards at Charlotteville, from January 13, 1779, to October 12th of the same year, and received 4000 acres of land from the State.

LIEUTENANT JOHN WILSON,

Of the Virginia Line, was commissioned Lieutenant in the 4th Regiment March 12, 1777, and was killed at the battle of the Eutaw Springs, September 8, 1781. His heirs received 2666⅔ acres of land from the State.

LIEUTENANT CHARLES YARBOROUGH,

Appointed Lieutenant in Colonel William Washington's Virginia Cavalry, Oct. 16, 1780, and served to the end of the war.

LIEUTENANT JOHN McKINLEY,

Of the Virginia Line. Captain Uriah Springer, of Colonel John Gibson's Frontier Detachment, swears that McKinley entered the army early in 1776 as Sergeant in Captain Stephen Ashby's Company of State troops, and served till December following, when he was commissioned as Lieutenant in the 13th Continental Regiment, and served till early in 1778. He joined Colonel Crawford's expedition against the Indians in 1782 and was killed. (2. 27. 1064.)

LIEUTENANT MICHAEL McDONALD

Served as a Lieutenant in the British navy. He deserted and entered the Continental service with the same rank, March 23, 1777, and served to January 1, 1781, in Putnam's and Nixon's Regiments as a private soldier, for fear the British would see him as an officer. (2. 27. 1079.)

ADJUTANT SIMON SUMMERS,

Of the Virginia Line, was appointed Lieutenant and Adjutant in the 6th Virginia Regiment on the 21st March, 1776, and was paid for services as such to the 10th February, 1781. His service extended to the end of the war, and was pensioned under act

15th May, 1828, as Lieutenant, and under act 7th June, 1832, as Adjutant.

CAPTAIN WILLIAM E. GODFREY,

Of the Pennsylvania Line, was taken prisoner by the British and carried to New York, where he remained seven months. He was Captain in Colonel Flower's Corps of Artillery Artificers from July 1, 1777, to Jan. 1, 1782, when he became supernumerary.

LIEUTENANT EDMUND GAMBLE,

Of the North Carolina State Cavalry, was commissioned by Gov. Caswell, and served to the end of the war.

CAPTAIN AUGUSTUS WILLETT,

Of the Pennsylvania Line, served in Montgomery's expedition against Canada in 1775, and on the 10th May, 1780, he was commissioned a Major in the 4th Battalion of Pennsylvania Militia, and was made a Lieutenant-colonel of the same May 1, 1783.

CAPTAIN SAMUEL JONES,

Of the Virginia Line, served in the 11th Regiment as Lieutenant from September 1, 1777, to January 1, 1780; and as Captain from January 1, 1780, to January 1, 1781.

HENRY KING,

Of the Maryland Line, enlisted as Sergeant May 25, 1778, and served as such to the 20th of October of the same year. He served as Commissary's Clerk from October 21 to December 31, 1778, and as the same from this latter date to April 19, 1780; and as Assistant Commissary of Issues from May 10, 1780, to September 10, 1781, in General Smallwood's Brigade.

LIEUTENANT ISAAC BOWMAN

Served as Lieutenant and Quartermaster in Col. George R. Clark's "Illinois" Regiment from May, 1779. He was taken prisoner and kept as such from November, 1779, to April, 1780, and was sold by the Indians to a trader named Turnbull, who carried him to New Orleans and Cuba. He escaped, and made his way home to Virginia.

LIEUTENANT EZRA CHAPMAN,

Of the Connecticut Line, entered the service in Captain

Horton's company of Colonel Baldwin's Artificers, August 6, 1777, and died in service September 1, 1778.

ENSIGN CLEMENT SEWELL,

Of the Maryland Line, entered the service in March, 1777, in Captain Ford's Company, of the 1st Maryland Regiment. He was promoted to Ensign September 12, 1777. He received a severe wound in the leg at the battle of Germantown, October 4, 1777, which disabled him from field service for a long time. His services were recognized to the end of the war, and a pension was granted him, per act 15th May, 1828.

CAPTAIN WILLIAM DAVENPORT,

Of the Virginia Line, entered the service as Lieutenant, and resigned his commission as such in December, 1779. Brigadier-general Muhlenberg, under date July 24, 1783, certifies that William Davenport served upwards of three years as Lieutenant, and lastly as Captain, in the Virginia Line. He received 4000 acres of land from the State.

ENSIGN JAMES BROADUS,

Of the Virginia Line, entered the service as a private February 1, 1776, was promoted to Sergeant and Ensign, and served to the surrender of Cornwallis at Yorktown, October 19, 1781, but held his commission to the close of the war, subject to duty.

COLONIAL JOHN H. STONE,

Of the Maryland Line, was appointed a Captain in January, 1776, and in December of the same year he was appointed Colonel. He was severely wounded at the battle of Germantown, and by reason of his disability he was obliged to resign August 1, 1779. He died October 5, 1804.

CAPTAIN JOHN DAVIS,

Of the Pennsylvania Line, was appointed Captain November 15, 1776, in the 9th Pennsylvania Regiment, and was in service as such in South Carolina January 11, 1782. His service has been accredited to the end of the war.

NOTES ON THE SERVICES OF OFFICERS.

NEHEMIAH STOKELY,

Of the Pennsylvania Line, entered the service as Captain, in the 8th Pennsylvania Regiment, under Colonel Bradshaw, in 1776, and became supernumerary in April, 1779.

CAPTAIN DAVID NOBLE,

Of the Massachusetts Line, raised a company in 1775, and entered into the service in Colonel Patterson's Regiment, attached to General Sullivan's Brigade, and died in the service in July, 1776.

LIEUTENANT SAMUEL JONES,

Of the Virginia Line. There were two of this name, one of the 11th and the other of the 15th Regiment. The one of the 15th Regiment was dismissed from the service June 6, 1778, and restored by General Washington on the 11th of the same month (see Washington's orders of those days, and Report No. 12, 1st Session 34th Congress).

CAPTAIN SAMUEL RANSON,

Of the Pennsylvania Line, was Captain of a company raised by Congress for the defence of Westmoreland, per act August 23, 1776. He continued to act in concert with the Continental army till the threatened invasion of Wyoming by the British and Indians, in 1778. He was killed in the bloody battle of Wyoming, July 3, 1778.

COLONEL WILLIS REDDICK,

Of the militia of Nansemond county, Va. His house, containing military stores, was burnt by the British in 1779.

DOCTOR FRANCIS LE BARON GOODWIN

Was Surgeon of Colonel Henry Jackson's 9th Massachusetts Regiment, and served from 1779 to the close of the year 1782, which service entitled him to the benefits of the act of January, 17, 1781.

CAPTAIN WILLIAM HARRISON

Was appointed in 1776 a Lieutenant in Captain Edward Veasey's Company, of Colonel Smallwood's Maryland Regiment. Captain Veasey was killed at the battle of Long Island, August

27, 1776, when Lieutenant Harrison succeeded to the command of the company, and died in 1777, of wounds received in service.

Rev. David Griffith,

Of the 3d Virginia Regiment, served as Surgeon and Chaplain of the Regiment from February 28, 1776, to March 18, 1779, as certified by Brigadier-general George Weedon, under date of September 25, 1780.

Captain Abraham Hite

Served as Paymaster to the 8th Virginia Regiment from January 1, 1779, to the reduction of Charleston, May 12, 1780, when he was made a prisoner. No one was appointed in his place, and his service is accredited to the end of the war.

Captain Mayo Carrington

Was appointed Assistant Quartermaster-general in the Virginia Line December 10, 1779, and acted in that capacity till the 27th March, 1781, and likewise acted as Quartermaster to General Woodford's Brigade from July 16th to December 10, 1779.

Lieutenant James Morton

Was appointed Quartermaster to the 4th Virginia Continental Regiment April 1, 1778, and so continued till January 1, 1782.

Ensign John Spitfathom

Was in service at the battle of Great Bridge, December 12, 1775, and continued in active service in the northern campaigns until December 17, 1780, when he was made Ensign, and so continued until the arrangement of the army in 1782.

Captain Henry Bedinger,

Of the Virginia Line, entered the service in June 1775, in Captain Hugh Stephenson's Company of Riflemen, and was appointed Sergeant before he left the recruiting rendezvous at Shepherdstown, Va. He marched with his company to the siege of Boston, and served till his company was discharged, in June, 1776. He was, July 9, 1776, made a Lieutenant in Captain Abraham Shepherd's Company, in Colonel Hugh Stephenson's Regiment of Riflemen. In August, 1776, Colonel Stephenson

A LIST OF CLAIMS AGAINST VIRGINIA.

died, and Colonel Moses Rawlings assumed the command of the regiment. Captain Bedinger was with his regiment at the defence of Fort Washington, November 16, 1776. He was there captured and detained a prisoner of war "four years wanting sixteen days." His service is accredited to the end of the war, and he received a pension in Berkeley county, Va., under act May 15, 1728, as a captain, to which he had been promoted while a prisoner.

A List of Claims brought against the State of Virginia by Officers of her Line on Continental Establishment.

Lieutenant-colonels.

Thomas Posey, for pay from September 11, 1782, to March 10, 1783, and balance of subsistence from January 1, 1782, to March 10, 1783.
Samuel Cabell, claim referred to John Pierce, Postmaster-general.
John Webb, for depreciation of his pay, and his account for commutation.
Oliver Towles, for pay and commutation.

Majors.

Samuel Finley, claim for pay in 1776, 1782, and 1783.
William Taylor, deranged in 1781, claim for commutation.
Joseph Crocket, claim for twelve month's pay as a supernumerary Captain
William Croghan, sundry accounts.

Captains.

Abraham Kilpatrick, old money account.
Clough Skelton, recruiting account.
Francis Minnis, for pay in 1783.
Erasmus Gill, ration account.
John Mountjoy, twelve months' pay as supernumerary.
James Williams, subsistence account.
Nathan Reid, subsistence account.
Strother Jones, account for commutation.
John B. Johnson, account for pay, &c.
Presley Nevill,   do.   do.
Lewis Thomas, for pay and subsistence in 1782.
John Fitzgerald, do.   do.   in 1783.
Simon Morgan, account for pay, &c.

Lieutenants.

William Brownlee, for commutation.
Charles Jones, account as Paymaster up to 1783.

A LIST OF CLAIMS AGAINST VIRGINIA.

Nicholas Taliaferro, recruiting account.
William Triplett, for commutation.
John Gordon, for pay in 1782 and 1783.
William Patterson, for sundry expenses.
Christopher Greenup, recruiting account.
Charles Erskine, for pay in 1782 and 1783 as Lieutenant of Dragoons.
William Stevenson, for pay in 1782 and 1783 as Lieutenant of Artillery.
Albion Throckmorton, for pay in 1783 as Cornet in Lee's Legion.
James Wallace, for pay in 1782, and commutation.
George Blakemore, for expenses as Lieutenant.

James Bedford, Sergeant, recruiting account.
William Dinsmore, for pay as private in 1782 and 1783.
A. McMahan, for pay as Sergeant of Dragoons.
John Rogers, for pay as private in 1782 and 1783.
James Bowser, for pay as private in 1782 and 1783.
Elias Honey, pay as Matross in 1782 and 1783.
Henry Craddock, balance due as Sergeant.
George Gillaspie, pay as Musician.
Daniel Wilkinson, pay as private.
Robert Brown, do. do.
Lewis Peyton, do. do.
James Brook, do. do.
Samuel Horton, pay as Dragoon.
Joseph Cooker, pay as Matross.
Spencer Cooper, do. do.
Thomas Smith, pay as Drum-major.
Nicholas Nell, pay as Sergeant.
John Ayres, pay as private.

Zadoc Robertson, pay as Matross.
Martin Whitsell, do. do.
Jacob Shoemaker, do. do.
Daniel Carn, do. do.
James Dixon, pay as Dragoon,
Charles Neal. do. do.
William Smothers, pay as Matross.
George Moxley, pay as Corporal of Dragoons.
Joseph Timberlake, pay as private of guards.
Nathan Fortune, pay as Dragoon.
Jacob Gore, pay as Sergeant of Dragoons.
John Plodd, pay as Dragoon.
Adam Andrew, do. do.
John Demoss, pay as private.
John Reasoner, do. do.
John Trotter, do. do.
John McDowell, do. do.
Alexander Scott, pay as Matross.
Elisha Dickerson, pay as Dragoon in 1782.
William Wood, pay as Corporal of Artillery.

PROMISES AND CONTRACTS

OF THE CONTINENTAL CONGRESS WITH THE OFFICERS OF THE REVOLUTIONARY ARMY.

IN CONGRESS, August 14, 1776.

Whereas, it has been the wise policy of the States to extend the protection of their laws to all those who should settle among them, of whatever nation or religion they might be, and to admit them to a participation of the benefits of civil and religious freedom; and the benevolence of this practice, as well as its salutary effects, have rendered it worthy of being continued in future times; and whereas, his Britannic majesty, in order to destroy our freedom and happiness, has commenced against us a cruel and unprovoked war; and unable to engage Britons sufficient to execute his sanguinary measures, has applied for aid to foreign princes, who are in the habit of selling the blood of their people for money, and from them has procured and transported hither considerable numbers of foreigners. And it is conceived that such foreigners, if apprised of the practice of these States, would choose to accept of lands, liberty, safety, and a communion of good laws and mild government, in a country where many of their friends and relations are already happily settled, rather than continue exposed to the toils and dangers of a long and bloody war, waged against a people guilty of no other crime than that of refusing to exchange freedom for slavery; and that they do this the more especially, when they reflect that after they have violated every Christian and moral precept by invading and attempting to destroy those who have never injured them or their country, their only reward, if they escape death and captivity, will be a return to the despotism of their prince, to be by him again sold to do the drudgery of some other enemy to the rights of mankind. And whereas, the parliament of Great Britain have thought fit, by a late act, not only to invite our troops to desert our service, but to direct a compulsion of our people, taken at sea, to serve against their country:

Resolved, therefore, That these States will receive all such foreigners who shall leave the armies of his Britannic majesty in America, and shall choose to become members of any of these States, and they shall be protected in the free exercise of their respective religions, and be invested with the rights, privileges, and immunities of natives, as established by the laws of these States, and moreover, that this Congress will provide for every such person fifty acres of unappropriated lands, in some of these States, to be held by him and his heirs in absolute property.

Congress proceeding to take into further consideration the expediency of inviting, from the service of his Britannic majesty, such foreigners as are engaged therein, and expecting that among the officers having command in the said foreign corps there may be many of liberal minds, possessing just sentiments of the rights of human nature, and of the inestimable value of freedom, who may be prompted to renounce so dishonorable a service by the feelings of humanity, and a just indignation at the office to which they are devoted by an infamous contract between two arbitrary sovereigns, and at the insults offered them, by compelling them to wage war against an innocent people who never offended them, nor the nation to which they belong, but are only contending for their just rights; and willing to tender to them also, as they had before done to the soldiers of their corps, a participation of the blessings of peace, liberty, property, and mild government:

Resolved, That this Congress will give to all such of the said foreign officers as shall leave the armies of his Britannic majesty in America, and chose to become citizens of these States unappropriated lands, in the following quantities and proportions, to them and their heirs in absolute dominion; to a colonel, 1000 acres; to a lieutenant-colonel, 800 acres; to a major, 600 acres; to a captain, 400; to a lieutenant, 300 acres; to an ensign, 200 acres; to every non-commissioned officer, 100 acres; and to every other officer or person employed in the said foreign corps, and whose office or employment is not here specially named, in the like proportion to their rank or pay in the said corps; and moreover, that where any officers shall bring with them a number of said foreign soldiers, this Congress, besides the lands before promised to the said officers and soldiers, will give to such officers further rewards, proportioned to the number they shall bring over, and suited to the nature of their wants: provided that such foreign officers or soldiers shall come over from the armies of his Britannic majesty before these offers shall be recalled.

IN CONGRESS, September 16, 1776.

Resolved, That, in addition to a money bounty of twenty dollars to each non-commissioned officer and private soldier, Congress make provision for granting lands, in the following proportions, to the officers and soldiers who shall engage in the service, and continue therein to the close of the war, or until discharged by Congress, and to the representatives of such officers and soldiers as shall be slain by the enemy. Such lands to be provided by the United States, and whatever expense shall be necessary to procure such land; the said expense shall be paid and borne by the States, in the same proportion as the other expenses of the war, viz.: to a colonel, 500 acres; to a lieutenant-colonel, 450 acres; to a major, 400 acres; to a captain, 300 acres; to a lieutenant, 200 acres; to an ensign, 150 acres; each non-commissioned officer and soldier, 100 acres.

IN CONGRESS, May 15, 1778.

Resolved, unanimously, That all military officers, commissioned by Congress, who now are, or hereafter may be, in the service of these United States, and shall continue therein during the war, and not hold any office of profit under these States, or any of them, shall, after the conclusion of the war, be entitled to receive annually, for the term of seven years, if they live so long, one-half of the present pay of such officers: *Provided*, That no general officer of the cavalry, artillery, or infantry, shall be entitled to receive more than the one-half part of the pay of a colorel of such corps respectively: And provided, That this resolution shall not extend to any officer in the service of the United States, unless he shall have taken an oath of allegiance to, and shall actually reside within, some one of the United States.

Resolved, unanimously. That every non-commissioned military officer and solidier who hath enlisted, or shall enlist, into the service of these States for and during the war, and shall continue therein to the end thereof, shall be entitled to receive the further reward of eighty dollars at the expiration of the war.

IN CONGRESS, November 24, 1778.

Whereas, from the alteration of the establishment, and other causes, many valuable officers have been, and may be, omitted in the new arrangement as being supernumerary, who, from their conduct and services, are entitled to the honorable notice of Congress, and to a suitable provision, until they can return to civil life with advantage: *Resolved, therefore,* That Congress gratefully acknowledge the faithful services of such officers, and that all supernumerary officers be entitled to one year's pay of their commissions respectively, to be computed from the time such officers had leave of absence from the Commander-in-Chief on this account; and Congress do earnestly recommend to the several States to which such officers belong, to make such further provision for them as their respective circumstances and merit may entitle them to.

IN CONGRESS, May 22, 1779.

Resolved, That all Continental officers who are or may be exchanged, and not continued in the service, be, after such exchange, considered as supernumerary officers, and entitled to the pay provided by the resolution of Congress of the 24th of November last.

IN CONGRESS, August 24, 1780.

Resolved, That the resolution of May 15, 1778, granting seven years' half-pay to the officers of the army who should continue in the service to the end of the war, be extended to the widows of those officers who have died, or shall hereafter die, in the service; to commence from the time of such officer's death, and continue for the term of seven years; or if there be no widow, or, in case of her death or intermarriage, the said half-pay be given to the orphan children of the officer dying as aforesaid, if he shall have left any: and that it be recommended to the legislatures of the respective States, to which such officers belong, to make provision for paying the same on account of the United States; that the restricting clause in the resolution of May 15, 1778, granting half-pay to the officers for seven years, expressed in these words, "and not hold any office of profit under these States, or any of them," be, and the same is hereby, repealed.

IN CONGRESS, October 8, 1780.

Whereas, by the foregoing arrangement (*reform of the army*, to take effect January 1, 1781), many deserving officers must become supernumerary, and it is proper that regard be had to them: *Resolved*, That from the time the reform of the army takes place, they be entitled to half-pay for seven years in specie, or other current money equivalent, and also grants of lands at the close of the war, agreeably to the resolution of September 16, 1776.

IN CONGRESS, October 21, 1780.

Resolved, That the Commander-in-Chief, and commanding officer in the Southern department, direct the officers of each State to meet and agree upon the officers for the regiments to be raised by their respective States, from those who incline to continue in the service, and where it cannot be done by agreement, to be determined by seniority, and make return of those who are to remain; which is to be transmitted to Congress, together with the names of the officers reduced, who are to be allowed half-pay for life.

Resolved, That the officers who shall continue in the service to the end of the war shall also be entitled to half-pay during life, to commence from the time of their reduction.

IN CONGRESS, November 28, 1780.

Resolved, That the said half-pay for life be extended to all Major-generals and Brigadier-generals who shall continue in service to the end of the war.

Resolved, That the resolution of October 21 was so meant and intended.

IN CONGRESS, January 17, 1781.

Resolved, That all officers in the hospital department and medical staff, hereinafter mentioned, who shall continue in service to the end of the war, or be reduced before that time, as supernumeraries, shall be entitled to, and receive, during life, in lieu of half-pay, the following allowance, viz.: The director of the hospital equal to the half-pay of a Lieutenant-colonel.

Chief physicians and surgeons of the army and hospitals, and hospital physicians and surgeons, purveyor, apothecary, and regimental surgeons, each equal to the half-pay of a Captain.

IN CONGRESS, May 8, 1781.

Resolved, That every chaplain, deemed and certified to the Board of War to be supernumerary, be no longer continued in service, and be entitled to have their depreciation made good, and to the half-pay of Captains for life.

IN CONGRESS, May 26, 1781.

Resolved, That the officers of the Flying-Camp, lately returned from captivity, be allowed depreciation by their respective States in the same manner as officers in the line of such States: That is settling the accounts of officers returned from captivity, and who are entiled to the benefit of the resolutions of November 24, 1780, and May 22, 1779, the auditors allow the year's pay mentioned in said resolutions in bills of the new emission.

IN CONGRESS, December 31, 1781.

Resolved, That all officers of the line of the army below the rank of Brigadier-general, who do not belong to the line of any particular State, or separate corps of the army, and are entitled by acts of Congress to pay and subsistence, shall have the same, with the depreciation of their pay made good to January 1, 1782.

Resolved, That the Secretary of War be, and he is hereby directed to make returns to Congress, on or before the 20th day of January, 1782, of the names and rank of all the officers necessary to be retained in service, that are included in the preceding resolution.

Resolved, That all officers included in the foregoing description, and whose names shall not be inserted in the returns directed to be made by the preceding resolution, shall be considered as retiring from service January 1, 1782; provided always, that nothing contained in these resolutions shall be construed so as to prevent or hinder any officer that shall retire as aforesaid from enjoying all the emoluments that he may, upon retiring be entitled to by any former acts of Congress.

IN CONGRESS, March 22, 1783.

WHEREAS, The officers of the several lines under the immediate command of his Excellency, General Washington, did, by their late memorial, transmitted by their committee, represent to Congress that the half-pay granted by sundry resolutions was regarded in an unfavorable light by the citizens of some of these States, who would prefer a compensation for a limited term of years, or by a sum in gross, to an establishment for life; and did, on that account solicit a commutation of their half-pay for an equivalent, in one of the two modes above mentioned, in order to remove all subject of dissatisfaction from the minds of their fellow-citizens: and whereas, Congress are desirous, as well of gratifying the reasonable expectations of the officers of the army, as of removing all objections which may exist in any part of the United States to the principle of the half-pay establishment, for which the faith of the United States hath been pledged; persuaded that these objections can only arise from the nature of the compensation, not from any indisposition to compensate those whose services, sacrifices, and sufferings have so just a title to the approbation and rewards of their country. Therefore,

Resolved, That such officers as are now in service, and shall continue therein to the end of the war, shall be entitled to receive the amount of five years' full pay in money, or securities on interest at six per cent. per annum, as Congress shall find most convenient, instead of the half-pay promised for life by the resolution of October 21, 1780; the said securities to be such as shall be given to other creditors of the United States: *Provided*, It be at the option of the lines of the respective States, and not of officers individually in those lines, to accept or refuse the same: *And provided, also*, That their election shall be signified to Congress through the Commander-in-Chief, from lines under his immediate command, within two months, and through the commanding officer of the Southern army from those under his command, within six months from the date of this resolution: That the same commutation shall extend to the corps not belonging to the lines of any particular States, and who are entitled to half-pay for life as aforesaid; the acceptance or refusal to be determined by corps, and to be signified in the same manner, and within the same time, as above mentioned: That all officers belonging to the hospital department, who are entitled to half-pay by the resolution of January 17, 1781, may collectively agree to accept or refuse the aforesaid commutation, signifying the same, through the Commander-in Chief, within six months from this time: That such officers as have retired at different periods, entitled to half-pay for life, may collectively, in each State of which they are inhabitants, accept or refuse the same; their acceptance or refusal to be signified by agents authorized for that purpose, within six month from this period: That with respect to such retiring officers, the commutation, if accepted by them, shall be in lieu of whatever may be now due to them since the time of their retiring from service, as well as of what might hereafter become due; and that, so soon as their acceptance shall be signified, the Superintendent of Finance be, and he is hereby directed to take measures for the settlement of their accounts accordingly, and to issue to them certificates bearing interest at six per cent.: That all officers entitled to half-pay for life, not included in the preceding resolution, may also collectively agree to accept or refuse the aforesaid commutation, signifying the same within six months from this time.

IN CONGRESS, May 16, 1783.

Resolved, That the commutation in lieu of half-pay, as well as to chaplans as to the officers of the hospital departments and medical staff, shall be calculated by what they are respectively entitled to agreeably to the resolutions of the 17th Jan. and 8th May, 1781.

IN CONGRESS, January 26, 1784.

Resolved, That half-pay cannot be allowed to any officer, or to any class or denomination of officers, to whom it has not heretofore been expressly promised.

IN CONGRESS, February 11, 1784.

Resolved, That Congress agree to the following Report:

"That, by a resolve of November 24, 1778, it was provided that all deranged officers should be entitled to one year's pay; and it was further provided, that officers who had been prisoners with the enemy, and then were, or thereafter might be exchanged, should, if appointed by authority of the State, be entitled to return into the service in the same rank they would have had if they had not been captured, under certain restrictions, and that they should receive half-pay till the time of their entering again into the service. Under this act, certain officers claim half-pay to the end of the war, and the commutation for half-pay from that period during life; on which the committee observe, that the half-pay first mentioned was promised as a temporary support to such officers as should be reappointed by their respective States, and to none besides; and that all other Continental officers who have been prisoners with the enemy and deranged, are entitled to one year's pay, and nothing besides. That such was the intention of Congress is explained by the subsequent acts of May 22, 1779, and May 26, 1781. There is no act under which those officers can claim the commutation for half-pay. It is provided by a resolve of June 28, 1782, that 'there shall be such additional pay and emoluments to the pay of Captains and subalterns serving as Aides de-Camp to Major and Brigadier Generals, and to Brigade-majors, as shall make their pay and emoluments equal to the pay and emoluemnts of a Major in the line of the army.' Under these resolutions certain Aides and Brigade-majors, who are Captains or subalterns in the line, claim commutation equal to that of a Major in the line. This claim appears for sundry reasons to be ill-founded. The offices which these gentlemen held out of the line were temporary, and the additional pay and emoluments were certainly promised to them while they continued to serve in those offices, and no longer. If they are supposed to found their claim to the commutation of a Major, under the head of additional emoluments, their claim must be ill-founded, for it is clear, from the terms of the resolution, that pay and emoluments do not signify the same thing, but the commutation is the substitute for pay alone, or half-pay, and not for rations, nor any other emolument. On the whole, the Committee are of opinion that the Paymaster-general, in settling the accounts of the army, in all claims which may be brought for half-pay or commutation, should be determined by the Act of the 26th January, 1784."

IN CONGRESS, June 3, 1784.

Resolved, That an interest of six per cent. per annum be allowed to all creditors of the United States for supplies furnished or services done, from the time the payment becomes due.

IN CONGRESS, March 8, 1785.

Resolved, That the officers who retired under the resolve of December 31, 1781, are equally entitled to the half-pay or commutation with those officers who retired under the resolves of the 3d and 21st October, 1780.

IN CONGRESS, August 11, 1790.

And be it further enacted, That Caleb Brewster, lately a lieutenant, who was wounded and disabled in the service of the United States, be allowed three hundred and forty-eight dollars and fifty-seven cents, the amount of his necessary expenses for sustenance and medical assistance, while dangerously ill of his wounds, including the interest to the 1st of July, 1790. And that the said Brewster be allowed a pension, equal to his half-pay as Lieutenant, from the 3d of November, 1783, he first having returned his commutation of half-pay.

OFFICERS ENTITLED TO HALF-PAY. 411

A LIST OF OFFICERS OF THE CONTINENTAL ARMY OF THE REVOLUTION, WHO WERE EITHER KILLED IN SERVICE, BECAME SUPERNUMERARY, OR SERVED TO THE END OF THE WAR, AND ACQUIRED THE RIGHT TO HALF-PAY, COMMUTATION, AND BOUNTY LAND UNDER THE PRECEDING ACTS OF CONGRESS.

Allen, Ethan, Colonel, N. H.
Angell, Israel, do. R. I.
Adams, Peter, Lieut. Col., Md.
Anderson, Richard C., Lt. Col., Va.
Armstrong, James, Colonel, N. C.
Armstrong, John, Lieut. Col., N. C.
Allen, Ichabod, Col., Mass. Killed by the Indians at Cherry Valley, Nov. 11, 1778.
Adams, Winburn, Lieut. Col., N. H. Died Sept. 19, 1777.
Allen, David, Surgeon's Mate, N.H.
Addrick, George, Captain, do.
Adams, John, Lieutenant, do.
Adams, Samuel, do. do.
Ashley, Moses, Major, Mass.
Allen, Noah, do. do.
Allen, Nathaniel C., Captain, do.;
Abbott, Stephen. do. do.
Ames, Jotham, Lieutenant, do.
Andrews, William, do. do.
Austin, John. do. do.
Adams, Henry, Surgeon, do.
Adams, Samuel, do. do.
Adams, Levi, Ensign, do.
Abbott, Josiah, do. do.
Allen, Jacob, Captain, Mass. Died Sept. 19, 1777.
Andrews, Joseph, Lieutenant, Mass. Died Sept. 11, 1780.
Arnold, Noyes, Lieutenant, Mass. Died Aug. 22, 1778.
Andrews, Joseph, Lieutenant, Mass. Died Dec. 1, 1777.
Arnold, Thomas, Captain, R. I.
Allen, William, do. do.
Allen, Timothy, do. Conn.
Adams, David, Surgeon, do.

Anderson, Thomas, Lieut., Conn.
Avery, Simeon, do. do.
Allen, Robert, do. do.
Alden, Judah, Captain, Conn. Died Aug. 22, 1777.
Aorson, Aaron, Captain, N. Y.
Adams, Jonas, Lieutenant, do.
Anspack, Peter, do. do.
Appleton, Abraham, do. N. J.
Anderson, James, do. do.
Anderson, William, do. do.
Anderson, Joseph J., Captain, N. J.
Anderson, Ephraim, Adjutant, do.
Adams, William, Surgeon, Penn.
Allison, Richard, Mate, do.
Armstrong, John, Major, do.
Alexander, William, do. do.
Armstrong, James, do. do.
Armstrong, John, Lieut. do.
Ashton, Joseph, do. do.
Allison, Robert, do. do.
Anderson, Thomas, do. Delaware.
Adams, William, do. Maryland.
Anderson, Richard, Captain, do.
Anderson, John, Captain, Virginia.
Allen, David, Lieutenant, do.
Archer Peter F., do. do.
Archer, Richard, do. do.
Ashby, Benjamin, do. do.
Armstrong, Wm., Captain, N. Car.
Armstrong, Thomas, do. do.
Ashe, Samuel, do. do.
Alexander, Wm., Lieut., do.
Alexander, Nath'l, Surg. Mate, S.C.
Axon, Samuel J., do. do.
Allison, Henry, Lieut., Georgia.
Ashe, John B., Lieutenant-colonel North Carolina.

OFFICERS ENTITLED TO HALF-PAY.

Adams, Nathan, Captain, Delaware. Died March 27, 1776.
Anderson, ——, Major, Maryland. Killed at Guilford Court-House, March 15, 1781.
Armstrong, Mark, Capt., Maryland. Killed at the siege of "Ninety-Six," June 18, 1781.
Arundell Dohickey, Captain, Virginia. Killed July 8, 1776.
Avebing, Phillippe, Lieut. Dragoons. Pennsylvania.
Baron De Kalb, Maj. Gen. Killed at the battle of Camden, Aug. 16, 1780.
Bunner, Rudolph, Col., Penn. Killed at Monmouth, June 28, 1778.
Byles, Thomas L., Major, Pennsylvania. Died Feb. 1, 1779.
Bush, John, Lieut., South Carolina. Killed at the siege of Savannah, Oct. 9, 1779.
Barron, John, Lieut., Mass. Killed at Concord, April 19, 1775.
Beatty, Wm., Captain, Md. Killed at Hobkirk's Hill, April 24, 1781.
Beall, Zachariah, Captain, N. Hampshire. Died Oct. 27, 1777.
Bell, Frederick M., Captain, New Hampshire. Died Oct. 8, 1777.
Bryant, David, Captain, Massachusetts. Died Sept. 11, 1777.
Bond, William, Colonel, Massachusetts. Died Aug. 31, 1776.
Bragdon, Josiah, Lieut., Massachusetts. Died April 30, 1778.
Brown, Stephen, Capt., Connecticut. Died Nov. 16, 1777.
Barber, David, Lieut., Connecticut. Died Dec. 25, 1777.
Baker, Francis, Colonel, New Jersey. Died Jan. 6, 1783.
Barron, William, Lieut., Virginia. Died March 26, 1778.
Blair, John, Lieut., Va. Died Aug. 18, 1780.

Bunting, William B., Lieut., Virginia. Died April 1, 1777.
Bell, Wm. M., Capt., N. Hampshire.
Bayley, Mountjoy, Capt., Md.
Brownson, Gideon, Major, N. H.
Blodget, Caleb, Lieutenant, do.
Blanchard, James, do. do.
Beach, Samuel, do. do.
Blake, Thomas, do. do.
Butterfield, Jonas, do. do.
Blackwell, Thomas, Captain, Va.
Brooke, Edmund, Lieut., do.
Boynton, Joseph, do. N. H.
Bacon, Oliver, do. do.
Barrett, Oliver, do. do.
Barnett, James, do. Virginia.
Bigelow, Timothy, Colonel, Mass.
Baldwin, Jeduthan, do. do.
Bailey, John, do. do.
Bradford, Gamaliel, do. do.
Bassett, Berachiah, do. do.
Brooks, John, do. do.
Baird, Absalom, Surgeon, Penn.
Baylis Hodijah, Major, Mass.
Ballard William H., do. do.
Burnham, John, do. do.
Bradford, Wm., Major, R. Island.
Barton, William, Colonel, do.
Buxton, James, Captain, Mass.
Bannister, Seth, do. do.
Burbeck, Henry, do. do.
Bowman, Phinehas, do. do.
Blanchard, John, do. do.
Benson, Joshua, do. do.
Bailey, Adams, do. do.
Bailey, Luther, do. do.
Bradford, Robert, do. do.
Burley, William, do. do.
Bates, Joseph, do. do.
Bogart, Nicholas N., Sur. Mate, R.I.
Butler, Zebulon, Colonel, Conn.
Bradley, Philip B., do. do.
Ballard, Asa, Lieutenant, Mass.
Bolcom, Joseph, do. do.
Brown, Ebenezer, do. do.
Bancroft, James, do. do.

OFFICERS ENTITLED TO HALF-PAY. 413

Brown, Ezekiel, Surgeon, Mass.
Bartlett, Daniel, do. do.
Ballentine, Eben, Sur. Mate, do.
Brigham, Origen, do. do.
Bills, Jabez, Lieutenant, do.
Benjamin, Samuel, do. do.
Bailey, Thomas, do. do.
Bussey, Isaiah, do. do.
Buffington, Samuel, do. do.
Bliss, Joseph, do. do.
Bowles, Ralph H., do. do.
Barlow, Joel, Chaplain, do.
Barnet, John, do. do.
Blake, Edward, Lieutenant, do.
Bowman, Samuel, do. do.
Bradley, Levi, do. do.
Brown, Zephaniah, Captain, R. I.
Burlingame, Chandler, Lieut., do.
Bugbee, Edward, do. do.
Bushnell, David, Captain, Conn.
Betts, Stephen, do. do.
Bulkley, Edward, do. do.
Buel, John H., do. do.
Benton, Selah, do. do.
Bernard, John, do. do.
Bates, David, do. do.
Baldwin, Caleb, do. do.
Billings, Stephen, do. do.
Baldwin, Abraham, Chapl'n, do.
Brunson, Isaac, Surg. Mate, do.
Beekman, Jerrick, Captain, N. Y.
Bowman, Nathaniel, Major, N. J.
Bull, Aaron, Lieutenant, Conn.
Bennet, James, do. do.
Beach, David, do. do.
Bradley, Daniel, do. do.
Benjamin, Aaron, do. do.
Beers, Nathan, do. do.
Belding, Simeon, do. do.
Beaumont, Wm., do. do.
Barnum, Eli, do. do.
Ball, John, do. do.
Brooks, David, Asst. Clothier-general, New York.
Burrall, Jona., Dep. P. M., Gen., New York.

Burr, Aaron, Lieut. Colonel, N. Y.
Bruin, Jacobus, do. do.
Bauman, Sebastian, Major, do.
Bless, Theodore T., Captain, do.
Bevier, Philip D., do. do.
Blecker, Leonard, do. do.
Bull, William, do. do.
Browne, Joseph, Surgeon, Penn.
Bard, John, Captain, Georgia.
Barr, John, Ensign, New York.
Bradford, James, Lieut., do.
Burnett, Robert, do. do.
Brewster, Caleb, do. do.
Brewster, James, do. do.
Bagley, Josiah, do. do.
Bowen, Prentice, do. do.
Barrett, James, do. do.
Brindley, Francis, do. do.
Belknap, William, do. do.
Barber, William, Major, N. Jersey.
Burrows, John, do. do.
Bunnell, James, Captain, do.
Barton, William, do. do.
Ballard, Jeremiah, do. do.
Burnett, Wm., Surgeon, do.
Burnel, Wm., do. do.
Blair, John, Lieutenant, do.
Burrows, Eden, do. do.
Bonham, Absalom, Lieut., do.
Buck, Joseph, do. do.
Bishop, John, Ensign, do.
Brooks, Almarin, do. do.
Brodhead, Daniel, Colonel, Penn.
Butler, Richard, do. do.
Butler, William, Lieut. Col., do.
Bayard, Stephen, do. do.
Beatty, Reading, Surgeon, do.
Binney, Barnabas, do. do.
Burk, Edmund, Captain, do.
Bartholomew, Benj., do. do.
Butler, Thomas, do. do.
Bunner, Jacob, do. do.
Bush, John, do. do.
Bowen, Thomas B., do. do.
Boude, Thomas, do. do.
Bicker, Henry, do. do.

OFFICERS ENTITLED TO HALF PAY.

Brady, Samuel, Captain, Penn.
Bankson, John, do. do.
Bowen, Jacob, do. do.
Bush, George, do. do.
Bryce, John, do. do.
Boyer, Peter, do. do.
Bond, Thomas, jr., Surgeon, do.
Bennet, Caleb P., Lieut., Delaware.
Bryson, Samuel, do. Penn.
Butler, Edward, do. do.
Beatty, Eukuries, do. do.
Ball, Blackall W., do. do.
Butler, Percival, do. do.
Blauer, George, do. do.
Bevins, Wilder, do. do.
Barclay, John, do. do.
Boyd, John, do. do.
Benstead, Alex., do. do.
Beall, William L., Major, Maryland
Brown, William, do. do.
Brooks, Benjamin, do. do.
Belt, John Sprigg, Captain, do.
Brice, Jacob, do. do.
Bruff, James, do. do.
Benson, Perry, do. do.
Beall, Lloyd, do. do.
Boyer, Michael, do. do.
Baltzell, Charles, do. do.
Bruce, William, do. do.
Bonham, Malachi, Lieut. do.
Burgess, Bazel, do. do.
Britton, Joseph, do. do.
Burgess, Joshua, do. do.
Beal, Samuel, do. do.
Boyd, Thomas. do. do.
Baques, James, do. do.
Beatty, Thomas, do. do.
Baldwin, Henry, do. do.
Baker, Henry, do. do.
Brevitt, John, do. do.
Baylor, George, Colonel, Virginia.
Buford, Abraham, do. do.
Ball, Burgess, Lieut. Col., do.
Bruin, Peter B., Major, do.
Belfield, John, do. do.
Bedinger, Henry, Captain, do.

Biggs, Benjamin, Capt. Virginia.
Breckenridge, Alex., do. do.
Butler, Lawrence, do. do.
Beale, Robert, do. do.
Boyer, Michael, do. do.
Breckenridge, Robt. do. do.
Blackwell, Joseph, do. do.
Bell, Thomas, do. do.
Barrett, William, do. Virginia.
Burwell, Nathaniel, do. do.
Bowne, Thomas, do. do.
Barbee, Thomas, do. do.
Booker, Samuel, do. do.
Blackwell, John, do. do.
Bentley, William, do. do.
Buckner, Thomas, do. do.
Bowyer, Thomas, do. do.
Baldwin, Cornelius, Surgeon, do.
Belmain, Alex., Chaplain, do.
Bradford, Samuel K., Lieut., do.
Baskerville, Samuel, do. do.
Ball, Daniel, do. do.
Bohannon, Ambrose, Lieut. and Paymaster, Virginia.
Beck, John, Lieutenant, Virginia.
Bowyer, Henry, do. do.
Bell, Henry, do. do.
Bradford, Charles, do. do.
Brown, Jacob R., do. do.
Bowen, John, do, do.
Brooke, Francis T., do. do.
Brooke, John, do. do.
Booker, Lewis, do. do.
Bedinger, Daniel, do. do.
Baylis, Henry, Ensign, do.
Blyth, Joseph, Surgeon, N. C.
Boyd, Adam, Chaplain, do.
Blount, Reading, Major, do.
Brevard, Alex., Captain, do.
Ballard, Kedar, do. do.
Bacott, Peter, do. do.
Budd, Samuel, do. do.
Bradley, Gee, do. do.
Baily, Benjamin, do. do.
Bell, Robert, Lieutenant, do.
Brevard, Joseph, do. do.

OFFICERS ENTITLED TO HALF-PAY.   415

Bush, William, Lieut., N. Carolina.
Brownson, Nath., Purveyor, S. Car.
Brownfield, Robt. Sur. Mate, do.
Beekman, Bernard, Colonel, do.
Baker, Richard, Captain,   do.
Buchanan, John,   do.   do.
Baker, Jesse,   do.   do.
Beekman, Sam. Lieutenant, do.
Bradwell, Nathaniel, do.   do.
Budd, John S.,   do.   do.
Brown, Charles,   do.   do.
Booker, Gideon, Captain, Georgia.
Brossard, Celeron, do.   do.

Cuthbert, Alex., Captain, Georgia.
Cook, Parris,   do.   do.
Collins, Corn., Lieutenant,   do.
Cowan, Edward, do.   do.
Carne, John, Apothecary,   S. Car.
Cooper, Leonard, Captain,   do.
Clarke, Thomas, Colonel,   N. Car.
Carter, Benjamin, Captain,   do.
Child, Francis,   do.   do.
Coleman, Benjamin, do.   do.
Craddock, John,   do.   do.
Callender, Thomas, do.   do.
Clark, Thomas, Lieutenant,   do.
Croucher, Anthony, do.   do.
Clendennin, John,   do.   do.
Campbell, John,   do.   do.
Campen, James,   do.   do.
Caldwell, James, Chaplain, New Jersey. Shot by a sentinel at Elizabethtown Point, Nov. 24, 1781.
Colburn, Andrew, Lieut. Col., New Hampshire. Killed at the battle of Stillwater, Sept. 19, 1777.
Cranston, Abner, Major, Massachusetts. Killed May 29, 1777.
Carpenter, Benajah, Captain, Rhode Island. Killed at the battle of Long Island, Aug. 27, 1776.
Coon, James, Lieut., Connecticut. Killed Sept. 6, 1780.
Campbell, Richard, Col., Va. Killed at Eutaw Springs, Sept. 8, 1781.

Chronicle, William, Major. Killed at the battle of King's Mountain, Oct. 7, 1780.
Calderwood, James, Capt., Virginia. Killed Sept. 11, 1777.
Carson, John, Lieutenant, Maryland. Killed Sept. 12, 1781.
Casey, Benjamin, Captain, Virginia. Killed Sept. 1, 1777.
Cooper, Apollis, Lieutenant, Virginia. Killed Sept. 11, 1777.
Conway, James, Lieut., Va. Killed Dec. 28, 1776.
Caruthers, John, Lieut., Pa. Killed Oct. 4, 1777.
Carmichael, Alexander, Lieut., Pa. Killed Sept. 11, 1777.
Campbell, John, Capt., Va. Killed at Moore's Creek, Feb. 26, 1776.
Cabell, Samuel J., Lt. Col.,Virginia
Carrington, Edward, do.   do.
Clark, Jonathan,   do.   do.
Croghan, William, Major,   do.
Call, Richard,   do.   do.
Cowherd, Francis, Captain, do.
Carter, John C.,   do.   do.
Carrington, Maze,   do.   do.
Cocke, Colin,   do.   do.
Curry, James,   do.   do.
Coleman, Whitehead, do.   do.
Carnes, Patrick, Captain, Virginia.
Craike, James, Physician,   do.
Clements, Mace, Surgeon,   do.
Chrystie, Thomas, do.   do.
Claiborne, Richard, Lieut.,   do.
Carrington, George, do.   do.
Clay, Matthew,   do.   do.
Crute, John,   do.   do.
Cannon, Luke,   do.   do.
Coleman, Jacob,   do.   do.
Clark, Edmund,   do.   do.
Coleman, Samuel,   do.   do.
Crawford, John,   do.   do.
Coverly, Thomas,   do.   do.
Clayton, Philip,   do.   do.
Crittenden, John,   do.   do.

OFFICERS ENTITLED TO HALF-PAY.

Campbell, Archibald, Lieut., Va.
Conway, Joseph, do. do.
Craddock, Robert, do. do.
Chiderson, Richard, Captain, Md.
Carlisle, John, do. do.
Clagett, Horatio, do. do.
Coates, John, do. do.
Campbell, William, do. do.
Cheever, John, Lieutenant, do.
Clements, Henry, do. do.
Cross, Joseph, do. do.
Chapman, Henry H., do. do.
Compton, Edmund, do. do.
Carey, John D., do. do.
Crawford, Jacob, do. do.
Cox. Daniel P., Captain, Delaware.
Cutting, John B., Apothecary, do.
Campbell, James, Lieutenant, do.
Conway, John, Lieut. Col., N. J.
Cumming, John N., do. do.
Cape, John, Lieutenant, do.
Cox, Richard, Major, do.
Campfield, Jabez, Surgeon, do.
Corn, Samuel, Lieutenant, do.
Chambers, James, Colonel. Penn.
Craig, Thomas, do. do.
Craig, Isaac, Major, do.
Church, Thomas, do. do.
Craig, John, Captain, do.
Craig, Samuel, do. do.
Carnahan, James, do. do.
Christie, James, do. do.
Campbell, Thomas, do. do.
Claypoole, Abra'm G., do. do.
Coltman, Robert, do. do.
Cobea, John, do. do.
Carberry, Henry, do. do.
Christie, John, do. do.
Clark, John, do. do.
Crosley, Jesse, Lieutenant, do.
Cramer, Jacob, do. do.
Collier, Joseph, do. do.
Crawford, Edward, do. do.
Campbell, James, do. do.
Crawford, John, do. do.
Clockner, Christian, do. do.

Coventry, John, Hos. Mate, Penn.
Cowel, John, do. do.
Cochran, John, Director Gen., N. Y.
Clinton, James, Brig. Gen., do.
Cortlandt, Philip, Colonel, do.
Cochran, Robert, Lieut. Col., do.
Clarkson, Matthew, Major, do.
Codwise, Christopher, Lieut., do.
Clinton, Alexander, do. do.
Colbreath, Wm., Lt. & Qr. Mr. do.
Crimshier, John D., Lt. & Pay'r, do.
Crosby, Ebenezer, Surgeon of Guards, New York.
Cunningham, Henry, Lieut., N. Y.
Conine, Philip, do. do.
Connolly, Michael, do. de.
Cady, Palmer, do. do.
Cragie, Andrew, Apothecary, do.
Cook, Samuel, Surgeon, do.
Campbell, George, do. do.
Carpenter, Nehemiah, Lieut., do.
Chapman, Albert, Major, Conn.
Clift, Wills, do. do.
Chamberlain, Ephraim, Capt., do.
Comstock, Samuel, do. do.
Clift, Samuel, do. do.
Chapman, Elijah, do. do.
Chipman, John, do. do.
Converse, Thomas, do. do.
Coleman, Noah, Surgeon, do.
Crosby, Ebenezer, do. do.
Campbell, John, Lieutenant, do.
Cunningham, Henry, do. do.
Colfax, William, do. do.
Chapman, Joseph, do. do.
Curtis, Giles, do. do.
Colton, George, Ensign. do.
Clark, Joseph, do. do.
Cole, Abner, do. do.
Cleveland, John, do. do.
Crane, John, Colonel, Mass.
Cobb, David, Lieut. Col., do.
Carr, Samuel, Major. do.
Cogswell, Thomas, do. do.
Cogswell, Amos, Captain, do.
Cook, David, do. do.

OFFICERS ENTITLED TO HALF-PAY. 417

Coburn, Asa, Captain, Mass.
Clark, Silas, do. do.
Cooper, Ezekiel, do. do.
Clapp, Caleb, do. do.
Clayes, Peter, do. do.
Chambers, Matthew, do. do.
Cushing, Nathaniel, do. do.
Crane, John, Surgeon, do.
Cheever, Abijah, do. do.
Coggswell, Wm. Surg'n's Mate, do.
Carleton, Moses, Lieutenant. do.
Carleton, Osgood, do. do.
Castaing, Peter, do. do.
Cogswell, Samuel, do. do.
Condy, Thomas, H., do. do.
Crane, John, do. do.
Cole, Thomas, do. do.
Clapp, Joshua, do. do.
Carey, Jonathan, do. do.
Callender, John, do. do.
Cooper, Samuel, do. do.
Crawley, Florence, do. do.
Cushing, Thomas, do. do.
Crook, Joseph, do. do.
Chapin, Samuel, do. do.
Cilley, Joseph, Colonel, New Hamp.
Carr, James, Major, do.
Cherry, Samuel, Captain, do.
Cass, Jonathan, do. do.
Cilley, Jonathan, Lieut. do.
Clapp, Daniel, do. do.
Church, Reuben, Ensign, do.

Davidson, John, Major, Maryland.
Dorsey, Richard, Captain, do.
Dyson, Thomas A., Lieut., do.
Davis, Resin, Captain, do.
Denny, Robert, Lieutenant, do.
Denwood, Levin, Surgeon, do.
Dearborn, Henry, Colonel, N. H.
Dunston, Moses, Captain, do.
Dennitt, John, do. do.
Dustin, Moody, do. do.
Dunning, Michael, do. do.
Duponceau, Peter S., Captain.
  Steuben's Staff.
Davidson, William, General, N.
  Car. Killed at Cowan's Ford,
  February 1, 1781.
Dimon, David, Lieut. Colonel,
  Conn. Killed Sept. 17, 1777.
Douglas, William, Colonel, Conn.
  Killed May 27, 1777.

Davis, Isaac, Captain, Mass. Killed
  April 19, 1775.
Dickinson, Edmund B., Major, Va.
  Killed at the battle of Mon-
  mouth, June 28, 1778.
Dye, Jonathan, Lieutenant, Vir-
  ginia. Killed Sept. 11, 1777.
Drake, Thomas, Lieutenant, Vir-
  ginia. Killed Jan. 21, 1777.
Dunn, Peter, Captain, Va. Killed
  Sept. 26, 1777.
Donovan, Richard, Adjutant, Md.
  Killed at Camden, Aug. 16, 1780.
Dobson, Henry, Capt., Maryland.
  Killed Sept., 8, 1781.
Duvall, Edward, Lieut., Md. Killed
  at Camden. Aug. 16, 1780.
De Hart, Jacob, Aid-de-Camp,
  Penn. Killed July 21, 1780.
Davis, Joseph, Captain, Penn.
  Killed April 23, 1779.
Durkee, John, Colonel, Conn. Died
  at "Bean Hill," March 1, 1782.
Davenport, Hezekiah, Lieut., Conn.
  Killed April 27, 1777.
Dunham, Silas, Lieutenant, Conn.
  Killed Dec. 7, 1777.
Dill, James, Lieut., Penn. Killed
  Sept. 11, 1777.
Darby, Samuel, Major, Mass.
Drew, Seth, do. do.
Dix, Nathan, Captain, Mass.
Daniels, Japhet, do. do.
Day, Luke, do. do.
Day, Elijah, Lieutenant, do.
Dean, Walter, do. do.
Davis, John, do. do.
Danforth, Joshua, do. do.
Dodge, Levi, do. do.
Dana, Benj., do. do.
Duffield, John, Surgeon, do.
Davis, James, Lieutenant, do.
Davis, Ebenezer, do. do.
Dexter, John S., Major, R. Island.
Dexter, Daniel S., Captain, do.
Durkee, John, do. Conn.
Dagget, Henry, do. do.
Douglass, Richard, do. do.
Durrance, David, do. do.
Dole, James, Lieutenant, do.
De Forrest, Samuel, do. do.
Denslow, Martin, do. do.
Dimmick, Benj., do. do.

OFFICERS ENTITLED TO HALF-PAY.

Deming, Pownal, Lieut., Conn.
Draper, George, Surgeon, N. Y.
Davidson, Jas., Commissary, do.
Davis, John, Major, do.
Dunscomb, Edw'd, Captain, do.
De Witt, Sim., Geographer, do.
Doughty, John, Captain, do.
Doughty, Major, do.
Dodge, Henry, Lieutenant, do.
Dodge, Samuel, do. do.
Denniston, Daniel, do. do.
Demler, Henry, do. do.
Denniston, Geo. I., do. do.
Dubois, Henry, Captain, do.
D'Aurier, Charles, do. do.
De Rousse, Pierre Regnier, Lieut. Colonel, New York.
Dayton, Elias, Brig. Gen., N. J.
Dayton, Jonathan, Captain, do.
De Hart, Cynes, do. do.
Darby, Ephraim, Lieut., do.
Donnell, Nathaniel, Capt., Penn.
Dunn, Isaac B., do. do.
Davis, John, do. do.
Doyle, John, do. do.
Douglas, Thomas, do. do.
Duncan, James, do. do.
Davidson, James, Surgeon, do.
Darcy, John, Surg. Mate, do.
Detrick, Michael, do. do.
Doty, Samuel, Lieutenant, do.
De Marcellin, Anth., do. do.
Davis, Llewellyn, do. do.
Doxon, Sankee, do. do.
Dover, Andrew, do. do.
Dunn, Abner M., do. do.
Driskill, Joseph, do. Del.
Davis, William, Colonel, Virginia.
Dabney, Charles, Lt. Col., do.
Drake, William, do. do.
Dandridge, John, Captain, do.
Dandridge, Robert, do. do.
Dandridge, Alex., Lieut., do.
Davenport, Opie, Captain, do.
Delaplane, James, do. do.
Dix, Thomas, do. do.

Dickerson, Edmund, Captain, Va.
Dick, Alexander, Lieut., do.
Dobson, Robert, do. do.

Elbert, Samuel, Colonel, Georgia.
Egbert, Jacob V., Surg. Mate, do.
Elliott, Bernard, Captain, S. C.
Evans, George, Lieut., do.
Evans, Thomas, Capt., N. Carolina.
Eggleston, Jos., Major, Virginia.
Eaton, ——, Major, Georgia. Killed at Augusta, Ga., May 21, 1781.
Ellis, Paul, Captain, Mass. Killed at Monmouth, June 28, 1778.
Eno, Martin, Ensign, Conn. Killed Oct. 11, 1780.
Eppes, Francis, Lieut. Colonel, Va. Killed at the battle of Long Island, Aug. 27, 1776.
Eddins, Samuel, Captain, Va.
Edwards, Le Roy, do. do.
Edmunds, Thomas, do. do.
Eppes, William, Lieutenant, do.
Eskridge, William, do. do.
Eastin, Philip, do. do.
Erskine, Charles, do. do.
Evans, William, do. do.
Eustace, John, do. do.
Eccleston, John, Major, Maryland.
Edgerly, Edward, Captain, do.
Ewing, James, do. do.
Evans, Elijah, do. do.
Elbert, John L., Surgeon, Md.
Edmiston, Samuel, Lieut., do.
Edwards, Evan, Major, Penn.
Eames, Worley, Captain, do.
Everly, Michael, Lieut., do.
Erwin, James, do. do.
Elmer, Moses G., Sur. Mate, N. J.
Elmer, Ebenezer, Surgeon, do.
Edgar, David, Captain, do.
Elliott, John, Surg. Mate, N. York.
English, Samuel, Lieut., do.
Ellsworth, Peter, do. do.
Ellis, John, Chaplain, Connecticut.
Ells, Edward, Captain, do.

OFFICERS ENTITLED TO HALF-PAY. 419

Ennis, Wm., Captain, R. Island.
Eustis, William, Surgeon, Mass.
Emerson, Nehemiah, Capt., do.
Englis, Andrew, do. do.
Eaton, Benjamin, Lieut., do.
Eggleston, Azariah, do. do.
Everett, Pelatiah, do. do.
Essenden, William, do. do.
Edwards, Thomas, do. do.
Eldridge, Samuel, do. do.
Emery, Ephraim, do. do.
Evans, Israel, Chapl'n, N. H.
Ellis, Benjamin, Captain, do.

Fish, Nicholas, Major and Inspector, New York.
Fairlie, James, Lieut. and Aid-de-Camp, New York.
Flemming, George, Captain, N. Y.
Fowler, Theodocius, do. do.
Fink, Andrew, do. do.
French, Abner, do. do.
Frelick, Joseph, Lieutenant, do.
Furman, John, do. do.
Fondy, Duoy, Ensign, do.
Fondy, John, do. do.
Farwell, Isaac, Captain, N. H.
Fogg, Jeremiah, do. do.
Frye, Isaac, do. do.
Frost, George P., do. do.
Fernald, Tobias, Colonel, Mass.
Fisk, Joseph, Surgeon, do.
Finley, Samuel, Surgeon, Mass.
Finley, James E. B., do. do.
Felt, Jonathan, Captain, do.
Francis, Thomas, do. do.
Frost, Samuel, do. do.
Fox, Joseph, do. do.
Fuller, John, do. do.
Fowles, John, do. do.
Fenno, Ephr., Lt. & Qr. Mr., do.
Frye, Nathaniel, Lieutenant, do.
Freeman, Thos. D., do. do.
Freeman, Const. V., do. do.
Foster, Thomas, do. do.
French, Elijah, Ensign, do.
Frink, Samuel, do. do.
Floyd, Ebenezer, do. do.
Frye, Frederick, [do. do.
Foster, Elisha, do. do.
Fitch, Andrew, Captain, Conn.

Fanning, Charles, Lieut., Conn.
Farmer, Thomas, do. do.
Frothingham, Eben., Lieut., do.
Forman, Jonathan, Lt. Col., N. J.
Faulkner, Peter, Ensign, do.
Fishbourne, Benjamin, Aid-de-Camp and Captain, Penn.
Franks, David S., Aid-de-Camp and Major, Penn.
Fontleroy, Moore, Major, Penn.
Finney, Walter, Captain, do.
Finley, John, do. do.
Finley, Joseph L., do. do.
Freeman, Jeremiah, Captain, do.
Ferguson, William, do. do.
Fullerton, Richard, Lieut., do.
Fick, David, do. do.
Forrest, Uriah, Lt. Col., Maryland.
Furnival, Alex., Captain, do.
Finley, Ebenezer, do. do.
Fickle, Benjamin, Lieut., do.
Ford, Hezekiah, do. do.
Febiger, Christian, Colonel, Va.
Finnie, William, do. do.
Flemming, Thomas, do. do.
Flemming, Charles, Lt. Col. do.
Finley, Samuel, Major, do.
Fitzhugh, Perrigrine, Capt., Va.
Fitzgerald, John, do. do.
Field, Reuben, do. do.
Fox, Thomas, de. do.
Fitzhugh, William, Cornet, do.
Fenn, Thomas, Lieutenant, do.
Foster, John H., Ensign, do.
Fawn, William, Captain, N. C.
Fenner, Robert, do. do.
Fergus, James, Surgeon, do.
Fenner, Richard, Lieut., do.
Ford, John, do. do.
Finney, Thomas, do. do.
Flagg, Henry C., Apothecary, S. C.
Faysoux, Peter, Surgeon, do.
Farrar, Field, do. do.
Frierson, John, Lieutenant, do.
Field, James, do. do.
Ford, Tobias, Ensign, do.
Frazer, John, Lieutenant, Georgia
Fitzpatrick, Pat., do. do.
Flagg, Ebenezer, Major, R. I. Killed by the Tories under Col. Delancy, in Westchester county, N. Y., May 13, 1781.

OFFICERS ENTITLED TO HALF-PAY.

Fleming, ——, Captain. Killed at the battle of Princeton, Jan. 3, 1777.
Forbes, John, Captain, S. C. Killed at the battle of Guilford, Mar. 15, 1781.
Ford, Benjamin, Lieut. Col., Md. Killed at the battle of Hobkirk's Hill, April 25, 1781.
Francis, Ebenezer, Colonel, Mass. Killed at the battle of Hubbardtown, July 7, 1777.
Faey, Joseph, Ensign, N. Hampshire. Killed Sept. 19, 1777.
Foster, Ebenezer, Ensign, Massachusetts. Killed at Bemis's Heights, Oct. 19, 1777.
Fellows, David, Ensign, Connecticut. Killed Dec. 10, 1779.

Greene, Christopher, Lt. Col., R. I. Killed in Westchester Co., N. Y., by Col. Delancy's Tories, May 13, 1781.
Goodwin, Nathaniel, Captain, Conn. Killed May 1, 1777.
Grimes, William, Captain, Virginia. Killed Aug. 1, 1777.
Gould, David, Surgeon, Va. Died July 12, 1781.
Gardiner, Thomas, Colonel. Killed at the battle of Bunker Hill, June 17, 1775.
Goodrich, Ezekiel, Lieutenant, Mass. Killed Oct. 7, 1777.
Gray, Hugh, Lieut., Mass. Killed Aug. 3, 1777.
Glenny, William, Lieut., New York. Killed Oct. 30, 1781.
Greene, Ebenezer, Captain, N. H.
Gillman, Nicholas, do. do.
Gookin, Daniel, Lieut., do.
Greaton, John, Brig. Gen., Mass.
Glover, John, do. do.
Goodwin, Francis, L. B., Surgeon's Mate, Mass.
Graham, Isaac G., Surgeon's Mate, Mass.
Gibbs, Caleb, Major. Mass.
Goodale, Nathan, Captain, do.
Green, Francis, do. do.
Greenleaf, William, Lieut., do.
Garret, Andrew, do. do.
Green, John, Lieut., Mass.
Gardner, James, do. do.
Gordon, William, do. do.
Givens, Robert, do. do.
Gilbert, Benjamin, do. do.
George, John, do. do.
Gridley, John, do. do.
Graves, Asa, Ensign, do.
Greaton, John W., do. do.
Greaton, Rich. H., do.
Greene, Nathaniel, Maj. Gen., R. I.
Greenman, Jeremiah, Lieut., do.
Green, Morley J., do. do.
Grosvenor, Thos., Lt. Col., Conn.
Gray, Ebenezer, do. do.
Gibbs, Samuel, Lieut. do.
Griswold, Andrew, do. do.
Glenny, William, do. do.
Gorham, Nehemiah, do. do.
Grover, Phineas, do. do.
Goodell, Silas, do. do.
Gore, Obadiah, do. do.
Gregory, Matthew, do. do.
Grant, Benoni, do. do.
Goodrich, Ozias, Ensign, do.
Gansevort, Peter, Colonel, N.York.
Giles, Aquilla. Lieut. Col. and Aid-de-Camp, New York.
Graham, John, Major, N. York.
Gano, John, Chaplain, do.
Gano, David, Captain, do.
Gray, Silas, do. do.
Goodwin, Henry, do. do.
Graham, Charles, do. do.
Gregg, James, do. do.
Giles, James, Lieutenant, do.
Graham, Steph., Hospital Mate, New York.
Guion, Isaac, Capt. Lieut., N. Y.
Gildersleeve, Finch, Lieut., do.
Grier, James, Lieut. Col., Penn.
Gill, Erasmus, Captain, do.
Gray, William, do. do.
Gosmer, Peter, do. do.
Guthrey, George, Lieut,, do.
Gries, Henry, do. do.
Gamble, James, do. do.
Griffith, Levi, do. do.
Glentworth, James, do. do.
Gilchrist, James, do. do.
Gilder, Reuben, Surgeon, Del.
Gist, Mordecai, Brig. Gen., Md.
Gunby, John, Colonel, do.

OFFICERS ENTITLED TO HALF-PAY. 421

Gibson, Jonathan, Captain, Md.
Gassaway, John, do. do.
Gaither, Henry, do. do.
Gist, John, do. do.
Gale, John, do. do.
Gray, James W., do. do.
Gerry, Robert, Lieut. do.
Gassaway, Nicholas, do. do.
Gassaway, Henry, do. do.
Goldsboro', Wm., do. do.
Grometh, Jacob, do. do.
Gates, Horatio, Maj. Gen., Virginia
Gist, Nathaniel, Colonel, do.
Gibson, John, do. do.
Green, John, do. do.
Gaskins, Thomas, do. do.
Grayson, William, do. do.
Gilchrist, George, Major, do.
Gunn, James, Captain, do.
Gamble, Robert, do. do.
Gillison, John, do. do.
Gaines, Wm., Fleming, Lieut., Va.
Green, Gabriel, do. do.
Glascock, Thomas, do. do.
Gray, William, do. do.
Green, Robert, do. do.
Gray, Francis, do. do.
Gordon, Ambrose, do. do.
Garnett, Benjamin, do. do.
Gibson, John, Ensign, do.
Gibbs, Churchill, Lieut., do.
Green, James W., Surgeon, N. Car.
Gerard, Francis, Lieutenant, do.
Graves, Francis, do. do.
Grimke, John F., Lieut.Col., S. Car.
Gadsden, Thomas, Captain, do.
Goodwin, Uriah, do. do.
Goodwin, John, Lieutenant, do.
Grayson, John, do. do.

Houston, James, Surgeon, Georgia.
Habersham, John, Major, do.
Handley, George, Captain, do.
Hicks, Isaac, do. do.
Hillary, Christopher, Lieut., do.
Hayes, Arthur, do. do.
Huger, Isaac, Brigader-gen'l, S. C.
Henderson, Wm., Lieut. Col., do.
Harleston, Isaac, Major, do.
Hyrne, Edmund M., do. do.
Hart, Oliver, Surgeon's Mate, do.
Rixt, William, Captain, do.

Hart, John, Lieutenant, S. C.
Hamilton, John, do. do.
Hazzard, William, do. do.
Howe, Robert, Maj. Gen., N.Car.
Harney, Shelby, Colonel, do.
Hogg, Thomas, Major, do.
Hadley, Joshua, Captain, do.
Hall, Clement, do. do.
Holling, Solomon, Surgeon, do.
Hill, John, Lieutenant, do.
Hays, Robert, do. do.
Holmes, Hardy, do. do.
Hargrave, Wm., do. do.
Harrison, Chas., Colonel, Virginia.
Heth, William, do. do.
Hawes, Samuel, do. do.
Hopkins, Samuel Lieut. Col., do.
Holmer, Christian, Major, do.
Hopkins, David, do. do.
Hill, Thomas, do. do.
Hayes, John, do. do.
Hogg, Samuel, Captain, do.
Holt, Thomas, do. do.
Heth, Henry, do. do.
Hughes, John, do. do.
Hite, Abraham, do. do.
Hord, Thomas, do. do.
Holmes, David, Surgeon, do.
Hughes, Jasper, Cornet, do.
Heth, John, Lieutenant, do.
Holt, James, do. do.
Harris, John, do. do.
Hamilton, James, do. do.
Hunt, John, do. do.
Hackley, John, do. do.
Hite, George, do. do.
Harrison, Lawrence, do. do.
Harrison, John, do. do.
Higgins, Peter, do. do.
Hall, Josiah Carvel, Colonel, Md.
Howard, John Eager, do. do.
Hardman, Henry, Major, do.
Hanie, Ezekiel, Surgeon, do.
Hoops, Adam, Captain, do.
Hugo, Thomas B., do. do.
Hamilton, George, do. do.
Hamilton, John A., do. do.
Handy, George, do. do.
Hanson, Isaac, Lieutenant, do.
Hanson, Samuel, Lieutenant, Md.
Hanson, William, do. do.
Hill, Phillip, do. do.

OFFICERS ENTITLED TO HALF-PAY.

Harris, Arthur, Lieutenant, Md.
Hamilton, John, do. do.
Hawkins, Henry, do. do.
Hartshorn, John, do. do.
Halkerstone, Robert, do. do.
Hamilton, Edward, do. do.
Hall, David, Colonel, Delaware.
Hosman, Joseph, Lieutenant, do.
Hyatt, John V., do. do.
Hand, Edward, Brig. Gen., Penn.
Hampton, Richard, Colonel, do.
Hay, Samuel, Lieut. Colonel, do.
Harmar, Josiah, do. do.
Hubley, Adam, do. do.
Hamilton, James, Major, do.
Humphrey, Jacob, Captain, do.
Hubley, Bernard, do. do.
Heard, John, do. do.
Hopkins, David, do. do.
Henderson, William, do. do.
Harris, Robt.,Surgeon's Mate,do.
Henderson, Gustavus, do. do.
Hughes, John, Lieutenant, do.
Hicks, Jacob, do. do.
Hallet, Jonah, do. do.
Honeymoon, Wm., do. do.
Humphreys, John, do. do.
Howell, Ezekial, do. do.
Huston, William, do. do.
Henderson, Andrew, do. do.
Herbert, Stewart, do. do.
Harper, John, do. do.
Hammond, David, do. do.
Henley, Henry, do. do.
Hunter, Andrew, Chaplain, N. J.
Harris, Jacob, Surgeon, do.
Holmes, John, Captain, do.
Holmes, Jonathan, do. do.
Holmes, William, do. do.
Howell, John, do. do.
Heard, James, do. do.
Hendry, Samuel, do. do.
Halsey, Luther, Lieut., do. do.
Heyre, Jacob, Ensign, New Jersey.
Hopper, John, do. do.
Hamilton, Alex., Lieut. Col., N. Y.
Hay, Udny, do. do.
Hay, Samuel, do. do.
Hubbell, Isaac, Captain, Lieutenant and Paymaster, New York.
Hanson, Dirck, Captain, N. Y.
Hughes, James Miles, do. do.

Hallett, Jonathan, Captain, N. Y.
Hamtramck, John F., do. do.
Hicks, Benjamin, do. do.
Hardy, Joseph, do. do.
Hutton, Christopher, Lieut., do.
Harvey, Elisha, do. do.
Hardenburg, Abraham,do. do.
Hardenburg, John L., do. do.
Hyatt, Abraham, do. do.
Hunt, Thomas, do. do.
Hanmer, Francis, do. do.
Hammond, Abijah, do. do.
Henry, Nathaniel, do. do.
Herring, Benjamin, Ensign, do.
Huntington, Jedediah, Brig. Gen., Connecticut.
Huntington, Ebenezer, Lieut. Col., Conn.
Humphreys, David, Lt. Col., Conn.
Holdridge, Hezekiah, do. do.
Halte, Joseph, do. do.
Halte, Samuel, Captain, do.
Hogeland, Jeronimus, do. do.
Hill, Ebenezer, do. do.
Hall, Stephen, do. do.
Hinckley, Ichabod, do. do.
Humphrey, Elijah, do. do.
Hodge, Asel, do. do.
Hopkins, Elisha, do. do.
Heart, Jonathan, do. do.
Howley, Gideon, Lieutenant, do.
Hobart, John, do. do.
Halte, Samuel, do. do.
Holt, Silas, do. do.
Hubbard, Hezekiah, do. do.
Hosmer, Timothy, Surgeon, do.
Hosmer, Prentice, Lieut., do.
Hall, Talmadge, Paymaster, do.
Heath, Peleg, Lieutenant, Conn
Higgins, William, do. do.
Hall, Philemon, do. do.
Hubble, Solomon, do. do.
Henshaw, William, do. do.
Hyde, James, do. do.
Harman, James, Ensign, do.
Heart, John, do. do.
Holden, John, Captain, R. Island.
Hughes, Thomas, do. do.
Humphrey, William, do.
Hubbart, John, Lieut., do.
Hunter, Robert, Ensign, do.
Heath, William, Maj. Gen., Mass.

OFFICERS ENTITLED TO HALF-PAY. 423

Hull, William, Lieut. Col., Mass.
Holbrook, David, Captain, do.
Hollister, Jesse, do. do.
Hastings, John, do. do.
Holden, Aaron, do. do.
Houdin, Michael G., do. do.
Hunt, Thomas, do. do.
Henley, Samuel, do. do.
Heywood, Benjamin, do. do.
Hobby, John, do. do.
Hartshorn, Thomas, do. do.
Haskell, Einathan, do. do.
Hastings, Walter, Surgeon, do.
Hart, John, do. do.
Holland, Park, Lieutenant, do.
Hooker, Zibeon, do. do.
Hammond, Abijah,do. do.
Hunt, Ephraim, do. do.
Hiwell, John, do. do.
Holbrook, Nathan, do. do.
Hill, Jeremiah, do. do.
Haskell, Jonathan, do. do.
Holden, Levi, do. do.
Holden, John, do. do.
Hollidge, John, do. do.
Holland, Ivory, do. do.
Hildreth, William, do. do.
Hoey, Benjamin, do. do.
Hull, James, do. do.
Howe, Richard S., Ensign, do.
Horton, Elisha, do. do.
Hamlin, Africa, do. do.
Hard, John, Ensign, Mass.
Henry, Robert R., Surgeon, N. H.
Hutchins, Nathaniel, Capt., do.
Harvey, John, Lieutenant, do.
Howe, Bazaleel, do. do.
Herkimer, ——, General, N. York.
Killed at the battle of Oriskany, Aug. 6, 1777.
Huger, Benjamin, Major, S. Carolina. Killed at Charleston Neck, May 11, 1779.
Hilton, William, Lieut., North Carolina. Killed July 15, 1779.
Hawking, Moses, Captain,Virginia. Killed at Germantown, Oct. 4, 1777.
Humphries, John, Captain. Virginia. Killed at Quebec, Dec. 31, 1775.
Harrison, James, Lieutenant, Va. Killed Oct. 7, 1777.

Hardman John, Captain, Maryland. Killed Sept. 1, 1780.
Hendricks, William, Captain, Penn. Killed Dec. 31, 1775.
Huston, Alexander, Captain, Penn. Killed at Brandywine, September 11, 1777.
Hammond, Benjamin, Lieut., Penn. Killed Feb. 20, 1778.
Hopes, Robert, Captain, Penn. Killed at Brandywine, Sept. 11, 1777.
Holliday, James, Lieut., Penn Killed at Brandywine, Sept. 11, 1777.
Hume, Alexander, Lieut., South Carolina. Killed at the storming of Savannah, Oct. 9, 1779.
Holmes, David, Surgeon, Connecticut. Died March 20, 1779.
Howe, Solomon, Surgeon, Connecticut. Died June 10, 1778.
Harris, John, Lieut., Connecticut. Died Dec. 7, 1777.
Hopkins, Weigh, Captain, Sheldon's Horse. Killed July 15, 1779.
Hale, Nathan, Captain, Connecticut. Sent by Gen. Washington to reconnoitre the British on Long Island in 1776. He was captured by them and hanged as a spy Sept. 22, 1776.
Haslett, John, Colonel, Del. Killed at the battle of Princeton, January 3, 1777.
Holland, Thomas, Captain Delaware. Killed at Germantown. Oct. 4, 1777.
Henley, ——, Major, Aid to Gen. Heath. Killed at Montressor's Island, Sept. 21, 1776.
Hale, ——, Colonel. Died a prisoner on Long Island, 1780.

Irwin, Henry, Colonel, North Carolina. Killed at Germantown, Oct. 4, 1777.
Ingersoll, George, Lieut., Mass.
Irvine, William, Brig. Gen., Penn
Irvine, James, do. do.
Irvine, Andrew, Captain, do.
Irwin, John, do. do.
Irvine, Matthew, Surgeon, do.

424   OFFICERS ENTITLED TO HALF-PAY.

Inglis, John, Captain, N. Carolina.
Ivey, Curtis, Lieutenant,   do.
Irish, Nathaniel, Captain of Artificers, Pennsylvania.

Jackson, Ephraim, Colonel, Mass. Killed Dec. 19, 1777.
Johnson, Philip, Colonel, N. Jersey. Killed at the battle of Long Island, August 27, 1776.
Jouett, Matthew, Captain, Virginia. Died Nov. 15, 1777.
Jackson, Henry, Colonel, Mass.
Jackson, Michael,   do.   do.
Jackson, Thomas, Captain, do.
Jackson, Simon,   do.   do.
Jackson, Daniel, Lieut.,   do.
Jackson, Ebenezer,   do.   do.
Jackson, Michael,   do.   do.
Johnson, William,   do.   do.
Jeffred, Samuel,   do.   do.
Jenkins, Joel,   do.   do.
Jackson, Amasa, Ensign,   do.
Jackson, Charles,   do.   do.
Johnson, Jonathan, Lt. Col., Conn.
Jackson, Thomas F., Lieut., Adjutant, and Aid, Conn.
Judd, William, Captain, Conn.
Judson, David,   do.   do.
James, Elijah, Lieut.,   do.
Jansen, Cornelius T., Capt., N. Y.
Johnson, John,   do.   do.
Johnson, Robert, Surgeon,   do.
Johnston, James, Lieut.,   do.
Johnston, Francis, Colonel, Penn.
Jackson, Jeremiah, Captain,   do.
Jones, James, Surgeon,   do.
Jones, David, Chaplain,   do.
Jones, James M., Lieut.,   do.
Janney, Thomas,   do.   do.
Johnston, Andrew,   do.   do.
Jaquette, Peter, Cap., Delaware.
Jennifer, Daniel, Surgeon,   Md.
Jordan, John, Capt. of Cav.,   do.
Jones, John C., Captain,   do.
Jamison, Adam, Lieut.,   do.
Jameson, John, Lieut. Col., Va.
Joines, Levin,   do.   do.
Johnston, William, Captain, do.
Jones, Churchill,   do.   do.
Jones, Strother,   do.   do.
Johnston, John B.,   do.   do.

Jones, Albrighton, Lieut.,   Va.
Johnston, Peter,   do.   do.
Jones, Charles,   do.   do.
Jones, Samuel, Captain,   N. Car.
Jones, Phillip, Lieutenant,   do.
Jackson, William, Captain, S. C.
Jordan, William, Lieut., Georgia.

Knox, Henry, Major-general, Mass.
Knapp, Moses, Lieut. Col.,   do.
King, Zebulon, Captain,   do.
Killam, Joseph,   do.   do.
Kindry, William, Lieut.,   do.
Kirby, Ephraim,   do.   R. Island.
Kimberly, Ephraim, Capt., Conn.
King, Joshua, Lieutenant,   do.
Keeler, Isaac,   do.   do.
Keeler, Thaddeus, do.   do.
Keeler, Aaron, Ensign,   Conn.
King, John,   do.   do.
Knapp, Joshua,   do.   do.
Kingsbury, Jacob, do.   do.
Keese, John, Assistant Deputy Quartermaster-general, N. Y.
Kemper, Daniel, Deputy Clothier-general, New York.
Kemper, Jacob, Captain,   N. Y.
Kirkpatrick, David, Lieut.,   do.
Kenney, Abraham,   do.   N. J.
Kersey, William,   do.
Kennedy, Samuel, Captain, Penn.
Keene, Lawrence,   do.   do.
Kirkwood,   do.   Del.
Kidd, Charles, Lieut., Maryland.
Kilty, William, Surgeon,   do.
Kilty, John, Captain,   do.
Keene, Sam'l Y., Sur. Mate, do.
Kirkpatrick, Abram., Captain, Va.
Kendall, Kurtis,   do.   do.
Kays, Robert,   do.   do.
King, Elisha, Lieutenant.   do.
Kirk, Robert,   do.   do.
Kingsbury, John, Captain, North Carolina.
Knapp, John, Lieut., S. Carolina.
Kolb, Josiah,   do.   do.
Kennedy, Jas.,   do.   do.
Knowlton, Thomas, Colonel, Conn. Killed September 16, 1776.
Kingman, Elward, Ensign, Mass. Killed Sept. 26, 1777.

OFFICERS ENTITLED TO HALF-PAY. 425

Kirkland, Nathaniel, Lieut., Conn. Killed Oct. 12, 1777.
Kennedy, Samuel, Surgeon, Penn. Killed June 28, 1778.
Laurens, John, Lieut., Col., S. C. Killed in a skirmish on the Combahee, Aug. 27, 1781.
Ledyard, William, Colonel. Massacred by Major Bloomfield, a tory, under the Command of Arnold, the traitor, Sept. 6, 1781, at Fort Griswold.
Locke, Francis, Colonel. Killed at Charlotte, S. C., Sept. 25, 1780.
Lewis, Robert, Capt., Conn. Killed March 22, 1777.
Lamar, Marian, Major, Penn. Killed Sept. 21, 1777.
Lemon, James, Lieut., Penn. Killed Sept. 11, 1777, at Brandywine
Lucas, Thomas, Lieut., Penn. Killed Oct. 4, 1777, at Germantown.
Leitch, Andrew, Major, Va. Killed at Harlem Plains, Sept. 28, 1776.
Lewis, William, Lieut., Va. Killed Sept. 14, 1778.
Livermore, Daniel, Capt., N. H.
Lyon, Thomas, Lieut., do.
Lightall, William, do. do.
Lyford, Thomas, do. do.
Leavitt, Nehemiah, do. do.
Lincoln, Benj., Maj. Gen., Mass.
Littlefield, Noah M., Lt. Col., do.
Lincoln, Rufus, Captain, do.
Lunt, Daniel, do. do.
Lee, Daniel, do. do.
Learned, Simon, do. do.
Lord, Simeon, do. do.
Loughton, Wm., Sur. Mate, do.
Lovejoy, Obadiah, Lieut., do.
Liewell, John, do. do.
Lunt, James, do. do.
Lily, Reuben, do. do.
Leland, Joseph, do. do.
Lilly, John, do. do.
Lyman, Cornelius, Ensign, do.
Lord, Jeremiah, do. do.
Leonard, Jacob, do. do.
Lewis, Elijah, Captain, R. Island.
Leavenworth, Eli, Major, Conn.
Lyman, Daniel, do. do.

Lay, Asa, Captain, Conn.
Lee, Noah, do. do.
Loomis, Lebbeus, Lieut., do.
Lyon, Asa, do. do.
Lord, William, do. do.
Lynn, William, do. do.
Lord, James, do. do.
Lamb, John, Colonel, N. York.
Livingston, James, do. do.
Livingston, Hy. B., do. do.
Lawrence, Judge advocate General, New York.
Lewis, Morgan, Colonel and Qr. Mr., New York.
Livingston, Brokolst, Lt. Col., N. Y.
Lutterloh, Henry F., Col., N. York.
Ledyard, Isaac, Sur. Mate, do.
Logan, Samuel, Major, do.
Livingston, Abra'm, Capt., do.
Livingston, Robt. H., do. do.
Lewis, Samuel, Lieut., do.
Leycraft, William, do. do.
Leycraft, George, do. do.
Lansing, Garret G., do. do.
Leggett, Abraham, do. do.
Lawrence, Jonathan, Capt., do.
Lane, Derrick, Capt., N. J.
Leonard, Nathaniel, do. do.
Lloyd, Richard, do. do.
Luce, Francis, Ensign, do.
Lusk, William, Captain, Penn.
Lambert, Le Chevalier, Lt., do.
Lee, Andrew, Lieut., do.
Leroy, George, do. do.
Lytle, Andrew, do. do.
Lodge, Benjamin, do. do.
Lloyd, James, do. do.
Latimer, Henry, Surgeon, Del.
Learmonth, John, Captain, do.
Lansdale, Thos., Major, Maryland.
Lucket, Thos. H., do. do.
Lynch, John, do. do.
Lingan, James M., Captain, do.
Lamar, Abraham, do. do.
Lamar, William, do. do.
Lynn, David, do. do.
Lowe, John T., Lieut., do.
Lynn, John, do. do.
Lee, Henry, Lieut. Col., Virginia.
Lawson, Robert, General, do.
Lee, Philip R. F., Captain, do.
Long, Gabriel, do. do.

OFFICERS ENTITLED TO HALF-PAY.

Lewis, William, Major, Virginia.
Lapsley, Samuel, Capt., do.
Loveley, Wm. L., do. do.
Lind, Arthur, Lieut., do.
Lawson, Benj., do. do.
Ludeman, John W., do. do.
Linton, John, do. do.
Long, Reuben. do. do.
Lovell, James, do. do.
Lamb, Gideon, Colonel, N. C.
Lytle, Archibald, Lt. Col.. do.
Lytle, William, Captain, do.
Lewis, Micajah, do. do.
Lawrence, Nathan'l, do. do.
Lamb, Abner, do. do.
Lockman, Chas., Sur. Mate, S. C.
Liddell, George, Captain, do.
Lining, Charles, do. do.
Legare, James, do. do.
Lloyd, Edward, Lieut., do.
Liston, Thomas, do. do.
Lloyd, Benjamin, do. do.
Langford, Daniel, do. do.
Lowe, Philip, Major, Georgia.
Lane, Joseph, do. do.
Lucas, John, Captain, do.

Mercer, Hugh, Brig. Gen., Va. Killed at Princeton, Jan. 3, 1777.
McPherson, John, Aid-de-Camp to General Montgomery. Killed at Quebec, Dec. 31, 1775.
Mattocks, John, Capt. Killed at King's Mountain, Oct. 7, 1780.
Montgomery, Richard, Brig. Gen., New York. Killed at Quebec, Dec. 31, 1775.
Mumford, Augustus, Major, R. I. Killed at Plowed Hill, August 27, 1775.
Morris, Joseph, Major, N. J. Killed at Princeton, Jan. 3, 1777.
McMyers, Andrew, Captain, N. J. Killed at Germantown, Oct. 4, 1777.
Miller, John, Capt., Penn. Killed at Fort Washington, Nov. 16, 1776.
Motte, Chas., Major, S. C. Killed at the storming of Savannah, Oct. 9, 1779.
Moore, Willard, Major, Mass. Killed at Bunker Hill, June 17, 1775.

McClary, Andrew, Major, N. H. Killed at Bunker Hill, June 17, 1775.
Munroe, Edmund, Captain, Mass. Killed at Monmouth, June 28, 1778.
McCauley, Nathaniel, Lieut., N. H. Killed Aug. 30, 1779.
Martin, Peter, Lieut., Penn. Killed at Brandywine, Sept. 11, 1777.
Morris, Benj., Ensign, Penn. Killed at Brandywine, Sept. 11, 1777.
Mason, Caleb, Ensign, Md. Killed at Camden, Aug. 16, 1780.
McClintock, Alex., Lieut., Pa. Killed at Brandywine, Sept. 11, 1777.
Magee, William, Ensign, Pa. Killed Sept. 20, 1777.
McLain, Robert A., Ensign. Penn. Killed Sept. 27, 1777.
Morrill, Amos, Major, N. H.
McGregor, David, Captain, do.
Munroe, Josiah, do. do.
Morrow, Joshua, Lieut. do.
Mason, Lemuel, do. do.
Mills, Joseph, do. do.
McGaffey, Neal, do. do.
McLowry, Alex., Ensign, do.
Marshall, Thos., Colonel, Mass.
Maxwell, Hugh, Lt. Col., do.
Millen, James, do. do.
Marshall, Chris., Capt., do.
Maynard, Jonathan, do. do.
Means, James, do. do.
McFarland, Moses, do. do.
Mills, William, do. do.
Mills, John, do. do.
Miller, Jeremiah, do. do.
Moore, William, do. do.
McLane, Daniel, Lieut., do.
Morton, Silas, do. do.
Marble, Henry, do. do.
Maynard, William, do. do.
Mason, David, Lieut., Mass.
Merrick, Samuel, do. do.
Mellish, Samuel, do. do.
Maynard, John, do. do.
Miller, Joseph, do. do.
Morgan, Benj., Sur. Mate, do.
McKay, Daniel, Ensign, do.
Macomber, Eben., Capt., R. Island.
Masury, Joseph, Lieut., do.

OFFICERS ENTITLED TO HALF-PAY. 427

Meigs, Return J., Colonel, Conn.
Mather, Timothy, Surgeon, do.
Munson, Eneas, Sur. Mate, do.
Munson, Theophilus, Capt. do,
Munson, William, do. do.
Moulton, William, do. do.
Morris, James, do. do.
McGregor, John, do. do.
Mix, John, Lieut., do.
Mix, Timothy, do. do.
Manifield, John, do. do.
Meigs, John, do. do.
Miller, Charles, do. do.
McDougall, Alex., Maj. Gen., N. Y.
McDougall, Rebald S., Major, do.
Morris, Lewis, do. do.
McKnight, Chas., Surgeon, do.
Menema, Daniel, do. do.
Moore, Henry, Hos. Mate, do.
Machin, Thomas, Captain, do.
Marshall, Elihu, do. do.
Motte, Gershom, do. do.
Moodle, Andrew, do. do.
Mansfield, Samuel, do. do.
Morris, Wm. W., Lieut., do.
Magee, Peter, do. do.
Monty, Francis, do. do.
Miles, John, do. do.
Maxwell, Anthony, do. do.
Mott, Ebenezer, do. do.
Marsh, John, Ensign, do.
Morrell, Joseph, do. do.
Mason, John, Chaplain, N. Jersey.
Mitchell, Alex., Captain, do.
Martin, Absalom, do. do.
Meade, Giles, do. do.
Meeker, Usal, Lieutenant, do.
McEwen, John, Ensign, do.
Moylan, Stephen, Colonel, Penn.
Magaw, Robert, do. do.
Murray, John, Lieut. Col., do.
Mentges, Francis, do. do.
Maus, Matthew, Surgeon, do.
Magaw, William, do. do.
Martin, Hugh, do. do.
McCalla, Thomas, do. do.
McDowell, John, do. do.
McCoskey, Alex., do. do.
McCoffrey, Sam. A., do. do.
McMordie, Robt., Chaplain, do.
McClure, James, Captain, do.
McCurdy, Wm., do. do.

McIntire, Thomas, Capt., Penn.
McConnell, Matthew, do. do.
McMurray, William, do. do.
McKey, William, do. do.
McCully, George, do. do.
McClellan, John, do. do.
McGowan, John, do. do.
Miller, William, do. do.
Martin, William, do. do.
Moutgomery, Sam., do. do.
Marshall, John, do. do.
McCullom, John, Lieut., do,
McPherson, Jas. F., do. do.
McGuire, Matthew, do. do.
McDowell, William, do. do.
McKnight, David, do. do.
McKinney, John, do. do.
McMichael, James, do. do.
McElhatton, Wm., do. do.
McLean, James, do. do.
McFarlane, James, do. do.
Marshall, David, do. do.
Milligan, James, do. do.
Markland, John, do. do.
Moore, William, do. do.
Martin Robert, do. do.
Mahon, John, do. do.
Murrin, William, do. do,
Mytinger, Jacob, do. do.
Marcellin, Chevalier, do. do.
Manning, Lawrence, do. do.
Marshall, Benjamin, Lieut., do.
Morrisou, James, Ensign, do.
McLean, Allen, Major, Del.
Mitchell, Nathaniel, do. do.
Moore, James, Captain, do.
McKennon, Wm., do. do.
McWilliams, Steph., Lieut., do.
McHenry, James, Major, do.
McAllister, Archibald, Capt., do.
McFadden, James, do. do.
Myers, Christian, do. do.
McPherson, Samuel, do. do.
Muse, Walter, do. do.
Marberry, Joseph, do. do.
Mason, Thomas, do. do.
Morris, Jonathan, do. do.
Mitchell, John, do. do.
Morgan, David, Lieut., do.
McCoy, John, do. do.
McPherson, Mark, do. do.
Myers, Lawrence, do. do.

428 OFFICERS ENTITLED TO HALF-PAY.

Muhlenberg, Peter, Brig. Gen., Va.
Morgan, Daniel, do. Virginia.
Mathews, George, Colonel, do.
Marshall, Thomas, do. do.
McClenahan, Alex., do. do.
Mathews, Thos., Lt. Col., do.
Montgomery, John, do. do.
Meade, Richard K., do. do.
Mosely, William, Major, do.
Minnis, Holman, Captain, do.
Minnis, Callowhill. do. do.
Minnis, Francis, do. do.
Mallory, Philip, do. do.
Morgan, Simeon, do. do.
Muir, Francis, do. do.
Moss, Henry, do. do.
Morrow, Robert, do. do.
Morton, Hezekiah, do. do.
Mabin, James, do. do.
Meredith, William, do. do.
Meade, Everard, do. do.
Mercer, John F., do. do.
Minor, Thomas, do. do.
Mosely, Benj., (1) Lieut., do.
Mosely, Benj., (2) do. do.
Meriwether, David, do. do.
Meriwether, James, do. do.
Miller, Thomas, do. do.
Mills, John, do. do.
Miller, Jarran, do. do.
Morton, James, do. do.
Miller, David, do. do.
Miller, William, do. do.
Martin, Thomas, do. do.
McGuire, William, do. do.
Massey, John, Cornet, do.
Middleton, Baziel, Surgeon, do.
Monroe, George, do. do.
Murfree, Hardy, Lieut., Col., N. C.
McRae, Griffith I., Major, do.
Mills, James, Captain, do.
Monfort, Joseph, do. do.
Moore, Elijah, do. do.
McNees, John, do. do.
McClure, William, Surgeon, do.
McLain, William, Sur. Mate, do.
Marshall, Dixon, Lieut., do.
Moore, James, do. do.
Moultrie, Wm., Maj. Gen., S. C.
Marion, Francis, Colonel, do.
Mayzick, Daniel, Major, do.
Mitchell, Ephraim, do. do.

Mason, Richard, Captain, S. C.
Milling, Hugh, do. do.
Martin, John, do. do.
Mitchell, James, do. do.
Martin, James, Surgeon, do.
McGuire, Merry, Lieut., do.
Moore, Henry, do. do.
Mayzick, Stephen, do. do.
McIntosh, Lachlin, Brig. Gen., Ga.
McIntosh, John, Colonel, Georgia.
Moore, Francis, Major, do.
Mosby, Littleby, Captain, do.
Milton, John, do. do.
Melvin, George, do. do.
McIntosh, William, do. do.
McIntosh, Lachlin, Lieut., do.
Meanly, John, do. do.
Mitchell, John, do. do.
Morrison, John, do. do.
Mosby, Robert, Lieut., Georgia.
Maxwell, Josiah, do. do.

Neil, Daniel, Captain, New Jersey.
Killed at Princeton, Jan. 3, 1777.
Nash, Francis, Brig. Gen., North Carolina. Killed at Germantown, Oct. 4, 1777.
Neutville, William, Surgeon, S. C.
Nelson, John, Major, do.
Nelson, John, Captain, Virginia.
Nevil, John, Colonel, do.
Nelson, William, Lieut.Col., do.
Nevil, Presley, do. do.
Norvell, Lipscomb, Captain, do.
Nixon, Andrew, do. do.
Nelson, Roger, Lieutenant, do.
Norris, Jacob, do. Md.
Nichola, Lewis, Colonel, Penn.
North, Caleb, Lieut. Col., do.
North, George, Lieutenant, do.
Nice, John, Captain, do.
Neely, Benjamin, do. do.
Nestell, Peter, do. N. York.
Newkirk, Charles, do. do.
Niven, Daniel, do. do.
Norton, Nathaniel, do. do.
Nicholson, Geo. C., do. do.
Neely, Abraham, do. do.
Noyes, John, Surgeon, Conn.
Norton, Benjamin, Lieut., do.
Nixon, John, Brig. Gen., Mass.
Nixon, Thomas, Colonel, do.

OFFICERS ENTITLED TO HALF-PAY. 429

Newell, Ezra, Lieut. Colonel, Mass.
North, William, Captain, do.
Nason, Nathaniel, do. do.
Nelson, Henry, Lieut. do.

Olney, Jeremiah, Colonel, R. I.
Olney, Coggeshall, Major, do.
Oliver, Robert, do. Mass.
Oliver, Alexander, Lieut., do.
Olmstead, James, do. do.
Ogden, Mathias, Colonel, N. J.
Ogden, Aaron, Captain, do.
Otto Bodo, Surgeon, do.
Orr, John, Lieutenant, N. J.
Osman Benjamin, do. do.
Oldham, Edward, Captain, Md.
Oldham, Conway, do. Virginia.
Oliver, William, do. do.
O'Neal, Ferdinand, do. do.
Overton, John, do. do.
Oliphant, David, Surgeon, S. C.
Orgive, George, Lieut., do.
Ousby, Thomas, do. do.

Putnam, Rufus, Brig. Gen., Mass.
Patterson, John. Colonel, do.
Peters, Andrew, do. do.
Pope, Isaac, Major, do.
Porter, William, do. do.
Perkins, William, do. do.
Pettingill, Joseph, do. do.
Pillsbury, Daniel, Captain, do.
Pray, John, do. do.
Pike, Benjamin, do. do.
Pierce, Silas, do. do.
Pritchard, Thomas, do. do.
Porter, Benj. J., Sur. Mate, do.
Porter, Moses, Lieutenant, do.
Phelan, Edward, do. do.
Price, William, do. do.
Pardee, Aaron, do. do.
Phelan, John, do. do.
Phelan, Patrick, do. do.
Pierce, Benjamin, do. do.
Pratt, Joel, do. do.
Parker, Elias, do. do.
Pierce, John, do. do.
Parker, Benjamin, do. do.
Parker, Levi, do. do.
Potter, Joseph, Captain, N. H.
Page, Moses, Lieutenant, do.
Perkins, Jonathan, do. do.

Payne, Francis, Lieutenant, N. H.
Pennyman, Adna, do. do.
Plumb, William, Chaplain, R. I.
Peck, William, Major, do.
Peckham, Benj. L., Captain, do.
Patton, Thomas, do. do.
Pratt, William, Lieutenant, do.
Putnam, Israel, Maj. Gen., Conn.
Parsons, Samuel H., do. do.
Prior, Abner, Major, do.
Potter, Stephen, Captain, do.
Phelps, Seth, do. do.
Parsons, David, do. do.
Pendleton, Daniel, do. do.
Perry, Sylvanus, Lieutenant, do.
Pike, William, do. do.
Pomeroy, Ralph, do. do.
Pinto, Solomon, do. do.
Pride, Reuben, do. do.
Pickering, Timothy, Colonel, N. Y.
Platt, Richard, Major, do.
Popham, William, Captain, do.
Pemberton, Robert, do. do.
Pell, Samuel, T., do. do.
Pawling, Henry, do. do.
Parsons, Charles, do. do.
Prior, Abner, Surg. Mate, do.
Peck, Biel, Lieut., do.
Provost, Robert, Ensign, do.
Peters, William, do. do.
Phillips, Jonathan, Captain, N. J.
Platt, William, do. do.
Parrott, Silas, Lieutenant, do.
Paul, James, do. do.
Peck, John, do. do.
Porter, Andrew, Lieut. Col., Penn.
Peres, Petor, Surgeon, do.
Platt, Samuel, Surg. Mate, do.
Proctor, Francis, Lieut. Col., do.
Parr, James, Major, do.
Power, William, Captain, do.
Prye, Thomas, do. do.
Paulient, Antoine, do. do.
Patterson, John, do. do.
Patton, Robert, do. do.
Pierson, John, do. do.
Parker, Alexander, do. do.
Pike, Zebulon, do. do.
Power, William, do. do.
Purcell, Henry D., Lieut., do.
Pugh, Jonathan, do. do.
Peasely, Zacheus, do. do.
Piercy, Henry, do. do.

OFFICERS ENTITLED TO HALF-PAY.

Pettigrew, James, Lieut., Penn.
Pratt, John, do. do.
Peebles, Robert, do. do.
Peterson, Grabriel, do. do.
Porter, Robert, do. do.
Parker, Robert, do. do.
Purvis, George, Captain, N. J.
Patten, John, do. do.
Platt, John, do. do.
Platt, John, Lieutenant, do.
Pratt, Edward, Captain, Md.
Price, Benjamin, do. do.
Price, Thomas, jr., Lieut., do.
Pendergast, William, do. do.
Pindell, Richard, Surgeon, do.
Porterfield, Charles, Lt. Col., Va.
Posey, Thomas, do. do.
Powell, Levin, do. do.
Pelham, Charles, Major, do.
Poulson, John, do. do.
Pendleton, Nathaniel, Capt., do.
Pierce, William, do. do.
Parsons, William, do. do.
Pemberton, Thomas, do. do.
Pendleton, James, do. do.
Parker, Thomas, do. do.
Parker, Alexander, do. do.
Payne, Tarleton, do. do.
Porterfield, Robert, do. do.
Payne, Thomas, do. do.
Powell, Peyton, Lieutenant, do.
Pryor, John, do. do.
Parsons, Thomas, do. do.
Porter, William, do. do.
Perkins, Archelaus, do. do.
Power, Robert, Cornet, do.
Perry, John, do. do.
Payne, Josiah, Ensign, do.
Patton, John, Colonel, N. C.
Pearl, James, Captain, do.
Pinckney, Charles C., Colonel, S. C.
Pinckney, Thomas, Lt., Col., do.
Purcell, Henry, Chaplain, do.
Prescott, Joseph, Surgeon, do.
Pollard, Richard, Captain, do.
Proveaux, Adrian, do. do.
Poyas, John E., Hos. Mate, do.
Payne, Thomas, Lieut., Georgia.
Parre, Nathaniel, do. do.
Parker, Moses, Lt. Col., Mass.
 Killed at Bunker Hill, June 17, 1775.

Patton, William, Lieut., Penn.
 Killed at Germantown, Oct. 4, 1777.
Peyton, Robert, Lieut., Va., Killed at Brandywine, Sept. 11, 1777.
Phillips, Noah, Ensign, Connecticut. Killed March 16, 1778.
Parmelie, Josiah, Capt., Connecticut. Killed March 24, 1778.
Pierce, Timothy, Lieutenant, Penn. Killed July 3, 1778.
Pugh, Willis, Ensign, Virg'a. Killed May 1, 1777.

Quarles, James, Captain, Virginia.
Quarles, Thomas, do. do.
Quarles, Wm. P., Lieutenant, do.
Quarles, Robert, do. do.
Quirk, Thomas, do. do.

Reid, George, Lieut., N. Hamp.
Robinson, Caleb, Major, do.
Robinson, Noah, Captain, de.
Rowell, William, do. do.
Rice, Nathan, Major, Mass.
Rouse, Oliver, Captain, do.
Rennick, Timothy, do. do.
Richardson, Abiah, Surgeon, do.
Rice, Oliver, Lieutenant, do.
Ripley, Hezekiah, do. do.
Reab, George, do. do.
Richards, William, do. do.
Row, John, Ensign, do.
Rawson, Jeduthan, do. do.
Rogers, John, Lieutenant, do.
Russell, Thomas, do. do.
Riley, John, Captain, Conn.
Reed, Enoch, do. do.
Robinson, Peter, do. do.
Rose, John, do. do.
Rodgers, Hezekiah, do. do.
Richards, William, do. do.
Rogers, Jedediah, do. do.
Rice, Nehemiah, do. do.
Russell, Cornelius, Lieut., do.
Ransom, Elijah, do. do.
Rhea, Aaron, do. do.
Richards, Samuel, do. do.
Robinson, Elias, do. do.
Rogers, Joseph, Ensign, do.
Rose, John, Surgeon, do.
Rosecrans, James, Major, N. York.

OFFICERS ENTITLED TO HALF-PAY. 431

Randall, Thomas, Captain, N. Y.
Robecheau, James, do. do.
Reed, Jacob, do. do.
Reed, John, do. do.
Reed, Thomas, Surgeon, do.
Ryckman, Wilhelm, Lieut., do.
Ross, John, Major, New Jersey.
Reading, Sam'l. do. do.
Reckles, Anthony, Lieut., do.
Reed, John, do. do.
Rencastle, John, do. do.
Rhea, Jonathan, do. do.
Read, John, Ensign, do.
Robinson, Thomas, Lt. Col., Penn.
Rogers, John R.B., Surgeon, do.
Rogers, William, Chaplain. do.
Rogue, John, Surgeon's Mate, do.
Reid, James R., Major, do.
Rose, John, do. do.
Riely, John, Captain, do.
Rice, William, do. do.
Reeves, Enos, Lieutenant, do.
Robinson, Andrew, do. do.
Reed, Samuel, do. do.
Robbins, John, do. do.
Reed, Archibald, do. do.
Roche, Edward, do. Delaware.
Ramsey, Nathaniel, Col., Md.
Rawlings, Moses, Lt. Col., do.
Richmond, Christopher, Capt., do.
Roxburg, Alexander, do. do.
Reed, Philip, do. do.
Reese, Frederick, do. do.
Revelly, Francis, do. do.
Rudolph, Michael, do. do.
Relly, William, do. do.
Ricketts, Nicholas, Lieut., do.
Reybold, Jacob, do. do.
Rawlings, Isaac, do. do.
Rutledge, Joshua, do. do.
Rasin, William, do. do.
Rouse, Thomas, Ensign, do.
Russell, William, Colonel, Virginia.
Read, Isaac, do. do.
Richardson, Holt, Lt. Col., do.
Rose, Robert, Surgeon, do.
Ridley, Thomas, Major, do.
Reid, Nathan, Captain, do.
Ragsdale, Drury, do. do.
Ransdell, Thomas, do. do.
Roy, Beverly, do. do.
Russell, Albert, Lieut., do.

Roney, John, Lieut., Virginia.
Rankin, Robert, do. do.
Rudder, Epaphroditus, do. do.
Rhea, Matthew, do. do.
Robertson, William, do. do.
Robertson, John, do. do.
Reed, Jesse, Captain, N. Car.
Ralford, Robert, do. do.
Read, James, do. do.
Rhodes, Joseph T., do. do.
Read, William, Surgeon, S. Car.
Ramsay, Jesse H., Surg. Mate, do.
Roux, Albert, Captain, do.
Roberts, Richard B., do. do.
Russell, Thomas C., Lieut., do.
Rothmaler, Erasmus, do. do.
Roberts, Moses, Captain, Massachusetts. Killed Feb. 11, 1780.
Riker, Abraham, Lieutenant, N. Y. Killed May 7, 1780.
Heinick, Christopher, Surgeon, Penn. Died Sept. 21, 1778.
Redpith, John, Lieutenant, N. Car. Killed Oct. 13, 1777.
Ramsey, John, Surgeon, Penn. Died Nov. 4, 1776.
Roberts, Owen, Colonel, S. Carolina. Died June 20, 1779.

Scammell, Alexander, Colonel, N. H. Shot by the Hessian Cavalry, at Yorktown, Va., Sept. 30, 1781, and died Oct. 6, 1781.
Stirling, Lord, Maj. Gen., N. York. Died at Albany, Jan. 15, 1783. His proper name was Wm. Alexander.
Shubrick, Richard, Captain, S. Carolina. Killed Nov. 8, 1777.
Smith, William, Lieut., Va. Killed at Germantown, Oct. 4, 1777.
Smith, Samuel, Lieut., Penn. Killed May 27, 1777.
Shile, Peter, Lieut., Penn. Killed Nov. 5, 1777.
Stoddard, Nathan, Captain, Conn. Killed May 27, 1777.
Stoddard, Josiah, Captain, Conn.
Shaw, Sylvanus, Captain, R. Island. Killed Oct. 22, 1777.
Shortridge, Benj., Captain, N. Hampshire. Killed July 8, 1778.

OFFICERS ENTITLED TO HALF PAY.

Skillings, John, Captain, Mass. Killed April 2, 1777.
Steele, Aaron, Lieut., Mass. Killed Nov. 24, 1777.
Starke, John, Brig. Gen. N. Hamp.
Stafford, Samuel, Lt. Col., do.
Stockton, Eben., Surgeon, do.
Scott, William, Major, do.
Senter, Asa, Captain, do.
mith, Simeon, do. do.
Starke, Archibald, Lieut., do.
Stevens, Ebenezer, do. do.
Sheppard, Wm., Colonel, Mass.
Sproat, Ebenezer, do. do.
Stacy, William, Lt. Col. do.
Smith, Calvin, do. do.
Sumner, Job, Major, do.
Spurr, John, do. do.
Scott, William, do. do.
Shute, Daniel, Captain, do.
Sargeant, Winthropp, Captain and Aid, Mass.
Sewall, Henry, Captain, Mass.
Smith, Josiah, do. do.
Smith, Sylvanus, do. do.
Smith, John K., Captain, Mass.
Smith, Ebenezer, do. do.
Satterlee, Wm., do. do.
Sluman, John, do. do.
Stratton, Aaron, do. do.
Storrey, William, do. do.
Storer, Ebenezer, Captain and Paymaster, Mass.
Shaw, Samuel, Captain, Mass.
Stone, Jonathan, do. do.
Seward, Thomas, do. do.
Sloan, Sturgeon, do. do.
Stevens, William, do. do.
Savage, Joseph, do. do.
Sturdivant, Isaac, Lieut., do.
Smith, John, do. do.
Smith, Joseph, do. do.
Smith, Josiah, do. do.
Stocker, Ebenezer, do. do.
Selden, Charles, do. do.
Sampson, Crockett, do. do.
Spring, Simeon, do. do.
Stone, Nathaniel, do. do.
Savage, Henry, do. do.
Sheppard, William, do. do.
Sawyer, James, do. do.

Scammon, Sam'l L., Ensign, Mass.
Scott, James, do. do.
Sever, James, do. do.
Swan, Caleb, do. do.
Stafford, John R., do. do.
Sherburne, Henry, Colonel, R. I.
Sayles, David, Captain, do.
Sherman, Henry, Lieutenant, do.
Sherburne. Benjamin, do. do.
Sheldon, Elisha, Colonel of Dragoons, Conn.
Swift, Heman, Colonel, Conn.
Starr, Josiah, do. do.
Sumner, John, do. do.
Sherman, Isaac, Lieut. Col. do.
Skinner, Thomas, Surgeon, do.
Simpson, John, do. do.
Storrs, Justus, do. do.
Smith, David, Major, do.
Sill, Richard, Captain, do.
Shumway, John, Captain, Conn.
Starr, David, do. do.
Savage, Abijah, do. do.
Stevens, John, do. do.
Strong, David, do. do.
Stanton, William, do. do.
Stevens, Aaron, do. do.
Simon, Spaulding, do. do.
Sanford Samuel, do. do.
Smith, Ezra, Lieutenant, do.
Smith, William, do. do.
Sherman, John, do. do.
Shipman, Benoni, do. do.
Starr, Thomas, do. do.
Shutliff, Benjamin, do. do.
Seymour, Horace, do. do.
Smith, Joel, Ensign, do. do.
Stevens, Ebenezer, Colonel, do.
Steuben, Baron De, Maj. Gen., do.
Smith, Wm. S., Lieut. Col., do.
Sweet, Caleb, Surgeon, N. York.
Schuyler, Nich., do. do.
Smith, Wm. P., Surg. Mate, do.
Santford, John, Captain, do.
Smith, Israel, do. do.
Stewart, James, do. do.
Swartwout, Corn., do. do.
Bytez, George, Major, do.
Strachan, William, Lieut., do.
Schuyler, Dirck, do. do.
Scudder, William, do. do.

OFFICERS ENTITLED TO HALF-PAY. 433

Shaw, John,	Lieut.,	N. York.
Smith, Isaac,	do.	do.
Smith, John,	do.	do.
Snow, Ephraim,	do.	do.
Stagg, John,	do.	do.
Stake, John,	do.	do.
Stedliford, Gerard,	do.	do.
Swartwout, Henry,	do.	do.
Swartwout, Barn'd, Ensign, do.		
Spencer, Oliver,	Colonel,	N. J.
Shreeve, Israel,	do.	do.
Seely, Samuel,	do.	do.
Stout, Abraham,	do.	do.
Snowden, Jonathan,	do.	do.
Sears, Peter,	do.	do.
Shute, Samuel M.,	Lieut.,	N. J.
Stout, Wesell T.,	do.	do.
Sproal, Moses,	do.	do.
Shute, William,	Ensign,	do.
Sedam, Cornelius,	do.	do.
St. Clair, Arthur,	Maj. Gen.,	Penn.
Stewart, Walter,	Colonel,	do.
Stewart, Christop'r,	Lt. Col.,	do.
Stewart, Alex.,	Surgeon,	do.
Smith, Wm. H.	Surg. Mate,	do.
Stevenson, George,	do.	do.
Stotesbury, John,	Captain,	do.
Stevenson, Stephen,	do.	do.
Simonds, Jonas,	do.	do.
Sproat, William,	do.	do.
Simpson, Michael,	do.	do.
Steele, John,	do.	do.
Sample, Robert,	do.	do.
Smith, Samuel,	do.	do.
Stake, Jacob,	do.	do.
Seely, Isaac,	do.	do.
St. Clair, Daniel,	Lieut.,	do.
Smith, Peter,	do.	do.
Smith, Nathaniel,	do.	do.
Smith, James,	do.	do.
Stewart, William,	do.	do.
Shrader, Philip,	do.	do.
Stricker, John,	do.	do.
Sullivan, John,	do.	do.
Spear, Edward,	do.	do.
Stoy, John,	do.	do.
Stediford, Gerard,	do.	do.
Skillington, Elijah, do. Delaware.		
Smallwood, Wm.,	Maj. Gen.,	Md.
Stone, John H.,	Colonel,	do.
Smith, Samuel,	Lt. Col.,	do.
Swan, Jno.,	Maj. of Drag.,	do.
Selhuan, Jonathan,	Major,	do.

Smith, Joseph,	Captain,	Md.
Spurrier, Edward,	do.	do.
Smith, John,	do.	do.
Somerville, James,	do.	do.
Smith, James,	do.	do.
Smith, John,	do.	do.
Smith, Alex.,	Surg. Mate.	do.
Shugart, Martin,	Lieutenant,	do.
Sears, John,	Lieutenant,	do.
Smith, Edward M.,	do.	do.
Smote, William,	do.	do.
Skerritt, Clement,	do.	do.
Stoddard, Wm. T.,	do.	do.
Sewell, Clement,	Ensign,	do.
Scott, Charles,	Brig. Gen.,	Va.
Stephenson, David,	Major,	do.
Snead, Smith,	do.	do.
Skelton, Clough,	Captain,	do.
Stith, John,	do.	do.
Sansum, Philip,	do.	do.
Springer, Uriah,	do.	do.
Singleton, Anthony.	do.	do.
Stribling, Sigismund,	do.	do.
Stubblefield, Beverly,	do.	do.
Stokes, John,	do.	do.
Swearingen, Joseph,	do.	do.
Sayres, Robert,	do.	do.
Scott, Joseph,	do.	do.
Slaughter, Philip,	do.	do.
Summers, Simon,	Lt. & Adj.,	do.
Stockley, Charles,	Lieut.,	do.
Springer, Jacob,	do.	do.
Selden, Samuel,	do.	do.
Smith, James,	do.	do.
Smith, Jonathan,	do.	do.
Scarborough, John,	do.	do.
Southall, Stephen,	do.	do.
Stevans, William,	do.	do.
Starke, Richard,	do.	do.
Smith, Francis,	do.	do.
Smith, William S.,	do.	do.
Steele, John,	do.	do.
Stewart, Philip,	do.	do.
Smith, Ballard,	do.	do.
Sayres, Thomas,	do.	do.
Stribling, Erasmus,	do.	do.
Smith, Larkin,	do.	do.
Skinner, Alex.,	Surgeon,	do.
Smith, Nathan,	do.	do.
Savage, Joseph,	do.	do.
Southall, Stephen,	Lieut.,	do.
Settle, Strother,	do.	do.
Scott, Charles,	Cornet,	do.

484   OFFICERS ENTITLED TO HALF-PAY.

Sumner, Jethro, Brig. Gen., N. C.
Sharpe, Anthony, Captain, N. C.
Stewart, Charles,   do.   do.
Summers, John,   do.   do.
Slaughter, John,   do.   do.
Slade, Stephen, Lieutenant, do.
Steed, Jesse,   do.   do.
Shaw, Daniel,   do.   do.
Scarlock, James,   do.   do.
Saunders, William, do.   do.
Scott, William, Lieut. Col., S. C.
Shubrick, Thomas, Captain and Aid, South Carolina.
Smith, John C., Captain, S. Carolina
Sunn, Frederick, Surgeon, do.
Springer, Sylves, Sur. Mate, do.
Stevens, William S., do.   do.
Smith, Robert, Chaplain,   do.
Smith, Aaron, Lieut.,   do.
Sharpe, James B., Surgeon, Ga.
Steadman, James, Lieut.,   do.
Shick, Frederick,   do.   do.
Scott, William, Captain,   do.

Threadgill, Thomas, Captain, Ga.
Templeton, Andrew, do.   do.
Tetard, Benjamin, Surgeon, do.
Tennell, Francis, Lieut.,   do.
Tucker, Thomas T., Surgeon, S. C.
Theus, Simeon, Captain,   do.
Turner, George,   do.   do.
Tate, William,   do.   do.
Tatum, Howell,   do.   N. C.
Thaxton, James, Lieut. Col.,   do.
Tatum, James, Lieutenant,   do.
Towles, Oliver, Lt. Colonel, Va.
Taylor, Richard,   do.   do.
Temple, Benjamin,   do.   do.
Trezvant, John, Surgeon,   do.
Trant, Lawrence,   Captain, do.
Talliaferro, Benjamin, do.   do.
Terry, Nathaniel,   do.   do.
Thomas, Lewis,   do.   do.
Throckmorton, Alb., Cornet,   do.
Tannehill, Josiah,   Lieut.,   do.
Talliaferro, Nicholas,   do.   do.
Tatum, Zechariah,   do.   do.
Trabue, John,   Ensign,   do.
Tabb, Augustine,   do.   do.
Tilghman, Tench, Lt. Col.,   Md.
Tillard, Edward,   do.   do.
Tillotson, Thomas, Surgeon, do.
Tannehill, Adamson, Capt.,   do.

Trueman, Alexander, Capt., Md.
Trueman, John, Lieutenant,   do.
Towson, William,   do.   do.
Tilton, James, Surgeon, Delaware.
Taylor, Christopher, Sur. Mate, Pa.
Thompson, Joseph,   do.   do.
Tudor, George,   Major,   do.
Talbott, Jeremiah, do.   do.
Turnbull, Charles, Captain,   do.
Talbott, Samuel,   do.   do.
Thornbury, Francis, Lieut.,   do.
Tilden, John B.,   do.   do.
Thompson, William,   do.   do.
Tunison, Garrett, Surgeon, N. J.
Tharp, John,   Lieutenant, do.
Thomas, Edward D., do.   do.
Tuttle, William, Ensign,   do.
Troup, Robert, Lieut. Col., N. York.
Trumbull, John, Dept. Adjt. General, New York.
Ten Eyck, John D., Captain, N. Y.
Ten Broock, John C., do.   do.
Titus, Jonathan,   do.   do.
Taulman, Peter,   do.   do.
Tiebout, Henry,   do.   do.
Thompson, Alexander, Lieut., do.
Tappan, Peter,   do.   do.
Ten Eyck, Abraham,   do.   do.
Thompson, Andrew,   do.   do.
Talmadge, Samuel,   do.   do.
Tuthill, Azariah,   do.   do.
Tapp, William,   do.   do.
Trumbull, Jona., Lt. Col.,   Conn.
Talmadge, Benjamin, Major, do.
Throop, Benjamin,   do.   do.
Ten Eyck, Henry, Captain,   do.
Taylor, Timothy,   do.   do.
Trowbridge, John, Lieut.,   do.
Thompson, Isaiah,   do.   do.
Throop, John R.,   do.   do.
Tanner, Ebenezer, Lieut.,   Conn.
Tiffany, Isaiah,   do.   do.
Tupper, Benjamin, Colonel, Mass.
Thompson, Joseph, Lt. Col.,   do.
Trescott, Lemuel, Major,   do.
Taylor, Othniel, Captain,   do.
Thomas, Joseph,   do.   do.
Thorp, Eliphalet,   do.   do.
Trotter, John,   do.   do.
Turner, Jonathan, do.   do.
Treadwell, Wm.,   do.   do.
Tisdale, James,   do.   do.
Thatcher, James,   Surgeon, do

OFFICERS ENTITLED TO HALF-PAY. 435

Thompson, Thaddeus, Sur., Mass.
Thomas, John, do. do.
Townsend, David, do. do.
Tupper, Anselem, Lieut., do.
Tucker, Joseph, do. do.
Trowbridge, Luther, do. do.
Thatcher, Nathaniel, do. do.
Taylor, Tertius, do. do.
Tufts, Francis, do. do.
Thayer, Bartholo., do. do.
Town, Jacob, do. do.
Torrey, William, do. do.
Taylor, William, do. do.
Turner, Thomas, Captain, do.
Turner, Malbra, Lieutenant, do.
Titcomb, Benjamin, Lt. Col., N. H.
Taulman, Thomas, Lieut., do.
Taylor, Nathan, do. do.
Thompson, Joshua, do. do.
Thomas, John, Major-general, Mass. Died at Chambli, May 30, 1776.
Thomas, Joseph, Lieut. Colonel, New Hampshire. Killed at Bemis's Heights, Sept. 19, 1777.
Turner, Jacob, Captain, N. C. Killed at Germantown, Oct. 4, 1777.
Templeman, Andrew, Captain, Ga. Killed at the siege of Charleston, May 12, 1780.
Vose, Joseph, Colonel, Mass.
Vose, Elijah, Lieut. Col., do.
Vose, Thomas, Captain, do.
Van Schaick, Goosse, Colonel, N.Y.
Varick, Richard, Lieut. Col. and Mus. Mr. Gen., New York.
Van Dyck, Corn., Lt. Col., N.York.
Van Woert, Henry, Lt. and Qr. Mr., New York.
Vosburg, Peter J., Captain, N Y.
Van Rennselaer, Nicholas, Captain, New York.
Vandeburg, Henry, Captain, N. Y.
Van Reunselaer, Jeremiah, Lieut., New York.
Vacher, John F., Surgeon, N. Y.
Van Wolkenburg, Barth, Lt., do.
Van Hovenbarach, Rudolph, Lt. New York.
Van Wagener, Tunis, Lieut., N. Y.
Vandeburg, Bartholomew, Lieut., New York.

Van Horne, David, Captain, N. Y.
Van Wagener, Garret, Surg., Pa.
Van Lear, William, Captain, do.
Van Horne, Isaac, do. do.
Vernon, Frederick, Major, do.
Von Heer, Bartholomew, do. do.
Vernon, Job., Captain, do.
Van Court, John, Lieutenant, do.
Vaughan, Joseph, Lieut., Col., Del.
Vaughan, Joseph, Captain, do.
Vaughan, Claiborne, Surg. Mate, Virginia.
Vanderwall, Marks, Lieut., Va.
Van Metre, Joseph, do. do.
Vance, Robert, do. do.
Vance, John, Lieutenant, N. C.
Vickers, Samuel, Surgeon, S. C.
Van Brunne, John De La., Lieut., Md. Killed Sept. 12, 1781.
Voorhees, Peter, Captain, New Jersey. Killed Oct. 26, 1779.
Vaughan, William, Lieut., Delaware. Killed March 22, 1777.
Van Vielland, Cornelius, Lieutenant. Killed at the storming of Savannah, Oct. 9, 1779.
Warner, Seth., Colonel, N. H.
Wheatcomb, Benj., Major, do.
Washburn, Azel, Surgeon, do.
Walcott, Giles, Captain, do.
Weare, Nathan, Lieutenant, do.
Wilkins, Robert B., Lieut., N. H.
Wesson, James, Colonel, Mass.
Whitney, Daniel, Lt. Col., do.
Whitewell, Sam., Surgeon, do.
Warren, John, do. do.
Winslow, Nathaniel, Major, do.
Wiley, John, do. do.
Walker, Robert, Captain, do.
Woodbridge, Chris., do. do.
White, Hatfield, do. do.
Williams, Abraham, do. do.
Williams, John, do. do.
White, Moses, do. do.
Webb, George, do do.
Wattles, Mason, do. do.
Williams, Joseph, do. do.
Watson, William, do. do.
Wade, Abner, do. do.
Wigglesworth, Wm., do. do.
Whitney, John, Lieutenant, do.
White, Solomon, do. do.
White, Edward, do. do.

OFFICERS ENTITLED TO HALF-PAY.

White, Henry, Lieutenant, Mass.
Warren, Adriel, do. do.
Wells, James, do. do.
Williams, Robert, do. do.
Williams, Eben., do. do.
Warren, John, do. do.
Walker, Edward, do. do.
Willington, Elishu, do. do.
Webber, Daniel, do. do.
Wales, Joseph, do. do.
Wilds, Ebenezer, do. do.
Wells, Benjamin, do. do.
Wing, Jonathan, Ensign, do.
Wardell, Joseph, do. do.
Waterman, Jedediah, do. do.
Ward, Samuel, Lt. Col., R. Island.
Wheaton, Joseph, Lieut., do.
Welch, John, do. do.
Webb, Samuel B., Colonel, Conn.
Wyllis, Samuel, do. do.
Watrous, John R., Surgeon, do.
Woodbridge, Theod., Major, do.
Wyllis, John P., do. do.
Waldridge, Amos, do. do.
Wright, Joseph A., do. do.
Warner, Robert, do. do.
Webb, John, Captain, do.
Wadsworth, Elijah, do. do.
Walker, Joseph, do. do.
Webb, Nathaniel, do. do.
Weed, Thaddeus, do. do.
Wells, Roger, do. do.
Williams, Sam. W., do. do.
Woolcut, Erastus, do. do.
White, John, Lieut. do.
Wilcox, Joseph, do. do.
Whiting, Nath. H., do. do.
Woodward, Peter, do. do.
Whiting, Fred. J., do. do.
Wetsell, Michael, do. do.
Williams, Henry A., do. do.
Wales, Ebenezer, do. do.
Whitney, Joshua, do. do.
Walmsley, William, Ensign, do.
White, Anthony Walton, Col., N. Y.
Weisenfels, Frederick, Lt. Col, do.
Willett, Marinus, do. do.
Wendell, Jacob H., Lt. and Adj., do.
Woodruff, Samuel, Surgeon, do.
Woodruff, Henlock, do. do.
Wendell, John H., Captain, do.
Wright, Jacob, do. do.
Welp, Anthony, do. do.

Wright, Jotham, Lieutenant, N.Y.
Woodruff, Ephraim, do. do.
Weisenfels, Charles F., do. do.
Willson, Robert, Ensign do.
White, Andrew, Lieutenant, do.
Wetherby, Benj., Captain, N. J.
Weyman, Abel, do. do.
Walker, George, Lieut., do.
Whitlock, Ephraim, do. do.
Wayne, Anthony, Brig. Gen., Penn.
Weaver, Jacob, Captain, do.
Woelper, John D., do. do.
Wilkins, Robert, do. do.
Wilson, James, do. do.
Walker, Andrew, do. do.
Wilson, William, do. do.
Wilkins, John, Sur. Mate, do.
Wharry, Robt., do. do.
Weidman, John, Lieut., do.
Weitzell, Jacob, do. do.
Wigton, John, do. do.
White, Francis, do. do.
Ward, John, do. do.
Webster, John B. do. do.
Wilson, John, Captain, Delaware.
Williams, Otho H., Brig. Gen., Md.
Weltner, Lodowick, Colonel, do.
Woolford, Thomas, do. do.
Winder, Levin, Lieut. Col., do.
Williams, Lylburn W., Capt., do.
Watkins, Gassaway, do. do.
Waters, Richard, do. do.
Warfield, Walter, Surgeon, do.
Wilkinson, Young, Lieutenant, do.
Ware, Francis, do. do.
Wilmott, Robert, do. do.
Wright, Nathan, do. do.
Winchester, George, do. do.
Waring, Bazel, do. do.
Weedon, Geo., Brig. Gen., Virginia.
Woodford, Wm., do. do.
Wood, James, Colonel, do.
White, Anthony W., do. do.
Washington, Wm., Lt. Col., do.
Wallace, Gustavus B., do. do.
Warmock, Frederick, do. do.
Webb, John, do. do.
Wagener, Andrew, Major, do.
Willis, John, do. do.
Wallace, James, Surgeon, do.
West, Charles, Major, do.
Woodson, Tarleton, do. do.

FOREIGN OFFICERS.

Wright, James, Captain, Virginia.
Watts, John, do. do.
Woodson, Robert, do. do.
Warman, Thomas, do. do.
White, William, do. do.
Williams, James, do. do.
Wallace, James, Lieut., do.
White, John, do. do.
Worsham, Richard, do. do.
Washington, Geo. A., do. do.
Walters, Richard, do. do.
Walker, David, do. do.
Winlock, Joseph, do. do.
Whiting, Francis, do. do.
Wilson, Willis, do. do.
Wallace, William B., do. do.
Williams, David, do. do.
Whittaker, William, do. do.
Walton, William, Captain, N. Car.
Williams, William, do. do.
Williams, Nathaniel, do. do.
Williamson, John, do. S. Car.
Warley, George, do. do.
Warley, Felix, do. do.
Warley, Joseph, do. do.
Wickley, John, do. do.
Ward, John P., Lieutenant, do.
Ward, William, do. do.
Withers, William R., Ensign, do.
Wright, John G., Surgeon, Georgia.
Wagnon, John P., Lieut., do.
Warren, Joseph, Major Gen., Mass. Killed at Bunker Hill, June 17, 1775.
Wooster, David, Major Gen., Conn. Mortally wounded at the invasion of Danbury by Tryon's forces, April 27, 1777. Died May 2. 1777.
Wilmott, William, Captain, Md. Killed by a British foraging party in a skirmish on John's Island, S. C., Nov. 14, 1782. The blood of Capt. Wilmott was the last spilled in battle in the Revolution.
Woodhull, Nathaniel, Gen., N. Y. Died Sept. 20, 1776, from a wound received in battle on Long Island.
Wilson, Jonathan, Captain, Mass. Killed at Concord, April 19, 1775.
Walker, Benjamin, Capt. Killed at Bunker Hill, June 17, 1775.
Wise, Samuel, Major, S. C. Killed at Savannah, Oct. 9, 1779.
Witherspoon, James, Brigade-major. Killed at Germantown, Oct. 4, 1777.
Williams, Nathan, Lieut., Maryland. Killed at Camden, Aug. 16, 1780.
Wallace, Andrew, Captain, Virginia. Killed at the battle of Guilford, March 15, 1781.
Wilson, John, Lieutenant, Virginia. Killed at Eutaw Springs, Sept. 8, 1781.
Wait, Joseph, Lieutenant-colonel. Died Sept. 28, 1776.
Webster, Amos, Lieutenant. Died Oct. 7, 1777.
Whiting, Charles, Captain. Killed July 10, 1779.
Yeomans, John, Lieutenant, Mass.
Young, Joseph, Surgeon, N. Y.
Young, Guy, Captain, do.
Young, Marcus, Lieutenant, Penn.
Yates, George, Surgeon's Mate, Va.
Yancey, Leighton, Captain, do.
Yancey, Robert, do. do.
Young, Henry, do. do.
Yarborough, Charles, Lieut., do.
Yarborough, Edward, Capt., N. C.

FOREIGN OFFICERS IN THE REVOLUTIONARY SERVICE OF THE UNITED STATES.

Baron De Kalb, of Germany. Killed at Camden, Aug. 16, 1780.
Count Casimir Pulaski, of Lithuania in Poland. Killed at Savannah, Oct. 9, 1779.
Lieut. Col. Baron De Boze, of Pulaski's Legion. Killed at Egg Harbor, in 1778.
Ferdinand J. S. De Brahm, Major of Engineers.

FOREIGN OFFICERS.

Thaddeus Kosciusko, of Poland.
Lewis Du Pontier, Captain.
Le Brun De Bellecour, Captain.
Chevalier De Fontiveaux, Lieut.
James Decatours, do.
James McDougall, Cornet.
Peter Raffencau, do.
Charles Roth, Lieutenant.
Felix Texier, Surgeon.
Marquis De La Fayette, Maj. Gen.
Count De Rochambeau, General-in-Chief.
Count Deuxponts, Col. of Infantry.

Duke De Lavel Montmorency, Col
Count Caustine, Colonel.
Duke De Lauzum, Col. of Cavalry.
General Choizy.
Viscount Viomenil,
Marquis De St. Simon.
Count Fersen, Aid-de-Camp.
Count Charles Dumas.
Marquis De Chastellux.
Baron, De Viomenil.
Count De Grasse, Admiral.
Count De Barras, do.
Count De Estaing, do.

REMARKS ON THE HALF-PAY ACTS.—THE RISE AND PROGRESS OF THE REVOLUTION.—THE END, ETC.

On reference to the act of October 21, 1780, and other subsequent acts, it will be perceived that the Continental Congress created a *national debt* for the purpose of carrying on a war waged against the country for the purpose of bringing it into unconditional subjection to a foreign tyrant. This *national debt* was made due and payable to all military officers who would espouse the cause of the country, engage in the war, and continue therein to the end.

The Revolutionary war, in opposition to the encroachments of Great Britain on the civil rights of the American Colonies, commenced on the 19th April, 1775, by the shedding of human blood at Lexington, in the State of Massachusetts, and finally closed with the evacuation of New York by the British, on the 25th November, 1783. As the news of war spread with the velocity of the hurricane, it roused the energies of the soul to the highest tone of feeling, and to deeds of the most lofty action. The lawgiver left the senate-house, the lawyer the court, the judge the bench, the mechanic his shop, the husbandman his plough, and rushed forward to the seat of danger; while the wild war-cry of vengeance took the wings of the tempest.

The time had come when all must "hang together" in one common cause, or else "*hang separately.*" They hung together, cemented by the great principle, that, "Whenever any form of government becomes destructive of its ends, it is the right of the people to alter or abolish it." The bright star of victory led them onward and onward, through the dark shades of war, casting light and hope athwart the path of the war-worn American soldier.

On the 6th July, 1775, the Provincial Congress announced its intention to resist Great Britain in the following words: "We are reduced to the alternative of choosing an unconditional submission to the tyranny of wicked ministers, or resistance by force. The latter is our choice. We have counted the cost of this contest, and find nothing so dreadful as voluntary slavery."

On the 4th of July, 1776, the same Congress, within hearing of the fierce thunders of war, declared that these United Colonies *are*, and of right ought to be, free and independent. But where now was the revenue of the country? How shall this infant nation procure the means of driving from her soil her cruel invaders? A well-fed, numerous, and powerful foe were about taking possession of the strong-holds of the country to awe into subjection the patriot army. Commerce had already been driven from her harbors, and her vessels captured and plundered on the high seas. "Appealing to the Supreme Judge of the world for the rectitude of her intentions," she sent forth Commissioners "in the name and by the authority of the good people of these United Colonies" to negotiate loans from friendly powers, to replenish the military chests of the country, and provide the means of war. Means were provided, plans of operation were matured, the war went on, and patriots flocked to the standard.

On the 16th September, 1776, Congress promised land. This encouraged enlistments, increased the ranks, and new light enlightened the cause. This land, however, was promised for the services to the end of the war: but distant as the reward appeared, thousands, hoping to realize it, left private fortunes to suffer at home, and came up to the aid of the nation.

The war progressed. Dark clouds often hung over and obscured the American cause. The patriot army were often found fleeing before a dark and powerful British host, yet sullen and dangerous in its flight. By deeds of daring, sanguinary battles, and miraculous escapes from destruction, the American army, still bearing her cause in characters of blood on her banners, reached the eventful period of 1780.

ON THE HALF-PAY ACTS, ETC. 441

In the spring of this year, a great portion of the army, whose terms of enlistment for three years had expired, were about to leave the army, and abandon the cause of liberty as hopeless. Time had not yet obliterated the remembrance of the gloomy encampment at Valley Forge. Traitors were abroad in the land, who, with the insidious tory, conducted fearful conspiracies against the cause of liberty. Officers could not maintain themselves with proper decency in the service, and resignations, actual and threatened, were frequent, much dreaded, and deplored. The enemy, ever vigilant and active, conspired to weaken and thin the American ranks by encouraging desertion. The arch traitor and prototype of the infamous Catiline, had raised his arm to blast forever, with one fell swoop, the struggling germ of liberty in America; but the "Supreme Judge of the world," to whom the voice of patriotism had ascended for the justice of its intentions, in mercy averted the blow, and hurled the fiend and his foul instrumentality in fury down, and the same army, which had been made the devoted object of destruction, halted at Tappan, and suspended between Heaven and earth the deluded instrument by which the downfall of liberty had been attempted.

Amid those impending evils, the Commander-in-Chief, prolific in expedients, suggested a remedy as follows: "I have no scruple in declaring that I most firmly believe the independence of the United States never will be established till there is an army on foot *for the war.*"

On the 21st of October, 1780, seventeen days after those words were penned, Congress resolved: "That the officers who shall continue in service to the end of the war shall be entitled to half-pay during life, to commence with the time of their reduction. Here Congress entered into a solemn contract with the officers of the army, and on the faith of the Colonies therein represented, created a *national debt*, which could not be annulled, or discharged by any subsequent legislation, except by an act giving a full and perfect *equivalent* for the half-pay for life. As the value of an annual salary cannot be calculated in the lifetime of the annuitant, no equivalent therefore can be rendered for it. Some officers did by their memorial solicit a commutation of their half-pay for an *equivalent*, but Congress, by its act of March 22, 1783, reserved to itself the power of determining that equivalent ; and as no equivalent could be equitably calculated, the memorial of the officers should have been rejected, as a proposition admitting of no equitable grounds of action. The officers asked for a *fish*, but Congress gave them a *stone*. They received as the commutation of their half-pay securities on interest, which they supposed to be a fish, but when offered for sale, brought only the price of a stone, and therefore must have been the equivalent of a stone. It is true the officer thankfully received his commutation certificate, thinking that in the worst view of the case he ought to get for it the full value, less the interest, that would accrue. But Congress fixed no time for the payment of those certificates. The officer carried about in his pocket a certificate from the Continental treasury stating that five years' full pay, with interest, from November 4, 1783, was due him, which he offered for sale. But, says the capitalist, when is it to be paid, and by whom ? Some military leader may spring up and plunge the country into another war. The stock is unsafe.

These certificates, immediately after their issue, sank in value, and at once reached a depreciation of eight dollars for one in specie ; and from the close of the war in 1783 to the organization of the government under the new constitution in 1787, no man could tell how or when those certificates were to be redeemed. In 1790 and 1791, they were funded in a stock bearing three per cent. interest, and were finally paid in full by the government, but not until the officer had lost all his interest in them, by circumstances brought about by the condition of his country, over which he could have no control.

As the commutation act of March 22, 1783, was a failure, and did not discharge any legal obligations entered into by Congress, it therefore becomes the duty of the country to revive the half-pay acts of the Continental Congress, and restore to the revolutionary officer, his heirs, or legal representatives, the benefits of the original contracts. Petitions for the revival of these half-pay acts have been before Congress ever since 1790. Congress having restored some officers to the benefits of the act of October 21, 1780, by special acts of August 11, 1790, and subsequently, a precedent is formed for the others. But it may be said that the act of August 11, 1790, was a pension act alone. This could not have been the case with respect to officers who served to the end of the war, for all officers, as well as privates, under the numerous general acts prior to the act of 1790, were entitled to pensions for wounds received in the service according to their degree of disability, and no special legislation was therefore necessary, except to revive the act of October 21, 1780, and require the recipient of its benefits to refund the amount of commutation awarded him by the provisions of the act of March 22, 1783.

Many officers and privates, per special acts from 1790 to 1800, and subsequently were placed on the pension-rolls, but it will be observed at once that officers who served to the *end of the war*, were not, by the spirit of the law, really pensioned, but restored to their half-pay by refunding their commutation. This was done because the degree of disability of the officer would not, under the existing invalid pension laws of the day, entitled him to an annual rate of pension equal to his half-pay. He therefore petitioned to be restored to his half-pay by refunding his commutation, because this was more beneficial to him than would have been the pension to which he would have been entitled under existing laws.

It, of course, is admitted that to invalids alone the acts of 1790 restored the half-pay, but it must be seen that the invalid officer had pension laws in his favor, and sometimes sums of money granted him, while the other officers had nothing to lean upon for the least aid. The invalid officer, therefore, while pension laws existed in his favor, had no more right to a restoration of his half-pay than another who had not been wounded in the service. All the officers and privates were seriously disabled in the service, and were disqualified from returning to the pursuit of peaceful occupations after the hardships of an eight years' war, with any of the advantage and success which they previously enjoyed.

In the spring of 1808 the subject of the revival of the half-pay acts of the old Congress was earnestly agitated. Circulars were sent through the country, bearing the signatures of distinguished Revolutionary officers, which formed the basis of a general petition to Congress in 1810, from which the following is gathered: "By a resolution of Congress, passed the 11th of August, 1779, it was ordained, 'That the half-pay provided by the resolution of the 15th of May, 1778, be extended to continue for life;' and on the 22d March, 1783, it was resolved, 'That such officers as are now in service, and shall continue therein to the end of the war, shall be entitled to receive the amount of five years' of full pay in money or securities on interest at six per cent. per annum, as Congress shall find most convenient, instead of the half-pay for life.'

"The circumstances under which the proposal of commutation originated and was partially acceded to, the desperate state of public credit, and the imperious necessity which compelled many of the holders of certificates of public debt to part with them at a price far below their nominal value, are too well known to require a recapitulation.

"That the benevolent intentions of the Congress of 1779 have not been realized, that many meritorious officers, bowed down with infirmities and advanced in years are now struggling with adversity, are facts so notorious as of late to attract the public attention.

"So equitable is the claim on the honor and faith of Government to make good the original promise; so great the zeal latterly displayed in Congress on this interesting subject, and so ample are the means of full remuneration, that it has been deemed proper by a number of Revolutionary officers, to call the attention of their brethren in the several States, and to suggest the expediency of a memorial on the subject being prepared in each State, circle, or district, during the recess of Congress, to be presented to the Senate and House of Representatives as soon as circumstances will permit after their next meeting."

This language bears the signatures of no less distinguished officers than Colonel Stephen Bayard, Colonel Isaac Craig, and Surgeon William Magaw, of the Pennsylvania Line, and Capt. Adamson Tannehill, of Maryland, and speaks forth a true history of the times not to be misunderstood.

There has not been a session of Congress in the history of the Government under the New Constitution, at which the subject of the restoration of the half-pay acts of the old Congress has not been brought up in some shape or other; and at the first session of the thirty-fourth Congress, the following bill in substance, for the restoration of the half-pay for life, passed the House of Representatives, but was lost in the Senate at the second session:

"An Act to provide for the Settlement of the Claims of the Officers of the Revolutionary Army, and of the Widows and Orphan Children of those who died in the Service.

"*Be it enacted by the Senate and House of Representatives of the United States of America in Congress assembled*, That the officers of the army of the Revolution, who were entitled to half-pay for life under the resolutions of Congress of the 3d and 21st of October, 1780, the 17th of January, 1781, the 8th of May, 1781, and the 8th of March, 1785, shall be entitled to receive the same, although such officer may have received, in lieu thereof, the commutation of full pay for five years, under the resolution of Congress of the 22d of March, 1783.

"SEC. 2. *And be it further enacted*, That it shall be the duty of the proper accounting officer of the Treasury, when applied to for that purpose by any one who by this act is entitled to receive, or his or her guardian, to ascertain what is due to such officer, from the time he became entitled to the said half-pay until his death, if that occurred before the 3d day of March,

1826; but if he died after that time, then up to the 3d day of March, 1826.

"SEC. 3. *And be it further enacted,* That it shall be the duty of the Secretary of the Treasury, when the amount due to an officer has been ascertained, as aforesaid, to pay the same, as hereinafter directed, after deducting therefrom the amount received for commutation, under the resolution of the 22d of March, 1783.

"SEC. 4. *And be it further enacted,* That the benefit of the resolution of the 24th of August, 1780, shall be extended to the widows and orphan children of all officers who died in the service at any period during the war of the Revolution, whether such officers belonged to the Continental Line, or to any volunteer corps called into service under the authority of any State, but no payment shall be made under this clause, except to the widows and orphan children of such deceased officers.

"SEC. 5. *And be it further enacted,* That Surgeons' Mates shall be entitled to the benefit of the resolution of the 17th of January, 1781, and receive the same pay as hospital physicians and surgeons.

"SEC. 6. *And be it further enacted,* That it shall be the duty of the Secretary of War, under the direction, and with the approbation of the President of the United States, to prescribe such rules of evidence as may be necessary to carry into effect the provisions of this act, according to its true intent and meaning.

"SEC. 7. *And be it further enacted,* That all payments made by authority of this act shall be without interest.

"SEC. 8. *And be it further enacted,* That in every case the said accounting officer, before he shall order any claim to be paid, shall require satisfactory proof that the person or persons, in whose name the same may be presented, is or are the *bona fide* owner or owners thereof, and that the claim has not been sold, transferred, peldged, or mortgaged, or any part thereof, to any person or persons, whomsoever; and all sales, transfers, mortgages, or pledges of any such claims are hereby declared void, and of no effect whatever.

"SEC. 9. *And be it further enacted,* That this act shall not extend to the case of any officer, or his representatives, who have received half-pay for life under any special act of Congress.

"SEC. 10. *And be it further enacted,* That all persons who apply and receive the benefit of this act, shall receive the same in full satisfaction of all claims under any of the resolutions of Congress hereinbefore recited, and for all losses alleged to have been sustained by depreciation in the value of the certificates received as commutation under the resolution of Congress of the 22d of March, 1783.

SEC. 11. *And be it further enacted,* That all claims which shall be allowed under the 1st and 5th Sections of this act shall be paid to the officer, if alive, and if he be dead, to his widow and children equally, and if there be no widow living, then to his child, children, or grand-children—the issue of any deceased child taking among them the share of their deceased parent—and to no other persons.

SEC. 12. *And be it further enacted,* That this act shall continue and be of force for the term of ten years, and no longer, and all claims not presented, with the evidence, for their adjudication within that time shall be forever barred."

On reference to the preceding list of Continental officers who died in service, and who continued in service to the end of the war, the names of those officers whose heirs are entitled to the benefits of the preceding bill will be seen; and should the bill pass Congress and become a law, they, or any other persons interested for them, may determine their claim, on reference to the rank of the officer, and to the pay-table of the Continental army, given in a preceding page.

The acts of the Continental Congress to which the 1st, 4th, and 5th Sections of this bill refer are given in this work; and in order to understand the 2d Section, it will be necessary to quote an act of Congress approved May 15, 1828, which is as follows:

"*Be it enacted by the Senate and House of Representatives of the United States of America, in Congress assembled*, That each of the surviving officers of the army of the Revolution, in the Continental Line, who was entitled to half-pay by the resolve of October 21, 1780, be authorized to receive, out of any money in the treasury not otherwise appropriated, the amount of his full pay in said line, according to his rank in the line, to begin on the 3d day of March, 1826, and to continue during his natural life: *Provided*, That under this act no officer shall be entitled to receive a larger sum than the full pay of a captain in said line."

Attorney-general Wirt, in his opinion under date of the 12th of February, 1825, fixes the close of the Revolutionary war at the ratification of the definitive treaty of peace, April 23, 1783; but in the adjustment of commutation claims under act March 22, 1783, originating in the act of October 21, 1780, the war is considered as having closed with the final disbanding of the troops, November 3, 1783, and consequently the five years' full pay referred to in the act of March 22, 1783, commenced November 4, 1783. Five years' full pay being equal to ten years' half-pay, the officers by their commutation certificates received their ten years' half-pay from November 4, 1783, to November 4, 1793, therefore the half-pay bill pending in Congress proposes to give the officer his half-pay from November 4, 1793, where the commutation certificate dropped him, to March 3, 1826, where the act of May 15, 1828, took him up—or it proposes to give him his half-pay from November 4, 1783, to March 3, 1826, deducting his five years' full pay or ten years' half-pay per act March 22, 1783. It must, however, be recollected, that where the officer died before March 3, 1826, his heirs will only receive his half-pay from November 4, 1793, to the day of his death; and when the officer died between November 4, 1783, and November 4, 1793, his heirs will receive nothing, because the commutation certificate has covered the whole period. But it is the meaning and spirit of the pending bill, as expressed in the report which accompanies it, that the half-pay of the officer shall commence from the time of his *reduction*, which means the time he quit the service. Many officers were *reduced* and *retired* from the service, or became *supernumerary* under the various arrangements of the army from 1778 to 1783, so that, if the officer died at any period within ten years after the time of his reduction, his heirs are not now entitled to anything, for, as before stated, the commutation certificate has covered the ground.

Section 4 of the bill will be almost, if not entirely inoperative, for there are at this day but few relicts of officers who lost their lives prior to 1782. Some children may be found. This section, it will be seen, is not confined to Continental officers alone, like the others, but gives the pay to the officers of any corps called into service by the authority of any State, such as militia, &c.

If any officer, living at the passage of the act of May 15, 1828, was not entitled to pension under that act, his heirs will have no claim under this bill should it become a law; because the said bill and the act of 1828 both have their foundation in the half-pay acts of the Continental Congress. But should Congress, instead of the whole amount of the commutation certificate, determine to deduct what it sold for only, then all will get something.

Senator Crittenden, of Kentucky, on the subject of the bill in question, and relative to the act of March 22, 1783, remarks: "What was the condition of the government when it made this proposition to the officers? They came out of the war victorious and naked. They came out of the war triumphant and penniless. The government was in no condition to execute its obligations. Promises of half-pay they could not satisfy. They sought for themselves some little exemption and procrastination of this obligation by giving the promise of full pay for five years, the payment of the principal to be postponed for ten years. By these hopes your needy, naked, and hungry officers, as many of them were, were tempted to accept the terms.—

They have received the commutation. If they give credit for that on the account, when you become able and prosperous, where is there any restraint in the Constitution to prevent your satisfying your sense of moral obligation by paying the full balance? Is it no debt, because it is not recoverable by law? No national debt is recoverable by law. The creditor must depend on the sovereignty and on the gratitude of the government. It is to measure its own obligation. There is no legal tribunal before which you could go and drag this nation to answer. *Your courts of law have decided that, as to a debt barred, and which is no longer one of legal obligation, if the party promise to pay it, the previous debt, barred though it be, is an ample consideration for the subsequent promise.* That was your condition. You were unable to pay, as you had promised, half-pay for life; you gave something like security for a smaller sum. Your honest creditor accepted it. You have paid that; and if you feel any moral obligation to do so, you are able to pay the balance. Will you do it? It is not a case of mere gratuity, certainly, nor a case of a mere debt of gratitude. That is not it; it is a money obligation, which, under your invitation, your creditor departed from, and took for it that which was not an ample consideration—that which was not a fair equivalent. Half-pay for life was given up for full-pay for five years. Now, when the government is rich and prosperous, and abundantly able to pay, the House of Representatives, at least, have said, 'We will settle with these men fairly; we will credit them for the sum they received as full pay for five years, and if there be any of the half-pay for life due to any of them, we will pay that.' I say this is not a gratuity. There was a moral obligation, to satisfy this debt of the Revolution. It was out of that we derived our very being as an independent sovereign government. We may well look back on all the transactions of that day as somewhat more hallowed than the ordinary transactions of life, or even the ordinary transactions of government. It was a sacred generation; a day sacred to liberty. Everything belonging to it ought to be sanctified in our view and to our feelings.

"I beg gentlemen to recollect that it was under a resolution of 1783 that this commutation of five years' full pay was accepted; and it was *ten years* from that time before the *principal became due*. What was the condition of those certificates during that time? The country was under the government of the Confederation, a weak and feeble government, impoverished, without power and without means. What was to be its destiny the wisest men could not tell—the wisest could not foresee; and the humblest and the most uniformed might well dread its termination—its falling to pieces from mere inability and want of cohesion at any time. They accepted these certificates, payable ten years afterwards. Of credit it had none. What was the value of a certificate payable ten years afterwards upon such a security? Could prompt payment be calculated upon at the time it fell due? Was it calculated upon, or did these certificates depreciate to a mere nominal value? They did so depreciate. What was the needy soldier to do? He was no longer in the army; his means consisted in his certificate, perhaps nothing or little else. What was he to do with it, and what did he in point of fact do with it? Nine out of ten sold these certificates for a nominal price. They were afterwards funded by the government, to be sure, after the adoption of the present Constitution; but during that term of ten years they depreciated day by day, and were sold for what the poor officer could get for them."

"George Washington," says Senator Seward, of New York, "by temper, knowledge, and impartiality, was qualified to be witness, advocate, and umpire between the officers of the army of the Revolution and the American government and people. In all human history, he is the only man who could acceptably fill and discharge the duties of these conflicting characters. I have therefore abstained from drawing into the case any facts or arguments, or authorities, other than those derived from his own immortal words. Standing on them, I claim that the half-pay for life pledged to the officers was a debt, a just debt, a constitutional one, with all the attributes of a common debt— a debt of honor and of gratitude, the equivalents of which were the blood of the officers and the independence of the country; that it was a perpetual debt, therefore, which could never be cancelled until it was fully and fairly paid. It was not fully and fairly paid by the promise of commutation; which promise was never executed, nor attempted to be executed, until after nine years' procrastination, in no degree resulting from any fault of the officers, but solely from the misfortunes and embarrassments of the country which was the debtor; and that when the attempt to execute it was then made, the payment made reached only those brokers who had speculated in the ruin of the officers, and not the officers themselves, who were the creditors.

"I reject the idea of a contract or bargain between the creditors and the country in the transaction of commutation, for there was no equality of position or advantage between the parties. Their relations were reversed. The army had been the defenders of the country—the country had now become the protector and guardian of the army. I agree that the embarrassments of the country excused it from paying or sustaining the commutation certificates nine years, and that it did wisely and well in then paying them to the holders; but the debt being one of gratitude and honor, it remained, nevertheless, and remained due to the officers who, under the pressure of poverty, resulting from the public distress—not any fault of their own—had sold their certificates for nominal values. The obligation to pay the officers, or to reimburse them to the extent of their annuities for life, revived with the renewed or restored ability and strength of the country. In the blaze of the revolutionary light now thrown upon the subject, the subtilties and refinements which have obscured and perplexed it disappear; such as this, that equal debts are due to other classes of officers more meritorious than those now to be paid; that equal debts are due to the militia and to the common creditors of the country; that it ought to be paid, not to the children of the officers, but to the officers themselves; and if to children, then equally to grandchildren, when children do not survive; and that it ought to be paid neither to the officers nor to the children, but to the creditors; and that some persons who are rich and great will be made richer by an act whose general operation will be to benefit and bless the poor and lowly, and that some of the officers who, in the person of their children, will be the recipients of this benefaction, were personally unworthy, and that agents and speculators will profit by it. *The bill stands on the policy established by Washington, after a full trial of opposing theories and speculations.*

"So far as practicable, consistently with reconciling conflicting objections, the bill is guarded against alleged abuses and dangers. Either these claims stand on the basis of a moral obligation which imperatively requires the assumption of Congress, or they stand on the basis of a debt actually existing, but needing provision for its payment. In either case Congress may rightfully direct the discharge of the obligation or the debt in the manner most agreeable to equity and good conscience. To those, if there be any, who cannot consent to pay these claims, amounting in the aggregate to two and a half millions, because they fear that many others will remain unpaid, I recall the sorrow of Lord Bacon on a similar occasion: 'Would to God that 1 were hooded, that I saw less, or that I could perform more, for now I see occasion of service, but cannot fly, because I am tied to another fist.' To those, if any, who shall object the lapse of time, I reply, in the language of one who, though he had served his king too well, and was starving on his unperformed engagements, was rebuked for unreasonable importunity: 'Your good promises sleep, which it may seem now no time to awaken, but that I do not find any general calendar of observation of time serveth for a court.' To those, if there be such, who know no policy in the finance of a free country always prosperous and rich because always at peace, but that parsimony which unjustly confiscates in civil administration that it may have the necessary means for war and oppression, I beg leave to say, that it was justly held in Rome that a State was contained in two words, *præmium* and *poena*, and that this principle has come to be a part of our own religion by our acceptance of the precept which teaches that governors are sent by the Supreme Ruler for the punishment of evil doers, and for the praise of them that do well.

"Mr. President, we have framed statues of brass and iron which present. Washington to the beholder as a general, as a statesman, as a magistrate, and as a citizen. We have pierced the skies with monuments of marble and of granite in honor of his name. We have imposed it upon villages, towns, cites, a State, and a capital that is becoming the glory of the world ; but, if I do not altogether mistake his genius, the fulfilment of his predictions and promises,—made when he was taking leave of the companions of his labors and sufferings, that this country would be just, and would ultimately redeem the pledges it had given them,—will be more acceptable to his serene and awful shade than all the tributes which have been paid, and all that are yet to be paid, by a redeemed nation and a grateful world."

THE UNITED STATES COURT OF CLAIMS.

Half-pay claims, under the various resolutions of the Continental Congress have been, and now are being prosecuted in the United States Court of claims, sitting at Washington, ever since its establishment by Congress, and interest is charged by the claimants per act June 3, 1784, on each annual payment of the half-pay for life, as it fell due during the life of the officer, and on the whole thus due at the time of his death up to the present time, or until payment is made by the government.

The first case tried in this court on this principle, was that of the heirs of Surgeon Absalom Baird, of Pennsylvania, who was a surgeon in Colonel Jeduthan Baldwin's Corps of Artificers, and furnishes the most interesting and important information to the heirs of all the officers of the medical department and the different corps of artificers of the Revolutionary army, and establishes an important precedent relating to the great question of Revolutionary half-pay, which is at this time engaging the attention of the whole country.

The facts in the case, found among the papers filed in the court, are as follows:

That Absalom Baird was a commissioned surgeon in the army of the Revolution, and by acts of Congress, particularly that of January 17, 1781, became entitled to half-pay for life and other emoluments.

That his regiment was dissolved, and he was discharged from service on the 29th of March, 1781; and his stipulated annuity commenced running on that day.

That, as amounts became due, he made immediate and frequent applications to the proper officers for payment, and was denied.

That, by the laws and regulations of the old Congress, interest was allowed on all claims and to all creditors of the United States, from the time that sums became due.

That Dr. Baird, therefore, ought of right to have received his accruing half-pay, and interest upon any amounts refused or withheld.

That, by the commutation act, passed March 22, 1783, it was provided that the officers shall have, at the end of the war, five years' full pay, in lieu of half-pay for life, in money or securities.

That, by this new contract Dr. Baird became entitled, not only to the arrears of half-pay then due him, but also to five years' full pay, being the granted commutation of his half-pay for life.

That he was denied the benefit of this substitution. Payment was refused, and after repeated demands, and continued efforts with the accounting officers, he at length, on the 28th of January, 1794, presented his petition to Congress for relief. The case was continued without action by the House until December 21, 1796, when it was ordered that Dr. Baird have leave to withdraw his petition.

That the claim was never abandoned, nor was there any *laches* or unreasonable delay in the prosecution of it.

That Dr. Baird removed to Western Pennsylvania, and there died, in October, 1805.

That the claim was continued to be prosecuted by his children, but no action could be had until June 23, 1836, when an act was passed granting five years' full pay as *commutation*, but *without* interest.

That under this law $2400 were paid, but the petitioners believing that a large sum was still due, on the 12th of December, 1837, presented themselves again to Congress, praying further and full relief.

That on the 9th of February, 1855, a bill granting the heirs of Dr. Baird the sum of $16,230, in full of arrears of pay due to them for the services of their said ancestor, was reported in their favor.

That the said bill did not pass into a law, and has been referred by a resolution of Congress to this honorable court, for the purpose of an examination into the *merits and legal validity of the claim.*

That the half-pay of Dr. Baird was the sum of $240 per annum, receivable at the end of every year. If not discharged upon demand, at the time when payable, interest upon the amount due was the legal compensation to the creditor. Not only universal custom, but positive law, in all commercial countries, has established this principle.

That the proper distinction between grasping usury and fixed interest is well settled and understood.

That the first act of Parliament limiting the rate per cent. in England, was passed in 1546, near the close of the reign of Henry VIII. Since that time, with a short interval, in which superstition revived, the whole matter has been subject to statutory regulations. In fact, it may be considered doubtful, whether always, at common law, compensation for the "*detainer*" of money was not allowed as damages. One authority (2d Blackstone's Reports, page 761) may be referred to as most brief in its terms: "Interest is due upon all liquidated sums from the time the principal becomes due and payable."

That the revolutionary government has always acted upon this just basis; and the United States since, in the case of the Virginia officers, gave a pertinent example, in the act of July 5, 1832, by directing, "*to be paid to those officers, or their representatives, interest upon each year's half-pay, from the time the same became due.*"

That, assuming this rule of justice and upright policy to be clearly established, the following exhibit is made: From March 29, 1781, to October 20, 1805, the day of Dr. Baird's death, the total of his half-pay then due would amount to more than $5280, and the interest accrued on the yearly deferred payments would be $4150; making an aggregate of debt, at that time, of $10,030, by the terms of the government contract, expressed in the resolutions, and according to the settled rules of computation.

That death closed this annuity on the 20th October, 1805; and at the date of that event, the representatives of Dr. Baird had an immediate right to this sum, by the laws of the land. With merely simple interest current, up to June 23, 1836, it would amount to $28,485; and deducting $2400, allowed by the act of that date, would still leave $26,085 *then* fairly due.

That in Thorndike *vs.* United States, Justice Story observes: "If the present were a contract between private citizens, there can be no doubt that the court would be bound to give interest upon the contract up to the time of payment; and if by law the amount due on the contract could be pleaded as a tender or a set-off to a private debt, it would be a good bar in the full extent of the principal and interest due at the time of such tender or set off. Nay, more; if the note or promise were made by a citizen to the government, the latter might enforce its claim to the like extent. Can it make any difference, in the construction of the contract, that the government is the debtor instead of the creditor? In reason and equity it ought to make none, and there is not a scintilla of law to justify any. If a suit could be maintained against the government, I do not perceive why it would not be as much the duty of the court to render judgment in such suit, for the principal and the interest, in the same manner and to the same extent as it would in the case of a private citizen.— *The United States have no prerogative to claim one law upon their own contracts as creditors and another as debtors. If, as creditors, they are entitled to interest, as debtors they are bound also to pay it.*"

That Attorney-general Wirt says : "Interest is in the nature of damages for withholding money which the party ought to pay, and would not or could not ;" and in this brief sentence is contained the main point of the case now presented to this honorable court.

That it is claimed, that from and after March 29, 1781, the day on which he was reduced, Dr. Baird was entitled by governmental contract to half-pay during his life, payable at the end of every year; and according to the rule directed by the act of July 5, 1832, in the case of the Virginia officers or their representatives, with interest on each year's half-pay from the time the same became due.

In the above light the case came up before the court for a trial, the Solicitor of the court, on the part of the United States, at the same time filing his opposing brief, and after the arguments on both sides, the case was submitted, and Chief-justice Gilchrist delivered the following opinion of the court :

The petitioner alleges that his father, Dr. Absalom Baird, was a commissioned surgeon in the army of the Revolution, and in that capacity was entitled by law to half-pay for life, and other emoluments.

Whether this allegation be true, is the first inquiry in the case.

It is not denied that he was a surgeon of a regiment of artificers, and was discharged from the service, upon the reduction of his regiment, on the 29th of March, 1781.

Whether this corps constituted a part of the army, so as to entitle the surgeon, upon its reduction to half-pay for life, is a point to be determined by an examination into the manner in which it was considered by the legislative authority at the time, and into the language of the resolution upon the subject.

The resolution of September 30, 1780, provides for "the pay and establishment of the officers of the Hospital Department and Medical Staff," and specifies the pay of the director, chief physicians, and surgeons of the army and hospitals, purveyor and apothecary, physicians and surgeons of the hospitals, assistant purveyors and apothecaries, regimental surgeons, surgeons' mates in the hospitals, surgeons' mates in the army, and steward and wardmaster for each hospital. As Dr. Baird rendered medical services to the United States, and in their employ, and in a position, at least, connected with the army, and as this was the only provision for the payment for medical services, and as he was entitled to compensation, he would seem to be necessarily included in the class of "regimental surgeons," particularly if there be any thing to corroborate this view of the case.

We think it cannot be denied that Dr. Baird was an "officer," and the resolution of the 21st of October, 1780, provides that the "officers reduced" shall be entitled to "half pay for life." This resolution had regard to the reform of the army, which was to take place on the 1st of January, 1781. Subsequent to this date, on the 17th of January, a resolution was passed, the preamble to which is as follows: "Whereas, by the plan for conducting the hospital department, passed in Congress the 30th day of September last, no proper establishment is provided for the *officers of the medical staff*, after their dismission from the public service, which, considering the customs of other nations, and the late provision made for the officers of the army, after the conclusion of the war, they appear to have a just claim to; for remedy whereof, and for amending several parts of the above-mentioned plan," it was provided that all officers in the hospital department and medical staff, hereinafter mentioned, who shall continue in service to the end of the war, or be reduced before that time as supernumeraries, shall be entitled to receive during life, in lieu of half-pay, the following allowance, &c. It was then provided that "regimental surgeons" should receive an allowance equal to half-pay of a captain. It is not at all probable that Congress intended to exclude from the benefit of this resolution the surgeon of the corps of artificers. Still, in order to entitle Dr. Baird to half-pay for life, he must be brought fairly within the class of regimental surgeons by reason of his connection with this corps. On the 12th of November, 1779, Congress resolved "that the eleven companies of artificers raised by the Quartermaster-general be reformed and incorporated and arranged in such a manner as the Commander-in-Chief shall deem proper." On the 3d of October, 1780, a resolution was passed providing for the reduction of certain regiments on the first of January then next, and that after that day the regular army of the United States should consist of "four regiments of cavalry or light-dragoons, four regiments of artillery, forty-nine regiments of infantry, and one regiment of artificers;" and that the regiment of artificers should consist of eight companies, and each company of sixty non-commissioned officers and privates.

These resolutions appear to us to be entirely conclusive. We do not see how any doubt can remain on the subject. This body of artificers is called a regiment, and is declared to be a part of the regular army. The surgeon of it, therefore, is a regimental surgeon, and if any thing more be necessary in order to constitute him such, we are at a loss to understand what it can be.

If these views be correct, as we think they are, when the regiment was reduced on the 29th of March, 1781, the surgeon of the regiment had a right to half-pay for life, which no subsequent legislation by Congress could, upon any principle of justice or legal reasoning, take away from him. It was a right earned by meritorious services, and conferred upon him in consideration of the sacrifice of his time and his talents for the good of the cause all had at heart. To say that any subsequent or declaratory legislation by Congress, as to the character of this corps, could deprive Dr. Baird of his half-pay to which he was entitled, would be to declare, not only that the precedents which a sense of justice had established in regard to the binding force of contracts might properly be disregarded—not only to maintain that the opinion and interest of one party to a contract might be substituted for the assent of both—but to assert, that notwithstanding all that had been said and done, there was no contract between Dr. Baird and Congress.

But we think that an analysis of the action that has been had upon the subject will show that there has not even been any declaratory law or resolution of Congress, which tends to the conclusion that Dr. Baird was not entitled to half-pay.

On the 19th of March, 1790, General Knox, the Secretary of War, reported a resolution to Congress, "That the petition of the late officers of the artillery artificers for the commutation of the half-pay cannot be granted, the United States in Congress assembled having decided against the same on the 19th October, 1785." He says that the principles upon which this decision was founded, will appear by the reports of the late Commissioner of Army Accounts, and a Committee of Congress, which he submits.

The report of the Commissioner was in consequence of the petitions of John Jordan and Thomas Wiley, late Captains in the Pennsylvania Corps of Artillery Artificers, for a commutation in lieu of half-pay for life. The substance of the report is, that Congress confined the promise of half-pay to *military* officers only, and that the officers of artificers were not military officers.

It may be remarked of the report, that it does not even by implication controvert Dr. Baird's claim, because it was made in relation to a class of officers to which confessedly he did not belong. No one ever supposed that a surgeon, either in the army or the navy, was in the strict sense of the word a military officer; and it is not upon that ground the present claim rests. The duty of a surgeon is to attend upon the sick and wounded, to employ his skill as well upon those who are enfeebled by disease, as upon those who are wounded in battle. The surgeon is no more a military officer when attached to an infantry regiment, than when on duty in the regiment of artificers, and he is as much a military officer in the latter case as when he is on duty at a garrison, or on a recruiting station. We are aware of no reason why Dr. Baird might not properly have been ordered upon any duty which any regimental surgeon might have been required to perform.

The report of the Committee of Congress, to which General Knox refers, denies the claim of Captain Jordan and Willey upon the same ground, that they were not military officers, and the same remarks are applicable to it.

General Knox also refers to a former report of his, dated on the 30th of July, 1788, in which he states, that the artificers were a part of the civil branch of the Ordnance Department; and also, that when the officers of this corps were commissioned as officers of "artillery and artificers," the manner of filling up the commissions must have been an error, as it was not authorized by any act of Congress. It is true, that there may have been no act of Congress pointing out the manner in which the commissions should be filled up; but it is not so clear that the mode in which they were filled up was authorized. His report states, that "the artificers did not in any instance act in the field as artillerists;" but it states, also, that "they were mostly stationed at the arsenal at Carlisle, and employed in making cartridges of various kinds for the use of the artillery in the field." It is not, then, a forced construction of their position which induced them to regard themselves as officers of "artillery and artificers," although whether they were properly so regarded or not has no bearing on the present case, as we shall hereafter have occasion to remark.

We are not called upon to decide whether Captain Jordan and Willey were or were not "military officers" in a sense which would entitle them to a commutation of half-pay. Whatever the decision might be, it could not have the slightest effect upon the question whether Dr. Baird was or was not a commissioned surgeon in the army of the Revolution. It may, however, be remarked, that as the resolution of October 3, 1780, provided that the regular army of the United States should consist of certain regiments of cavalry, artillery, infantry, and "one regiment of artificers," it is extremely difficult to understand how anything like logical reasoning can lead to the conclusion that the officers of the regiment, forming a part of the regular army, were not military officers, so as to entitle them to commutation. The "cotemporaneous construction," on which stress was laid in the argument, and which led the committee to decide that they were not military officers, is entitled to just so much weight as its intrinsic merits deserve, and no more. *Mankind are as competent now to judge of the meaning of words as they were then; and the executive and military departments of that day did not assume to possess any superior knowledge. There is no more mystery in the acts of Congress passed seventy years ago than in those of the present day, nor is any greater skill required to construe them.* But, at any rate, the case of Captain Jordan and Willey has no bearing whatever on the case of Dr. Baird.

For these reasons we are of opinion that Dr. Baird was entitled to half-pay for life, from the time of the reduction of his regiment, on the 29th of March, 1781.

The next question in the case is, whether the claimant is entitled to *interest.*

On the 3d of June, 1784, Congress passed the following resolution: "That an interest of six per cent. per annum shall be allowed to all creditors of the United States for supplies furnished or services done from the time that the payment became due." No language could be more express or free from doubt than this. It is directly applicable to the present case. Dr. Baird had rendered services to the United States, for which he was entitled to half-pay for life. *His half-pay became due at the expiration of a year from the time of his reduction, and at the end of each successive year thereafter.* The resolution was passed, from a feeling that it was just and right that interest should be paid from the time that half-pay became due, and it was a *voluntary contract on the part of the United States*, constituting a legal claim against them, which no subsequent legislation could release without the assent of the other party. It may be added, that up to the year 1837, there was paid interest on 1510 claims of widows and orphans, and claims of officers for personal services, the *statutes of limitations as to such claims having been suspended.* The proceedings in relation to the claim for commutation do not appear to be very material in relation to the case in its present position. On the 23d of March, 1783, a resolution was passed providing that the officers and others entitled to half-pay for life, "shall be entitled to receive at the end of the war their five years' full pay, in lieu of half-pay for life, in money—that is specie—or in securities on interest, as Congress should find most convenient." On the 28th of January, 1794, Dr. Baird applied for the benefit of this provision, but died in the year 1805, having, as is said in the report of the Committee of Claims of the 5th of February, 1855, "become wearied and disheartened with delay." In the year 1818, his son, Thomas H. Baird, having become of age, petitioned Congress for relief, and on the 3d of March, 1835, the committee reported that, "Dr. Absalom Baird was entitled to the benefit of the provision of the resolution of January 17, 1781, extending the grant of half-pay for life to the officers of the hospital department and medical staff." No action was had upon the resolution until the 22d June, 1836, when an act was passed granting five years' full pay as commutation, under the resolution of 1783, *but without interest.*

Now this claim does not depend for its validity upon any admission contained in the act of 1836. But the Congress which passed that act must have considered that Dr. Baird had a legal claim of some kind, otherwise their conduct in granting him five years' full pay was wholly indefensible. It is, however, relied upon as a final settlement of the claim. Upon any principle known to the law, this position is wholly untenable. It is easy enough to declare, *ex-cathedra,* that it was a final settlement; but it is extremely difficult to imagine, in the absence of all evidence, what reasons can be urged for holding that the payment of a sum of money is of itself a discharge of a debt for a larger amount. *A plea of payment of a small sum in satisfaction of a larger, is bad even after verdict.* This principle is familiar to every lawyer. A debt may be paid by a fair and well-understood compromise, carried faithfully into effect; but here there was no compromise. If it were a case between individuals, no one would dream of applying such a term to it. The United States are either bound by principles of law applicable to them, or they are not so bound. If they are not bound, there is an end of the discussion, for then all reasoning is fruitless. If they are bound by principles of law, it is impossible to regard the payment of five years' full pay without interest as a satisfaction of this claim. There is no evidence that either party so regarded it, and unless we set at defiance every principle of law, we cannot hold that one party to a contract, without the assent of the other, can discharge his debt by the payment of a smaller sum than the amount due.

If A owes B a thousand dollars by his promissory note, payable in ten years, with interest, and if, when the note becomes due, A pays five hundred dollars, but refuses to pay the remainder and the interest, upon the principle here contended for, the payment of five hundred dollars discharges the debt. Such a proposition, to be refuted, needs only to be stated.

If Dr. Baird was entitled to commutation under this resolution, he should have received either the money or securities, as Congress should find most convenient. They did not find it convenient to pay the money at the time, and of course he was entitled to interest. He asked either for the money or securities on interest, but Congress permitted fifty-three years to elapse after the passage of the resolution, and then gave him merely the sum of $2400, to which he was entitled in the year 1783. Mr. Ready's report, of the 5th of February, 1855, considers only the question whether interest should be allowed on the five years' full pay as commutation from the end of the war, the time when it became due, and the committee decided that interest was due. But as our opinion is that Dr. Baird was entitled to half-pay for life, from the 29th of March, 1781, the matter relating to the commutation need not be further inquired into.

The evidence in the case proves, that Dr. Baird was surgeon of the regiment of artificers from the 20th of March, 1780, and served in that capacity until the regiment was reduced, on the 29th of March, 1781. It is admitted by the solicitor, and the evidence proves, that the case *does not come within any of the acts or resolutions in the nature of acts of limitation*, which requires claims to be presented within a specified period, and *is not barred by any of them*. It is admitted that Dr. Baird died on the 27th of October, 1805; and it is proved that the claimant, Thomas H. Baird, was appointed administrator of his estate on the 9th day of March, 1819.

The amount of Dr. Baird's half-pay was $240 per annum, payable at the end of every year. *He was entitled to this sum up to the 27th of October, 1805, the day of his death, and interest on the payments as they became due, according to the express provisions of the resolution of June 3, 1784.*

There was, therefore, due him at the time of his death the sum of $10,074$\frac{74}{100}$. *Upon this sum interest is due from the 27th of October, 1805, to the 1st of June, 1856, deducting therefrom the sum of $2400, paid under the act of June 23, 1836.*

It will be seen that the accounting officers of the Government, cotemporaneous with the commutation act of 1783, decided that, from the nature of the corps in which Dr. Baird served, and on the ground that he was not a "regimental surgeon," he was not entitled to the benefits of that act.

His title to commutation was never admitted until the second session of the 23d Congress, when a favorable report was made; and it was not until June 23, 1836, that a bill passed granting him this commutation.

Every one will agree that, inasmuch as Dr. Baird did not receive his commutation of half-pay until June 23, 1836, interest was justly due on it from the Revolutionary period up to that time, as has been allowed in nearly every similar case from 1794 to the present day.

But the difference between Dr. Baird's case and that of the other officers of the Revolutionary army is, that the other officers received their commutation at the time it was first made due, and therefore *were not* entitled to interest for *time delayed* in the issuing of their commutation certificates, while Dr. Baird did not receive his till 1836, and therefore *was entitled* to interest for *time delayed* from 1783 to 1836.

And Dr. Baird has been restored to his half-pay from March 29, 1781, to October 27, 1805, when he died, with interest on each annual payment to the day of his death, and has been allowed interest also on the whole sum, thus accumulated at the time of his death, up to June 1, 1856, when payment was made, deducting from the whole amount the sum of $2400, as commutation received in 1836.

To this restoration of the half-pay for life with interest, Dr. Baird has no better right than the other officers, who now claim the action of Congress and the Court of Claims in his case as a precedent for their own.

For the information of the many thousands of the heirs of Revolutionary officers and others in the United States interested, a great many of whom may have, as yet, heard little or nothing of the proceedings, we have reported the action of Congress and the opinion of the Court of Claims on these half-pay cases somewhat at length, for our limits, and may further remark that, from what has been admitted on all sides, and assuming the opinion of Attorney-general Berrieh, under date of October 2, 1830, in the case of Colonel Harrison, to be correct, viz., "*No interest is due unless the claimant shall have paid interest; in which case, indeed, interest becomes strictly a portion of the principal of his claim,*" the right of the officers to a restoration of their half-pay, and an allowance of interest on the deferred payment from the Revolutionary period, cannot be disputed ; for the officers, in the sale of their securities, did pay a heavy interest in depreciation, equal in amount, in a majority of cases, to seven-eighths of the *face* of their certificates.

THE SOCIETY OF THE CINCINNATI.

This institution is so intimately connected with affairs at the close of the Revolution, and with preparations for the return of the country to the pursuits of peace, after emerging from the conflicts of an eight years' war, that some account of it, in this connection, may be proper, and to many instructive.

It was in the period of the government of ancient Rome by the "Tribunes of the People," before the appointment of the Decemviri, that Coriolanus, an eloquent and powerful senator. was expelled from the commonwealth, and took shelter with Tullus Attius, a distinguished Volscian leader, who espoused his quarrel. In consequence, the league between this country and the Romans was broken, and a powerful Volscian army was sent to invade Rome, headed by the expatriated Coriolanus, who, yielding to the tears and entreaties of Veturia his mother and Volumnia his wife, withdrew his army from Rome.

But a restoration of peace to the commonwealth, and a cessation of hostilities without, only gave opportunity for intrigue and dissension within. Spurius Cassius, fired with wild ambition, and wanting to make himself despotic by means of the people, was found guilty of a number of conspiracies against the Constitution of the State, and was thrown headlong from the Tarpian Rock by the very persons whose interests he represented.

The Agrarian law, a measure for dividing the lands of the commonwealth equally among the people, now agitated the country, and Manlius and Fabius, consuls of a former year, accused of making unjustifiable delays in putting it off, were summoned by the Tribunes to appear before the people.

This law was a grant the Senate could not think of giving up to the people, and the many excuses and delays made about it,

SOCIETY OF THE CINCINNATI. 469

incensed the people so as to threaten the destruction of the commonwealth.

In this alarming state of things, they were obliged once more to have recourse to a dictator, and LUCIUS QUINTUS CINCINNATUS, an illustrious Roman, who had given up all views of ambition, and retired to his little farm, was waited upon by the deputies of the Senate, who found him at his plough, dressed in the mean attire of a laboring husbandman. He appeared but little elevated at the address of ceremony and pompous robes they brought him, and upon declaring to him the Senate's pleasure, he testified a natural preferment of the charms of a country retirement to the fatiguing splendors of office, and said to his wife, as the deputies were leading him away, "I fear, my Attilla, that for this year, our little fields must remain unsown." Thus, taking a tender leave, he departed to the city, where both parties were inflamed against each other. By strict attention to the interests of his country, instead of gaining the confidence of factions, he won the esteem of all; and by prevailing on the Tribunes to put off the Agrarian law for a time, restored tranquillity to the people, and again retired from the splendors of power to his "little farm."

"The Æqui and the Volsci," writes Goldsmith, "who, though still worsted, still were for renewing the war, made new inroads into the territories of Rome. Minutius, one of the consuls who succeeded Cincinnatus, was sent to oppose them; but being naturally timid, and rather more afraid of being conquered than desirous of victory, his army was driven into a defile between two mountains, from which, except through the enemy, there was no egress. This, however, the Æqui had the precaution to fortify, by which the Roman army was so hemmed in on every side, that nothing remained but submission to the enemy, famine, or immediate death. Some knights, who found means of getting away privately through the enemy's camp, were the first who brought the account of this disaster to Rome. Nothing could exceed the consternation of all ranks of the people when informed of it: the Senate, at first, thought of the other consul;

but not having sufficient experience of his abilities, they unanimously turned their eyes on Cincinnatus, and again resolved to make him dictator. Cincinnatus, the only person on whom Rome could now place her whole dependence, was found, as before, by the messengers of the Senate laboring in his little field with cheerful industry. He was at first astonished at the ensigns of unbounded power with which the deputies came to invest him, but still more at the approach of the Senate, who came out to meet him. A dignity so unlooked for, however, had no effect on the simple integrity of his manners.

"Upon entering the city, the dictator put on a serene look, and entreated all those who were able to bear arms to repair before sunset to the Campus Martius with the necessary provisions for five days. He put himself at the head of these, and marching all night with great expedition, arrived before day within sight of the enemy. Upon his approach he ordered his soldiers to raise a loud shout, to apprise the consul's army of the relief that was at hand. The Æqui were not a little amazed when they saw themselves between two enemies, but still more when they perceived Cincinnatus making the strongest intrenchments beyond them to prevent their escape, and inclosing them as they had inclosed the consul. To prevent this, a furious combat ensued; but the Æqui being attacked on both sides, and unable to resist or fly, begged a cessation of arms; they offered the dictator his own terms; he gave them their lives, but obliged them, in token of servitude, to pass under the yoke.— Their captains and generals he made prisoners of war, being reserved to adorn his triumph. As for the plunder of the enemy's camp, that he gave entirely to his own soldiers, without reserving any part for himself, or permitting those of the delivered army to have a share.

"Thus, having rescued a Roman army from inevitable destruction, having defeated a powerful enemy, having taken and fortified their city, and still more, having refused any part of the spoil, he resigned the dictatorship, after having enjoyed it but fourteen days. The Senate would have enriched him, but he declined their offers, choosing to retire once more to his farm and cottage, content with temperance and fame."

It has been beautifully said that "Providence moves through time as the gods of Homer through space—it takes one step and ages have rolled away;" and though it has rolled twenty-three centuries between the illustrious farmer of Rome and our own immortal farmer of Mount Vernon, yet, in the night-march of the former to the aid of the despairing army of Minutius, and in that of the latter, over the storm-lashed and icy billows of the Delaware, on the Hessian encampment at Trenton, the same "Arcturus, Orion, Pleiades, and the chambers of the South," known also in the days of the patient man of Uz, still perpetuated by the same moving Providence, enlightened both armies; and the gaze of both generals has rested upon the same constellations, so that time, by similitude of circumstances and character, seems to have been so far annihilated as to bring the two to stand contemporaneously on the great platform of human liberty, and to a personal recognition of each other in the great Society of Peace, bearing the name of the one and presided over by the other, whose valedictory proclaimed, that, "Having finished the work assigned me, I retire from the great theatre of action, and bidding an affectionate farewell to this august body, under whose orders I have so long acted, I here offer my commission, and take leave of all the public employments of life"—and of whom it was said, when the "clods of the valley" were about to cover all of him that was mortal: "Our virtuous Chief, mindful only of the common good, in a moment of tempting personal aggrandizement, hushed the discontents of growing sedition; and, surrendering his power into the hands from which he had received it, converted his sword into a ploughshare, teaching an admiring world that to be truly great, you must be truly good."

The following is the Constitution of the Society of the Cincinnati, agreed upon at the "Cantonment of the American Army, on Hudson River, May 13, 1783."

SOCIETY OF THE CINCINNATI.

It having pleased the Supreme Governor of the Universe, in the disposition of human affairs, to cause the separation of the Colonies of North America from the domination of Great Britain, and after a bloody conflict of eight years, to establish them free, independent, and sovereign States, connected, by alliances founded on reciprocal advantages, with some of the greatest princes and powers of the earth.

To perpetuate, therefore, as well the remembrance of this vast event, as the mutual friendships which have been formed under the pressure of common danger, and in many instances cemented by the blood of the parties, the officers of the American army do hereby, in the most solemn manner, associate, constitute, and combine themselves into one SOCIETY OF FRIENDS, to endure as long as they shall endure, or any of their eldest male prosterity, and in failure thereof, the collateral branches, who may be judged worthy of becoming its supporters and members.

The officers of the American army, having generally been taken from the citizens of America, possess high veneration for the character of that illustrious Roman, LUCIUS QUINTUS CINCINNATUS; and being resolved to follow his example, by returning to their citizenship, they think they may, with propriety, denominate themselves THE SOCIETY OF THE CINCINNATI.

The following principles shall be immutable, and form the basis of the Society of the Cincinnati:

An incessant attention to preserve inviolate those exalted rights and liberties of human nature, for which they have fought and bled, and without which the high rank of a rational being is a curse instead of a blessing.

An unalterable determination to promote and cherish, between the respective States, that union and national honor so essentially necessary to their happiness, and the future dignity of the American empire.

To render permanent the cordial affection subsisting among the officers. This spirit will dictate brotherly kindness in all things, and particularly extend to the most substantial acts of beneficence, according to the ability of the Society, towards those officers and their families who unfortunately may be under the necessity of receiving it.

The General Society will, for the sake of frequent communications, be divided into State Societies, and those again into such districts as shall be directed by the State Society.

The societies of the districts to meet as often as shall be agreed upon by the State Society; those of the State on the fourth day of July annually, or oftener, if they shall find it expedient; and the General Society on the first Monday in May, annually, so long as they shall deem it necessary, and afterwards, at least once in every three years.

At each meeting the principles of the institution will be fully considered, and the best measures to promote them adopted.

The State Societies will consist of all the members resident in each State respectively; and any member removing from one State to another, is to be considered, in all respects, as belonging to the Society of the State in which he shall actually reside.

The State Societies to have a president, vice-president, secretary, treasurer, and assistant treasurer, to be chosen annually by a majority of votes, at the State meeting.

Each State shall write annually, or oftener, if necessary, a circular letter to the other State Societies, noting whatever they may think worthy of observation, respecting the good of the Society, or the general union of the States, and giving information of the officers chosen for the current year. Copies of these letters shall be regularly transmitted to the secretary-general of the Society, who will record them in a book to be assigned for that purpose.

The State Society will regulate every thing respecting itself and the societies of the districts, consistent with the general maxims of the Cincinnati; judge of the qualifications of the members who may be proposed; and expel any member who by conduct inconsistent with a gentleman and a man of honor, or by an opposition to the interests of the community in general, or the Society in particular, may render himself unworthy to continue a member.

In order to form funds which may be respectable, and assist the unfortunate, each officer shall deliver to the treasurer of the State Society one month's pay, which shall remain forever to the use of the State Society; the interest only of which, if necessary, to be appropriated to the relief of the unfortunate.

Donations may be made by persons not of the Society, and by members of the Society, for the express purposes of forming permanent funds for the use of the State Society; and the interest of these donations appropriated in the same manner as that of the month's pay.

Moneys, at the pleasure of each member, may be subscribed in the societies of the districts, or the State Societies, for the relief of the unfortunate members, or their widows and orphans, to be appropriated by the State Society only.

The meeting of the General Society shall consist of its officers, and a representation from each State Society, in number not exceeding five, whose expenses shall be borne by their respective State Societies.

In the general meeting, the president, vice-president, secretary, assistant secretary, treasurer, and assistant treasurer-general, shall be chosen, to serve until the next meeting.

The circular letters which have been written by the respective State Societies to each other, and their particular laws, shall be read and considered, and all measures concerted which may conduce to the general intendment of the society.

It is probable that some persons may make donations to the General Society, for the purpose of establishing funds for the further comfort of the unfortunate; in which case such donations must be placed in the hands of the treasurer-general, the interest only of which is to be disposed of, if necessary, by the general meeting.

All the officers of the American army, as well as those who have resigned with honor, after three years' service in the capacity of officers, or who have been deranged by the resolutions of Congress, upon the several reforms of the army, as those who shall have continued to the end of the war, have the right to become parties in this institution; provided that they subscribe one month's pay, and sign their names to the general rules, in their respective State Societies,—those who are present with the army immediately, and others within six months after the army shall be disbanded, extraordinary cases excepted. The rank, time of service, resolutions of Congress by which they have been deranged, and place of residence, must be added to each name; and as a testimony of affection to the memory and the offspring of such officers as have died in the service, their eldest male branches shall have the same right of becoming members as the children of the actual members of the Society.

Those officers who are foreigners, not resident in any of the States, will have their names enrolled by the secretary-general, and are to be considered as members in the societies of any of the States in which they may happen to be.

And as there are, and will at all times be, men in the respective States, eminent for their abilities and patriotism, whose views may be directed to the same laudable objects with those of the Cincinnati, it shall be a rule to admit such characters as honorary members of the Society, for their own lives only: Provided always, that the number of honorary members in each State does not exceed a ratio of one to four of the officers or their descendants.

Each State Society shall obtain a list of its members, and, at the first annual meeting, the State secretary shall have engrossed, on parchment, two copies of the institution of the Society, which every member present shall sign; and the secretary shall endeavor to procure the signature of every absent member; one of those lists to be transmitted to the secretary-general, to be kept in the archives of the Society, and the other to remain in the hands of the State secretary. From the State lists, the secretary-general must make out, at the first general meeting, a complete list of the whole Society, with a copy of which he will furnish each State secretary.

The Society shall have an Order, by which its members shall be known and distinguished, which shall be a medal, of gold, of a proper size to receive the emblems, and suspended by a deep-blue ribbon, two inches wide, edged with white, descriptive of the union of America and France, viz :

The principal figure, CINCINNATUS; three senators presenting him with a sword and other military ensigns: on a field in the background his wife standing at the door of their cottage; near it a plough and implements of husbandry. Round the whole, *Omnia reliquit sevare Rempublicam*. On the reverse: Sun rising; a city with open gates, and vessels entering the port; Fame crowning Cincinnatus with a wreath, inscribed *Virtutis Præmium*. Below, Hands joined, supporting a Heart, with the motto, *Esto Perpetua*. Round the whole, *Societas Cincinnatorum Instituta*, A. D. 1783.

The Society, deeply impressed with a sense of the generous assistance this country has received from France, and desirous of perpetuating the friendships which have been formed and so happily subsisted between the officers of the allied forces, in the prosecution of the war, direct, that the President-general transmit, as soon as may be, to each of the characters hereafter named, a medal containing the order of the Society, viz.:

His Excellency the Chevalier De La Luzerne, Minister Plenipotentiary;

His Excellency the Sieur Gerard, late Minister Plenipotentiary:

Their Excellencies the Count D'Estaing,
   the Count De Grasse,
   the Count De Barras,
   the Chevalier De Touches,
     Admirals and Commanders in the Navy;

His Excellency the Count De Rochambeau, Commander-in-Chief; And the Generals and Colonels of his army, and acquaint them that the Society does themselves the honor to consider them as members.

SOCIETY OF THE CINCINNATI. 477

Resolved, That a copy of the foregoing institution be given to the senior officer of each State Line, and that the officers of the respective State Lines sign their names to the same, in the manner and form following; viz:

We, the subscribers, officers of the American army, do hereby voluntarily become parties to the foregoing institution, and do bind ourselves to observe, and be governed by, the principles therein contained. For the performance whereof we do solemnly pledge to each other our sacred honor.

Done in the Cantonment on Hudson River, in the year 1783.

General Heath, General Baron De Steuben, and General Knox, were appointed to wait on His Excellency General Washington, with a copy of the Institution, and request him to honor the Society by placing his name at the head of it.

The following are the names of the different officers of the General Society from its formation, with the dates of their election:

PRESIDENTS.

George Washington,	1783.
Alexander Hamilton,	1800.
Charles C. Pinckney,	1805.
Thomas Pinckney,	1825.
Aaron Ogden,	1829.
Morgan Lewis,	1839.
William Popham,	1844.
Henry A. S. Dearborn,	1848.

SECRETARIES.

Henry Knox,	1783.
William Jackson,	1800.
Alexander W. Johnston,	1829.

TREASURERS.

Alexander McDougall,	1783.
William McPherson,	1800.
Allen McLane,	1823.
John Markland,	1832.
Joseph W. Scott	1838.

VICE-PRESIDENTS.

Horatio Gates,	1784.
Thomas Mifflin,	1787.
Charles C. Pinckney,	1800.
Henry Knox,	1805.
J. Brooks,	1811.
Aaron Ogden,	1825.
Morgan Lewis,	1829.
William Schute,	1839.
Horace Binney,	1844.
Hamilton Fish,	1848.

ASSISTANT SECRETARIES.

Otho H. Williams,	1784.
George Turner,	1787.
William McPherson,	1790.
Nathan Dorsey,	1800.
Thomas McEwen.	1829.

478   SOCIETY OF THE CINCINNATI.

The following form of subscribing to the State Societies was adopted in 1783, and following it we will give the names of the original members in some of the State Societies, viz.:

"To JOHN PIERCE, ESQ., Paymaster Gen. to the army of the United States.

"SIR:—Please pay to ———, Treasurer for the ——— State Association of the Cincinnati, or his order, one month's pay of our several grades respectively, and deduct the same from the balance which shall be found due to us on the final liquidation of our accounts; for which this shall be your warrant."

LIST OF ORIGINAL MEMBERS OF THE NEW YORK STATE SOCIETY OF THE CINCINNATI.

Jonas Addoms, Lieutenant, 2d Regiment, New York Artillery.
Peter Anspach,   do.   do.   do.   do.
Aaron Aorson, Captain, 1st Regiment New York.
Josiah Bagley, Lieutenant,   do.   do.
John Bard, Captain, 2d Regiment, Georgia.
Sebastian Bauman, Major, 2d Regiment, New York Artillery.
Jerrick Beekman, Lieutenant,   do.   do.   do.
William Belknap, Lieutenant, Livingston's Regiment.
Walter Bicker, Captain, Patton's Regiment.
Leonard Bleeker, Captain, 1st New York Regiment.
James Bradford, Lieutenant and Adjutant, New York Artillery.
James Brewster, Captain-lieutenant,   do.   do.
David Brooks, Assistant Clothier-general.
Joseph Browne, Surgeon, 7th Pennsylvania Regiment.
Robert Burnett, Lieutenant, New York Artillery.
Jonathan Burrall, Deputy Paymaster-general.
Caleb Brewster, Captain-lieutenant, New York Artillery.
Aaron Burr, Lieutenant-colonel, Malcom's Regiment, New York.
Duncan Campbell, Lieutenant-colonel, Livingston's Regiment, New York.
John Cape, Lieutenant, 1st Regiment, New Jersey.
Nehemiah Carpenter, Ensign, New York Artillery.
James Chrystie, Captain, 2d Pennsylvania Regiment.
Matthew Clarkson, Major.
James Clinton, Brigadier-general.
George Clinton, Honorary Member.
Alexander Clinton, Lieutenant, New York Artillery.
Christopher Codwise, Lieutenant,   do.   do.
Robert Cochran, Lieutenant colonel, 2d Regiment, New York.

John Cochran, Director of Hospital.
William Colbreath, Lieutenant and Quartermaster, 2d Regiment, N. Y.
Michael Connolly, Lieutenant, 2d Regiment, New York.
John Conway, Lieutenant-colonel, 1st Regiment, N. J.
Samuel Cooper, Lieutenant, Crane's Artillery.
Andrew Cragie, Surgeon, General Hospital.
John D. Crimshier, Paymaster, Lamb's New York Artillery.
Ebenezer Crosby, Surgeon, Washington's Life Guard.
Henry Cunningham, New York Artillery.
James Davidson, Commissary, Hospital Department.
Henry Demler, Lieutenant, New York Artillery.
Daniel Denniston,   do.   do.   do.
George J. Denniston, Lieutenant, 3d New York Regiment.
Pierre Regnier De Rousse, Lieutenant-colonel, 2d Regiment, New York.
Simeon De Witt, Geographer.
Samuel Dodge, Lieutenant, 2d Regiment New York.
Samuel Dodge, Ensign,   do.   do.
John Doughty, Captain, New York Artillery.
Henry Dubois, Captain, 2d New York Regiment.
Edward Dunscomb, Captain, 4th do.   do.
Baron Charles D'Aurier, French officer.
John Elliott, Surgeon's Mate, 1st Regiment, New York.
Andrew English, Captain-lieutenant, 1st Massachusetts Regiment.
James Fairlie, Lieutenant, 2d New York Regiment, and Aid-de-Camp to Major-general Baron Steuben.
Ephraim Fenno, Captain-lieutenant, New York Artillery.
Nicholas Fish, Major and Brigade Inspector, New York.
George Fleming, Captain, New York Artillery.
John Fondy, Ensign, 1st New York Regiment.
Duoy Fondy,   do.   do.   do.
Joseph Foote, Lieutenant, 1st Massachusetts Regiment.
Theodocius Fowler, Captain, 2d New York Regiment.
Joseph Frelick, Lieutenant,   do.   do.
John Furman, Lieutenant, 1st New York Regiment.
John Gano, Brigade Chaplain, New York.
David Gano, Captain-lieutenant, New York Artillery.
Peter Gansevoort, Colonel, 3d New York Regiment.
Benjamin Gilbert, Lieutenant, 1st New York Regiment.
James Giles, Lieutenant, 2d Regiment New York Artillery.
Aquilla Giles, Lieutenant-colonel and Aid-de-Camp.
John Graham, Major, 1st New York Regiment.
Charles Graham, Captain, New York Line.
Stephen Graham, Hospital Mate.

Silas Gray, Captain, 4th New York Regiment.
John W. Greaton, Captain, Massachusetts Line.
John Green, Naval Captain.
James Gregg, Captain, 1st New York Regiment.
James Grier, Lieutenant-colonel, Pennsylvania Line.
John Grier, Lieutenant, 6th Pennsylvania Regiment.
Isaac Guion, Captain-lieutenant, Lamb's Artillery.
Hoysted Hacker, Naval Captain.
Mordecai Hale, Surgeon's Mate.
Jonathan Hallett, Captain, 2d Regiment, New York.
Luther Halsey, Captain New Jersey Line.
Alexander Hamilton, Lieutenant-Colonel and Aid-de-Camp.
Abijah Hammond, Lieutenant, New York Artillery.
John F. Hamtramck, Captain 2d Regiment, New York.
Francis Hanmer, Lieutenant, 5th New York Regiment.
Abraham Hardensburg, Lieutenant, 1st New York Regiment.
Joseph Hardy, Captain of Marines.
Samuel Hay, Lieutenant-colonel, New York Line.
Nathaniel Henry, Lieutenant, 2d New York Regiment.
Benjamin Herring, Ensign, 1st New York Regiment.
Abel Holden, Captain 6th Massachusetts Regiment.
Bazaleel Howe, Lieutenant, New Hampshire Line.
Isaac Hubbell, Captain-lieutenant, and Paymaster, N. Y. Artillery.
James Miles Hughes, Captain, Malcom's Regiment, and Aid-de-Camp to General Gates.
Thomas Hunt, Lieutenant, 4th New York Regiment.
Christopher Hutton, Lieutenant and Adjutant, 2d New York Regiment.
Ephraim Hunt, Lieutenant, 4th Massachusetts Regiment.
Abraham Hyatt, Lieutenant, New York Line.
Thomas T. Jackson, Lieutenant, New York Artillery.
Cornelius T. Jansen, Captain 1st New York Regiment.
James Johnson, Lieutenant, 2d New York Regiment.
Robert Johnson, Physician, General Hospital.
John Keese, Assistant Deputy Quartermaster-general.
Jacob Kemper, Captain-lieutenant, Stevens' Artillery.
Daniel Hemper, Deputy Clothier-general.
John Lamb, Colonel, 2d Regiment Artillery.
Garret Lansing, Ensign, 1st New York Regiment.
John Lawrence, Judge-advocate-general.
Nathaniel Lawrence, Lieutenant, 2d North Carolina Regiment.
Jonathan Lawrence, Captain of Sappers and Miners.
George Leycraft, Lieutenant, Lamb's Artillery.
William Leycraft,   do.   do.   do

SOCIETY OF THE CINCINNATI. 481

Benjamin Ledyard, Major, New York Line.
Isaac Ledyard, Surgeon's Mate.
Morgan Lewis, Colonel and Quartermaster-general.
Brokolst Livingston, Lieutenant-colonel.
Henry B. Livingston, Colonel, 4th New York Regiment.
Samuel Logan, Major, 5th New York Regiment.
Lebbeus Loomis, Lieutenant and Adjutant, Col. Swift's Conecticut Regt.
Henry E. Lutterloh, Colonel, New York Line.
Abraham Leggett, Lieutenant, 5th New York Regiment.
Alexander McDougall, Major-general.
Renald S. McDougall, Major and Aid-de-Camp.
Charles McKnight, Surgeon.
Daniel McLane, Lieutenant, Massachusetts Line.
Thomas Machin, Captain, 2d Regiment, New York.
Peter Magee, Lieutenant, 1st New York Regiment.
Samuel Mansfield, Captain of Artillery.
John Marsh, Ensign, 1st New York Regiment.
Elihu Marshall, Captain, New York Line.
Daniel Menema, Surgeon, 2d New York Regiment.
Andrew Moodie, Captain, Lamb's Artillery.
Joseph Morrell, Ensign, 1st New York Regiment.
William W. Morris, Lieutenant, 2d Regiment Artillery.
Ebenezer Macomber, Captain, Rhode Island Line.
Peter Nestell, Captain-lieutenant, New York Artillery.
Charles Newkirk, Captain-lieutenant, 2d Regiment, New York.
James Nicholson, Naval Captain.
Daniel Niven, Captain of Engineers.
William North, Captain, Mass., Line, and Aid-de-Camp to Gen. Steuben.
Nathaniel Norton, Captain, New York Line.
Daniel Parker, Captain-Lieutenant, Crane's Artillery.
Charles Parsons, Captain, 1st New York Regiment.
Henry Pawling, Captain, 2d New York Regiment.
Samuel T. Pell,   do.   do.   do.
Robert Pemberton, Captain, Connecticut Regiment.
Nathaniel Pendleton, Captain, Virginia Line, and Aid-de-Camp, to General Greene.
William Peters, Ensign, 2d New York Regiment.
Richard Platt, Major and Aid-de-Camp.
William Popham, Captain and Aid de-Camp.
Henry Pray, Captain, 1st Massachusetts Regiment.
William Price, Lieutenant, Massachusetts Artillery.
Abner Prior, Surgeon's Mate, 2d New York Regimen
Thomas Randall, Captain of Artillery.

John Reed, Lieutenant, New York Artillery.
Jacob Reed, Captain, do. do.
John R. B. Rogers, Surgeon, 1st Pennsylvania Regiment.
Wilhelmus Ryckman, Lieutenant, 1st New York Regiment.
Baron De Steuben, Major-general.
John Santford, Captain, Spencer's Connecticut Regiment.
Derick Schuyler, Ensign, 2d New York Regiment.
Philip Schuyler, Major-general.
William Scudder, Lieutenant, 1st New York Regiment.
John Shaw, Lieutenant, New York Artillery.
Israel Smith, Captain, 2d New York Regiment.
William S. Smith, Lieutenant-colonel.
Isaac Smith, Lieutenant, New York Artillery.
Ephraim Snow, Lieutenant, 1st New York Regiment.
John Stagg, Lieutenant, Spencer's Regiment.
John Stake, Lieutenant of Light Dragoons.
Jehosaphat Starr, Ensign, Colonel Webb's Regiment.
Gerard Stediford, Lieutenant, 4th Pennsylvania Regiment.
Ebenezer Stevens, Lieutenant-colonel, New York Artillery.
James Stewart, Captain, New York Line.
William Strachan, Lieutenant, New York Artillery.
Caleb Swan, Ensign, Massachusetts Line.
Bernardus Swartwout, Ensign, 2d New York Regiment.
Cornelius Swartwout, Captain-lieutenant, New York Artillery.
Caleb Sweet, Surgeon, 1st New York Regiment.
George Sytez, Captain, do. do.
William Stewart, Captain, Hazen's Regiment.
Ebenezer Storer, Lieutenant and Paymaster, Brewer's Regiment.
Silas Talbott, Lieutenant-colonel, Pennsylvania Line.
Samuel Tallmadge, Lieutenant, 2d New York Regiment.
William Tapp, Lieutenant, 3d New York Regiment.
Peter Taulman, Captain-lieutenant, Sappers and Miners.
John C. Ten Broeck, Captain, 1st New York Regiment.
Adam Ten Broeck, Ensign, do. do.
Alexander Thompson, Lieutenant, New York Artillery.
Henry Tiebout, Captain, 1st New York Regiment.
Thomas Tillotson, Physician and Surgeon-general.
William Torrey, Lieutenant, Massachusetts Line.
Robert Troup, Lieutenant-colonel and Aid-de-Camp.
John Trumbull, Colonel and Deputy Adjutant-general.
Thomas Turner, Captain, Massachusetts Line.
John F. Vacher, Surgeon, New York Line.
Philip Van Courtlandt, Colonel, 2d New York Regiment.

SOCIETY OF THE CINCINNATI.   483

Cornelius Van Dyck, Lieutenant-colonel, 1st New York Regiment.
Henry Vandeburg, Captain, 2d New York Regiment.
Bartholomew Vandeburg, Ensign, 2d New York Regiment.
John Van Dyck, Captain-lieutenant, New York Artillery.
Rudolph Van Hovenburgh, Lieutenant, 2d New York Regiment.
David Van Horne, Captain, Pennsylvania Line.
Jeremiah Van Rennselaer, Lieutenant and Paymaster, 1st New York Regt.
Goosse Van Schaick, Colonel, 1st New York Regiment.
Garret Van Wagenen, Surgeon, 8th Pennsylvania Regiment.
Tunis Van Wagenan, Lieutenant, 2d New York Regiment.
Richard Varick, Lieutenant-colonel and Deputy Mus. Mr. General.
Veter Vosborough, Captain, Livingston's Regiment.
Nicholas Van Rennselaer, Lieutenant, 1st New York Regiment.
John Waldron, Captain-lieutenant, New York Artillery.
Benjamin Walker, Captain, 2d New York Regiment.
Jedediah Waterman, Ensign, 8th Massachusetts Regiment.
James Walson, Captain, New York Line.
Samuel B. Webb, Colonel, 3d Connecticut Regiment.
Charles F. Weisenfels, Lieutenant, 2d New York Regiment.
Frederick Weisenfels, Lieutenant-colonel, New York Line.
Jacob H. Wendell, Lieutenant and Adjutant, 1st New York Regiment.
John H. Wendell, Captain,   do.
Michael Wetzell, Lieutenant, New York Artillery.
Andrew White, Lieutenant, 2d Regiment, New York.
Anthony Walton White, Colonel, 1st Regiment Light Dragoons.
Marinus Willett, Lieutenant-colonel, 5th New York Regiment.
Robert Wilson, Ensign, 1st New York Regiment.
Jacob Wright, Captain, 2d New York Regiment.
Ephraim Woodruff, Lieutenant,   do.
Peter Woodward, Lieutenant, Connecticut Line.

MEMBERS OF THE PENNSYLVANIA SOCIETY OF THE CINCINNATI, IN THE ORDER IN WHICH THEY SUBSCRIBED, IN DECEMBER, 1783.

John Armstrong, Lieutenant, 3d Pennsylvania Regiment.
Thomas Wylis, Captain, Pennsylvania Artillery Artificers.
Francis White, Lieutenant, 1st Pennsylvania Regiment.
James McLean, Lieutenant of Invalids.
Samuel Doty, Captain-lieutenant, Pennsylvania Artillery.
W. Ferguson, Captain,   do.
David Zeigler, Captain.
F. Mentges, Lieutenant-colonel and Inspector, Southern Army.
J. Pratt, Lieutenant, 3d Pennsylvania Regiment.

Richard Fullerton, Lieutenant and Adjutant, 1st Pennsylvania Regiment.
George Bush, Captain, 3d Pennsylvania Regiment.
John Stricker, Lieutenant, do.
Erkuries Beatty, Lieutenant, do.
William Moore, Lieutenant, 1st Regiment Dragoons.
Robert McConnell, Captain-lieutenant of Artillery.
Jab. Weitzel, Lieutenant, 1st Pennsylvania Regiment.
William Wilson, Captain, do.
James Armstrong, Captain, Lee's Legion.
John Baukson, Captain, 1st Pennsylvania Regiment.
J. McFarlane, Lieutenant, do.
John Markland, Lieutenant, do.
John Bush, Captain, 3d Pennsylvania Regiment.
Thomas Doyle, Lieutenant, 1st Pennsylvania Regiment.
Joseph Harmar, Lieutenant-colonel, do.
R. Allison, Surgeon's Mate, 2d Pennsylvania Regiment.
Andrew Lytle, Lieutenant, 1st Pennsylvania Regiment.
T. Seely, Captain, 2d Pennsylvania Regiment.
John Doyle, Captain, 1st Pennsylvania Regiment.
Jas. F. McPherson, Lieutenant, 1st Pennsylvania Regiment.
William Magaw, Surgeon, do.
Anty. Wayne, Brigadier-general, Pennsylvania Line.
William McHatton, Captain of Invalids.
C. De Marcellin, Lieutenant, 2d Pennsylvania Regiment.
Le Roy, Lieutenant. do.
Le Chevalier De Lambert, Lieutenant d'Artillerie.
H. Henly, Lieutenant, 1st Pennsylvania Regiment.
Andrew Henderson, Lieutenant, 2d Pennsylvania Regiment.
Joseph Ashton, Captain-lieutenant, Pennsylvania Artillery.
Edward Speer, Lieutenant, 1st Pennsylvania Regiment.
Robt. McMordie, Chaplain, 1st Pennsylvania Brigade.
John Stoy, Captain-lieutenant, 2d Pennsylvania Regiment.
Walter Stewart, Colonel and Inspector of Northern Army.
Enos Reeves, Lieutenant, 1st Pennsylvania Regiment.
James Morris Jones, Lieutenant, do.
Jno. McDowell, Surgeon, Pennsylvania Line.
E. Edwards, Major, 4th Pennsylvania Regiment.
P. Peres, Surgeon, German Regiment.
Andrew Porter, Lieutenant-colonel, Com't Pennsylvania Regt. Artillery.
Francis Nichols, Lieutenant-colonel.
Francis Proctor, Major of Artillery.
William Murrin, Lieutenant, 2d Pennsylvania Regiment.
Hen. D. Purcell, do. do.

Andw. Walker, Captain, 3d Pennsylvania Regiment.
Stewart Herbert, Lieutenant,   do.
J. Mackinney,   do.   do.
Francis Johnston, Colonel, Pennsylvania.
Ja: Chrystie, Captain, 2d Pennsylvania Regiment.
Henry Bicker, Captain, 11th Pennsylvania Regiment.
Wilder Bevins, Lieutenant.
Benj. Lodge, Lieutenant, 1st Pennsylvania Regiment.
Thomas Dugan, Lieutenant, 2d Pennsylvania Regiment.
T. Robinson, Lieutenant-colonel,   do.
Jas. Gamble, Lieutenant, Pennsylvania Artillery.
Henry Piercy, Lieutenant, 2d Pennsylvania Regiment.
Alexr. Parker, Captain,   do.
Jas. Chambers, Colonel, Pennsylvania.
Matthew Maus, Surgeon, Invalid Regiment.
Fredk. Vernon, Major, 1st Pennsylvania Regiment.
J. Grier, Major, 3d Pennsylvania Regiment.
John B. Webster, Captain-lieutenant.
J. Moore, Major, 1st Pennsylvania Regiment.
A. G. Claypoole, Captain, 3d Pennsylvania Regiment.
Daniel Brodhead, Colonel, 1st Pennsylvania Regiment.
Matthew McConnell, Captain of Invalids.
James Glentworth, Lieutenant, 2d Pennsylvania Regiment.
J. Stake, 3d Pennsylvania Regiment.
W. Van Lear, Captain, 5th Pennsylvania Regiment.
T. B. Bowen, Captain, 1st Pennsylvania Regiment.
W. Macpherson, Major.
David S. Franks, Major.
Jesse Crosley, Captain-lieutenant, Pennsylvania Artillery.
Jno. Stricker, Captain-lieutenant, 4th Pennsylvania Artillery.
Stephen Moylan, Colonel, 4th Regiment Light Dragoons.
Zebn. Pike, Captain,   do.   do.
John Davis, Captain.
Isaac Craig, Major, Pennsylvania Artillery.
Stephen Bayard, Lieutenant-colonel, 3d Pennsylvania Regiment.
W. Finney, Captain, 1st Pennsylvania Regiment.
S. Montgomery, Captain, 3d Pennsylvania Regiment.
John R. B. Rogers, Surgeon,   do.
Wm. McCurdy, Captain, 1st Pennsylvania Regiment.
Jno. Reily, Captain, Invalid Regiment, Pennsylvania.
Thos. Proctor, Colonel, Pennsylvania Artillery.
Chas. Turnbull, Captain,   do.
James Lloyd, Captain-lieutenant, Artillery.

James Hamilton, Major, 2d Pennsylvania Regiment.
Ph. Liebery, Captain of Invalids.
Jean Aug. De Florat, Captain, and Assistant Engineer.
Jno. Wigton, Lieutenant, 3d Pennsylvania Regiment.
John Harper, Lieutenant, 5th Pennsylvania Regiment.
John Christie, Captain, 3d Pennsylvania Regiment.
Benj. Bartholomew, Captain, 5th Pennsylvania Regiment.
Saml. A. McCoffrey, Surgeon, Pennsylvania Artillery Artificers.
John Jordan, Captain,   do.   do.
Isaac Van Horne, Captain, 2d Pennsylvania Regiment.
Js. Campbell, Lieutenant, 1st Pennsylvania Regiment.
Jno. McClelan, Captain,   do.
J. McCullam, Lieutenant and Adjutant, 4th Pennsylvania Regiment.
Reading Beatty, Surgeon, Pennsylvania Artillery.
Wm. Sproat, Captain, 3d Pennsylvania Regiment.
Richd. Butler, Colonel,   do.
Isaac B. Dunn, Major,   do.
W. McDowell, Lieutenant, 1st Pennsylvania Regiment.
Edw. Crawford, Lieutenant, 3d Pennsylvania Regiment.
John Rose,   do.   do.
Wm. Martin, Captain, Pennsylvania Artillery.
John Marshall, Captain, 2d Pennsylvania Regiment.
Jas Parr, Major.
C. North, Lieutenant-colonel, 2d Pennsylvania Regiment.
Ln. Davis, Lieutenant, 3d Pennsylvania Regiment.
Francis Murray, Lieutenant-colonel.
Wm. Rogers, Chaplain, 3d Pennsylvania Brigade.
James R. Reid, Major.
John Patterson, Captain.
John Van Court, Lieutenant, Pennsylvania Artillery.
Jno. Stotesbury, Captain.
Jas. Pettigrew, Lieutenant, 2d Pennsylvania Regiment.
Peter Smith, Lieutenant, 3d Pennsylvania Regiment.
John Armstrong, jr., Major.
Edmund Bourke, Captain, 1st Pennsylvania Regiment.
T. Boude,   do.   do.
George Stevenson, Hospital Mate.
Robt. Parker, Captain, Pennsylvania Artillery.
Jas. McMichael, Lieutenant, 1st Pennsylvania Regiment.
Levi Griffith, Lieutenant, 5th Pennsylvania Regiment.
James Montgomery, Captain.
Thomas Douglas, Captain of Artillery.
Barnabas Binney, Hospital Surgeon.

SOCIETY OF THE CINCINNATI.

Thos. Bond, jr., Purveyor.
Edwd. Hand, Major-general.
T. Campbell, Captain.
Wm. Lusk,   do.
George North, Lieutenant.
Andw. Irvine, Captain, 1st Pennsylvania Regiment.
John Nevill, Colonel, 4th Virginia Regiment.
John Boyd, Captain-lieutenant, 3d Pennsylvania Regiment.
Jacob Mytinger, Lieutenant, Von Heer's Cavalry.
Jno. Michon, Lieutenant, 2d Pennsylvania Regiment.
Robt. Sample, Captain, 10th Pennsylvania Regiment.
Alex. Benstead, Lieutenant,   do.
Wm. Henderson, Captain, 1st Pennsylvania Regiment.
Robert Wilkin, Captain, 2d Pennsylvania Regiment.
Adm. Hubley, jr., Lieutenant-colonel, 11th Pennsylvania Regiment.
Worsley Emes, Captain, Pennsylvania Artillery.
Nat. Irish, Captain, Pennsylvania Artillery Artificers.
Thomas M. McCalla, Surgeon, 4th Regiment Light Dragoons.
Ezekiel Howell, Lieutenant, Pennsylvania Artillery.
Robt. Coltman, Captain,   do.   do.
John Bryce,   do.   do.   do.
Matthew McGuire, do.   do.   do.
Robert McGaw, Colonel, 6th Pennsylvania Regiment.
James G. Heron, Captain, Hazen's Regiment.
Wm. Sade, Captain, 11th Penn. Regiment, and Assistant Geographer.
Wm. Wilkins, Captain of Invalids.
James Gilchrist, Lieutenant, 5th Pennsylvania Regiment.
Thos. McIntire, Captain.
Blackall Wm. Ball, Lieutenant, 3d Pennsylvania Regiment.
John Humphrey, Lieutenant, 4th Pennsylvania Regiment.
William Power, Captain of Artillery.
James Smith, Captain-lieutenant, Pennsylvania Artillery.
L. Keene, Captain, 3d Pennsylvania Regiment, and Aid-de-Camp.
A. St. Clair, Major-general.
Jer. Jackson, Captain.
Job Vernon,   do.
Robert Patton, do.
Sam'l Smith,   do.
Rob't Martin, Lieutenant, 1st Pennsylvania Regiment.
Philippe Avabing, Lieutenant of Dragoons.
John Craig, Captain of   do.
Ber'd Kibley, Captain, German Regiment.

James Davidson, Surgeon, 5th Pennsylvania Regiment.
J. Talbott, Major, 6th do. do.
George Tudor, do. 5th do. do.
Sam'l Bryson, Lieutenant, 4th do. do.
Wm. Price, Captain, German Regiment.
Jonah Hallett, Lieutenant, Partizan Legion.
Wm. Williams, Captain of Invalids.
Philip Shrawder, Captain, German Regiment.
Samuel Talbott, Captain, 2d Pennsylvania Regiment.
Barthol'w Von Heer, Major, Light Dragoons.
Sam'l Reed, Lieutenant, 1st Pennsylvania Regiment.
Gabriel Peterson, Lieutenant, 3d Pennsylvania Regiment.
Daniel St. Clair, do. do. do.
John Weidman, Lieutenant, German Regiment.
William McMurray, Captain of Sappers and Miners.
Jeremiah Freeman, Captain, Pennsylvania Artillery.
Hugh Martin, Surgeon, 8th Pennsylvania Regiment,
Joseph L. Finley, Captain, 3d Pennsylvania Regiment.
Jno. Nice, do. 6th do. do.
Will. Mackey, do. 9th do. do.
John Hughes, Lieutenant, 4th do. do.
J. B. Tilden, do.
Richard Humpton, Colonel.
J. Simonds, Captain, Pennsylvania Artillery.
Jacob Bower, do.

MEMBERS OF THE MARYLAND SOCIETY OF THE CINCINNATI.

W. Smallwood, Major-general.
M. Gist, Brigadier-general.
O. H. Williams, do.
N. Ramsey, Lieutenant-colonel.
John Eccleston, Major.
Joshua Barney, Captain, Navy.
John Nicholson, do. do.
H. Hardman, Major.
John Davidson, Major.
William D. Beall, do.
William Brown, do.
John Cotes, Captain.
Richard Dorsey, do.
David Morrow, Surgeon.
Ezekiel Hayne, do.
Thomas Boyd, Lieutenant.
Samuel Morrow, Surgeon.
James Armstrong, Chaplain.

Thomas Mason, Captain.
Samuel McPherson, Captain.
Henry Baldwin, Lieutenant.
James Brocco, do.
J. Hamilton. Captain.
William Campbell, do.
George Hamilton, do.
John L. Elbert, Surgeon.
N. Ricketts, Lieutenant.
David Hopkins, Captain.
Basil Burgess, Lieutenant.
Thomas Price, do.
James Smith, Captain.
Jonathan Morris.
Edward Hall, Lieutenant.
Isaac Rawlings, do.
Edward Oldham, Captain.
William Reily, do.

SOCIETY OF THE CINCINNATI.

John Kilty, Captain.
John Jordan, do.
Perry Benson, do.
Lloyd Beall, do.
Abraham Lamar, do.
Michael Boyer, do.
John J. Jacobs, Lieutenant.
Edward Dyer, Captain.
Philip Reed, do.
Samuel Hanson, Lieutenant.
Arthur Harris, do.
Samuel B. Beall, do.
Edward Spurrier, Captain.
James Peale, do.
J. Brevitt, Lieutenant.
William Pendergast, do.
Thomas Rouse, do.
William Kilty, Surgeon.
Francis Revelly, Captain.
Thomas Bealty, Lieutenant.
Mark McPherson, do.
Henry Gaither, Captain.
John Sears, Lieutenant.
Christopher Richmond, Captain.
Edward Compton, Lieutenant.
Jno. H. Stone, Colonel.
Samuel F. Keene, Surgeon's Mate.
John Sprigg Belt, Captain.
Samuel Smith, Lieutenant-col.
John Gunby, Colonel.
James Craike, Physician.
John Hughes, Captain.
Benjamin Price, do.
James Bruff, do.
William Bruce, do.
Elisha Harrison, Surgeon's Mate.
A. Tannehill, Captain.
J. D. Carey, Lieutenant.
James Mann, Surgeon.
John Gassaway, Captain.
Thomas A. Dyson, Lieutenant.
Henry Clements, do.
Samuel Edmiston, do.
John T. Lowe, do.
William Smoote, do.
Elihu Hall, do.
Malachi Bonham, do.
Hezekiah Ford, do.
Gerard Wood, Surgeon's Mate.
Henry H. Chapman, Lieutenant.
Isaac Hanson, do.
Benjamin Fickle, do.

R. Anderson, Captain.
John Smith, do.
James W. Gray, do.
John Mitchell, do.
Nathan Wright, Lieutenant.
William Goldsborough, do.
Walter Muse, Captain.
James Baques, Lieutenant.
Clement Skerrett, do.
Henry Gassaway, do.
Robert Gerry, do.
Edward Pratt, Captain.
Horatio Clagett, Captain.
John Swan, Major.
James M. Lingan, Captain.
Rezin Davis, do.
James McFadon, Lieutenant.
Mountjoy Bailey, Captain.
Paul Bentalou, do.
John Carlisle, Major.
R. McAllister, Captain.
John Gale, Major.
Richard Waters, Captain.
Moses Rawlings, Colonel.
George Handy, Captain.
John Trueman, Lieutenant.
Gassaway Watkins, Captain.
Joseph Smith, do.
Levin Denwood, Surgeon.
Alexander Trueman, Captain.
Joseph Cross, Lieutenant.
John Smith, Captain.
James Somerville, do.
Robert Denny, Lieutenant.
James G. Heron, Captain.
Daniel Jennifer, Surgeon.
John E. Howard, Colonel.
J. C. Hall, do.
R. Pindell, Surgeon.
J. Seliman, Major.
Tench Tilghman, Lieut.-Colonel.
Levin Winder, do.
Walter Warfield, Surgeon.
Thomas Woolford, Lieut. Colonel.
Benjamin Brooks, Major.
Thomas Lansdale, do.
L. W. Williams, Captain.
James Ewing, do.
Richard Chiderson, do.
James Winchester, do.
Samuel T. Wright, do.
G. Winchester, Lieutenant.

D. Luckett, Lieutenant.
Osborn Williams, do.
John Lynn, do.
Joshua Rutledge, do.

Philip Hill, Lieutenant.
P. Fitzhugh, Captain.
Nathan Wright, Lieutenant.
John Lynch, Major.

ACTS OF THE LEGISLATURE OF VIRGINIA.

RELATING TO BOUNTY LANDS, HALF-PAY AND COMMUTATION, AND TO THE ASSUMPTION OF THE PAYMENT OF THE HALF-PAY CLAIMS OF VIRGINIA BY THE GENERAL GOVERNMENT, PER ACT OF CONGRESS, APPROVED JULY 5, 1832.

Congress, by acts of the 16th and 18th of September, 1776, and others subsequent thereto, stipulated grants of land to the officers and soldiers of the Continental army, and to certain officers of the medical department. At that period, Congress had no land at its disposal, for all of it belonged to the States; and it would have been compelled to purchase lands to make good its contracts, had it not been for the liberality of the States.

IN CONGRESS, September 13, 1783.

The committee, consisting of Mr. Rutledge, Mr. Ellsworth, Mr. Bedford, Mr. Gorham, and Mr. Madison, to whom was referred the act of the Legislature of Virginia, of the 2d of January, 1781, and the report thereon, report that they have considered the several matters referred to them, and observe that the Legislature of Virginia, by the act of the 2d of January, 1781, resolved that they would yield to the Congress of the United States for the benefit of the said States, all right, title, and claim which the said commonwealth hath to the lands northwest of the river Ohio, upon the following conditions, viz:

1. That the territory so ceded should be laid out and formed into States, containing a suitable extent of territory, not less than one hundred nor more than one hundred and fifty miles square, or as near thereto as circumstances will admit; and that the States so formed should be distinct republican States, and admitted members of the federal Union, having the same

rights of sovereignty, freedom, and independence as the other States.

2. That Virginia should be allowed and fully reimbursed by the United States her actual expenses in reducing the British posts at the Kaskaskias, at St. Vincent's, the expenses of maintaining garrisons, and supporting civil government there since the reduction of the said posts, and, in general, all the charges she has incurred on account of the country on the northwest side of the Ohio River since the commencement of the present war.

3. That the French and Canadian inhabitants, and other settlers of the Kaskaskias, St. Vincent's, and the neighboring villages, who have professed themselves citizens of Virginia, should have their possessions and titles confirmed to them, and should be protected in the enjoyment of their rights and liberties; for which purpose troops should be stationed there, at the charge of the United States, to protect them from the encroachments of the British forces at Detroit or elsewhere, unless the events of the war should render it impracticable.

4. As Colonel George Rogers Clarke planned and executed the secret expedition by which the British posts were reduced, and was promised, if the enterprise succeeded, a liberal gratuity in lands in that country, for the officers and soldiers who first marched thither with him; that a quantity of land, not exceeding 150,000 acres, should be allowed and granted to said officers and soldiers, and the other officers and soldiers that have since been incorporated into the said regiment, to be laid off in one tract, the length of which not to exceed double the breadth, in such place on the northwest side of the Ohio River as the majority of the officers should choose, and to be afterwards divided among the said officers and soldiers, in due proportion, according to the laws of Virginia.

5. That in case the quantity of good lands on the southeast side of the Ohio, upon the waters of the Cumberland River, and between the Green River and Tennessee River, which have been reserved by law for the Virginia troops upon Continental

establishment, should, from the North Carolina line bearing in further upon the Cumberland lands than was expected, prove insufficient for their legal bounties, the deficiency should be made up to the said troops in good lands, to be laid off between the rivers Scioto and Little Miami, on the northwest side of the Ohio, in such proportions as have been engaged to them by the laws of Virginia.

6. That all the lands within the territory so ceded to the United States, and not reserved for, or appropriated to, any of the before-mentioned purposes, or disposed of in bounties to the officers and soldiers of the American army, should be considered as a common fund for the use and benefit of such of the United American States as have become, or shall become, members of the confederation or federal alliance of the said States, Virginia inclusive, according to their usual respective proportions in the general charge and expenditure, and should be faithfully and *bona fide* disposed of for that purpose, and for no other use or purpose whatever.

7. And therefore, that all purchases and deeds from any Indian or Indians, or from any Indian nation or nations, for any lands within any part of the said territory which have been, or should be, made for the use or benefit of any private person or persons whatsoever, and royal grants within the ceded territory, inconsistent with the chartered rights, laws, and customs of Virginia, should be deemed and declared absolutely void, and of no effect, in the same manner as if the said territory had still remained subject to, and part of, the Commonwealth of Virginia.

8. That all the remaining territory of Virginia, included between the Atlantic Ocean and the southeast side of the river Ohio, and the Maryland, Pennsylvania, and North Carolina boundaries, should be guaranteed to the Commonwealth of Virginia by the said United States.

Whereupon your committee are of opinion, that the first condition is provided for by the act of Congress of the 10th of October, 1780.

That in order to comply with the second condition, so far as has been heretofore provided for by the act of October 10, 1780, it is agreed that one commissioner should be appointed by Congress, one by the State of Virginia, and another by those two commissioners; who, or a majority of whom, should be authorized and empowered to adjust and liquidate the account of the necessary and reasonable expenses incurred by the said State, which they may judge to be comprised within the true intent and meaning of the said recited act.

With respect to the third condition, the committee are of opinion that the settlers therein described should have their possessions and titles confirmed to them, and be protected in the enjoyment of their rights and liberties.

Your committee are further of opinion that the fourth, fifth, and sixth conditions, being reasonable, should be agreed to by Congress.

With respect to the seventh condition, your committee are of opinion that it would be proper for Congress to declare the purchases and grants therein mentioned, absolutely void and of no effect; and that the sixth condition, engaging how the lands beyond the Ohio shall be disposed of, is sufficient on this point.

As to the last condition, your committee are of opinion that Congress cannot agree to guarantee to the Commonwealth of Virginia the land described in the said condition, without entering into a discussion of the right of the State of Virginia to the said land; and that, by the acts of Congress, it appears to have been their intention to avoid all discussion of the territorial rights of individual States, and only to recommend and accept a cession of their claims, whatsoever they might be, to vacant territory. Your committee conceived this condition of a guarantee to be either unnecessary or unreasonable; inasmuch as, if the land above mentioned is really the property of the State of Virginia, it is sufficiently secured by the confederation; and if it is not the property of that State, there is no reason or consideration for such guarantee.

Your committee, therefore, upon the whole, recommend, that if the Legislature of Virginia make a cession conformable to this report, Congress accept such cession.

The Legislature of Virginia did, at their session commenced October 20, 1783, cede to the United States the said territory, on the principles recited in the aforesaid act of September 13, 1783.

VIRGINIA BOUNTY LANDS.

Virginia, holding immense tracts of unappropriated land, very soon adopted the idea suggested by Congress, of granting land bounties to her officers and soldiers, both in the *State* and Continental establishments; and having it more in her power, she was more liberal than Congress in those grants.

By act of May, 1779, chapter 6, concerning officers, soldiers, sailors, marines, a bounty of one hundred acres is allowed to each private at the end of the war; and to the officers, the like quantity as is allowed to officers of the same rank in the Virginia regiments on Continental establishment. By the same law, two hundred acres are given to each volunteer soldier who served under Colonel George Clarke, until the reduction of the posts in the Illinois country, and to each soldier who should reenlist for the protection of the Illinois country, one hundred acres, and the like quantity to each trooper of cavalry who should enlist for the war, for the defence of the eastern frontier.

A quantity of land not exceeding 150,000 acres, was reserved to satisfy the officers and soldiers under Col. George Rogers Clarke, in the cession of the northwestern territory to the United States.

The act of May, 1779, chapter 18, prescribes the evidence on which warrants for land bounties shall issue, and by the same chapter, a tract of country, bounded by the Green River, the Cumberland Mountains, the North Carolina Line, the Tennessee River, and the Ohio River, was reserved for the officers and soldiers. A considerable part of this territory having fallen into North Carolina, by the extension of the boundary line between that State and Virginia, a further tract of land, included within the rivers Mississippi, Ohio, and Tennessee, and the

Carolina boundary line, was substituted by the act of November, 1781, chapter 19, in lieu of that so fallen into North Carolina. By the same act, section 9, a provision is made for surveying their lands; section 12 declares that the bounties in lands given to the officers in the Virginia line in Continental service, and the regulations for surveying, shall be extended to the State officers; section 13 gives the cavalry the same advantages as the infantry; and section 14 entitles the officers and seamen of the navy to the same advantages as those in the land service.

But the act of October, 1782, is more explicit as to the navy, and declares that the "officers, seamen, and marines, and their representatives, shall be entitled to the same bounty in lands and other emoluments as the officers and soldiers of the Virginia Line on Continental establishment."

ACT OCTOBER, 1779, CHAPTER 9.

Be it enacted by the General Assembly, That every person acting as chaplain, surgeon, or surgeon's mate, to any regiment or brigade of officers and soldiers raised in this Commonwealth, and upon Continental establishment, and who hath or shall hereafter serve in that office the space of *three years, or during the war*, shall be entitled to and have the like quantity of lands as is by law allowed to commissioned officers receiving the same pay and rations.

Chapter 21 of the Act of October, 1779, fixes the quantity of land referred to in chapter 9, as follows:

Be it enacted, That the officers who shall serve in the Virginia Line on Continental establishment, or in the army or navy on State establishment, *to the end of the present war*, and the non-commissioned officers, soldiers, and sailors, upon either of the said establishments, their airs or legal representatives, shall respectively be entitled to and receive the proportion and quantities of land following: That is to say, every *Colonel*, 5,000 acres; every *Lieutenant-Colonel*, 4,500 acres; every *Major*, 4,000 acres; every *Captain*, 3,000 acres; every *subaltern*, 2,000 acres; every *non-commissioned officer*, who, having enlisted for the war, shall have served *to the end thereof*, 400 acres ; and every *soldier* and *sailor*, under the like circumstances, 200 acres ; every *non-commissioned officer*, who, having enlisted for the term *of three years*, shall have served out the same, or to the end of the present war, 200 acres ; and every *soldier* and *sailor*, under the like circumstances, 100 acres ; every officer of the navy, the same quantity of land as an officer of equal rank in the army. And where any *officer, soldier, or sailor*, shall have fallen or died in the service, his *heirs or legal representatives* shall be entitled to and receive the same quantity of land as would have been due to such officer, soldier, or sailor respectively, had he been living.

ACT OCTOBER, 1780, CHAPTER 3.

And each recruit, and also all our soldiers, now in service, that have already enlisted, or may hereafter enlist, by the first day of April next, to serve *during the war*, and who shall continue to serve faithfully to the *end thereof*, shall then *receive a healthy sound negro*, between the ages of ten and thirty years, or *sixty pounds in gold or silver*, at the option of the soldier, in lieu thereof, to be paid for or procured by equal assessment on property ; and moreover, be entitled to 300 acres of land, in lieu of all such bounties given by any former laws.

OCTOBER, 1780, CHAPTER 27.

Be it enacted, That there shall be allowed to a *Major general* 15,000 acres of land, and to a *Brigadier-general*, 10,000 acres of land, to be reserved to them and their heirs, in the same manner and on the same conditions, as is by law heretofore directed for the officers and soldiers of the Virginia Line in Continental service ; and there shall be, moreover, allowed to all the officers of this State, on Continental or State establishments, or to the *legal representatives* of such officers, according to their respective ranks, an additional bounty in lands, in the proportion of *one-third of any former bounty heretofore granted them.*

And be it further enacted, That the legal representatives of any officer on Continental or State establishments, who may have died in the service before the bounty of lands granted by this or any former law, shall be entitled to demand and receive the same, in like manner as the officer himself might have done when living, agreeable to his rank.

ACT MAY, 1782, CHAPTER 47.

And be it further enacted, That any officer or soldier who hath not been *cashiered or superseded*, and who hath served the term of *three years* successively, shall have an absolute and unconditional title to his respective apportionment of the land appropriated as aforesaid; and for *every year* which every such officer or soldier may have continued, or shall hereafter continue in service, *beyond the term of six years*, to be computed from the time he last went into service, he shall be entitled to *one sixth* part in addition to the quantity of land appropriated to his rank respectively.

ACT OCTOBER, 1782, CHAPTER 35.

And that all officers, seamen, and marines, or their representatives, shall be entitled to the same bounty in lands and other emoluments as the officers and soldiers of the Virginia Line on Continental establishment.

ACT OCTOBER, 1783, CHAPTER 4.

And be it further enacted, That the surveys under the direction of the superintendents, and the claimants having a right to survey from the priority of their numbers, shall proceed in the first place to survey all the good lands, to be judged of by the superintendents, in that tract of country lying on the Cumberland and Tennessee rivers, as set apart by law for the said officers and soldiers, and then proceed in like manner to survey on the northwest side of the Ohio River, between the rivers Scioto and Little Miami, until the deficiency of all military bounties in lands shall be fully and amply made up.

ACT OCTOBER, 1784, CHAPTER 16.

Be it enacted, That the Governor, with the advice of the Council, shall be, and he is hereby, authorized and empowered to suspend, for such time as he may think the tranquillity of the government may require, the surveying or taking possession of those lands that lie on the northwest side of the river Ohio, or below the mouth of the river Tennessee.

In consequence of this last act the Governor of Virginia issued two proclamations, suspending surveys, the latter of which is as follows :

PROCLAMATION.

Whereas, in pursuance of the act of the General Assembly entitled "An act authorizing the Governor, with the advice of the Council, to suspend, when necessary, the surveying of certain lands in the western country," his Excellency the Governor, with the advice of the Council of State, on the 6th day of January, in the year of our Lord 1785, did suspend the taking possession and surveying of any lands on the northwest side of the Ohio, or below the mouth of the river Tennessee, until authority for that purpose should hereafter be given, *it appearing that the tranquillity of the government did at that time require such suspension;* but whereas the United States in Congress assembled, on the 9th day of May, in the year of our Lord 1786, did resolve "that the surveyors, appointed pursuant to the ordinance for ascertaining the mode of disposing of lands in the western territory, should proceed in the execution thereof, within the east and west lines therein mentioned," and the superintendents of the surveys to be made on the lands allotted to the Virginia Line on Continental establishment, have requested that so much of the said proclamation as relates to the lands on the northwest side of the Ohio, should be annulled, and I have therefore thought fit, with the advice of the Council of State, hereby to annul so much of the said proclamation as relates to the lands on the northwest side of the Ohio. EDMUND RANDOLPH.

In the year 1784, the superintendent appointed by the deputation of officers, proceeded to Kentucky for the purpose of laying off and surveying the lands in the military districts of the Kentucky reserve, but found them in the possession of the Indians, and claimed by them. The settlers in the country earnestly represented to the Legislature of Virginia, that, if the surveys were persisted in, the infant and defenceless settlements in Kentucky would be involved in all the horrors and calamities of an Indian war. Accordingly, at the October session of 1784, the Legislature authorized the Governor of Virginia to suspend, for such time as he may think the tranquillity of the government may require, the surveying or taking possession of those lands which lie on the northwest side of the Ohio River, or below the mouth of the Tennessee River, and which have been reserved for the officers and soldiers of the Virginia Line, and the Illinois Regiment. In pursuance of this authority, the Governor of Virginia, on the 6th of January, 1785, issued his proclamation suspending the surveys. Thus Virginia, by her own act, put it out of the power of her officers and soldiers, after the 6th of January, 1785, to locate their warrants. This inhibition by the State authority continued until the 10th of January, 1786, when the prohibition was continued by the act of the General Government.

At that date, the treaty of Hopewell was concluded between the United States and the Chickasaw Indians, guaranteeing to the Indians, as part of their habitation and hunting-ground, all the lands below the Tennessee River, and providing that if any citizen of the United States, or any person not being an Indian, shall attempt to settle in any of the lands thereby allotted to the Chickasaws to live and to hunt on, such person shall forfeit the protection of the United States of America, and the Chickasaws may punish him or not, as they please.

The treaty of Hopewell remained in force until 1818, when the Indian title was extinguished. After that period Kentucky would not permit the location of military warrants to be made.

"From 1792 to 1800, that portion of Kentucky," says the Auditor of that State, "east of the high lands between the Tennessee and the Cumberland rivers, and reserved for the officers and soldiers of the Virginia State and Continental Lines, was not held in much estimation by the early land speculators and settlers, owing to the fact of the fear of Indian hostility, and likewise a belief that all the good lands on the rivers and creeks had been appropriated by the military claims, and the remainder thereof was poor and barren. Kentucky valued them thus:

OFFICERS RECEIVING LAND WARRANTS.

In 1795, at $30 per 100 acres; in 1796, at $40 per 100 acres; and in 1800, at $20 per 100 acres.

Owing to all these difficulties, military warrants in vast numbers have remained unlocated, and Congress at different times have appropriated vast quantities of western lands to satisfy the demand, but so enormous has been the quantity required, that up to 1844, 650,000 acres of warrants still remained unsatisfied and unlocated.

A List of Officers for whose Revolutionary Services Virginia Military Land Warrants were Issued prior to December 31, 1784.

Generals.

George Rogers Clarke,
Horatio Gates,
Robert Lawson,
Hugh Mercer,
Daniel Morgan,
Peter Muhlenberg,
Charles Scott,
Baron Steuben,
George Weedon,
William Woodford.

Colonels.

George Baylor,
Theodoric Bland,
William Brent,
Abraham Buford,
Richard Campbell,
William Crawford,
William Davis,
Christian Febiger,
William Finnie,
Thomas Fleming,
Nathaniel Gist,
William Russell,
Gregory Smith,
Hugh Stephenson,
John Gibson,
John Green,
William Grayson,
Charles Harrison.
William Heth,
Thomas Marshall,
George Mathews,
Alexander McClenahan,
George Muter,
John Nevill,
Isaac Reed,
Oliver Towles,
James Wood,

Lieutenant colonels.

John Allison,
Richard E. Anderson,
Robert Ballard,
Otway Bird,
Samuel J. Cabell,
Edward Carrington,
Jonathan Clark,
Nathaniel Cocke,
Joseph Crocket,
John Cropper,
Charles Dabney,
William Darke,
Elias Edmunds,
Charles Flemming,
Thomas Gaskins,
Samuel Hawes,
Samuel Hopkins,
John Jameson,
Levin Joines,
Henry Lee,

OFFICERS RECEIVING LAND WARRANTS.   501

Thomas Mathews,
Richard K. Meade,
John Montgomery,
Presley Nevill,
William Nelson,
Charles Porterfield,
Levin Powell,
Thomas Posey,
Holt Richardson,

Charles Simms,
William B. Taliaferro,
Richard Taylor,
Benjamin Temple,
Gustavus B. Wallace,
Frederick Warnock,
William Washington,
John Webb.

Other Officers.

Alexander, George,
Allen, David,
Allen, Edward,
Allen, John,
Anderson, John,
Anderson, Robert,
Archer, Joseph,
Archer, Peter F.,
Armistead, Thomas,
Armistead, William,
Ashby, Stephen,
Ashby, Benjamin,

Ballard, William,
Barbee, Thomas,
Balmain, Alexander,
Baylor, Walker,
Baskerville, Samuel,
Barron, James,
Ball, Burgess,
Baynham, John,
Barbour, James,
Bowyer, Thomas,
Bowyer, Michael,
Banks, James,
Baytop, James,
Baytop, John,
Ballard, William,
Baytop, Thomas,
Baylis, William,
Baylis, Henry,
Barnett, William,
Barnett, Chiswell,
Barksdale, John,
Ball, Daniel,
Bailey, John,
Baldwin, Cornelius,
Bentley, William,
Beale, Robert,
Bedinger, Henry,
Bell, Thomas,
Bernard, William,

Bennett, William,
Beck, John,
Beale, Robert,
Berry, George,
Bilfield, John,
Bell, Henry,
Biggs, Benjamin,
Blackwell, Joseph,
Blackwell, John,
Blackwell, Samuel,
Blackmore, George,
Blanden, Seth,
Blair, John,
Browne, Thomas,
Booker, Samuel,
Booker, Lewis,
Bohannan, Ambrose,
Bowyer, Henry,
Boush, Charles,
Bowen, John,
Boswell, Meacham,
Brodie, Ludwick,
Browne, Windsor,
Brookes, Walker,
Bradford, Samuel K.,
Breckinridge, Alexander,
Brown, Jacob,
Brownlee, William,
Brown, William,
Brown, John,
Brittain, John,
Breckinridge, Robert,
Bruin, Peter B.,
Brooke, Edmund,
Brooke, Francis,
Brooke, John,
Brown, Robert,
Broadus, James,
Broadus, William,
Bradley, James,
Brashier, Richard,
Bradley, Christopher,

502 OFFICERS RECEIVING LAND WARRANTS.

Butler, Lawrence,
Burton, Hutchins,
Burfort, Thomas,
Bucker, Thomas,
Butler, Samuel,
Bullock, Rice,
Burwell, Nathaniel,

Christie, Thomas.
Campbell, William,
Campbell, Samuel,
Campbell, Archibald,
Carrington, Mayo,
Carrington, George,
Carrington, Clement,
Callender, Eleazer,
Carter, John C.,
Calmes, Marquis,
Cannon, Luke,
Casey, Benjamin,
Carney, Martin,
Carey, Samuel,
Catlett, Thomas,
Carnes, Patrick,
Call, Richard,
Calvert, Joseph,
Chamberlayne, George,
Chapman, John,
Chilton, John,
Cherry, William,
Chaplin, Abraham,
Clay, Matthew,
Clements, Mace,
Clayton, Philip,
Clay, Thomas,
Clark, Richard,
Clark, William,
Clark, Edmund,
Clark, John,
Claiborne, Richard,
Cleverius, James,
Coleman, Samuel,
Coleman, Jacob,
Coleman, Whitehead,
Coleman, John,
Coleman, Richard,
Coleman, Wyatt,
Cowherd, Francis,
Cowne, Robert,
Coverley, Thomas,
Cotterill, William,
Conway, Joseph,
Coke, Calvin,

Coke, Pleasant,
Cooper, Leonard,
Croghan, William,
Craddock, Robert,
Crawford, John,
Crump, Abner,
Crittenden, John,
Cramo, James,
Craig, James,
Crute, John,
Cunningham, William,
Cubberton, James,
Curry, James,

Dandridge, John,
Dandridge, Robert,
Dandridge, Alexander,
Davis, Joseph,
Dawson, Henry,
Darby, Nathaniel,
Dade, Francis,
Davenport, Opie,
Dedham, Archibald,
Delaplane, James,
Dix, Thomas,
Digges, Dudley,
Dickerson, Edmonds,
Dixon, Anthony F.,
Dick, Alexander,
Dicklawman, Christopher,
Dobson, Robert,
Drew, Thoms H.,
Drew, John,
Draper, George,
Dudley, Henry,
Dudley, Robert,
Duff, Edward,
Durall, Daniel,
Dye, Jonathan,

Easton, Philip,
Easton, Richard,
Edmonds, Thomas,
Eddins, Samuel,
Edwards, Leroy,
Edmonson, Benjamin,
Eggleston, Joseph,
Eggleston, William,
Eppes, Williams,
Erskine, Charles,
Eppes, William,
Eskridge, William,

OFFICERS RECEIVING LAND WARRANTS. 503

Eustance, John (1),
Eustance, John (2),
Evans, George,
Evans, William,
Ewell, Charles,
Ewell, Thomas,
Ewing, Alexander,

Fontleroy, Henry,
Fontleroy, Griffith,
Finn, Thomas,
Findley, Samuel,
Ferguson, Robert,
Fields, Reuben,
Fitzgerald, John (1),
Fitzgerald, John (2),
Fitzhugh, William,
Fitzhugh, Perigrine,
Fleet, John,
Fleet, Henry,
Flemming, John,
Fowler, William,
Fox, Thomas,
Fox, Nathaniel,
Foster, James,
Foster, Robert,
Foster, John,
Frazey, Falvy,

Gault, Patrick,
Gault, John M.,
Gaines, William F.,
Garland, Peter,
Gamble, Robert,
George, William,
Gerault, John,
George, Robert,
Gibson, John, jun.,
Gilchrist, George,
Gill, Samuel,
Gibbs, Churchill,
Gillison, John,
Giles, John,
Glasscock, Thomas,
Gordon, Arthur,
Gordon, Ambrose,
Goodwin, Dinwiddie,
Green, John,
Green, Robert,
Green, Samuel B.,
Green, Gabriel,
Graves, William,
Gray, Godfrey,

Gray, William,
Griffith, David (1),
Graham, Walter,
Gratton, John,
Gray, Francis,
Gray, James,
Gray, George,
Griffith, David (2),
Greer, Charles,
Guthrie, George,

Hardiman, John,
Hayes, John,
Harrison, John P.,
Harrison, John,
Harrison, Valentine,
Harrison, Charles,
Harrison, James,
Harrison, Richard,
Harrison, William R.,
Harper, James,
Hackley, John,
Hamilton, James,
Hays, Thomas,
Harcum, Rhodam,
Harris, John (1),
Harris, Jordan,
Harris, John (2),
Haney, Holland,
Hawkins, John,
Hawkins, Moses,
Harvie, John,
Heth, John,
Heth, Henry,
Healy, Martin,
Henderson, David,
Herbert, Thomas,
Hill, Thomas,
Hill, Bailor,
Hite, George,
Hite, Abraham,
Hite, Isaac,
Higgins, Peter,
Higgins, Robert,
Holmes, Benjamin,
Hoomes, Thomas C.,
Hoomes, David,
Hoomes, Isaac,
Holt, John H.,
Holt, Thomas,
Holt, James,
Hourd, Thomas,
Hoffler, William,

OFFICERS RECEIVING LAND WARRANTS.

Holdcombe, John,
Hockaday, Philip,
Holland, George,
Howell, Vincent,
Hogg, Samuel,
Holmer, Christian,
Hughes, Pratt,
Hughes, John,
Hughes, Jasper,
Hughes, Henry,
Hudson, John,
Humphreys, John,
Hurt, John,
Huffman, Philip,

Inniss, James,

James, Michael,
Jennings, John,
Jones, Samuel,
Jones, Strother,
Jones, Lewis (1),
Jones, Lewis (2),
Jones, Charles,
Jones, Peter,
Jones, Albrighton,
Jones, Churchill,
Jones, Cadwalader,
Jouett, Matthew,
Jouett Robert,
Johnson, Gideon,
Johnson, William,
Johnson, John B.,
Johnson, William,
Johnson, Peter,
Jolifee, John,
Jordan, John,
Jones, Gabriel,

Kays, Robert,
Kautsman, John,
Kennedy, James,
Kemp, Peter,
Kemp, James,
Kelly, Thaddy,
Kerny, John,
Kinley, Benjamin,
Kennon, John,
Keith, Isham,
Keller, Abraham,
Kendall, Custis,
Kirk, Robert,

King, Elisha,
King, Miles,
Kirkpatrick, Abraham,
Knight, John,
Knox, James,

Lapsley, Samuel,
Lapsley, John,
Lawson, Benjamin,
Langham, Elias,
Larty, John,
Lawson, Claiborne,
Lewis, William,
Lewis, George,
Lewis, Addison,
Lewis, Stephen,
Lewis, Audrew,
Lee, John,
Lee, Jond,
Lee, Phil. Francis F.,
Leigh, John,
Leitch, Andrew,
Lipscomb, Bernard,
Lipscomb, Reuben,
Lindsey, William,
Lightburn, Richard,
Livingston, Justice,
Linton, John,
Lilley, Thomas,
Lipscomb, Yancey,
Lovely, William L.,
Long, William,
Long, Reuben,
Longworth, Burgess,
Long, Gabriel,
Longsford, William,
Ludiman, William J.,
Lucas, James,
Lucas, Nathaniel,
Lynd, Arthur,

Marks, John,
Marshall, John,
Marshall, Thomas,
Marshall, Humphrey,
Marshall, James M.,
Mallory, Philip,
Maury, Abraham,
Mabin, James,
Mann, David,
Marston, John,
Massey, Thomas

OFFICERS RECEIVING LAND WARRANTS.

Marks, Isaiah,
Markham, James,
Martin, Thomas,
Mazaret, John,
Magill, Charles,
McDowell, John,
McWilliams, Joshua,
McMahon, William,
McClung, Walter,
McGuire, William,
McAdam, Joseph,
McCarty, Richard,
McAdams, John,
McElhany, John,
Meriwether, Thomas,
Meriwether, David,
Meriwether, James (1),
Meriwether, James (2),
Meriwether, James (3),
Meade, Everard,
Mercer, John F.,
Meredith, William,
Mills, John,
Miller, David,
Miller, Jarran,
Miller, Thomas,
Miller, William,
Minnis, Francis,
Minnis, Holman,
Minnis, Callowhill,
Middleton, Bazil,
Moody, Edward,
Moody, James,
Morton, James,
Mosely, Benjamin (1),
Mosely, William,
Mosely, Benjamin (2),
Moon, Alexander,
Moore, William,
Moore, John,
Moore, Peter,
Moore, Elson,
Moss, Henry,
Morrow, Robert,
Morton, Hezekiah,
Morgan, Simeon,
Morgan, Spencer,
Montague, Richard,
Montgomery, James,
Moxley, Rhodam,
Mountjoy, William,
Muir, Francis,
Munroe, James,

Muir, John,
Murray, Abraham,
Monroe, George,

Nelson, John (1),
Nelson, John (2),
Nelson, Roger,
Nixon, Andrew,
Norvell, Lipscomb,
Noland, Pierce,
Nuttall, Iverson,

Oldham, Conway,
Oliver, William,
O'Neal, Ferdinand,
Overton, Thomas,
Overton, John,
Payne, Thomas,
Payne, Tarlton,
Payne, Joseph,
Payne, Josiah,
Parker, Thomas,
Parker, Richard,
Parker, Nicholas,
Parker, William H.,
Parker, Alexander,
Parker, Josiah,
Parker, Thomas,
Parsons, William,
Patterson, Thomas,
Payton, Dade,
Page, Carter,
Peyton, John,
Peyton, Valentine,
Peyton, Henry,
Peyton, George,
Peyton, Robert,
Pendleton, James,
Pendleton, Nathaniel,
Pelham, Charles,
Pemberton, Thomas,
Pearson, Thomas,
Perry, John,
Pettus, John R.,
Perault, Michael,
Perkins, Archelaus,
Phillips, Samuel,
Pierce, William,
Porterfield, Robert,
Pointer, William,
Poulson, John,
Powell, Robert,

OFFICERS RECEIVING LAND WARRANTS.

Powell, Thomas,
Powell, Peyton,
Powell, Francis,
Powers, Robert,
Poythress, William,
Porter, William (1),
Porter, William (2),
Pope, Matthews,
Prior, John,
Pride, William R.,
Pugh, Willis,
Purvis, James,

Quarles, James,
Quarles, Henry,
Quarles, Thomas,
Quarles, Robert,
Quarles, William P.,
Quarles, John (1),
Quarles, John (2),
Quirk, Thomas,

Ragsdale, Drury,
Randolph, Robert,
Rankin, Robert,
Ransdell, Thomas,
Read, Nathaniel,
Read, Edmund,
Read, Clement,
Renner, John,
Reddick, Jason,
Reddick, Willis,
Rhea, Matthew,
Rice, George,
Rice, Nathaniel,
Richardson, Walker,
Ridley, Thomas,
Rickman, William,
Robertson, William,
Robertson, James,
Robins, John (1),
Robins, John (2),
Roberts, John,
Rose, Robert,
Robinson, John,
Roane, Christopher,
Rogers, John,
Rogers, William,
Roy, Beverly,
Rooney, John,
Russell, John,
Russell, Albert,
Russell, Charles,

Russell, Andrew,
Rust, Benjamin,
Rucker, Angus,
Rudder, Epaphroditus,
Rydman, John.

Saunders, William,
Saunders, Joseph,
Saunders, Celey,
Savage, Joseph,
Savage, Nathaniel,
Sansum, Philip,
Sayres, Robert,
Scott, Charles,
Scott, Walter,
Scott, Joseph, jr.,
Scott, John (1),
Scott, John (2),
Scott, Joseph, sen.,
Sayers, Thomas,
Settle, Strother,
Seldon, Samuel,
Shepherd, Abraham,
Shearman, Martin,
Skelton, Clough,
Shield, John,
Shackelford, William,
Singleton, Joseph,
Singleton, Anthony,
Skinner, Alexander,
Slaughter, John,
Slaughter, Philip,
Slaughter, William,
Slaughter, Lawrence,
Slaughter, George.
Slaughter, Augustine,
Smith, Obadiah,
Smith, William,
Smith, Granville,
Smith, Nathan,
Smith, Francis,
Smith, Gregory,
Smith, Jonathan,
Smith, William S.,
Smith, Ballard,
Smith, Larkin,
Smart, Richard.
Snead, Smith,
Southall, Stephen,
Spottswood, John,
Spencer, William,
Spencer, John,
Spiller, William,

OFFICERS RECEIVING LAND WARRANTS. 507

Springer, Jacob,
Springer, Uriah,
Stith, John (1),
Stith, John (2),
Stephenson, David,
Steele, John,
Steele, William,
Stokely, Charles,
Steed, John,
Stribling, Sigesmund,
Stribling, Erasmus,
Stubblefield, George,
Stubblefield, Beverly,
Stoakes, John,
Stephens, William,
Stephens, Edward,
Stuart, Philip,
Starke, William,
Starke, Richard,
Stott, William,
Summers, Simon,
Summerson, Gavin,
Swoope, John,
Swearingen, Joseph,
Swan, John,

Tabb, Augustine,
Taliaferro, Benjamin,
Taliaferro, Nicholas,
Taylor, Benjamin,
Taylor, Richard,
Taylor, Reuben,
Taylor, Francis,
Taylor, Isaac,
Taylor, William,
Taylor, Thornton,
Tatem, Zechariah,
Tannehill, Josiah,
Terry, Nathaniel,
Thompson, William,
Thompson, George,
Thornton, Presley,
Thomas, Lewis,
Throckmorton, Albion,
Thweatt, Thomas,
Tebbs, Thomas,
Tinsley, Samuel,
Tompkins, Robert,
Tompkins, Henry,
Tompkins, Christopher,
Tompkins, Daniel R.,
Townes, John,
Todd, Robert,

Trant, Lawrence,
Tresvant, John,
Trabue, John,
Travis, Edward,
Triplett, George,
Tutt, Charles,
Turner, John,
Tupman, John,
Tyler, John,

Upshur, Thomas,
Upshur, James,

Van Metre, Joseph,
Vance, Robert,
Vanse, William,
Vaughan, Claiborne,
Vaughan, John,
Valentine, Edward,
Valentine, Jacob,
Vanderwall, Marks,
Volluson, Armand,
Vawters, William,
Vowles, Charles,
Vowles, Henry,
Vowles, Walter,
Warman, Thomas,
Wallace, William B.,
Wallace, James (1),
Wallace, James (2),
Wallace, Adam,
Wallace, Andrew,
Walker, Jacob,
Walker, David,
Walker, Levin (1),
Walker, Levin (2),
Waggoner, Andrew,
Walters, Richard C.,
Watts, John,
Walls, George,
Washington, George,
Waddy, Sharpleigh,
Welch, Nathaniel,
Webb, Isaac,
West, Charles,
White, Robert,
White, John (1),
White, John (2),
White, Tarpley,
White, William (1),
White, Thomas,
White, William (2),
White, William (3),

Whittaker, William,
Whiting, Henry,
Whiting, Francis,
Wilson, Willis (1),
Wilson, Willis (2),
Winston, Benjamin,
Winston, John,
Winston, William,
Williams, James,
Williams, Edward,
Williams, David,
Williams, Jarrett,
Williams, John,
Willis, John W.,
Willis, Henry,
Winlock, Joseph,
Woodson, Frederick,

Woodson, Hughes,
Woodson, Tarleton,
Woodson, Robert,
Worsham, John,
Worsham, Richard,
Worsham, William,
Wright, Wescott,
Wright, James,
Wright, Patrick,
Wyatt, Carey,

Yarborough, Charles,
Yancey, Leighton,
Yancey, Robert,
Young, Henry,

NOTE.—After the Revolution, the greater part of these officers emigrated to the military land districts in Ohio, Kentucky, and Tennessee, where their representatives now reside.

VIRGINIA HALF-PAY.
ACT MAY SESSION, 1779.

Be it enacted, That all general officers of the army, being citizens of this Commonwealth, and all field-officers, captains, and subalterns, commanding, or who shall command in the battalions of this Commonwealth, on Continental establishment, or serving in the battalions raised for the immediate defense of this State, or for the defense of the United States; and all chaplain, physicians, surgeons, and surgeons' mates, appointed to the said battalions, or any of them, being citizens of this Commonwealth, and not being in the service of Georgia or of any other State, provided Congress do not make some tantamount provision for them, who shall serve henceforward, or from the time of their being commissioned, until the end of the war; and all such officers who have or shall become supernumerary on the reduction of any of the said battalions, and shall again enter into the said service, if required so to do, in the same or any higher rank, and continue therein until the end of the war, shall be entitled to half-pay during life, to commence from the determination of their command or service.

VIRGINIA HALF-PAY.

ACT NOVEMBER SESSION, 1781.

Be it enacted, That the officers and seamen of the navy of this State, as they stand arranged by a late regulation, shall be entitled to the same advantages as the officers belonging to this State in the land service, agreeable to their respective ranks.

The officers of Virginia under those acts prosecuted their claims for half-pay to judgment in the courts of the State, and Congress assumed the payment of those judgments, etc., by the following

ACT, APPROVED JULY 5, 1832.

SEC. 1. *Be it enacted by the Senate and House of Representatives of the United States of America, in Congress assembled,* That the proper accounting officers of the Treasury do liquidate and pay the accounts of the Commonwealth of Virginia against the United States, for payments to the officers commanding in the Virginia Line in the war of the Revolution, on account of the half-pay for life promised the officers aforesaid by that Commonwealth, the sum of one hundred and thirty-nine thousand five hundred and forty-three dollars and sixty cents.

SEC. 2. *And be it further enacted,* That the Secretary of the Treasury be, and he is hereby, required and directed to pay to the State of Virginia the amount of the judgments which have been rendered against the said State for and on account of the promise contained in an act passed by the General Assembly of the State of Virginia, in the month of May, A. D. 1779, and in favor of the officers, or representatives of the officers, of the regiments and corps hereafter recited, and not exceeding in the whole the sum of two hundred and forty-one thousand three hundred and forty-five dollars, to wit:

1. To the officers, or their legal representatives, of the regiment commanded by the late Colonel George Gibson, the amount of the judgments which they have obtained, and which are now unsatisfied.

2. To the officers, or their legal representatives, of the regiment denominated the Second State Regiment, commanded, at times, by Colonels Brent and Dabney, the amount of the judg-

ments which they have obtained, and which are now unsatisfied.

3. To the officers, or their legal representatives, of the regiments of Colonels Clarke and Crockett, and Captain Rogers' troop of cavalry, who were employed in the Illinois service, the amount of the judgments which they have obtained, and which are now unsatisfied.

4. To the officers, or their legal representatives, serving in the regiment of State Artillery commanded by the late Colonel Marshall, and those serving in the State Garrison Regiment commanded by Colonel Muter, and those serving in the State Cavalry, commanded by Major Nelson, the amount of the judgments which they have obtained, and which are now unsatisfied.

5. To the officers, or their legal representatives, who served in the navy of Virginia during the late war of the Revolution, the amount of the judgments which they have obtained, and which are now unsatisfied.

SEC. 8. *And be it further enacted*, That the Secretary of the Treasury be, and he is hereby, directed and required to adjust and settle those claims for half-pay of the officers of the aforesaid regiments and corps, which have not been paid or prosecuted to judgment against the State of Virginia, and for which said State would be bound on the principles of the half-pay cases already decided in the Supreme Court of Appeals of said State; which several sums of money herein directed to be settled or paid, shall be paid out of any money in the treasury not otherwise appropriated by law.

On the 12th of August, 1848, Congress appropriated a further sum of $81,273.17, for the payment of those Virginia half-pay claims, and made it the duty of the agent of the State to first deposit authenticated copies of the acts or judgments under which the money was paid by the State of Virginia.

By act of Congress, approved March 3, 1835, the adjustment of those claims was transferred from the Secretary of the Treasury to the Commissioner of Pensions.

VIRGINIA HALF-PAY.

We will add a few cases showing the large sums paid to the heirs or legal representatives of officers entitled to half-pay under this act:

Name	Rate		Total
John Allison, Lieutenant-colonel	$360	per annum	$7,989.04
William Armistead, Captain of Cavalry	300	"	8,987.53
Thomas Armistead, Capt. of Artillery	240	"	4,148.38
Robert Andrews, Chaplain	240	"	7,284.88
John Archer, Lieutenant, Navy	182.50	"	2,153.00
John Applewhaite, Surgeon, Navy	182.50	"	9,138.70
John Allen, Captain of Artillery	300	"	6,270.41
William Armistead, Paymaster	180	"	7,352.38
William Broadus, Lieutenant	160	"	6,148.08
Rice Bullock, Lieutenant	160	"	7,057.53
Samuel Butler, Lieutenant of Artillery	200	"	6,360.00
John Baily, Captain	240	"	10,548.16
Richard Brashears, Captain	240	"	9,697.31
Machin Boswell, Captain	240	"	3,081.86
Wm. Ballard, Lieutenant of Artillery	200	"	4,646.00
Samuel Barron, Captain, Navy	243.33	"	6,906.40
James Bradley, Captain of Artillery	300	"	1,407.12
William Brent, Colonel	450	"	1,960.27
Isaac Browning, Lieutenant	160	"	6,606.90
James Banks, Sailing-master	152.08	"	1,880.42
John Brittain, do.	152.08	"	2,253.42
Wm. Bennett, do.	152.08	"	2,982.92
Thomas Bonewell, do.	152.08	"	1,680.81
John Baytop, Lieutenant	180	"	2,704.65
Laban Baily, Sailing-master	152.08	"	2,021.20
Charles S. Bouch, Lieutenant, Navy	182.50	"	5,066.00
Philip Bartlett, Surgeon	182.50	"	4,779.50
William Booth, Sailing-master	152.08	"	4,549.48
Robert Brown, Lieutenant of Artillery	200	"	6,579.72
James Barron, Commodore			32,382.50
Richard Barron, do.			11,215.78
James Banks, do.			5,734.12
John Baily, Captain, Bardstown, Ky			9,480.68
Gideon Johnson, Quartermaster, Warrenton, Va			4,303.82
Edward Worthington, Captain, Shelby county, Ky			7,149.50
Churchill Gibbs, Lieutenant, Madison, Va			7,961.53
Corbin Griffin, Captain, Williamsburg, Va			10,930.19
John Cox, Captain, Norfolk, Va			13,715.22

REVOLUTIONARY PENSION LAWS.

Prior to the year 1818, Congress passed no pension laws except for the relief of those officers and soldiers who were disabled in the service; consequently, all those who were not disabled, and died between the close of the Revolutionary war and the year 1818, could receive no pension, for all the pension laws required that the soldier shall be living at the date of the passage of the law.

The pension acts now in force are as follows:

ACT MARCH 18, 1818.

SEC. 1. *Be it enacted by the Senate and House of Representatives of the United States, in Congress assembled,* That every commissioned officer, non-commissioned officer, musician, and private soldier, and all officers in the hospital department and medical staff, who served in the war of the Revolution to the end thereof, or for the term of *nine months,* or longer, at any period of the war, on the Continental establishment, and every commissioned officer, non-commissioned officer, mariner, or marine, who served at the same time, and for a like term, in the naval service of the United States, who is yet a resident citizen of the United States, and who is, or hereafter, by reason of his reduced circumstances in life, shall be in need of assistance from his country for support, and shall have substantiated his claim to a pension in the manner hereinafter directed, shall receive a pension from the United States: if an officer, of twenty dollars per month during life; if a non-commissioned officer, musician, mariner, marine, or private soldier, of eight dollars per month during life: *Provided,* no person shall be entitled to the provisions of this act until he shall have relinquished his claim to every pension heretofore allowed him by the laws of the United States.

Sec. 2. *And be it further enacted*, That, to entitle any person to the provisions of this act, he shall make a declaration, under oath or affirmation, before the district judge of the United States of the district, or before any judge or court of record of the county, State, or territory in which the applicant shall reside, setting forth, if he belonged to the army, the company, regiment, and line to which he belonged; the time he entered service, and the time and manner of leaving the service; and, in case he belonged to the navy, a like declaration, setting forth the name of the vessel and particular service in which he was employed, and the time and manner of leaving the service, and shall offer such other evidence as may be in his power; and on its appearing, to the satisfaction of the said judge, that the applicant served in the Revolutionary war as aforesaid, against the common enemy, he shall certify and transmit the testimony in the case, and the proceedings had thereon, to the Secretary for the Department of War, whose duty it shall be, if satisfied the applicant comes under the provisions of this act, to place such officer, musician, mariner, marine, or soldier, on the pension list of the United States, to be paid in the same manner as pensions to invalids who have been placed on the pension list are now paid, and under such restrictions and regulations, in all respects, as are prescribed by law.

Sec. 3. *And be it further enacted*, That every pension, by virtue of this act, *shall commence on the day that the declaration under oath or affirmation, prescribed in the foregoing section, shall be made.*

Sec. 4. *And be it further enacted*, That, from and after the passage of this act, no sale, transfer, or mortgage, of the whole, or any part, of the pension in pursuance of this act, shall be valid; and any person who shall swear or affirm falsely in the premises, and he be thereof convicted, shall suffer as for willful and corrupt perjury.

The above act relates to the Continental army alone, or those forces raised by Congress and serving in the regular army of the United Colonies, and those serving in the Continental navy.

Soon after the passage of this act, applications for pensions numbering about eight thousand had accumulated, so that on the 1st May, 1820, Congress appears to have been alarmed into the passage of an act to the effect that after March 4, 1820, no person shall be entitled to the further benefits of this act "until he shall have exhibited to some court of record, in the county, city, or borough in which he resides, *a schedule subscribed by him*, containing his whole estate and income." Being poor, yet possessing too much of the spirit of '76, to permit their "goods and chattels" to be exposed to the gaze of the public, many refused a compliance with the provisions of this act; and others possessed of some estates could not affirm that they stood in "need of the assistance of their country for a support." Many of those who had been admitted to pension prior to the passage of the act of May 1, 1820, made out their schedules as required, but in the opinion of the Secretary of War a large number of them were not entitled to the "assistance of their country for a support," and were consequently dropped from the rolls and ceased to be pensioners.

The provisions of this act of May 1, 1820, as the government afterwards discovered, operated strongly on some as an invitation to squander their property, so as to bring themselves fairly within the provisions of the act of 1818; and for this purpose many were known to make over their property to friends or children for mere imaginary considerations.

The knowledge of these facts brought forth from Congress another act, approved March 1, 1823, authorizing the secretary of War "to restore to the list of pensioners the name of any person who may have been, or may hereafter be, stricken therefrom, if such person has heretofore furnished, or hereafter shall furnish, evidence that he is in such indigent circumstances as to be unable to support himself without the assistance of his country, and that he has not disposed of, or transferred his property, or any portion thereof, with a view to obtain a pension;" and enacting, "that no pension hereafter to be allowed on claims or schedules heretofore filed under the act or acts to which this act is a supplement, or under the provisions of this act, shall commence before the passage thereof; and all other pensions hereafter to be allowed, under the acts aforesaid, *shall commence from the time* of completing the proof."

After the passage of this act of 1823, and after so many of the old soldiers had been "driven off the field" by the act of 1820, and allowed a little more time to die, the Secretary of War became more liberal in his opinions with respect to the "schedules," and large numbers of them were by degrees restored to the rolls—but not until they were deprived of from three to five years' pension by Congress legislating in a state of "alarm."

ACT, APPROVED MAY 15, 1828.

SEC. 1. *Be it enacted by the Senate and House of Representatives of the United States of America, in Congress assembled*, That each of the surviving officers of the army of the Revolution, in Continental line, who was entitled to half-pay by the resolve of October twenty-first, seventeen hundred and eighty, be authorized to receive out of any money in the treasury not otherwise appropriated, the amount of his full pay in said line according to his rank in the line, to begin on the third of March, one thousand eight hundred and twenty-six, and to continue during his natural life : *Provided*, That under this act no officer shall be entitled to receive a larger sum than the full pay of a captain in said line.

SEC. 2. *And be it further enacted*, That whenever any of said officers has received money of the United States, as a pensioner, since the third day of March, eighteen hundred and twenty-six, aforesaid, the sum so received shall be deducted from what said officer would otherwise be entitled to under the first section of this act; and every pension to which said officer is now entitled shall cease after the passage of this act.

SEC. 3. *And be it further enacted*, That every surviving non-commissioned officer, musician, or private, in said army, who enlisted therein for and during the war, and continued in service until its termination, and thereby became entitled to receive a reward of eighty dollars, under a resolve of Congress, passed May 15, 1778, shall be entitled to receive his full monthly pay in said service, out of any money in the Treasury not otherwise appropriated; to begin on the third day of March, 1826, and to continue during his natural life : *Provided*, That no non-commissioned officer, musician, or private, in said army, who is now on the pension list of the United States, shall be entitled to the benefits of this act.

SEC. 4. *And be it further enacted*, That the pay allowed by this act shall, under the direction of the Secretary of the Treasury, be paid to the officer or soldier entitled thereto, or to their authorized attorney, at such places and days as said Secretary may direct; and that no foreign officer shall be entitled to said pay, nor shall any officer or soldier receive the same, until he furnish to said Secretary satisfactory evidence that he is entitled to the same in conformity to the provisions of this act; and pay allowed by this act shall not, in any way, be transferable, or liable to attachment, levy, or seizure, by any legal process whatever, but shall inure wholly to the personal benefit of the officer or soldier entitled to the same by this act.

SEC. 5. *And be it further enacted*, That so much of said pay as accrued by the provisions of this act, before the third day of March, 1828, shall be paid to the officers and soldiers entitled to the same, as soon as may be, in the manner and under the provisions before mentioned; and the pay which shall accrue after said day shall be paid semi-annually, in like manner, and under the same provisions.

This act was passed without regard to any "property qualification," and being founded on the half-pay acts of the Continental Congress and the "Gratuity Act" of May 15, 1778, no one could claim its provisions, unless he was adjudged to be entitled to "commutation" per act March 22, 1783, or to the gratuity of $80 per act May 15, 1778. Though precisely a half century had rolled between the passage of the acts of May 15, 1778, and May 15, 1828, yet several hundreds of the time-worn and old "non-commissioned officers, musicians, and privates" came forth to receive the last token of their country's regard under the latter act; many of whom had been "dropped" by the "alarm" act of May 1, 1820.

Invalid pensioners, placed on the rolls by the provisions of former acts of Congress, were required to relinquish their pensions before they could be entitled under this act, and because the provisions of this act, were in a majority of instances, more beneficial to them than their pensions, they received its benefits, deducting therefrom the amount of their pensions, which had been received by them since March 3, 1826.

But, on the 31st May, 1830, Congress passed an act declaring that the 2d section of the act of May 15, 1828, "shall not be construed so as embrace invalid pensioners; and that the pension of invalid soldiers shall not be deducted from the amount receivable by them under the said act."

But the act of May 31, 1830, was not construed by the Executive to restore the soldier to his invalid pension from March 3, 1826, the time from which it had been deducted, but only from the date of the passage of the said act of May 31, 1830; so that he was allowed to enjoy his two pensions only from the date of this latter act; which circumstance gave rise to numerous applications to Congress for a restoration of the invalid pension, which had been, contrary to the spirit of the law, deducted from his full pay between the periods of March 3, 1826, and May 31, 1830. Congress by special acts restored the invalid pension thus deducted in a number of cases.

The act of May 31, 1830, related to invalid officers alone, and on the 14th of July, 1832, Congress passed an act making the same provision for the soldier; both of which acts were, by the Attorney-general, declared to be altogether prospective, so that the soldier did not enjoy his two pensions until after July 14, 1832.

All staff officers were excluded from the benefits of the act of May 15, 1828, except they, at the same time, held a commission in the *line*, in which case the amount of their pay, under said act, is determined by their rank in said *line*, without regard to their pay in the staff.

ACT APPROVED JUNE 7, 1832.

SEC. 1. *Be it enacted by the Senate and House of Representatives of the United States of America, in Congress assembled,* That each of the surviving officers, non-commissioned officers, musicians, soldiers, and Indian spies, who shall have served in the Continental line, or State troops, volunteers, or militia, at one or more terms, a period of two years, during the war of the Revolution, and who are not entitled to any benefit under the act for the relief of certain surviving officers and soldiers of the Revolution, passed the fifteenth day of May, eighteen hundred and twenty-eight, be authorized to receive, out of any money in the treasury not otherwise appropriated, the amount of his full pay in the said line, according to his rank, but not exceeding, in any case, the pay of a captain in the said line; such pay to commence from the fourth day of March, eighteen hundred and thirty-one, and shall continue during his natural life; and that any such officer, non-commissioned officer, musician, or private, as aforesaid, who shall have served in the Continental line, State troops, volunteers, or militia, a term or terms in the whole less than the above period, but not less than six months, shall be authorized to receive, out of any unappropriated money in the treasury, during his natural life, each according to his term of service, an amount bearing such proportion to the annuity granted to the same rank for the service of two years, as his term of service did to the term aforesaid; to commence from the fourth day of March, one thousand eight hundred and thirty-one.

SEC. 2. *And be it further enacted,* That no person, receiving any annuity or pension under any law of the United States providing for Revolutionary officers and soldiers, shall be entitled to the benefits of this act, unless he shall have relinquished his further claim to such pension; and in all payments under this act, the amount which may have been received under any other act, as aforesaid, since the date at which the payments under this act shall commence, shall first be deducted from such payment.

SEC. 3. *And be it further enacted,* That the pay allowed by this act shall, under the direction of the Secretary of the Treasury, be paid to the officer, non-commissioned officer, musician, or private, entitled thereto, or his or their authorized attorney, at such places and times as the Secretary of the Treasury may direct; and that no foreign officer shall be entitled to said pay, nor shall any officer, non-commissioned officer, musician, or private, receive the same until he furnish the said Secretary satisfactory evidence that he is entitled to the same, in conformity to the provisions of this act; and the pay hereby allowed shall not be in any way transferable, or liable to attachment, levy, or seizure, by any legal process whatever, but shall inure wholly to the personal benefit of the officer, non-commissioned officer, musician, or soldier, entitled to the same.

SEC. 4. *And be it further enacted,* That so much of the said pay as accrued before the approval of this act, shall be paid to the person entitled to the same as soon as may be, in the manner and under the provisions above mentioned; and the pay which shall accrue thereafter shall be paid semi-annually, in the manner above directed; and in case of the death of any person embraced by the provisions of this act, or of the act to which it is supplementary, during the period intervening between the semi-annual payments directed to be made by said acts, the proportionate amount of pay which shall accrue between the last preceding semi-annual payment and the death of such person, shall be paid to his widow, or if he leave no widow, to his children.

SEC. 5. *And be it further enacted,* That the officers, non-commissioned officers, mariners, or marines, who served for a like term in the naval service, during the Revolutionary war, shall be entitled to the benefits of this act, in the same manner as is provided for the officers and soldiers of the army of the Revolution.

This act grants a pension to the officers, soldiers, and sailors, of every grade, who were engaged in military service during the Revolution for a period of two years, or for any period not less than six months; but excludes privateers. To those who served for a time less than six months, nothing has been given, though for four or five months they may have been in the most meritorious service and in the fiercest engagements.

All staff officers whose claims were rejected under act May 15, 1828, are admitted under this. Thus: assume the case of a person who has served for two years as lieutenant and adjutant, the act of 1828 only gave him $320 per annum; but he could have, at any time since the passage of the act of 1832, applied, or his children can now apply, for the benefits of this act for his services as adjutant, and receive pension from March 4, 1831, to the day the officer died, at $480 per annum.

By this act and that of May 15, 1828, the act of March 18, 1818, has been rendered disadvantageous, and consequently inoperative; and though, to a private soldier, the act of 1818 grants a pension of $96 per annum, and the act of 1832 only $80, yet the provisions of the latter act since its passage are more beneficial than those of the former; because, on the day of the passage of the said act of 1832, the sum of one year's pension by enactment was made *to have accrued* and become due, from March 4, 1831, to March 4, 1832, which the pensioner could receive as soon after the 7th day of June, 1832, as he could establish his claim—and at the time of the passage of the act of 1828, the sum of two years' pension was declared *to have accrued* and become due, from March 3, 1828, to March 3, 1828, which the annuitant could also receive as soon after the 15th day of May, 1828, as he could establish his claim.

On the contrary, let it be assumed that on the 15th day of May, 1828, a person applies under the act of 1818 for a pension at $96 per annum, his pension, then, by law, could only commence on the day of the "completion of the proof," and no back pay will have accrued to him.

REVOLUTIONARY PENSION LAWS. 521

The same is true with respect to the act of 1832, which gives the one year's back pay, consequently after May 15, 1828, and June 7, 1832, all applications under the act of 1818 ceased to be made.

Again, let it be assumed that a private applies in 1850 for a pension under the act of 1818 at $96 per annum, his pension can only commence from the time he completes his testimony in 1850, while, on the contrary, if he or his heirs apply in the said year of 1850 for pension under the act of 1828 or 1832, at the lower rate of $80 per annum, he or they will then receive the whole amount of back pension from March 3, 1826, or from March 4, 1831, as the case may be, which is far more beneficial than the pension under act 1818, to commence only in 1850.

The second section of the act of 1832 requires the reduction of all invalid and other pensions, and a total relinquishment thereof, before receiving its benefits; but Congress, on the 19th of February, 1833, removed this restriction; so that, since that time, invalids have received two pensions where their service has been of sufficient duration to admit them to pension per act 1832.

On the 4th of July, 1836, with respect to the act of 1832, Congress enacted as follows: That if any person entitled to the benefits of the act of June 7, 1832, "have died since March 4, 1831, and before the date of said act, the amount of pension which would have accrued from March 4, 1831, to the time of his death, and become payable to him by virtue of that act, if he had survived the passage thereof, shall be paid to his widow; and if he left no widow, to his children, in the manner prescribed in the act hereby amended."

Foreign officers, commissioned by the Continental Congress or any State authority, are entitled to pension under this act, but those not so commissioned have no claim.

On the 14th of July, 1832, Congress again enacted, that in the execution of the act of 1832 "the time of imprisonment as a prisoner of war shall be taken and computed as a part of the period of service." The time the party was a prisoner *on parole* is also allowed as a part of his time of service.

On the 2d of March, 1833, Congress also enacted, that in the execution of the act of 1832, "whenever it shall be made to appear that any applicant for a pension under the said act entered the army of the Revolution, in pursuance of a contract with the government, made previous to April 11, 1783, and continue in service until that period, it shall be the duty of the Secretary of War to compute the period of such applicant's service from the time he then entered the army, and until the date of the Definitive Treaty of Peace, and allow him a pension accordingly."

ACT APPROVED JULY 4, 1836.

SEC. 3. *And be it further enacted*, That if any person who served in the war of the Revolution, in the manner specified in the act passed June 7, 1832, have died, leaving a widow whose marriage took place *before the expiration of the last period of his service*, such widow shall be entitled to receive, during the time she may remain unmarried, the annuity or pension which might have been allowed to her husband, by virtue of the act aforesaid, if living at the time it was passed.

The marriage of a widow does not destroy her claim to pension under this act, provided she was a widow a second time on the day of its passage.

Pensions under this act commence on the 4th day of March, 1831, as did those under the act of June 7, 1832.

On the 7th of July, 1838, Congress declared that pensions under this act "shall not be withheld from any widow whose husband has died since the passage of said act, or shall hereafter die," if she shall be otherwise entitled to the benefits of the act of July 4, 1836.

The Attorney-general, under date of the 13th of April, 1837, declares that "the right of the widow under the act is to be regarded as a *vested interest accruing on the passage of the law*, and not defeated by the omission to apply for it; and it goes as such, on her death, to her personal representatives," that is, children; and where the widow, in consequence of a second marriage, has two sets of children, the pension is to be divided equally among them all.

But, assuming that a widow entitled to pension per act July 4, 1836, dies, for instance, in 1840, without having received her pension, and leaving a number of children, who, or a portion of whom, do not apply for their mother's pension until 1857, after some of the children have died, between 1840 and this latter date; then those *now living*, will receive the pension. The representatives of those children of the widow, who died between the death of said widow in 1840, and the time of the application for the pension in 1857, have no claim. The same is true with respect to the following widows' acts and the act of 1832, on the principle that grand-children have no claim; and that on the death of the husband and widow, leaving no children, the claim dies with them—but under the act of May 15, 1828, in default of children the pension goes to executors or administrators, but forms no part of the assets of estate in their hands.

A widow who, on her own application, has been divorced from her husband, has no claim to pension.

All persons applying for pension under this act must prove that their parents were *legally* married.

ACT APPROVED JULY 7, 1838.

SEC. 1. *Be it enacted by the Senate and House of Representatives of the United States of America, in Congress assembled,* That if any person who served in the war of the Revolution in the manner specified in the act passed June 7, 1832, have died, leaving a widow, *whose marriage took place after the expiration of the last period of his service, and before January* 1, 1794, such widow shall be entitled to receive, for and during the term of *five years from the 4th day of March,* 1836, the annuity or pension which might have been allowed to her husband, by virtue of the said act, if living at the time it was passed: *Provided,* That in the event of the marriage of such widow, said annuity or pension shall be discontinued.

All widows whose husbands served in the Revolutionary war, as stated in the act, and who were married after the *last term* of his service, and *prior* to January 1, 1794, can claim pension under this act, provided they were widows at the passage thereof.

No pension can be granted to a widow for any part of the time her husband may have received one.

On the 3d of March, 1843, Congress passed an act extending the provisions of the act of 1838 one year from March 4, 1843.—On the 17th of June, 1844, they extended them four years from March 4, 1844, and on the 2d of February, 1848, they extended them from March 4, 1848, for life—leaving a period of two years, from March 4, 1841, to March 4, 1843, for which no provision of law has yet been made, and for which period the old ladies received nothing. A bill is now pending in Congress which proposes to give those two years' pension to the children of the old ladies, provided they themselves are not living.

Those who became widows after the passage of the act of July 7, 1838, have no claim to its provisions, nor to the supplementary acts of 1843 and 1844, but they can claim under act of February 2, 1848, provided they were living at the passage thereof.

The act of July 7, 1838, gives $80 per annum to the widow of a soldier who served two years, and $20 dollars per annum for a service of six months in the Continental and State lines, militia, &c., as the act of June 7, 1832, gives to the husband; but on the first of July, 1848, Congress enacted that any widow whose husband had served in the *Continental line* for a period of nine months, and whose marriage took place prior to January 1, 1794, should receive the same rate of pension per annum that her husband would have been entitled to under the act of March 18, 1818; consequently many pensions under the act of February 2, 1848, were increased from very low rates to $96 per annum in the case of privates, and to $240 per annum in some few cases of officers, commencing July 1, 1848.

ACT APPROVED JULY 29, 1848.

SEC. 1. *And be it enacted by the Senate and House of Representatives of the United States of America, in Congress assembled,* That the widows of all officers, non-commissioned officers, musicians, soldiers, mariners, marines, and Indian spies, who shall have served in the Continental line, State troops, volunteers, militia, or in the naval service, in the Revolutionary war with Great Britain, shall be entitled to a pension, during such widowhood, of equal amount per annum that their husbands would have been entitled to, if living, under existing pension laws; to commence on the 4th day of March, 1848, and to be paid in the same manner that other pensions are paid to widows; but no widow now receiving a pension shall be entitled to receive a further pension under the provisions of this act; and no widow married after January 1, 1800, shall be entitled to receive a pension under this act.

This act, as well as all other acts, requires that the widow shall be a widow and living at the date of its passage; and places on the pension rolls all those whose marriage took place between January 1, 1794, and January 1, 1800.

If the widow did not receive her pension under this act while living, her children can apply after her death for the amount from March 4, 1848, to the day she died.

Grandchildren, executors, or administrators, have no claim; but the rule now is to apply through an administrator, or executor, for the benefit of the children—pension money being no part of the assets in the hands of an administrator, nor "liable to attachment, levy, or seizure, by any legal process whatever."

ACT APPROVED FEBRUARY 3, 1853.

SEC. 2. *And be it further enacted,* That the widows of all officers, non-commissioned officers, musicians, and privates of the Revolutionary army, who were married subsequent to January, A. D. 1800, shall be entitled to a pension in the same manner as those who were married before that date.

This act places on the pension list all widows who were married between January 1, 1800, and February 3, 1853, if they were widows and alive on this latter date.

The Secretary of the Interior decided that pensions under this act shall "commence from the date of its passage;" and consequntly the pensions of all who have claimed its benefits have been made to commence February 3, 1853; but it is contended that Congress, by the words *"shall be entitled to a pension in the same manner as those who were married before that date,"* means that the pension should commence on the 4th of March, 1848, as under the act of July 29, 1848.

A bill is now pending in Congress placing the commencement of pensions under this act back to March 4, 1848, which, if it becomes a law, will give the widows their pensions from March 4, 1848, to February 3, 1853, or the same to their children, if they should not be living.

This is the last pension act that has been passed by Congress.

When a person entitled to pension applies to the Commissioner of Pensions, at Washington, to be placed on the pension-roll, a "certificate of pension" is issued to him, and made payable at the United States Pension Agency, in the State nearest the pensioner's residence, to which he applies every six months for his semi-annual stipend.

A LIST OF REVOLUTIONARY OFFICERS,
SHOWING SOME EVENTS IN THEIR LIVES, AND THE DATES WHEN THEY DIED.

GEORGE WASHINGTON.

Elected Commander-in-Chief of the American army June 15, 1775—Takes command of the army at Cambridge, July 2, 1775—At the Evacuation of Boston, March 17, 1776—At the Battle of Long Island, August 27, 1776—Invested by Congress with dictatorial powers, December 27, 1776—At the Battle of Trenton, December 26, 1776—At the Battle of Princeton, January 3, 1777—At the Battle of Brandywine, September 11, 1777—At the Battle of Germantown, October 4, 1777—At the Battle of Monmouth, June 28, 1778—At the siege of Yorktown, October 19, 1781—Makes his farewell address to the army, November 2, 1783—Takes possession of New York, November 25, 1783—Last meeting with his officers, December 4, 1783—Resigns his commission, December 23, 1783—Chosen President of the United States,

March 4, 1789—Inaugurated at New York, April 30, 1789—Chosen President for a second term from March 4, 1793—Returns to private life, March 4, 1797—Died at Mount Vernon, December 14, 1799.

MAJOR-GENERAL CHARLES LEE.

Second in command to the Commander-in-Chief—At Cambridge with General Washington, July 2, 1775—Captured by the British at Baskinridge, N. J., December, 1776—Exchanged, May 6, 1778—At the Battle of Monmouth, June 28, 1778—Left the army in 1780—Died in Philadelphia, October 2, 1782.

MAJOR-GENERAL HORATIO GATES.

Joins the army in 1775—Accompanies General Washington to Cambridge in July, 1775—Takes the command of the northern army in June, 1776—Burgoyne surrenders to him, October 17, 1777, at Saratoga—Is defeated at Camden, August 16, 1780—Serves to the end of the war—Goes to reside on Manhattan Island in 1790—Elected to the Legislature of New York in 1800—Died at his residence, April 10, 1806.

MAJOR-GENERAL NATHANIEL GREENE.

Commands the "Army of Observation" in Rhode Island in 1775—Promoted to Major-general in August, 1776—At the battles of Trenton, Princeton, Brandywine, and Germantown—Appointed Quartermaster-general in March, 1778—At the Battle of Monmouth, June 28, 1778—Resigns as Quartermaster-general in 1780—Takes the command of the southern department, December 8, 1780—Makes his famous retreat through the Carolinas in February, 1781—Defeated at Guilford, March 15, 1781—Fought Lord Rawdon, near Camden, in April, 1781, and defeated—Besieged "Fort Ninety-Six" in May, 1781, unsuccessful—Is victorious at Eutaw Springs, September 8, 1781—Served to the end of the war and went to Rhode Island—Visited his estate in Georgia in 1785—Died there, June 19, 1786—Buried in a vault in Savannah.

MAJOR-GENERAL WILLIAM MOULTRIE.

Defends Sullivan's Island in 1776—Whips the British at Beaufort in 1779—At the siege of Charleston in 1780—Taken prisoner there, May 12, 1780—Several times Governor of South Carolina. Died at Charleston, September 7, 1805.

MAJOR-GENERAL HENRY KNOX

Was a bookseller in Boston—Volunteer at the Battle of Bunker Hill—Everywhere distinguished thoughout the war—Commands the artillery—With General Washington in all his battles—Commissioned Major-general after the capture of Cornwallis—Was author and suggester of the Cincinnati Society—Made Secretary of War in 1785—Died at Thomaston, Maine, October 25, 1806.

MAJOR-GENERAL BENJAMIN LINCOLN,

Commissioned Major-general February 19, 1777—Severely wounded at Saratoga, October 7, 1777—Captured at Charleston, May 12, 1780—Exchanged in November, 1780—at Yorktown, October 19, 1781, and received Cornwallis' sword—Made Secretary of War in 1781—Collector of the port of Boston in 1789—Died at Hingham, May 9, 1810.

MAJOR-GENERAL JOHN SULLIVAN,

Plans the Battle of Three Rivers, and directs General Thompson to make the attack—His forces are captured—Is at the Battle of Long Island—Fights Clinton and De Heister at Flatbush, and is defeated and captured—Exchanged for General Prescott—At the Battle of Brandywine, September 11, 1777—At Trenton, December 26, 1776—At Princeton, January 3, 1777—Conducts the expedition against the Six Nations of Cherry Valley and Wyoming in 1779—Elected to Congress in 1780—Attorney-general of New Hampshire in 1783—Governor of the State in 1786—Died January 23, 1795.

MAJOR-GENERAL ARTHUR ST. CLAIR,

Commissioned Colonel in 1776—Marches for Canada—Appointed Brigadier-general in August, 1776—Fights at Trenton and Princeton—Appointed Major-general in February, 1777—Commands at Ticonderoga—Protects Congress at Philadelphia in 1781—Marches for Yorktown—Joins Greene at Savannah—Elected to Congress in 1786—President of Congress in 1787—Governor of the Northwestern Territory from 1788 to 1802—

Pensioned per special act of Congress passed March 9, 1818—Placed on the pension-roll, March 10, 1818, to commence from March 4, 1817—Died at Laurel Hill, August 30, 1818.

MAJOR-GENERAL LORD STIRLING
(WILLIAM ALEXANDER).

Born in New York—Commissioned Brigadier in 1776—Fights bravely on Long Island, August 27, 1776—Is captured—Fights desperately at Brandywine and Monmouth—In command at Albany—Upsets the Conway Cabal—Died at Albany, January 15, 1783.

MAJOR-GENERAL LA FAYETTE

Joins the Revolutionary army in 1777—Fights bravely at Brandywine and Monmouth—Goes to France in 1778—Returns in 1780—Goes in pursuit of Benedict Arnold—Defeats his plans—Coops Cornwallis at Yorktown—Returns to France—Takes part in the Revolution of that country—Comes to America in 1824—Is enthusiastically received—Returns to France—Died in 1834.

MAJOR-GENERAL BARON DE KALB

Came to America in 1777, with Lafayette—Commissioned Major-general September 15, 1777—Commands at Elizabethtown and Amboy—Heads the Maryland troops in 1780—Marches in April, 1780, to reinforce General Lincoln in the South—Fights Lord Rawdon's forces at Camden—Killed in that battle, August 16, 1780.

MAJOR-GENERAL JOHN THOMAS

Joins the Revolutionary army in 1775—Made a Brigadier—Commands at the siege of Boston—Appointed Major-general in March, 1776—Joins the army before Quebec—Died of the smallpox at Chambli, May 30, 1776.

MAJOR-GENERAL ALEXANDER MCDOUGALL

Joins the army in 1775—Made a Brigadier in August, 1776—Made a Major-general in October, 1777—Commands at White Plains and Germantown in 1777—Elected to Congress in 1781—Died June 8, 1786.

Major-General Baron De Steuben

Joins the army at Valley Forge—Made Inspector-general—Commands at Monmouth, June 28, 1778—Made Major-general—Commands in Virginia and at Yorktown in 1781—Receives 16,000 acres of land in Oneida Co., N. Y.—Congress, per act June 4, 1790, grants him an annuity of $2500 for life, to commence January 1, 1790—Died at Steubenville, N. Y., November 28, 1795.

Major-General Philip Schuyler,

Appointed Major-general in June, 1775—Commands in the Province of New York—Superseded by Gates in 1777—Services faithful and honorable—Elected to Congress—Elected to the U. S. Senate in 1789 and 1797—Died at Albany, November 18, 1804.

Major-General David Wooster,

Made Brigadier in 1775—Commands the Connecticut forces—Made Major-general of the militia of that State—Mortally wounded at Ridgefield by the British, April 27, 1777—Died May 2, 1777.

Major-General Israel Putnam

Leaves his plough in the furrow, and joins the army in 1775—Heads the Connecticut troops at Bunker Hill—Distinguishes himself—At the Battle of Long Island, August 27, 1776—Commands on the Highlands in 1777—Captures Nathan Palmer as a spy—Governor Tryon threatens "Old Put" with "particular thunder"—"Old Put" hangs Palmer—Commands at West Point in 1779—Is there disabled from active service—Died May 29, 1790.

Major-General William Heath,

Commissioned a Brigadier in 1775—Made a Major-general, August 9, 1776—Commands at King's Bridge—Had the custody of Burgoyne's captive army—Commands on the Hudson in 1779—Serves to the end of the war—Last of the surviving Major-generals—Died January 24, 1814.

Major-General Joseph Spencer,

Made Major-general August 9, 1776—In the expedition against Rhode Island in 1778—Resigns in 1779—Elected to Congress from Connecticut—Died January 13, 1789.

MAJOR-GENERAL THOMAS MIFFLIN

Joined the army at Cambridge in 1775—Made a Brigadier in 1776—Made Major-general in February, 1777—Served with distinction throughout the war—Elected to Congress in 1783 and made President—In the Convention of 1787—First Governor of Pennsylvania under the new constitution—Quells the "Whiskey boys" in 1794—Died January 20, 1800.

MAJOR-GENERAL JOHN STARK

Joins the army in 1775—Fights at Bunker Hill, Trenton, and Princeton—Whips the British at Bennington in 1777—Serves in Rhode Island in 1778 and 1779, and in New Jersey in 1780—Commands the Northern Department at Saratoga in 1781—Serves to the end of the war—Congress, per act December 28, 1818, places him on the pension list at $60 per month, to commence August 16, 1817—Died May 8, 1822.

COLONEL ETHAN ALLEN

Joins the army in 1775—Raises a regiment of "Green Mountain Boys"—Makes a descent on Ticonderoga—Captures the garrison there, May 10, 1775—Attacks Montreal and is captured—Is exchanged in 1778—Visits Valley Forge—Retires from the army—Died February 13, 1789.

GENERAL JOHN ARMSTRONG,

Of Pennsylvania—Made Brigadier in 1776—Defends Fort Moultrie and Charleston in 1776—Fights at Brandywine and Germantown in 1777—Resigns in the fall of 1777—Elected to Congress—Died March 9, 1795.

COLONEL CHARLES ARMAND.

French officer—Made Colonel, May 10, 1777—Fights at Red Bank in 1777—Opposes the tories in Westchester Co., N. Y., and captures Baramore—Stationed at Ridgefield, Conn., in 1779—Fights under Gates in the South—Pursues Cornwallis to Yorktown—Made a Brigadier in 1783—Went to France—Died January 30, 1793.

GENERAL JOHN ASHE,

Of North Carolina—Destroys Fort Johnson in 1775—Denounced as a rebel—Made a Brigadier in 1776—Joins Lincoln in 1778—Surprised and defeated at Briar Creek—Died October 24, 1781.

MAJOR JOHN ARMSTRONG,

Of Pennsylvania—Joins the army in 1775—Appointed Aid-de-Camp to General Hugh Mercer—With Gates at Burgoyne's surrender—Adjutant-general in 1780—Remained with Gates to the close of the war—Died April 1, 1843.

COLONEL THEODORICK BLAND,

Entered the army in 1775—A meritorious officer—Commands the "Convention Troops" of General Burgoyne in 1779—Elected to Congress in 1780—In the Convention of 1787—Died June 1, 1790.

COLONEL ELIAS BOUDINOT,

Appointed Commissary-general of Prisoners in 1776—Served till 1779—Elected to Congress—President in 1782—Member of Congress in 1789—First President of the American Bible Society—Died October 24, 1821.

MAJOR WILLIAM BRADFORD,

Of the Pennsylvania Flying-Camp in 1776—Commissary of Musters in 1777 and 1778—Paymaster in 1778 and 1779—Died in Philadelphia, August 23, 1795.

COLONEL ELEAZER BROOKS,

Of Massachusetts—Commands at White Plains in 1776—At the Battle of Stillwater in 1777—Died November 9, 1806.

GENERAL JOHN CADWALLADER,

Fights at Princeton, Germantown, and Monmouth—Puts down the conspirators in the "Conway Cabal"—Wounds Conway—Died February 10, 1786.

GENERAL GEORGE R. CLARKE,

Of Virginia—Commands in the Western Department during the Revolution—Made Brigadier in 1781—Died February 18, 1818.

General James Clinton,

Fought with Montgomery at Quebec in 1775—Defends Fort Clinton in 1777—With Sullivan's expedition in 1779—Serves to the end of the war—Died December 22, 1812.

Colonel Peter Gansevoort,

Of New York—Appointed Major July 19, 1775—Commands the 2d New York Regiment—Made Lieutenant-colonel, March 19, 1776—Made Colonel November 21, 1776—Defends Fort Stanwix against St. Leger in 1777—In Sullivan's Expedition in 1779— Captures Mohawk Castle—Served to the end of the war—Died July 2, 1812.

Colonel John Gibson,

Serves in the Western frontier—Commands the Western Department in 1780 and 1781—Served to the end of the war—Pensioned per act 18th March, 1818—Resided in Allegany county, Pa.—Died April 10, 1822.

Colonel George Gibson,

Commands the "Border Sharp-shooters" in 1775—Joins the army at Williamsburg—His regiment destroyed at Germantown—Heads the Spanish Powder Expedition to New Orleans—Fights at Trenton under Washington—Commands the "Prison Station" at York, Pa., in 1780—Marches his prisoners to Elizabethtown for exchange—Mortally wounded at St. Clair's defeat in 1791—Died December 11, 1791.

Colonel John E. Howard,

Of Maryland—Brave and distinguished—Fights at Germantown, —White Plains, Monmouth, Camden, Cowpens, Hobkirk's Hill —Served to the end of the war—Governor of Maryland—Died October 12, 1827.

Brigadier-General Jedediah Huntington,

Of Connecticut—Marches his regiment to Cambridge in 1775— Distinguished throughout the war—Died September 25, 1818.

Colonel James Jackson,

Of Georgia—Makes a descent on Savannah—Pursues Tarleton and captures some of his forces—Fights at the Cowpens—

Serves to the end of the war—United States Senator—Died January 9, 1806.

Colonel Francis Johnston,

Of Pennsylvania—Serves with Wayne throughout the war—Distinguishes himself—Secretary of the Cincinnati Society in 1783—Died February 22, 1815.

Brigadier-General John Lacy,

Of Pennsylvania—Made Captain January 6, 1776—Serves under Wayne—Commands the militia of Bucks county—Made Brigadier January 9, 1778—Left the service in 1781—See names of his company, *Ante*—Died February 17, 1814.

Colonel Henry Lee,

Of Virginia—Commands a Cavalry Legion—Is called "Lighthorse Harry"—Distinguished in the South—The scourge of Tarleton—Serves to the end of the war—Elected to Congress in 1786—Quells a "Baltimore mob" in 1814—Died March 25, 1818.

Colonel Return J. Meigs,

Of Connecticut—Captured at Quebec in 1775—Exchanged in 1776—Made a Colonel in 1777—Captures twelve British vessels in Long Island Sound—At the storming of Stony Point in 1779 Served to the end of the war—Died January 28, 1823.

Colonel Daniel Morgan,

Of Virginia rifle renown—Served everywhere—Surrendered nowhere—Served to the end of the war—Died July 6, 1802.

Brigadier-General Peter Muhlenburg,

Commissioned Colonel in 1776—Made a Brigadier in 1777—Distinguished to the close of the war—Died October 1, 1807.

Brig. Gen. Samuel H. Parsons,

Of Connecticut—Made Brigadier in August, 1776—Distinguished to the end of the war—Drowned in the Ohio River, near Pittsburg, November 17, 1789.

Colonel Timothy Pickering,

Marches to Lexington in 1775—Commands a regiment in Washington's retreat through New Jersey—Fights at Brandywine and Germantown—Made Quartermaster-general in 1780—Faithful to the end of the war—Afterwards distinguished—Died January 29, 1829.

GENERAL COUNT CASSAMIR PULASKI,
Comes to America in 1777—Commands "Pulaski's Legion"—Ordered to the South in 1779—Reinforced by Armand's Corps—Killed at the siege of Savannah, October 9, 1779.

COLONEL GOSSÉ VAN SHAICK,
Of New York—Joined the army in 1775—Commands the 1st Regiment of New York—Fights at Monmouth—Whips the Onondaga Indians in 1779—Served to the end of the war—Died December 12, 1784.

BRIGADIER-GENERAL WILLIAM SMALLWOOD,
Of Maryland—Made Colonel in 1776—Brigadier, March 27, 1777—Major-general in 1780—Distinguished throughout the war—Governor of Maryland—Died February 14, 1792.

COLONEL WILLIAM WASHINGTON,
Of Virginia—Commands the Dragoons—At the Battles of Long Island, Trenton, and Princeton—Brave and distinguished everywhere—Whips Gray at Tappan in 1778, and Tarleton at the Cowpens—Fights desperately at Eutaw Springs and Hobkirk's Hill—Was at last captured; not by his fault, but by misfortune—Prisoner on parole to the end of the war—Died March 6, 1810.

GENERAL O. H. WILLIAMS,
Of Maryland—Joins Cresap's Riflemen in 1775—At the capture of Fort Washington—Captured and imprisoned in New York—Exchanged for Major Ackland—Serves under Gates in 1780—Distinguished in the South—Served to the end of the war—Died July 16, 1794.

BRIGADIER-GENERAL ANTHONY WAYNE,
Of Pennsylvania—Made Colonel in 1775—Brigadier in 1776—Distinguished throughout the war—Died in December, 1796.

COLONEL MARINUS WILLETT,
Of New York—Commands at St. John's in 1775 and 1776—At Fort Constitution in 1777—Desperately defends Fort Schuyler, or Stanwix, in the same year—Fights at Monmouth in 1778—

With Sullivan's expedition in 1779—Commands in the Mohawk Valley in 1780, 1781, and 1782—Distinguished throughout the war—Died August 23, 1830.

COLONEL RICHARD VARICK,

Of New York—Joins the army in 1776—Made Mustermaster-general—Serves till 1780—Faithful to the end of the war in other capacities—Mayor of New York city from 1791 to 1801—President of the American Bible Society—Died July 30, 1831.

GENERAL JAMES VARNUM,

Of Massachusetts—Joins the army in 1775—Commissioned Brigadier in 1777—At Valley Forge in 1777 and 1778—Resigns in 1778—Died January 10, 1790.

BRIGADIER-GENERAL WILLIAM IRVINE,

Of Pennsylvania—Captured at Three Rivers, June 8, 1776—Sent to Quebec—Exchanged May 6, 1778—Commands the Second Pennsylvania Brigade until the 6th December, 1780—Then succeeds Colonel John Gibson in the western department—Served to the end of the war—Died August 12, 1804.

BRIGADIER-GENERAL FRANCIS MARION,

Of South Carolina—Distinguished as a partisan warrior—A terror to the British cavalry—Renowned as the "Swamp Fox"—Faithful and invincible to the end of the war—Died February 9, 1795.

A LIST SHOWING THE DEATHS OF OTHER OFFICERS.

Generals.

	Time of Death.		Time of Death.
Thomas Sumpter,	June 1, 1832.	Charles Scott,	Oct. 23, 1820.
Andrew Pickens,	Aug. 17, 1817.	William Woodford,	Nov. 13, 1780.
Enoch Poor,	Sept. 8, 1780.	Artemas Ward,	Oct. 28, 1800.
Joseph Reed,	Mar. 4, 1785.	Thomas Blount,	Feb. 8, 1812.
Mordecai Gist,	July 9, 1792.	George Clinton,	April 20, 1812.
Hugh Mercer,	Jan. 8, 1777.	Edward Hand,	—, 1803.
Edward Stevens,	Aug. 17, 1820.	John Nixon,	Mar. 24, 1815.
William Maxwell,	Nov. 12, 1798.	William North,	Jan. 4, 1828.
Lachlin McIntosh,	—, 1806.	Count De Rochambeau,	—, 1807.
Peleg Wadsworth,	Nov. 16, 1829.	John Morin Scott,	Sept. 14, 1784.

TIME OF THEIR DEATHS.

Colonels.

Name	Time of Death	Name	Time of Death
Moses Allen,	Feb. 8, 1779.	Uriah Forrest,	April —, 1805.
John Armstrong,	—, 1795.	Christopher Gadsden,	—, 1805.
Hezekiah Broad,	Mar. 17, 1824.	Francis Gurney,	May 25, 1815.
John Brooks,	—, 1825.	William Guynn,	Oct. 1, 1819.
Andrew Brown,	Feb. 4, 1797.	Alexander Hamilton,	July 12, 1804.
Benjamin Bird,	Oct. 5, 1823.	Benoni Hathaway,	April 19, 1823.
Aaron Burr,	Sept. 14, 1836.	Joseph Hawley,	Mar. 10, 1786.
Thomas Butler,	Sept. 7, 1805.	Edward Heston,	May 14, 1824.
Richard Butler,	Nov. 4, 1791.	Levi Holden,	April 19, 1823.
Richard Caswell,	Nov. 20, 1789.	David Humphrey,	Feb. 19, 1818.
John Cropper,	Jan. 15, 1812.	Andrew Irvine,	May 4, 1789.
Oliver Ellsworth,	Nov. 26, 1807.	Jared Irwin,	Mar. 1, 1818.
Robert Kirkwood,	Nov. 4, 1791.	Samuel Prioleau,	Mar. 23, 1813.
Thaddeus Kosciusko,	Oct. 16, 1817.	Rufus Putnam,	May 4, 1824.
Henry Laurens,	Dec. 8, 1792.	Paul Revere,	—, 1818.
Ezra Lee,	Oct. 29, 1821.	Winthrop Sargeant,	—, 1820.
Christopher Lippett,	—, 1824.	Francis Barber,	Jan. 6, 1783.
Robt. R. Livingston,	—, 1813.	Zebulon Butler,	July 28, 1795.
William Livingston,	July 25, 1790.	Edward Carrington,	Oct. 28, 1810.
John Manly,	July 12, 1793.	John Lamb,	May 31, 1800.
Thomas Mathews,	April 20, 1812.	Aaron, Ogden,	April —, 1839.
Henry Miller,	April 5, 1824.	Eleazer Oswald,	Oct. 1, 1795.
Mathias Ogden,	Mar. 31, 1791.	William Polk,	Jan. 14, 1835.
Jeremiah Olney,	Nov. 10, 1812.	John Sevier,	Sept. 24, 1815.
John Orr,	—, 1823.	Isaac Shelby,	July 18, 1826.
John Paulding,	Dec. 30, 1819.	Ebenezer Stevens,	Sept. 2, 1823.
Charles Petit,	Sept. 6, 1806.	William Thompson,	Nov. 22, 1796.
Edward Preeble,	Aug. 25, 1807.	James Wilkinson,	Dec. 28, 1825.

Pensioned Officers.

Name		Place	Time of Death
William Wells, Captain,		Dist. Columbia,	Mar. 16, 1812.
Peter Faulkner, Ensign,		do.	Sept. 27, 1823.
Peter Mills,	Captain,	do.	Oct. 10, 1830.
David M. Randolph,	do.	do.	Sept. 23, 1830.
Stephen B. Balch,	do.	do.	Sept. 22, 1833.
William Gamble, Major,		do.	Jan. 15, 1833.
John B. Cutting, Apothecary,		do.	Feb. 3, 1831.
Clement Sewell, Ensign,		do.	Jan. 7, 1839.
Philip Stewart, Lieutenant,		do.	Aug. 14, 1830.
Joseph Wheaton,	do.	do.	Nov. 23, 1828.

REVOLUTIONARY OFFICERS:

MAINE—ACT MARCH 18, 1818.

		Time of Death.
Moses Banks, Lieutenant,	Cumberland Co.,	Oct. 10, 1823.
Peter W. Brown, Ensign,	do.	Feb. 28, 1850.
David Cook, Captain,	do.	Oct. 27, 1823.
Thomas Cummings, Lieutenant,	do.	Oct. 24, 1824.
Silas Chadbourne, do.	do.	June 15, 1823.
William Hasty, do.	do.	June 23, 1831.
Richard Hunnewell, do.	do.	May 14, 1828.
Hezekiah Harding, do.	do.	May 1, 1825.
William McKinney, do.	do.	Jan. 27, 1823.
John Starbird, Ensign,	do.	Nov. 4, 1824.
James Webb, do.	do.	Sept. 1, 1825.
Bela Nichols, Lieutenant,	Hancock Co.,	Nov. 18, 1831.
Jesse Sturtevant, do.	do.	Sept. 1, 1818.
George White, Captain,	do.	May 20, 1826.
Daniel Webber, Lieutenant,	do.	Feb. 1, 1827.
William Briggs, Captain,	Kennebec Co.,	Aug. 11, 1819.
Samuel Davis, Lieutenant,	do.	Mar. 6, 1826.
James Johnson, Captain,	do.	June 12, 1830.
Abijah Poole, Lieutenant,	do.	May 9, 1820.
Bradley Richards, Ensign,	do.	June 12, 1821.
James Shaw, do.	do.	April —, 1822.
Samuel Stubs, do.	do.	Mar. 3, 1822.
Joseph Wadsworth, Captain,	do.	July 4, 1824.
John Wingate, Surgeon,	do.	July 25, 1819.
Eleazer Bearce, Lieutenant,	Lincoln Co.,	May 3, 1827.
Thomas Berry, do.	do.	Jan. 27, 1828.
Thomas Boffee, Ensign,	do.	Jan. 10, 1820.
Samuel Jennison, Lieutenant,	do.	Sept. 1, 1826.
James Lord, do.	do.	Feb. 13, 1830.
John Lemont, Captain,	do.	Feb. 23, 1827.
Samuel Payson, do.	do.	June 19, 1819.
John Polereski, Major,	do.	June 8, 1830.
Christopher Woodbridge, Captain,	do.	Mar. —, 1825.
Abner Wade, do.	do.	Oct. —, 1827.
Gabriel Johonet, Lieut. Col.,	Penobscot Co.,	Oct. 9, 1820.
Nathan Parsons, Ensign,	do.	Nov. —, 1834.
Elisha Skinner, Surgeon,	do.	Nov. —, 1827.
Abraham Tourtelott, Lieutenant,	do.	Dec. 6, 1820.
Samuel Thomas, Captain,	do.	Feb. 13, 1823.
Nathaniel Coffin, Lieutenant,	Waldo Co.,	July 23, 1823.
James Keith, Major,	Washington Co.,	May 14, 1829.

TIME OF THEIR DEATH.

		Time of Death.
William Frost, Lieutenant,	York Co.,	June 2, 1827.
John Grant, Quartermaster,	do.	Nov. —, 1825.
Jeremiah Hill, Captain,	do.	June 11, 1820.
James Heart, Lieutenant,	do.,	Sept. —, 1827.
George Jacobs, do.	do.	June 4, 1831.
Nathaniel Leavitt, do.	do.	Feb. —, 1825.
Noah M. Littlefield, Lieut. Colonel,	do.	Oct. 25, 1821.
Jabez Lane, Captain,	do.	Oct. 25, 1826.
William Morris, Lieutenant,	do.	Dec. 20, 1822,
Nathaniel Nason, Captain,	do.	July 27, 1818.
Jonathan Newell, do.	do.	Jan. 5, 1821.
Isaac Pope, do.	do.	June —, 1820.

ACT MAY 15, 1828.

Henry Dearborn, Lieut. Col.,	Kennebec Co.,	June 6, 1829.
Nathaniel Frye, Lieutenant,	Oxford Co.,	April 17, 1833.
Nathaniel Hutchins, Captain,	do.	Jan. 10, 1832.
Joseph Boynton, Lieutenant,	York Co.,	June 24, 1830.
Daniel Gookin, do.	do.	Sept. 24, 1831.

NEW HAMPSHIRE—ACT MARCH 18, 1818.

Jonathan Holton, Lieutenant,	Cheshire Co.,	Nov. 19, 1821.
Aaron Smith, Ensign,	do.	June 6, 1819.
John Orr, Lieutenant,	Hillsboro' Co.,	Dec. 23, 1822.
Joseph Hilton, Lieutenant,	Rockingham Co.,	Nov. 26, 1826.
Jeremiah Pritchard, do.	do.	Dec. 2, 1813.
Joseph Reed, Brigadier-general,	——— —,	Sept. —, 1798.
Nathan Sanborn, Captain,	——— —,	Aug. 13, 1814.
John Bergin, Ensign,	Coos County,	April 28, 1828.
Obadiah Mann, Lieutenant,	do.	Feb. 4, 1825.
Caleb Baldwin, Captain,	Cheshire Co.,	Sept. 5, 1823.
Isaac Morton, Lieutenant,	do.	Dec. —, 1827.
Thomas Kemp, do.	Grafton Co.,	May 25, 1825.
Isaac Moray, do.	do.	Oct. 17, 1830.
Jonathan Perkins, do.	do.	Aug. 11, 1824.
Benjamin Whitcomb, Major,	do.	July. 22, 1828.
Archelaus Bachelor, Lieutenant,	Hillsboro' Co.,	Dec. 18, 1823.
Samuel Curtis, Surgeon,	do.	Mar. 31, 1822.
Benjamin Stone, Captain,	do.	Feb. 13, 1820.
James Taggert, Lieutenant,	do.	Jan. 25, 1826.
Nathan Brown, Captain,	Rockingham Co.,	May 29, 1825.
Daniel Moore, do.	do.	July 19, 1820.
James Wedgewood, Lieutenant,	do.	May 18, 1826.

540   REVOLUTIONARY OFFICERS:

		Time of Death.
Joshua Fernald, Ensign,	Strafford Co.,	Jan. 11, 1830.
John Gilman, Lieutenant,	do.	June 25, 1821.
Jeremiah Gilmau, Captain,	do.	Mar. 24, 1823.
Nathan Holt, Lieutenant,	do.	Jan. 6, 1820.
Samuel Nute, do.	do.	Mar. 21, 1823.
Adna Pennyman, do.	do.	Nov. 4, 1830.
Noah Robinson, Captain,	do.	Feb. 10, 1827.
Samuel Stackpole, Lieutenant,	do.	July 18, 1823.
Mark Wiggins, Captain,	do.	Feb. 23, 1821.
Reuben Sanderson, Lieutenant,	Sullivan Co.,	Dec. 31, 1822.

ACT MAY 15, 1828.

Oliver Bacon, Lieutenant,	Cheshire Co.,	Mar. 25, 1836.
Benjamin Ellis, Captain,	do.	Nov. 29, 1831.
Moses White, do.	Coos Co.,	May 23, 1833.
Moses Page, Lieutenant,	Grafton Co.,	Oct. 5, 1832.
William Cogswell, Surgeon,	Rockingham Co.,	Jan. 1, 1831.
James Carr, Major,	Strafford Co.,	Mar. 11, 1829.

MASSACHUSETTS—ACT MARCH 18, 1818.

Azariah Eggleston, Lieutenant,	Berkshire Co.,	Jan. 12, 1822.
David Hull, do.	do.	Dec. 8, 1831.
Zachariah Watkins, Lieutenant,	Berkshire Co.,	June 24, 1896.
Thomas Williams, do.	do.	May 13, 1828.
James Cooper, Captain,	Bristol Co.,	Oct. 20, 1819.
Jacob Haskin, Lieutenant,	do.	Jan. 4, 1819.
Elisha Harvey, Captain,	do.	Feb. 11, 1821.
John Medbury, Lieutenant,	do.	Nov. 2, 1825.
Benjamin Richmond, Ensign,	do.	July 1, 1825.
Oliver Soper, Captain,	do.	Aug. 8, 1821.
Ebenezer Cleveland, Captain,	Essex County.	Nov. 26, 1822.
Ephraim Emery, Lieutenant,	do.	Sept. 27, 1827.
Aaron Francis, do.	do.	Oct. 17, 1825.
Samuel Goodrich, do.	do.	Mar. 27, 1820.
Samuel Huse, do.	do.	Oct. 22, 1820.
John Merritt, Captain,	do.	June 28, 1818.
Robert Nemblett, Lieutenant,	do.	Oct. 9, 1819.
Joseph Noyes, do.	do.	June 28, 1834.
Daniel Parker, Ensign,	do.	Feb. 2, 1822.
John Tucker, Lieutenant,	do.	Jan. 16, 1831.
Jonathan Woodman, Ensign,	do.	Nov. 18, 1831.
Edward Wigglesworth, Colonel,	do.	Dec. 8, 1826.
Henry White, Lieutenant,	do.	Dec. 16, 1822.
William Stickney, do.	do.	Aug. 25, 1833.

TIME OF THEIR DEATHS. 541

		Time of Death.
John Clarke, Lieutenant,	Franklin Co.,	Jan. 29, 1829.
Foxwell Thomas, do.	do.	Sept. 10, 1829.
Tehan Noble, Captain,	Hampden Co.,	Mar. 2, 1825.
Josiah Lyman, Major,	Hampshire Co.,	Nov. 18, 1822.
Samuel Sheldon, Lieutenant,	do.	Mar. 23, 1829.
Noahdiah Warner, do.	do.	Oct. 16, 1824.
William Bancroft, Ensign,	Middlesex Co.,	Dec. 17, 1827.
Solomon Bowman, Lieutenant,	do.	July 1, 1823.
James Berry, do.	do.	Nov. 3, 1823.
James Bancroft, Captain,	do.	Mar. 17, 1831.
Joseph Cheever, Lieutenant,	do.	Oct. 23, 1830.
Josiah Carey, Ensign,	do.	Jan. 25, 1821.
John George, Lieutenant,	do.	Jan. 22, 1821.
Eliphalet Hastings, Ensign,	do.	Nov. 16, 1824.
Thomas Locke, Lieutenant,	do.	Feb. 18, 1831.
Pelatiah Russell, do.	do.	Jan. 21, 1831.
Nathaniel Sartwell, do.	do.	Jan. 24, 1822.
Nathan Smith, Captain,	do.	Feb. 17, 1825.
John Williams, do.	do.	July 1, 1822.
John Winship, Ensign,	do.	Oct. 9, 1822.
John Child, Lieutenant,	Norfolk Co.,	Sept. 3, 1825.
Samuel Daggett, do.	do.	Nov. 19, 1831.
James Hall, Captain,	do.	April 3, 1819.
Ichabod Holbrook, Lieutenant,	do.	Mar. 31, 1823.
Zadock Howe, do.	do.	Nov. 7, 1819.
David Holbrook, Captain,	do.	Jan. 13, 1834.
Nathan Thayer, Ensign,	do.	Sept. 24, 1827.
Elijah Vose, Lieutenant-colonel,	do.	Mar. 21, 1822.
Barnabas Ashley, Captain,	Plymouth Co.,	May 8, 1833.
Joseph Cotton, Ensign,	do.	Mar. 7, 1829.
William Curtis, Lieutenant,	do.	Oct. 11, 1821.
George Dunham, Captain,	do.	Dec. 19, 1819.
Isaac Hartwell, Lieutenant,	do.	June 12, 1831.
Benjamin Warren, Captain,	do.	June 10, 1825.
Seneca Wadsworth, Lieutenant,	do.	Aug. 29, 1824.
Elias Bacon, do.	Suffolk Co.,	July 20, 1828.
Elisha Brewer, Captain,	do.	July 23, 1827.
Josiah Bartlett, Surgeon,	do.	Mar. 3, 1820.
Benjamin Brown, Ensign,	do.	Mar. 5, 1833.
Percival Hall, Surgeon's Mate,	do.	Sept. 24, 1825.
Abijah Hastings, Ensign,	do.	Feb. '25, 1826.
John Johnson, Captain,	do.	June 20, 1818.

542 REVOLUTIONARY OFFICERS:

Time of Death.

James Perkins, Lieutenant,	Suffolk Co.,	Mar. 4, 1830.
Thomas Welch, Surgeon,	do.	Feb. 9, 1831.
Robert Williams, Lieutenant,	do.	Sept. 10, 1818.
William Dennison, do.	do.	Jan. 24, 1834.

Invalid Officers.

Thomas Alexander, Captain,	County unknown,	Mar. 23, 1801.
John Blunt, do.	do.	May 18, 1804.
Thomas M. Baker, do.	do.	Nov. 14, 1809.
Samuel Clark, do.	do.	Nov. 26, 1801.
Joshua Clapp, Ensign,	do.	Nov. 4, 1810.
John Crane, Colonel,	do.	Aug. 21, 1805.
Ebenezer Learned, Colonel,	do.	April 1, 1801.
James Reed, Brigadier-general,	do.	Feb. 13, 1807.
James Wesson, Colonel,	do.	Nov. —, 1809.
John Reed, Captain,	do.	Sept. —, 1797.
Moses McFarlane, Captain,	do.	Mar. —, 1790.
Daniel Bartlett, Surgeon,	Worcester Co.,	Dec. 25, 1819.
Joseph Balcom, Lieutenant,	do.	Nov. 11, 1827.
Benjamin Felton, Captain,	do.	Jan. 26, 1830.
John Holden, Lieutenant,	do.	Mar. 13, 1828.
William Moore, Captain,	do.	Aug. 16, 1819.
John Maynard, Lieutenant,	do.	Jan. 31, 1823.
Elias Mann, Ensign,	do.	May 21, 1823.
Eliphalet Perley, do.	do.	April 15, 1822.
William Warner, Captain,	do.	July 21, 1822.
William Warren, Lieutenant,	do.	July 29, 1831.

ACT MAY 15, 1828.

Nehemiah Emerson, Captain,	Essex Co.,	Dec. 11, 1832.
Thomas Francis, do.	do.	Nov. 9, 1833.
William Greenleaf, Lieutenant,	do.	Mar. 28, 1833.
Samuel Buffington, do.	Hampshire Co.,	Mar. 2, 1830.
Daniel Jackson, do.	Middlesex Co.,	Dec. 11, 1833.
Sylvanus Smith, do.	do.	May 12, 1830.
James Tisdale, Captain,	Norfolk Co.,	Nov. 13, 1832.
William Forry, Lieutenant,	Plymouth Co.,	Oct. 19, 1828.
Daniel Shute, Captain,	Suffolk Co.,	April 18, 1829.
David Townsend, Surgeon,	do.	April 13, 1829.
Robert Williams, Lieutenant,	do.	Nov. 16, 1834.

NEW YORK—RESIDENCE UNKNOWN.

INVALID, AND ACT MARCH 18, 1818.

John Thomas, Surgeon,	Oct. 30, 1819.
Philip Corey, Ensign,	Dec. 9, 1833.

TIME OF THEIR DEATHS. 543

	Time of Death.
Darius Howe, Lieutenant,	Feb. 23, 1833
Benjamin B. Stockton, Surgeon,	June 9, 1829.
John Blanchard, Captain,	Aug. 9, 1821.
Nathaniel Hall, Lieutenant,	Nov. 4, 1821.
Arthur Fenner, do.	Aug. 23, 1827.
Seth Smith, do.	July 6, 1830.
Ezekiel Goodale, do.	July 10, 1827.
Jesse Pryor, do.	Feb. 10, 1822.
Nathaniel Alexander, Captain,	Feb. 16, 1829.
Josiah Brown, Lieutenant,	Aug. 12, 1826.
Andrew Fink, Major,	Feb. 3, 1820.
John Banks, Com. Mil. Stores.	July 13, 1818.
Lewis J. Costigin, Lieutenant,	Mar. 9, 1822.
Henry Brewster, do.	Mar. 15, 1830.
Elijah James, do.	Feb. 22, 1823.
Joseph McCracken, Major,	May 5, 1825.
Thomas Boyce, Ensign,	June 7, 1826.
Selah Benton, Captain,	May 12, 1812.
Henry Crane, Major,	Aug. —, 1808.
Frederick Fisher, Colonel,	June 9, 1809.
Jacob Gardner, Captain,	May 9, 1808.
Robert Harris, Lieutenant,	May 17, 1806.
Isaac Keeler, do.	Aug. 26, 1808.
Jeremiah Mullan, Captain,	Mar. 18, 1801.
Francis Monty, Lieutenant,	Feb. 8, 1809.
Silas Talbott, Lieutenant-colonel,	June 30, 1813.
Henry Zimmerman, Ensign,	May 8, 1807.
Gideon Waring, Captain,	April 4, 1808.
Silas Gray, Captain,	Jan. 19, 1820.
Edward Weaver, Ensign,	Jan. 29, 1828.
Horatia Ross, Captain,	Oct. 26, 1828.
John Rose, Ensign,	Dec. 2, 1818.
John Shepard, Captain,	Jan. 20, 1822.
Asa Pixley, Ensign,	Mar. 26, 1825.
Daniel Shays, Captain,	Sept. 29, 1825.
Othniel Taylor, do.	Aug. 15, 1819.
Benjamin Wells, Lieutenant,	June 3, 1828.
Giles Wolcott, Captain,	June 4, 1819.
John Belknap, do.	Oct. 26, 1825.
William Irwin, Lieutenant,	Jan. 16, 1834.
Frederick Frye, Ensign,	Jan. 30, 1828.
James Bostwick, do.	Nov. 19, 1829.

REVOLUTIONARY OFFICERS:

	Time of Death.
Eli Parsons, Lieutenant,	Sept. 26, 1830.
James Butterfield, Captain,	Oct. 31, 1818.
Amos Bostwick, Ensign,	Nov. 19, 1829.
Jacob Fox, Lieutenant,	Nov. 27, 1824.
Levi Spalding, Captain,	Mar. 1, 1835.
John Waterman, Ensign,	Dec. 16, 1825.
Abel Wright, Lieutenant,	June 9, 1827.
Joel Jenkins, Ensign,	June 23, 1827.
Joseph Rogers, do.	Sept. 3, 1818.
Lewis Dubois, Colonel,	Mar. 4, 1824.
Aquila Giles, Major,	Mar. —, 1830.
Mason Wattles, Captain,	July 23, 1819.
William Wilcox, Aid-de-Camp,	Dec. 20, 1828.
John Wiley, Captain,	Dec. 24, 1819.
John Winans, do.	July 19, 1828.
Gershom Beardsly, Surgeon's Mate,	Nov. 13, 1828.
Asa Graves, Ensign,	Oct. 6, 1823.
Asa Danforth, Captain,	Sept. 2, 1818.
Stephen Cutter, Lieutenant,	Sept. 7, 1824.
John Knapp, Ensign,	July 19, 1829.
Benjamin Throop, Major,	May 16, 1822.
Lewis Goslin, Lieutenant,	Aug. 7, 1823.
Lyman Hitchcock, Major,	Feb. 15, 1819.
Lathrop Allen, Captain,	Aug. 12, 1826.
Melancthon L. Woolsey, Lieutenant,	June 29, 1819.
James Bennet, do.	Nov. 14, 1819.
Samuel Johnson, Ensign,	Feb. 10, 1826.
Joseph Fox, Captain,	Mar. 24, 1820.
William Johnson, do.	Feb. 20, 1819.
John M. Fought, Lieutenant,	April 9, 1836.
James Fairlie, Aid-de-Camp,	Oct. 10, 1830.
William North, Captain,	Jan. 3, 1836.
Thomas Tillotson, Captain and Physician,	May 5, 1832.
Lebbeus Loomis, Lieutenant,	Jan. 10, 1836.
Jonas Adoms, do.	July 16, 1837.
Sebastian Bauman, Major,	Oct. 19, 1803.
Walter Bicker, Captain,	April 6, 1821.
Leonard Bleecker, do.	Mar. 12, 1844.
David Brooks, Clothier-general,	Aug. 30, 1838.
Jonathan Burrall, Paymaster-general,	Nov. 18, 1834.
Caleb Brewster, Captain,	Feb. 13, 1827.
Duncan Campbell, Lieutenant,	Mar. —, 1807.

TIME OF THEIR DEATHS.

	Time of Death.
James Christie, Captain,	June —, 1807.
Mathew Clarkson, Major,	April 25, 1825.
Robert Cochran, Lieutenant-colonel,	Feb. 23, 1802.
Ebenezer Crosby, Surgeon,	July 16, 1788.
Daniel Denniston, Lieutenant,	Feb. 8, 1834.
Simeon De Witt, Geographer,	Dec. 3, 1834.
Samuel Dodge, Lieutenant,	Oct. 27, 1795.
Henry Du Bois, Captain,	Jan. —, 1804.
Edward Dunscomb, do.	Nov. 12, 1814.
Nicholas Fish, Major,	June 20, 1833.
George Fleming, Captain,	Oct. 2, 1822.
Theodocius Fowler, do.	Oct. 16, 1841.
James Giles, Lieutenant,	Aug. —, 1825.
John Graham, Major,	May 7, 1832.
Isaac Guion, Captain,	Sept. 12, 1823.
Mordecai Hale, Surgeon's Mate,	Dec. 9, 1832.
Abijah Hammond, Lieutenant,	Dec. 30, 1832.
John F. Hamtramck, Captain,	Feb. —, 1805.
Samuel Hay, Lieutenant-colonel,	Dec. —, 1803.
James M. Hughes, Captain,	Dec. 27, 1802.
Daniel Kemper, Dep. Clo. Gen.,	Aug. 6, 1847.
Garret Lansing, Ensign,	May 27, 1831.
Jonathan Lawrence, Captain,	April 27, 1802.
George Leycraft, Lieutenant,	April —, 1811.
William Leycraft, do.	June 7, 1827.
Morgan Lewis, Col. and Qr. Mr.,	April 7, 1844.
Samuel Lewis, Lieutenant,	Aug. 25, 1822.
Brockolst Livingston, Lieut. Colonel,	Mar. 18, 1823.
Henry B. Livingston, Colonel,	Nov. 7, 1831.
Abraham Leggett, Lieutenant,	Jan. 16, 1842.
Charles McKnight, Surgeon,	Nov. 16, 1791.
Thomas Machin, Captain,	April 3, 1816.
Samuel Mansfield, Captain,	Feb. 8, 1810.
Elihu Marshall, do.	April 10, 1506.
Andrew Moodie, Captain,	Sept. 18, 1787.
William W. Morris, Lieutenant,	April 5, 1832.
Ebenezer Macomber, Captain,	April 5, 1829.
James Nicholson, do.	Sept. 2, 1804.
Samuel T. Pell, do.	Dec. 29, 1786.
Nathaniel Pendleton, do.	Oct. 21, 1821.
Richard Platt, Major,	Mar. 4, 1830.
Jacob Reed, Captain	May 31, 1832.

546 REVOLUTIONARY OFFICERS:

	Time of Death.
John R. B. Rogers, Surgeon,	Jan. 29, 1833.
John Shaw, Lieutenant,	July 14, 1826.
William S. Smith, Lieutenant-colonel,	Jan. 10, 1816.
John Smith, Lieutenant,	June 15, 1801.
John Stagg, do.	Dec. 28, 1803.
Gerard Steddiford, do.	April 5, 1820.
William Stewart, Captain,	Feb. 5, 1831.
Ebenezer Storer, do.	Jan. 20, 1846.
Peter Taulman, do.	Dec. 16, 1835.
John C. Ten Broeck, Captain,	Aug. 10, 1835.
Alexander Thompson, Lieutenant,	Sept. 28, 1809.
Robert Troup, Lieutenant-colonel,	Jan. 14, 1832.
John Trumbull, Colonel,	Nov. 10, 1843.
John F. Vacher, Surgeon,	Dec. 4, 1807.
Philip Van Courtlandt, Colonel,	Nov. 5, 1831.
John Van Dyk, Captain,	Feb. 28, 1840.
David Van Horn, do.	May 12, 1807.
Jeremiah Van Rensselaer, Paymaster,	Feb. 17, 1810.
Henry Van Woert, Lt. and Qr. Mr.	July 30, 1831.
Nicholas Van Rensselaer, Lieutenant,	Mar. 29, 1848.
Benjamin Walker, Captain,	Jan. 13, 1818.
Jedediah Waterman, Ensign,	Sept. 25, 1826.
Samuel B. Webb, Colonel,	Dec. 3, 1807.
Frederick Weisenfels, Lieut. Col.,	May 14, 1806.
Jacob H. Wendell, Lieut. and Adj.,	Mar. 23, 1826.
John H. Wendell, Captain,	July 10, 1732.
Anthony W. White, Colonel,	Feb. 10, 1803.

NEW JERSEY—INVALIDS.

Josiah Burnett, Ensign,	Dec. 3, 1812.
Thomas Combs, Captain,	Mar. 10, 1798.
William Crane, Lieutenant,	Mar. —, 1814.
Garretson Hendrickson, do.	Dec. 21, 1801.
Cornelius Hennion, Captain,	Mar. 28, 1800.
George McFarland, Ensign,	Mar. 19, 1792.
William Oliver, Lieutenant,	Jan. —, 1803.
John Van Anglen, Captain,	Oct. 14, 1812.
Daniel Denniston, Lieutenant, Bergen Co.,	Feb. 3, 1824.
John Hopper, Ensign, do.	Nov. 14, 1819.
Samuel Hendry, Captain, Burlington Co.,	Oct. 15, 1823.
George Norris, Lieutenant, do.	April 9, 1818.

TIME OF THEIR DEATHS. 547

		Time of Death.
Almarin Brooks, Ensign,	Cumberland Co.,	Jan. 25, 1824.
James Johnson, do.	do.	July 1, 1828.
Alexander Orr, Lieutenant,	do.	Jan. 27, 1832.
Levi Holden, Captain,	Essex Co.,	April 19, 1823.
Silas Parrott, Lieutenant,	do.	Oct. 5, 1819.
John Phillips, Ensign,	Hunterdon Co.,	May 25, 1831.
Isaac Sherman, Lieut. Colonel,	do.	Feb. 16, 1819.
John Quay, Lieutenant,	Monmouth Co.,	Feb. 2, 1827.
David Rhea, Major,	do.	June 14, 1821.
Henry Stricker, Ensign,	do.	April 30, 1821.
William Schenck, Lieutenant,	do.	July 1, 1827.
Wessel T. Stout, Captain,	do.	Nov. 11, 1818.
John Kinney, Ensign,	Morris Co.,	July 17, 1832.
Joseph Lindsley, Captain,	do.	July —, 1822.
Nathaniel Solomon, Ensign,	do.	July 23, 1827.
John Sparks, Captain,	Salem Co.,	April 30, 1826.
Peter Welsh, Lieutenant,	Sumerset Co.,	Aug. 22, 1831.
Ephraim Woodruff, do,	Sussex Co.,	July 9, 1820.
ACT MAY 15, 1828.		
William Colfax, Captain,	Bergen Co,	Sept. 7, 1838.
Usal Meecker, Lieutenant,	do.	Sept. 3, 1829.
Cyrus De Hart, Captain,	Essex Co.,	Sept. 7, 1831.
Aaron Ogden, do.	do.	April —, 1839.
James Heard, Major,	Middlesex Co.,	Mar. 26, 1831.
John Craig, Captain,	Warren Co.,	Nov. 29, 1829.
PENNSYLVANIA—INVALIDS.		
James Irvine, Brig. General,	Philadelphia Co.,	April 28, 1819.
Matthew McConnell, Captain,	do.	Mar. 11, 1816.
Archibald Steele, Lieut. and adjt.,	do.	Oct. 19, 1832.
Thomas Campbell, Captain,	York Co.,	Mar. —, 1815.
Solomon Bush, Lieut. Colonel,	——— ———,	April —, 1795.
Luke Brodhead, Lieutenant,	——— ———,	May —, 1806.
Thomas Blair, do.	——— ———,	Aug. —, 1814.
Wilder Bevins, do.	——— ———,	Aug. 3, 1809.
Charles Clarke, do.	——— ———,	Mar. —, 1813.
Jesse Crosby, do.	——— ———,	Oct. —, 1791.
Silas Clark, Captain,	——— ———.	Aug. 13, 1800.
Thomas Doyle, Captain,	——— ———,	Feb. 6, 1802.
Samuel Ewing, Ensign,	——— ———,	April 8, 1804.
John Gilchrist, Lieutenant,	——— ———,	Mar. —, 1791.
David Hammond, do.	——— ———,	June —, 1801.
Nathan Hubble, Major,	——— ———,	April —, 1802.

REVOLUTIONARY OFFICERS:

		Time of Death.
Samuel Lindsay, Lieutenant,	———— ——,	April 16, 1800.
James McLean, do.	——— ——. ——,	Oct. 28, 1804.
John McGowan, Captain,	———— ——,	Nov. —, 1806.
William Mackey, do.	———— ———,	Nov. 4, 1812.
Kenneth McCoy, Lieutenant,	———— ——,	June —, 1809.
William McHatton, do.	———— ——,	April 26, 1807.
Robert Power, Cornet,	———— ——,	Jan. 20, 1811.
William Russell, Ensign,	———— ——,	Mar. 4, 1803.
William Rice, Lieutenant,	———— ——,	June —, 1805.
John Stone, do.	——— ——— ———,	Mar. —, 1792.
William Scott, do.	———— ——,	Sept. 6, 1797.
James Speed, do.	———— ——,	June —, 1811.
James Johnson, Colonel,	———— ——,	Oct. 3, 1807.
William Whitman, Lieutenant,	———— ——,	Oct. 12, 1808.
Joseph Wood, Lieut.-Col.,	———— ——,	Mar. —, 1789.

ACT MARCH 18, 1818.

William Blakeney, Captain,	Alleghany Co.,	July 14, 1821.
Michael Huffnagle, do.	do.	Dec. 31, 1819.
David Steel, do.	do.	Feb. 4, 1819.
Jacob Springer, Ensign,	do.	June 16, 1823.
Nathan Bostwick, do.	Bradford Co.,	Aug. 10, 1829.
William Moore, Captain,	Chester Co.,	June 6, 1824.
William Schofield, Lieutenant,	do.	Feb. 3, 1822.
John Parkhurst, Captain,	do.	May 13, 1832.
Thomas Buchanan, do.	Cumberland Co.,	Oct. 13, 1823.
Samuel Bearsley, do.	Dauphin Co.,	Mar. 22, 1830.
Levi Griffith, Lieutenant,	Fayette Co.,	Jan. 30, 1825.
Thomas Lucas, Captain,	Franklin Co.,	Nov. 3, 1823.
James Hook, do.	Greene Co.,	Jan. 23, 1824.
John Holliday, do.	Huntington Co.,	Aug. 19, 1823.
Joseph Chapman, Lieutenant,	Luzerne Co.,	Aug. 9, 1822.
John Jenkins, do.	do.	Mar. 19, 1827.
Samuel Davis, do.	Mifflin Co.,	April 6, 1824.
Eden Boroughs, do.	Northampton Co.,	Feb. 26, 1825.
John Cook, Ensign,	Northumberl'd Co.,	Feb. 21, 1823
Robert Lyon, Lieutenant,	do.	Aug. 19, 1823.
Enoch Anderson, Captain,	Philadelphia Co.,	Mar. 4, 1820.
Shubert Armitage, Lieutenant,	do.	Dec. 27, 1823.
Nathaniel Donnell, Major,	do.	May 29, 1821.
Walter Dyer, Lieutenant,	do.	April 2, 1819.
John Lockman, Surgeon,	do.	Aug. 16, 1819.
Henry Malcolm,	Philadelphia Co.,	April 18, 1831.

TIME OF THEIR DEATHS. 549

		Time of Death.
Joseph Parker, Captain,	Philadelphia Co.,	Dec. 7, 1831.
John Savidge, do.	do.	April 20, 1825.
George Wonder, Ensign,	do.	Sept. 25, 1828.
John Clark, Major,	York Co.,	April 27, 1819.

ACT MAY 15, 1828.

Gabriel Peterson, Lieutenant,	Alleghany Co.,	Feb. 12, 1832.
John McCoy, do.	Erie Co.,	June 30, 1831.
Edward Crawford, do.	Franklin Co.,	Mar. 6, 1833.
Robert Allison, do.	do.	April 24, 1836.
John Weidman, do.	Lebanon Co.,	June 8, 1830.
Thomas Craig, Colonel,	Lehigh Co.,	Jan. 14, 1832.
Hugh Means, Ensign,	Mercer Co.,	Feb. 12, 1835.
Daniel St. Clair, Lieutenant,	Mifflin Co.,	Feb. 18, 1833.
John Boyd, do.	Northumberl'd Co.,	Feb. 13, 1832.
Andrew Dover, do.	Philadelphia Co.,	Dec. 12, 1831.
John Paul Schott, Captain,	do.	July 18, 1829.
James E. Smith, do.	do.	Jan. 14, 1835.
John B. Webster, do.	Somerset Co.,	Mar. 19, 1834.

DELAWARE—INVALID,

Edward Armstrong, Lieutenant,	New Castle Co.,	May 14, 1824.
William McKennon, Captain,	do.	Feb. —, 1803.

ACT MARCH 18, 1818.

Benjamin McLane, Ensign,	New Castle Co.,	Sept. 28, 1823.

ACT MAY 15, 1828.

James Jones, Surgeon,	Kent Co.,	April 29, 1830.
Peter Jaquette, Captain,	New Castle Co.,	Sept. 13, 1834.
Allen McLane, Major,	do.	May 22, 1829.

MARYLAND—INVALID.

George H. Vaughn, Lieutenant,	Baltimore Co.,	Dec. 2, 1820.
Richard Anderson, Captain,	Frederick Co.,	June 23, 1835.
Roger Nelson, Lieut. of Cavalry,	do.	June 7, 1815.
Perry Benson, Captain,	Talbott Co.,	Oct. 2, 1827.
Joseph Ford, do.	Baltimore Co.,	Dec. —, 1812.
John Truman, Lieutenant,	do.	Feb. 4, 1809.

ACT MARCH 18, 1818.

John Gassaway, Captain,	Anne Arundel Co.,	Mar. —, 1819,
Walter Lane Price, Lieutenant,	do.	April 13, 1832.
Osborn Williams, do.	do.	Dec. 19, 1819.
Young Wilkerson, do.	do.	Sept. 15, 1827.
John P. Ahl, Surgeon's Mate,	Baltimore Co.,	July 13, 1827.
Vachel Burgess, Captain,	do.	Mar. 30, 1824.
George Cole, Ensign,	do.	Aug. 21, 1828.

REVOLUTIONARY OFFICERS:

		Time of Death.
Samuel H. Gatchell, Captain,	Baltimore Co.,	—— —, 1825.
David Hopkins, Major,	do.	Mar. 7, 1824.
John Phelan, Captain,	do.	Sept. 14, 1827.
William Starr, Lieutenant,	do.	June 6, 1823.
Richard Wilson, Captain,	do.	June 27, 1818
Robt. Halkerstone, Lieutenant,	Charles Co.,	Feb. 17, 1825.
Thomas Lingan, do.	Montgomery,	May 28, 1825.
Patrick Simms, Lieut. Colonel,	Prince George Co.,	Jan. 7, 1819.
Adam Ott, Lieutenant,	Washington Co.,	Aug. 10, 1827.

ACT MAY 15, 1828.

William Lamar, Captain,	Alleghany Co.,	Jan. 8, 1838.
David Lynn, do.	do.	April 11, 1835.
Gassaway Watkins, Captain,	Howard Co.,	July 14, 1840.
Hezekiah Foard, Lieutenant,	Cecil Co.,	Feb. 16. 1833.
Richard Waters, Captain,	Dorchester Co.,	Aug. 25, 1829.
Philip Reed, do.	Kent Co.,	Nov. 2, 1829.
William D. Beale, Major,	Prince George Co.,	Sept. 24, 1829.
Joseph Cross, Lieutenant,	do.	Sept. 16, 1830.

VIRGINIA—INVALID.

Thomas Coverely, Ensign,	Amelia Co.,	Sept. 22, 1827.
Andrew Wagoner, Captain,	do.	May 27, 1812.
Pitman Wyatt, do.	—— ——,	June 17, 1801.

ACT MARCH 18, 1818.

William Godman, Captain,	Berkeley Co.,	July 10, 1825.
William Somerville, do.	do.	Mar. 18, 1826.
William Linton, do.	Brooke, Co.,	Feb. 28, 1827.
Francis Gray, Ensign,	Campbell Co.,	April 24, 1827.
John Rice, Lieutenant,	do.	June 30, 1830.
Joseph Scott, Captain,	do.	April 23, 1828.
Joseph Blackwell, do.	Fauquier Co.,	Sept. 8, 1823.
Gideon Johnson, do.	do.	Dec. 6, 1825.
Nathaniel Henry, Lieutenant,	Frederick Co.,	June 14, 1824.
Rees Pritchard, Ensign,	Hampshire Co.,	Sept. 25, 1830.
James Cochran, do.	Harrison Co.,	Nov. 13, 1830.
Matthias Hite, Lieutenant,	do.	Jan. 9, 1823.
Andrew McCausland, do.	Henrico Co.,	Oct. 22, 1820.
John Ashton, Ensign,	King George Co.,	Aug. 26, 1831.
Henry Micon, do.	do.	Dec. 17, 1821.
Robert Nicholson, Lieutenant,	Southampton Co.,	May 21, 1819.
Samuel P. Bell, Lieutenant,	Wood Co.,	Mar. 28, 1828.
James Neal, Captain,	do.	Feb. 2, 1821.

TIME OF THEIR DEATHS. 551

ACT MAY 15, 1828.

		Time of Death.
Samuel Wapples, Lieutenant,	Accomac Co.,	Aug. 11, 1834.
William Robertson, do.	Augusta Co.	Nov. 12, 1831.
Nathan Reid, Captain,	Bedford Co.,	Nov. 6, 1830.
John Watts, do.	do.	June 8, 1830.
Henry Bowyer, Lieutenant,	Boutetourt Co.,	June 13, 1832.
John Crawford, do.	Dinwiddie Co.,	Mar. 3, 1833.
William Eskridge, do.	Frederick Co.,	Oct. 9, 1830.
Robert White, Captain,	do.	Nov. 2, 1831.
Peter Foster, Lieutenant,	Hanover Co.,	Mar. 11, 1833.
William Price, do.	Henrico Co.,	June 27, 1830.
William Broadus, do.	Jefferson Co.,	Oct. 7, 1830.
William B. Harrison, Cornet,	Loudon Co.,	Feb. 28, 1835.
James Burton, Captain,	Orange Co.,	Aug. 21, 1829.
Francis Cowherd, do.	do.	Mar. 25, 1833.
William White, do.	do.	July 20, 1828.
John Mills Lieutenant,	Ohio Co.,	Nov. 23, 1833.
Hezekiah Morton, Captain,	Prince Edward Co.,	June 30, 1831.
Luke Cannon, Lieutenant,	Prince William Co.,	Feb. 7, 1829.
John Withers, do.	Rappahannock Co.,	Oct. 10, 1834.
Thomas Minor, Captain,	Spottsylvania Co.,	July 31, 1824.

NORTH CAROLINA—INVALIDS, AND ACT 1818.

Thomas Childs, Captain,	Anson Co.,	Sept. 15, 1820.
Thomas Harris, Major,	Iredell Co.,	Aug. 31, 1826.
William Hall, Captain.	Nash Co.,	June 3, 1825.
Thomas Shute, Ensign,	Craven Co.,	Jan. 15, 1819.
Reuben Mitchell, Lieutenant,	Chatham Co.,	June —, 1826.
John Pendergrass, do.	do.	June 8, 1830.
David Poe, do.	do.	May —, 1820.
Thomas Granberry, Captain,	Gates Co.,	May 20, 1830.
Ethelred Dance, Ensign,	Nash Co.,	Feb. 4, 1828.
Frederick Albarty, do.	Surry Co.,	Aug. 29, 1831.
Peter Jones, Captain,	Warren Co.,	Feb. 10, 1833.

ACT MAY 15, 1828.

Kedar Ballard, Captain,	Gates Co.,	Jan. 16, 1834.
William McLean, Surg. Mate,	Lincoln Co.,	Oct. 25, 1828.
Thomas Callender, Captain,	New Hanover Co.,	Aug. 20, 1828.

SOUTH CAROLINA—ACT MARCH 18, 1818.

Nathaniel Cudworth, Major,	Charleston Distr.,	Jan. 21, 1826.
Henry Gray, Lieutenant,	do.	July 20, 1824.
John Glover, Ensign,	Edgefield District,	Mar. 27, 1821.

REVOLUTIONARY OFFICERS:

		Time of Death.
Peter Bacot, Captain,	Georgetown Dist.,	Aug. 13, 1821.
John Low, Lieutenant,	Spartenburg, Dist.,	June 8, 1826.
John Bird, do.	Union District,	Dec. 4, 1843.
Richard M. Head, Cornet,	York District,	May 15, 1827.

ACT MAY 15, 1828.

Alexander Garden, Lieutenant,	Charlestown Dist.,	Feb. 24, 1829.
James Legare, do.	do.	Jan. 14, 1831.
Benjamin Carter, Captain,	Kershaw District,	Jan. 20, 1830.

GEORGIA—INVALIDS.

John Kendrick, Lieutenant,	—————,	Dec. 14, 1802.
Alexander Irvine, do.	—————,	Mar. —, 1799.
John Lindsay, Major,	—————,	June —, 1808.
Hugh Lawson, Captain,	—————,	Feb. 20, 1802.
James Lewis, Lieutenant,	—————,	Jan. —, 1807.

ACT MARCH 18, 1818.

Peter Deveaux, Aid-de-Camp,	Chatham Co.,	Oct. 6, 1826.
Nathan Holbrook, Lieutenant,	do.	Sept. 8, 1819.
Abraham P. Jones, do.	Putnam Co.,	Jan. 28, 1831.
William Stephens, do.	do.	Jan. 28, 1825.
Thomas Russell, do.	Richmond Co.,	Sept. 28, 1819.
Richard Worsham, do.	Wilkes Co.,	Feb. 17, 1826.

KENTUCKY—ACT MARCH 18, 1818.

William Tucker, Lieutenant,	Adair Co.,	May 23, 1829.
Nathaniel G. Morris, Captain,	Bracken Co.,	Sept. 15, 1824.
Matthew Lyon, Lieutenant,	Caldwell Co.,	Aug. 1, 1822.
William Porter (1), do.	do.	Jan. 6, 1828.
Jonathan McConnell, do.	Casey Co.,	May 10, 1829.
John Roberts, Surgeon,	Franklin Co.,	April 21, 1821.
Joseph Spencer, Captain,	Grant Co.,	Aug. 27, 1829.
George Berry, do.	Logan Co.,	Oct. 29, 1823.
James Carr, Lieutenant,	do.	Mar. 13, 1833.
George McCormick, Major,	Mercer Co.,	Jan. 30, 1830.
Samuel Woods, Lieutenant,	do.	Feb. 8, 1826.
John Geoghan, Ensign,	Nicholas Co.,	Feb. 20, 1823.
John Johnson, do.	Scott Co.,	May 27, 1825.
John McHatton, Captain,	do.	Feb. 21, 1831.
Robert Yancey, do.	Woodford Co.,	Nov. 17, 1824.

ACT MAY 15, 1828.

Thomas Triplett, Captain,	Bath Co.,	Feb. 28, 1833.
William Porter (2), Lieutenant,	Butler Co.,	July 8, 1828.
John McKinney, Lieutenant,	Butler Co..	Nov. 25, 1838.

TIME OF THEIR DEATHS.

			Time of Death.
Wynne Dixon,	do.	Henderson Co.,	Nov. 24, 1829.
Robert Breckinridge, do.		Jefferson Co.,	Sept. 11, 1833.
Joseph Crockett, Major,		Jessamine Co.,	Nov. 7, 1829.
Robert Kirk, Lieutenant,		Livingston Co.,	Aug. 28, 1828.
Charles Pelham, Major,		Mason Co.,	Aug. 29, 1829.
David Williams, Lieutenant,		Mercer Co.,	Nov. 8, 1831.
Charles Ewell, Captain,		McCracken Co.,	April 1, 1830.
John Howell,	do.	Ohio Co.,	Sept. 18, 1830.
William Taylor, Major,		Oldham Co.,	April 14, 1830.
Abraham Buford, Colonel,		Scott Co.,	June 29, 1833.
Elliott Rucker, Lieutenant,		Shelby Co.,	Mar. 19, 1832.
George Triplett,	do.	Spencer Co.,	Sept. 15, 1833.
Thomas Blackwell, Captain,		Union Co.,	April 28, 1831.
William Meredith,	do.	Warren Co.,	Feb. 20, 1833.
John Nelson,	do.	Fayette Co.,	May 27, 1838.

TENNESSEE—ACT MARCH 18, 1818.

Clement Hall, Captain,		Davidson Co.,	Aug. 4, 1824.
James Tatum, Lieutenant,		do.	Sept. 10, 1821.
Matthew Wood, Captain,		Giles Co.,	Oct. 28, 1832.
Samuel Walker,	do.	Roan Co.,	July 6, 1830.
William Harrison, Lieutenant,		Rutherford Co.,	June 22, 1833.
Dixon Marshall,	do.	Smith Cq.,	Aug. 22, 1824.
John P. Wagnor,	do.	Sumner Co.,	Aug. 22, 1828.
Joshua Hadley, Captain,		do.	Feb. 8, 1830.

OHIO—INVALIDS.

Benjamin Hillman, Lieutenant,	Delaware Co.,	Aug. 31, 1821.
Alexander Foreman, Captain,	Pickaway Co.,	Dec. 25, 1831.

ACT MARCH 18, 1818.

Francis Costigan, Lieutenant,		Adams Co.,	July 27, 1821.
David Sackett,	do.	Ashtabula Co.,	June 6, 1838.
Benjamin Brown, Captain,		Athens Co.,	Oct. 1, 1821.
John Martin,	Lieutenant,	do.	May 14, 1837.
Bartholomew Thayer, do.		Coshocton Co.,	April 11, 1826.
John Crosier,	do.	Cuyahoga Co.,	April 26, 1823.
Samuel Eldred,	do.	do.	Dec. 18, 1826.
John Thompson, Colonel,		Franklin Co.,	April 17, 1834.
Isaac Thompson, Lieutenant,		Geauga Co.,	April 25, 1823.
John Lafier, Ensign,		Hamilton Co.,	Oct. 30, 1823.
John Mott,	Lieutenant,	Knox Co.,	May 31, 1831.
Augustine Anderson, do.		Morgan Co.,	Jan. 18, 1834.
Elijah Blackman, Captain,		Portage Co.,	May 15, 1822.
Daniel Tilden, Lieutenant,		do.	Sept. —, 1832.

		Time of Death.
Thomas Miller, Ensign,	Ross Co.,	July 17, 1821.
Nathan Wheeler, do.	Scioto Co.,	July 15, 1823.
John Elliott, Lieutenant,	Starke Co.,	Aug. 29, 1826.
John Cotton, do.	Trumbull Co.,	Feb. 1, 1831.
Jonathan Devol, do.	Washington Co.,	Aug. 19, 1824.

ACT MAY 15, 1828.

Nathan Lamme, Captain,	Greene Co.,	Jan. 15, 1834.
Thomas Cooke, do.	Guernsey Co.,	Nov. 5, 1831.
Samuel Baskerville, Lieutenant,	Madison Co.,	Aug. 29, 1830.
Elias Langham, do.	do.	April 3, 1830.
Jonathan Cass, Captain,	Muskingum Co.,	Aug. 14, 1830.
Isaac Van Horne, do.	do.	Feb. 2, 1834.
James Curry, do.	Union Co.,	July 5, 1834.

INDIANA—ACT MAY 15, 1828.

Zebulon Pike, Captain,	Dearborn Co.,	July 27, 1834.

MISSISSIPPI—ACT MAY 15, 1828.

Peter B. Bruin, Major,	Claiborne Co.,	Jan. 27, 1827.

ILLINOIS—ACT MARCH 18, 1818.

John Wood, Ensign,	Wabash Co.,	Nov. 4, 1832.
John Edgar, Captain,	Randolph Co.,	Dec. 19, 1830.

This brings us to the close of our task of recording some of the names, deeds, and sufferings of the principal heroes of the Revolution who defied, scorned, and breasted the foe, and at last hurled down the crowned tyrant of American liberty.

If we have rescued one name from oblivion, and restored it to the hearts and remembrance of the American people, we shall be happy.

Time has waged a fearful war on the memorials of the days that "tried men's souls," and they lie scattered everywhere, throughout the country, at the feet of the desolator; and he who will not, if possible, gather, preserve, and record the precious fragments, must, to a great extent, be guilty of an indirect war on the history of a blood-purchased nation.

With the mighty names and minds of our Revolutionary fathers we can now only converse in history. Though dead, they act, they speak, and "still live" in the hearts of the nation; but many whose "merits deserved a temple, scarce found a tomb," and to them.

"How vain! how frail! how transitory!
This world with all its pomp and show!
Its mighty names, renown'd in story—
They've gladly left them all below."

THE END.

INDEX

to

SAFFELL'S LIST

of

Virginia Soldiers in the Revolution

By
J. T. McALLISTER
Hot Springs, Va.

INDEX

to

SAFFELL'S LIST

of

VIRGINIA SOLDIERS IN THE REVOLUTION

by
J. T. McAllister
Hot Springs, Va.

Copywright, 1913
by
McAllister Publishing Co.,
of
Virginia Hot Springs

Explanation of the Index of Virginia Revolutionary Soldiers given by W. T. R. Saffell in the Third Edition of his work published in Baltimore in 1894.

241-245:

Where name is found with page number from 241 to 255 inclusive it means that the person mentioned was either an officer or private in COL. CHAS. HARRISON'S Virginia and Maryland Regiment of artillery as it stood from November 30, 1776, to April, 1782.

(Some of these are necessarily Maryland names).

256-269:

If the page number is from 256 to 269, inclusive the person was either an officer or a private in COL. DANL. MORGAN'S 11th and 15th Virginia Regiments as they stood from May 31, 1777 to November 30, 1778.

270-275:

If the page number is from 270 to 275 inclusive it gives the names of the officers and privates of COL. ALEXANDER SPOTTSWOOD'S Second Virginia Regiment as it stood from January to June, 1777.

276-279:

Pages 276 to 279 inclusive give the names of the officers and privates of the Third Virginia Regiment commanded by LT. COL. WM. HETH, as it stood from September, 1777, to May, 1778, to which are to be added the following names, found on page 280.

Alva, John,	Kendall, Francis,
Florence, George,	Line, Abraham,
Groves, William,	Tillis, John.

280-284:

If a name is given on pages 280 to 284 inclusive, *except the six names set out just above,* it indicates that the person named was an officer or private of COL. JOHN GIBSON'S Detachment, serving in the Western Department from January 1, 1780, to December 6, 1781.

285-287:

From pages 285 to 287, inclusive, together with the following twenty-six persons, the names are of officers or privates who served in COL. NATHL. GIST'S Regiment in 1777.

(The following are the twenty-six names above referred to):

Brady, Joseph,	Minnaham, Morris,
Brady, Perrigrine,	Myers, Frederick,
Cliffon, Joshua,	Oliver, James,
Crook, John,	Peterson, Israel,
Dawson, Benjamin,	Powell, Levi,
Davis, Jesse,	Rains, Henry,
Etholl, Benjamin,	Rains, James,
Foster, William,	Reynolds, Robert,
Hill, Richard,	Reinglespauser, Henry,
Hobingstock, Christian,	Rump, Jacob,
Jones, Samuel,	Stevens, Thomas,
Knight, John,	Verdin, Thomas,
McGee, James,	Williams, Joseph.

288:

If on page 288, except the twenty-six names above referred to, and the following four names, to-wit:

Gregory, William,	Patterson, Thomas,
Johnson, James,	Towles, Oliver,

the person referred to was an officer of LT. COL. LEE'S Legion of Cavalry.

289:

The names given on 289, together with the four names just above mentioned, are the names of a Virginia Officer, whose commission was dated in 1776.

411-437:

If the page number is from 411 to 437, it shows that the person mentioned was a Virginia Officer of the Continental Army, who was either killed in service, became a supernumerary, or served to the end of the war and acquired the right to half pay, commutation and bounty land under the Act of Congress.

500-508:

If the page number is from 500 to 508, inclusive, this indicates that the person named was an officer for whose service Virginia Land Warrants were issued prior to December 31, 1784.

As this in an Index and not an attempt to reproduce the Saffell list, no effort has been made to give the name of the office held by any person, but the foregoing statements will, in many cases, show whether the party was an officer or not.

WHERE A STAR FOLLOWS THE NAME OF A PERSON IN THE INDEX IT INDICATES THAT A PERSON OF SIMILAR NAME IS SHOWN IN THE PUBLICATION KNOWN AS McALLISTER'S DATA ON THE VIRGINIA MILITIA IN THE REVOLUTION, WHERE, IN MANY INSTANCES, THERE IS A CONSIDERABLE AMOUNT OF INFORMATION IN REGARD TO THE ACTUAL SERVICE OF THE PARTIES, THEIR RESIDENCES AND, IN MANY INSTANCES, THE NAMES OF THE DECENDANTS OF THE SOLDIER.

The Index to the names of Virginia Officers given in Palmer's Calendar of Virginia State Papers will be found at the back of this book.

A

Abbett, Reuben, 284.
Abbott, Ransdell, 274.
Abell, Matthias, 256.
Absalom, Edmund, 266.
Adams, Jacob, 284.
Adams, James, 255, 283.
Adams, Jervis, 241.
Adams, John, 249, 249, 260*.
Adams, Malleroy, 276.
Adams, Matthew, 255.
Adams, William, 279*.
Adderson, Thomas, 243.
Addison, Richard, 259, 263.
Adkerson, Master, 244.
Alderson, Richard, 272.
Aldridge, John, 281.
Alexander, Andrew, 277.
Alexander, George, 501.
Alexander, James, 242, 247.
Alexander, John, 248, 248, 254, 281.
Alexander, Morgan, 270.
Alexander, William, 251.
Algood, John, 265.
Allen, David, 411, 501.*
Allen, Edward, 501.
Allen, John, 252, 252, 501.*
Allen, Matthew, 246, 247.
Allen, Moses, 278.
Allen, Reuben, 275.
Allen, Robert, 277.
Allenworth, James, 260.
Allford, John, 281.
Allington, John, 282.
Allison, George, 275.
Allison, John, 500.
Almand, John, 274.
Alphin, Thomas, 243, 255.
Alright, John, 260.
Alva, John, 280.
Alverson, James, 277.
Alvey, Robert, 276.
Amberson, James, 284.
Anderson, Andrew, 263.*
Anderson, George, 250-251.*
Anderson, John, 260-262-268-275-411-501.*
Anderson, Richd. C., 411.*
Anderson, Richard E., 500.
Anderson, Robert, 501.*
Anderwin, Presley, 242.
Anglin, Isaac, 285.
Andrews, Claiborne, 264.
Andrews, Robert, 270.
Antill, Jacob, 271.
Apperson, Richard, 289.
Archer, Benjamin, 281.
Archer, Jeremiah, 282.
Archer, Joseph, 274-501.
Archer, Peter E., 501.
Archer, Peter F., 411.
Archer, Richard, 411.
Archer, Sampson, 286.
Armistead, Thomas, 501.
Armistead, William, 501.
Armond, John, 257-264.
Armstead, William, 289.
Armstrong, Abell, 287.
Armstrong, George, 276.
Armstrong, James, 278-288.*
Arrell, David, 277.
Arnold, John, 285.
Arthur, Reuben, 278.
Artiss, Isaac, 287.
Arundell, Dohickey, 412.
Ash, Benjamin, 263.
Ash, James, 262.
Ashby, Benj, 411-501.
Ashby, Bladen, 281.
Ashby, John, 270.
Ashby, Stephen, 501.
Ashley, Thomas, 265.
Aspinwald, John, 253.
Atchison, John, 277.
Atchison, William, 260.
Athey, John, 279.
Atkinson, Major, 245.
Atkinson, Reuben, 245-245.
Avery, Billy H., 289.
Ayres, John, 276.

B

Baaer, Moses, 271.
Bacon, Burwell, 242-254.
Bacon, Burwick, 243.
Bacon, Robert, 284.
Bagley, William, 281.
Bailey, James, 251-268.
Bailes, Jesse, 271.
Bailey, John, 501.*
Bailey, Simon, 281.
Bailey, William, 278-279-283.
Baity, Pat, 283.
Baker, Christopher, 281.
Baker, Fennel, 267.
Baldwin, Caleb, 287.
Baldwin, Cornelius, 414-501.
Ball, Aaron, 243-243-254.
Ball, Burgess, 414-501.
Ball, Daniel, 414-501.
Ball, Joseph, 248.
Ballard, Dudley, 273.
Ballard, Robert, 500.
Ballard, Thomas, 274.
Ballard, William, 501-501.
Balmain, Alexander, 501.
Banks, James, 501.
Banks, Thomas, 268.
Barbee, Thomas, 414-501.
Barber, Thomas, 255.
Barbour, James, 501.
Barham, Hart, 267.
Barker, Charles, 277.
Barker, Henry, 270.
Barker, John, 266.*
Barksdale, John, 289-501.*
Barnes, James, 246.
Barnes, John, 256-264-269.
Barnes, William, 247.
Barnett, Chiswell, 501.
Barnett, Henry, 274.
Barnett, James, 289-412.*
Barnett, John, 284.
Barnett, William, 501.*
Barnes, William, 246.
Barr, William, 283.
Barrand, Peter, 261.

Barrett, William, 414.*
Barrom, Fielding, 247-253-254.
Barrom, William, 412.
Barron, James, 501.
Barry, Augustine, 269.
Barry, Simon, 262.
Barthorn, Hugh, 286.
Bartlett, Archibald, 285.
Bartlett, Benj, 265.
Bartlett, William, 260.
Bartley, James, 246.
Bartley, John, 259-263.
Bartley, William, 242-254.
Barton, James, 256.
Basdell, Jeffrey, 286.
Basey, William, 286.
Basham, Jerry, 266.
Baskerville, Samuel, 414-501.
Bassett, Philip, 257.
Bates, John, 262-268-277.
Bates, Joseph, 256.
Bates, Thomas, 246-262.
Battershell, Freeman, 281.
Baughan, William, 255.
Bawcut, William, 278.
Baxter, James, 275.
Baylis, Henry, 414-501.
Baylis, William, 501.*
Baylor, George, 414-500.
Baylor, Walker, 501.
Baynham, John, 289-501.
Bayton, Thomas, 251.
Baytop, James, 501.
Baytop, John, 501.
Baytop, Thomas, 501.
Beal, Richard, 276.
Beale, Robert, 414-501-501.
Bealer, Charles, 269.
Beall, Robert, 280.
Bean, John, 284.
Bearley, Reuben, 258.
Beason, William, 261.
Beavan, John, 258.
Beavers, James, 246.
Beazley, James, 274.

Beck, John, 280-414-501.
Becket, Humphreys, 260.
Beckett, Robert, 282.
Bedinger, Daniel, 414.
Bedinger, Henry, 414-501.
Beetly, James, 263.
Beham, James, 284.
Belcher, Edwin, 266-272.
Belcher, George, 266.
Belcher, Isaac, 271.
Belcher, Jacob, 271.
Belcher, Joel, 272.
Belcher, Robert, 266.
Belcher, Thomas, 271.
Belcher, William, 264-272.
Belfield, John, 414.
Bell, Henry, 414-501.
Bell, John, 261-289.*
Bell, Robert, 270.*
Bell, Thomas, 286-414-501.*
Bell, William, 277.
Belmain, Alex, 414.
Belvin, Robert, 242-254.
Bendure, Thomas, 281.
Benham, Peter, 279.*
Bennet, Artes, 244-245.
Bennett, William, 501.*
Bent, Samuel, 285.
Bentley, Jerry, 266.
Berry, Augustus, 261.
Berry, George, 280-501.
Bernard, William, 501.
Bentley, William, 414-501.
Berry, John, 284.
Best, Lewis, 267.
Bethel, Valentine, 252.
Bevins, John, 273.
Bevins, Matthew, 263.
Bibbey, John, 268.
Bibb, William, 250.*
Biggs, Benjamin, 414-280-284-501.
Bilby, Richard, 283.
Bilfield, John, 501.
Bills, William, 261.
Bird, Henry, 265.
Bird, Otway, 500.
Bird, William, 257.*
Bishard, John, 242.

Bishop, Joseph, 250.
Bishop, Solomon, 271.
Bishop, Thomas, 271.
Black, Richard, 263.
Blackburn, Joseph, 281.
Blackburn, Julius, 285.
Blackmore, George, 271-501.
Blackwell, John, 278-414-501.*
Blackmore, Thomas, 271.
Blackwell, Joseph, 278-414-501.
Blackwell, Samuel, 501.
Blackwell, Thomas, 262-412.
Blenningham, Morris, 278.
Blair, John, 242-243-253-412-501.*
Blair, Robert, 259-263.
Bland, Christian, 246-427.
Bland, Theodoric, 500.
Bland, William, 276.
Blanden, Seth, 501.
Blankenship, Benj'm, 244-245.
Blankenship, George, 264.
Blundell, Elijah, 265.
Blunder, Charles, 278.
Boberts, Thomas, 261.
Bodkin, Charles, 282.
Bogan, Benjamin, 259-263.
Bohannon, Ambrose, 241-244-245-253-414-501.
Bolden, John, 264-269.
Bonner, Richard, 270.
Booker, Edward, 271.*
Booker, Abraham, 281.
Booker, Lewis, 250-251-253-414-501.
Booker, Richison, 266.
Booker, Samuel, 265-414-501.
Booth, Michael, 267.
Booten, William, 273.
Boswell, Meacham, 501.
Botts, Archibald, 258-258.
Bourk, Tobias, 260.
Bourn, John, 274.
Boush, Charles, 501.
Bouton, Richard, 254.
Boutwell, Samuel, 275.
Bowdree, Lewis, 245.
Bowdry, Lewis, 244-254.
Bowen, Henry, 280-414-501.
Bowen, James, 263.

Bowen, John, 271-414-501.
Bowen, Joseph, 277.
Bowers, Morris, 244-245.
Bowers, Phillips, 244-245.
Bowers, Thomas, 271.
Bowing, James, 259.
Bowles, Zachariah, 255.
Bowler, Mark, 275.
Bowling, Jesse, 273.
Bowling, Robert, 277.
Bowling, Thornberry, 274.
Bowls, Zachariah, 251.
Bowne, Thomas, 414.
Bowyer, Michael, 501.
Bower, Thomas, 414-501.
Boyer, Elias, 244-245.
Boyer, Michael, 414.
Bradford, Charles, 414.
Bradford, Samuel, 245.
Bradford, Samuel K., 237-253-414-501.
Bradford, William, 278.
Bradley, Christopher, 501.
Bradley, James, 501.
Bradley, Richard, 272.
Bradshaw, Robert, 272.*
Brady, Joseph, 288.
Brady, Hezekiah, 287.
Brady, Luke, 279.
Brady, Perrigrine, 288.
Bramford, Joseph, 257.
Bramham, Evan, 274.
Brashier, Richard, 501.
Brawner, John, 265.
Bray, James, 242.
Brazer, William, 284.
Breckenridge, Alexander, 287-414-501.
Breckenridge, Robert, 414-501.
Breedlove, John, 271.
Breedlove, Thomas, 274.
Breedlove, William, 278.
Brent, John, 271.
Brent, William, 500.
Brewer, Abraham, 259.
Brewer, Jesse, 274.
Bridgeman, Thomas, 265.
Bridgewater, Levid, 282.

Bridges, John, 276.
Brian, John O., 286.
Brisby, John, 281.
Briscoe, Reuben, 279.
Brittain, John, 256, 501.
Britton, John, 283.
Broach, Charles, 246.
Broad, Robert, 282.
Broadfield, Charles, 263.
Broadus, Edward, 274.
Broadus, James, 273-501.
Broadus, Richard, 262-268.
Broadus, William, 501.
Brodie, Ludwick, 501.
Brock, Uriah, 249-249.
Brook, Edmund, 501.
Brooke, Francis, 501.
Brooke, Francis T., 414.
Brooke, John, 414-501.
Brooke, Thomas, 242.
Brookes. Walker, 501.
Brooks, Charles, 284.
Brooks, George, 274.
Brooks, Thomas, 272.
Broomes, Benjamin, 283.
Browder, Isham, 270.
Brower, James, 257.
Browers, John, 277.
Brown, ———, 255.
Brown, Charles, 275.
Brown, Isaac, 260-261.
Brown, Jacob, 501.
Brown, Jacob R., 414.
Brown, James, 264-271-274.*
Brown, John, 282-282-286-501.*
Brown, Nell, 249.
Brown, Neil, 249.
Brown, Robert, 250-501.
Brown, Thomas, 278.*
Brown, William, 281-501.*
Browne, Thomas, 501.
Browne, Windsor, 501.
Brownlee, Thomas, 281.
Brownlee, William, 501.
Bruce, John, 258.
Bruin, Peter Bryan, 262.
Bruin, Peter B., 414-501.
Brumagen, William, 284.

Brundage, Solomon, 285.
Bruton, William, 279.
Bryan, James, 269.
Bryan, Thomas, 264.
Bryan, Thomas, 257.
Bryant, Jesse, 265.
Bryant, William, 277.
Bryon, Robert, 248.
Bryron, Robert, 248.
Bucker, Thomas, 502.
Buher, Jacob, 284.
Buckner, Samuel, 289.
Buckner, Thomas, 414.
Buite, Thomas, 284.
Buford, Abraham, 256-414-500.*
Buford, William, 265.
Buller, Claiborne, 270.
Bullin, Luke, 249.
Bullins, Luke, 250.
Bullock, Obadiah, 263.
Bullock, Rice, 502.
Buly, Christopher, 260.
Bunting, William B., 412.
Burd, Thomas, 256.
Burfort, Thomas, 502.
Burgh, Tobias, 262.
Burk, John, 263.*

Burk, William, 259-263.
Burn, Christian, 278.
Burn, Robert, 276.
Burnett, James, 289.
Burnett, John, 283.
Burns, Isham, 249-250.
Burton, Hutchins, 289-502.
Burton, James, 273.
Burton, Thomas, 272.
Burriss, John, 269.
Burris, Thomas, 276.
Burroughs, George, 270.
Burrows, Jacob, 274.
Burwell, Nathaniel, 242-243-253-414-502.
Bushell, John, 244-255.
Bushiel, John, 243.
Butler, Lawrence, 265-414-502.
Butler, Samuel, 502.
Butler, Thomas, 267.
Butt, Simon, 268.
Butts, Zachary, 261.
Buzan, Philip, 282.
Bvram, Matthew, 261.
Byrom, Anthony, 261.
Byas, Adam, 271.

C

Cabell, Samuel J., 415-500.
Cadell, John, 273.
Cahill, John, 258.
Cain, John, 287.
Calderwood, James, 256-415.
Call, Richard, 415-502.
Callahan, Major, 243-244.
Callendar, Eleazer, 502.
Calloway, Samuel, 282.
Calmes, George, 262.
Calmes, Marquis, 270-502.
Calvert, Jonathan, 241.
Calvert, Joseph, 502.
Camp, William, 241-242.
Campbell, Alexander, 268.
Campbell, Archibald, 416-502.
Campbell, John, 260-263-269-281-415.
Campbell, Richard, 415-500.*
Campbell, Samuel, 502.*
Campbell, Thomas, 252-252.

Campbell, William, 259-502.*
Canard, William, 282.
Cannary, William, 273.
Cannon, Luke, 263-415-502.
Carbury, Peter, 285.
Cardonas, John, 284.
Carey, Samuel, 502.
Carey, John, 263.
Carle, Richard, 251.
Carnes, Patrick, 288-415-502.
Carney, Martin, 502.
Carpenter, Christopher, 283-283.
Carpenter, John, 285.
Carr, James, 284.
Carr, James, T., 272.
Carrier, Thomas, 269.
Carroll, John, 272.
Carrington, Clement, 288-502.
Carrington, Edward, 241-415-500.*
Carrington, George, 288-415- 502.*

Cowran, Bryan, 284.
Cox, Bradford, 263.
Cox, Jeremiah, 274.
Cox, John, 272.
Cox, Presley, 275.
Cox, Samuel, 277.*
Cox, William, 268.
Coxon, William, 280.
Craddock, Henry, 266.*
Craddock, Robert, 266-416-502.
Craig, James, 502.*
Craig, William, 283.
Craigg, Thomas, 283.
Craike, James, 415.
Crame, James, 502.
Crawford, Charles, 283.
Crawford, John, 270-415-502.*
Crawford, Nehemiah, 286.
Crawford, Robert, 283.
Crawford, William, 500.
Creamore, William, 268.
Creaton, William, 264.
Creimer, William, 251.
Cremer, William, 250.
Critchfield, John, 264.
Crittenden, John, 258-415-502.
Crockett, Joseph, 500.
Croghan, William, 415-502.
Crook, James, 264.
Crook, John, 288.
Crook, Jonathan, 278.

Crook, Joseph, 270.
Croncher, James, 275.
Cropper, John, 256-267-500.
Crosby, Hick, 277.
Crosby, William, 287.
Cross, Samuel, 242-243-254.
Cross, Thomas, 243-243-254.
Crosson, John H., 257.
Crown, Absalom, 260.
Croxton, Richard, 250-255.
Crumley, Thomas, 265.
Crumm, John, 263.
Crump, Abner, 502.
Cruswell, Samuel, 284.
Crutchlow, Edward, 281.
Crute, John, 256-415-502.
Cryster, John, 262-268.
Cubberton, James, 502.
Cullins, John, 279.*
Cumberford, James, 283.
Cunningham, Charles, 257-264.
Cunningham, William, 502.
Curd, Joseph, 289.
Curly, Dennis, 285.
Curry, James, 415-502.
Curtis, James, 266.
Curtis, Thomas, 287.
Curtiss, Wiliam, 265.
Custard, John, 281.
Cutlip, Abraham, 285.
Cyrus, Bartholomew, 264.

D

Dabney, Charles, 418-500.*
Dade, Francis ,502.
Daily, Patrick, 260.
Dandridge, Alex, 418-502.
Dandridge, John, 247-248-418-502.
Dandridge, Robert, 249-252-253-418-502.
Dane, Benjamin, 281.
Daniel, Josiah, 286.
Daniels, Joseph, 262.
Darby, Nathaniel, 502.
Dark, William, 500.
Darrington, Elisha, 285.

Darvill, William, 246.
Davenport, Opie, 418-502.
Davidson, Adonijah, 273.
Davidson, William, 278.
Davies, Daniel, 260.
Davies, Nathan, 272.
Davis, Abraham, 265.
Davis, George, 275.
Davis, Humphrey, 275.
Davis, Isaac, 257.*
Davis, Jacob, 271.
Davis, James, 263-278.*
Davis, John, 256.*

Davis, Jesse, 288.*
Davis, Joseph, 256-257-268-502.*
Davis, Thomas, 266.*
Davis, William, 264-269-274-275-278-418-500.*
Dawbin, William, 273.
Dawson, Benjamin, 274-287-288.
Dawson, Henry, 280-502.*
Dawson, James, 272 282.
Dawson, Robert, 273.
Dawson, William, 289.
Day, Benjamin, 270.
Day, Richard, 266.
Dean, Edward, 248.
Dean, Peter, 273.
Deans, Edward, 248.
Dearing, James, 274.
Dearon, Peter, 276.
Death, William, 256-263.
Deaton, George, 272.
Deaton, Jabby, 271.
Deadham, Archibald, 502.
Deer, Elijah, 274.
Dalaplane, James, 417-502.
Dampsey, John, 256-261.
Denison, Joseph, 284.
Denny, William, 272.
Dennington, Daniel, 278.
Dennis, William, 262.
Dent, John, 280.
Denton, John, 250.
Derry, John, 265.
Devore, Isaac, 284.
Dichie, William, 250.
Dick, Alexander, 418-502.
Dick, James, 267.
Dickerson, Edmund, 417.
Dickerson, Edmonds, 502.
Dickerson, John, 257.*
Dickerson, Robert, 273.
Dickert, Nicholas, 281.
Dickinson, Edmund B., 417.
Dicklawman, Christopher, 502.
Didlake, James, 246-247.
Diener, Jacob, 249-249.
Digges, Dudley, 502.
Dillard, James, 289.*

Dillon, Jesse, 251.
Dillon, William, 273.
Dindell, Alex., 261.
Dinny, William, 248.
Dison, Robert, 264.
Dix, Thomas, 242-249-253-417-502.
Dixon, Anthony F., 502.
Dixon, John, 281.
Dobbs, Kedah, 268.
Dobson, Robert, 418-502.
Dogan, Henry, 257-265.
Dogans, William, 278.
Dolbey, William, 268.
Dolman, Thomas, 245-245 253.
Dolin, Michael, 286.
Dollar, William, 271-273.
Donovan, Matthew, 258-259.
Dorothy, Patrick, 279.
Dorsey, Nicholas, 249-250-255.
Douglas, William, 282.*
Dougherty, John, 284.
Doughrah, Ephriam, 270.
Dowdie, James, 262.
Dowel, Wm., 280.
Downer, Thomas, 275.
Downey, Cornelius, 281.
Doyle, John, 256.
Doyle, Robert, 278.
Drake, Andrew, 260.
Drake, Michael, 277.
Drake, Thomas, 417.
Drake, William, 418.
Draper, George, 502.
Dressdell, Alexander, 260.
Drew, John, 502.
Drew, Thomas H., 502.
Drinker, Joseph, 271.
Drishell, Francis, 273.
Drummond, John, 282.
Drury, Matthew, 252-252.
Drewry, Samuel, 252-253-254.
Dudley, Henry, 502.
Dudley, Robert, 502.
Duff, Abden, 268.
Duff, Edward, 502.
Duffey, James, 268-283.
Duggan, Thomas, 282.

Dukins, James, 277.
Dullin, Daniel, 259.
Dunaway, John, 265-275.
Dunbar, James, 259-260.
Duncan, Charles, 262.
Duncan, Christopher, 260.
Dunlap, John, 273.
Dunlap, Samuel, 272.
Dunn, Andrew, 282.
Dunn, Charles, 268.
Dunn, David, 267.
Dunn, John, 252-252.
Dunn, Peter, 289-417.
Dunnagan, David, 283.

Dunnavant, Claiborne, 271.
Dunnavant, Daniel, 271.
Dunnavant, Leonard, 271.
Dunnavant, Philip, 271.
Durall, Daniel, 502.
Durret, Clayborne, 275.
Dust, Adam, 282.
Duvlin, James, 273.
Dye, Jonathan, 417-502.
Dyer, Francis, 243-244-255.
Dyer, Peter, 272.
Dyer, Samuel, 243-244-255.
Dyson, Stephen, 264.

E

Eady, Thomas, 282.
Eakle, Harmon, 282.
Early, John, 262-267.
Eastin, Philip, 418-502.
Eastin, Richard, 502.
Eaton, Joseph, 242.
Ebb, James, 257.
Ebbs, Emanuel, 266.
Eddens, Samuel, 242-250-251.
Eddins, Samuel, 418-502.
Edmonds, Thomas, 502.
Edmonson, Benjamin, 502.
Edmonson, William, 259.
Edwards, Charles, 265.
Edwards, Edmund, 267.
Edwards, John, 263.*
Edwards, Le Roy, 418-502.
Edwards, Spencer, 262-268.
Edmunds, Elias, 500.
Edmunds, Richard, 267.
Edmunds, Thomas, 418.
Edmundson, William, 260.
Edzard, James, 269.
Eggleston, Joseph, 288-418-502.
Eggleston, William, 502.
Elcheson, William, 261.
Elliott, Samuel, 262-268.
Elliott, William, 242-272.*
Ellis, Mathew, 250.
Ellerton, Joseph, 256.

Elmore, John, 255.
Elmore, Moses, 278.
Elmore, Thomas, 244-243-271.
Elsmore, John, 279.
Elsmore, William, 277.
Emmons, William, 242-243.
Emmett, George, 281.
English, John, 284.
English, William, 282.
Eppes, William, 418-502-502.
Eppes, Francis, 418.
Erskine, Charles, 256-418-502.
Ermin, Thomas, 285.
Estes, Elisha, 274.
Eskridge, Joseph, 272.
Eskridge, William, 274-418-502.
Eustance, John, 503-503.
Eustace, John, 418.
Etholl, Benjamin, 288.
Ethrington, John, 276-276.
Evans, Arnold, 281.
Evans, Charles, 283.
Evans, David, 266.
Evans, Edward, 282.
Evans, George, 503.
Evans, Griffith, 245-241.
Evans, James, 257-264.
Evans, John, 265-269-282.
Evans, Philip, 244-245.
Evans, Richard, 259-269.

Evans, William, 283-418-503.*
Evies, Thomas, 245.
Everhart, Andrew, 260-261.
Everett, John, 264.

Everett, Thomas, 280.
Ewing, Alexander, 503.
Ewell, Charles, 503.
Ewell, Thomas, 503.

F

Fagg, John, 268.
Farrell, John, 257.
Farlough, John, 247.
Farron, Cattesly, 272.
Farron, James, 272.
Farrow, William, 273.
Feagan, John, 258-259.
Febiger, Christian, 419-500.
Feely, Timothy, 258-262.
Felkins, John, 278.
Felts, Isham, 267.
Fenn, Thomas, 252-252-419.
Fenton, Arthur, 271.
Ferguson, Daniel, 287.
Ferguson, Robert, 272-503.
Feris, William, 278.
Ferrell, William, 252-253.
Ferrill, John, 264.
Field, Reuben, 419.
Fielding, Edward, 262-268.
Fields, Reuben, 503.
Fields, Robert, 269.
Filey, William, 256.
Figg, Thomas, 242.
Findley, Samuel, 503.
Finley, Archibald, 260-261.
Finley, Samuel, 419.
Finn, Philip, 281.
Finn, Thomas, 503.
Finnigan, Patrick, 283.
Finnet, John, 274.
Finney, John, 283.*
Finney, Robert, 244-245.
Finnie, William, 419-500.
Fish, Felty, 261.
Fisher, John, 248-248-255.
Fisher, Thomas, 270.
Fitzgerald, George, 282.·
Fitzgerald, James, 261.
Fitzgerald, John, 253-419-503-503.

Fitzhugh, Perrigrine, 419-503.
Fitzhugh, William, 248-248-419-503.
Fitzpatrick, Solomon, 259.
Fitzsimmons, Christian, 258.
Flack, George, 268.
Flaherty, James, 262.
Flaugherty, Samuel, 258.
Fleet, Henry, 503.
Fleet, John, 503.
Fleetwood, Isaac, 262.
Fleming, James, 277.
Fleming, William, 242.
Flemming, Charles, 419-500.
Flemming, John, 503.
Flemming, Thomas, 419-500.
Flennan, Thomas, 274.
Flipper, Joseph, 275.
Fleshner, John, 254.
Flishner, Johan, 246.
Flood, Burwell, 264.
Flood, Thomas, 287.
Flora, William, 268.
Florence, George, 280.
Folkes, John, 253.
Fountleroy, Griffith, 503.
Fountleroy, Henry, 503.
Fox, Joseph, 269.
Fox, Nathaniel, 289-503.
Fox, Thomas, 277-419-503.
Forbes, Thomas, 273.
Forehand, John, 286.
Forrest, Anthony, 262.
Foster, Achilles, 274.
Foster, James, 503.
Foster, Joel, 274.
Foster, John, 256.
Foster, John H. 419.
Foster, Robert, 503.
Foster, Thomas, 286.*
Foster, William, 251-288-503.

Fowler, Joseph, 284.
Francis, Christian, 250-251.
Fraser, Alexander, 284.
Frazier, James, 265.*
Frazier, William, 242.
Frazey, Falvy, 503.
Freeland, John, 285.
Freeman, Isaac, 242.
Freeman, Philip, 264.
Freeman, Stephen, 266.
Freeman, William, 248-248.
Fritts, George, 244-245-253.
Fritz, Felty, 269.
Fryer, Richard, 273.
Fullam, Peter, 257-265.
Fuller, Joseph, 282.
Furlough, James, 247.

G

Gale, Thomas, 263.
Gallahue, Charles, 257.
Gamble, Robert, 421-503.
Gamble, William, 259-263.
Gainer, Charles, 262.
Gaines, Thomas, 261-269.
Gaines, William Flemming, 251-253-421-503.
Garland, James, 242.*
Garland, Peter, 289-503.
Garner, Joseph, 262.
Garnett, Anthony, 269.
Garnett, Benjamin, 421.
Garrett, Henry, 278.
Garret, William, 271.
Garvey, Henry, 279.
Gaskins, Jesse, 265.
Gaskins, Job, 267.
Gaskins, Littleton, 265.
Gaskins, Thomas, 421-500.*
Gassaway, James, 271.
Gassaway, John, 271.
Gates, Horatio, 421-500.
Gault, John M., 503.
Gault, Patrick, 503.
Gammels, Nathan, 273.
Gentry, James, 250-251-252-255.*
George, Robert, 503.
George, William, 503.*
Gerault, John, 503.
Gibbs, Churchill, 421-503.
Gibbs, Edward, 271.
Gibbs, Herod, 272.
Gibbs, Miles, 271.
Gibbs, William, 264.*

Gibbons, James, 274.
Gibson, James, 285.*
Gibson, John, 283-289-421-421-500-503.*
Gilchrist, George, 421-503.
Gilbert, James, 257.
Gilbert, John, 282.
Giles, James, 260.
Giles, John, 503.
Gilham, Peter, 259.*
Gill, Erasmus, 272.
Gill, Samuel, 503.
Gillaspy, Thomas, 287.
Gillaspy, William, 281.
Gillihan, Clement, 284.
Gillison, John, 421-503.
Gillock, John, 274.*
Gilmore, George, 257.
Gilver Thomas, 278.
Gimber, William, 277.
Gist, John, 285.
Gist, Nathaniel, 421-500.*
Glass, Hugh, 259-263.
Glascock, Thomas, 421-503.
Glynn, Samuel, 263.
Godbolt, John, 258.
Godfrey, John, 284.
Godfrey, Robert, 277.
Godman, William, 245.
Goodrum, Thomas, 267.
Goodwin, Benjamin, 280.
Goodwin, Dinwiddie, 289-503.
Goff, Adam, 272.
Goff, Daniel, 264.
Goff, Philip, 273.

Goley, John, 277.
Goldsberry, Mark, 253.
Golman, Francis, 275.
Gordon, Ambrose, 421-503.
Gordon, Arthur, 503.
Gordon, James, 270.
Gordon, George, 277.
Gorman, Bernard, 256.
Grossett, John, 283.
Gould, David, 420.
Gowden, William, 275.
Graham, Walter, 503.
Graham, William, 270.*
Grant, Daniel, 262.
Grant, John, 246-262.
Grant, William, 257-264.
Gratton, John, 503.
Gravatt, John, 275.
Graves, John, 252.
Graves, William, 503.*
Gray, Benjamin, 257-265.
Gray, Francis, 257-265-421-503.
Gray, George, 252-252-503.
Gray, Godfrey, 503.
Gray, James, 266-281-282-503.
Gray, John, 248.*
Gray, William, 421-503.*
Gray, Wilson, 286.
Grayson, William, 421-500.*
Gregory, John, 266-289.
Gregory, William, 288.

Green, Gabriel, 421-503.
Green, John, 421-500-503.*
Green, Robert, 261-269-421-503.
Green, Samuel B., 503.*
Green, William, 267.
Greenway, George, 259.
Greer, Charles, 503.
Grew, Michael, 257.
Griffin, Ignatius, 253.
Griffin, Thomas, 285.
Griffin, William, 275.
Griffith, David, 276-503-503.
Griffith, Reuben, 249-250.
Grimes, James, 277.
Grimes, William. 420.
Groome, Charles, 252.
Groves, Abraham, 260.
Groves, William, 259-263-280.
Grow, Isham, 264.
Grubbs, Thomas, 242-244.
Gruttage, John, 287.
Guilder, Daniel, 287.
Gully, George, 277.
Gunn, James, 421.
Gunner, James, 282.
Gunter, Charles, 243-244-255.
Guthrie, George, 288-503.
Guttery, John, 284.
Guy, Samuel, 257-264.
Guy, William, 264.

H

Hackley, John, 421-503.
Haddocks, John, 278.
Hagan, Charles, 286.
Hagerty, John, 283.
Hagerty, Nicholas, 283.
Hagerty, Patrick, 270.
Hagley, William, 246.
Hailey, Thomas, 283.
Haily, Daniel, 268.
Haines, John, 256.
Hainey, Holland, 253.
Hains, William, 243.
Hainy, Michael, 283.

Hale, Caleb, 281.
Haley, John, 281.
Haley, William, 287.
Halley, Daniel, 256.
Halfpain, John, 259-263.
Halfpenny, Isaac, 284.
Hall, Frederick, 244.
Hall, Jesse, 266.
Hall, John, 272.*
Hall, Solomon, 250.
Haller, William, 273.
Ham, Stephen, 274.
Hamilton, Gawin, 251.*

Hamilton, James, 421-503.'
Hamilton, John, 282.*
Hammersly, Abraham, 277.
Hamrick, Benjamin, 278.
Handley, Joseph, 264.
Haney, Holland, 503.
Hansford, William, 283-283.
Handshaw, George, 263.
Handy, George, 288.
Hanna, John, 285.
Hansbrough, James, 276.
Hanshaw, George, 259.
Harbert, William, 283.
Harcum, Rhodam, 503.
Hardiman, John, 503.
Harding, James, 246-254.
Hardy, James, 272.
Hardy, William, 268.
Harfield, David, 273.
Harley, John, 257.
Harling, George, 282.
Harper, James, 273-503.
Harper, Nathaniel, 260.
Harrigan, Jeremiah, 271.
Harris, Burn, 276.
Harris, David, 262-268.
Harris, Edward, 276.
Harris, George, 260.
Harris, James, 269-285.
Harris, John, 242-243-244-255-258-258-421-503-503.*
Harris, Jordan, 503.
Harris, Joseph, 259.
Harris, Rowly, 274.
Harris, William, 273-285.*
Harrison, Col. ———, 255.
Harrison, Andrew, 258-259-267-274.
Harrison, Bobert, 266.
Harrison, Charles, 241-250-421-500-503.
Harrison, James, 268-423-503.*
Harrison, John, 269-283-421-503.
Harrison, John P., 503.
Harrison, Joseph, 270.
Harrison, Lawrence, 280-421.
Harrison, Lovell, 270.
Harrison, Patrick, 269.

Harrison, Peyton, 272.
Harrison, Richard, 503.*
Harrison, Thomas, 286.*
Harrison, Valentine, 272-503.
Harrison, William, 288-503.*
Hart, Ludwick, 283.
Hart, Robert, 241-254.
Hart, Samuel, 258.
Hart, William, 242-254.
Hartlett, Walter, 285.
Hartley, Daniel, 269.
Harvey, Charles, 282.
Harvey, Edward, 286.
Harvey, Richard, 262-268.
Harvie, John, 503.
Hastey, John, 268.
Hastings, John, 278.
Hasty, Clement, 262.
Hasty, John, 262.
Hawes, Samuel, 275-421-500.*
Hawkins, Elisha, 274.
Hawkins, John, 276-503.
Hawkins, Moses, 423-503.*
Haycraft, Joshua, 261.
Haycroft, Joshua, 259.
Hayes, John, 421-503.*
Hayley, Daniel, 277.
Haynie, Holland, 251.
Hays, John, 280.*
Hays, Thomas, 503.
Hazel, Henry, 249.
Head, John, 253.
Heally, William, 262.
Healy, Martin, 503.
Healy, William, 268.
Heatherly, Thomas, 272.
Heatly, James, 259.
Henderson, David, 503.
Henderson, John, 267.*
Henderson, Samuel, 248-248.
Henper, Nathaniel, 261.
Henry, John, 252.*
Henry, Thomas, 286.
Henry, William, 257-264.
Henson, Richard, 252-253.
Henthoon, Philip, 283.
Henwood, Elijah, 273.

Herbert, Thomas, 503.
Herndon, Benjamin, 275.
Hernly, Thomas, 261.
Hervey, Joseph, 274.
Heth, Henry, 421-503.
Heth, John, 259-421-503.
Heth, William, 276-421-500.
Hews, Joseph, 267.
Hickey, John, 259.
Hickock, William, 284.
Hicks, James, 281.
Hicks, William, 261.*
Hildrup, John, 273.
Higgins, Peter, 421-503.
Higgins, Robert, 503.
Hill, Abraham, 268.
Hill, Bailor, 503.
Hill, Caleb, 266.
Hill, Curtis, 263.
Hill, George, 275.
Hill, Richard, 250-288.*
Hill, Shedrack, 274.
Hill, Thomas, 421- 503.*
Hill, William, 289.*
Hillier, John, 286.
Hinds, John, 283.
Hinds, William, 260-261.
Hines, James, 247-248-254-265.
Hines, John, 279.*
Hite, Abraham, 421-503.
Hite, George, 421-503.
Hite, Isaac, 503.
Hiveler, Joseph, 281.
Hix, Henry, 273.
Hix, James, 273.
Hobbs, Frederick, 270-270.
Hobinstock, Christian, 288.
Hobson, Edward, 272.
Hobson, Nicholas, 289.
Hockaday, John, 289.
Hockaday, Philip, 504.
Hodge, William, 259.
Hoffler, William, 503.
Hogg, Samuel, 421-504.
Hogg, William, 261.
Hogland, Elert, 269.
Holcombe, John, 504.*

Holder, John, 273.
Holdway, Henry, 269.
Holland, George, 504.
Holland, Thomas, 277.
Holliday, James, 276.*
Holliday, Joseph, 289.
Holliday, Philip, 289.
Holliday, Robert, 257-264.
Holliday, Thomas, 280.
Holly, John, 260.
Holmer, Christian, 241- 421-504.
Holmes, Bartlett, 266.
Holmes, Benjamin, 503.
Holmes, David, 280-421.
Holmes, Edward, 261.
Holmes, James, 261.
Holmes, John, 275.
Holmes, William, 275.
Holt, James, 421-503.
Holt, John H.   503.
Holt, Micajah, 266.
Holt, Thomas, 266-421-503.*
Hood, John, 272.
Hood, Joseph, 287.
Hood, Joshua, 272.
Hood, Thomas, 246-247.*
Hood, William, 256.
Hoomes, Isaac, 503.
Hoomes, James, 269.
Hoomes, David, 503.
Hoomes, Thomas C., 503.
Hoorish, James, 284.
Hopewell, John, 260.
Hopewell, Thomas, 287.
Hopkins, David, 421.
Hopkins, Samuel, 289-421-500.
Hopper, John, 251.
Hord, Thomas, 421.*
Horsfield, Isaac, 283.
Horn, Simon, 272.
Houge, Francis, 245.
Hough, Joseph, 272.
House, James, 246.
Hourd, Thomas, 503.
Howard, John, 242-254-286.
Howard, Peter, 265.
Howe, Robert, 242-243.

Howell, Vincent, 269-504.
Howell, William, 256-269.
Huggard, Obadiah, 272.
Hudson, Benjamin, 244.
Hudson, John, 504.*
Hudson, Rush, 275.
Hudson, William, 275.
Huffman, John, 268.
Huffman, Philip, 504.
Hull, John, 284.
Hughes, Francis, 276.
Hughes, Henry, 504.
Hughes, Jasper, 421-504.
Hughes, Jesse, 242.
Hughes, John, 242-421-504.
Hughes, Nathan, 254.
Hughes, Nathaniel, 243.
Hughes, Pratt, 504.
Hughes, Reuben, 243-243-254.
Hughes, Robert, 283-284. *
Hughes, Sylvester, 275.
Hughes, Thomas, 272.*

Hughs, Hugh, 285.
Humphries, John, 423.
Hundly, Joshua, 265.
Hungerford, Thomas, 279.
Hunt, George, 267.
Hunt, John, 421.
Hunt, Samuel, 272.
Hunt, William, 258-259.*
Hunter, Robert Hart, 247.
Hunter, John, 267.*
Hunter, William, 281.
Humphries, John, 504.
Hurley, John, 258.
Hurley, Matthew, 283.
Hurly, Sylvester, 261.
Hurt, John, 504.
Hutchins, Thomas, 289.
Hutchinson, Richard, 256.
Hutchinson, Samuel, 282.
Hutt, Read, 275.
Hutton, William, 248.

I

Ingram, Jerry, 267.
Inniss, James, 504.
Irons, Henry, 282.
Irwin, Edward, 289.

Irwin, Matthew, 288.
Irvine, William, 280.
Ivis, Thomas, 246.

J

Jaco, William, 286.
Jacobs, Roly, 260.
Jacobs, William, 260.
Jackson, Burwell, 271.
Jackson, James, 274.
Jackson, John, 275.
Jackson, Matthew, 265.
Jackson, Thomas, 284.
James, Chris, 267.
James, Daniel, 276.
James, John, 269.
James, Michael, 504.
James, Thomas, 282.*

Jameson, John, 424-500.
Jarrel, Dennis, 263.
Jeffrey, George, 277.
Jeffrace, William, 265.
Jeffs, Thomas, 259-263.
Jenkins, Job, 259-263.
Jenkins, John, 243-243.
Jenkins, Richard, 242-273.
Jenkins, William, 259-260-266-280.
Jennings, John, 504.
Johannes, William, 284.
Johns, Samuel, 260.
Johns, George, 277.

Johnson, Cornelius, 282.
Johnson, Jacob, 286.
Johnson, James, 242-243-275-284-286-289.
Johnson, Gideon, 504.
Johnson, John, 259-274.
Johnson, John H., 257-504.
Johnson, Leonard, 271.
Johnson, Moses, 271.
Johnson, Peter, 288-504.
Johnson, Phil, 247-247-246.
Johnson, Richard, 263.*
Johnson, Samuel, 246.
Johnson, Thomas, 286.*
Johnson, William, 254-504-504.*
Johnston, Francis, 282.
Johnston, John, 263.
Johnston, John B., 424.
Johnston, Peter, 424.
Johnston, William, 258-258-424.
Joines, Levin, 424-500.
Jolifee, John, 504.
Jones, Albridgeton, 256.
Jones, Albrighton, 424-504.
Jones, Ambrose, 287.

Jones, Cadwalader, 504.ʳ
Jones, Charles, 424-504.
Jones, Churchill, 424-504.
Jones, Daniel, 263.*
Jones, Elias, 243.
Jones, Elisha, 244-255.
Jones, Gabriel, 504-*
Jones, George, 276.
Jones, Jesse, 268.
Jones, John, 246-248-248-252-252-289.*
Jones, Lewis, 504-504.
Jones, Peter, 244-245-289-504.
Jones, Richard, 278-278.*
Jones, Robert, 271.
Jones, Samuel, 256-266-288-504.
Jones, Strother, 285-424-504.
Jones, Thomas, 244-259-275-284.*
Jones, Wood, 271.
Jones, William, 273-277.*
Joyce, Edward, 285.
Jordan, John, 246-288-289-504.
Jouett, Matthew, 424-504.
Jouett, Robert, 504.*
Jump, Vaughan, 270.

K

Kairns, Michael, 283.
Kahill, John, 259.
Kane, William, 256.
Karland, Peter, 263.
Kautsman, John, 504.
Kays, Robert, 424-504.
Keane, Thomas, 278.
Kear, Alexander, 270.
Kearly, John, 263.
Kearns, James, 276.
Kearns, John, 258.
Kearns, William, 262-268.
Keith, Alexander, 271.
Keith, Isham, 277-504.
Keller, Abraham, 504.
Kelly, James, 281.
Kelly, Jesse, 264.
Kelly, John, 242-247-260-261.

Kelly, Gordon, 286.
Kelly, Patrick, 282.
Kelly, Robert, 249-250.
Kelly, Thaddy, 504.
Kelly, Timothy, 287.
Kelly, Thomas, 282.
Kelly, William, 242-247.
Kelshaw, John, 277.
Kem, John, 265.
Kemp, James, 504.
Kemp, Peter, 504.
Kendall, Custis, 504.
Kendall, Francis, 280.
Kendall, Kurtis, 424.
Kennedy, James, 504.
Kennedy, Timothy, 261.
Kennon, John, 270-504.
Kenny, Isaac, 247.

Kenny, Joseph, 287.
Kent, Daniel, 259.
Kent, William, 277.
Kenton, Benjamin, 262.
Kerny, John, 504.
Kersey, Alexander, 243-254.
Ketlar, John, 246.
Key, Richard, 275.
Kidd, Benjamin, 243-244-254.
Kidd, James, 273.
Kimmey, Isaac, 247-254.
Kinard, John, 282.
King, Elisha, 424-504.
King, John, 276-278.
King, Miles, 504.
King, Samuel, 256.
King, Stephen, 257.
King, William, 278.*

King, Zechariah, 273.*
Kingore, William, 286.
Kinley, Benjamin, 504.
Kinsey, Alexander, 244.
Kinsey, Sol., 267.
Kinsey, Thomas, 285.
Kirk, John, 287.
Kirk, Robert, 424-504.*
Kirkland, Jesse, 267.
Kirkland, Rowland, 270.
Kirkpatrick, Abraham, 424-504.
Kittare, Peter, 287.
Kittler, John, 254.
Knapp, John, 282.
Knight, John, 278-280-504.
Knowles, William, 285.
Knox, James, 504.
Kock, Benjamin, 262.

L

Lacy, Henry, 251.
Lacey, Nat., 278.
Lajournade, Alex., 241.
Lambert, Charles, 276.
Lambert, George, 287.
Land, Charles, 272-276.
Lane, James, 280.
Lander, Charles, 279.
Langfitt, Francis, 257.
Langham, Elias, 246-504.
Langham, William, 244-245.
Lapsley, John, 504.
Lapsley, Samuel, 285-426-504.*
Larks, Isaiah, 261.
Larru, Peter, 279.
Larty, John, 504.
Lawler, John, 277.
Lawler, Thomas, 262-268-276.
Lawless, Augustine, 251.
Lawless, John, 262-268.
Lawman, Charles, 244.
Lawrence, John, 265.
Laws, John, 262-268.
Lawson, Benjamin, 250-251-426-504.
Lawson, Claiborne, 504.

Lawson, Robert, 425-500.*
Layland, Peter, 248.
Lazier, Hyatt, 283.
League, James, 266.
Leany, Daniel, 281.
Lee, James, 276.
Lee, John, 262-268-285-504.*
Lee, Jond, 504.
Lee, Henry, 288-425-500.*
Lee, Phil, Francis F., 504.
Lee, Richard, 278-279-425.
Lee, Thomas, 261.
Lefevers, John, 281.
Lefler, George, 281.
Legg, John, 278.*
Legget, William, 263.
Leigh, Bartlett, 252-253.
Leigh, John, 504.
Leigh, Thomas, 248-248.
Leitch, Andrew, 425-504.
Lemasters, Joseph, 281.
Lemon, Samuel, 284.
Lenegar, Edward, 254.
Lent, William, 279.
Leversage, William, 268.

Levy, Jeremiah, 249-250.
Lewin, John, 285.
Lewis, Addison, 504.
Lewis, Andrew, 504.*
Lewis, George, 504.
Lewis, John, 265.*
Lewis, St. John, 243.
Lewis, Stephen, 504.
Lewis, William, 264-269-288-425-426-504.*
Lial, William, 246.
Lightburn, Richard, 504.
Lilley, Thomas, 504.
Lind, Arthur, 276-277-426.
Line, Abraham, 280.
Linegar, Edward, 244-245.
Lindsey, William, 504.
Linton, John, 287-426-504.*
Linton, Michael, 279.
Linsey, Hezekiah, 281.
Lipscomb, Bernard, 504.
Lipscomb, Benori, 265.
Lipscomb, John, 246.
Lipscomb, Major, 246.
Lipscomb, Morning, 266.
Lipscomb, Reuben, 504.
Lipscomb, Thomas, 266.
Lipscomb, Yancey 504.
Lisk, John, 281.
Livingston, Justice, 504.
Livingston, Thomas, 275.
Loyd, James, 246.
Lock, Joseph, 248-248-254.
Locke, John, 286.
Lockhart, James, 287.
Lockhart, John, 283.
Long, Andrew, 275.
Long, Evans, 269.
Long, Gabriel, 268-425-504.
Long, George, 268.
Long, James, 274.
Long, Jeremiah, 275.
Long, Michael, 275..

Long, Nicholas, 269.
Long, Reuben, 268-426-504.
Long, William, 504.*
Longsford, William, 504.
Longsworth, Burgess, 504.
Lorman, Charles, 255.
Love, Samuel, 279.
Love, William, 284.
Loveley, Wm. L., 426-504.
Lovell, George, 266.
Lovell, James, 426.
Lovell, John, 259-263.
Loven, Priesly, 270.
Lovett, Joseph, 285.
Low, James, 284.
Lowe, Robert, 273.
Lowry, Peter, 257.
Loyd, William, 269.
Loyde, Nicholas, 258.
Loysett, Michael, 258-258.
Lucas, Charles, 264.
Lucas, Nathaniel, 504.
Lucas, Thomas, 256.
Lucas, William, 257.*
Luck, James, 265-504.
Luckett, David, 285.
Ludeman, John, W., 426.
Ludiman, William J., 504.
Lumpkin, Moore, 266.
Lush, Sebastian, 279.
Lussy, Josiah, 271.
Lussy, Shedrack, 272.
Lutredge, John, 242.
Lynd, Arthur, 504.
Lyle, Charles, 250-255.
Lyle, John, 250-255.*
Lynch, James, 259.
Lynch, John, 253-254.
Lynch, Peter, 267.
Lynch, Patrick, 267.
Lyon, Enoe, 265.
Lyon, John, 258-263.

M

McAdams, Alex., 284.
McAdams, John, 505.
McAdam, Joseph, 505.
McAdams, Robert, 286.
McAllister, Charles, 249.
McAnnally, Michael, 263.
McCallister, Charles, 250.
McCarney, Robert, 283.
McCart, John, 258-258.
McCartny, Peter, 284.
McCarty, Daniel, 276.
McCarty, Richard, 505.
McChinney, Daniel, 274.
McClain, Thomas, 278.
McClenahan, Alex, 428-500.*
McClenahan, Thomas, 274.
McClung, Walter, 505.
McCord, Samuel, 284.
McCoy, Eneas, 283.
McCullock, John, 270.
McCurkle, Samuel, 269.
McCutchen, John, 281.
McDaniel, John, 287.*
McDaniel, Roderick, 283.
McDonald, Aug., 279.
McDonald, Edward, 283.
McDonald, Laurence, 250.
McDonald, Thomas, 261.
McDorman, James, 246-254.
McDougle, Matthew, 268.
McDowell, John, 256-505.
McEagan, James, 285.
McElhany, John, 505.
McElhenny, John, 285.
McEnnolly, Michael, 259.
McEntire, Charles, 263.
McElroy, William, 281.
McFarland, Benjamin, 277.
McFarland, James, 254.
McGee, James, 288.
McGery, Bennet, 265.
McGinnis, Edward, 276.
McGowan, Daniel, 271.
McGowan, William, 286.

McGuire, Conner, 278.
McGuire, Dennis, 277.
McGuire, John, 263.
McGuire, Patrick, 281.
McGuire, William, 428-505.
McHugh, Matthew, 285.
McIlwain, Thomas, 284.
McIntosh, Alexander, 283.
McIntosh, William, 273.
McIvory, Patrick, 273.
McKay, John, 256.
McKinney, Felix, 283.
McKinnie, James, 279-281.
McKinney, Dennis, 286.
McKinney, Vincent, 275.
McKinsey, John, 265.
McKinsey, Murdock, 263.
McXennon, Martin, 249-249-253.
McKenny, John, 267.
McKensey, John, 273.
McKentree, William, 271.
McLane, Lachlin, 283.
McLaughlin, Hugh, 287.
McMahon, George, 264.
McMahon, Joseph, 264.
McMahon, Roger, 257.
McMahon, William, 505.
McMaklan, John, 262.
McMasters, Michael, 287.
McMicken, Robert, 278.
McMullan, James, 281.
McMullan, John, 259.
McNemera, Michael, 247.
McRector, ———, 277.
McTyree, William, 252-252.
McWilliams, Hazel, 287.
McWilliams, Joshua, 505.
McWilliams, Robert, 272.
Mabin, James, 428-504.
Machie, William, 250.
Madden, Anthony, 260-261.
Madden, Michael, 285.
Madden, Samuel, 278.
Madison, Ambrose, 270.*

24

Madison, William, 266.
Maddox, Notley, 246.
Magill, Charles, 262-505.
Maginnis, Peter, 264.
Maiden, David, 266.
Maiden, William, 271.
Maidy, Anthony, 259.
Mains, Francis, 284.
Mains, John, 282.
Mallory, Francis, 271.
Mallory, Philip, 428-504.
Malone, Michael, 264-269.
Maloy, James, 259.
Mangum, David, 267.
Manly, James, 281.
Mann, David, 504.
Mann, Robert, 272.
Manning, Lawrence, 288.
Mansfield, Thomas, 272.
Markham, James, 505.
Markham, John, 270.
Marks, John, 504.*
Marks, Isaiah, 505.
Marlow, Edward, 259-261.
Marlow, George, 257.
Marshall, George, 275.
Marshall, Humphrey, 504.
Marshall, James M., 504.
Marshall, John, 262-267-504.*
Marshall, Richard, 257-264.
Marshall, Thomas, 276-428-500-504.*
Marshall, William, 275-275.
Marston, John, 504.
Martin, John, 258-285.*
Martin, Mathew, 265.
Martin, Robert, 285.*
Martin, Thomas, 428-505.*
Martin, William, 274-284.*
Marvel, John, 275.
Mason, David, 257-266.*
Mason, Samuel, .277.
Massey, Edmund, 266.
Massey, John, 428.
Massey, Thomas, 504.
Massie, Thomas, 289.*
Mathews, Daniel, 276.
Mathews, George, 428-500.*

Mathews, John, 264-279.*
Mathew, Thos, 428-501.*
Matthews, Benjamin, 267.
Matthews, Richard, 258.*
Matthews, William, 279.
Matthias, Griffy, 275.
Matthias, Henry, 268.
Mattingly, John, 257-264.
Maury, Abraham, 504.
Mazaret, John, 505.
May, George, 279.
May, John, 242.
Meacham, Wm., 244.
Mead, Duncan, 259.
Meade, Everard, 271-428-505.
Meade, John, 263.
Meade, Richard, 428-501.
Means, John, 258-258.
Medley, William, 274.
Melone, John, 259.
Melton, Charles, 287.
Melvin, John, 264.
Mercer, Hugh, 426-500.
Mercer, John F., 276-428-505.
Meredith, William, 247-252-252-253-428-505.*
Merick, John, 282.
Meriwether, David, 428-505.
Meriwether, James, 428-504-504-504.*
Meriwether, Thomas, 505.*
Merritt, Rousy, 286.
Meruny, Thomas, 287.
Merryman, Francis, 273.
Merryman, Thomas, 273.
Metheny, Luke, 287.
Michell, John, 282.
Michie, William, 251.
Micon, Henry, 279.
Middleton, Bazil, 505.
Middleton, Bazil, 428.
Middleton, Henry, 249-249.
Middleton, Samuel, 260.
Middleton, William, 288.
Midson, John, 264.
Miller, David, 428-505.
Miller, Isaac, 269.

Miller, Jarran, 428-505.
Miller, John, 278-428.
Miller, Ludwick, 287.
Miller, Thomas, 258-259-287-428-505.
Miller, Wm., 244; 428; 505.*
Mills, Robert, 257.
Mills, John, 284-505.
Millington, Nathan, 268.
Minnaham, Morris, 288.
Minor, Thomas, 428.*
Minnis, Callowhill, 428-505.
Minnis, Francis, 428-505.
Minnis, Holman, 428-505.
Mishwonger, John, 282.
Mitcham, William, 245.
Mitchell, Archibald, 278.
Mitchell, James, 278.*
Mitchell, John, 262-268-286.*
Mitchell, Peter, 256.
Mitchell, Reaps, 270.
Mitchell, Robert, 259.
Mitchell, Thomas, 261-269.*
Mitchell, William, 286.*
Moffett, William, 278.
Molloy, James, 263.
Monohon, Michael, 271.
Moody, Edward, 505.
Moody, George, 272.
Moody, James, 505.
Moon, Alexander, 505.
Moore, Burren, 269.
Moore, Elson, 505.
Moore, Francis, 275.
Moore, George, 286.*
Moore, John, 505.
Moore, Peter, 505.
Moore, Thomas, 283.*
Moore, William, 278-505.*
Monroe, Alexander, 286.
Monroe, Andrew, 277.
Monroe, George, 428-505.*
Montague, Richard, 505.
Montgomery, Humphrey, 285.
Montgomery, James, 505.
Montgomery, John, 428-501.
Moreland, John, 279.

Morgan, ———, 260-267-268.
Morgan, Charles, 250-251-255-262-284.
Morgan, Daniel, 256-428-500.*
Morgan, James, 242-273.
Morgan, John, 252-262.
Morgan, Randall, 261.
Morgan, Simon, 428-505.
Morgan, Spencer, 505.
Morris, Isaac, 266.
Morris, John, 264.
Morris, Thomas, 274.
Morris, William, 264-274.*
Morrison, John, 284.*
Morrow, Ralph, 282.
Morrow, Robert, 428-505.
Morton, Gerard, 274.
Morton, Hezekiah, 428-505.
Morton, James, 428-505.*
Mosely, Benjamin, 245-428-428-505-505.
Mosely, Thomas, 282.
Mosely, William, 428-505.
Moss, Henry, 271-428-505.
Moss, John, 273.*
Moss, Thomas, 276.*
Mountjoy, William, 276-505.
Moxley, Rhodam, 505.
Mudd, Richard, 256.
Muhlenburg, Peter, 428-500.*
Muir, Francis, 287-428-505.
Muir, John, 505.
Mullan, Daniel, 264.
Munroe, James, 505.
Munroe, John, 277.
Murfrey, John, 263.
Murfrey, Samuel, 263.
Murran, George, 275.
Murray, Abraham, 505.
Murray, Daniel, 282.
Murray, James, 279.
Murray, William, 289.
Murphy, James, 281.
Murphy, Lewis, 279.
Murphy, Leander, 257-264.
Murphy, Martin, 269.
Murphy, Michael, 261-284.

Murritt, Charles, 253.
Murry, Richard, 275.
Mush, Robert, 266.
Muse, George, 275.

Musgrove, James, 247.
Muter, George, 500.
Myers, Frederick, 288.

N

Nance, Frederick, 263.
Nance, Zachariah, 247.
Narvel, Aquilla, 257-264.
Nash, Tarpley, 274.
Neal, Joseph, 285.
Neal, Thomas, 253.
Neal, William, 266.*
Nedley, Bartholomew, 281.
Needham, John, 283.
Nelmes, Charles, 248-248-254.
Nelson, John, 265-286-428-505-505.*
Nelson, Roger, 428-505.
Nelson, William, 428-501.
Nevil, John, 428-500.
Nevil, Presley, 428-501.
Nevines, Thomas, 256.
Newton, Benjamin, 266.
Newell, John, 267.

Neyland, Thomas, 256.
Nicholas, George, 273.*
Nichols, James, 258.
Nichols, Francis, 270.
Nichols, Jesse, 267.
Nicholas, James, 258.
Nicholson, John, 276.
Nix, Francis, 258.
Nixon, Andrew, 505.
Nixon, Andrew, 428.
Noland, James, 261-269.
Noland, Pierce, 505.
Norman, John, 279.
Norvell, Lipscomb, 428-505.
Nugent, John, 262.
Nunnally, John, 266.
Nuss, William, 287.
Nuttall, Iverson, 505.

O

Oakman, William, 281.
Oast, James, 267.
O'Bannon, Aaron, 271.
O'Brian, Christopher, 287.
O'Brian, James, 287.
O'Bryan, James, 259.
O'Donald, Roger, 255.
Ogan, Thomas, 259.
Ogden, George, 246.
Ogleby, George, 257.
Oglesvy, Robert, 285.
Ogilby, John, 271.
O'Hara, Patrick, 270.
Oldham, Conway, 429-505.
Oldmond, Tarlton, 267.
Oldrid, William, 258.
Oliver, James, 288.
Oliver, John, 244-245.*
Oliver, William, 276-429-505.

Olvason, John, 262.
O'Neal, Ferdinand, 288-429-505.
O'Neal, Luke, 287.
O'Neal, Thomas, 244-245.
O'Neal, William, 244-245.
Ord, Robert, 265.
Ore, John, 268.
Orem, Henry, 287.
Organ, Thomas, 258.
Orr, William, 281.
Osburn, Samuel, 283.
Ously, John, 260.
Overline, William, 284.
Overton, John, 429-505.
Overton, Thomas, 505.
Owsly, Thomas, 261.
Owens, William, 281-282.
Owsly, Jonathan, 261.

P

Pable, Andrew, 265.
Page, Carter, 505.
Pain, Jacob, 267.
Palmer, Henry, 272.
Palmer, Jeffrey, 265.
Palmer, William, 258.*
Parchment, Peter, 281.
Parish, Peter, 287.
Parker, Alexander, 274-430-505.*
Parker, David, 264.
Parker, Jeremy, 273.
Parker, John, 270.
Parker, Josiah, 505.*
Parker, Nicholas, 505.
Parker, Peter, 282.
Parker, Richard, 250-270-505.*
Parker, Thomas, 274-275-430-505-505.
Parker, Warren, 252-252.
Parker, William H., 505.
Parks, James, 264.*
Parkson, John, 264.
Parlor, James, 284.
Parr, Thomas, 241-247-254.
Parris, John, 265.
Parrish, Henry, 270.
Parrott, John, 286.
Parsons, Thomas, 265-430.
Parsons, William, 289-430-505.
Pasgoe, John, 258.
Patridge, Richard, 270.
Patten, Alexander, 277.
Patten, George, 276.
Patterson, Benjamin, 289.
Patterson, Perry, 274.
Patterson, Samuel, 287.*
Patterson, Thomas, 288-505.
Paul, Aaron, 259-263.
Paul, Edward, 283.
Payne, Joseph, 505.
Payne, Josiah, 430-505.
Payne, Tarleton, 430-505.
Payne, Thomas, 430-505.

Payton, Dade, 505.
Peal, Jacob, 251.
Peal, Jesse, 243-243.
Peale, Jacob, 250.
Pearce, John, 267.
Pearce, William, 267.
Pearle, Richard, 287.
Pearson, John, 283.
Pearson, Thomas, 505.
Peek, Edward, 246.
Pelham, Charles, 430-505.
Pemberton, Thomas, 430-505.
Pendleton, James, 246-247-430-505.
Pendleton, Nathaniel, 430-505.
Penery, Robert, 282.
Pennell, Thomas, 272.
Perault, Michael, 505.
Perkins, Archelaus, 430-505.
Perkins, Harden, 289.
Perkins, Joshua, 263.
Perry, John, 430-505.
Peterson, Israel, 288.
Petrie, Alexander, 246.
Pettus, John, R. 505.
Peyton, George, 505.
Peyton, Henry, 288-505.*
Peyton, John, 279-505.
Peyton, Robert, 430-505.
Peyton, Valentine, 277-505.*
Phelps, George, 284.
Philbert, Obadiah, 279.
Phillips, David, 259-261.
Phillips, Samuel, 262-268-505.
Philips, Thomas, 282.
Pickett, Abraham, 243.
Pierce, William, 242-253-430-505.
Piggat, Abraham, 255.
Pigott, Abraham, 244.
Piggot, William, 244-245.
Pines, Lewis, 274.
Plain, Moses, 260-261.
Poe, Jesse, 275.
Poe, Virgil, 275.

Pointer, William, 505.
Poisal, Jacob, 281.
Pole, Peter, 286.
Pollard, Joseph, 272.
Pollock, Thomas, 256.
Poock, Michael, 282.
Pool, Jacob, 277.
Pope, Matthews, 506.
Pope, Thomas, 266.
Pope, William, 257.*
Porter, John, 246-271.
Porter, William, 271-430-506-506.
Porterfield, ———, 260.
Porterfield, Charles, 259-269-430-501.*
Porterfield, Robert, 256-258-258-430-505.
Portis, Kirby, 266.
Poor, Joshua, 286.
Posey, Thomas, 430-501.*
Posey, William, 276.
Posey, Zephaniah, 257-265.
Potts, David, 261-261.
Potts, John, 261.
Potts, Jonathan, 261-262.
Poulson, John, 430-505.
Powell, Charles, 250-251-255.
Powell, Francis, 506.
Powell, Levi, 288.*
Powell, Levin, 430-501.
Powell, Peyton, 258-258-430 506.

Powell, Robert, 278-430-505.
Powell, Thomas, 506.
Powell, William, 247-251-252-258.*
Power, Robert, 288.
Powers, Robert, 506.
Powers, William, 249-250.*
Poythress, William, 249-249-506.
Pratt, John, 282.
Preston, Daniel, 279.
Preston, Robert, 272.
Price, David, 276.
Price, John, 272.*
Price, Richard, 272.
Price, Thomas, 285.*
Pride William R., 506.
Prim, James, 276.
Primm, James, 276.
Prior, John, 246-247-506.
Proctor, Isaac, 265.
Prudon, Henry, 263.
Pryor, John, 430.*
Pryor, William, 267.*
Purcel, Henry, 261.
Pugh, David, 260.
Pugh, Lewis, 265.
Pugh, Willis, 430-506.
Puller, Ledford, 270.
Punter, Henry, 242.
Pursell, Henry, 249.
Purvis, James, 506.
Puaintance, John, 259.

Q

Quarles, Henry, 506.
Quarles, James, 430-506.*
Quarles, John, 506-506.*
Quarles, Nathaniel, 268.
Quarles, Robert, 430-506.
Quarles, Thomas, 430-506.

Quarles, Wm. P., 430-506.
Quinn, James, 274.
Quinn, John, 259-266.
Quint, John, 257-265.
Quirk, Thomas, 430-506.

R

Race, Andrew, 279.
Ragan, Bartholomew, 286.
Ragin, Brice, 271.
Ragin, Daniel, 270.
Ragin, Philip, 270,

Ragon, Brice, 282.
Ragsdale, Drury, 245-431-506.
Ragsdate, Drudy, 253.
Rains, Henry, 288.
Rains, James, 288.

Ramsey, Thomas, 275.
Rand, Walter, 264.
Randolph, John, 244.
Randolph, Robert, 506.
Rankin, Robert, 269-431-506.
Rankins, James, 281.*
Ransdell, Edward, 262.
Ransdell, Thomas, 262-267-431-506.
Ratliff, Francis, 242.
Rattray, Alexander, 287.
Ravenscroft, Francis, 287.
Ravenscroft, Thomas, 281.
Ray, David, 260.
Raynolds, Waitman, 287.
Read, Clement, 506.
Read, Edmund, 506.*
Read, Isaac, 431.*
Read, John, 259.*
Read, Nathaniel, 506.
Read, Peter, 258.
Reader, Shadrack, 258-258.
Reardon, John, 273.
Reardon, Yelverton, 257.
Reaves, Samuel, 284.
Reddick, Jason, 506.
Reddick, Willis, 506.
Redman, Aaron, 260-261.
Redman, Michael, 259.
Redwood, John, 266.
Reed, Isaac, 500.
Reed, Thomas, 277.*
Reed, William, 271.
Reese, Randall, 266.
Reid, John, 271.*
Reid, Nathan, 431.
Relph, Ephriam, 280.
Renner, John, 506.
Reynolds, Aaron, 276.
Reynolds, James, 283.*
Reynolds, John, 253.
Reynolds, Robert, 288.
Rhea, Matthew, 431-506.
Rhodes, Jacob, 284.
Rhodes, John, 253.
Rhodes, Thomas, 287.
Rhodes, William, 272.
Rice, George, 248-264-506.

Rice, Nathaniel, 506.
Rice, Thomas, 278.
Rich, Daniel, 257-265.
Richards, Clements, 261-269.
Richardson, Holt, 431-501.*
Richardson, Morning, 245.
Richardson, Nightingale, 286.
Richardson, Walker, 253-506.
Richardson, Water, 247-248.
Richeson, John, 284.
Richerson, George, 252.
Richerson, ———, 244.
Richison, William, 256.
Ricker, Angus, 506.
Ricketts, Thomas, 281.
Rickman, William, 506.
Riddle, Wildender, 275.
Ridle, Richard, 275.
Ridley, Thomas, 431-506.
Riland, John, 246.
Riley, Edward, 277.
Riley, John, 278-284.
Rind, Cornelius, 263.
Rineker, Edward, 287.
Rineker, Jesse, 287.
Ringlespauser, Henry, 288.
Rippey, Elijah, 256.
Ritchie, John, 284.
Rival, Holiday, 268.
Roach, John, 253.
Roach, Joseph, 271.
Roach, Richard, 283.
Roan, Charles, 271.
Roane, Christopher, 506.
Roberson, Thomas, 257.
Roberts, Barnard, 272.
Roberts, Elias, 285.
Roberts, John, 259-506.*
Roberts, Joseph, 257.
Roberts, Thomas, 259.
Roberts, William, 281.*
Robertson, Benjamin, 275.
Robertson, James, 273-506.*
Robertson, John, 257-431.*
Robertson, Nathaniel, 273.
Robertson, Thomas, 272.
Robertson, William, 431-506.

Robeson, John, 284.
Robins, John, 506-506.
Robinson, Charles, 284.
Robinson,, Daniel, 256.
Robinson, Hugh, 242.
Robinson, John, 260-506.*
Robinson, Mach, 262.
Robinson, Thomas, 248-248-281.
Robison, Joseph, 265.
Rock, John, 284.
Roe, William, 261-269.
Rogers, Barnard, 260.
Rogers, Francis, 286.
Rogers, John, 276-506.
Rogers, Michael, 276.
Rogers, Patrick, 282.
Rogers, Richard, 250-251-255.
Rogers, William, 506.
Roland, William, 268.
Romaine, Abel, 260.
Romaine, James, 260.
Roney, John, 431.
Rooke, John, 284.
Roeny, Christian, 263.
Rooney, John, 506.
Rose, Alexander, 289.
Rose, George, 268.
Rose, Jesse, 278.
Rose, Robert, 431-506.
Rose, William, 264.
Ross, Isaac, 282.
Ross, John, 283.*

Rosser, John, 242.
Rounsifer, Richard, 260.
Routon, Richard, 242-243.
Row, Joseph, 283.
Roy, Beverly, 278-431-506.
Rucks, Benjamin, 263.
Rudder, Epaphroditus, 431-506.
Rudolph, Michael, 288.
Ruffin, Thomas, 289.
Rump, Jacob, 288.
Rush, Henry, 272.
Russell, Albert, 431-506.
Russell, Andrew, 506.
Russell, Baptist, 260.
Russell, Charles, 506.
Russell, George, 267-278.
Russell, Henry, 274.
Russell, John, 279-506.*
Russell, Matthew, 267.
Russell, William, 246-277-431-500.
Rust, Benjamin, 506.
Rutherford, Thomas, 277.
Ryalls, James, 265.
Ryalls, Samuel, 265.
Ryan, James, 256.
Ryan, John, 256.
Ryan, William, 285.*
Ryanhart, Daniel, 281.
Rydman, John, 506.
Rynalds, Alexander, 268.
Rycroft, Thomas, 262-268.

S

Sacrey, Isaac, 275.
Sacrey, James, 275.
Sadler, John, 271.
Sage, Edward, 250.
Sale, John, 287.*
Sale, Leonard, 274.
Salter, James, 281.
Salter, John, 277-278.
Sampson, George, 268.
Sampson, Joseph, 269.
Sanford, James, 274.
Sanford, Richard, 244-245-274.

Sanford, Thomas, 245-245.
Sanford, William, 245-245-274.*
Sanford, Richard, 253.
Sanford, Samuel, 254.
Sandifer, James, 247.
Sandifer, Samuel, 246-254.
Sanders, John, 253.*
Sanders, Presley, 274.
Sansum, Philip, 433-506.
Saunders, Celey, 506.
Saunders, John, 273.
Saunders, Joseph, 506.

Saunders, William, 506.
Savage, Joseph, 433-506.
Savage, Nathaniel, 506.*
Savage, Samuel, 287.
Sayres, Robert, 433-506.*
Sayres, Thomas, 433-506.
Scandle, William, 275.
Scarborough, John, 433.
Scolfield, ———, 286.
Scott, Charles, 433-433-500-506.*
Scott, Henry, 282.
Scott, John, 276-506-506.*
Scott, Joseph, 433-506-506.
Scott, Reuben, 255.
Scott, Robert, 247-248.
Scott, Walter, 506.*
Scurlock, Alexander, 264.
Seay, James, 271.
Seay, Jacob, 273.
Seay, Hezekiah, 271.
Seavell, James, 283.
Sebra, William, 265.
Selavan, Dennis, 284.
Selden, Samuel, 433.
Selden, Samuel, 506.
Settle, Strother, 433-506.
Severe, Robert, 260.
Shacklett, Edward, 242-243-254.
Shackelford, Henry, 242.
Shackelford, Mag., 242.
Shackelford, William, 506.
Shackelty, George, 259.
Shain, Timothy, 259.
Shannon, Patrick, 286.
Shannon, William, 249-249.
Sharman, Robert, 256.
Sharpe, James, 251.
Sharwood, Richard, 255.
Shaugh, Henry, 264.
Shaver, John, 281.
Shaw, James, 281.*
Shay, Dennis, 286.
Shay, Humphrey, 274.
Shea, Dennis, 277.
Shea, John, 284.
Shea, Michael, 259.
Shearman, Martin, 506.

Shearman, Robert, 257.
Shearwood, Richard, 244.
Sheckelty, George, 263.
Shee, Michael, 263.
Shett, William, 266.
Sheets, Adam, 261-269.
Sheerer, Richard, 277.
Shehan, Timothy, 263.
Shelton, David, 242.
Shelton, Joel, 272.
Shelton, Thomas, 274.*
Shepherd, James, 276.
Shepherd, ———, 269.
Shepherd, Abraham, 506.
Sheppard, Edward, 284.
Sheridan, Thomas, 256.
Sherry, John, 263.
Sherry, Thomas, 259.
Shields, James, 286.
Shields, John, 256-506.
Shivers, Thomas, 264.
Shores, Thomas, 264.*
Shumate, William, 262-268.
Shurles, Benjamin, 249-249.
Sidebottom, John, 279.
Silence, William, 275.
Simmons, Aaron, 286.
Simmons, Henry, 268.
Simmons, James, 267.
Simmons, Spartley, 266.
Simmons, Thomas, 271.
Simmons, Williamson, 267.
Simms, Charles, 501.
Simpkins, Garret, 285.
Simpkins, James, 285.*
Simpkins, William, 285.
Simpson, Jeremiah, 282.
Singleton, Anthony, 244-245-253-433-506.
Singleton, Isreal, 265.
Singleton, John, 267.
Singleton, Joseph, 265-506.
Sisson, Robert, 275.
Skelton, Clough, 433-506.
Skelton, David, 254.
Skerrett, Clement, 241.
Skinner, Alexander, 288-433-506.

Skinner, Henry, 284.
Skinner, Thomas, 257.
Slate, James, 273.
Slate, John, 267.
Slaughter, Augustine, 506.
Slaughter, George, 506.*
Slaughter, John, 506.*
Slaughter, Lawrence, 506.
Slaughter, Philip, 256-260-268-433-506.
Slaughter, William, 506.
Smart, Richard, 506.
Smithey, Abraham, 244.
Smithey, Robert, 255.
Smith, Adam, 243.
Smith, Alex., 272.
Smith, Ballard, 433-506.
Smith, David, 282.
Smith, Francis, 266-283-433-506.
Smith, George, 271-276.
Smith, Granville, 506.
Smith, Gregory, 500-506.
Smith, Jacob, 269.
Smith, James, 283-285-433.*
Smith, John, 259-280-281-282-282-283.*
Smith, John V., 275.
Smith, Jonathan, 275-433-506.*
Smith, Joseph, 274-286-287.*
Smith, Larkin, 289-433-506.
Smith, Michael, 283.
Smith, Nathan, 433-506.*
Smith, Obadiah, 506.*
Smith, Peter, 247.
Smith, Robert, 253.
Smith, Samuel, 283.
Smith, Thomas, 252-259-285-287.*
Smith, William, 252-252-257-261-283-431-506-506.*
Smith, William S., 433.
Snead, Holman, 242.
Snead, Smith, 433-506.
Snead, Thomas, 287.
Sneed, John, 250-251-255.
Snow, John, 274.
Soden, John, 267.
Sollers, William, 249-250-254-277.

Solomon, James, 286.
Southall, Stephen, 433-433-506.
Sparham, James, 244-245.
Sparks, Samuel, 258-263.
Sparrow, Richard, 283.
Speak, George, 286.
Speake, Hezekiah, 286.
Speake, William, 286.
Speed, John, 266.
Spelcy, Darby, 253.
Spence, Henry, 265.
Spence, James, 265.
Spence, John, 265.
Spencer, Amos, 257-265.
Spencer, Beverly, 246-247.
Spencer, George, 262.
Spencer, John, 243-506.*
Spencer, William, 506.
Spender, William, 276.
Spiller, William, 506.
Spindler, Richard, 287.
Spinner, John, 272.
Spitfathom, John, 287.
Splaune, Thomas, 272.
Spottswood, Alexander, 270.*
Spottswood, John, 506.
Spratt, Daniel, 285.
Spratliff, Richard, 242-243.
Springer, Jacob, 284-433-507.
Springer, Peter, 282.
Springer, Uriah, 280-283-433-507.
Springfield, Peter, 252-254.
Squires, James, 285-287.
Squires, Henry, 283.
Stacy, Jeremiah, 278.
Stacy, John, 270.
Stacey, Stephen, 266.
Stackhouse, John, 282.
Stackpole, James, 284.
Stafford, Joshua, 268.
Stanard, Larkin, 289.*
Stakes, Robert, 259.
Stanton, John, 258-258.
Stark, William, 289.
Starke, Richard, 433-507.
Starke, William, 507.
Steed, John, 507.

Steele, John, 433-507.*
Steele, William, 507.
Stephens, Edward, 507.*
Stephens, John, 265-286.*
Stephens, William, 507.
Stephenson, Arthur, 277.
Stephenson, David, 256-433-507.
Stephenson, Hugh, 500.
(?)Stevens, Baron, 500.*
Stevens, Thomas, 288.
Stevens, William, 433.
Stevenson, William, 242-243-251-253.
Stewart, James, 242-254.
Stewart, Philip, 433.
Still, Joshua, 282.
Stilwell, Joseph, 265.
Stith, John, 433-507-507.
St. John, Lewis, 243-254.
Stoakes, Christopher, 242-254.
Stoakes, John, 507.
Stockley, Chas., 433.
Stokely, Charles, 507.
Stoker, Edward, 281.
Stokes, John, 289-433.
Stokes, Robert, 263.
Stone, Bayles, 262.
Stone, Josias, 286.
Story, Daniel, 266.
Story, Le is, 266.
Stott, Isaac, 284.
Stott William, 507.
Straughn, John, 262.
Strickland, Alexander, 259.
Strickland, John, 261-269.
Stribling, Erasmus, 433-507.

Stribling, Sigismund, 433-507.
Strother, James, 273.
Strother, John, 273.
Streets, Samuel, 282.
Stubblefield, Beverly, 289-433-507.
Stubblefield, George, 507.^
Stubbs, Joseph, 272.
Stump, Lewis, 260-261.
Stump, Jacob, 260.
Stuart, Philip, 507.
Stutherd, Thomas, 260-261.
Sublett, Benjamin, 266.+
Suddoth, William, 257-264.
Suddoth, William, 262.
Sugars, William, 276.
Sullinger, John, 275.
Sullivan, James, 248-248.
Sullivan, John, 282.
Sullivan, Michael, 252.
Summers, Simon, 433-507.
Summers, William, 249-249.
Summerson, Gavin, 507.
Sutch, Geo., 283.
Sutherland, William, 276.
Suttle, William, 249.
Suttles, William, 250.
Sutton, Benjamin, 260-269.
Sutton, Martin, 287.
Sutton, Rowland, 261-269.
Sweepstone, John, 287.
Swan, John, 507.*
Swearingen, Joseph, 433-507.
Swoope, John, 507.
Sykes, Barney, 270.
Symes, Isaiah, 268.

T

Tabb, Augustine, 434-507.
Tabor, Thomas, 244.
Talbert, Levy, 272.
Taliaferro, Benjamin, 507.
Taliaferro, William B., 501.
Talliaferro, Benjamin, 289-434.
Talliaferro, Nicholas, 434-507.

Talman, James, 263.
Tandy, William, 269.
Tannehill, Josiah, 280-434-507.
Tannehill, Thomas, 283.
Tanner, Paul, 277.
Tate, James, 286.*
Tate, John, 276.*

Tatum, Zachariah, 434-507.
Taylor, Benjamin, 507.
Taylor, Edward, 244.
Taylor, Francis, 273-507.*
Taylor, Isaac, 507.*
Taylor, James, 253-272-286.*
Taylor, Reuben, 507.
Taylor, Richard, 266-280-434-501-507.*
Taylor, Samuel, 275.
Taylor, Thomas, 286.
Taylor, Thornton, 279-507.
Taylor, William, 273-507.*
Team, Joseph, 278.
Teate, John, 270.
Tebbs, John, 279.
Tebbs, Thomas, 272.
Temple, Benjamin, 434-501.
Templar, James, 276.
Terry, Nathaniel, 434-507.
Thindall, Jeremiah, 276.
Thomas, Edward, 285.
Thomas, Elijah, 281.
Thomas, Evan, 272.
Thomas, Even, 279.
Thomas, Henry, 281.
Thomas, James, 271.*
Thomas, John, 258-259-269-278.*
Thomas, Joseph, 274-281.*
Thomas, Lewis, 280-434-507.
Thomas, Thomas, 261.*
Thomas, Woodlies, 271.
Thompkins, Drudy, 267.
Thompson, George, 507.*
Thompson, James, 257-258-263-264-287.*
Thompson, John, 270-279.*
Thompson, Smith, 287.*
Thompson, Turner, 274.
Thompson, William, 507.
Thornton, Joseph, 261.
Thornton, Pat, 284.
Thornton, Presley, 507.
Throckmorton, Alb., 434.
Throckmorton, Albion, 288-507.
Thraikill, John, 276.
Thurman, William 279.

Thweatt, Thomas, 507.
Tillar, Henry, 266.
Tillis, John, 280.
Tillory, John, 265.
Tinchman, Henry, 261-269.
Tinnel, Benjamin, 279.
Tinsley, Jonathan, 286.
Tinsley, Samuel, 507.
Tittle, James, 281.
Todd, Robert, 507.
Toe, Edwin, 261.
Toland, Elias, 260.
Toles, John, 264.
Tompkins, Christopher, 507.
Tompkins, Henry, 507.
Tompkins, Daniel R., 507.
Tompkins, Robert, 507.*
Tomlin, John, 260-261.
Tomlin, Stephen, 278.
Tomlinson, George, 287.
Tomlinson, William, 267.
Towers, John, 279.
Towles, Oliver, 288-434-500.*
Townes, John, 258-267-507.*
Trabue, William, 263-434-507.
Trant, Lawrence, 434-507.
Trapp, Thomas, 270.
Travis, Edward, 507.
Trent, Thomas, 266.
Tresvant, John, 507.
Trezvant, John, 434.
Triplett, George, 507.
Trivet, Samuel, 271.
Trusfield, William, 257.
Tubbs, John, 285.
Tucker, James, 251.*
Tucker, John, 271.
Tuder, John, 267.
Tufnell, James, 278.
Tuning, Harden, 275.
Tupman, John, 507.
Turbutt, John, 285.
Turner, David, 263.*
Turner, Hezekiah, 276.
Turner, John, 507.*
Turner, Stephen, 267.
Turner, William, 274.*

Turvey, William, 278.
Tutt, Chas., 289-507.
Tyrie, James, 251.

Tyler, Charles, 257-279.
Tyler, John, 507.*

U

Underhill, Howell, 268.
Upchurch, Michael, 267.

Upshur, James, 275-507.*
Upshur, Thomas, 507.

V

Valentine, Edward, 507.
Valentine, Jacob, 507.
Vance, Joseph, 263.
Vance, Robert, 280-435-507.
Vanderwall, Marks, 435.
Van Metre, Joseph, 435-507.
Vann, Henry, 283.
Vanse, William, 507.
Vasser, George, 272.
Vasser, Joel, 265.
Vasser, Daniel, 265.
Vaughan, Claiborne, 507.
Vaughan, John, 275-507.

Vaughan, William, 250.
Vaughn, Lystra, 278.
Vaughn, Sherwood, 285.
Vawters, William, 507.
Veal, Solomon, 260.
Veatch, Elijah, 281.
Verdin, Thomas, 288.
Vilet, John, 284.
Vindervall, Marks, 507.
Vollusion, Armand, 507.
Vowles, Charles, 507.
Vowles, Henry, 507.
Vowles, Walter, 507.

W

Waddy, Sharpleigh, 507.
Wagener, Andrew, 436.
Waggoner, Andrew, 507.*
Walden, James, 264.
Walker, David, 437-507.*
Walker, Edward, 284.*
Walker, George, 248-248-255.*
Walker, Jacob, 507.
Walker, John, 278.*
Walker, Levin, 507-507.
Walker, Thomas, 282.*
Walker, William, 242-282.*
Wallace, Adam, 507.*
Wallace, Alexander, 286.
Wallace, Andrew, 437-507.*
Wallace, Gustavis B., 256-436-501.
Wallace, Henry, 244.
Wallace, James, 270-436-437-507-507.

Wallace, John, 282.
Wallace, William B., 437-507.
Wallace, William Gibbs, 277.
Waller, William, 264.
Walls, George, 507.
Walter, Anthony P., 266.
Walter, Jacob, 282.
Walter, Peter, 282.
Walters, John, 267.
Walters, Richard, 437.
Walters, Richard C., 507.
Walton, John, 278.
Ward, Lawrence, 264.
Ward, Moses, 284.
Ward, Thomas, 246-247.
Ward, William, 267-274.
Warman, Thomas, 437-507.*
Warmock, Frederick, 436.
Warner, John, 273.

Warnock, Frederick, 501.
Warren, James M., 261.
Warren, Samuel, 274.
Washington, George, 507.
Washington, Geo. A., 437.
Washington, William, 436-501.
Waters, James, 246.
Waters, Richard, 241-245-246.
Waters, William, 273.
Watterson, Robert, 268.
Watts, John, 437-507.*
Watson, James, 281.*
Watson, John, 282.
Watson, Thomas, 285.
Weatherholt, Jacob, 281.
Weatherly, Thomas, 266.
Webb, Henry, 279.
Webb, Isaac, 507.*
Webb, John, 244-245-265-436-501.*
Webb, Mathew, 265.
Webster, Thomas, 271.
Weedon, George, 436-500.
Wefield, George, 286.
Weir, James, 256.
Welch, Benj., 248-248.
Welch, James, 273.
Welch, John, 264.
Welch, Michael, 248.
Welch, Nathaniel, 507.
Welch, Patrick, 259.
Welch, Thomas, 258-259.
Welch, William, 285.
Welsh, Jonathan, 284.
Welsh, Sill, 248-248-255.
Wells, John, 251-276.*
Wells, Thomas, 243.
West, Capt. ———, 269.
West, Beriah, 244-245.
West, Chas., 276-436-507.
West, Henry, 286.
Wesson, Isaac, 250-251.
Whaley, William, 267.
Wharton, Ben., 267.
Whatley, George, 257.
Whealy, James, 283.
Whealy, Thomas, 283.
Wheeler, John, 282.

White, Anthony W., 436.
White, Daniel, 287.⊤
White, George, 257-265.
White, James, 251-277.*
White, John, 275-437-507-507.*
White, Joseph, 259-263-282.
White, Nicholas, 258-258.
White, Robert, 266-274-507.*
White, Tarpley, 507.
White, Thomas, 507.
White, William, 282-437-507-507-507.*
Whiteall, William, 261.
Whitehall, William, 261.
Whitehurst, Levi, 268.
Whiteman, Charles, 276.
Whiting, Francis, 437-508.
Whiting, Henry, 508.
Whitaker, Joseph, 266.
Whitaker, Thomas, 282.
Whitt, Isham, 266.
Whittaker, William, 437-508.
Wickliffe, Arrington, 257.
Wickliffe, Benjamin, 257-264.
Wickliffe, Moses, 257-264.
Wilday, Moll, 265.
Wilds, John, 250.
Wilhite, Jesse, 269.
Wilkes, James, 277.
Wilkins, Samuel, 247.
Wilkins, Thomas, 248-248.
Wilkinson, Bernard, 267.
Wilkinson, John, 278.
Wilkinson, Drury, 245.
Wilkerson, Drury, 244.
Wilkerson, Thomas, 267.
Wilks, Burwell, 267.
Williams, Charles, 244.*
Williams, Daniel, 269.
Williams, David, 260-437-508.
Williams, Edward, 508.
Williams, George, 272-273-274.
Williams, Henry, 267-289.
Williams, James, 437-508.
Williams, Jarrett, 508.
Williams, John, 251-262-267-283-287-508.*

37

Williams, Jonathan, 279.
Williams, Joseph, 288.
Williams, Seth, 268.
Williams, Walker, 243.
Williams, Walter, 244-255.
Williams, William, 277.
Williamson, Drury, 254.
Williamson, William, 277.
Willis, Henry, 508.
Willis, John, 436.*
Willis, John W., 508.
Wills, Thomas, 263.
Wilson, David, 249.
Wilson, Edward, 257-265.
Wilson, James, 269-286.
Wilson, John, 437.*
Wilson, Joseph, 285.
Wilson, Stacy, 271.
Willis, ———, 266-437-508-508.
Wiltshire, Charles, 263.
Winder, John, 258.
Wing, Gideon, 249-250-254.
Wingate, Elias, 247-248.
Winlock, Joseph, 283-437-508.
Winn, Thomas, 282.
Winston, Benjamin, 508.
Winston, Wm., 288-508.
Winter, George, 257-264.
Winters, Stephen, 284.
Wise, Clark, 269.
Wolf, George, 261-269.
Wood, Edward, 281.
Wood, James, 436-500.*
Wood, John, 261-269-279.*
Wood, Robert, 278.
Wood, Timothy, 268.
Wood, William, 281.*
Woodham, Richard, 258-259.

Woodford, Gen. ———, 267.*
Woodford, Wm., 436-500.
Woodman, John, 284.
Woodruff, Jesse, 275.
Woods, John, 281.
Woods, Joseph, 284.
Woods, Thomas, 280.
Woods, William, 284.
Woody, William, 273.*
Woodson, Frederick, 508.
Woodson, Hughes, 508.*
Woodson, Tarleton, 436-508.*
Woodson, Robert, 437-508.
Woosley, Aaron, 264.
Woosley, Moses, 266.
Woosley, William, 266.
Wooster, John, 286.
Wooton, Thomas, 252.
Worsham, Henry, 272.
Worsham, John, 270-508.
Worsham, Joshua, 271.
Worsham, Richard, 437-508.
Worsham, William, 508.*
Worthington, Wm., 248.
Wotten, Thomas, 252.
Wray, Richard, 272.
Wren, John, 249-250.
Wright, Daniel, 277.
Wright, James, 262-264-437-508.
Wright, Patrick, 508.
Wright, Thomas, 269.*
Wright, Wescott, 508.
Wright, William, 277.*
Wyatt, Carey, 508.
Wyatt, Elisha, 265.
Wymer, Charles, 285.
Wynn, John, 287.

Y

Yancey, Leighton, 437-508.
Yancey, Robert, 437-508.
Yarboro, John, 275.
Yarborogh, Charles, 437-508.
Yarnton, Oliver, 244.
Yarrington, Oliver, 245.
Yates, George, 437.
Yewless, Michael, 286.

Young, Frederick, 270.
Young, Henry, 437-508.*
Young, John, 279-284.*
Young, Robt., 257-263.
Young, Samuel, 276.
Young, Walter, 277.
York, Jeremiah, 283.

Index to Officers in the 1st, 2nd, 3rd, 4th, 5th, 6th, and 11th Virginia Regiments as given in Volume I. of Palmer's Calendar of Virginia State Papers, giving the date of commission and the number of the page on which the name appears.

Anderson, Capt: John, 3rd Rgt., Com. Aug. 12, 1777—410.
Archer, Lt. Field, 2nd Rgt., Com. Feb. 18, 1781—410.
Archer, Ensign Richard, 3rd Rgt., Com. Nov. 28, ———410.
Ashby, Lt. Benjamin, 3rd Rgt., Com. March 18, 1779—410.
Barbee, Lt. Thomas, 6th Rgt., Com. March 22, 1779—413.
Barbour, Ens. James, 6th Rgt., Com. Oct. 14, ———413.
Barnes, Ensign ———, 11th Rgt., Com. ———. —, ———302.
Baskerville, Lt. Samuel, 6th Rgt., Com. Sept. 14, ———413.
Beale, Capt. Robert, 3rd Rgt., Com. June 19, 1779—410.
Bedinger, Ens. Danl., 4th Rgt., Com. Feb| —, 1781—412.
Bedinger, Lt. Henry, 3rd Rgt., Com. Sept. 23, 1777—410.
Bently, Capt. William, 3rd Rgt., Com. ——— —, 1779—410.
Blackman, Lt. Geo., 2nd Rgt., Com. Feb. 18, 1781—410.
Blackwell, Capt. John, 3rd Rgt., Com. Sept. 15, 1777—410.
Blackwell, Lt. Joseph, 6th Rgt., Com. Nov. 30, ———413.
Booker, Capt. Saml., 4th Rgt., Com. Aug. 1, 1777—412.
Brackenridge, Lt. Robert, 5th Rgt., Com. April 4, ———412.
Brown, Ensign Jacob, 5th Rgt., Com. Sept. 15, 1778—413.
Browne, Lt, Thos.. 1st Rgt., Com. Oct. 18, 1777—410.
Bruin, Capt. ———, 11th Rgt.—302.
Burford, Lt. Thomas, 1st Rgt., Com. July 16, 1780—410.
Butler, Capt. Lawrence, 4th. Rgt., Com. May 14, 1779—412.
Campbell, Ens. Archibald, 4th. Rgt., Com. Oct. 17, 1780—412.
Campbell, Lt. Col. Richard, 4th Rgt., Com. Feb. 20, 1778—412.
Cannon, Lt. Luke, 4th Rgt., Com. Aug. 15, 1779—412.
Carr, Ensign John, 1st Rgt., Com. ——— —, ———410.
Carrington, Capt. Mayo, 6th Rgt., Com. May 12, 1779—413.
Clark, Ensign Edmund, 6th Rgt. Com. Mar. 21, 1780—413.
Clay, Lieut. Mathew, 5th Rgt., Com. April 23, ———413.
Cocke, Capt. Colin, 2nd Rgt., Com. Dec. 9, 1779—410.
Conway, Lieut. Jos., 1st. Rgt., Com. July 15, 1780—410.
Courtney, Lt. Philip, 1st. Rgt., Com. Feb. 18, 1781—410.
Coverley, Lt. Thomas, 5th. Rgt., Com. May 26, ———413.
Cowherd, Capt. Francis, 2nd Rgt. Com. May 29, 1781—410.
Craddock, Lt. Robert, 4th Rgt., Com. Sept. 25, ———412.
Crane, Capt. James, 4th. Rgt., Com. April 5, 1780—412.
Crawford, Lt. John, 2nd Rgt., Com. ——— —. ———410.
Croghan, Maj. Wm., 4th Rgt., Com. May 16, 1778—412.
Crute, Lt. John, 4th Rgt., Com. Nov. 30, 1779—412.
Culbertson, Capt. James, 5th Rgt., Com. May 12, 1779—412.
Currey, Capt. James, 4th Rgt., Com. Sept. 24, 1779—412.

Darby, Lt. Nathaniel, 5th Rgt., Com. Mar. 9, ———412.
Davies, ———, 1st Lt., 11th Rgt.—302.
Davies, Col. Wm., 1st Rgt., Com. Mar. 20, 1778—410.
Delaplain, Lt. James, 2nd Rgt., Com. Aug. 1, 1780—410.
Denholm, Capt. Archibald, 1st Rgt., Com. June 25, 1779—410.
Drew, Ensign ———, 1st Rgt., Com. ——— —, ———410.
Easton, Lt. Philip, 4th Rgt., Com. Aug. 10, ———412.
Edmonds, Capt. Thomas, 3rd Rgt., Com. Mar. 18, 1777—410.
Edwards, Capt. Leroy, 3rd Rgt., Com. ——— —, ———410.
Evans, Lt. William, 6th. Rgt., Com. Sept. 10, ———413.
Erskine, Lt. Charles, 4th Rgt., Com. April 5, 1780—412.
Eskridge, Lt. Wm., 2nd Rgt., Com. Dec. 9, ———410.
Eustace, Ens. John, 3rd Rgt., Com. Oct. 7, 1780—410.
Fealy, Lt. Timothy, 3rd Rgt,. Com. Nov. 6, 1777—410.
Febiger, Col. Christian, 2nd Rgt., Com. Sept. 26, 1777—410.
Feely, Ensign ———, 11th Rgt.—302.
*Fields, Lt. Reuben, 4th Rgt., Com. Jan. 10, 1778—412.
Finley, Capt. ———, 11th Rgt., (Prisoner)—302.
Finley, Capt. Samuel, 4th Rgt., Com. Dec. —, 1776—412.
Fitzgerald, Capt. John, 6th Rgt., Com. May 10, 1780—413.
*Foster, Ens. John, 2nd Rgt., Com. Feb. 18, 1781—410.
Foster, Lt. Robert, 4th Rgt., Com. April 20, ———412.
Fox, Lieut. Thomas, 6th Rgt., Com. Oct. 30, ———413.
*Gaskins, Lt. Col. Thomas, 3rd Rgt., Com. May 16, 1778—410.
George, Capt. ———, 11th Rgt.—302.
Giles, Ensign John, 3rd Rgt., Com. Oct. 24, ———410.
Gillison, Capt. John, 6th Rgt., Com. Feb. 6, 1777—413.
Gray, Lt. Francis, 6th Rgt., Com. Oct. 15, ———413.
Green, Ens. Gabriel, 6th Rgt., Com. Oct. 12, ———413.
Green, Ensign James, 6th Rgt., Com. Oct. 13, ———413.
Green, Ensign Robert, 6th Rgt., Com. Oct. 11, ———413.
Greene, Col John, 6th Rgt., Com. Jan. 26, 1778—413.
Hackley, Lt. John, 6th Rgt., Com. ——— —, ———413.
Hamilton, Lt. James, 6th Rgt. Com. Jan. 13, 1778—413.
Harris, Ensign John, 1st Rgt., Com. Feb. 11, 1781—410.
*Hawes. Col. Samuel, 6th Rgt., Com. Mar. 1, 1778—413.
Hayes, Ensign Robert, 4th Rgt., Com. ——— —, ———412.
Hays, Ensign Andrew, 5th Rgt., Com. Feb. 15, ———413.
Heth, Ensign, John, 2nd Rgt., Com., Mar. 8, 1780—410.
Higgins, Lt. Peter, 2nd Rgt., Com. ——— —, 1779—410.
Higgins, Capt. Robert, 2nd Rgt., Com. Mar. 1, 1777—410.
Hoard, Capt. Thomas, 6th Rgt., Com. Feb. 18, ———413.
Hogg, Lt. Saml., 1st Rgt., Com. Dec. 18, 1777—410.
Holt, Lt. James, 4th. Rgt., Com. Aug. 12, 1779—412.
Holt, Capt. Thomas, 1st Rgt., Com. Mar. 12, 1779—410.
Hopkins, Lt. Col. Saml., 1st. Rgt., Com. June 19, 1778—410.
Huffman, Lt. Phillip, 4th Rgt., Com. Mar. 9, 1779—412.

Johnson, Capt. John Boswell, 1st Rgt., Com. Feb. 15, 1781—410.
*Johnston, Capt. ———, 11th Rgt.—302.
*Johnston, Capt. Wm., 3rd Rgt., Com. Feb. 9, 1777—410.
Jones, Lt. Albridgton, 4th Rgt., Com. Sept. 24, ———412.
Jones, Lt. Charles, 6th Rgt., Com. ——— —, ———413.
Jordan, Lt. John, 2nd Rgt., Com. Sept. 3, 1777—410.
King, Lt. Elisha, 1st Rgt., Com. Feb. 15, 1781—410.
Kirkpatrick, Capt. Adrah, 4th Rgt., Com. Aug. 10, 1777—412.
Kelly, Lt. Wm. D. O., 6th Rgt., Com. ——— —, ———413.
Kendall, Capt. Custis, 5th Rgt., Com. May 26, 1778—412.
*Lamb, Capt. Nathan, 6th Rgt., Com. Sept. 10, ———413.
Lawson, Lt. Benj., 2nd Rgt., Com. Aug. 30, 1779—410.
Lewies, Maj. Wm., 3rd, Rgt., Com. May 12, 1779—410.
Livingston, Lt. Robert, 3rd Rgt., Com. ——— —, 1779—410.
Long, Capt. ———, 11th Rgt.—302.
Long, Ensign ———, 11th Rgt.—302.
Long, Lt. Reuben, 3rd Rgt., Com. May 10, 1779—410.
Lovely, Capt. Wm. E., 4th Rgt., Com. Feb. 18, 1781—412.
Ludiman, Ensign John W., 6th Rgt., Com. May 23, ———413.
McGuire, Ensign Wm., 3rd Rgt., Com. Oct. —, 1780—410.
Morgan, Col. ———, 11th Rgt.—302.
Morton, Lt. James, 4th Rgt., Com. ——— —, ———412.
Moss, Lt. Henry, 2nd Rgt., Com. July 11, 1777—410.
Mosseley, Lt. Benj., 5th Rgt., Com. Aug. 29, 1779—413.
Mallory, Capt. Philip, 4th. Rgt. Com. Mar. 10, 1780—412.
Marks, Capt. Josiah, 2nd Rgt., Com. May 10, 1779—410.
Marshall, 1st Lt., 11th Rgt.—302.
Martin, Lt. Thomas, 5th Rgt., Com. Jan. 4, 1778—412.
*Mathews, Col. Geo., 3rd Rgt., Com. Feb. 10, 1777—410.
Mayborn, Lt. James, 3rd Rgt., Com. Dec. 23, 1777—410.
Merriwether, Lt. David, 1st Rgt., Com. May 7, 1779—410.
Miller, Lt. David, 3rd Rgt., Com. May 1, 1779—410.
Miller, Ensign Garvin, 4th Rgt., Com. July 4, 1779—412.
Miller, Lt. Thomas, 2nd Rgt., Com. Sept. 24, 1779—410.
Minnis, Capt. Francis, 1st Rgt., Com. April 25, 1780—410.
Nelson, Capt. John, 6th Rgt., Com. ——— —, ———413.
Nevill, Col. John, 4th Rgt., Com. Dec. 11, 1777—412.
Norvell, Lt. Lipscomb, 3rd Rgt., Com. Feb. 20, 1780—410.
Overton, Capt. John, 1st Rgt., Com. Oct. 4, 1777—410.
Parker, Capt. Alexander, 2nd Rgt., Com. June 1, 1777—410.
Parker, Capt. Thomas, 5th Rgt., Com. April 23, 1778—412.
Parker, Lt. Thomas, 2nd Rgt., Com. Oct. 13, 1777—410.
Payne, Capt. Thomas, 5th Rgt., Com. Dec. 9, ———412.
Pearson, Lt. Thomas, 6th Rgt., Com. ——— —, ———413.
Pendleton, 1st Lt. ———, 11th Rgt.—302.
Pendleton, Capt. Nathaniel, 3rd Rgt., Com. Mar. 13, 1777—410.
Perkins, Ensign Hercules, 5th Rgt., Com. Sept. 11, 1780—413.

Piles, 1st Lieut. ———. 11th Rgt.—302.
Porterfield, 2nd Lt., 11th Rgt.—302.
Porterfield, Capt. ———, 11th Rgt.—302.
Porterfield, Capt. Robert, 2nd Rgt., Com. April —. 1780—410.
*Posey, Maj. Thos., 1st Rgt., Com. April 30, 1778—410.
Powell, 1st Lieut. ———. 11th Rgt.—302.
Powell, Ensign Preston, 3rd Rgt., Com. July 4, 1779—410.
Quarles, Ensign P., 1st Rgt., Com. Oct. 6, 1780—410.
Ransdale, Lt. Thomas, 3rd Rgt., Com. July 1, 1777—410.
Ransdel, 2nd Lt. ———, 11th Rgt.—302.
Reed, Capt. Nathan, 1st Rgt., Com. Jan. 20, 1777—410.
Rice, Capt. ———, 11th Rgt.—302.
Riddick, Capt. Willis, 4th Rgt., Com. —— ——, ———412.
Robbins, Lt. John, 5th Rgt., Com. Aug. 25, ———413.
Robertson, Lt. John, 6th Rgt., Com. —— —, ———413.
Robertson, Lt. William, 5th Rgt., Com. Nov. 24, ———413.
Rodgers, Capt. Wm., 5th Rgt., Com. April 1, 1778—412.
Roney, Lt. John, 3rd Rgt., Com. July 23, 1779—410.
Roy, Lt. Beverly, 3rd Rgt., Com. Nov. 28, 1777—410.
Russell, Col. Wm., 5th Rgt., Com. Dec. 19, 1776—412.
Sansum, Lt. Philip, 1st Rgt., Com. Oct. 4, 1777—410.
Sayers, Ensign Thomas, 5th Rgt., Com. Feb. 12, 1781—413.
Scarborough, Lt. John, 5th Rgt., Com. Dec. 26, ———413.
Scott, Ensign John, 1st Rgt., Com. Feb. 10, 1781—410.
Scott, Capt. Joseph, Sen., 5th Rgt., Com. Aug. 9, 1777—412.
Scott, Capt. Jos., Jr., 1st Rgt., Com. June 3, 1780—410.
Scott, Ensign William, 4th Rgt., Com. —— —, ———412.
Seldon, Lt. Saml., 1st Rgt., Com. June 25, 1779—410.
Shepherd, Capt. ———. 11th Rgt., (1st Parol)—302.
*Skelton, Capt. Clough, 6th Rgt., Com. Jan. 24, 1778—413.
Slaughter, 1st Lt. ———, 11th Rgt.—302.
Smith, Lt. Ballard, 1st Rgt., Com. May 12, 1779—410.
Smith, Lt. Jonathan, 5th Rgt., Com. Sept. 24, ———413.
Smith, Ensign Thomas, 6th Rgt., Com. Mar. 5, 1780—413.
Smith, Ensign Wm., 2nd Lt., 6th Rgt., Com. Sept. 9, 1778—413.
Snead, Capt. Charles, 5th Rgt., Com. —— —, ———412.
Snead, Maj. Thos., 2nd Rgt., Com. Dec. 9, 1779—410.
Spitsfaddon, Ensign John, 4th Rgt., Com. Dec. 17, 1780—412.
Spottswood, Capt. John, 6th Rgt., Com. Feb. 25, ———413.
*Steel, Lt. John, 5th Rgt., Com. Feb. 18, 1781—413.
Stephenson, Maj. David, 6th Rgt., Com. May 1, 1778—413.
Stevens, Lt. William, 3rd Rgt., Com. June 19, 1779—410.
Stith, Capt. John, 2nd Rgt., Com. Mar. 12, 1777—410.
Stockley, Lt. Charles, 5th Rgt., Com. Feb. 25, ———412.
Stokes, Capt. John, 2nd Rgt., Com. Feb. —, 1778—410.
Stubblefield, Lt. Beverly, 2nd Rgt., Com. Aug. 7, 1777—410.
Taliaferro, Capt. Benj., 2nd Rgt., Com. Sept. 22, 1777—410.

Taliaferro, Lt. Nicholas, 6th Rgt., Com. Feb. 18, 1781—413.
Tatum, Ensign Zachariah, 5th Rgt., Com. Dec. 13, ———413.
Teagle, Capt. Severn, 5th Rgt., Com. June 25, ———412.
Terry, Capt. Nathaniel, 1st Rgt., Com. Dec. 15, 1779—410.
Thweat, Capt. Thomas, 1st Rgt., Com. Mar. 26, 1777—410.
Towles, Lt. Col. Oliver, 5th Rgt., Com. Feb 11, 1778—412.
Townes, Lt. John, 6th Rgt., Com. July 1,———413.
Towns, Ensign ———, 11th Rgt.—302.
Vandervall, Lt. Marks, 1st Rgt., Com. Feb. 4, 1778—410.
Walker, Lt. Richard, 1st Rgt., Com. Mar. 2, 1778—410.
Wallace, Lt. Col Gustavus B., 2nd Rgt., Com. Mar. 20, 1778—410.
Warman, 1st Lieut. ———, 11th Rgt.—302.
*Warman, Lt. Thomas, 3rd Rgt., Com. Sept. 23, 1777—410.
Washington, Ensign Geo. A., 2nd Rgt., Com. ——— ———, ———410.
Williams, Ensign ———, 11th Rgt.—302.
William, Lt. David, 3rd Rgt., Com. July 2, 1779—410.
Williams, Capt. James, 6th Rgt., Com. Sept. 19, ———413.
Willis, Maj. John, 5th Rgt., Com. May 12, 1779—412.
Wilson, Lt. John, 4th Rgt., Com. April 1, 1778—412.
Wilson, Lt. Willis, 4th Rgt., Com. Nov. 29, ———412.
Woodson, Capt. Robert, 5th Rgt,. Com. May 27, 1778—412.
Worsham, Lt. Richard, 1st Rgt., Com. Mar. 12, 1779—410.
Wright, 2nd Lt. ———, 11th Rgt.—302.
Wright, Capt. James, 3rd Rgt., Com. July 2, 1779—410.
Young, 2nd Lt. ———, 11th Rgt.—302.
Young, Capt. Henry, 5th Rgt., Com. Dec. 28, 1776—412.

END

www.ingramcontent.com/pod-product-compliance
Lightning Source LLC
Chambersburg PA
CBHW071132300426
44113CB00009B/951